CW01496407

International Criminal Justice Series

Volume 16

Series editors

Gerhard Werle, Berlin, Germany
Moritz Vormbaum, Berlin, Germany

Series Information

The *International Criminal Justice Series* aims to create a platform for publications in the whole field of international criminal justice. It, therefore, deals with issues relating, among others, to:

- the work of international criminal courts and tribunals;
- transitional justice approaches in different countries;
- international anti-corruption and anti-money laundering initiatives;
- the history of international criminal law.

The series concentrates on themes pertinent to developing countries. It is peer-reviewed and seeks to publish high-quality works emanating from excellent scholars, in particular from African countries.

Editorial Office

Prof. Dr. Gerhard Werle
Humboldt-Universität zu Berlin
Faculty of Law
Unter den Linden 6,
10099 Berlin, Germany
gerhard.werle@rewi.hu-berlin.de
moritz.vormbaum@rewi.hu-berlin.de

More information about this series at http://www.springer.com/series/13470

Kelly Pitcher

Judicial Responses to Pre-Trial Procedural Violations in International Criminal Proceedings

Kelly Pitcher
Department of Criminal Law
    and Criminal Procedure
Leiden University
Leiden
The Netherlands

ISSN 2352-6718   ISSN 2352-6726   (electronic)
International Criminal Justice Series
ISBN 978-94-6265-218-7   ISBN 978-94-6265-219-4   (eBook)
https://doi.org/10.1007/978-94-6265-219-4

Library of Congress Control Number: 2017954483

Published by T.M.C. ASSER PRESS, The Hague, The Netherlands www.asserpress.nl
Produced and distributed for T.M.C. ASSER PRESS by Springer-Verlag Berlin Heidelberg

Printed on acid-free paper

This T.M.C. ASSER PRESS imprint is published by Springer Nature
The registered company is Springer-Verlag GmbH Germany
The registered company address is: Heidelberger Platz 3, 14197 Berlin, Germany

Acknowledgements

This book is the result of doctoral research conducted between 2009 and 2016 at the University of Amsterdam. During this time, I benefitted from the able guidance of professors Tom Blom and Göran Sluiter, and the support of the Department of Criminal Law and Criminal Procedure, for which I am grateful. To Egbert, Edie, Robert and Pieter and to my family, I am grateful for everything.

Contents

Abbreviations

ACHR	American Convention on Human Rights
ASP	Assembly of States Parties (International Criminal Court)
CCP	Code of Criminal Procedure (The Netherlands)
DRC	Democratic Republic of Congo
ECCC	Extraordinary Chambers in the Courts of Cambodia
ECHR	European Convention on Human Rights
ECnHR	European Commission of Human Rights
ECtHR	European Court of Human Rights
EU	European Union
FRY	Federal Republic of Yugoslavia
HRC	Human Rights Committee (United Nations)
IACtHR	Inter-American Court of Human Rights
ICC	International Criminal Court
ICCPR	International Covenant on Civil and Political Rights
ICTR	International Criminal Tribunal for Rwanda (United Nations)
ICTs	International Criminal Tribunals
ICTY	International Criminal Tribunal for the former Yugoslavia (United Nations)
NATO	North Atlantic Treaty Organization
PACE	Police and Criminal Evidence Act 1984 (England and Wales)
RPE	Rules of Procedure and Evidence
SCSL	Special Court for Sierra Leone
SFOR	Stabilization Force
SPSC	Special Panel for Serious Crimes in East Timor
STL	Special Tribunal for Lebanon
TRCP	Transitional Rules of Criminal Procedure (SPSC)
UN	United Nations

UNCAT   United Nations Convention against Torture
UNGA   United Nations General Assembly
UNTAES   United Nations Transitional Administration for Eastern Slavonia,
          Baranja and Western Sirmium

Chapter 1
Introduction

Abstract In this chapter the central research question is introduced (how should judges at the international criminal tribunals respond to procedural violations committed in the pre-trial phase of the proceedings?), as well as several sub-questions, concerning: the proper rationale(s) for judicial responses to pre-trial procedural violations; the extent to which the determination of whether to attach legal consequences to established procedural violations should entail the exercise of judgement, whereby the judge has due regard to the particular circumstances of the case (which may be contrasted to an approach whereby the judicial response is more or less automatic) and, on a related note, the extent to which it should entail a balancing approach, whereby the court (also) takes into account factors that seemingly have nothing to do with that which warranted the court's attention in the first place, and which militate against a (potentially) far-reaching response thereto; and, finally, who bears (and indeed, who should bear) responsibility for pre-trial procedural violations—the state whose law enforcement authorities 'actually' committed the procedural violation or the international criminal tribunal that sought the cooperation of that state and is now seeking to rely on the results of the measures executed by such authorities on their behalf. In addition to introducing the central research question and the aforementioned sub-questions, this chapter delineates the scope of the study, whereby the object thereof is limited to the law and practice of the ICTY, ICTR and ICC, and several definitions are provided.

Keywords public interest · discretion · balancing · goals of international criminal justice · features/goals of international criminal procedure · compliance with human rights law · comparative criminal procedure · right to a fair trial · right to an effective remedy · inter-state cooperation in criminal matters · exclusion of evidence · stay of proceedings · sentence reduction · financial compensation · express acknowledgement

K. Pitcher, *Judicial Responses to Pre-Trial Procedural Violations in International Criminal Proceedings*, International Criminal Justice Series 16,
https://doi.org/10.1007/978-94-6265-219-4_1

Contents

1.1   Framing the Issue[1]

On 3 November 1999, the Appeals Chamber of the International Criminal Tribunal for Rwanda (hereafter: ICTR) imposed a permanent stay of proceedings in the case of *Barayagwiza*, by which the criminal proceedings against Jean-Bosco Barayagwiza, who was charged with genocide, conspiracy to commit genocide, complicity in genocide, direct and public incitement to commit genocide, crimes against humanity and war crimes, were brought to a halt. According to the Appeals Chamber, such a procedural step, which would bar prosecution for the same charges at a later date, was necessary in light of serious violations of the accused's rights while detained in Cameroon, by national authorities at the ICTR Prosecutor's request pending preparation of the indictment against him, whereby the Prosecutor had failed in her duty of due diligence to ensure the protection thereof. What made the case so 'egregious' as to warrant such a procedural step, was 'the combination of delays that seemed to occur at virtually every stage of the Appellant's case', including a 'failure to hear the *writ of habeas corpus*' and the 'prolonged detention of the Appellant without an indictment'.[2] Indeed, the fundamental rights of the Appellant had been 'repeatedly violated', whereby, moreover, the 'Prosecutor's failure to prosecute this case was tantamount to negligence'.[3] To (nevertheless) try an accused in such circumstances would, the Appeals Chamber argued, be to place an 'imprimatur' on such violations,[4] and 'cause irreparable damage to the integrity of the judicial process'.[5]

The decision to stay the proceedings against Jean-Bosco Barayagwiza was met with widespread public condemnation in Rwanda, whereby the Rwandan government is reported to have responded by threatening to suspend all cooperation with the ICTR.[6] Upon request of the Prosecutor (which appears to have been prompted

---

[1] This section is based on the introduction to an earlier piece of writing by the same author. See Pitcher 2013.

[2] *Prosecutor v Barayagwiza* (Decision) ICTR-97-19-AR72, A Ch (3 November 1999) para 109.

[3] Ibid., para 106.

[4] Ibid., para 112.

[5] Ibid., para 108.

[6] See *Prosecutor v Barayagwiza* (Decision (Prosecutor's Request for Review or Reconsideration)) ICTR-97-19-AR72, A Ch (31 March 2000) para 34. See also e.g. Schabas 2000, 565; and Cogan 2002, 135.

by said adverse reaction),[7] the decision was reviewed, with the newly constituted[8] Appeals Chamber finding that the stay of proceedings and release of the Accused were no longer appropriate. According to the Appeals Chamber, the 'new facts' established upon review 'diminish[ed] the role played by the failings of the Prosecutor as well as the intensity of the violation of the rights of the Appellant'.[9] Instead, the Accused would be entitled to either financial compensation upon acquittal, or sentence reduction upon conviction. Upon conviction, Barayagwiza's sentence was reduced from one of life imprisonment to thirty-two years, in light of the aforementioned rights violations.[10]

The potential for controversy when a court attaches legal consequences to the violation of procedural standards in the pre-trial phase of criminal proceedings is not unique to the context of the international criminal tribunals (hereafter: ICTs). In the context of national criminal proceedings also, 'issues associated with police misconduct are always potentially politically sensitive', since '[e]ven if the public may be quick to condemn police misconduct, it may be equally quick to condemn judicial responses to … [police] misconduct that are perceived as having the effect of 'letting the guilty go free on technicalities".[11] Judicial responses that may be so perceived include the (permanent) stay of proceedings, the imposition of which effectively means the end of the case, and, where the other evidence in the case is not sufficient to convict, the exclusion of (unlawfully obtained) evidence. Other (less drastic) judicial responses, such as sentence reduction, may also lead to public condemnation if perceived as detracting from the effectiveness of punishment or its expressive value, especially where the underlying crime is of a particularly serious nature.

The fact that issues related to the violation of procedural standards in the pre-trial phase of criminal proceedings are likely to be politically sensitive may raise the question of whether this—the (predicted) public reaction to the judicial response,

---

[7] *Prosecutor v Barayagwiza* (Decision (Prosecutor's Request for Review or Reconsideration)) ICTR-97-19-AR72, A Ch (31 March 2000) paras 34–35.

[8] See Schabas 2000, 563, n 1.

[9] *Prosecutor v Barayagwiza* (Decision (Prosecutor's Request for Review or Reconsideration)) ICTR-97-19-AR72, A Ch (31 March 2000) para 71. While the Appeals Chamber denied that they had been pressurized into changing their decision to release Barayagwiza (para 34 of the decision states that: 'The Appeals Chamber wishes to stress that the Tribunal is an independent body, whose decisions are based solely on justice and law. If its decision in any case should be followed by non-cooperation, that consequence would be a matter for the Security Council.'), there is broad consensus in the literature that the decision was influenced by the Rwandan Government's threats. See e.g. Schabas 2000, 567; Cogan 2002, 135; Fairlie 2003, 57–58; and Naymark 2008, 3–4.

[10] *Prosecutor v Nahimana, Barayagwiza and Ngeze* (Judgement and Sentence) ICTR-99-52-T, T Ch I (3 December 2003) para 1107; *Prosecutor v Nahimana, Barayagwiza and Ngeze* (Judgement) ICTR-99-52-A, A Ch (28 November 2007) para 1097.

[11] Choo 2008, 106. Choo uses the term 'misconduct' to denote 'in the words of the Criminal Justice Act 2003 [an Act of the Parliament of the United Kingdom], 'the commission of an offence or other reprehensible behaviour", whereby the term 'reprehensible' denotes 'some element of culpability or blameworthiness'. Ibid., referring to the English Court of Appeals' interpretation of the term 'misconduct' within the meaning of s 112(1) Criminal Justice Act 2003 in *R v Renda* [2006] 1 WLR 2948 [24].

i.e. the attachment of legal consequences, to procedural violations—is something to which a judge faced with an application for relief in this respect should have regard. Similarly, the question may arise as to whether the fact that the offence with which the accused is charged is particularly serious is a factor to which the judge faced with such an application should attach importance, i.e. whether the public interest in 'ensuring that those that are charged with grave crimes should be tried'[12] should inform the determination to be made. While such questions are just as likely to arise in the national context as in the context of international criminal proceedings (the potential for controversy when a court attaches legal consequences to the violation of procedural standards in the pre-trial phase of criminal proceedings not being unique to the latter context), they may take on a different meaning at the international level, in light of the fact that the goals of international criminal justice are not limited to the conviction of the guilty (and, correspondingly, the acquittal of the innocent), but include such 'special' or 'idiosyncratic' (socio-political) goals as 'reconciliation and restoration of peace and security', 'establishment of a historical record', 'promoting international rule of law' and 'justice for victims',[13] and in light of the ICTs' dependence on state cooperation for such essential activities as the apprehension of persons suspected or accused of crimes falling within their jurisdiction and for the carrying out of investigations, i.e. for their proper functioning, thereby making them vulnerable to political backlash. Put differently, while the potential for controversy when a court attaches a legal consequence to the violation of procedural standards in the pre-trial phase of criminal proceedings is not unique to the context of international criminal proceedings, at the international level, the stakes may be higher. And aside from the issue of political sensitivity, the fact that the ICTs do not have their own enforcement agencies (and are reliant on state cooperation for the aforementioned activities), coupled with the fact that their governing documents are (largely) silent on how such activities are to be executed, raises challenging questions on both a conceptual and practical level for a judge faced with an application for relief in respect of procedural violations committed in the pre-trial phase of international criminal proceedings.

1.2   Purpose of the Book

The issues raised above go to fundamental questions about the proper rationale(s) for judicial responses to procedural violations committed in the pre-trial phase of international criminal proceedings; about the extent to which the determination of whether to attach legal consequences to established procedural violations should entail the exercise of judgement, whereby the judge has due regard to the particular circumstances of the case, i.e. about the extent to which it should be discretionary in

---

[12] To borrow from Lord Steyn in *R v Latif; R v Shahzad* [1996] 1 WLR 104, 113.

[13] Vasiliev 2014, 171–182.

nature (which may be contrasted to an approach whereby the judicial response is more or less automatic) and, on a related note, about the extent to which it should entail a 'balancing' approach, whereby the court (also) takes into account factors that seemingly have nothing to do with that which warranted the court's attention in the first place, and which militate against a (potentially) far-reaching response thereto; and, finally, about who bears (and indeed, who should bear) responsibility for procedural violations committed in the pre-trial phase of international criminal proceedings—the state whose law enforcement authorities 'actually' committed the procedural violation or the international criminal tribunal that sought the cooperation of that state and now seeking to rely on the results of the measures executed by such authorities on their behalf.

Such questions lie at the heart of the present study, the purpose of which is to provide an in-depth examination of the judicial response at the ICTs to procedural violations committed in the pre-trial phase of the proceedings, i.e. of the law and practice of the ICTs with respect to the question of how to address such procedural violations. That examination will be both descriptive and normative in nature; descriptive in that it will entail setting out, or 'taking stock' of the law and practice of the ICTs with respect to the question of how to address the violation of procedural standards in the pre-trial phase of the proceedings, and normative in that (ultimately) it will entail arguing what the law and practice ought to be (and underlying this normative aim, it should be recalled, is the assumption that certain particularities of international criminal proceedings may warrant a different approach to the matter than at the national level). Both aspects of the examination are entailed by the central research question of this book, which is: How should judges at the international criminal tribunals respond to procedural violations committed in the pre-trial phase of the proceedings? Indeed, in order to be able to answer this question, it is necessary to know what the law and practice with respect to the question of how to address procedural violations committed in the pre-trial phase of international criminal proceedings *is*. Moreover, answering the central research question would appear to require an assessment of the 'soundness' of the existing law and practice of the ICTs in this regard. To this end, two analytical tools have been employed in this book: human rights law (in particular, that pertaining to the position of the suspect or accused), and national criminal procedure. Regarding the former tool, it is widely accepted that the ICTs are required to observe, i.e. are bound by, internationally recognized human rights norms.[14] Accordingly, such norms constitute a suitable tool by which to critically evaluate the law and practice of the ICTs with respect to the question of how to address procedural violations committed in the pre-trial phase of the proceedings.[15] Regarding the latter tool, it may be observed that 'comparative criminal procedure' is a 'widely recognized

---

[14] See most recently Zeegers 2016. See also Gradoni 2013, 74–95. The matter of applicability of human rights to the ICTs is addressed further in Chap. 2.

[15] Vasiliev et al. 2013, 27.

metric' in the discipline of international criminal procedure.[16] As has been observed, 'international criminal justice scholars' often resort to the method of comparative criminal procedure, due to the fact that 'international criminal tribunals do not have a historically predetermined and coherent legal-cultural tradition to fall back on'.[17] The ICTs, it bears emphasizing, are not bound by the procedural law and practice of domestic jurisdictions as such (although their rules of procedures and evidence have certainly been influenced by it),[18] so that reliance on this parameter should not result in 'strong value judgements on … contested issues'.[19] Put differently, the procedural law and practice of domestic jurisdictions does not constitute an *evaluative* tool as such. It does, however, provide an analytical tool by which to '[establish] whether certain procedures adopted by the tribunals 'make sense'',[20] and to assess the quality of reasoning adopted by the ICTs in this regard, in terms of cogency, coherence and consistency; correspondingly, the procedural law and practice of domestic jurisdictions (and the theoretical accounts thereof) may serve as inspiration or guidance to the ICTs in the application of their own law.

1.3 Delineation and Definitions

This is a book about international criminal procedure, which may be defined as 'the specialized body of international law that governs the conduct of criminal proceedings, including matters of both procedure and evidence, in the context of the international legal order', and which has as its 'principle objective … the effective and fair enforcement of substantive international criminal law'.[21] Logically, the focus is on the law and practice of the three international criminal tribunals: the International Criminal Tribunal for the former Yugoslavia (hereafter: ICTY) and the ICTR (together: the ad hoc Tribunals),[22] and the International Criminal Court (hereafter: ICC). As has been observed, the 'international nature of their procedural law' and the 'fact that they conduct international criminal trials' is beyond question.[23] The same cannot be said of the 'hybrid', 'mixed' or 'special' tribunals, for example, the Special Court for Sierra Leone (SCSL), the Special Panel for Serious Crimes in East Timor (SPSC), the Extraordinary Chambers in the Courts of

---

[16] Ibid., 27.

[17] Ibid., 27–28.

[18] See e.g. Mégret 2013, 70.

[19] Vasiliev et al. 2013, 28.

[20] Ibid., 28.

[21] Vasiliev et al. 2013, 13–14.

[22] The law and practice of the Mechanism for International Criminal Tribunals (MICT) has not been included in this book; the MICT's practice remains very limited, with the Arusha branch of the Mechanism only having commenced functioning on 1 July 2012, and the branch in The Hague only having commenced functioning on 1 July 2013.

[23] Vasiliev 2014, 72–73.

Cambodia (ECCC) and the Special Tribunal for Lebanon (STL); such tribunals (purport to) rely upon domestic procedural law (as well as procedural standards established at the international level) for their procedures.[24] Accordingly, their procedural law and practice has not been included in this book.

In particular, this is a book about how judges at the ICTs (should) respond to procedural violations committed in the pre-trial phase of the proceedings, i.e. about the procedural law and practice of the ICTs with respect to the question of how to address such violations. 'Procedural violation' may be defined as the non-observance of procedural standards (and 'procedural standards' denotes the standards governing international criminal procedure, i.e. the ICTs' own governing documents (their respective statutes and rules of procedure and evidence) and relevant human rights standards, pertaining to the position of the suspect or accused) and, in general, it is to be preferred over such terms as 'impropriety' or 'misconduct'; the latter terms may suggest something more than the non-observance of procedural standards, i.e. they might connote deliberate wrongdoing or bad faith, whereas this book is not limited to such instances.[25] In this book the focus is on (the judicial response to) the non-observance of procedural standards *at the pre-trial stage of international criminal proceedings*, i.e. with what may be termed 'pre-trial illegality' or 'unlawfulness'. This encompasses those procedural violations that at the national level would be described as *police* illegality or unlawfulness; at the international level, this term—'police' illegality or unlawfulness—is apt to mislead though, since the ICTs do not have their own enforcement agencies, i.e. police forces (and are reliant on state cooperation for such activities as the apprehension of persons suspected or accused of crimes falling within their jurisdiction and for the carrying out of investigations). It also encompasses the violation by the prosecution of its pre-trial obligations, of which disclosure to the defence (of the prosecution's case against the accused or of potentially exculpatory material) is a prime example.[26] As to the term 'judicial

---

[24] The SCSL Statute authorizes the judges to, in adopting rules of procedure and evidence, draw upon Sierra Leone's own criminal procedure, as laid down in the Criminal Procedure Act 1965 (Article 14(2)). As for the SPSC, s 3(1) TRCP provides that the panels shall apply 'the law of East Timor', as well as 'where appropriate, applicable treaties and recognised principles and norms of international law, including the established principles of the international law of armed conflict'. Pursuant to Article 12 of the ECCC Agreement, '[t]he procedure shall be in accordance with Cambodian law. Where Cambodian law does not deal with a particular matter, or where there is uncertainty regarding the interpretation or application of a relevant rule of Cambodian law, or where there is a question regarding the consistency of such a rule with international standards, guidance may be sought in procedural rules established at the international level.' Finally, the STL Statute authorizes the judges to, in adopting rules of procedure and evidence, draw upon the Lebanese Code of Criminal Procedure.

[25] See in this regard n 11. Nevertheless, it bears noting that this is not always how such terms are employed in the literature.

[26] The fact that, at the ICTs, disclosure is an *ongoing* obligation, meaning that, 'as new material comes into the possession of the [p]rosecution, it should be assessed as to its potentially exculpatory nature and disclosed accordingly' (*Prosecutor v Karadžić* (Decision on Prosecution's Request for Reconsideration of Trial Chamber's 11 November 2010 Decision) IT-95-5/18, T

response', it is to be preferred over such terms as 'remedy' and 'sanction', which may denote a particular rationale for responding to procedural violations; thus, 'remedy' may denote a judicial response intended to 'cure the prejudice suffered by … [a] party', whereas 'sanction' denotes a judicial response intended to 'punish a party for failing to respect the rule of law'.[27] Ascertaining the rationale that the ICTs are pursuing (and, ultimately, of course, which rationale(s) they should be pursuing) is an aim of this book, so that a more neutral term is fitting. The phrase 'attaching legal consequences to (procedural violations)' is neutral, also, and is, accordingly, also employed in this book.

As stated, this book adopts two analytical tools for the purpose of assessing the soundness of the existing law and practice of the ICTs with respect to the question of how to address pre-trial procedural violations: human rights law (in particular, that pertaining to the position of the suspect or accused), and national criminal procedure. Regarding the former, it bears emphasizing that, as international organizations, the ICTs are bound by human rights norms that form part of general international law (i.e. customary international law and general principles of law).[28] The ICTs may, moreover (and perhaps more importantly), be said to be bound by 'internationally recognised' human rights on account of their own law and practice. For example, pursuant to Article 21(3) of the ICC Statute, the ICC is required to apply and interpret the law applicable to it (as provided for in Article 21(1) and (2) of the ICC Statute) in a manner consistent with 'internationally recognized human rights'.[29] As to the latter analytical tool—national criminal procedure—two jurisdictions have been selected for the purpose of the comparative exercise: The Netherlands, and England and Wales. These jurisdictions have been selected on the basis of their instructiveness with regard to the issue under consideration in this book,[30] and on the basis that they are representative samples of the inquisitorial and

---

(Footnote 26 continued)

Ch III (10 December 2010) para 11; thus, it does not mean that the prosecution 'can delay the disclosure of such material already in its possession, or identify and disclose potentially exculpatory material on a "rolling basis"'. Ibid.), does not alter the fact such disclosure should, in principle, be effected prior to the commencement of trial, i.e. that prosecution disclosure is, essentially, a pre-trial obligation.

[27] De los Reyes 2005, 595.

[28] See e.g. Gradoni 2013, 81.

[29] While the source of obligation differs for the ad hoc Tribunals, according to Gradoni, this has 'no bearing on the status of human rights norms within the legal systems of international criminal tribunals'. See Gradoni 2013, 83.

[30] Put differently, they have been selected on the basis of their ability to 'teach us something'. See Oderkerk 2001, 313. Oderkerk states that a system can 'teach us something' when the topic under analysis has 'reached a higher level of development'. Certainly, Dutch and English courts have more experience than do the ICTs with the topic, and in both jurisdictions there is a substantial body of literature on the matter. Indeed, the law and practice of the two jurisdictions selected (and the theoretical accounts and (critical discussions) thereof in the scholarship) provide a rich source of reference material for the comparative exercise to be undertaken in this book.

adversarial models of procedure, respectively,[31] whereby it is to be noted that such models form the basis of international criminal procedure.

Finally, it bears emphasizing that this is not a book about the standards governing the pre-trial phase of international criminal proceedings as such;[32] it is a book about the *judicial response to the violation of* such standards. In other words, its purpose is not to ascertain when a standard of procedure may (or should) be considered to have been violated, such as to warrant a judicial response thereto. Most of the literature to address the question of how judges at the ICTs respond (and *should* respond) to procedural violations committed in the pre-trial phase of the proceedings does so from the perspective of a specific type of procedural violation, for example, unlawful arrest or detention, unlawfully obtained evidence, or late and non-disclosure, whereby the general features of the legal consequences that may be attached thereto are generally not addressed and whereby (logically) the focus tends to be on a particular legal consequence. This book seeks to add to the existing scholarship, by addressing the matter of how judges at the ICTs respond to the violation of procedural standards principally from the perspective of the legal consequences that may be attached thereto, i.e. their general features, including the standard to be applied for each response or consequence (and whether that standard requires, or otherwise lends itself to, a consideration of the particular circumstances of the case in determining whether to attach the legal consequence in question) and their underlying rationale(s).

1.4 Outline

This book is divided into eight chapters, including the current—introductory—chapter and the conclusion. In Chaps. 2–4, the tools employed for the purpose of assessing the soundness of the law and practice of the ICTs with respect to the question of how to address procedural violations committed in the pre-trial phase of the proceedings—human rights law and national criminal procedure—are set out, while that law and practice is itself set out in Chaps. 5 and 6. Accordingly, Chaps. 2 through 6 are descriptive in nature, not normative; indeed, the purpose of Chaps. 2–4 is not to argue what the human rights law, or what the law and practice in the domestic jurisdictions in question should be, but rather to set out what it *is* with a view to assessing the law and practice of the ICTs with respect to the question of how to address procedural violations committed in the pre-trial phase of the proceedings, as described in Chaps. 5 and 6, in light thereof. That assessment lies at the heart of Chap. 7, and it is there that arguments are made as to what the law ought to be.

---

[31] Of course, the reality is more nuanced. The Dutch procedural model, for example, is best described as 'moderately inquisitorial'.

[32] For such a (comprehensive) study, see De Meester 2014.

A brief description of the contents of each chapter is in order. Chapter 2 sets out the human rights framework with respect to the question of how to address procedural violations committed in the pre-trial phase of criminal proceedings. Several rights enshrined in the comprehensive human rights treaties are relevant to this question, in particular, the right to a fair trial (which sheds light on when it is necessary to address procedural violations committed in the investigative phase *within the criminal trial*) and the right to an effective remedy; both are examined in this chapter, as well as how they relate to one another. In addition, the human rights law with respect inter-state cooperation in criminal matters (where procedural violations have been committed in that context, that is) is considered; although inter-state cooperation in criminal matters differs from the cooperation between states and the ICTs, the former has 'greatly impacted on the latter',[33] such that the human rights law in respect thereof may be employed as an evaluative tool in respect of the ICTs' law and practice in this regard. In the examination of the right to a fair trial, consideration is given to the question of *when* unlawful conduct on the part of the police in the course of the investigation will impact on the fairness of the proceedings (i.e. trigger the protection of the right), and to the extent to which the determination of whether there has been a violation of the right depends on the particular circumstances of the case, and also whether public interest considerations may inform this determination. Finally, in one of the domestic jurisdictions examined in this book—the Netherlands—another aspect of human rights law has entered the discussion on how to address procedural violations committed by the police or the public prosecutor in the context of criminal proceedings: the positive obligations arising under the ECHR. The argument is that certain responses to such procedural violations, i.e. a stay of proceedings, the exclusion of evidence and a significant reduction of sentence, may be inconsistent with the positive obligations arising from, for example, Article 2 (which protects the right to life) and Article 3 (which prohibits torture and inhuman and degrading treatment and punishment) of the ECHR, because they prevent the court from 'punishing effectively' the person responsible. Proponents of this argument therefore read into such positive obligations a 'duty to punish'. The question of whether a duty to punish can be read into such positive obligations is also addressed in Chap. 2.

Chapters 3 and 4 set out the law and practice with respect to the question of how to address procedural violations committed in the pre-trial phase of criminal proceedings in the Netherlands, and England and Wales, respectively. They do so by means of an overview of the consequences that the judge may attach to such procedural violations. In both chapters, consideration is given to the extent to which the determination of whether to attach legal consequences to established procedural violations entails the exercise of judgement, whereby the judge has due regard to the particular circumstances of the case, i.e. the extent to which it should be discretionary in nature (which, as stated, may be contrasted to an approach whereby the judicial response is more or less automatic), and, in light of the context in which

---

[33] Zeegers 2016, 115.

the ICTs operate, also to how courts respond to procedural violations committed in an international context. The examination in Chaps. 3 and 4 is not limited to a description of the relevant law and practice, however; it also includes a description of the (possible) theoretical accounts thereof, as well as an evaluation of the law and practice in light of such accounts.

Chapters 5 and 6 set out the law and practice of the ICTs with respect to the question of how to address procedural violations committed in the pre-trial phase of the proceedings. In Chap. 5, such law and practice is set out by means of an overview of the consequences that the judge may attach to such procedural violations which (potentially) have *general* application, i.e. are applicable in respect of a wider range of pre-trial procedural violations, including their general features. Those consequences are: a stay of proceedings, the exclusion of evidence, financial compensation, sentence reduction and 'express acknowledgement' of the violation. It also compares the law and practice of the ad hoc Tribunals to that of the ICC. In Chap. 6, the law and practice of the ICTs with respect to the question of how to address procedural violations committed in the pre-trial phase of the proceedings is addressed in two specific contexts: arrest and detention, and disclosure. The purpose of this 'contextual' chapter is to complement the overview provided in Chap. 5, and thereby provide a fuller picture of the law and practice of the ICTs with respect to the question of how to address procedural violations committed in the pre-trial phase of the proceedings. As stated, this book is concerned with the judicial response to procedural violations committed in the pre-trial phase of international criminal proceedings, which covers not only what at the national level would be described as 'police illegality' or 'unlawfulness', of which unlawful arrest or detention is an obvious example,[34] but also the violation by the prosecution of its pre-trial obligations, of which disclosure to the defence is, it may be recalled, a prime example. In this chapter also, the law and practice of the ad hoc Tribunals and that of the ICC are compared.

In Chap. 7, the law and practice of the ICTs with respect to the question of how to address procedural violations committed in the pre-trial phase of the proceedings, as set out in Chaps. 5 and 6, is evaluated in light of the human rights standards set out in Chap. 2, and compared to the national law and practice (and the theoretical accounts thereof) set out in Chaps. 3 and 4, in an assessment of its soundness; compliance with human rights law, and the quality of reasoning of the ICTs in this regard, in terms of cogency, coherence and consistency. Points of concern are identified and suggestions for improvement are made, and conclusions are drawn as to the most suitable rationale(s) for responding to procedural violations committed in the pre-trial phase of international criminal proceedings, the merits of a discretionary approach to the question of how to address such violations and to the impact of certain particularities of international criminal proceedings on the determination of this question. Finally, Chap. 8 concludes with a brief summary of the foregoing chapters and the main points of analysis.

---

[34] Another example is unlawfully obtained evidence.

References

Choo AL-T (2008) Abuse of Process and Judicial Stays of Criminal Proceedings, 2nd edn. Oxford University Press, Oxford

Cogan JK (2002) International Criminal Courts and Fair Trials: Difficulties and Prospects. Yale J Int'l L 27:111 et seq.

De los Reyes C (2005) Revisiting Disclosure Obligations at the ICTR and its Implications for the Rights of the Accused. Chinese JIL 4:583 et seq.

De Meester K (2014) The Investigation Phase in International Criminal Procedure. In Search of Common Rules. DPhil thesis, University of Amsterdam

Fairlie MA (2003) Due Process Erosion: The Diminution of Live Testimony at the ICTY. Cal W Int'l L J 34:47 et seq.

Gradoni L (2013) The Human Rights Dimension of International Criminal Procedure. In: Sluiter G et al. (eds) International Criminal Procedure. Principles and Rules. Oxford University Press, Oxford, pp 74–95

Mégret F (2013) The Sources of International Criminal Procedure. In: Sluiter G et al. (eds) International Criminal Procedure. Principles and Rules. Oxford University Press, Oxford, pp 68–73

Naymark D (2008) Violations of the Rights of the Accused at International Criminal Tribunals: The Problem of Remedy. JILIR 4:1 et seq.

Oderkerk M (2001) The Importance of Context: Selecting Legal Systems in Comparative Legal Research NILR 48:293 et seq.

Pitcher KM (2013) Addressing violations of international criminal procedure. In: Abels D et al. (eds) Dialectiek van nationaal en internationaal strafrecht. Boom Juridische uitgevers, The Hague, pp 257–308

Schabas WA (2000) International Decisions: Barayagwiza v. Prosecutor (Decision, and Decision (Prosecutor's Request for Review or Reconsideration)). AJIL 94:563 et seq.

Vasiliev S (2014) International Criminal Trials. A Normative Theory. Volume 1: Nature. DPhil thesis, University of Amsterdam

Vasiliev S et al. (2013) Introduction. In: Sluiter G et al. (eds) International Criminal Procedure. Principles and Rules. Oxford University Press, Oxford, pp 1–37

Zeegers KJ (2016) International Criminal Tribunals and Human Rights Law. Adherence and Contextualization. TMC Asser Press, The Hague

Chapter 2
Human Rights Framework

Abstract This chapter sets out the human rights framework with respect to the question of how to address pre-trial procedural violations. Several rights enshrined in the comprehensive human rights treaties are relevant to this question, in particular, the right to a fair trial and the right to an effective remedy; both are examined in this chapter. In addition, the human rights law with respect to inter-state cooperation in criminal matters (where procedural violations have been committed in that context, that is) is considered. In the examination of the right to a fair trial, consideration is given to the question of when unlawful conduct on the part of the police in the course of the investigation will impact on the fairness of the proceedings, and to the extent to which the determination of whether there has been a violation of the right depends on the particular circumstances of the case and whether public interest considerations may inform this determination. Finally, in one of the domestic jurisdictions examined in this book another aspect of human rights law has entered the discussion on how to address pre-trial procedural violations: the positive obligations arising under the ECHR. The argument is that certain responses to such procedural violations may be inconsistent with the positive obligations arising from certain substantive rights protected by the ECHR, because they prevent the court from punishing effectively the person responsible. The question of whether a duty to punish can be read into such positive obligations is therefore also addressed in this chapter.

Keywords right to a fair trial · Article 6 ECHR · (evidence obtained by) torture and other ill-treatment · (evidence obtained by violation of) right of access to counsel in investigative phase · (evidence obtained by violation of right not to incriminate oneself) · (evidence obtained by violation of) right to privacy · Entrapment · Non-disclosure · use of the (unlawfully obtained) evidence · balancing · public interest considerations · right to an effective remedy · Article 13 ECHR · inter-state cooperation in criminal matters · non-enquiry

© T.M.C. ASSER PRESS and the author 2018

K. Pitcher, *Judicial Responses to Pre-Trial Procedural Violations in International Criminal Proceedings*, International Criminal Justice Series 16,
https://doi.org/10.1007/978-94-6265-219-4_2

Contents

2.1 Introduction

The purpose of this chapter is to set out the human rights framework with respect to the question of how to address procedural violations committed in the pre-trial phase of criminal proceedings, as relevant to the central research question of this book: how should judges at the ICTs respond to procedural violations committed in the pre-trial phase of the proceedings? Before setting out the human rights framework, however, it is important to address the matter of applicability of human rights to the ICTs. Much has been written on this topic[1] and while it is widely accepted that the ICTs are required to observe human rights standards pertaining to the position of the suspect or accused, the precise reason for this has been subject to extensive discussion on account of such tribunals not being states and not being party to the universal and/or regional instruments that 'provide the basic legal materials out of which human rights obligations are usually fashioned'.[2] The most convincing argument for such an obligation appears to be that the ICTs are international organizations and therefore bound by human rights standards that form part of general international law (i.e. customary international law and general principles of law).[3] Through this law, the ICTs, as international organizations, are bound by norms 'similar or identical in content' to those provided for in the human rights instruments.[4] The ICTs may, moreover (and perhaps more importantly), be said to be bound by 'internationally recognised' human rights on account of their own law and practice. For example, pursuant to Article 21(3) of the ICC Statute, the ICC is required to apply and interpret the law applicable to it (as provided for in Article 21 (1) and (2) of the ICC Statute) in a manner consistent with 'internationally

---

[1] See e.g. Zappalà 2003, 5–7; Gradoni 2006, 2013, 81–83; and most recently, Zeegers 2016.

[2] Gradoni 2013, 81.

[3] See e.g. Gradoni 2013, 81.

[4] Gradoni 2013, 81.

recognized human rights'.[5] It is reasonable to assume that a right is 'internationally recognized' when it is provided for in a universal human rights instrument such as the ICCPR. This may raise questions as to whether the standards set forth in regional instruments such as the ECHR and ACHR and, more particularly, the case law of the corresponding supervisory bodies, can be considered to be binding on the ICTs. Despite (any) such questions, these standards (and, in particular, those contained in the ECHR) have been included in this chapter on the understanding that the norms contained in such regional instruments largely reflect those contained in the ICCPR, as a consequence of which the case law of the corresponding supervisory body can reasonably be regarded as providing authoritative interpretations of the norms that bind the ICTs. Moreover, it is to be noted that the case law of the ECtHR is 'over-represented' in the case law of the ICTs, thereby confirming its value as an evaluative tool.

Several rights enshrined in the ICCPR and the ECHR are relevant to the question of how judges at the ICTs should respond to procedural violations committed in the pre-trial phase of the proceedings. The right to a fair trial, provided for in Articles 14 and 6 of the ICCPR and ECHR, respectively, is an obvious starting point for addressing the aforementioned question; examination of this provision will shed light on the question on when it is necessary to address pre-trial procedural violations *within the criminal trial*. Other rights are also relevant to the question of how judges at the ICTs should address procedural violations committed in the pre-trial phase of the proceedings, although they do not require a response within the criminal trial; they *may* be provided within that context, though. The right to an effective remedy, provided for in Articles 2(3) and 13 of the ICCPR and ECHR, respectively, is often mentioned in case law and scholarly discussions on how to address procedural violations committed in the pre-trial phase of criminal proceedings,[6] and there is the right to compensation in case of unlawful arrest or detention, provided for in Articles 9(5) and 5(5) of the ICCPR and ECHR, respectively (which is a specific manifestation of the general right to an effective remedy). Each of these provisions is addressed below.

In setting out the human rights framework with respect to the question of how to address pre-trial procedural violations, it is important to bear in mind the specific context in which the ICTs operate: they are largely dependent on state cooperation as regards the apprehension of suspects or accused and as regards the carrying out of investigations. This raises issues that do not arise, or arise to a lesser degree, in a purely domestic context. For this reason it is important to also consider the relevant human rights law on inter-state cooperation in criminal matters. Thus, domestic courts may be confronted with acts by *foreign* public authorities that are (alleged to

---

[5] While the source of obligation differs for the ad hoc Tribunals, according to Gradoni, this has 'no bearing on the status of human rights norms within the legal systems of international criminal tribunals'. See Gradoni 2013, 83.

[6] Most importantly, both of these rights have been cited in the relevant case law of the ICTs. Such case law is set out in Chaps. 5 and 6, and in order to be able to evaluate it, it is necessary to set out the relevant human rights law.

be) incompatible with the fundamental rights of the accused. In this regard it may
be observed that inter-state cooperation in criminal matters, for example, extradition
or the provision of mutual legal assistance,[7] is no longer a novelty: states
increasingly cooperate with one another in order to combat terrorism and other
serious crime. Inter-state cooperation in criminal matters is of particular relevance
to the law and practice of the ICTs. Zeegers points out that, '[a]lthough inter-state
cooperation differs from the cooperation between States and the [international
criminal tribunals], the former has greatly impacted on the latter'.[8] Accordingly, the
human rights case law on unlawfulness in the context of inter-state cooperation in
criminal matters is also set out below, after first examining that on unlawfulness in a
purely domestic context. This case law, which is scarce, concerns not only cases
brought against the state to have *requested* cooperation (the requesting, adjudicating
state), but also those brought against the state to have *been requested* to cooperate
(the requested state) and, as regards the latter category of cases, the use in extradition proceedings of evidence alleged to have been obtained unlawfully (in a third
state). While it is the case law regarding the responsibility of the requesting state
that is most (obviously) relevant to the context of the ICTs, it is also relevant to
consider the case law on the responsibility of the requested (or cooperating) state,
since such case law may also shed light, albeit indirectly, on the responsibility of
the requesting state in such cases: a finding that the requested state does not bear
responsibility for certain conduct may well be connected to the responsibility that
the requesting state bears, or should bear.[9] Because the case law discussed is not
limited to cases brought against the requesting, adjudicating state, it is not
addressed under the right to a fair trial,[10] but rather forms part of the general human
rights framework. It may be noted at the outset that inter-state cooperation in
criminal matters is widely acknowledged to be characterized by the
under-protection of the (rights of the) suspect or accused, a fact that has been
subject to much criticism in the literature.[11] Such under-protection makes a proper

---

[7] For the distinction between extradition and mutual legal assistance, and the definition of mutual
legal assistance, see Currie 2000, 144–146.

[8] Zeegers 2016, 115.

[9] The case of *Soering v UK* (App no 14038/88 (ECtHR, 7 July 1989)) is perhaps the most
(in)famous case to address the responsibility of the requested state (for a flagrant denial of justice
in the requesting state), but that case did not concern pre-trial procedural violations and as such is
not addressed here.

[10] Invoking the right to a fair trial in respect of unlawfulness in the requested state is not a
straight-forward matter: see Klip 2012, 424. Moreover, the right to a fair trial does not appear to
apply to extradition proceedings: such proceedings so not involve the determination of a criminal
charge as such. However, see *Soering v UK* App no 14038/88 (ECtHR, 7 July 1989), para 113.

[11] See generally Orie 1983; Currie 2000; Van Hoek and Luchtman 2005; Hodgson 2011; Klip
2012, 422–428; Bachmaier Winter 2013; and Vogler 2013.

understanding of the human rights law and practice on the effects of unlawful conduct on the part of *national* public authorities all the more important: surely this is the minimum protection to which an accused (who is the subject of inter-state cooperation) is entitled.

Finally, in one of the domestic systems examined in this book—the Netherlands —another aspect of human rights law has entered the discussion on how to address procedural violations committed in the pre-trial phase of criminal proceedings: the positive obligations arising under the ECHR. The argument is that certain responses to such procedural violations, i.e. a stay of proceedings, the exclusion of evidence and a significant reduction of sentence, may be inconsistent with the positive obligations arising from, for example, Article 2 (which protects the right to life) and Article 3 (which prohibits torture and inhuman and degrading treatment and punishment) of the ECHR, because they prevent the court from 'punishing effectively' the person responsible. Proponents of this argument therefore read into such positive obligations a 'duty to punish'.[12] Failure to discharge such a duty may lead to liability for the state (acting through its judicial authorities). The question of whether a duty to punish can be read into such positive obligations is therefore also addressed below, in Sect. 2.3.

On the basis of the foregoing, then, the structure of this chapter is as follows. First, the human rights case law on the question of how to address pre-trial procedural violations committed in the pre-trial phase of criminal proceedings in a purely domestic context will be set out, through the provisions identified above as being relevant to the question of how judges at the ICTs should respond to procedural violations committed in the pre-trial phase of the proceedings, and which pertain to the position of the suspect or accused.[13] Next, the human rights case law on the question of how to address pre-trial procedural violations in an international context will be set out, again through the standards that pertain to the position of the suspect or accused.[14] In Sect. 2.3, an overview will be provided of the obligations that human rights law imposes on states to address (serious) human rights violations occurring within their jurisdiction (to the extent that such obligations could bear on the question of how judges at the ICTs should respond to procedural violations committed in the pre-trial phase of the proceedings). Such standards may be said to provide protection to other persons than the suspect or accused in criminal proceedings, i.e. to the victims of crime. Finally, this chapter will conclude, in Sect. 2.4, with a brief summary of the main features of the human rights framework and the main points of analysis.

---

[12] This argument is set out in more detail in Chap. 3.

[13] See Sect. 2.2.1 through 2.2.3.

[14] See Sect. 2.2.4.

2.2 Protection of the Suspect or Accused

As stated, several rights enshrined in the ICCPR and the ECHR are relevant to the
question of how judges at the ICTs should respond to procedural violations committed in the pre-trial phase of the proceedings. The right to a fair trial, provided for
in Articles 14 and 6 of the ICCPR and ECHR, respectively, is an obvious starting
point for addressing the aforementioned question. Other rights are also relevant to
the question of how judges at the ICTs should address pre-trial procedural violations, although they do not require a response within the criminal trial; they may be
provided within that context, though. These are: the right to an effective remedy,
provided for in Articles 2(3) and 13 of the ICCPR and ECHR, respectively, and the
right to compensation in case of unlawful arrest or detention, enshrined in Articles
9(5) and 5(5) of the ICCPR and ECHR, respectively. Each of these provisions is
addressed below, starting with the right to a fair trial.

2.2.1 Right to a Fair Trial

2.2.1.1 Introduction

Articles 14 of the ICCPR and 6 of the ECHR provide for the right to a fair trial and
afford the individual a number of procedural guarantees for the adjudication of
disputes which involve 'the determination of his civil rights and obligations or of
any criminal charge against him'.[15] In determining a criminal charge, the domestic
court may be confronted with acts by public authorities, i.e. the police or prosecutor, that are (alleged to be) incompatible with declared standards of conduct,
including the fundamental rights of the accused. In the first place, this may occur
when the prosecutor seeks to adduce evidence obtained unlawfully by the police in
the course of a criminal investigation. In this regard it should be noted that the
domestic court's obligation to do that which is necessary to protect the fairness of
the proceedings may require it *not* to use evidence obtained unlawfully, whether the
evidence concerned consists of a single item or the case as a whole.[16] Although (as
will be seen below) Article 6 of the ECHR itself does not prescribe rules on the
admissibility of evidence, such rules (which entail what the domestic court is
required to do in order to avoid liability under Article 6) may nonetheless be
inferred from the interpretation by the European Court of Human Rights (hereafter:

---

[15] For the distinction between substantive and procedural rights, see Strasser 1988, 595–604.

[16] The consequence of the non-use of the case as a whole is more akin to the national criminal
procedure remedy of a stay of proceedings, whereby the proceedings are brought to a halt, than to
that of exclusion of evidence. See n 171 and accompanying text.

ECtHR) of Article 6.[17] Nor does Article 14 of the ICCPR prescribe rules on the admissibility of evidence, but while the United Nations Human Rights Committee (hereafter: HRC) has stated that '[i]n order to safeguard the rights of the accused under paras 1 and 3 of Article 14, judges should have authority to consider any allegations made of violations of the rights of the accused during any stage of the prosecution',[18] which, according to Safferling, 'may imply that the court is permitted or even obliged to exclude evidence that was obtained improperly',[19] no such rules can be inferred from its case law *on Article 14*. As such, the remainder of this section (on the right to a fair trial) will focus on the ECHR and corresponding case law of the ECtHR. Even where no evidence is obtained (let alone adduced), courts may be called upon to examine (what is alleged to constitute) unlawful conduct on the part of public authorities, including that which is inconsistent with fundamental rights, on account of its potential impact on the fairness of the proceedings. This may concern police *or* prosecutorial unlawfulness. The question may arise as to whether, in order for unlawful conduct on the part of the police in the conduct of the investigation to impact on the fairness of the proceedings, any evidence obtained actually needs to be used in subsequent trial proceedings.[20] This question is addressed below.[21]

The structure of this subsection is as follows. First, some general observations will be made about the manner in which the ECtHR has approached the determination of Article 6 of the ECHR where it was argued (by the applicant) that unlawful conduct on the part of the police or public prosecutor impacted on the fairness of the proceedings.[22] This is in order to assist the reader in understanding the case law of the ECtHR to be set out below on the determination of Article 6 of the ECHR where it was argued that unlawful conduct on the part of the police or public prosecutor impacted on the fairness of the proceedings, according to specific categories of conduct.[23] After setting out such case law, this subsection will address the question raised above of whether, in order for unlawful conduct on the part of

---

[17] At the supranational level the relevant institution may be called on to examine the acts (of obtaining evidence) themselves, as well as the use by domestic courts of evidence obtained by such acts. Thus, on the one hand the ECtHR's case law formulates standards on how public authorities may investigate crime and obtain evidence, and on the other, it formulates standards on how domestic courts may fairly use evidence. See, for a similar analysis, Ölçer 2008, 36–37.

[18] HRC, 'General Comment no 13. Article 14 (Administration of justice)' in Compilation of General Comments and General Recommendations Adopted by Human Rights Treaty Bodies (1994) UN Doc HRI/GEN/1/Rev.1, 14, para 15.

[19] Safferling 2003, 293.

[20] Regardless of the answer to this question, it is a requirement at the supranational level that in order to be able to claim 'victim status' in connection with Article 6, the proceedings must not have ended in an acquittal or have been discontinued, i.e. they must have ended in a conviction. See e.g. *Osmanov and Husseinov v Bulgaria* App no 54178/00 (ECtHR, Decision of 4 September 2003), 4–5.

[21] See Sect. 2.2.1.4.

[22] See Sect. 2.2.1.2.

[23] See Sect. 2.2.1.3.

the police in the course of the investigation to impact on the fairness of the proceedings, any evidence obtained thereby actually needs to be used in subsequent trial proceedings.[24] Following this, the extent to which the ECtHR can be said to endorse a discretionary or 'balancing' approach to the question of how to address procedural violations committed in the pre-trial phase of criminal proceedings will be addressed.[25] In Chap. 1, it may be recalled, the question of the extent to which the determination of whether to attach legal consequences to established procedural violations should entail the exercise of judgement, whereby the judge has due regard to the particular circumstances of the case, i.e. the extent to which it should be *discretionary* in nature (which may be contrasted to an approach whereby the judicial response is more or less automatic) and, on a related note, that of the extent to which it should entail a 'balancing' approach, whereby the court (also) takes into account factors that seemingly have nothing to do with that which warranted the court's attention in the first place, and which militate against a (potentially) far-reaching response thereto, were said to lie at the heart of the present study.

2.2.1.2 Fair Trial Analysis

On account of its status and internal structure, Article 6 of the ECHR has proven a challenging provision to determine when alleged to have been violated.[26] Regarding its status, it may be observed that Article 6 is not subject to the qualifications that the rights in Articles 8–11 of the ECHR are, which allow a certain degree of interference with such rights. At the same time, however, it does not fall within the category of non-derogable rights provided for in Article 15 of the ECHR. Article 6 is, therefore, an unqualified but derogable right. According to Goss, this status 'raises a number of normative questions: should the Article 6 guarantee(s) be interpreted as 'absolute', with no infringement thereof being capable of justification? Should some infringements of Article 6 be justifiable? If so, what standard applies, and should it be similar to the standards used for the qualified rights?'[27] Regarding its internal structure it may be observed that Article 6 is structurally complex. It consists of three paragraphs, whereby it is unclear how such paragraphs relate to one another: are references to 'fair trial rights' or 'the right to a fair trial' 'shorthand for all of the various rights and guarantees, express and implied, that may be found in Article 6(1), Article 6(2), and the provisions of Article 6(3)', or do Article 6(2) and Article 6(3) 'merely [provide] definitional assistance and elaboration on the meaning of Article 6(1)'?[28] According to Goss, in attempting to solve 'the puzzle of Article 6', i.e. the questions arising from its status and internal

---

[24] See Sect. 2.2.1.4.

[25] See Sect. 2.2.1.5.

[26] Article 14 ICCPR has a similar status and internal structure.

[27] Goss 2014, 118 (footnote in original omitted).

[28] Ibid., 118–119.

structure, the ECtHR has employed a number of different 'analytical tools', including the 'proceedings as a whole' test (whereby the determination of Article 6 is dependent on whether the proceedings as a whole were fair), 'counter-balancing' (whereby the question is whether a potential violation has been offset by other (counter-balancing) measures in the same proceedings), the 'never fair' method (whereby some infringements of Article 6 rights and some rights violations render a trial irretrievably unfair), the 'sole or decisive' (evidence) test, and balancing and proportionality analysis (whereby restrictions on Article 6 rights may be justified on account of public interest considerations).[29] As will be seen below, such tools have also been applied in cases in which Article 6 was alleged to have been violated on account of unlawful conduct on the part of police or prosecutorial authorities in the context of criminal proceedings. However, it may be observed at the outset that, in the context of unlawfully obtained evidence, the ECtHR has frequently adopted (or purported to adopt) a 'holistic' approach, whereby the determination of Article 6 is dependent on whether the proceedings as a whole were fair. Such an approach sits well with the notion that '[w]hile the right to a fair trial under Article 6 is an unqualified right, what constitutes a fair trial cannot be the subject of a single unvarying rule but must depend on the circumstances of the particular case'.[30] The adoption of a holistic approach in this context can moreover be explained by reference to the cautious approach traditionally adopted by the Court towards the assessment of evidence. One of the first cases to express the margin of appreciation with respect to the assessment of evidence was *Schenk v Switzerland*, in which the ECtHR held that while Article 6 of the ECHR guarantees the right to a fair trial, 'it does not lay down any rules on the admissibility of evidence as such, which is therefore primarily a matter for regulation under national law'.[31] Accordingly, it could '[not] exclude as a matter of principle and in the abstract that unlawfully obtained evidence of the present kind may be admissible' and only had to ascertain whether the Applicant's trial *as a whole* was fair.[32] The ECtHR reiterated this position in *Khan v United Kingdom*:

> It is not the role of the Court to determine, *as a matter of principle, whether particular types of evidence – for example, unlawfully obtained evidence – may be admissible* ... The question which must be answered is whether the proceedings as a whole, including the way in which the evidence was obtained, were fair. This involves an examination of the "unlawfulness" in question and, where violation of another Convention right is concerned, the nature of the violation found.[33]

---

[29] Ibid., 124.

[30] *O'Halloran and Francis v UK* App nos 15809/02 and 25624/02 (ECtHR, 29 June 2007), para 53.

[31] *Schenk v Switzerland* App no 10862/84 (ECtHR, 12 July 1988), para 46.

[32] Ibid., para 46 (emphasis added).

[33] *Khan v UK* App no 35394/97 (ECtHR, 12 May 2000), para 34 (emphasis added).

Initially, therefore, the ECtHR refused to lay down a *general principle* with respect to the admissibility of unlawfully obtained evidence, by '[disavowing] any authority to determine, as a matter of principle, whether particular types of evidence —for example, unlawfully obtained evidence—may be admissible',[34] only ruling on the question of whether in the particular circumstances of the case the use of such evidence was contrary to the right to a fair trial. In doing so, the ECtHR adopted a 'holistic' approach, whereby the question of whether the proceedings have been fair requires the examination of a number of factors, including 'the unlawfulness in question and, where the violation of another Convention right is concerned, the nature of the violation found', 'whether the rights of the defence have been respected' and, in particular, 'whether the applicant was given an opportunity to challenge the authenticity of the evidence and to oppose its use' (i.e. whether sufficient procedural safeguards were in place), 'the quality of the evidence', i.e. whether the circumstances in which it was obtained 'casts doubt on its reliability or accuracy' and whether it required corroboration, 'whether the evidence in question was or was not decisive for the outcome of the proceedings', and 'the weight of the public interest in the investigation and punishment of the particular offence in issue'.[35] While the ECtHR has continued to take a holistic approach, repeatedly referring to its judgment in *Schenk* that the admissibility of evidence is primarily a matter for regulation under national law and that its role is to determine whether the proceedings, as a whole, have been fair, subsequent decisions have 'sometimes … been more overtly interventionist' than previous ones (in which the ECtHR treated issues of admissibility as matters for domestic courts),[36] in that the ECtHR has held (explicitly) that the use of certain types of unlawfully obtained evidence automatically, or nearly so, renders the proceedings unfair, i.e. regardless of the aforementioned factors. Thus, in a number of decisions it appears to have adopted the 'never fair' method.[37] These decisions are discussed in the following section.

---

[34] Jackson 2012, 136.

[35] This last factor is discussed below, in Sect. 2.2.1.5.

[36] Jackson 2012, 136.

That the ECtHR is not entirely deferential to states with respect to the assessment of evidence is, by now, widely accepted in the literature, although accounts of the ECtHR's approach in this regard range from the (cautious) observation that despite Article 6(1) ECHR not requiring 'that any particular rules of evidence are followed in national courts in either criminal or non-criminal cases', the ECtHR 'has set certain parameters within which a state must operate' (Harris et al. 2014, 418; see also Ashworth 2012, 159–160), to referring to it as 'interventionist' and 'active', and, in certain circumstances, as providing for an exclusionary rule (See e.g. Ölçer 2013, 372; and Ambos 2009, 383; for other 'less cautious' accounts, see Chedraui 2010, 206–208; Goss 2014, 60; and Ashworth 2014, 336). A number of authors have pointed to the language of the ECtHR, that it is primarily, but not solely a matter of national law, as support for the proposition that the ECtHR is not entirely deferential.

[37] Goss 2014, 161–163.

2.2.1.3 Types of (Unlawful) Conduct

The purpose of this subsection is to set out the ECtHR's case law on the determination of Article 6 of the ECHR where it was argued (by the applicant) that unlawful conduct on the part of the police or public prosecutor impacted on the fairness of the proceedings. Such case law will be set out according to the following categories of conduct on the part of such authorities (some of which are, in and of themselves, unlawful, while others are not): torture or other ill-treatment; denial of access to counsel in the investigative phase; coercion, compulsion and deception in the context of 'questioning'; covert surveillance or interception of communication; entrapment; and non-disclosure.

Torture or Other Ill-Treatment

In the first place, the ECtHR has held that 'the use of evidence obtained in violation of Article 3 [of the ECHR] in criminal proceedings raises serious issues as to the fairness of such proceedings'. More specifically in relation to torture within the meaning of Article 3 of the ECHR, it has held that:

> [I]ncriminating evidence – whether in the form of a confession or real evidence – obtained as a result of acts of violence or brutality or other forms of treatment which can be characterised as torture – should *never* be relied on as proof of the victim's guilt, irrespective of its probative value. Any other conclusion would only serve to legitimate indirectly the sort of morally reprehensible conduct which the authors of Article 3 of the Convention sought to proscribe or, as it was so well put in the United States Supreme Court's judgment in the *Rochin* case [...], to "afford brutality the cloak of law".[38]

The reference to the 'use of evidence ... in criminal proceedings' and the phrase 'should never be relied on as proof of the victim's guilt', which appears in the ECtHR's assessment of the alleged violation of Article 6, imply that only where evidence obtained by torture is actually *used* by the domestic court, that is, relied on as proof of the accused's guilt or in the determination of punishment,[39] will the ECtHR find a violation of Article 6 of the ECHR.[40] Once it has been used, however, the probative value, i.e. weight, of such evidence, whether confessional or

---

[38] *Jalloh v Germany* App no 54810/00 (ECtHR, 11 July 2006), para 105 (emphasis added), as referred to in *Harutyunyan v Armenia* App no 36549/03 (ECtHR, 28 June 2007), para 63; *Leviņţa v Moldova* App no 17332/03 (ECtHR, 16 December 2008), para 100; *Baran and Hun v Turkey* App no 30685/05 (ECtHR, 20 May 2010), para 69; *Gäfgen v Germany* App no 22978/05 (ECtHR, 1 June 2010), paras 166 and 167; and *Othman (Abu Qatada) v UK* App no 8139/09 (ECtHR, 17 January 2012), para 264.

[39] *Gäfgen v Germany* App no 22978/05 (ECtHR, 1 June 2010), paras 179, 180 and 186.

[40] In setting out the Court's general principles with respect to unlawfully obtained evidence, the ECtHR in *Gäfgen v Germany* (App no 22978/05 (ECtHR, 1 June 2010)), refers to 'the admission of statements ... as evidence to establish the relevant facts in criminal proceedings' (para 166), and 'the use at the trial of real evidence' (para 167). Also telling in this regard is the ECtHR's observation that 'an issue arises under Article 6 in respect of evidence obtained as a result of

real,[41] is irrelevant.[42] Nor is it relevant whether, for example, sufficient procedural safeguards were in place, or whether the evidence was decisive.[43] Moreover, regarding the use of confessional evidence, i.e. statements, obtained as a result of torture, the foregoing applies regardless of who made the statement, i.e. the defendant him- or herself, or a third party, such as a witness or co-defendant.[44] For evidence obtained as a result of torture, therefore, the ECtHR, through its interpretation of Article 6, prescribes an absolute exclusionary rule.[45] Such a rule is also

---

(Footnote 40 continued)

methods in violation of Article 3 only if such evidence was not excluded from use at the applicant's trial' (para 172).

In addition to formulating this requirement in its general principles, the ECtHR has in numerous cases found the *use* of evidence obtained by violation of Article 3 ECHR to be contrary to Article 6 ECHR. See e.g. *Jalloh v Germany* App no 54810/00 (ECtHR, 11 July 2006), paras 108 and 122; *Harutyunyan v Armenia* App no 36549/03 (ECtHR, 28 June 2007), para 66; *Levinţa v Moldova* App no 17332/03 (ECtHR, 16 December 2008), para 105; *Gladyshev v Russia* App no 2807/04 (ECtHR, 30 July 2009), para 79; *Baran and Hun v Turkey* App no 30685/05 (ECtHR, 20 May 2010), para 72; *Stanimirović v Serbia* App no 26088/06 (ECtHR, 18 October 2011), para 52; *Hajnal v Serbia* App no 36937/06 (ECtHR, 19 June 2012), para 115; *Kaçiu and Kotorri v Albania* App nos 33192/07 and 33194/07 (ECtHR, 25 June 2013), paras 118 and 129; and *Cēsnieks v Latvia* App no 9278/06 (ECtHR, 11 February 2014), para 69.

Finally, the existence of such a requirement is widely recognised in the literature. See e.g. Jackson and Summers 2012, 163; and Chedraui 2010, 212.

[41] See *Jalloh v Germany* App no 54810/00 (ECtHR, 11 July 2006), para 105; *Baran and Hun v Turkey* App no 30685/05 (ECtHR, 20 May 2010), para 69; and *Gäfgen v Germany* App no 22978/05 (ECtHR, 1 June 2010), paras 166 and 167.

[42] See e.g. *Jalloh v Germany* App no 54810/00 (ECtHR, 11 July 2006), para 105; *Harutyunyan v Armenia* App no 36549/03 (ECtHR, 28 June 2007), para 63; *Baran and Hun v Turkey* App no 30685/05 (ECtHR, 20 May 2010), para 69; *Gäfgen v Germany* App no 22978/05 (ECtHR, 1 June 2010), paras 166–167; and *Stanimirović v Serbia* App no 26088/06 (ECtHR, 18 October 2011), para 51.

[43] See e.g. *Levinţa v Moldova* App no 17332/03 (ECtHR, 16 December 2008), paras 100 (referring to *Harutyunyan v Armenia* App no 36549/03 (ECtHR, 28 June 2007), paras 63 and 66) and 105; *Gäfgen v Germany* App no 22978/05 (ECtHR, 1 June 2010), para 166; and *Stanimirović v Serbia* App no 26088/06 (ECtHR, 18 October 2011), para 51.

[44] *Kaçiu and Kotorri v Albania* App nos 33192/07 and 33194/07 (ECtHR, 25 June 2013), para 128, referring to *Harutyunyan v Armenia* (App no 36549/03 (ECtHR, 28 June 2007), where the ECtHR found that the use of witnesses' statements obtained as a result of torture, as well as the Applicant's own statements obtained by such means, rendered the trial against the Applicant unfair (paras 64–66), and to *Othman (Abu Qatada) v UK* (App no 8139/09 (ECtHR, 17 January 2012)), where the ECtHR ruled that the admission of co-defendants' statements, which had been obtained by torture and incriminated the Applicant, would constitute a breach of Article 6 ECHR in the event of the applicant's deportation to, and trial in Jordan (paras 285 and 287). See also *El Haski v Belgium* App no 649/08 (ECtHR, 25 September 2012), para 85.

[45] This position was confirmed in *Harutyunyan v Armenia* App no 36549/03 (ECtHR, 28 June 2007), paras 63 and 66; *Levinţa v Moldova* App no 17332/03 (ECtHR, 16 December 2008), paras 99–100 and 105; *Tangiyev v Russia* App no 27610/05 (ECtHR, 11 December 2012), paras 73–76; and *Kaçiu and Kotorri v Albania* App nos 33192/07 and 33194/07 (ECtHR, 25 June 2013), para 118. In all of these cases, the use of evidence obtained by torture was found to violate Article 6 ECHR.

prescribed by Article 15 of the UNCAT[46] and the HRC.[47] The ECtHR has referred to various rationales for excluding such evidence. According to the Court, evidence obtained as a result of torture 'should never be relied on as proof of the victim's guilt, irrespective of its probative value', and admitting such evidence 'would only serve to legitimate indirectly the sort of morally reprehensible conduct which the authors of Article 3 of the Convention sought to proscribe'.[48] Other 'compelling reasons for the exclusion of torture evidence' include unreliability, unfairness, offensiveness 'to ordinary standards of humanity and decency', incompatibility 'with the principles which should animate a tribunal seeking to administer justice'[49] and the need 'to protect the integrity of the trial process [and court] and, ultimately, the rule of law itself'.[50]

While it is fair to say that the ECtHR prescribes an absolute exclusionary rule in respect of evidence obtained by torture (in the sense that, once it is established that evidence obtained by torture was used at trial, a finding that Article 6(1) of the ECHR is inevitable, regardless of, for example, its probative value, whether its use could be challenged and how it was used), there may be room for it to conclude that the trial was fair notwithstanding the use of such evidence, on the basis of the extent to which the torture can be considered to have been causal for the evidence. In *Harutyunyan v Armenia*, the Applicant alleged that his confessions, and those of two witnesses, were used at his trial, which had been obtained by torture. The Government accepted that the Applicant and two witnesses had been subjected to torture. In response to the Government's attempt to justify the use of the confessions by arguing that the Applicant had confessed to the investigator and not to the police officers who had tortured him, i.e. that the statement had not been obtained as a (direct) result of the mistreatment, the ECtHR opined that:

> ... where there is compelling evidence that a person has been subjected to ill-treatment, including physical violence and threats, the fact that this person confessed – or confirmed a coerced confession in his later statements – to an authority other than the one responsible

---

[46] It certainly excludes *statements* obtained by torture, and it may also exclude real evidence obtained as a result of torture. See Pattenden 2006, 9–10.

[47] HRC 'General Comment no 32. Article 14: Right to equality before courts and tribunals and to a fair trial' (23 August 2007) UN Doc CCPR/C/GC/32, para 6.

[48] *Jalloh v Germany* App no 54810/00 (ECtHR, 11 July 2006), para 105. According to Jackson and Summers, this statement demonstrates that the use of evidence obtained as a result of torture 'is prohibited, not necessarily because the evidence is in itself unreliable, although this may well be a factor, but principally because the use of such evidence is seen as fatally undermining the fairness of the proceedings and the legitimacy of the criminal justice system'. In their view, therefore, the ECtHR's justification for the exclusion of evidence obtained as a result of torture is primarily non-epistemic in nature. See Jackson and Summers 2012, 162.

[49] *Othman (Abu Qatada) v UK* App no 8139/09 (ECtHR, 17 January 2012), para 264, referring to Lord Bingham's opinion in *A v Secretary of State for the Home Department (No 2)* [2005] 3 WLR 1249 [52].

[50] *Othman (Abu Qatada) v UK* App no 8139/09 (ECtHR, 17 January 2012), para 264. Thus, the ECtHR provides both epistemic and non-epistemic justifications for the exclusion of evidence obtained as a result of torture.

for this ill-treatment should not *automatically* lead to the conclusion that such confession or later statements were not made *as a consequence of* the ill-treatment and the fear that a person may experience thereafter.[51]

While in the particular circumstances of the case the fact that the Applicant had confessed to a different authority than the one responsible for his mistreatment did *not* lead to the conclusion that the statements were *not* made as a consequence of the mistreatment,[52] this statement suggests that where a confession is made to a different authority than the one responsible for the mistreatment (amounting to torture), there is room to conclude that it was not made as a result of the mistreatment. In other words, the absolute exclusionary rule referred to above only appears to apply to evidence obtained as a *direct* result of torture.

As to the use of incriminating evidence obtained by methods falling short of torture but nonetheless falling within the ambit of Article 3, while the use of confessional evidence, i.e. statements, obtained as a result of methods amounting to 'inhuman and degrading treatment' automatically renders the trial unfair, regardless of the probative value of such evidence and *how* it was used,[53] this rule appears to be subject to the same qualification as above, i.e. it applies only to (confessional) evidence obtained as a direct result of such treatment.[54] Thus, in *Gäfgen v Germany*

---

[51] *Harutyunyan v Armenia* App no 36549/03 (ECtHR, 28 June 2007), para 65 (emphasis added).

[52] Ibid., para 65.

[53] Thus, whether obtained as a (direct) result of torture of inhuman and degrading treatment within the meaning of Article 3 ECHR, the use of *confessional* evidence in criminal proceedings automatically renders the trial unfair. See *Gäfgen v Germany* App no 22978/05 (ECtHR, 1 June 2010), paras 166 and 173; *Stanimirović v Serbia* App no 26088/06 (ECtHR, 18 October 2011), para 51; *Hajnal v Serbia* App no 36937/06 (ECtHR, 19 June 2012), paras 112–115; *Tangiyev v Russia* App no 27610/05 (ECtHR, 11 December 2012), para 73; *Kaçiu and Kotorri v Albania* App nos 33192/07 and 33194/07 (ECtHR, 25 June 2013), paras 117 and 124; *Nasakin v Russia* App no 22735/05 (ECtHR, 18 July 2013), paras 97–100; *Ryabtsev v Russia* App no 13642/06 (ECtHR, 14 November 2013), paras 91–94; and *Cēsnieks v Latvia* App no 9278/06 (ECtHR, 11 February 2014), paras 65–66 and 69.

See, however, *Haci Özen v Turkey* App no 46286/99 (ECtHR, 12 April 2007), paras 102–105 and *Gladyshev v Russia* (App no 2807/04 (ECtHR, 30 July 2009), para 79), in which the use of statements obtained as a (seemingly, direct) result of inhuman and degrading treatment did not automatically render the trial (as a whole) unfair. It is worth noting that the first two cases were decided before the Grand Chamber issued its judgment in *Gäfgen*, i.e. before the Grand Chamber clarified its findings in *Jalloh* regarding the use of evidence obtained as a result of inhuman and degrading treatment. Admittedly, in *Haci Özen*, the ECtHR does not say whether the statements were obtained as a direct result of the ill-treatment. In *Gladyshev*, however, it does appear to have been of the view that the confession evidence in question was obtained as a result of the ill-treatment (para 79).

As with evidence obtained by torture, in order for evidence obtained by inhuman and degrading treatment (within the meaning of Article 3 ECHR), whether confessional or real, to impact on the fairness of the proceedings, the evidence has to have been *used*, that is, relied on as proof of the accused's guilt or in the determination of punishment. See n 39–40 and accompanying text.

[54] The ECtHR's statement in *Harutyunyan v Armenia* (see n 51 and accompanying text) does not appear to be limited to torture; it simply refers to 'physical violence and threats'.

the Grand Chamber appears to have endorsed the approach in *Harutyunyan v Armenia*. In the former case, the Applicant confirmed a confession obtained by methods constituting inhuman treatment within the meaning of Article 3 of the ECHR, to a different authority (in this case, the domestic court) than the one responsible for the mistreatment (the police). In such cases, there is room to conclude that the confession was not made as a result of the mistreatment.[55] Indeed, having had regard to the particular facts and circumstances of the case, the Grand Chamber concluded that it was not satisfied that 'the breach of Article 3 in the investigation proceedings had a bearing on the applicant's confession at the trial'.[56] In *Alchagin v Russia*, while the authority to which the Applicant confessed appears to have been the same as the one that had previously mistreated him (the police), the ECtHR's acceptance of the Government's submission that, 'at the moment when the applicant made his confession statement, he enjoyed the benefit of legal advice by defence counsel of his own choice'[57] and, presumably, though not explicitly, of the Government's submission that the Applicant, therefore, could not have been mistreated at the time of making his statement,[58] suggests the lack of a direct link between the mistreatment (which, according to the ECtHR, amounted to inhuman and degrading treatment within the meaning of Article 3 of the ECHR)[59] and the confession, along the lines of the approach in *Harutyunyan v Armenia*.[60] In *Stanimirović v Serbia*, the link between the ill-treatment in police custody and the confessions to the investigating judge also appears to have been indirect, such that the use of such confessions did not automatically render the trial as a whole unfair.[61] Where confessional evidence obtained as an *indirect* result of inhumane

---

[55] This line of reasoning is reminiscent of the US doctrine of attenuation, which recognises that the connection between the (impugned) evidence and the (unlawful) conduct of the investigative authorities may be so 'tenuous' that the exclusion of the evidence is not warranted.

[56] *Gäfgen v Germany* App no 22978/05 (ECtHR, 1 June 2010), paras 181–184. By this point in the judgment, the connection between the prohibited methods of investigation and the Applicant's conviction and sentence was already 'strained', the Grand Chamber having found that the impugned real evidence, i.e. the real evidence obtained as a direct result of the confession extracted by inhuman and degrading treatment, had not been used by the domestic court to convict the Applicant, 'but only to test the veracity of his confession'. See paras 179–180.

[57] *Alchagin v Russia* App no 20212/05 (ECtHR, 17 January 2012), para 70.

[58] Ibid., para 60.

[59] Ibid., para 57.

[60] The likeness of the findings in *Alchagin v Russia* to the findings of the Grand Chamber in *Gäfgen v Germany* appears to have been overlooked in the subsequent case of *Kaçiu and Kotorri v Albania* App nos 33192/07 and 33194/07 (ECtHR, 25 June 2013), in which *Alchagin v Russia* was branded 'an exception' to the case law on the use of confessional evidence obtained as a result of a breach of Article 3 ECHR (para 125). If such case law is understood as providing for an absolute exclusionary in respect of confessional evidence obtained as a direct result of torture, *Alchagin* is arguably in line with such case law. In *Cēsnieks v Latvia* App no 9278/06 (ECtHR, 11 February 2014), the ECtHR appears to have taken a similarly simplistic view of *Alchagin* (para 68), referring to it as though an exception that did not apply in the circumstances.

[61] *Stanimirović v Serbia* App no 26088/06 (ECtHR, 18 October 2011), para 52. See n 69 and accompanying text.

and degrading treatment is used, the observance of relevant safeguards is important to offset any presumption of unfairness caused by the use of such evidence (it is reasonable to assume that the same goes for confessional evidence obtained as an indirect result of torture). Thus, the Grand Chamber's conclusion in *Gäfgen* that the breach of Article 3 in the pre-trial phase had had no bearing on the Applicant's confession at the trial (and, by extension, that the use of that confession did not render the trial unfair) was based on the fact that, prior to this confession, 'the applicant had been instructed about his right to remain silent and about the fact that none of the statements he had previously made on the charges could be used as evidence against him',[62] that the Applicant, 'who was represented by defence counsel, stressed in his statements [at trial] that he was confessing freely out of remorse and in order to take responsibility for his offence ...',[63] and that the Applicant's confession at trial 'referred to many additional elements which were unrelated to what could have been proven by the impugned real evidence [obtained as a direct result of the initial pre-trial statement obtained in violation of Article 3 of the ECHR]'.[64] Similarly, in *Alchagin*, the ECtHR based its conclusion that the use of a confession obtained as an indirect result of the inhumane and degrading treatment did not render the trial 'wholly' unfair on the fact that 'at the moment when the applicant made his confession statement, he enjoyed the benefit of legal advice by defence counsel of his own choice',[65] 'that the ... statement had been cumulative to other extensive evidence against the applicant, including his own statement made during the jury trial',[66] and that 'the applicant was duly represented throughout the proceedings and was, therefore, afforded ample opportunity, which he took, to challenge before the domestic court the admissibility and the use of evidence obtained under pressure'.[67] In *Stanimirović* the ECtHR noted that, in addition to the fact that the Applicant's confession before the investigating judge was indeed a result of his ill-treatment by the police, the Applicant had not been 'able to consult properly (notably, in private) with his lawyer prior to making the confession before the investigating judge ... and made [further] statements before the investigating judge ... in the absence of his lawyer'.[68] According to the ECtHR, '[i]n such circumstances, ... regardless of the impact those statements had on the outcome of the criminal trial, their use rendered the trial as a whole unfair.'[69]

---

[62] *Gäfgen v Germany* App no 22978/05 (ECtHR, 1 June 2010), para 182.

[63] Ibid., para 183.

[64] Ibid., para 184.

[65] *Alchagin v Russia* App no 20212/05 (ECtHR, 17 January 2012), para 70.

[66] Ibid., para 71.

[67] Ibid., para 72.

[68] *Stanimirović v Serbia* App no 26088/06 (ECtHR, 18 October 2011), para 52.

[69] Ibid., para 52 (emphasis added). While the ECtHR's statement that 'regardless of the impact those statements had on the outcome of the criminal trial, their use rendered the trial as a whole unfair' implies that the use of the statements automatically rendered the trial unfair in that case, the ECtHR also attached importance to other factors, i.e. the lack of legal assistance at particular points. It was only '[i]n these circumstances', i.e. in view of the fact that the Applicant had not had

Regarding the use of *real* evidence obtained as a result of inhuman and degrading treatment, the ECtHR has held that the use of such evidence may require a different approach to that to the use evidence obtained by torture. In *Gäfgen v Germany* the ECtHR held that '[i]n its [earlier] *Jalloh* judgment, the Court left open the question whether the use of *real* evidence obtained by an act classified as inhuman and degrading treatment, but falling short of torture, always rendered a trial unfair ...'[70] However, in the latter case, the ECtHR did not explicitly refer to real evidence: 'It cannot be excluded that on the facts of a particular case the use of evidence ... will render the trial against the victim unfair, irrespective of the seriousness of the offence allegedly committed, the weight attached to the evidence and the opportunities which the victim had to challenge its admission and use at his trial.'[71] Nevertheless, in *Gäfgen* and in subsequent cases, the ECtHR (has) confirmed that the Grand Chamber's findings in *Jalloh* pertain to (the use of) real evidence.[72] Such findings imply that the use of real evidence obtained by ill-treatment not amounting to torture will not automatically render the trial unfair.[73] As with the use of confessional evidence that has been obtained as an indirect result of inhuman and degrading treatment, the observance of relevant safeguards is important to offset any risk to fairness presented by the use of real evidence obtained as a result of inhuman and degrading treatment. It follows that a failure to observe relevant safeguards may result in a finding that Article 6 of the ECHR has been violated. Thus, in *Jalloh*, the Grand Chamber's finding that the use in evidence of drugs obtained by the forcible administration of emetics to the Applicant, which constituted inhuman and degrading treatment within the meaning of Article 3 of the ECHR, rendered his trial as a whole unfair[74] was based on the fact that 'the drugs ... were the decisive element in securing the applicant's conviction',[75] and that 'any discretion on the part of the national courts to exclude that evidence [i.e. the drugs] could not come into play as they considered the administration of emetics

---

(Footnote 69 continued)

(proper) legal assistance, that their use rendered the trial as a whole unfair, regardless of their impact on the outcome of the trial. As such, the statements were not subject to automatic exclusion on account of their use alone.

[70] *Gäfgen v Germany* App no 22978/05 (ECtHR, 1 June 2010), para 167 (emphasis added), referring to *Jalloh v Germany* App no 54810/00 (ECtHR, 11 July 2006), paras 106–107.

[71] *Jalloh v Germany* App no 54810/00 (ECtHR, 11 July 2006), para 106.

[72] See e.g. *El Haski v Belgium* App no 649/08 (ECtHR, 25 September 2012), para 85. In addition, the ECtHR has consistently held that the use of *confessional* evidence obtained as a result of inhuman and degrading treatment automatically renders the trial unfair. See n 53 and accompanying text.

[73] See also *Gäfgen v Germany* App no 22978/05 (ECtHR, 1 June 2010), para 178.

[74] *Jalloh v Germany* App no 54810/00 (ECtHR, 11 July 2006), paras 82–83 and 108.

[75] According to Jackson and Summers, '[t]his implies that it may be permissible for the authorities to use evidence obtained by inhuman and degrading treatment providing that it is not decisive to the conviction'. See Jackson and Summers 2012, 164.

to be authorised by domestic law [thereby rendering the ability of the applicant to challenge the use of the drugs meaningless]'.[76]

Denial of Access to Counsel in Investigative Phase

Another area in which the ECtHR has adopted a more principled, 'interventionist' approach to the admissibility (or use) of (unlawfully obtained) evidence is the right of access to a lawyer in the investigative phase, which may be read into Article 6(3) (c) of the ECHR.[77] In *Salduz v Turkey*, the ECtHR held that,

> ... in order for the right to a fair trial to remain sufficiently "practical and effective" ... Article 6 § 1 requires that, as a rule, access to a lawyer should be provided as from the first interrogation of a suspect by the police, unless it is demonstrated in the light of the particular circumstances of each case that there are compelling reasons to restrict this right. Even where compelling reasons may exceptionally justify denial of access to a lawyer, such restriction – whatever its justification – must not unduly prejudice the rights of the accused under Article 6 ... The rights of the defence will in principle be irretrievably prejudiced when incriminating *statements* made during police interrogation without access to a lawyer are used for a conviction.[78]

Thus, the ability to contest an incriminating statement at trial, i.e. challenge its admissibility, is not sufficient to repair the prejudice caused by the denial of access to counsel at the time of police questioning if that statement ends up being used to convict the accused. In *Panovits v Cyprus*, in which the Applicant, who at the material time was a minor, was questioned without any assistance from his guardian or a lawyer, and had not been properly informed of his right to receive legal representation or of his right to remain silent, the ECtHR held that,

> ... although the applicant had the benefit of adversarial proceedings in which he was represented by the lawyer of his choice, the nature of the detriment he suffered because of the breach of due process at the pre-trial stage of the proceedings was not remedied by the subsequent proceedings, in which his confession was treated as voluntary and was therefore held to be admissible as evidence... despite the fact that the voluntariness of the applicant's statement taken shortly after his arrest was challenged and formed the subject of a separate

---

[76] *Jalloh v Germany* App no 54810/00 (ECtHR, 11 July 2006), para 107. In addition, the Grand Chamber noted that: '[T]he public interest in securing the applicant's conviction cannot be considered to have been of such weight as to warrant allowing that evidence to be used at trial. ... the [impugned] measure targeted a street dealer selling drugs on a relatively small scale who was eventually given a six-month suspended prison sentence and probation.' The implications of this statement are discussed below, in Sect. 2.2.1.5.

[77] In other words, the right is not explicitly provided for in Article 6 ECHR: it is an implied right. See e.g. Goss 2014, 91.

[78] *Salduz v Turkey* App no 36391/02 (ECtHR, 27 November 2008), para 55 (emphasis added). This marked a significant step away from ECtHR's earlier case law in this regard: See e.g. Ölçer 2013, 390.

trial within the main trial, and although it was not the sole evidence on which the applicant's conviction was based, it was nevertheless decisive for the prospects of the applicant's
defence and constituted a significant element on which his conviction was based.[79]

In that case, the ECtHR found violations of Article 6 of the ECHR both on account
of 'the lack of legal assistance … in the initial stages of police questioning' *and* of
'the use in trial of the applicant's confession obtained in circumstances which
breached his rights to due process', which 'irreparably undermined his rights of
defence'.[80] In *Salduz* also, the ECtHR based its finding that Article 6(1) had been
violated on both the lack of legal assistance at the time of questioning (such
restriction having been imposed by law, which applied to offences falling within the
jurisdiction of the State Security Courts) *and* on the use of the statements obtained
thereby to convict the Applicant.[81] To the extent that there was any confusion as to
whether the Grand Chamber's findings in *Salduz* meant that a suspect has a right to
counsel during questioning (and not just a right of consultation beforehand), subsequent case law confirms that it does.[82] For example, in *Panovits* the ECtHR held
that:

> As regards *the* applicant's complaints which concern the lack of legal consultation at the
> pre-trial stage of the proceedings, the Court observes that the concept of fairness enshrined
> in Article 6 requires that the accused be given the benefit of the assistance of a lawyer
> already at the initial stages of police interrogation. The lack of legal assistance *during an*
> applicant's interrogation would constitute a restriction of his defence rights in the absence
> of compelling reasons that do not prejudice the overall fairness of the proceedings.[83]

In *Dayanan v Turkey*, it was held that Article 6 'requires that, as a rule, a suspect
should be granted access to legal assistance *from the moment he is taken into police
custody or pre-trial detention*', i.e. that 'an accused person is entitled, as soon as he
or she is taken into custody, to be assisted by a lawyer, and not only while being
questioned.'[84] According to the Court, an accused should be able 'to obtain the
whole range of services specifically associated with legal assistance', meaning that
'counsel has to be able to secure without restriction the fundamental aspects of that
person's defence: discussion of the case, organisation of the defence, collection of
evidence favourable to the accused, preparation for questioning, support of an
accused in distress and checking of the conditions of detention'.[85] This suggests

---

[79] *Panovits v Cyprus* App no 4268/04 (ECtHR, 11 December 2008), paras 75 and 76.

[80] Ibid., paras 77 and 86.

[81] *Salduz v Turkey* App no 36391/02 (ECtHR, 27 November 2008), paras 56–58.

[82] Nevertheless, it is important to note that this reading of the ECtHR's case is not accepted in all
European jurisdictions. In the Netherlands, for example, the Dutch Supreme Court continues to
maintain that the ECtHR's case law does not unequivocally provide for such a right.

[83] *Panovits v Cyprus* App no 4268/04 (ECtHR, 11 December 2008), para 66 (emphasis added).
See also *Sebalj v Croatia* App no 4429/09 (ECtHR, 28 June 2011), paras 256–257; and *Navone
and Others v Monaco* App nos 62880/11, 62892/11 and 62899/11 (ECtHR, 24 October 2013),
paras 77–85.

[84] *Dayanan v Turkey* App no 7377/03 (ECtHR, 13 October 2009), paras 31–32 (emphasis added).

[85] Ibid., para 32.

that the purpose of providing counsel in the investigative phase is not solely to ensure respect of the right of an accused not to incriminate himself. The ECtHR appears to have recognised as much in *Salduz* itself, where it observed that 'international human rights standards' on the right of access to a lawyer during police custody '*also* contribute to the prevention of miscarriages of justice and the fulfilment of the aims of Article 6, notably equality of arms between the investigating or prosecuting authorities and the accused'.[86] Nevertheless, ensuring respect for the right not to incriminate oneself does appear to be the primary purpose of providing counsel in the investigative phase. According to Court in *Salduz*, the rationale of 'international human rights standards' on the right of access to a lawyer during police custody 'relates *in particular* to the protection of the accused against abusive coercion on the part of the authorities'.[87] Legal assistance is required in order to ensure respect for the right not to incriminate oneself because suspects find themselves 'in a particularly vulnerable position at that stage of the proceedings'.[88] Not receiving assistance at this stage can have far-reaching consequences. In this regard it should be noted that: 'National laws may attach consequences to the attitude of an accused at the initial stages of police interrogation which are decisive for the prospects of the defence in any subsequent criminal proceedings.'[89] In other words, it may be open to the domestic court to draw adverse inferences from silence.

The Grand Chamber's finding in *Salduz* that that '[e]ven where compelling reasons may exceptionally justify denial of access to a lawyer, such restriction—whatever its justification—must not unduly prejudice the rights of the accused under Article 6' and that the 'rights of the defence will in principle be irretrievably prejudiced when incriminating statements made during police interrogation without access to a lawyer are used for conviction'[90] should be taken to mean that even if the denial of access to a lawyer does not by itself render the proceedings unfair, the use of incriminating statements obtained thereby will.[91] This includes the incriminating statements of a third party obtained in violation of the principles established in *Salduz*, where it constitutes the sole and decisive evidence against the accused.[92] Nevertheless, the Grand Chamber's use of the words 'in principle' implies that there may be situations in which the use of incriminating statements made during police questioning without access to a lawyer will not render the proceedings unfair.[93]

---

[86] *Salduz v Turkey* App no 36391/02 (ECtHR, 27 November 2008), para 53 (emphasis added).

[87] Ibid., para 53 (emphasis added).

[88] Ibid., para 54.

[89] Ibid., para 52.

[90] Ibid., para 55.

[91] The implications of this analysis are discussed in more detail below, in Sect. 2.2.1.4.

[92] See *Şiray v Turkey* App no 29724/08 (ECtHR, 11 February 2014), para 29.

[93] Thus, Ölçer refers to a '*nearly* absolute rule of exclusion' in this regard. See Ölçer 2013, 390 (emphasis added). In *Ibrahim and Others v UK*, the ECtHR appears to have considered there to be such a situation. In that case the ECtHR found that despite the fact that statements made during police questioning without legal advice had been used at trial, Article 6(1) had not been violated.

In *Mehmet Şerif Öner v Turkey*, it was not the use of an incriminating statement that was fatal to the fairness of the proceedings (the Applicant having repeatedly denied the charges against him during police questioning, as a result of which there were no incriminating statements to speak of), but the use in evidence of the result of an identification parade, in which the Applicant had taken part in police custody, during which time he had not had access to counsel (such restriction having applied pursuant to the law denying access to counsel to suspects of crimes falling within the jurisdiction of the State Security Courts). According to the ECtHR, since the trial court had relied heavily on the result of the identification parade in convicting the Applicant, the Applicant had 'undoubtedly [been] affected by the restrictions on his access to a lawyer during the preliminary investigation', and '[n]either the assistance provided subsequently by a lawyer nor the adversarial nature of the ensuing proceedings could cure the defects which had occurred during the applicant's custody period.'[94] Finally, even if an incriminating statement obtained in the absence of counsel is excluded from evidence, the rights of the defence may still be irretrievably prejudiced by the defects in the custody period. In *Martin v Estonia*, the facts were as follows: while the county court had used the incriminating statements of the Applicant which had been obtained in the absence of a lawyer *of the Applicant's own choosing* to convict the Applicant, the court of appeal had excluded them. However, the court of appeal had also been of the view that despite the exclusion of the statements there was 'nothing to prevent the use of such general knowledge; the confession of murder was to a large extent the reason why [the applicant] was committed to trial charged with murder, and the investigations were carried out on the basis of that knowledge.'[95] The ECtHR held as follows:

> The Court considers that the exclusion of the pre-trial statements from the body of evidence reveals the importance that the Court of Appeal attaches to securing a suspect's defence rights from the early stages of the proceedings. Although tainted evidence as such can be left aside in the subsequent proceedings, in the present case the Court of Appeal's decision nevertheless demonstrated that the consequences of the breach of defence rights had not been totally undone.

(Footnote 93 continued)

See *Ibrahim and Others v UK* App nos 50541/08, 50571/08, 50573/08 and 40351/09 (ECtHR, 16 December 2014), paras 204–224, and also the Grand Chamber's judgment in that case (*Ibrahim and Others v UK* App nos 50541/08, 50571/08, 50573/08 and 40351/09 (ECtHR, 13 September 2016)) at para 260: 'In its summary of the general principles applicable to the case, the Court in *Salduz* ... referred to the overall fairness assessment that had to be carried out when determining whether there had been a breach of Article 6 rights. It said that the rights of the defence would "in principle" be irretrievably prejudiced when incriminating statements made during police interrogation without access to a lawyer were used for a conviction, indicating that the rule, while strict, was not absolute'.

[94] *Mehmet Şerif Öner v Turkey* App no (ECtHR, 13 September 2011), para 21.

[95] *Martin v Estonia* App no 35985/09 (ECtHR, 30 May 2013), paras 48 and 94–95.

In the light of the above considerations, the Court concludes that the applicant's defence
rights were irretrievably prejudiced owing to his inability to defend himself through legal
assistance of his own choosing.[96]

Of course, it might simply be argued that the (domestic) court of appeal did in fact
use the statement (contrary to its assertions), whereby it should be recalled that the
use of 'incriminating statements made during police interrogation without access to
a lawyer' to convict the accused will, in principle, irretrievably prejudice the rights
of the defence.[97] However, it might also be that, despite being excluded, the
statement determined the *framework* within which the charges were determined at
trial.[98] This raises the question of whether in cases in which a suspect has been
denied access to legal advice the unfairness caused thereby could always be offset
by the exclusion of incriminating statements. This issue is addressed below.[99]

Coercion, Compulsion and Deception in the Context of 'Questioning'[100]

In *Salduz v Turkey*, the right of access to a lawyer in the investigative phase of
criminal proceedings was expressly linked to the right not to incriminate oneself. In
underlining 'the importance of the investigation stage for the preparation of the
criminal proceedings, as the evidence obtained during this stage determines the
framework in which the offence charged will be considered at the trial', the Grand
Chamber noted the 'particular vulnerability' of an accused at this stage in this
regard, which in its view 'can only be properly compensated for by the assistance of
a lawyer whose task it is, among other things, to help to ensure respect of the right
of an accused not to incriminate himself'.[101] It is during police questioning that an
accused is at his or her most vulnerable and, because it is here that the parameters of
the case are set, it is of paramount importance that the accused is protected from
coercion or compulsion that undermines his or her right to remain silent.[102] When
'questioning' is undertaken outside of the formal interrogation context, for example
when undercover officers or informants are used to elicit information from the

---

[96] Ibid., paras 96 and 97.

[97] See n 78 and accompanying text.

[98] See n 226 and accompanying text.

[99] In Sect. 2.2.1.4.

[100] According to Jackson and Summers: 'The notion of coercion suggests that an unwilling person
has been persuaded by way of force or threats to do something, while compulsion suggests that a
person has been obliged to do something or his or her cooperation has been brought about by
force.' In their view, the facts of *Allan v UK* (App no 48539/99 (ECtHR, 5 November 2002),
discussed below) do not 'suggest that the applicant was coerced into or compelled to make a
confession'; rather 'he was deliberately tricked into making statements'. See Jackson and Summers
2012, 178. Ölçer similarly argues that *Allan v UK* is an example of deception, not coercion or
compulsion. See Ölçer 2013, 381 and 387.

[101] *Salduz v Turkey* App no 36391/02 (ECtHR, 27 November 2008), para 54.

[102] Ibid., para 54.

suspect (de facto questioning), similar concerns arise on account of the 'deception' involved. Before considering the impact of coercion, compulsion and deception in the context of 'questioning' on the fairness of the trial, however, a general overview of the right not to incriminate oneself will be provided, in order to assist the reader in understanding the ECtHR's findings on the right in said context.

Regarding 'the right not to incriminate oneself'[103] it is important to note that not every instance of (compelled) self-incrimination constitutes a violation of Article 6(1) of the ECHR. Thus, a particular procedure may 'engage' the right not to incriminate oneself (or, put differently, the right may be 'applicable' to a particular procedure) without rendering the trial unfair.[104] Only where the compulsion is 'improper', i.e. the (very) 'essence' of the right not to incriminate oneself is destroyed, will there be a violation of Article 6(1) of the ECHR.[105] In examining whether the compulsion is improper and the essence of the right destroyed, the ECtHR looks to 'the nature and degree of the compulsion, the existence of any relevant safeguards in the procedures and the use to which any material so obtained is put'.[106] In addition, the ECtHR has held that it may, in this regard, take into

---

[103] To the extent that the ECtHR distinguishes between testimonial and real evidence in this regard (as it did in *Saunders v UK* (App no 19187/91 (ECtHR, 17 December 1996), para 69), it should be noted that the right does not appear to be 'limited totally to the refusal to answer questions or make a statement'. See Harris, O'Boyle, Bates and Buckley (Harris et al. 2014, 422), referring to *Funke v France* App no 10828/84 (ECtHR, 25 February 1993); *JB v Switzerland* App no 31827/96 (ECtHR, 3 May 2001); and *Jalloh v Germany* App no 54810/00 (ECtHR, 11 July 2006). Accordingly, 'the statement of principle advanced by the ECtHR in *Saunders v UK* is misleading or at least incomplete'. See Choo 2012, 244. Conversely, the refusal to answer questions or make a statement is not necessarily protected by the right. See *O'Halloran and Francis v UK* App nos 15809/02 and 25624/02 (ECtHR, 29 June 2007), discussed below (see n 110–111 and accompanying text).

In order to reflect this (and to avoid confusion in this regard), this section will refer to the generic 'right not to incriminate oneself', rather than to the (more cumbersome) 'right to silence' and 'privilege against self-incrimination'. Regarding the relationship between the latter two rights, according to Trechsel: '[T]he two guarantees must be seen as representing two overlapping circles. The right to silence is narrower in that it refers to acoustic communication alone, the right not to speak. The privilege clearly goes further in that it is not limited to verbal expression... On the other hand, the scope of the right to silence goes beyond that of the privilege as it does not only protect against pressure to make statements detrimental to the person concerned, but any declaration at all.' Trechsel 2006, 342.

[104] See in this regard Choo 2013, 64.

[105] See the test set out in *John Murray v UK* App no 18731/91 (ECtHR, 8 February 1996), paras 45 and 49, as referred to in e.g. *Jalloh v Germany* App no 54810/00 (ECtHR, 11 July 2006), paras 100–101. See also Harris et al. 2014, 422–426.

[106] *Jalloh v Germany* App no 54810/00 (ECtHR, 11 July 2006), para 101.

According to Harris, O'Boyle, Bates and Buckley, this was not always the case. See Harris et al. 2014, 425, where the authors refer to *John Murray v UK* App no 18731/91 (ECtHR, 8 February 1996) and *Heaney and McGuinness v Ireland* App no 34720/97 (ECtHR, 21 December 2000), in which 'the Court adopted a 'degree of compulsion' criterion to be applied when deciding whether the compulsion was 'improper' so that the 'very essence' of the right to freedom from self-incrimination had been destroyed'.

account 'the weight of the public interest in the investigation and punishment of the offence at issue'.[107] Such factors should be distinguished from the factors that may be taken into account in determining whether the proceedings, as a whole, have been fair.[108] In view of the factors to be taken into account pursuant to the Grand Chamber's judgment in *Jalloh v Germany*, the question of what constitutes 'improper' compulsion, i.e. what destroys the essence of the right not to incriminate oneself such as to violate Article 6(1) of the ECHR, does not lend itself to easy answer. Prior to the Grand Chamber's judgment in *O'Halloran and Francis v United Kingdom*, which was delivered one year after its judgment in *Jalloh*, the ECtHR had, 'in all cases … in which "direct compulsion" was applied to require an actual or potential suspect to provide information which contributed, or might have contributed, to his conviction', found a violation of the applicant's right not to incriminate him- or herself.[109] However, according to the Grand Chamber in

---

[107] *Jalloh v Germany* App no 54810/00 (ECtHR, 11 July 2006), para 117. The ECtHR's consideration of the weight of the public interest in the context of Article 6 ECHR is discussed below, in Sect. 2.2.1.5.

[108] See n 35 and accompanying text. Ölçer speaks of a two-tiered analysis with respect to the ECtHR's case law on the use of unlawfully obtained evidence: 'In the first tier, the analysis seeks to determine if the [C]onvention rights were violated during the preliminary or pretrial investigation of the case in the form of violations of Article 3 ECHR (torture or inhuman and degrading treatment); Article 8 ECHR (right to privacy); Article 6(3)(c) ECHR (right to counsel) and the privilege against self-incrimination and the right to remain silent, also protected by Article 6 ECHR.' In the second tier of analysis, 'the [C]ourt looks to see if the admission (or use) of evidence obtained through the violation of a first tier norm violated Article 6 ECHR', whereby the ECtHR will often, though not always, engage in balancing, i.e. look to factors such as the gravity of the violated norm, the probative value of the evidence so obtained, whether the rights of the defence have been respected and, sometimes, public interest considerations. According to Ölçer, '[i]n determining in [the] first-tier analysis whether a Convention right was violated, the ECtHR, especially when dealing with implied rights … (such as the privilege against self-incrimination), will *also* look to broader factors, such as public interest concerns, needs brought about by the rise in organized crime, national security interests, the interests if witnesses, etc.' See Ölçer 2013, 373–375.

The factors that the ECtHR takes into account in order to establish whether the essence of the privilege against self-incrimination has been destroyed clearly resemble those that it takes into account in its second tier analysis. To state that a violation of the right not to incriminate oneself will automatically render the trial unfair may therefore be misleading, since the balancing that would otherwise take place in the second tier analysis simply appears to have been shifted to the first tier analysis. However, it is true that once it has been established that, on balance, the right not to incriminate oneself has been violated, no further balancing may take place.

[109] *O'Halloran and Francis v UK* App nos 15809/02 and 25624/02 (ECtHR, 29 June 2007), para 53. Thus, the ECtHR distinguishes between 'direct compulsion' and 'indirect compulsion': see *John Murray v UK* App no 18731/91 (ECtHR, 8 February 1996), paras 49 and 50. See also *O'Halloran and Francis v UK* App nos 15809/02 and 25624/02 (ECtHR, 29 June 2007), para 57; and Jackson and Summers 2012, 252–253.

As to the cases in which the application of direct compulsion to provide information, i.e. direct compulsion to *cooperate*, violated the right not to incriminate oneself, see *Funke v France* App no 10828/84 (ECtHR, 25 February 1993); *Saunders v UK* App no 19187/91 (ECtHR, 17 December 1996); *IJL, GMR and AKP v UK* App nos 29522/95, 30056/96 and 30574/96 (ECtHR, 19 September 2000); *Heaney and McGuinness v Ireland* App no 34720/97 (ECtHR, 21 December 2000); *Quinn v Ireland* App no 36887/97 (ECtHR, 21 December 2000); *JB v Switzerland* App no

O'Halloran and Francis, it did 'not … follow that any direct compulsion will automatically result in a violation', thereby referring to its judgment in *Jalloh*.[110] In that case, the compulsion in question had been direct (i.e. legal: a criminal sanction for failure to provide answers pursuant to Section 172 of the Road Traffic Act 1988), but '[h]aving regard to all the circumstances of the case' the Grand Chamber concluded that the essence of the applicants' right not to incriminate themselves had not been destroyed.[111] However, even before the *Jalloh*-criteria were introduced, the question of whether the essence of the right not to incriminate oneself has been extinguished was not clear-cut. As Hoyano notes,[112] while in *Funke v France* it appears to have been freedom from compulsion that constituted the essence of the right,[113] in *Saunders v United Kingdom* it appears to have been the use at trial of evidence so obtained.[114] On the basis of the ECtHR's case law on the right of access to a lawyer in the investigative phase, both Hoyano and Choo argue that (once again) freedom from compulsion appears to constitute the core of the right not to incriminate oneself.[115] Certainly the use at trial of self-incriminating evidence obtained by direct compulsion (as proof of the accused's guilt or in the determination of punishment) presents a threat to the fairness of the proceedings (as relevant to the question of whether the essence of the right not to incriminate oneself has been extinguished),[116] while in cases in which information is *not* provided, i.e. there is a failure to provide the information requested (notwithstanding the threat of a criminal sanction for such failure), and therefore *not* used at trial, there must at the time of the request for information have been a genuine prospect that such information (had it been provided) would be used at trial. In other words, criminal

---

(Footnote 109 continued)

31827/96 (ECtHR, 3 May 2001); *Kansal v UK* App no 21413/02 (ECtHR, 27 April 2004); and *Shannon v UK* App no 6563/03 (ECtHR, 4 October 2005). The case of *Jalloh v Germany* (App no 54810/00 (ECtHR, 11 July 2006)) is not included here because it concerned the use of force, rather than compulsion to cooperate. See in this regard Choo 2013, 45 and 117.

[110] *O'Halloran and Francis v UK* App nos 15809/02 and 25624/02 (ECtHR, 29 June 2007), para 53.

[111] Ibid., para 62. This decision has been subject to robust criticism in the literature: See e.g. Ashworth 2012, 151–152; and Choo 2013, 67–70.

[112] Hoyano 2014, 15.

[113] *Funke v France* App no 10828/84 (ECtHR, 25 February 1993), para 44.

[114] *Saunders v UK* App no 19187/91 (ECtHR, 17 December 1996), paras 75–76.

[115] See Hoyano 2014, 15; and Choo 2013, 86. See *Salduz v Turkey* App no 36391/02 (ECtHR, 27 November 2008), para 54 in this regard.

[116] That the use of (any) self-incriminating evidence is relevant to the violation itself is logical given the ECtHR's observation that '[t]he right not to incriminate oneself, in particular, presupposes that the prosecution in a criminal case seek to prove their case against the accused without resort to evidence obtained through methods of coercion or oppression in defiance of the will of the accused' (*Saunders v UK* App no 19187/91 (ECtHR, 17 December 1996), para 68) and moreover apparent from its enumeration of factors relevant to the question of 'whether a procedure has extinguished the very essence of the privilege against self-incrimination'. See n 106 and accompanying text.

proceedings against the person alleging a violation of the right not to incriminate oneself (on account of the imposition of a criminal sanction for failure to provide the information requested) must have been 'pending or anticipated'; the prospect of such criminal proceedings being pursued must not have been 'remote' or 'hypothetical'.[117]

Turning back now to the specific context of (police) questioning, there is a wide range of tactics that the police can resort to in order to bring about the cooperation of the suspect during questioning, but not all such tactics are inherently problematic from the point of view of the right not to incriminate oneself. Regarding de jure (that is, police) questioning of suspects, Choo observes that '[t]he environment in which a suspect is questioned with a view to obtaining relevant information is inherently coercive and liable to sap the suspect's free will', but that 'courts will not readily find that the questioning of a suspect by the police has infringed the privilege against self-incrimination'.[118] De facto questioning of suspects is, however, more problematic, as is apparent from the case law of the ECtHR. In *Allan v United Kingdom* the police had, among other things,[119] made use of a long-standing police informant to obtain information from the Applicant, who had been arrested for the murder of a supermarket store manager and who, in the police interviews that followed his arrest, had consistently exercised his right to remain silent. The police informant, who had been instructed by the police to 'push' the Applicant for what he could[120] had been placed in the Applicant's cell and fitted with recording devices. The recording thereby obtained was adduced in evidence at the Applicant's trial, and the police informant also gave evidence, testifying that the Applicant 'had admitted his presence at the murder scene' (although this admission did not form part of the recorded interview adduced in evidence). No evidence other than the admissions alleged by the police informant at trial connected the Applicant with the murder.[121] The police informant's evidence was deemed admissible by the trial judge and the evidence admitted before the jury (with directions on how to assess the reliability of such evidence, given the police informant's criminal record), which found the Applicant guilty of murder.[122] In assessing the use of the police informant and the admission of the informant's evidence at trial in the context of Article 6 of the ECHR, the ECtHR observed that:

---

[117] See *Weh v Austria* App no 38544/97 (ECtHR, 8 April 2004), paras 50–56. See also *Funke v France* App no 10828/84 (ECtHR, 25 February 1993). In both *Funke v France* (ECtHR, 25 February 1993) and *Heaney and McGuinness* (App no 34720/97 (ECtHR, 21 December 2000)) criminal proceedings were, at least, anticipated (if not pending), unlike in *Weh*.

[118] Choo 2013, 80.

[119] In addition to the use of a police informant, the Applicant's visits in custody from a female friend were recorded, as were his conversations with the other man arrested in connection with the killing of the supermarket manager. See *Allan v UK* App no 48539/99 (ECtHR, 5 November 2002), para 12.

[120] *Allan v UK* App no 48539/99 (ECtHR, 5 November 2002), para 13.

[121] Ibid., para 16.

[122] Ibid., paras 18–21.

While the right to silence and the privilege against self-incrimination are primarily designed to protect against improper compulsion by the authorities and the obtaining of evidence through methods of coercion or oppression in defiance of the will of the accused, the scope of the right is not confined to cases where duress has been brought to bear on the accused or where the will of the accused has been directly overborne in some way. The right, which ... is at the heart of the notion of a fair procedure, serves in principle to protect the freedom of a suspected person to choose whether to speak or to remain silent when questioned by the police. Such freedom of choice is effectively undermined in a case in which, the suspect having elected to remain silent during questioning, the authorities use subterfuge to elicit, from the suspect, confessions or other statements of an incriminatory nature, which they were unable to obtain during such questioning and where the confessions or statements thereby obtained are adduced in evidence at trial.[123]

Further, drawing on the case law of the Supreme Court of Canada, the ECtHR held that 'the right to silence would only be infringed where the informer [who allegedly acted to subvert the right to silence of the accused] was acting as an agent of the State at the time the accused made the statement'.[124] In finding a violation of Article 6(1) of the ECHR, the ECtHR attached importance to the fact that the Applicant had 'consistently availed himself of his right to silence', that the police informant had been placed in the Applicant's cell 'for the specific purpose of eliciting from the applicant information implicating him in the offence of which he was suspected', and that the admissions which formed the main or decisive evidence against the Applicant at trial 'were not spontaneous and unprompted statements volunteered by the applicant', but 'induced by the persistent questioning of [the police informant] ... in circumstances which can be regarded as the functional equivalent of interrogation, without any of the safeguards which would attach to a formal police interview, including the attendance of a solicitor and the issuing of the usual caution'.[125] While it could not identify any 'factors of direct coercion', the ECtHR considered that the Applicant 'would have been subjected to psychological pressures which impinged on the "voluntariness" of the disclosures allegedly made by the applicant to the [police informant]', on account of the fact that 'he was a suspect in a murder case, in detention and under direct pressure from the police in interrogations about the murder, and would have been susceptible to persuasion to take [the police informant], with whom he shared a cell for some weeks, into his confidence'.[126] In such circumstances, the ECtHR considered the information elicited by the police informant to have been obtained in defiance of the Applicant's will *and* 'its use at trial' to have 'impinged on the applicant's right to silence and privilege against self-incrimination',[127] thereby rendering the trial unfair contrary to Article 6(1) of the ECHR.[128] In finding a violation of Article 6(1), the ECtHR did

---

[123] Ibid., para 50.

[124] Ibid., para 51.

[125] Ibid., para 52.

[126] Ibid., para 52. The reliance on the notion of 'voluntariness' has been criticized in the literature. See e.g. Jackson and Summers 2012, 178.

[127] *Allan v UK* App no 48539/99 (ECtHR, 5 November 2002), para 52.

[128] Ibid., para 53.

not examine whether the prejudice caused by the use of the information elicited by the informant was compensated by, for example, the ability of the Applicant to challenge its admissibility at trial. Accordingly, this is another area in which the ECtHR appears to take a more interventionist stance towards the admissibility of evidence,[129] in the sense that the use of evidence obtained in circumvention of proper interrogation procedures (incorporating as they do certain safeguards) renders the proceedings unfair, i.e. regardless of, for example, whether the use of such evidence could be challenged or other safeguards were in place (a judge's direction, for example). Where, however, de facto questioning takes place outside of custody, the ECtHR's position is different. In the case of *Bykov v Russia*, a criminal investigation had been opened in respect of the Applicant on suspicion of conspiracy to murder after an acquaintance of the Applicant informed the police that the Applicant had ordered him to murder a former business associate and handed over the gun which he alleged to have received for this purpose. A covert operation was conducted for the purpose of obtaining evidence of the Applicant's intention to murder, in which the police staged the discovery of two dead men at the home the former business associate, and officially announced in the media that one of those killed had been identified as the former associate. The acquaintance who alleged to have been ordered to kill the former business associate was sent to see the Applicant, carrying with him a hidden radio-transmitting device for the purpose of recording his meeting with the Applicant. During the meeting, the acquaintance told the Applicant that he had carried out the murder. Despite attempts to challenge the admissibility of the recording at trial, it was admitted into evidence as lawfully obtained and relied on, together with other evidence, to convict the Applicant.[130] The Grand Chamber distinguished the case from *Allan v United Kingdom* as follows:

> In [*Allan*] the applicant was in pre-trial detention and expressed his wish to remain silent when questioned by the investigators. However, the police primed the applicant's cellmate to take advantage of the applicant's vulnerable and susceptible state following lengthy periods of interrogation. The Court, relying on a combination of these factors, considered that the authorities' conduct amounted to coercion and oppression and found that the information had been obtained in defiance of the applicant's will... in the present case the applicant had not been under any pressure to receive V. [the Applicant's acquaintance who alleged to have been ordered to murder the former business associate] at his "guest house", to speak to him, or to make any specific comments on the matter raised by V. *Unlike the applicant in the Allan case, the applicant was not detained on remand but was at liberty on his own premises attended by security and other personnel. The nature of his relations with V. – subordination of the latter to the applicant – did not impose any particular form of behaviour on him. In other words, the applicant was free to see V. and to talk to him, or to refuse to do so. It appears that he was willing to continue the conversation started by V. because its subject matter was of personal interest to him.* Thus, the Court is not convinced

---

[129] See also Jackson and Summers 2012, 175: 'The ECtHR has taken its most activist stance on the context of the use in criminal proceedings of evidenced obtained by coercion or compulsion in the course of custodial interrogation.

[130] *Bykov v Russia* App no 4378/02 (ECtHR, 10 March 2009), paras 43–44, 95–96 and 98.

that the obtaining of evidence was tainted with the element of coercion or oppression which in the *Allan* case the Court found to amount to a breach of the applicant's right to remain silent.[131]

Accordingly, having examined 'the safeguards which surrounded the evaluation of the admissibility and reliability of the evidence concerned, the nature and degree of the alleged compulsion, and the use to which the material obtained through the covert operation was put', the Grand Chamber found that 'the proceedings … considered as a whole, were not contrary to the requirements of fair trial'.[132]

Covert Surveillance and the Interception of Communication

'Covert surveillance' is an umbrella term for the (covert) measures that suspects may be subjected to by the authorities in order to obtain further information.[133] Such measures may raise issues under the right not to incriminate oneself, as is the case in the context of de facto questioning, which was dealt with above. This section is concerned with covert surveillance to the extent that it raises issues under the right to respect for private life, as enshrined in, for example, Article 8 of the ECHR, and the impact of such measures on the fairness of the trial.

While in *Schenk v Switzerland* the covert surveillance in question (the recording of a telephone conversation between the Applicant and a third (private) party, 'Pauty', who claimed he had been commissioned by the Applicant to kill his estranged wife) was not found to violate Article 8 of the ECHR,[134] it was acknowledged by the Court to have been obtained unlawfully (that is, contrary to Swiss law),[135] and accordingly its use at the Applicant's trial was considered in the context of Article 6(1) of the ECHR. According to the Court, the use of said evidence did not violate Article 6(1) because 'the rights of the defence were not disregarded', the Applicant having had 'the opportunity … of challenging its authenticity and opposing its use', and of putting questions to Pauty and the official in charge of the investigation.[136] In addition, the Court attached importance to the fact that 'the recording … was not the only evidence on which the conviction was based'.[137]

In *Khan v United Kingdom*, a conversation between the Applicant and 'B.' had been recorded by an electronic listening devise secretly installed by the police on

---

[131] Ibid., paras 101–102 (emphasis added).

[132] Ibid., para 104.

[133] Trechsel 2006, 541.

[134] In fact, the ECtHR was precluded from considering this issue, the ECnHR having declared the Applicant's complaint regarding Article 8 ECHR inadmissible. See *Schenk v Switzerland* App no 10862/84 (ECtHR, 12 July 1988), paras 37, 40 and 53.

[135] *Schenk v Switzerland* App no 10862/84 (ECtHR, 12 July 1988), paras 43, 46 and 47.

[136] Ibid., para 47.

[137] Ibid., para 48.

B.'s premises in connection with B.'s suspected involvement in dealing in heroin. The recording of the conversation was ruled admissible at trial, following which the Applicant entered a plea of guilty. In proceedings before the ECtHR, the Applicant alleged breaches of, inter alia, Articles 8 and 6 of the ECHR.[138] According to the ECtHR, the use of the covert listening device violated Article 8 on account of there having 'existed no statutory system to regulate the use of ... [such] devices', meaning that the interference could not be considered to be "in accordance with the law", as required by Article 8(2) of the ECHR.[139] Next, the ECtHR considered whether the use at the Applicant's trial of the evidence obtained in violation of Article 8 was compatible with Article 6(1) of the ECHR. In this regard it noted that:

> While Article 6 guarantees the right to a fair hearing, it does not lay down any rules on the admissibility of evidence as such, which is therefore primarily a matter for regulation under national law ... It is not the role of the Court to determine, as a matter of principle, whether particular types of evidence – for example, unlawfully obtained evidence – may be admissible or, indeed, whether the applicant was guilty or not. The question which must be answered is whether the proceedings as a whole, including the way in which the evidence was obtained, were fair. This involves an examination of the "unlawfulness" in question and, where violation of another Convention right is concerned, the nature of the violation found.[140]

In assessing whether the proceedings as a whole had been fair, the ECtHR first noted that 'in contrast to the position examined in the Schenk case, the fixing of the listening device and the recording of the applicant's conversation were not unlawful in the sense of being contrary to domestic criminal law'.[141] In other words, there was 'no allegation of police malpractice in relation to their internal guidelines', nor was there any 'human involvement directly with the defendant, such as to give rise to questions of entrapment or other forms of fundamental unfairness'.[142] Rather the 'unlawfulness "in question"' related 'exclusively to the fact that there was no statutory authority for the interference with the applicant's right to respect for private life' and, accordingly, 'such interference was not "in accordance with the law"' as required by Article 8(2) of the ECHR.[143] Next, it noted that while the recording 'was in effect the only evidence against the applicant and that the applicant's plea of guilty was tendered only on the basis of the judge's ruling that the evidence should be admitted', the 'relevance of the existence of evidence other

---

[138] The Applicant also alleged a violation of Article 13 ECHR, which is discussed below, in Sect. 2.2.2.

[139] *Khan v UK* App no 35394/97 (ECtHR, 12 May 2000), paras 27–28.

[140] Ibid., para 34.

[141] Ibid., para 36.

[142] Friedman 2002, 225.

[143] *Khan v UK* App no 35394/97 (ECtHR, 12 May 2000), para 38. See also para 28.

than the contested matter depends on the circumstances of the case'. In this case, the tape recording had been acknowledged to be 'very strong evidence', in respect of which there was no risk of unreliability. While in *Schenk* the Court had attached importance to the fact that the recording was not the only evidence on which the conviction was based, the Court (in *Khan*) argued that in *Schenk*, the recording had in fact had decisive or, at least, 'not inconsiderable' influence on the outcome of the criminal proceedings, thereby seemingly playing down the importance of this factor in that case, also pointing out that 'this element … [had] not [been] the determining factor in the Court's conclusion [in *Schenk*]'.[144] Finally, the ECtHR noted that, as in *Schenk*, the Applicant had 'had ample opportunity to challenge both the authenticity and the use of the recording'.[145] According to the ECtHR, therefore, the use at the Applicant's trial of the recording did not conflict with Article 6(1) of the ECHR.

In *PG and JH v United Kingdom* the use of covert listening devices at a third party's flat and in the police station was similarly found to violate Article 8 of the ECHR.[146] As to whether the use at the Applicants' trial of the recordings obtained thereby was compatible with Article 6(1) of the ECHR, the ECtHR adopted the 'holistic' approach taken in *Schenk* and *Khan*.[147] According to the Court, the use at trial of the recordings did not conflict with Article 6(1), because of the 'unlawfulness "in question"', which 'related exclusively to the fact that there was no statutory authority for the interference with the … right to respect for private life' and because the Applicants had had 'ample opportunity to challenge both the authenticity and the use of the recordings'.[148] In addition, the Court attached importance to the fact that the recordings in question were *not* the only evidence against the applicants, thereby distinguishing the case from *Khan*.[149]

---

[144] Ibid., para 37.

[145] Ibid., para 38. See also *PG and JH v UK* App no 44787/98 (ECtHR, 25 September 2001), para 79; *Allan v UK* App no 48539/99 (ECtHR, 5 November 2002), para 48; *Heglas v Czech Republic* App no 5935/02 (ECtHR, 1 March 2007), para 89; and *Goranova-Karaeneva v Bulgaria* App no 12739/05 (ECtHR, 8 March 2011), para 70.

[146] *PG and JH v UK* App no 44787/98 (ECtHR, 25 September 2001), paras 38 and 63. See also the following cases, in which the use of covert listening devices were found to violate Article 8 of the ECHR: *Allan v UK* App no 48539/99 (ECtHR, 5 November 2002), paras 35–36; *Chalkley v UK* App no 63831/00 (ECtHR, 12 June 2003), paras 24–25; *Heglas v Czech Republic* App no 5935/02 (ECtHR, 1 March 2007), paras 71–76; and *Bykov v Russia* App no 4378/02 (ECtHR, 10 March 2009), paras 72–83.

[147] See e.g. also *Allan v UK* App no 48539/99 (ECtHR, 5 November 2002), paras 42–43 and 46–48 and *Heglas v Czech Republic* App no 5935/02 (ECtHR, 1 March 2007), paras 89–93.

[148] *PG and JH v UK* App no 44787/98 (ECtHR, 25 September 2001), paras 78–79.

[149] Ibid., para 79. See also *Heglas v Czech Republic* App no 5935/02 (ECtHR, 1 March 2007), para 90 and n 144 and accompanying text. As Jackson and Summers point out, '[t]he reference [in *PG and JH*] to the other corroboratory evidence is confusing in that it seems to resurrect the sole and decisive type test, which the ECtHR appeared to reject in *Khan*.' See Jackson and Summers 2012, 175.

Finally, the case of *Heglas v Czech Republic* is worth noting here.[150] In that case, the ECtHR found that the obtaining by the authorities of a list of telephone calls relating to the mobile phone of the Applicant, and the recording of a conversation between the Applicant and a third party (who had been fitted with a listening device) violated Article 8 of the ECHR.[151] In its determination of whether, notwithstanding the use of the list and recording (i.e. the evidence obtained in violation of Article 8) at trial, the trial, as a whole, had been fair, the ECtHR attached importance to the fact that the Applicant had been able to contest both the recording and the list,[152] and that the Applicant's conviction had not been solely based on such items.[153] In addition, it held that in order to determine whether the proceedings as a whole had been fair, it was appropriate to take into account 'the weight of the public interest in the prosecution of a particular offence and the sanction of its author', and that this factor could be 'put in the balance with the interest of the individual that the incriminating evidence be gathered lawfully'.[154] However, it noted that such public interest considerations 'cannot justify measures emptying an applicant's rights of defence of their very substance, including [the privilege against self-incrimination] guaranteed by Article 6 of the Convention'. Apparently, this was not the case as the Court expressly took the public interest into account in determining whether Article 6 had been violated, observing in this regard that the offence was serious one, which caused injuries to a third party, and that the Applicant had been sentenced to nine-years imprisonment for his part therein.[155]

Entrapment

Previous sections dealt with the use of coercion, compulsion and deception in order to obtain the evidence necessary to secure a conviction for a crime already committed. The focus of the current section is on the use of deception in order to *bring about* the commission of a crime, with a view to subsequently prosecuting it.

---

[150] Although the facts of this case, which involved a third party (a friend of the Applicant's co-accused) being fitted with a listening device, and the Applicant subsequently confessing to the third party his role in the crime, raise issues under the right not to incriminate oneself, the Applicant does not appear to have argued the point before the ECtHR. Nor did the Court find a violation of that right. Accordingly, this case is dealt with in the current section, rather than the section titled 'Coercion, compulsion and deception in the context of 'questioning', above. Nevertheless, *Heglas* is sometimes cited in discussions on de facto questioning outside of custody. See e.g. *Bykov v Russia* App no 4378/02 (ECtHR, 10 March 2009), paras 100–101; and Jackson and Summers 2012, 180–181.

[151] *Heglas v Czech Republic* App no 5935/02 (ECtHR, 1 March 2007), paras 68 and 75–76.

[152] Ibid., para 89.

[153] Ibid., para 90.

[154] Ibid., para 87.

[155] Ibid., para 91.

The facts in *Teixeira de Castro v Portugal* were as follows. Two plain-clothes police officers approached VS, whom they suspected of 'petty drug-trafficking', on several occasions in the hope of identifying his supplier. Unaware that they were police officers, VS agreed to find a supplier and, after initially being unable to find one, VS mentioned the name of the Applicant. Through another of VS's acquaintances, FO, the police officers met with the Applicant, expressing their wish to buy 20 g of heroin. The Applicant agreed and procured the heroin from a third party. Upon handing over the heroin at VS's house, the police officers identified themselves and arrested the Applicant and VS, among others.[156] The Applicant was convicted for drug trafficking, the court having reached its verdict 'on the basis of the statements of the witness, FO, the co-defendant, VS, the applicant himself and, "mainly", of the two police officers'.[157] The verdict was upheld on appeal.[158] In proceedings before the ECtHR, the Applicant argued that he had not had a fair trial, contrary to Article 6 of the ECHR, on account of his incitement by plain-clothes police officers to commit an offence of which he was later convicted. The ECtHR first observed that: 'The general requirements of fairness embodied in Article 6 apply to proceedings concerning all types of criminal offence, from the most straightforward to the most complex. The public interest cannot justify the use of evidence obtained as a result of police incitement.'[159] As to what police incitement entails, according to the ECtHR, the question was whether the police officers' role had been confined to acting as an undercover agent, which would entail investigating the Applicant 'in an essentially passive manner', rather than an agent provocateur, which would entail exercising 'an influence such as to incite the commission of the offence'.[160] Answering this question in the negative, the ECtHR attached importance to the following circumstances: that the officers' intervention does not appear to have taken place as part of an anti-drug-trafficking operation ordered and supervised by a judge,[161] and that the competent authorities did not appear to have good reason to suspect the Applicant of drug-trafficking, on the basis of either prior or ongoing involvement therein, or a predisposition to commit such offences (or, more specifically, did not have any '*objective* suspicions' or evidence

---

[156] *Teixeira de Castro v Portugal* App no 25829/94 (ECtHR, 9 June 1998), paras 9–12.

[157] Ibid., para 20.

[158] Ibid., para 22.

[159] Ibid., para 36.

[160] Ibid., paras 38–39.

[161] Ibid., para 38. See also *Khudobin v Russia* App no 59696/00 (ECtHR, 26 October 2006), para 135; *Miliniené v Lithuania* App no 74355/01 (ECtHR, 24 June 2008), para 39; *Bannikova v Russia* App no 18757/06 (ECtHR, 4 November 2010), paras 48–50; *Veselov and Others v Russia* App nos 23200/10, 24009/07 and 556/10 (ECtHR, 2 October 2012), para 90; and *Nosko and Nefedov v Russia* App nos 5753/09 and 11789/10 (ECtHR, 30 October 2014), paras 52–53.

in this regard).[162,163] Regarding the second set of circumstances, the Court observed that:

> ... he had no criminal record and no preliminary investigation concerning him had been opened. Indeed, he was not known to the police officers ... Furthermore, the drugs were not at the applicant's home; he obtained them from a third party who had in turn obtained them from another person. Nor does the Supreme Court's judgment ... indicate that, at the time of his arrest, the applicant had more drugs in his possession than the quantity the police officers had requested thereby going beyond what he had been incited to do by the police.[164]

According to the ECtHR, the police officers' intervention, which went beyond the actions of an undercover agent, *and* 'its' use (i.e. the use of the evidence obtained by the intervention) in the criminal proceedings 'meant that, right from the outset, the applicant was definitively deprived of a fair trial', in violation of Article 6(1) of the ECHR.[165] In making this finding, the ECtHR confirmed that Article 6 is also concerned with the propriety of pre-trial proceedings.

The Court's approach in *Teixeira de Castro* was endorsed in *Ramanauskas v Lithuania*,[166] in which the Grand Chamber held that:

> Police incitement occurs where the officers involved – whether members of the security forces or persons acting on their instructions – do not confine themselves to investigating criminal activity in an essentially passive manner, but exert such influence on the subject as to incite the commission of an offence that would otherwise not have been committed, in order to make it possible to establish the offence, that is, to provide evidence and institute a prosecution.[167]

In addition, the Grand Chamber endorsed the *Teixeira* Chamber's findings pertaining to the question of whether the police officers' actions had been confined to those of an undercover agent.[168] Because (in *Ramanauskas*) there was no evidence that the Applicant had committed any (corruption-related) offences beforehand, and no (objective) evidence 'other than rumours ... to suggest that he had

---

[162] *Ramanauskas v Lithuania* App no 74420/01 (ECtHR, 5 February 2008), paras 56 and 67, interpreting *Teixeira de Castro v Portugal* App no 25829/94 (ECtHR, 9 June 1998), para 38. See also *Vanyan v Russia* App no 53203/99 (ECtHR, 15 December 2005), para 49; *Khudobin v Russia* App no 59696/00 (ECtHR, 26 October 2006), para 134; *Malininas v Lithuania* App no 10071/04 (ECtHR, 1 July 2008), para 36; *Bannikova v Russia* App no 18757/06 (ECtHR, 4 November 2010), paras 40–42; and *Nosko and Nefedov v Russia* App nos 5753/09 and 11789/10 (ECtHR, 30 October 2014), para 52. But see *Sequeira v Portugal* App no 73557/01 (ECtHR, 6 May 2003); and *Eurofinacom v France* App no 58753/00 (ECtHR, 7 September 2004).

[163] As Jackson and Summers note, these two sets of circumstances are closely linked. See Jackson and Summers 2012, 188–189. See also *Nosko and Nefedov v Russia* App nos 5753/09 and 11789/10 (ECtHR, 30 October 2014), paras 51–53.

[164] *Teixeira de Castro v Portugal* App no 25829/94 (ECtHR, 9 June 1998), para 38.

[165] Ibid., para 39.

[166] *Ramanauskas v Lithuania* App no 74420/01 (ECtHR, 5 February 2008), paras 55–56.

[167] Ibid., para 55.

[168] Ibid., paras 56 and 66–67.

been intending to engage in such activity', the Grand Chamber concluded that the actions of the individuals involved amounted to *police* incitement[169] and that 'such intervention and its use in the impugned criminal proceedings' violated Article 6(1) of the ECHR.[170]

The ECtHR's case law on the consequences to be attached to evidence obtained as a result of police incitement is clear: 'all [such] evidence ... must be excluded',[171] or 'a procedure with similar consequences must apply'.[172,173] As such, when faced with a claim that the accused was incited to commit an offence, the (domestic) court 'must carry out a careful examination of the material in the file'.[174] Where a domestic court convicts a person for an offence that (the ECtHR has established) was the result of police incitement (by failing to exclude the evidence or applying another appropriate procedure), a finding that Article 6(1) of the ECHR

---

[169] Thus, the ECtHR rejected the Government's argument that the prosecuting authorities 'had not been guilty of incitement', because the individuals to have intervened 'had acted on their own private initiative without having first informed the authorities'. It held that: 'The national authorities cannot be exempted from their responsibility for the actions of police officers by simply arguing that, although carrying out police duties, the officers were acting "in a private capacity".' This was because 'the initial phase of the operation ... took place in the absence of any legal framework or judicial authorisation', because 'the authorities legitimised the preliminary phase *ex post facto* and made use of its results' and because 'no satisfactory explanation ... [had] been provided as to what reasons or personal motives could have led ... [the officer] to approach the applicant on his own initiative without bringing the matter to the attention of his superiors ...'. Finally, it held that: 'To hold otherwise would open the way to abuses and arbitrariness by allowing the applicable principles to be circumvented through the "privatisation" of police incitement'. See *Ramanauskas v Lithuania* App no 74420/01 (ECtHR, 5 February 2008), paras 62–65. See, however, *Shannon v UK* App no 67537/01 (ECtHR, 6 April 2004).

[170] *Ramanauskas v Lithuania* App no 74420/01 (ECtHR, 5 February 2008), paras 67–68 and 73–74.

[171] See e.g. *Khudobin v Russia* App no 59696/00 (ECtHR, 26 October 2006), para 133; *Ramanauskas v Lithuania* App no 74420/01 (ECtHR, 5 February 2008), para 60; *Bannikova v Russia* App no 18757/06 (ECtHR, 4 November 2010), para 56; and *Sepil v Turkey* App no 17711/07 (ECtHR, 12 November 2013), para 36.
In this regard Ölçer points out (in the context of the ECHR) that in case of police incitement the prosecution is doomed to fail: without the police incitement the offence would not have been committed, there won't be any other evidence on which to base a conviction. See Ölçer 2008, 444. Similarly Kuiper (discussing the implications of the case law of the ECtHR on police incitement for Dutch criminal procedure) argues that there is a fine line between the exclusion of evidence and staying the prosecution. See Kuiper 2014, 360.

[172] See e.g. *Lagutin and Others v Russia* App no 6228/09, 19123/09, 19678/07, 52340/08 and 7451/09 (ECtHR, 24 April 2014), para 117; and *Furcht v Germany* App no 54648/09 (ECtHR, 23 October 2014), para 64.

[173] Also relevant in this regard is the ECtHR's finding that: 'The public interest cannot justify the use of evidence obtained as a result of police incitement'. See e.g. *Teixeira de Castro v Portugal* App no 25829/94 (ECtHR, 9 June 1998), para 36. See also *Ramanauskas v Lithuania* App no 74420/01 (ECtHR, 5 February 2008), paras 53–54.

[174] See e.g. *Ramanauskas v Lithuania* App no 74420/01 (ECtHR, 5 February 2008), para 60; *Bannikova v Russia* App no 18757/06 (ECtHR, 4 November 2010), para 56; and *Sepil v Turkey* App no 17711/07 (ECtHR, 12 November 2013), para 36.

has been violated will ensue. If, however, the ECtHR is unable to establish with a sufficient degree of certainty that the offence was the result of police incitement (due to, for example, lack of file disclosure) such a finding may still ensue if the applicant was unable 'to raise the issue of incitement at his trial, whether by means of an objection or otherwise'.[175,176]

Non-disclosure[177]

A failure on the part of the prosecution to disclose to the defence information relevant to the case against the accused may raise issues under the right to a fair trial, as provided for in, inter alia, Articles 14 of the ICCPR and 6 of the ECHR. Neither of these provisions expressly provides for a 'right to disclosure'; however, such a right has been read into the provisions in the case law. A right to disclosure has been read into Article 14(3)(b) of the ICCPR, i.e. the right of everyone charged with a criminal offence to have 'adequate time and facilities for the preparation of his defence', and linked to the principle of equality of arms. The HRC has stated that: '"Adequate facilities" must include access to documents and other evidence; this access must include all materials that the prosecution plans to offer in court against the accused or that are exculpatory', whereby 'exculpatory' material should be understood as including 'not only material establishing innocence but also other evidence that could assist the defence'.[178] At the ECtHR, the right to disclosure has

---

[175] *Ramanauskas v Lithuania* App no 74420/01 (ECtHR, 5 February 2008), paras 69–72. See also *Khudobin v Russia* App no 59696/00 (ECtHR, 26 October 2006), para 137; *Bannikova v Russia* App no 18757/06 (ECtHR, 4 November 2010), paras 51–52, 67; *Veselov and Others v Russia* App nos 23200/10, 24009/07 and 556/10 (ECtHR, 2 October 2012), para 94 and *Nosko and Nefedov v Russia* App nos 5753/09 and 11789/10 (ECtHR, 30 October 2014), para 55.

[176] In a number of ECtHR cases the ECtHR appears to have based its finding that Article 6(1) had been violated on the entrapment itself *and* on the failure to properly deal with the entrapment claim at trial. See e.g. *Ramanauskas v Lithuania* App no 74420/01 (ECtHR, 5 February 2008), paras 68–74, *Bannikova v Russia* App no 18757/06 (ECtHR, 4 November 2010), paras 51–52; and *Lalas v Lithuania* App no 13109/04 (ECtHR, 1 March 2011), paras 45–48. As one reporter has noted in respect of the ECtHR's findings in *Ramanauskas*, this is somewhat confusing: 'Surely the finding that the applicant was incited to commit the offence should have been determinative of the application; the failure of the Lithuanian courts to adjudicate on whether he was incited or not, while aggravating, should not have been relevant to the issue of whether there was a breach.' See (2008) Entrapment: incitement to commit an offence—state officials acting in a private capacity—Article 6. EHRLR 3:410, 412–413.

[177] As stated in Chap. 1, in this book the term 'procedural violations committed in the pre-trial phase of international criminal proceedings' encompasses not only those procedural violations that at the national level would be described as *police* illegality or unlawfulness, but the violation by the *prosecution* of its pre-trial obligations, of which of which disclosure to the defence (of the case against the accused or of any potentially exculpatory material) is a prime example. Accordingly, the human rights standards pertaining to the violation of disclosure standards are addressed here.

[178] HRC 'General Comment no 32. Article 14: Right to equality before courts and tribunals and to a fair trial' (23 August 2007) UN Doc CCPR/C/GC/32, para 33.

been expressly linked to the principle of the equality of arms[179] and that of adversarial proceedings,[180] both of which are inherent in the 'fair hearing' requirement of Article 6(1) of the ECHR. According to the ECtHR, 'it is a requirement of fairness under para 1 of Article 6 (Article 6-1) ... that the prosecution authorities disclose to the defence all material evidence for or against the accused'.[181] In addition, it may be read into the more specific rights under Article 6 (3), especially the right provided for under Article 6(3)(b) of the ECHR, which provides that: 'Everyone charged with a criminal offence has the ... [right] ... to have adequate time and facilities for the preparation of his defence'.[182]

However, the right to disclosure is not absolute; while Article 6(1) requires that 'the prosecution authorities should disclose to the defence all material evidence in their possession for or against the accused',

> ... the entitlement to disclosure of relevant evidence is *not an absolute right*. In any criminal proceedings there may be *competing interests*... which must be *weighed* against the rights of the accused. In some cases it may be necessary to withhold certain evidence from the defence so as to preserve the fundamental rights of another individual or to safeguard an important *public interest*. However, only such measures restricting the rights of the defence which are strictly necessary are permissible under Article 6 § 1. Moreover, in order to ensure that the accused receives a fair trial, any difficulties caused to the defence by a limitation on its rights must be sufficiently counterbalanced by the procedures followed by the judicial authorities.[183]

In other words, under Article 6 of the ECHR, the right to disclosure may be restricted on public interest grounds, provided that any prejudice caused thereby is offset by counterbalancing measures. However, it is not for the *prosecuting authorities* to determine whether the public interest justifies a restriction on disclosure; in *Rowe and Davis v United Kingdom*, the ECtHR held that 'a procedure, whereby the prosecution itself attempts to assess the importance of concealed information to the defence and weigh this against the public interest in keeping the information secret, cannot comply with the above-mentioned requirements of Article 6 § 1'.[184] In that case, the unlawfulness lay in the prosecution's failure to 'lay the evidence in question before the trial judge and to permit him to rule on the question of disclosure', which had deprived the Applicants of a fair trial.[185] As to the question of how, then, conflicts between the right to disclosure and the public interest are to be resolved, in *Jasper v United Kingdom* the ECtHR found that an ex parte application by the prosecution to the trial judge to withhold material in its

---

[179] See e.g. *Foucher v France* App no 22209/93 (ECtHR, 18 March 1997) para 36.

[180] See e.g. *PG and JH v UK* App no 44787/98 (ECtHR, 25 September 2001) para 67.

[181] *Edwards v UK* App no 13071/87 (ECtHR, 16 December 1992) para 36.

[182] Harris et al. 2014, 416.

[183] *Jasper v UK* App no 27052/95 (ECtHR, 16 February 2000), paras 51–52 (emphasis added). See also e.g. *Edwards and Lewis v UK* App nos 39647/98 and 40461/98 (ECtHR, 27 October 2004), para 46.

[184] *Rowe and Davis v UK* App no 28901/95 (ECtHR, 16 February 2000), para 63.

[185] Ibid., para 66.

possession on the grounds of public interest immunity, whereby the trial judge had examined the material in question, did not violate Article 6(1) of the ECHR.[186] In so finding, the Grand Chamber attached importance to the following factors: that 'the defence were kept informed and permitted to make submissions and participate in the above decision-making process as far as was possible without revealing to them the material which the prosecution sought to keep secret on public interest grounds';[187] that 'the material which was not disclosed ... formed no part of the prosecution case whatever, and was never put to the jury';[188] that the trial judge was 'fully versed in all the evidence and issues in the case and in a position to monitor the relevance to the defence of the withheld information both before and during the trial', whereby there had never been any suggestion that the trial judge was not impartial or independent.[189] In other cases, however, such ex parte applications have been found to violate Article 6(1) of the ECHR; in *Edwards and Lewis v. United Kingdom*, the ECtHR distinguished the facts from *Jasper v. United Kingdom*, noting that 'the undisclosed evidence related, or may have related, to an *issue of fact decided by the trial judge*' (at trial, both applicants had argued that they had been entrapped, and had asked the trial judge to consider whether prosecution evidence should be excluded for that reason),[190] whereas in *Jasper*, the undisclosed material had formed no part of the prosecution case whatsoever, and was never put to the jury. In also finding that there had been a violation of Article 6(1), the Grand Chamber referred to the Chamber's earlier judgment,[191] in which it—the Chamber —had attached importance to the fact that, 'in each case the judge, who subsequently rejected the defence submissions on entrapment, had already seen prosecution evidence which may have been relevant to the issue [of entrapment]',[192] and in which it had held that, '[u]nder English law, where public interest immunity evidence is not likely to be of assistance to the accused, but would in fact assist the prosecution, the trial judge is likely to find the balance to weigh in favour of non-disclosure'.[193]

---

[186] *Jasper v UK* App no 27052/95 (ECtHR, 16 February 2000).

[187] Ibid., para 55.

[188] Ibid., para 55.

[189] Ibid., para 56.

[190] *Edwards and Lewis v UK* App nos 39647/98 and 40461/98 (ECtHR, 27 October 2004), para 46, where the Grand Chamber reproduced the relevant parts of the Chamber's judgment (*Edwards and Lewis v UK* App nos 39647/98 and 40461/98 (ECtHR, 22 July 2003)).

[191] *Edwards and Lewis v UK* App nos 39647/98 and 40461/98 (ECtHR, 22 July 2003).

[192] *Edwards and Lewis v UK* App nos 39647/98 and 40461/98 (ECtHR, 27 October 2004), para 46.

[193] Ibid., para 46.

2.2.1.4 Use of Evidence

In most cases involving unlawfulness on the part of the police in carrying out a criminal investigation in which the ECtHR found a violation of Article 6(1), this finding has, in one way or another, been based on the fact that the evidence obtained thereby was used at trial, or otherwise relied on as proof of the accused's guilt or in the determination of punishment. Thus, in *Jalloh v Germany*, the Grand Chamber found that 'the use in evidence of the drugs obtained by the forcible administration of drugs obtained by the forcible administration of emetics to the applicant [which constituted inhuman and degrading treatment within the meaning of Article 3 of the ECHR] rendered his trial as a whole unfair'.[194] The risk to the fairness of the proceedings posed by such use (which was decisive in securing the Applicant's conviction) had not, in the circumstances, been offset by the observance of defence rights or justified by the public interest in the investigation and prosecution of the offence.[195] Earlier on in the judgment the Grand Chamber had observed that '*the use of evidence* obtained in violation of Article 3 [of the ECHR] in criminal proceedings raises serious issues as to the fairness of such proceedings'.[196] More specifically in relation to torture it held that:

> Incriminating evidence – whether in the form of a confession or real evidence – obtained as a result of acts of violence or brutality or other forms of treatment which can be characterised as torture – should *never* be relied on as proof of the victim's guilt, irrespective of its probative value. Any other conclusion would only serve to legitimate indirectly the sort of morally reprehensible conduct which the authors of Article 3 of the Convention sought to proscribe or, as it was so well put in the United States Supreme Court's judgment in the *Rochin* case [...], to "afford brutality the cloak of law".[197]

The reference to the 'use of evidence ... in criminal proceedings' and the phrase 'should never be relied on as proof of the victim's guilt', which appears in the ECtHR's assessment of the alleged violation of Article 6, imply that only where evidence obtained by torture is actually used by the domestic court, that is, relied on as proof of the accused's guilt or in the determination of punishment,[198] will the

---

[194] *Jalloh v Germany* App no 54810/00 (ECtHR, 11 July 2006), para 108.

[195] Ibid., para 107.

[196] Ibid., para 105 (emphasis added). See also *Gäfgen v Germany* App no 22978/05 (ECtHR, 1 June 2010), para 172.

[197] *Jalloh v Germany* App no 54810/00 (ECtHR, 11 July 2006), para 105 (emphasis added), as referred to in *Harutyunyan v Armenia* App no 36549/03 (ECtHR, 28 June 2007), para 63; *Levinţa v Moldova* App no 17332/03 (ECtHR, 16 December 2008), para 100; *Baran and Hun v Turkey* App no 30685/05 (ECtHR, 20 May 2010), para 69; *Gäfgen v Germany* App no 22978/05 (ECtHR, 1 June 2010), paras 166 and 167; and *Othman (Abu Qatada) v UK* App no 8139/09 (ECtHR, 17 January 2012), para 264.

[198] *Gäfgen v Germany* App no 22978/05 (ECtHR, 1 June 2010), paras 179, 180 and 186.

ECtHR find a violation of Article 6 of the ECHR.[199] The Court's approach in *Harutyunyan v Armenia* is telling in this regard: in assessing the Applicant's complaint that the use of evidence obtained by torture violated Article 6(1) of the ECHR, the Court considered it '*necessary first of all* to address the parties' arguments as to whether the [impugned statements] were used by the domestic courts as evidence in the criminal proceedings against the applicant', which, as Jackson and Summers point out, it did at length.[200] The implication of the requirement that only the use at trial of evidence obtained by torture will lead to a finding that Article 6(1) has been violated is that, by itself, the resort to torture in the investigation is not sufficient to render the entire proceedings unfair.[201] Thus, in a case in which torture was used in the investigation, it would not be contrary to Article 6(1) if the court were to rely on *other* evidence, i.e. evidence that cannot in any way be said to have been obtained by the torture, as proof of guilt. Once it has been established that the evidence obtained by torture was used by the domestic court, it matters not *how* it was used, i.e. whether it was it was decisive in the conviction. In other words, such use cannot be offset by the observance of procedural safeguards. In *Allan v United Kingdom*, the violation of Article 6(1) was also based on the use at trial of the evidence obtained in defiance of the will of the Applicant. More specifically, the use of the evidence obtained 'in defiance of the will of the applicant' impinged on the Applicant's right to silence and privilege against self-incrimination and, accordingly, violated Article 6(1).[202] In that case, the use of the evidence obtained in defiance of the will of the Applicant was sufficient to render the proceedings unfair (having impinged on the Applicant's right not to incriminate himself): it mattered not, for instance, whether the use of such evidence could be challenged.

In *Teixeira de Castro v Portugal*, the ECtHR found that the intervention amounting to police incitement *and* the use of the evidence obtained thereby in subsequent criminal proceedings violated Article 6(1) of the ECHR.[203] Also relevant in this regard is its finding that: 'The public interest cannot justify *the use of evidence* obtained as a result of police incitement.'[204] While in *Teixeira de Castro* the violation of Article 6(1) was, strictly speaking, based on the fact that evidence

---

[199] In numerous cases the ECtHR has found the *use* of evidence obtained by torture to be contrary to Article 6 ECHR. See e.g. *Harutyunyan v Armenia* App no 36549/03 (ECtHR, 28 June 2007), para 66; *Levinţa v Moldova* App no 17332/03 (ECtHR, 16 December 2008), para 105; *Baran and Hun v Turkey* App no 30685/05 (ECtHR, 20 May 2010), para 72; and *Kaçiu and Kotorri v Albania* App nos 33192/07 and 33194/07 (ECtHR, 25 June 2013), paras 118 and 129.

[200] *Harutyunyan v Armenia* App no 36549/03 (ECtHR, 28 June 2007), para 58 (emphasis added); and Jackson and Summers 2012, 163.

[201] For a different view, see Duff et al. 2007, 247.

[202] *Allan v UK* App no 48539/99 (ECtHR, 5 November 2002), paras 52–53. See also *Bykov v Russia* App no 4378/02 (ECtHR, 10 March 2009), para 99; and *Jalloh v Germany* App no 54810/00 (ECtHR, 11 July 2006), paras 109 and 122.

[203] *Teixeira de Castro v Portugal* App no 25829/94 (ECtHR, 9 June 1998), para 39. See also *Ramanauskas v Lithuania* App no 74420/01 (ECtHR, 5 February 2008), para 73.

[204] *Teixeira de Castro v Portugal* App no 25829/94 (ECtHR, 9 June 1998), para 36. See also *Ramanauskas v Lithuania* App no 74420/01 (ECtHR, 5 February 2008), para 54.

obtained by the intervention (amounting to police incitement) was used at trial, it is important to put this in perspective. Given that in cases of entrapment (or police incitement), the unfairness arises long before any trial, before charges are brought, even (as apparent from the Court's finding that the use of evidence obtained by entrapment meant that 'right from the outset' the Applicant was definitively deprived of a fair trial),[205,206] it appears to be not so much the use at trial of the evidence that is problematic from the perspective of Article 6, as the fact that the person concerned was tried in the first place (which would by definition have entailed the use of the evidence).[207,208]

In cases involving unlawful conduct on the part of public authorities in the pre-trial phase of criminal proceedings in which the ECtHR has *not* found a violation of Article 6(1), the use of evidence obtained thereby has nevertheless played a significant role. In cases in which such conduct constitutes a violation of Article 8 of the ECHR, the use at trial of the evidence obtained thereby appears to be the mechanism by which the determination of Article 6 is triggered,[209] although, to date, this fact alone (i.e. the fact that the evidence was used) has not been enough to found a violation of Article 6. In determining whether, notwithstanding the use at trial of evidence obtained in violation of Article 8, the proceedings as a whole have been fair, the ECtHR looks to the '"unlawfulness" in question', whether the rights of the defence were respected, 'in particular whether the applicant was given the opportunity of challenging the authenticity of the evidence and of opposing its use', and the quality of the evidence, 'including whether the circumstances in which it was obtained cast doubt on its reliability or accuracy'.[210] It also looks to how the evidence was used and in this regard has held that: 'While no problem of fairness necessarily arises where the evidence obtained was unsupported by other material, it may be noted that where the evidence is very strong and there is no risk of it being unreliable, the need for supporting evidence is correspondingly weaker'.[211]

---

[205] *Teixeira de Castro v Portugal* App no 25829/94 (ECtHR, 9 June 1998), para 39.

[206] Rainey et al. 2014, 280.

[207] See Roberts 2012, 181. Similarly, Ashworth has observed that 'conduct which amounts to entrapment goes beyond the mere collection of evidence and becomes the creation of an offence ...' See Ashworth 1977, 735.

It is perhaps telling in this regard that in the ECtHR's own guide on Article 6, entrapment is dealt with separately to unlawfully obtained evidence. See *Guide on Article 6. Right to a Fair Trial (Criminal Limb)*, Council of Europe/European Court of Human Rights (2014).

[208] Arguably, therefore, the appropriate response to entrapment is a stay of prosecution, rather than the exclusion of evidence. See Duff et al. 2007, 247. However, Kuiper (discussing the implications of the case law of the ECtHR on police incitement for Dutch criminal procedure) argues that there is a fine line between the exclusion of evidence and staying the prosecution in this context. See Kuiper 2014, 360.

[209] In *Khan, PG and JH* and *Heglas* this is what the Applicants argued, and the ECtHR proceeded on this basis.

[210] See e.g. *Bykov v Russia* App no 4378/02 (ECtHR, 10 March 2009), para 90.

[211] See e.g. *Bykov v Russia* App no 4378/02 (ECtHR, 10 March 2009), para 90.

Finally, there is a category of unlawful conduct on the part of the police which the ECtHR has found to violate Article 6(1), but whereby such finding does not appear to be dependent on the use at trial of evidence obtained thereby. Thus, in *Salduz* the restriction of access to counsel at the time of questioning and the failure of the respondent state to justify this restriction other than to say that such restriction 'was provided for on a systematic basis by the relevant legal provisions' appears to have been sufficient to found a violation of Article 6(1) of the ECHR.[212] In *Dayanan v Turkey*, it was not disputed by the parties that the Applicant had not had legal assistance while in police custody because, according to the Court, such legal assistance '*was not possible* under the law then in force' (the same law invoked by the Government in *Salduz*).[213] According to the ECtHR:

> A systematic restriction of this kind [referring to the law restricting access to counsel in connection with offences falling under the jurisdiction of the State Security Courts], on the basis of the relevant statutory provisions, is *sufficient in itself* for a violation of Article 6 to be found, notwithstanding the fact that the applicant remained silent when questioned in police custody [and that no statement was obtained].[214]

Thus, where no statement is obtained because the suspect has elected to remain silent, a restriction that '*expressly and systematically*' bars 'certain *categories of accused* from having access to a lawyer during the *entire period* of their pre-trial detention',[215] will be sufficient to render the entire proceedings unfair. This is because such a restriction would appear to make it impossible for a suspect to have legal assistance while in police custody.[216] Given the 'range of services' required by Article 6 in the context of legal assistance, which is not limited to assistance at the time of questioning and also includes 'discussion of the case', 'organization of the defence', 'collection of evidence favourable to the accused', 'support of an accused while in distress' and 'checking the conditions of detention',[217] it is, moreover, questionable whether in cases in which such a restriction applies the unfairness caused thereby could always be offset by the exclusion of incriminating statements. Where the failure to provide counsel is neither systematic nor based on statute,[218] i.e. the suspect *was* able to obtain the assistance of counsel, the determination of Article 6 *will* likely turn on whether any statement made during questioning (or whether any results obtained from other investigative action with

---

[212] *Salduz v Turkey* App no 36391/02 (ECtHR, 27 November 2008), para 56.

[213] *Dayanan v Turkey* App no 7377/03 (ECtHR, 13 October 2009), para 33 (emphasis added).

[214] Ibid., para 33 (emphasis added). See also *Bayram Güçlü v Turkey* App no 31535/04 (ECtHR, 18 February 2014), paras 23–26; *Hikmet Yilmaz v Turkey* App no 11022/05 (ECtHR, 4 June 2013), paras 22–23; and *Hüseyin Habip Taşkin v Turkey* App no (ECtHR, 1 February 2011), paras 21–23.

[215] See *Zdravko Petrov v Bulgaria* App no 20024/04 (ECtHR, 23 June 2011), para 47. See also *Smolik v Ukraine* App no 11778/05 (ECtHR, 19 January 2012), para 56; and *Simons v Belgium* App no 71407/10 (ECtHR, 28 August 2012), para 31.

[216] See n 213 and accompanying text.

[217] See n 85 and accompanying text.

[218] See n 215 and accompanying text.

the participation of the suspect) in the absence of counsel was used in evidence, whereby it should be recalled that the use of incriminating statements made during questioning in the absence of counsel will almost certainly render the proceedings unfair.[219] This implies the following (i.e. in cases in which the failure to provide counsel is neither systematic nor legislative). First, where no incriminating statement (made in the absence of counsel) is adduced, this failure alone is unlikely to be sufficient to render the proceedings unfair. Thus, in *Zdravko Petrov v Bulgaria* the failure to provide the Applicant with legal assistance in the first twenty-four hours after his arrest was not sufficient in itself to render the proceedings unfair, since, unlike in the *Dayanan* case, 'there were no legislative restrictions on access to legal assistance during pre-trial detention, and the applicant was able to obtain the assistance of counsel after one day'.[220] In that case, the domestic court had only based its judgment on statements obtained *after* he had been provided counsel (i.e. not on any statement obtained in the initial period after his arrest).[221] Second, where an incriminating statement made in the absence of counsel *is* adduced, the unfairness caused by the failure to provide counsel at the time of questioning will likely be offset by the exclusion thereof. After all, in such circumstances (i.e. where there is no systematic, legislative restriction on legal assistance) it cannot be discounted that the suspect will have obtained most of the 'services specifically associated with legal assistance',[222] in which case the prejudice caused by the failure to provide legal assistance attaches solely to the questioning, meaning that the prejudice can be offset by excluding the incriminating statement. That in cases in which the failure to provide counsel is neither systematic nor legislative the unfairness caused by the restriction may be able to be offset by the exclusion of any statement obtained thereby would appear logical given that the ECtHR expressly links the right of access to counsel in the investigative phase with the right not to incriminate oneself.[223] In this regard it should be noted that a suspect may incriminate himself in other ways than through the making of a statement. Thus, if *other* investigative action is carried out with the participation of the suspect (in the absence of counsel), the use of any results obtained thereby may well 'prejudice the rights of the defence irretrievably', regardless of whether any statement has been

---

[219] See n 93 and accompanying text.

[220] *Zdravko Petrov v Bulgaria* App no 20024/04 (ECtHR, 23 June 2011), para 47.

[221] Ibid., para 47.

[222] See n 85 and 217 and accompanying text.

[223] See *Salduz v Turkey* App no 36391/02 (ECtHR, 27 November 2008), paras 52–54. In a number of cases the use of the self-incriminating evidence formed part of the finding that the Applicant's right not to incriminate himself had been violated. See *Allan v UK* App no 48539/99 (ECtHR, 5 November 2002), paras 52–53. See also *Bykov v Russia* App no 4378/02 (ECtHR, 10 March 2009), para 99. Nevertheless, the ECtHR's case law on the right not to incriminate oneself in this regard is complex. See n 116–117 and accompanying text.

made, and regardless of whether any statement made has been used.[224]
Nevertheless, as suggested above,[225] there may be situations in which, notwithstanding the exclusion of incriminating statements on account of the absence of
counsel at the time of questioning (and of any 'poisonous fruits' in this regard), or
indeed of any other self-incriminating evidence obtained in such circumstances, it
will not be possible to say that the proceedings were fair. Even when an incriminating statement is excluded at trial, it is likely to have served as a 'blueprint' for
the remainder of the proceedings from the point of questioning onwards, setting the
parameters within which further investigations would be conducted and, ultimately
of course, within 'which the offence charged [would] be considered at the trial'.[226]
If other evidence was obtained as a result of the failure to provide access to counsel
at the time of questioning, such evidence could of course be excluded as 'poisonous
fruit'. But what if as a result of the incriminating statement the investigating
authorities have 'overlooked' potentially exculpatory evidence? If the court were to
rely on *other* evidence at trial, i.e. evidence that cannot in any way be said to have
been obtained by the failure to provide access to counsel at the time of questioning
and that tends to confirm the incriminating statement of the accused excluded from
consideration, can it reasonably be concluded that the proceedings were fair?

While the use of the evidence obtained by unlawful conduct on the part of public
authorities in the pre-trial phase of criminal proceedings enters the Article 6(1)
analysis in different ways, and it is therefore difficult to make any general statements in this regard, it is clear that in cases in which such conduct is alleged to
engage Article 6(1), the ECtHR attaches importance to the use of the evidence so
obtained. It may be that the use of the evidence obtained unlawfully is the necessary
'link' between the pre-trial phase and the trial phase of criminal proceedings
(particularly where the underlying unlawfulness does not involve one of the rights
enumerated in or otherwise flowing from Article 6). In other words, such use may
be necessary in order for unlawfulness in the course of the investigation to trigger
the protection of Article 6.[227,228] According to Ölçer, it is *the use of evidence*
obtained unlawfully that poses a risk to fairness within the meaning of Article 6,
which, depending on the risk posed (which, in turn, depends on the nature of the
unlawfulness in question) may be mitigated by its 'fair' use at trial, which involves
'balancing' (about which more will be said below). While the use of evidence
obtained in violation of Article 8 of the ECHR 'presents a low risk to trial fairness',
whereby such risk can be offset by its fair use, the use of evidence obtained by
inhuman and degrading treatment within the meaning of Article 3 'generally

---

[224] See n 94 and accompanying text, Nevertheless, it is worth noting that in that case the restriction
in question was systematic and based on statute (it concerned the same law as in *Salduz*), which
would have been sufficient in itself to render the proceedings unfair.

[225] See n 85–86, 216–217 and 222 and accompanying text.

[226] *Salduz v Turkey* App no 36391/02 (ECtHR, 27 November 2008), para 54.

[227] See Ölçer 2013, 375. See also, generally, Ölçer 2008.

[228] See n 20 and accompanying text.

presents a high risk to fairness', which means that 'more care must be taken in the balancing process, i.e. more must be done to restore or recuperate the balance of (overall) fairness'. The use of evidence obtained by torture 'presents so high a risk to fairness' that it cannot under any circumstances be offset by its fair use.[229] Given that, even in cases in which the underlying conduct involves the violation of Article 3 of the ECHR the ECtHR requires evidence obtained thereby to be used, it is reasonable to assume that the same applies to cases involving other types of unlawful conduct. Indeed, where such conduct involves the violation of Article 8 of the ECHR, the use of the evidence obtained thereby appears to be the mechanism by which the determination of Article 6(1) is triggered.[230] It is not, however, sufficient to found a violation of Article 6(1), as it is in cases of torture. In cases in which the underlying unlawful conduct does involve a fair trial right, it is more difficult to pinpoint the use of the evidence so obtained as the trigger for the Court's determination of Article 6(1) of the ECHR, and to ascertain the significance of such use for this determination more generally. In some cases, as in cases in which the underlying unlawful conduct amounting to torture within the meaning of Article 3 of the ECHR, the fact that evidence obtained unlawfully was used is sufficient to violate Article 6(1).[231] In the context of the violation of the right of access to counsel at the time of questioning this is because the use of evidence obtained thereby will, in principle, irretrievably prejudice the rights of the defence.[232] In entrapment cases the ECtHR is less explicit in this regard, but, as observed above, it appears to be not so much the use at trial of the evidence that is problematic in such cases, as the fact that the person concerned was tried at all (which would by definition have entailed the use of the evidence).[233] In *Allan v United Kingdom*, the use of the evidence formed part of the finding that the Applicant's right not to incriminate himself had been violated.[234]

A final observation regarding the use of evidence is due here. In those cases in which the use of the evidence obtained unlawfully has not been sufficient (on its own) to render the proceedings as a whole unfair, the ECtHR has, as stated above, looked to *how* it was used. However, its case law in this regard has not always been consistent.[235] Thus, whereas in *Schenk v Switzerland* the Court, in finding that Article 6 had not been violated, attached importance to the fact that the evidence obtained unlawfully had not formed the sole basis for the conviction,[236] in *Khan v*

---

[229] Ölçer 2013, 374.

[230] See n 209 and accompanying text.

[231] See e.g. *Teixeira de Castro v Portugal* App no 25829/94 (ECtHR, 9 June 1998) and *Salduz v Turkey* App no 36391/02 (ECtHR, 27 November 2008), para 55, although see n 93 and accompanying text. See also *Allan v UK* App no 48539/99 (ECtHR, 5 November 2002) and n 119–129 and accompanying text.

[232] *Salduz v Turkey* App no 36391/02 (ECtHR, 27 November 2008), para 55.

[233] See n 207 and 208 and accompanying text.

[234] See n 202 and accompanying text.

[235] See also Goss 2014, 171–173.

[236] See n 137 and accompanying text.

United Kingdom the Court appeared to distance itself from this 'sole or decisive rule'.[237] While in *PG and JH v United Kingdom* the Court appeared to revert back to its stance in *Schenk*,[238] in *Allan v United Kingdom* the Court cited with approval the approach in *Khan*, holding that: 'While no problem of fairness necessarily arises where the evidence obtained was unsupported by other material, it may be noted that where the evidence is very strong and there is no risk of its being unreliable, the need for supporting evidence is correspondingly weaker'.[239] In *Heglas v Czech Republic* and *Bykov v Russia*, the ECtHR cited with approval the approach in *Allan*.[240]

2.2.1.5 'Balancing' and Public Interest Considerations

It was seen above that, in the case law of the ECtHR, the use of evidence obtained unlawfully in the pre-trial phase of criminal proceedings does not automatically result in a violation of Article 6 of the ECHR. Accordingly, under the ECHR, there is no automatic exclusion for evidence obtained by violation of the suspect's or accused's Convention rights, let alone for evidence obtained by procedural viola-tions more generally. Nevertheless, the ECtHR does recognize an automatic exclusionary rule for evidence obtained by torture within the meaning of Article 3 of the ECHR, and a near automatic exclusionary rule for evidence obtained in violation of the right of access to a lawyer at the time of questioning under Article 6 (3)(c). However, for other Convention violations committed in the pre-trial phase of criminal proceedings the impact of the use of evidence obtained thereby on the fairness of the proceedings depends on such factors as whether the rights of the defence were observed, and *how* it was used. The ECtHR's practice of taking into account such factors is often referred to in the literature as 'balancing'. It is this practice that forms the focus of the present subsection.

In respect of evidence obtained by torture within the meaning of Article 3 of the ECHR, then, the ECtHR will not engage in balancing in order to determine whether its use amounted to a violation of Article 6 of the ECHR; the use of evidence obtained by torture will always do so. In respect of evidence obtained in violation of the right not to incriminate oneself, the ECtHR will similarly refrain from embarking on a balancing exercise for the purposes of the aforementioned deter-mination, although it is important to note that in order to determine whether the right has been violated *in the first place*, the ECtHR may have regard to such factors as the use to which the material obtained was put and the 'weight of the public

---

[237] See n 144 and accompanying text.

[238] See n 149 and accompanying text.

[239] *Allan v UK* App no 48539/99 (ECtHR, 5 November 2002), para 43.

[240] *Heglas v Czech Republic* App no 5935/02 (ECtHR, 1 March 2007), para 86; and *Bykov v Russia* App no 4378/02 (ECtHR, 10 March 2009), para 90.

interest in the investigation and punishment of the offence in issue'.[241] In respect of evidence obtained by violation of the right of access to a lawyer at the time of questioning, it will do so only exceptionally, it seems.[242] In respect of the prohibition of inhuman and degrading treatment within the meaning of Article 3 of the ECHR, the question of whether the use of evidence obtained thereby constitutes a violation of Article 6 depends firstly on whether the evidence obtained was confessional or real evidence, and, insofar as it concerns the latter, on whether the rights of the defence were observed—in particular, whether the defence could challenge the use of the evidence—and *how* it was used. Finally, in respect of violations of the right to privacy within the meaning of Article 8 of the ECHR, the ECtHR will also engage in balancing in order to determine whether the use of evidence obtained thereby amounted to a violation of Article 6; in addition to the aforementioned factors, the ECtHR also expressly looks to, and attaches significant importance to, the probative value (or the 'quality') of the evidence.[243] In one case, at least, it has also expressly looked to the public interest in the investigation and punishment of the particular offence in question. On the basis to the foregoing, it may be concluded that, for the purposes of the balancing exercise to be undertaken, i.e. the factors to be taken into account, in the determination of Article 6 of the ECHR (where such determination has been triggered by (alleged) unlawfulness in the pre-trial phase of criminal proceedings), the ECtHR distinguishes between different forms of unlawfulness; the factors that may be taken into account and/or the extent to which importance may be attached to them differs as between Convention violations.[244]

In the determination of Article 6 of the ECHR, where such determination has been triggered by (alleged) unlawfulness in the pre-trial phase of criminal proceedings, the ECtHR has taken into account, and in respect of some Convention violations, attached significant importance to, factors that seemingly have nothing to do with that which made the evidence problematic in the first place (the violation of a Convention right).[245] For example, in the context of violations of the prohibition of inhuman or degrading treatment within the meaning of Article 3 and the right to privacy within the meaning of Article 8, it has attached significant importance to the ability of the defence to challenge the use of the evidence obtained thereby. At the very least, this would appear to require that an exclusionary mechanism be provided for at the national level, which was in fact available to the accused in respect of the evidence in question. In addition, it has, in the context of the latter type of violations at least, attached significant importance to the

---

[241] *Jalloh v Germany* App no 54810/00 (ECtHR, 11 July 2006), para 117.

[242] See n 93 and accompanying text.

[243] This does not appear to be a decisive factor as regards the determination of whether the use at trial of real evidence obtained by inhuman or degrading treatment within the meaning of Article 3 ECHR violates Article 6 ECHR. See in this regard *Jalloh v Germany* App no 54810/00 (ECtHR, 11 July 2006).

[244] See similarly Ölçer 2013, 377–380.

[245] See similarly Ölçer 2013, 378.

probative value or 'quality' of the evidence; provided it is of high probative value (and that the rights of the defence have been observed), the use of evidence obtained by violation of Article 8 of the ECHR is unlikely to result in a violation of Article 6 before the ECtHR. Such factors create significant scope for the ECtHR to, in a given case, conclude that the use of the unlawfully obtained evidence did not violate the right to a fair trial. Another factor that has the potential to do so, is the public interest in the investigation and punishment of the crime in question. Arguably, public interest considerations already enter the fair trial analysis via consideration of the probative value or quality of the evidence,[246] even if the ECtHR does not *expressly* say so. In the paragraphs below, the relevant case law of the ECtHR[247] to expressly address the role of public interest considerations in the determination of Article 6 of the ECHR is set out.

In a number of decisions, the ECtHR appears to have rejected the inclusion of public interest considerations in its determination of Article 6. In *Saunders v United Kingdom*, the Applicant complained that the admission of self-incriminating statements obtained by compulsion (in the form of a legal requirement that the Applicant answer questions under pain of criminal sanction) at trial had violated the privilege against self-incrimination, which, he argued applied 'equally to all defendants regardless of the nature of the allegations against them or their level of education and intelligence'.[248] The ECtHR did not accept the Government's argument that the public interest in the investigation of corporate fraud justified a departure from the privilege.[249] According to the Grand Chamber,

> ... the general requirements of fairness contained in Article 6, including the right not to incriminate oneself, apply to criminal proceedings in respect of all types of criminal offences without distinction from the most simple to the most complex. The public interest cannot be invoked to justify the use of answers compulsorily obtained in a non-judicial investigation to incriminate the accused during the trial proceedings.[250]

In *Teixeira de Castro v Portugal* the Applicant complained that he had not had a fair trial on account of having been incited by plain-clothes police officers to commit an offence for which he was later convicted. In response to the Government's arguments in the context of Article 6 on the importance of fighting drug-trafficking,[251] the ECtHR held that:

---

[246] See in this regard Chap. 4, n 412 and accompanying text.

[247] That is, its case law on in the determination of Article 6 of the ECHR, where such determination has been 'triggered' by (alleged) unlawfulness in the pre-trial phase of criminal proceedings.

The ECtHR has condoned the 'balancing' of fair trial rights against public interest considerations in other contexts also. See e.g. *Al-Khawaja and Tahery v UK* App no 26766/05 and 22228/06 (ECtHR, 15 December 2011), para 146.

[248] *Saunders v UK* App no 19187/91 (ECtHR, 17 December 1996), para 60.

[249] Ibid., para 64.

[250] Ibid., para 74.

[251] *Teixeira de Castro v Portugal* App no 25829/94 (ECtHR, 9 June 1998), para 32.

The use of undercover agents must be restricted and safeguards put in place even in cases concerning the fight against drug trafficking. While the rise in organised crime undoubtedly requires that appropriate measures be taken, the right to a fair administration of justice nevertheless holds such a prominent place that it cannot be sacrificed for the sake of expedience. The general requirements of fairness embodied in Article 6 apply to proceedings concerning all types of criminal offence, from the most straightforward to the most complex. The public interest cannot justify the use of evidence obtained as a result of police incitement.[252]

In other decisions, while not rejecting the inclusion of public interest considerations in the determination of Article 6 outright, the ECtHR certainly appears to have been reluctant to do so. For example, in *Heaney and McGuinness v Ireland*, the Applicants complained that their convictions for failing to provide certain information contrary to Irish anti-terrorist legislation violated their right to silence and the privilege against self-incrimination guaranteed by Article 6 of the ECHR. In response to the Government's submission that the relevant provision of the legislation in question was 'a proportionate response given the security situation pertaining in the Irish State related to Northern Ireland and the consequent concerns to ensure the effective administration of justice and to preserve public peace and order',[253] the ECtHR held that 'the security and public order concerns relied on by the Government cannot justify a provision *which extinguishes the very essence of* the applicants' rights to silence and against self-incrimination guaranteed by Article 6 § 1 of the Convention'.[254] The ECtHR's findings in these cases regarding the inclusion of public interest considerations in the determination of Article 6 of the ECHR appear less 'robust' than those adopted in *Saunders* and *Teixeira* because while they certainly appear to limit the scope for doing so, they also imply that public interest considerations can justify measures that infringe the privilege against self-incrimination provided they do not extinguish its very essence.[255] In *Salduz v Turkey* the Grand Chamber appeared similarly reluctant to restrict the right of access to counsel in the investigative phase on account of public interest considerations:

Any exception to the enjoyment of this right should be clearly circumscribed and its application strictly limited in time. These principles [the importance of the investigation stage for the preparation of criminal proceedings, that the particular vulnerability of an accused at this stage can only be properly compensated for by the assistance of a lawyer

---

[252] Ibid., para 36. See also *Ramanauskas v Lithuania* App no 74420/01 (ECtHR, 5 February 2008), paras 53–54.

[253] *Heaney and McGuinness v Ireland* App no 34720/97 (ECtHR, 21 December 2000), para 33.

[254] Ibid., para 58 (emphasis added). See also *Quinn v Ireland* App no 36887/97 (ECtHR, 21 December 2000), para 59.

[255] Goss 2014, 193. Of course, the 'robustness' of these findings depends on what constitutes the essence of the privilege against self-incrimination. It may be that the ECtHR in *Saunders* considered 'the use of answers compulsorily obtained … to incriminate the accused during … trial proceedings' (see *Saunders v UK* App no 19187/91 (ECtHR, 17 December 1996), para 74) to constitute the essence of the privilege (although it did not explicitly say so), in which case the statement in *Saunders* may be no more robust than the one in *Heaney*.

whose task it is to help ensure respect for the right not to incriminate oneself] are particularly called for in the case of serious charges, for it is in the face of the heaviest penalties that respect for the right to a fair trial is to be ensured to the highest possible degree by democratic societies.[256]

In other decisions still, the ECtHR has neither rejected the inclusion of public interest considerations in the determination of whether Article 6 of the ECHR has been violated, nor been reluctant to do so; rather, it has expressly included such considerations in the determination, seemingly marking 'a significant step away from [its] older jurisprudence'.[257] In *Jalloh v Germany*, for example, in which the Applicant alleged a violation of, among other things, the privilege against self-incrimination and therefore Article 6, the ECtHR found that:

> In order to determine whether the applicant's right not to incriminate himself has been violated, the Court will have regard, in turn, to the following factors: the nature and degree of compulsion used to obtain the evidence; *the weight of the public interest in the investigation and punishment of the offence in issue*; the existence of any relevant safeguards in the procedure; and the use to which any material so obtained is put.[258]

Earlier on in the same judgment, the Grand Chamber enumerated the factors to which the ECtHR will have regard when examining 'whether a procedure has extinguished the very essence of the privilege against self-incrimination': 'the nature and degree of the compulsion, the existence of any relevant safeguards in the procedures and the use to which any material so obtained is put'.[259] Given that, only a few paragraphs earlier, the Grand Chamber noted that 'public interest concerns cannot justify measures which extinguish the very essence of an applicant's defence rights, including the privilege against self-incrimination',[260] the absence of public interest considerations in this summing-up is, perhaps, unsurprising.[261] Nevertheless, it is worth noting that the wording of the Grand Chamber does not preclude reliance on the public interest in this regard (since the Grand Chamber held that it would have regard '*in particular*, to the following elements…').[262] In *Jalloh* itself, the inclusion of public interest considerations in the determination of whether the privilege against self-incrimination had been violated worked *in favour* of the Applicant:

> As regards the weight of the public interest in using the evidence to secure the applicant's conviction, the Court observes that, as noted above, the impugned measure targeted a street dealer who was offering drugs for sale on a comparatively small scale and who was eventually given a six-month suspended prison sentence and probation. In the

---

[256] *Salduz v Turkey* App no 36391/02 (ECtHR, 27 November 2008), para 54.

[257] Ashworth 2012, 152.

[258] *Jalloh v Germany* App no 54810/00 (ECtHR, 11 July 2006), para 117.

[259] Ibid., para 101.

[260] Ibid., para 97

[261] See in this regard Goss 2014, 193–194.

[262] *Jalloh v Germany* App no 54810/00 (ECtHR, 11 July 2006), para 101 (emphasis added).

circumstances of the instant case, the public interest in securing the applicant's conviction could not justify recourse to such a grave interference with his physical and mental integrity.[263]

Nevertheless, *Jalloh* appears to have 'left open the possibility that the privilege [against self-incrimination] could be infringed in the public interest'.[264] Similarly, Ashworth notes that '[t]he implication of the Court's ... ruling [in *Jalloh*] is apparently that, in cases where the offence is very serious (unlike small-time drug dealing), official compulsion might be permissible without violating the privilege against self-incrimination.'[265] After all, while it may be true that once it has been established that the essence of a fair trial right has been extinguished the public interest in the investigation and punishment of the particular offence in issue may not subsequently be invoked in order to justify such a violation, in order to determine whether the essence of the privilege against self-incrimination has been extinguished *in the first place*, the public interest may be taken into account.[266] While in determining whether the essence of the privilege against self-incrimination and right to silence had been destroyed the ECtHR in *O'Halloran and Francis v United Kingdom* chose to 'focus on' the nature and degree of compulsion, the existence of relevant safeguards in the procedure and the use to which any material obtained was put,[267] with respect to the first factor the ECtHR cited with approval Lord Bingham's opinion in *Brown v Stott*, which explicitly took the public interest into account in the determination of whether the use of an admission pursuant to Section 172 of the Road Traffic Act 1988 would undermine the right to a fair trial.[268] Nevertheless, it is worth noting that, since *Jalloh*, the ECtHR has not *explicitly* referred to this factor as relevant to the question of whether the privilege against self-incrimination has been violated and in a number of judgments the enumeration of factors relevant to the determination of this question, which does not include the public interest, appears to be exhaustive.[269] While in *Heglas v Czech*

---

[263] Ibid., para 119.

[264] Jackson and Summers 2012, 258.

[265] Ashworth 2012, 152. See also Choo 2012, 249–254.

[266] See n 262 and accompanying text.

[267] *O'Halloran and Francis v UK* App nos 15809/02 and 25624/02 (ECtHR, 29 June 2007), para 55.

[268] Ibid., para 57, referring to *Brown v Stott* [2003] 1 AC 681, 705 (Lord Bingham). See also *Lückhof and Spanner v Austria* App no 58452/00 61920/00 (ECtHR, 10 January 2008), para 53, referring to *O'Halloran and Francis v UK* App nos 15809/02 and 25624/02 (ECtHR, 29 June 2007), para 57.
The (implicit) inclusion of public interest considerations by the ECtHR in *O'Halloran and Francis* is widely recognised. See e.g. Chedraui 2010, 225; Jackson and Summers 2012, 259–260; Ashworth 2012, 150–152; Harris et al. 2014, 426; and Goss 2014, 195.

[269] See e.g. *Bykov v Russia* App no 4378/02 (ECtHR, 10 March 2009), para 92; *Aleksandr Zaichenko v Russia* App no 39660/02 (ECtHR, 18 February 2010), para 38; *Pavlenko v Russia* App no 42371/02 (ECtHR, 1 April 2010), para 100; and *Niculescu v Romania* App no 25333/03 (ECtHR, 25 June 2013), para 111. See however *Sorokins and Sorokina v Latvia* App no 45476/04 (ECtHR, 28 May 2013), para 110.

Republic the ECtHR explicitly referred to the public interest as a factor relevant to the determination of whether the proceedings, as a whole, were fair, in that case the question appears to have been whether the use of evidence obtained *in violation of Article 8* violated Article 6.[270] While this finding may well shed light on the ECtHR's approach to the use of evidence obtained in violation of 8,[271] in view of the balancing already envisaged in the determination of the impact of the use of such evidence on the fairness of the proceedings,[272] which involves consideration of the probative value or quality of the evidence,[273] it is hardly surprising.

Non-disclosure is another area in which the ECtHR has explicitly considered the role of public interest considerations in the determination of Article 6. According to the Court in *Jasper v United Kingdom*, while Article 6(1) requires that 'the prosecution authorities should disclose to the defence all material evidence in their possession for or against the accused',

> ... the entitlement to disclosure of relevant evidence is not an absolute right. In any criminal proceedings there may be *competing interests*... which must be *weighed* against the rights of the accused. In some cases it may be necessary to withhold certain evidence from the defence so as to preserve the fundamental rights of another individual or to safeguard an important *public interest*. However, only such measures restricting the rights of the defence which are strictly necessary are permissible under Article 6 § 1. Moreover, in order to ensure that the accused receives a fair trial, any difficulties caused to the defence by a limitation on its rights must be sufficiently counterbalanced by the procedures followed by the judicial authorities.[274]

In other words, under Article 6 of the ECHR, the right to disclosure may be restricted on public interest grounds, provided that any prejudice caused thereby is offset by counterbalancing measures. However, it is not for the prosecuting authorities to determine whether the public interest justifies a restriction on disclosure; in *Rowe and Davis v United Kingdom*, the ECtHR held that 'a procedure, whereby the prosecution itself attempts to assess the importance of concealed information to the defence and weigh this against the public interest in keeping the information secret, cannot comply with the above-mentioned requirements of Article 6 § 1'.[275]

Having set out the relevant case law with respect to the right to a fair trial, which sheds light on the question of when it is necessary to address procedural violations

---

[270] See n 150–155 and accompanying text. In *Jalloh*, the Grand Chamber took the public interest into account in the determination of whether the use of the drugs obtained by inhuman and degrading treatment within the meaning of Article 3 violated Article 6.

[271] Ashworth 2012, 158–159.

[272] See e.g. *Khan v UK* App no 35394/97 (ECtHR, 12 May 2000) and *PG and JH v UK* App no 44787/98 (ECtHR, 25 September 2001). See also n 246 and accompanying text.

[273] See in this regard n 246 and accompanying text.

[274] *Jasper v UK* App no 27052/95 (ECtHR, 16 February 2000), paras 51–52 (emphasis added). See also e.g. *Edwards and Lewis v UK* App nos 39647/98 and 40461/98 (ECtHR, 27 October 2004), para 46.

[275] *Rowe and Davis v UK* App no 28901/95 (ECtHR, 16 February 2000), para 63.

committed in the pre-trial phase of criminal proceedings *within the criminal trial*, it is time to turn to those rights that do not require a response within the criminal trial to unlawfulness on the part of public authorities (including those charged with the investigation and prosecution of crime). The right to an effective remedy, provided for in Articles 2(3) and 13 of the ICCPR and ECHR, respectively, is often mentioned in case law and scholarly discussions on how to address procedural violations committed in the pre-trial phase of criminal proceedings,[276] and there is the right to compensation in case of unlawful arrest or detention, provided for in Articles 9(5) and 5(5) of the ICCPR and ECHR, respectively (which is a specific manifestation of the general right to an effective remedy). Each of these provisions is addressed below.

2.2.2 Right to an Effective Remedy

2.2.2.1 Requirements of the Right to an Effective Remedy

Article 2(3)(a) of the ICCPR confers a general right to an effective remedy on persons whose rights have been violated, including those of criminal defendants.[277] This provision is based on Article 13 of the ECHR, which provides that everyone whose rights and freedoms in the ECHR are violated 'shall have an effective remedy before a national authority notwithstanding that the violation has been committed by persons acting in an official capacity'.[278] According to Harris, O'Boyle, Bates and Buckley, this last part of the sentence ('notwithstanding … official capacity') should be construed as denying 'effect to national laws which provide immunity to public officials or the State for some wrongful acts'.[279] Clapham ascribes an additional meaning to this wording: according to him it indicates that states may also be obliged 'to provide a remedy for infringements of rights by non-state actors'.[280] This raises the question of whether Article 13 of the ECHR also applies to violations of the Convention by *foreign* officials. For example, in cases of inter-state cooperation in criminal matters, the requested State, in executing the request for cooperation, may have violated the rights of the suspect or accused. The question, then, is whether the suspect or accused may invoke the right to an effective remedy in the requesting, adjudicating, state in respect of violations committed in the requested State. While the wording of Article 13 does

---

[276] Most importantly, both of these rights have been cited in the relevant case law of the ICTs. Such case law is set out in Chaps. 5 and 6, and in order to be able to evaluate it, it is necessary to set out the relevant human rights law.

[277] Starr 2008, 703.

[278] Nowak 2005, 62.

[279] Harris et al. 2009, 567.

[280] Clapham 2006, 357–358.

not appear to preclude this,[281] the fact that the effectiveness of the remedy depends on the ability of the national authority to properly 'deal with the substance of the complaint'[282] raises obvious difficulties in this regard: is the requesting state really in a position to properly deal with the substance of a complaint concerning a violation committed by foreign officials, abroad? The same may, arguably, be said for the requested State. Thus, Van Hoek and Luchtman argue that 'the requested state is ... often not in a position to fully test the facts of the case'.[283] On the contrary, 'it is acting at the request of another state', as a result of which a referral of a complaint of a rights violation to the requested state for the purpose of obtaining an effective remedy will 'not necessarily provide an *effective* remedy'.[284]

Turning to the substantive requirements of the right to an effective remedy, it should be recalled that the English term 'remedy' has different meanings in the human rights context. It can refer to both 'access to (legal) recourse' (the procedural remedy) and to substantive redress (reparation). Regarding the latter, the HRC has stated that,

> Article 2, paragraph 3, requires that States Parties make reparation to individuals whose [ICCPR] rights have been violated. Without reparation to individuals whose [ICCPR] rights have been violated, the obligation to provide an effective remedy, which is central to the efficacy of article 2, paragraph 3, is not discharged.[285]

Article 2(3)(a) of the ICCPR encompasses both 'access to recourse' and reparation, whereby the former precedes the latter: 'Without access to recourse ... the victim of a human rights violation cannot demand or receive reparation'.[286] Similarly, the ECtHR has held in relation to Article 13 of the ECHR that it requires 'the provision of a domestic remedy allowing the 'competent national authority' both to deal with the substance of the complaint and to grant appropriate relief'.[287] According to the ECtHR, the effectiveness of the remedy depends on its ability to 'either' prevent the alleged violation or its continuation, or provide adequate redress for any violation that has already occurred.[288] It does not depend on the 'certainty of a favourable outcome for the applicant'.[289] Otherwise, however, states are

---

[281] There are, moreover, other reasons to argue this: efficiency. This argument is addressed below in the evaluation of the law and practice of the international criminal tribunals in Chap. 7.

[282] See n 287 and accompanying text.

[283] Van Hoek and Luchtman 2005, 25–26.

[284] Ibid., 26 (emphasis in original).

[285] HRC, 'General Comment no 31. The Nature of the General Legal Obligation Imposed on States Parties to the Covenant' (26 May 2004) UN Doc CCPR/C/21/Rev.1/Add. 13, para 16.

[286] Schleker 2009, 330.

[287] *Rotaru v Romania* App no 28341/95 (ECtHR, 4 May 2000), para 67. See also *Kudła v Poland* App no 30210/96 (ECtHR, 26 October 2000), para 157.

[288] *Kudła v Poland* App no 30210/96 (ECtHR, 26 October 2000), para 158.

[289] Ibid., para 157.

afforded 'a margin of appreciation in conforming with their obligations ... [under Article 13 of the ECHR],' no 'particular form of remedy' being required.[290]

Reparation is an umbrella term for many different forms of redress, including (but not limited to) restitution, compensation and satisfaction, which are usually cumulative.[291] However, this is not true for restitution and compensation.[292] In international law, restitution, which seeks to restore the situation before the violation occurred, constitutes the primary objective of reparation and compensation, which in this context refers to 'economic or monetary awards for certain losses, be they of material or immaterial, of pecuniary or non-pecuniary nature', is due when restitution cannot be obtained.[293] According to the Permanent Court of International Justice in the *Chorzów Factory* case,

> [t]he essential principle contained in the actual notion of an illegal act - a principle which seems to be established by international practice and in particular by the decisions of arbitral tribunals - is that reparation must, as far as possible, wipe-out all the consequences of the illegal act and re-establish the situation which would, in. all probability, have existed if that act had not been committed. [It must consist of r]estitution in kind, or, if this is not possible, payment of a sum corresponding to the value which a restitution in kind would bear.[294]

Compensation is required where restitution is 'materially impossible', or where it involves 'a burden out of all proportion to the benefit deriving from restitution instead of compensation'.[295] In any case, the principle formulated in *Chorzów Factory* requires full reparation, 'in that it permits no remedial shortfall (except in cases of impossibility); whatever damages cannot be corrected through in-kind restitution must otherwise be fully compensated'.[296]

As to the 'institutional' requirements of the right to an effective remedy, in *Leander v Sweden* the ECtHR held that the authority referred to in Article 13 of the ECHR 'need not be a *judicial* authority but, if it is not, the powers and the

---

[290] *Goranova-Karaeneva v Bulgaria* App no 12739/05 (ECtHR, 8 March 2011), para 57, referring to *Smith and Grady v UK* App nos 33985/96 33986/96 (ECtHR, 27 September 1999), para 135. See also *Horvath v Australia* Comm no 1885/2009 (HRC, 27 March 2014), para 8.2.

[291] International Commission of Jurists (2006) The Right to a Remedy and to Reparation for Gross Human Rights Violations. A Practitioners' Guide, 111. https://www.icj.org/wp-content/uploads/2012/08/right-to-remedy-and-reparations-practitioners-guide-2006-eng.pdf. Accessed 28 February 2017.

[292] Ibid., 111.

[293] Ibid., 123.

[294] *Case Concerning the Factory at Chorzów (Germany v Poland)* (Merits) PCIJ Rep Series A No 17, 47.
    It should be noted that remedies in international human rights law are drawn from other areas, including the traditional law on state responsibility. See e.g. Shelton 2005, 2.

[295] UN Principles on Responsibility of States for Internationally Wrongful Acts, Article 35(b) ('Resolution adopted by the General Assembly on the report of the Sixth Committee (A/56/589 and Corr.1), Responsibility of States for Internationally Wrongful Acts', UNGA Res 56/83 and Annex (28 Jan 2002) UN Doc A/RES/56/83).

[296] Starr 2008, 699.

guarantees which it affords are relevant in determining whether the remedy before it is effective'.[297] Moreover, the ECtHR has held that an accumulation of procedures may suffice: 'although no single remedy may itself entirely satisfy the requirements of Article 13 … the aggregate of remedies provided for under domestic law may do so'.[298] In other words, Article 13 does not require the state to provide one single remedy.[299]

2.2.2.2   Relationship to the Right to a Fair Trial

Since unlawfully obtained evidence (and procedural violations more generally) may raise issues under both the right to fair trial and the right to an effective remedy, it is important to examine the relationship between the two provisions. It was seen above that certain rights violations in the investigative phase impact on the fairness of the proceedings such as to violate the right to a fair trial, primarily through the use at trial of evidence obtained as a result of such violations. This sheds light on at least one aspect of the relationship between the provisions. In the case law of the ECtHR discussions on the use of unlawfully obtained evidence, whether consisting of a single item of evidence or the case as a whole, have taken place against the backdrop of Article 6 of the ECHR, not Article 13. Where the use of unlawfully obtained evidence does not undermine the fairness of the proceedings or the rights violation has not produced any evidence, or it has, but the evidence is not adduced at trial, and the protection afforded by the right to a fair trial for rights violations committed in the investigative phase is therefore not applicable, the right to an effective remedy may come into play.[300] Beyond this aspect of the relationship between the provisions, however, and given that the right to an effective remedy is often cited in case law and scholarly discussions on procedural violations in (international) criminal proceedings, the question may arise as to how suitable a place criminal proceedings are to provide an effective remedy within the meaning of Article 13 of the ECHR for rights violations committed during the investigative phase. A further question arises as to the logic of invoking the right to an effective remedy in order to elicit a response to such violations *within the criminal trial*.

As to the first question, it may be observed that the duty of domestic criminal courts to ensure the right to a fair trial (and to do that which is necessary in this regard) will not necessarily be sufficient for the purposes of the right to an effective

---

[297] *Leander v Sweden* App no 9248/81 (ECtHR, 26 March 1987), para 77 (emphasis added). See also Article 2(3)(b) ICCPR.

[298] *Leander v Sweden* App no 9248/81 (ECtHR, 26 March 1987), para 77.

[299] Regarding this point, however, Harris, O'Boyle, Bates and Buckley argue that while the 'approach based on 'aggregate remedies' may have been more defensible for sensitive cases such as *Leander* in the earlier years of the Court's 'life', when not all states had incorporated the Convention … it is harder to justify it today and it is submitted the Court should be reluctant to employ it.' See Harris et al. 2014, 773.

[300] For a similar analysis, see Ölçer 2008, 211.

remedy. This is particularly so where the underlying right to have been violated is a substantive right, such as the right to privacy.[301] While in *Khan v United Kingdom* the ECtHR found that the fact that evidence that had been obtained in violation of Article 8 of the ECHR was used by the domestic court did not render the trial unfair, it did find a violation of Article 13 of the ECHR. In response to the Applicant's allegation that Article 13 had been breached, the Government submitted that two remedies were available to satisfy the requirements of Article 13. First, the domestic courts had the discretion under Section 78 of the Police and Criminal Evidence Act 1984 (hereafter: PACE) to take into account the fact that evidence had been obtained in circumstances which involved an arguable breach of Article 8 of the ECHR. Second, it was open to the Applicant to complain to the Police Complaints Authority in respect of the allegations of police misconduct. In relation to the discretion to exclude evidence pursuant to Section 78 of PACE, the ECtHR noted that

> … the courts in the criminal proceedings were not capable of providing a remedy because, although they could consider questions of the fairness of admitting the evidence in the criminal proceedings, it was not open to them to deal with the substance of the Convention complaint that the interference with the applicant's right to respect for his private life was not "in accordance with the law"; still less was it open to them to grant appropriate relief in connection with the complaint.[302]

In relation to the Government's second submission, the ECtHR found that 'the system of investigation of complaints [did] not meet the requisite standards of independence needed to constitute sufficient protection against the abuse of authority and thus provide an effective remedy within the meaning of Article 13'. It therefore found that Article 13 had been violated.[303] Regarding the ECtHR's findings with respect to the exclusionary discretion under PACE, it should be noted that, at the time of the domestic criminal proceedings, the Human Rights Act 1998 had not been enacted. Prior to the enactment of the Human Rights Act 1998, individuals did not have a remedy before UK courts for breach of a Convention right. Moreover, English law did not recognise a general right to privacy. In this regard, it was 'not open' to the courts in the criminal proceedings 'to deal with the substance of the Convention complaint', let alone 'to grant appropriate relief in connection with the complaint'.[304]

Even if an individual is able to complain about breach of the right to privacy in the criminal proceedings, it is questionable whether the duty of domestic courts to ensure the fairness of the proceedings would always be sufficient for the purposes of the right to an effective remedy. In *Goranova-Karaeneva v Bulgaria* the Applicant complained that she had not had effective remedies in respect of her complaint

---

[301] See n 15 and accompanying text.

[302] *Khan v UK* App no 35394/97 (ECtHR, 12 May 2000), para 44.

[303] Ibid., para 47. See also *PG and JH v UK* App no 44787/98 (ECtHR, 25 September 2001), paras 82–88.

[304] *Khan v UK* App no 35394/97 (ECtHR, 12 May 2000), para 44.

under Article 8, relying on Article 13 of the ECHR in this regard.[305] In that case, the Applicant, a neurologist who was occasionally called upon to act as a court-appointed expert, alleged that she had been subjected to covert surveillance in breach of Article 8 of the ECHR. The covert listening devices in question had been installed by the police (pursuant to a court-issued warrant) in the Applicant's office pursuant to a tip-off that the Applicant had asked for money from a claimant in civil proceedings in exchange for her drawing up a report supporting the claim.[306] In response to the Applicant's complaint regarding Article 13, the ECtHR noted that the national courts dealing with the criminal case against the Applicant had examined her allegations that the covert surveillance had been unlawful. However, such courts were not capable of providing an effective remedy in this regard, since '[a]lthough they were competent to and indeed considered whether the surveillance had been carried out lawfully, they were concerned with its lawfulness only in so far as it could affect the fairness of the criminal proceedings against the applicant and the question of whether the material obtained could be admitted in evidence.' Moreover, 'even if this review could lead to a finding that the surveillance had been unlawful, such a finding could not in itself lead to any redress for the applicant'.[307] Presumably no redress was available before the domestic criminal court for breaches of the right to privacy that did *not* affect the fairness of the proceedings or the question of whether the material obtained could be admitted in evidence.[308] In this regard, Judges Garlicki and Mijović observed in their partially dissenting opinion that 'surveillance measures may have side-effects concerning private or family life', the assessment of which 'cannot be made within the framework of a criminal trial', and therefore that 'it may not be excluded that another (additional) remedy should be offered to the persons subjected to surveillance' (presumably outside of the framework of the criminal trial).[309] It should be recalled here that the right to an effective remedy consists of a procedural and a substantive component, whereby pursuant to the former, the competent national authority must be able to deal with

---

[305] The ECtHR did not find a violation of Article 8 ECHR in this case, but this does not preclude a finding that Article 13 ECHR has been violated, since that provision requires only that the applicant has an 'arguable claim' that he or she is the victim of the Convention violation. In other words, a violation of Article 13 ECHR is not dependent on the actual violation of another Convention right. See *Silver and Others v UK* App nos 5947/72; 6205/73; 7052/75; 7061/75; 7107/75; 7113/75; and 7136/75 (ECtHR, 25 March 1983), para 113, referring to *Klass and Others v Germany* App no 5029/71 (ECtHR, 6 September 1978), para 64.

[306] *Goranova-Karaeneva v Bulgaria* App no 12739/05 (ECtHR, 8 March 2011), para 7.

[307] Ibid., para 59.

[308] Interestingly, while the focus in *Khan v UK* appears to have been the absence of a procedural remedy (which, by definition, meant the absence of a substantive remedy—see the words 'still less'), in *Goranova-Karaeneva v Bulgaria*, the ECtHR addresses the two types of remedy separately.

[309] *Goranova-Karaeneva v Bulgaria* App no 12739/05 (ECtHR, 8 March 2011), Partly Dissenting Opinion of Judges Garlicki and Mijović. However, in their view, Article 13 ECHR had not been violated, since no such side effects had been 'mentioned as an "accompanying violation" of Article 8'.

the substance of the complaint.[310] In other words, it is not sufficient to provide substantive relief (in the absence of a procedural remedy that allows the national authority to deal with the *substance* of the complaint, it is, moreover, questionable whether any consequence to be attached to a rights violation can properly be called *substantive* relief).

Also relevant in this regard is the case of *Iliya Stefanov v Bulgaria*, in which the ECtHR found that the fact that the Applicant had never been 'formally charged, prosecuted or tried in relation to the material obtained during the search [and seizure carried out in the Applicant's office] is of no consequence for his complaint under Article 13' and that '[e]ven if the proceedings, which were stayed in 2001, are eventually discontinued and do not produce any negative consequences for him, this will not amount to appropriate relief for his complaint under Article 8.'[311] In that case, the Applicant alleged, among other things, that the search and seizure carried out in his office had been unlawful and unjustified and that he had not had effective remedies in this respect. The search and seizure had been ordered (pursuant to a court-issued warrant) in connection with allegations of extortion, whereby the Applicant had (allegedly) drawn up the documents that the victim of the (alleged) extortion was coerced into signing, promising, among other things, to pay money to his former employer.[312] That measures intended to ensure the fairness of the proceedings will not always be sufficient for the purpose of providing an effective remedy for rights violations is hardly surprising given that the right to an effective remedy is concerned with the specific harm caused by the violation in question, for example, a violation of the right to privacy, while Article 6 is only concerned with such harm insofar as it affects the fairness of the proceedings, i.e. the harm to the fairness of the proceedings. Nevertheless, this should not be taken to mean that such measures could *never* amount to appropriate relief for the purposes of the right to an effective remedy in respect of Article 8 breaches. Whether this is appropriate for such purposes may depend on the nature of the Article 8 breach and whether it affects trial fairness within the meaning of Article 6 of the ECHR. While some Article 8 breaches involve breaches of fair trial guarantees under Article 6 ('intrinsically' or otherwise), others do not (directly). Where the Article 8 breach 'intrinsically' involves breach of a fair trial guarantee, as for example in the case of unauthorized surveillance where a lawyer-client conversation is recorded,[313] and none of the aforementioned 'side-effects concerning private or family life' have arisen, the duty to do that which is necessary in order to ensure the fairness of the proceedings, for example the exclusion of evidence so obtained, may well constitute appropriate relief for the purposes of the right to an effective remedy in respect

---

[310] See n 286 and 287 and accompanying text.

[311] *Iliya Stefanov v Bulgaria* App no 65755/01 (ECtHR, 22 May 2008), para 58. In this regard the ECtHR relied on its findings in *Khan v UK* App no 35394/97 (ECtHR, 12 May 2000) and *PG and JH v UK* App no 44787/98 (ECtHR, 25 September 2001).

[312] *Iliya Stefanov v Bulgaria* App no 65755/01 (ECtHR, 22 May 2008), paras 5–16.

[313] Ormerod 2003, 75. See also Ölçer 2008, 60.

of the Article 8 breach.[314] In such circumstances, the right to an effective remedy in respect of the Article 8 breach is arguably absorbed by the safeguards of Article 6.

Where, however, the right alleged to have been violated is (more) intrinsically tied up with the notion of fair trial, the added value of the right to an effective remedy (in terms of legal protection against the violation of rights) is less evident. Procedural rights such as the right not to incriminate oneself 'lie at the heart of the notion of a fair procedure under Article 6'[315] and the violation thereof therefore falls squarely under the duty of the domestic criminal court to do that which is necessary in order to ensure the fairness of the proceedings. The same can be said for the other rights enumerated in, or otherwise flowing from, the right to a fair trial. Such rights are part and parcel of the notion of fair trial. Accordingly, violations thereof must be remedied within the criminal trial (on the basis of Article 6 of the ECHR): because any 'remedy' (within the meaning of Article 13) required for such violations must be given within the trial, Article 13 will not be of any added value in such circumstances. In other words, Article 6 of the ECHR already requires domestic criminal courts to address the violation of procedural rights (whether by the adoption of suitable compensatory measures, or by the exclusion of certain evidence), since such rights are inevitably tied up with the fairness of the proceedings, which the domestic courts are obliged to ensure pursuant to this provision. There may accordingly be said to be overlap between the duty to ensure that the suspect or accused receives a fair trial and the right to an effective remedy, insofar as the underlying violation for which legal protection is sought infringes on the fairness of the proceedings. In such circumstances, the effective remedy for the underlying violation is absorbed by the safeguards inherent in a criminal trial. If the underlying violation does *not* infringe on the fairness of the proceedings (and the domestic court is therefore not required to take action in order to ensure the right to a fair trial), the suspect or accused is nonetheless entitled to the legal protection afforded by the right to an effective remedy, although this remedy need not be given within the framework of the criminal trial,[316] bringing us to the second question raised above: the logic of invoking the right to an effective remedy in order to elicit a response to such violations *within the criminal trial*. Indeed, Article 13 of the ECHR only appears to require a remedy within the criminal trial insofar as the underlying violation infringes on the fairness of the proceedings, whereby it should be recalled that this protection is already inherent in the safeguards of the right to a fair trial. Thus, the fact that the suspect's rights have been violated in the context of

---

[314] See also Ormerod 2003 (70–71 (emphasis added)), where the author argues that '[b]reaches of the substantive Article 8 [ECHR] right should give rise to an effective remedy (which arguably they do [in England and Wales] in the form of damages) and not necessarily to a procedural right deriving from Article 6 [ECHR] fair trial guarantees, *unless that is shown to be effective.*'

[315] See e.g. *Saunders v UK* App no 19187/91 (ECtHR, 17 December 1996), para 68; *Allan v UK* App no 48539/99 (ECtHR, 5 November 2002), para 44; and *Jalloh v Germany* App no 54810/00 (ECtHR, 11 July 2006), para 100.

[316] For a similar analysis, see *R v P* [2002] 1 AC 146, 162, interpreting the ECtHR's findings in *Khan v UK* App no 35394/97 (ECtHR, 12 May 2000).

a criminal investigation, and/or that the violation of such rights in this context has resulted in a criminal prosecution (incriminating evidence having been obtained and subsequently adduced), does not mean that an effective remedy need be given within the criminal trial for that violation. In this regard it should be recalled that Article 13 simply requires 'the provision of a domestic remedy allowing the competent national authority both to deal with the substance of the relevant Convention complaint and to grant appropriate relief',[317] whereby the authority need not be a judicial one. Nor does it 'require a particular form of remedy, Contracting States being afforded a margin of appreciation in conforming with their obligations in that respect'.[318] Moreover, an accumulation of procedures may suffice for the purposes of Article 13.[319] For these reasons, invoking Article 13 of the ECHR for the purposes of obtaining (better) protection against rights violations committed during the criminal investigative phase *within the framework of the criminal trial* is unlikely to produce the desired result.

2.2.3 Right to Compensation in Case of Unlawful Arrest or Detention

Article 9(5) of the ICCPR prescribes that '[a]nyone who has been the victim of unlawful arrest or detention has an enforceable right to compensation'. Article 5(5) of the ECHR also provides for an enforceable right to compensation in case of unlawful arrest or detention.[320] The claim to compensation in Article 9(5) can be considered 'a specific type of domestic remedy within the meaning of [Article] 2(3) relating to liberty of person'.[321] Similarly, Article 5(5) of the ECHR 'is a specific manifestation of the more general obligation in Article 13 of the [ECHR] to provide an effective remedy where any of the guaranteed rights and freedoms have been violated'.[322] Trechsel observes in respect of this provision that '[t]he right to

---

[317] *Goranova-Karaeneva v Bulgaria* App no 12739/05 (ECtHR, 8 March 2011), para 57, referring to *Khan v UK* App no 35394/97 (ECtHR, 12 May 2000), para 44.

[318] *Goranova-Karaeneva v Bulgaria* App no 12739/05 (ECtHR, 8 March 2011), para 57, referring to *Smith and Grady v UK* App nos 33985/96 33986/96 (ECtHR, 27 September 1999), para 135.

[319] *Leander v Sweden* App no 9248/81 (ECtHR, 26 March 1987), para 77, referring to *Silver and Others v UK* App nos 5947/72; 6205/73; 7052/75; 7061/75; 7107/75; 7113/75; and 7136/75 (ECtHR, 25 March 1983), para 113.

[320] The right to compensation pursuant to Article 5(5) ECHR should not be confused with the ability of the ECtHR to award just satisfaction pursuant to Article 41 ECHR. The former exists vis-à-vis the high contracting state concerned. Non-adherence to Article 5(5) may give rise to an independent ground for complaint, which, if established, may lead to the application of Article 41.

[321] Nowak 2005, 237.

[322] Macovei 2002, 67.

compensation [thereunder] can be characterized as a kind of 'secondary right', dependent on and at the same time responsible for the extension of the primary right concerning personal liberty.'[323] The (procedural) remedy envisaged by these provisions is one before a court, 'leading to a legally binding award of compensation'.[324] Such compensation is usually financial,[325] 'but may be broader in scope than mere financial compensation'.[326] The claim to compensation prescribed in Article 9(5) of the ICCPR is available to every victim of unlawful arrest or detention, regardless of whether a violation of one of the provisions in Article 9(1)–(4) has been established. In other words, it is sufficient that the arrest or detention contradicts a provision of domestic law or international law.[327] By contrast, Article 5(5) of the ECHR only applies where any one or more of the paras (1)–(4) has been contravened, as established by either a domestic authority or the ECtHR.[328] Neither Article 9(5) of the ICCPR nor Article 5(5) of the ECHR applies to acquitted persons, whose pre-trial detention was based on reasonable suspicion of having committed a crime.[329] As to the amount of compensation, 'it is likely that' states are allowed a wide margin of appreciation.[330] However, a very low award of compensation might be entirely disproportionate to the duration of detention and, as such, might entail a violation of the right to compensation.[331] In this regard, Trechsel notes that the compensation must be 'substantial enough to highlight the value of personal liberty'.[332] While there is human rights case law to suggest that states are free to make an award of compensation dependent upon the ability of the person concerned to show *damage* resulting from the breach and upon the person concerned having suffered pecuniary or non-pecuniary damage,[333] there is also case law to suggest that an overly formalistic approach to, in particular, the question of whether non-pecuniary damage has been suffered, is problematic from the perspective of the right to compensation in case of unlawful arrest or detention.[334]

---

[323] Trechsel 2006, 498.

[324] Harris et al. 2014, 368.

[325] Ibid., 368. See also Macovei 2002, 69.

[326] *Bozano v France* App no 9990/82 (ECnHR, 15 May 1984), 119.

[327] Nowak 2005, 238.

[328] Harris et al. 2014, 367.

[329] Nowak 2005, 239.

[330] Harris et al. 2014, 368.

[331] Ibid., 368.

[332] Trechsel 2006, 501.

[333] *Wassink v Netherlands* App no 12535/86 (ECtHR, 27 September 1990), para 38.

[334] *Danev v Bulgaria* App no 9411/05 (ECtHR, 2 September 2010), para 35. See also *Georgi Marinov v Bulgaria* App 36103/04 (ECtHR, 15 March 2011), paras 47–48.

2.2.4   Procedural Violations in the Context of Inter-State Cooperation in Criminal Matters

It was stated above that in examining the human rights framework with respect to the question of how to address procedural violations committed in the pre-trial phase of criminal proceedings, it is important to be mindful of the specific context in which the ICTs operate: they are largely dependent on state cooperation as regards the apprehension of suspects or accused and as regards the carrying out of investigations. This raises issues that do not arise, or arise to a lesser degree, in a purely domestic context. For this reason it is important to also consider the relevant human rights law on inter-state cooperation in criminal matters; the purpose of this subsection is to set such case law out. It was observed above that inter-state cooperation in criminal matters is widely acknowledged to be characterized by the under-protection of the rights of the suspect or accused. Before setting out the aforementioned case law, it is worth considering this issue in more detail.

The under-protection of the rights of the suspect or accused may occur when the prosecuting authority in the state to have requested assistance (the requesting, adjudicating state) seeks to rely on evidence obtained unlawfully by the state to which the request was directed (the requested state). It may also arise in relation to a person brought into the jurisdiction of a state by extradition (for the purpose of prosecution), whereby in executing the request for extradition, the authorities of the requested state unlawfully arrested and/or detained said person. In both situations the adjudicating (i.e. requesting) state, acting through its judicial authorities, may be unwilling to enquire into, let alone take responsibility for, any unlawfulness (alleged) to have occurred in the execution of its request for cooperation.[335] The unwillingness of states to enquire into, and take responsibility for, unlawfulness in the execution of requests for cooperation is tied up with the notion of mutual recognition, pursuant to which states requesting assistance in criminal matters may 'presume the credibility and reliability' of the state to which the request is directed, thereby allowing states to work together effectively and efficiently.[336] In the European Union (hereafter: EU), this 'trust' is based 'upon an assumption that all Member States are human rights compliant'.[337] Hodgson is critical in this regard: while it 'is true that all EU Member States are members of the Council of Europe and have ratified the ECHR ... the EU has acknowledged that compliance levels are far from uniform and enforcement mechanisms are weak'.[338] In addition, she

---

[335] As to the responsibility of the requested state, Klip notes that this is difficult to determine. See Klip 2012, 424.

[336] Hodgson 2011, 617.

[337] Ibid., 618.

[338] Ibid., 618. The ECtHR also recognises this: 'the Court observes that the existence of domestic laws and accession to international treaties guaranteeing respect for fundamental rights in principle are not in themselves sufficient to ensure adequate protection against the risk of ill-treatment where ... reliable sources have reported practices resorted to or tolerated by the authorities which are

argues that the different legal systems across the EU pose particular problems for mutual recognition: 'Safeguards for the accused vary across jurisdictions, according to the roles and responsibilities of other legal actors at various points in the process —some are stronger during the investigation, others at the trial hearing. A defendant in a cross-jurisdiction case may have the best, or the worst, of both worlds.'[339] Efforts are now being made at the European level to improve the position of the suspect or accused who is the subject of inter-state cooperation, both through the human rights themselves (of which the ECtHR's case law on the right to counsel in the investigative phase is an example) and the mechanisms that enable cooperation between states.[340] Regarding the latter, Article 10 of the European Directive on the right of access to a lawyer in criminal proceedings and in European arrest warrant proceedings, and on the right to have a third party informed upon deprivation of liberty and to communicate with third persons and with consular authorities while deprived of liberty, for example, provides that 'Member States shall ensure that a requested person has the right of access to a lawyer *in the executing Member State* upon arrest pursuant to the European arrest warrant', and that:

> The competent authority in the executing Member State shall, without undue delay after deprivation of liberty, inform requested persons that they have the right to appoint a lawyer *in the issuing Member State*. The role of that lawyer in the issuing Member State is to assist the lawyer in the executing Member State by providing that lawyer with information and advice with a view to the effective exercise of the rights of requested persons.[341]

Further, Article 6 of the European Directive regarding the European Investigation Order in criminal matters provides that the state authority issuing the (investigation) order may only do so if the order is 'necessary and proportionate' for the purpose of criminal proceedings '[thereby] taking into account the rights of the suspected or accused person', and 'the investigative measure(s) indicated in the [European Investigation Order] could have been ordered under the same conditions in a similar domestic case'.[342] However, as Zeegers notes, 'these procedures are specific to cooperation within the EU', while the 'general international framework applicable to [inter-state cooperation in criminal matters] ... does not impose any

---

(Footnote 338 continued)

manifestly contrary to the principles of the Convention.' See *Saadi v Italy* App no 37201/06 (ECtHR, 28 February 2008), para 147; and *MSS v Belgium and Greece* App no 30696/09 (ECtHR, 21 January 2011), para 353.

[339] Hodgson 2011, 619.

[340] For a discussion of such 'efforts', see Hodgson 2011.

[341] Directive 2013/48/EU of the European Parliament and of the Council of 22 October 2013 on the right of access to a lawyer in criminal proceedings and in European arrest warrant proceedings, and on the right to have a third party informed upon deprivation of liberty and to communicate with third persons and with consular authorities while deprived of liberty (2013) OJ L 294/1, Article 10(1) and (4) (emphasis added).

[342] Directive 2014/41/EU of the European Parliament and of the Council of 3 April 2014 regarding the European Investigation Order in criminal matters (2014) OJ L 130/1, Article 6.

obligations on the requesting state related to the domestic safeguards that apply to the use of coercive measures'.[343] Traditionally, it seems, the law applicable to the execution of a request for coercive measures, has been the law of the requested state, according to the principle of *lex loci regit actum*.[344]

Turning now to the human rights case law on unlawfulness in the context of inter-state cooperation in criminal matters, it was stated above that an absolute exclusionary rule in respect of evidence obtained by torture flows from the case law of the ECtHR and from the UNCAT. The question that now needs to be answered is whether such a rule applies only to 'domestic' situations, whereby such evidence has been obtained by authorities of the same state to be adjudicating (through its judicial authorities) in criminal proceedings. Article 15 of the UNCAT provides that: 'Each State Party shall ensure that any statement which is established to have been made as a result of torture shall not be invoked as evidence in any proceedings, except against a person accused of torture as evidence that the statement was made.' Interpreting this provision literally, it seems that the exclusionary rule provided for therein also applies to torture evidence obtained abroad: it applies to any statement, in any proceedings.[345] Currie points to the importance of the prohibition of torture, its *jus cogens* status, to assert that Article 15 of the UNCAT prohibits the use of torture evidence obtained abroad.[346] While the ECtHR has not explicitly ruled on this issue, it is likely that under the ECHR also, the use of such evidence is prohibited. According to Ambos, 'analysis of the [ECtHR's] case law, especially with regard to the importance given to the protection of torture, implies that the Court would not rule any differently if the torture were obtained by third parties',[347] including, presumably, foreign authorities or private parties. If the importance attached to a particular right is an indicator that evidence obtained in violation thereof may not be used at trial (because it fatally undermines the fairness of the proceedings), it may well be that the use at trial of a statement obtained in another state in violation of the right to counsel in the investigative phase (and in any case at the time of questioning) will result in liability under Article 6 of the ECHR for the state using it. Thus, in pointing to the difficulties traditionally faced by cooperating states in protecting the rights of the suspect or accused, caused by 'differences in criminal procedural traditions', Hodgson notes the 'changing legal landscape' in Europe:

> ... the European Court of Human Rights ... has delivered a series of judgments that set out in the strongest terms the importance of prompt and effective custodial legal advice as part of the accused's right to a fair trial... This strand of ECtHR jurisprudence is more narrowly

---

[343] Zeegers 2016, 129, referring to the UN Model Treaty on Mutual Legal Assistance in Criminal Matters (UNGA Res 45/117 and Annex (14 December 1990) UN Doc A/RES/45/117).

[344] See e.g. Sluiter 2002, 204.

[345] See also Ambos 2009, 380; and Thienel 2006, 360.

[346] Currie 2000, 168.

[347] Ambos 2009, 385–386. See also Thienel 2006, 362–363.

prescriptive in setting out what is required, leaving no room for arguments based on procedural difference across legal traditions.[348]

Arguably, the terms adopted by the ECtHR and the narrow prescriptiveness of its case law implies that any statement obtained by the requested state in violation of the right to counsel would have to be excluded in proceedings in the requesting state in order to protect the fairness of the proceedings.[349] Nevertheless, it is to be noted that the European Directive on the right of access to a lawyer in criminal proceedings is somewhat equivocal in this regard:

> Without prejudice to national rules and systems on the admissibility of evidence, Member States shall ensure that, in criminal proceedings, in the assessment of statements made by suspects or accused persons or of evidence obtained in breach of their right to a lawyer or in cases where a derogation to this right was authorised in accordance with Article 3(6), the rights of the defence and the fairness of the proceedings are respected.[350]

Turning now to unlawfulness in the context of transnational cooperation alleged to be in violation of the right to privacy, in *S v Austria*,[351] the Applicant (bank) complained that an order issued by the Austrian authorities pursuant to a request by the German authorities for a search and seizure to be carried out on its premises in order to obtain certain documents and objects related to a client of the Applicant bank suspected of tax evasion, and which led to the Applicant bank handing certain material over to the Austrian authorities executing the order, violated, inter alia, Article 8 of the ECHR.[352] Thus, this case concerns the responsibility of the requested or cooperating state for alleged rights violations committed by its authorities in executing a request for cooperation. According to the treaty governing mutual legal assistance between Austria and Germany, in executing a German request for cooperation, the Austrian court 'was only required to examine whether the act requested was admissible under Austrian law, but not whether it was necessary, appropriate or proportionate'. Rather, the latter question was a matter for the German authorities. Indeed, the Austrian court did not examine this latter question, and deemed admissible the German request for cooperation on account of search and seizure being admissible under the Austrian Code of Criminal Procedure. The European Commission of Human Rights (hereafter: ECnHR) did not take issue with this stance of 'non-enquiry', noting only that the fact that the Austrian courts did not consider themselves competent to rule on the question of necessity,

---

[348] Hodgson 2011, 613.

[349] The ECtHR's judgement in *Stojkovic v France and Belgium* would seem to confirm this. See *Stojkovic v France and Belgium* App no 25303/08 (ECtHR, 27 October 2011) paras 55–57.

[350] See n 341, Article 12(2).

[351] *S v Austria* App no 12592/86 (ECnHR, 6 March 1989).

[352] It also alleged a violation of Article 6 ECHR, which the ECnHR rejected on the basis that Article 6 ECHR did not apply to proceedings in Austria relating to the German request for cooperation: such proceedings 'did not determine a criminal charge against the applicant bank' and did not 'determine the applicant bank's civil rights and obligations'. See, in this regard, Klip 2012, 424.

appropriateness and proportionality, 'does not mean that the search actually lacked these requirements'.[353] According to the ECnHR there was 'no indication that it was objectively unjustified or disproportionate' and the search was thus covered by Article 8(2) of the ECHR.[354] As the Applicant bank could not arguably claim that its right to privacy under Article 8 had been violated, its claim under Article 13, the right to an effective remedy, was found to be manifestly ill-founded.[355]

The case of *Chinoy v United Kingdom*[356] concerned the use by a domestic (UK) court in extradition proceedings (whereby the United States of America was the requesting State) of recordings made in France by US authorities of conversations between the Applicant, who was suspected by US authorities of drug offences, and others (including his family), which the Applicant claimed contravened French law. In proceedings before the ECnHR the Applicant argued, inter alia, that his right to respect for his private life, home, family and correspondence (provided for in Article 8 of the ECHR) had been interfered with, on account of the 'use' made by the UK authorities of the tape recordings (whereby such interference commenced with 'the existence of machinery for the receipt of the tapes by the authorities', continued with the 'actual receipt and subsequent internal use of the tapes in processing and assessing the case' and the 'reliance on and use of the tapes in processing and assessing the case' and ended with the 'reliance on and use of the tapes in the extradition proceedings')[357] and that his right to personal liberty had been violated on account of his detention having been based on unlawfully obtained evidence (the recordings). In dismissing the first complaint, the ECnHR attached importance to the fact the UK authorities had not been involved in the decision to record the conversations or in the recording itself.[358] Moreover, what the UK authorities *did* do, i.e. the use to which the recordings were put (which, according to the Commission was limited to: 'receipt of the materials from the United States authorities, examination of the material as to its relevance in the extradition proceedings, and production of the relevant parts as evidence in these proceedings'), did not amount to involvement on the part of those authorities such as to warrant liability under the Convention.[359] In this regard, the Commission noted that the domestic (UK) court had not relied on the recordings and transcripts involving the

---

[353] *S v Austria* App no 12592/86 (ECnHR, 6 March 1989), 4.

[354] Ibid., 4. It had previously found that the search had indeed constituted an interference with the right to privacy (thereby acknowledging that the right to respect for one's home encompasses the premises of legal persons), but that it had been in accordance with law, necessary in a democratic society and for the prevention of crime.

[355] Ibid., 4.

[356] *Chinoy v UK* App no 15199/89 (ECnHR, 4 September 1992).

[357] In this regard worth noting that Article 6 ECHR does not apply to extradition proceedings per se, because such proceedings do not involve the determination of a criminal charge or of civil rights or obligations.

[358] *Chinoy v UK* App no 15199/89 (ECnHR, 4 September 1992), 6.

[359] According to Van Hoek and Luchtman, this is not consistent with the findings of the Court in *Leander v Sweden* (App no 9248/81 (ECtHR, 26 March 1987), para 48) and *Amann v Switzerland*

Applicant's family.[360] In addition, the Commission attached importance to the public interest in inter-state cooperation in criminal matters (citing the 'international campaign against the drugs trade and the laundering of the proceeds of drug trafficking' and the 'United Kingdom's international treaty obligations' in this regard),[361] and to the fact that while the lawfulness of the recordings was doubtful, the domestic (UK) court had clearly considered them to be relevant.[362] In relation to the second complaint the Commission found 'no indication of arbitrariness in the decision of the United Kingdom courts to admit evidence which may have been obtained, and appears to have been accepted by the domestic courts as having been obtained, in breach of French law and/or the Convention'.[363] Accordingly, the Applicant's complaint under Article 8 of the ECHR was deemed inadmissible.[364]

Echeverri Rodriguez v The Netherlands[365] also concerned the use of intercepted communications, although in this case the (alleged) unlawfulness in question was of a different nature to that in *Chinoy v United Kingdom*. The recordings of the intercepted communications had been made by US authorities in the US in the context of an investigation opened (by US authorities) against a number of persons suspected of drug trafficking and money laundering offences, which such authorities subsequently disclosed to the Dutch investigative authorities, who (also) suspected one of those persons of drug offences. In the domestic (Dutch) proceedings against the Applicant, the defence argued that full disclosure had not been made as to the investigation in the USA, which was problematic because the defence suspected that a certain 'Mr. S.' might have been involved in the investigation as an 'infiltrator',[366] and that the Dutch authorities might have been involved in this investigation. In addition, the defence requested to question the individual responsible for disclosing the intercepted communications to the Dutch investigative authorities, a 'Ms. D.' The Dutch Court of Appeal denied the request. In proceedings

---

(Footnote 359 continued)

(App no 27798/95 (ECtHR, 16 February 2000), para 64), that the storage of data can give rise to separate responsibilities under Article 8(1) ECHR. See Van Hoek and Luchtman 2005, 17.

[360] *Chinoy v UK* App no 15199/89 (ECnHR, 4 September 1992), 6.

[361] Ibid., 7. See in this regard Vogler 2013, 33; and Van Hoek and Luchtman 2005, 17.

[362] *Chinoy v UK* App no 15199/89 (ECnHR, 4 September 1992), 7. According to Van Hoek and Luchtman the 'Commission seemed to balance the uncertainty with regard to the unlawfulness of the information against the clear relevance of the same to the extradition proceedings'. Van Hoek and Luchtman 2005, 17.

[363] *Chinoy v UK* App no 15199/89 (ECnHR, 4 September 1992), 8.

[364] According to Klip, this decision raises the question of 'whether a complaint against France might have been more successful', given that, while it is 'in the interest of the applicant to complain against all the possible states involved in the alleged violation', 'such a collective complaint may be declared inadmissible, because the applicant might not have exhausted the national remedies in all states against which the complaint is directed'. Klip 2012, 425.

[365] *Echeverri Rodriguez v Netherlands* App no 3286/98 (ECtHR, Decision of 27 June 2000).

[366] The suggestion is that the defence suspected that this Mr. S. incited or influenced the importation of the cocaine which led to the Applicant's arrest. *Echeverri Rodriguez v Netherlands* App no 3286/98 (ECtHR, Decision of 27 June 2000), 5.

before the ECtHR, the Applicant argued that his right to a fair trial had been violated on account of his request to question Ms. D. having been rejected, as a result of which he was unable to verify whether, if indeed an 'infiltrator' had been used, this use had been subject to the same limitations as those imposed by Dutch law. The ECtHR found as follows:

> Insofar as the applicant complains that the Court of Appeal refused to take oral evidence from the USA Assistant Attorney Ms. D. as she could have clarified issues in relation to the investigation carried out in the USA, the Court considers that the Convention does not preclude reliance, *at the investigating stage*, on information obtained by the investigating authorities from sources such as foreign criminal investigations. Nevertheless, the *subsequent* use of such information can raise issues under the Convention where there are reasons to assume that in this foreign investigation defence rights guaranteed have been disrespected.[367]

In convicting the Applicant, the Dutch Court of Appeal had not relied on the intercepted communications.[368] In other words, it had not used the intercepted communications at trial. They were 'only' used in the investigation. On the one hand the ECtHR appears to apply a 'more rigorous test' to the use *at trial* of evidence obtained abroad in the course of an investigation (than the one that applies to the use *in the investigation* of such evidence):[369] the way in which it was obtained must not 'disrespect' the rights of the defence. Thus, it recognises that the use of evidence obtained unlawfully abroad may render the subsequent trial in the requesting state unfair.[370] On the other hand, there must be 'reasons to assume' that in the investigation carried out abroad, defence rights were disrespected (either because the court, of its own accord, believes this to be the case or because the defence has made it sufficiently plausible that the evidence was obtained in such a manner). In other words, in the absence of such reasons, the presumption is that the evidence was obtained in a manner which respected the rights of the defence.[371]

---

[367] *Echeverri Rodriguez v Netherlands* App no 3286/98 (ECtHR, Decision of 27 June 2000), 8 (emphasis added).

[368] According to the ECtHR, it relied on: 'the applicant's statement before the Regional Court, statements taken from Mr. X. before the police and the investigating judge, statements taken from other persons before the police and/or the investigating judge, formal records and the results of a forensic examination of substances seized by the police on 3 August 1995'. *Echeverri Rodriguez v Netherlands* App no 3286/98 (ECtHR, Decision of 27 June 2000), 6.

[369] Vogler 2013, 33. See also Van Hoek and Luchtman 2005, 18.

[370] See also *PV v FRG*, which concerned the use at trial in Germany of witness evidence obtained in Turkey. The Applicant complained that that witness had never been heard by the domestic court and that he had not had the opportunity to examine the witness. While the ECnHR noted that 'the German authorities cannot be held responsible for the non-observance of provisions of the Turkish law by a Turkish court' and that the domestic court 'was not responsible for the examination of C on commission', it held that 'it is in principle conceivable that the use of the evidence thereby obtained could be contrary to that provision [Article 6(1) ECHR]'. See *PV v FRG* App no 11853/85 (ECnHR, 13 July 1987), 6 and 7.

[371] Accordingly, the test set forth by the ECtHR in *Echeverri* is a form of '*qualified* non-inquiry'. See Vogler 2013, 34.

In the circumstances, there were no reasons to assume that in the investigation in the USA, defence rights had been disrespected.

In *Sari v Turkey and Denmark* the applicant complained of the excessive length of the proceedings against him and therefore a violation of Article 6(1) of the ECHR. Shortly after a murder was committed in Denmark, the Applicant, who was suspected by the Danish authorities of having committed the murder, fled the country. The Danish authorities sought assistance from Turkey, where the Applicant was thought to be. Approximately two and a half years after fleeing Denmark, the Applicant was arrested in Istanbul, and for a further six and a half years, until the Applicant was convicted by a Turkish court for the murder, the Danish and Turkish authorities quarrelled over matters related to the transfer of jurisdiction over the crime to Turkey. In looking to the particular circumstances of the case the ECtHR found that the case was complex not on account of the nature of the offence but of the fact that the Applicant had fled Denmark, thereby making it necessary for the relevant national authorities to resort to inter-state cooperation.[372] It also found that the Applicant had contributed significantly to the delay by fleeing Denmark shortly after the murder and remaining at large for more than two years.[373] As to the conduct of the Danish authorities, the ECtHR found that the periods of inactivity on the part of such authorities was the joint responsibility of Denmark and Turkey and that any delay in transferring jurisdiction to the Turkish judiciary was the result of a system of mutual legal assistance which 'unfortunately' was time-consuming, making delay 'inevitable'.[374] Nor were the Turkish authorities to blame, any periods of inactivity in the cooperation process being the joint responsibility of Turkey and Denmark.[375]

In sum, while the ECnHR and the ECtHR have recognized that the way in which evidence was gathered abroad may render the subsequent trial in the requesting state unfair, it seems that only flagrant rights violations, i.e. rights violations that, on their face, pose a high risk to the fairness of the proceedings or are obviously offensive to other fundamental values, are capable of doing so, where evidence obtained thereby is used at trial;[376] after all, there must be 'reasons to assume' that in the investigation carried out abroad defence rights were 'disrespected'. In case of torture, where evidence obtained thereby is subsequently used at trial, there will be

---

(Footnote 371 continued)

This places a heavy burden on applicants in proceedings before the ECtHR to show unlawfulness. As Van Hoek and Luchtman observe, '[i]n most cases this is far from simple'. Van Hoek and Luchtman 2005, 18. See also Klip 2012, 425.

[372] *Sari v Turkey and Denmark* App no 21889/93 (ECtHR, 8 November 2001), paras 76–79.

[373] Ibid., paras 84–88.

[374] Ibid., paras 91 and 92.

[375] Ibid., para 96.

[376] Bachmaier Winter 2013, 140. In relation to state practice, Currie comes to a similar conclusion: 'State practice, as embodied in the judgements of criminal courts, would seem to posit ... an international exclusionary rule, but only in the most heinous or "shocking" cases.' See Currie 2000, 177–178.

reasons to assume that defence rights were disrespected.[377] Similarly, violation of the right of access to counsel at the time of questioning is likely to constitute a flagrant rights violation. In delay cases, the international dimension of the case, even when this is unrelated to the underlying offence, appears to be a factor militating against founding a violation of Article 6(1) of the ECHR.[378] This, and the ECtHR's application of a 'qualified' rule of non-enquiry[379] in cases concerning the use of evidence obtained abroad may well warrant the conclusion that the ECtHR attaches more importance to international cooperation than to the protection of individual rights.[380]

2.3 Protection of Others

In the introduction to this chapter it was stated that in one of the domestic jurisdictions examined in this book, the discussion (in both the literature and the case law) on how to address procedural violations committed in the pre-trial phase of criminal proceedings was informed not only by human rights standards that protect the suspect or accused in criminal proceedings, but also by human rights standards that purport to protect other persons, i.e. the victims of crime. According to proponents of an approach which (also) takes into account the latter set of human rights standards, certain judicial responses to pre-trial procedural violations *may* be inconsistent with the positive obligations arising from, for example, Articles 2 and 3 of the ECHR, because they prevent the effective punishment of the person responsible for the serious human rights violation, i.e. for the crime, in question.[381] Thus, a stay of proceedings prevents the case from proceeding to a verdict on the merits (and therefore the establishment of criminal responsibility), the exclusion of evidence may lead to an acquittal (if any remaining evidence is insufficient to found a conviction), and a significant reduction of sentence precludes the imposition of punishment commensurate with the criminal responsibility established. Such an approach appears to read into the positive obligations flowing from the substantive provisions of the ECHR a 'duty to punish', whereby the lack of punishment that

---

[377] Evidence obtained by torture cannot be said to have been obtained in compliance with the privilege against self-incrimination.

[378] Ibid., 19. See also Klip 2012, 425.

[379] See n 371 and accompanying text.

[380] Vogler 2013, 38. Currie appears to come to a similar conclusion in relation to state practice. See Currie 2000.

[381] See e.g. Kuiper 2014, 346–351; Van de Westelaken 2010, 151; and Vellinga-Schootstra and Vellinga 2008, 41–43.

results from the court attaching a certain consequence to a pre-trial procedural violation would amount to failure to discharge this duty.

The purpose of this section is to provide an overview[382] of the obligations that human rights law imposes on states on how to address (serious) human rights violations occurring within their jurisdiction (to the extent that such obligations could bear on the question of how to address pre-trial procedural violations), including whether, under human rights law, there exists a duty to punish. Given the central research question of this book, the question that must ultimately be answered here is whether any duty to prosecute imposed on states under human rights law can be said to apply to the international criminal tribunals. While it was observed above that the ICTs are bound by internationally recognized human rights, the duty to prosecute raises questions that warrant addressing the matter of its applicability to the ICTs separately. Accordingly, this matter is dealt with below, after first setting out the obligations of states in this regard.

2.3.1 States' Duties in Responding to Serious Human Rights Violations

It is, by now, widely accepted that states' human rights obligations are not limited to abstaining from conduct that violates the human rights of their subjects; such obligations may also require states to take action in order to ensure their subjects' enjoyment of such rights, i.e. to take measures to prevent human rights violations and to address adequately such violations when they occur. Such 'positive obligations' or 'affirmative duties' are derived from substantive rights such as the right to life and the prohibition of torture and inhuman and degrading treatment and punishment,[383] and states are required to discharge their positive obligations (to address adequately serious abuses when they occur) when state authorities have committed the human rights violation, as well as when a private individual has committed a serious abuse, such as murder.[384]

In order to ensure that its subjects are able to exercise their human rights effectively (or, put differently, in order to ensure that states discharge their positive obligations under the applicable human rights treaties), states are increasingly being required to take measures in the criminal law (enforcement) sphere. Thus, the

---

[382] It is beyond the scope of this book to provide a comprehensive analysis of the human rights law in this regard. For such an analysis see Seibert-Fohr 2009.

[383] That is, read in conjunction with the relevant provision on the obligation to protect human rights (for the HRC this is Article 2 ICCPR, for the ECtHR this is Article 1 ECHR). See also Seibert-Fohr 2009, 117.

Positive obligations also flow from other substantive provisions than the right to life and the prohibition of torture and inhuman and degrading treatment and punishment. See e.g. Mowbray 2004.

[384] See Seibert-Fohr 2009, 222.

bodies charged with supervising the compliance with, and implementation of, the comprehensive human rights treaties have called for the criminalization of certain types of (particularly serious) abuse,[385] and for the criminal investigation and prosecution thereof. Moreover, such bodies have in some cases looked to the *punishment*, i.e. criminal sanction, imposed in determining whether the state in question has discharged its positive obligations, and, in particular, its duty to prosecute, under the relevant human rights treaty. Under the comprehensive human rights treaties there is a duty to *investigate* human rights violations.[386] An investigation

> ... sheds light on the facts and identifies those responsible. The participation of the victims and their families is an important factor in the healing process. By conducting an investigation, a State demonstrates that it does not condone the abuse. It also re-establishes the validity of a right in principle, acknowledges the suffering of victims and condemns the injustice suffered by them. Acknowledgment is an important element of reconciliation. At the same time, the intention to avoid repetition is demonstrated.[387]

Moreover, there appears to be growing consensus that for particularly serious human rights violations the investigation required is a criminal one.[388] Indeed, the ECtHR has held in relation to the positive obligations that arise under the right to life, within the meaning of Article 2 of the ECHR, that: 'In order to be "effective" as this expression is to be understood in the context of Article 2 of the Convention, an

---

[385] At the HRC, See e.g. HRC, 'General comment no 20. Article 7 (Prohibition of torture, or other cruel, inhuman or degrading treatment or punishment)' in Compilation of General Comments and General Recommendations Adopted by Human Rights Treaty Bodies (1994) UN Doc HRI/GEN/1/Rev.1, 32, para 13 ('States parties should indicate when presenting their reports the provisions of their criminal law which penalize torture and cruel, inhuman and degrading treatment or punishment, specifying the penalties applicable to such acts, whether committed by public officials or other persons acting on behalf of the State, or by private persons. Those who violate Article 7, whether by encouraging, ordering, tolerating or perpetrating prohibited acts, must be held responsible. Consequently, those who have refused to obey orders must not be punished or subjected to any adverse treatment.'); at the ECtHR, See e.g. *Osman v UK* App no 23452/94 (ECtHR, 28 October 1998), para 115; and at the IACtHR See e.g. *Goiburú and Others v Paraguay* Series C no 153 (IACtHR, 22 September 2006), paras 91–92.

[386] See e.g. Seibert-Fohr 2009, 34, 190; and Shelton 2005, 153–155.

[387] Seibert-Fohr 2009, 209.

[388] Ibid., 191–192. In this regards she notes that: 'Apart from seeking out offenders and holding them accountable, States parties are also obliged to take additional measures to deal adequately with human rights violations. Regardless of whether there is a duty to prosecute, the Committee recognizes a duty to investigate and compensate victims' and that while an investigation 'is usually part of criminal proceedings', the duty to investigate 'exists independently'. Ibid., 34 n 129.

investigation into a death that engages the responsibility of a Contracting Party under that Article must firstly be adequate. That is, it must be *capable of leading to the identification and punishment of those responsible*.'[389] In light of this under-standing of 'criminal investigation', there may in cases of serious human rights violations be overlap between the duty to investigate and the duty to prosecute, whereby it is difficult to tell when the duty to conduct a criminal investigation ends, and the duty to prosecute begins. Indeed, under human rights law, there may be said to exist a duty to prosecute *serious* human rights violations, whereby the deter-mination of the seriousness of a violation is informed by the human right at issue, as well as the gravity of the violation.[390] Thus, a violation of the right to life need not give rise to a duty to prosecute; it depends on the facts and circumstances of the case.[391] Murder, it seems, does give rise to a duty to prosecute.[392] However, violation of another right than the right to life or the prohibition of torture and inhuman and degrading treatment and punishment, need not do so; other measures may suffice. In other words, there is no *comprehensive* duty to prosecute human rights violations, i.e. to prosecute *all* human rights violations, regardless of their seriousness. Whereas the lack of *punishment*, i.e. where no criminal sanction has been imposed, will not necessarily amount to a failure to discharge the duty to *investigate* if criminal proceedings have been initiated that have adequately brought to light the violation in question, it may, depending on the circumstances, amount to a failure to discharge the duty to *prosecute*. More will be said about this issue

---

[389] *Ramsahai and Others v The Netherlands* App no 52391/99 (ECtHR, 15 May 2007), para 324 (emphasis added). According to Seibert-Fohr, this should not be taken to mean that the ECtHR views criminal punishment as a personal remedy for the victim: 'When the Court requests an investigation capable of leading to the punishment of those responsible it has been cautious not to proclaim an individual right of the victim for the criminal punishment of the perpetrator. In those cases in which a lack or inadequacy of prosecution was criticized as contrary to the victim's rights it was not because of the lack of punishment... [rather] it was generally the failure to conduct an independent official investigation which was held to be in violation of the victim's rights. In *X. and Y. v The Netherlands* it was not the failure to punish but the lack of initiation of criminal proceedings which was held to be a violation of the victim's rights. It is thus the aspect of bringing to light a violation rather than criminal accountability which leads the Court to assume a right of the victim to investigation. The emphasis is clearly on the duty to investigate allegations of misconduct. The Court has not accepted that punishment is required in the interest of a particular victim.' Seibert-Fohr 2009, 148–149, referring to *X and Y v Netherlands* App no 8978/80 (ECtHR, 26 March 1985).

[390] Seibert-Fohr 2009, 200–201.

[391] Ibid., 201.

[392] See n 384 and accompanying text.

below. In principle, though, the duties of states to investigate and prosecute are obligations of means, not of result.[393] Indeed, the ECtHR has held that:

> An obligation to *investigate* "is not an obligation of result, but of means": not every investigation should necessarily be successful or come to a conclusion which coincides with the claimant's account of events; however, it should in principle be capable of leading to the establishment of the facts of the case and, if the allegations prove to be true, to the identification and punishment of those responsible.[394]

Further, the ECtHR has held that the obligation to *prosecute* serious human rights violations does not entail 'an absolute obligation for all prosecutions to result in conviction, or indeed in a particular sentence'.[395] In other words, punishment is not a necessary component of the duty to prosecute. For one thing, in prosecuting those alleged to be responsible for serious human rights violations, courts are required to respect due process or fair trial guarantees.[396] In this regard, Seibert-Fohr has observed that: 'It would not be in accordance with the right to a trial by an independent court and with the presumption of innocence if the outcome of a trial was predetermined by a duty to punish.'[397] Shelton also recognizes the importance of observing fair trial guarantees when prosecuting serious human rights violations, which she argues is essential for the credibility of the results of a prosecution: 'The emphasis in criminal trials on full and reliable evidence in accordance with due process usually makes the results more credible than those of other, more political proceedings, including truth commissions.'[398] In light of the central question of this research (how should judges at the international criminal tribunals respond to procedural violations committed in the pre-trial phase of the proceedings?), it may be noted that respect for 'due process' guarantees may be a

---

[393] Nevertheless, according to Seibert-Fohr, as the human rights bodies are increasingly seeking 'to ensure that those responsible for serious human rights violations serve an adequate sentence as a matter of general human rights protection', 'the assertion that the conduct of criminal proceedings is not an obligation of result, is losing ground'. Ibid., 138. More will be said about this below; see n 419–424 and accompanying text.

[394] *Kopylov v Russia* App no 3933/04 (ECtHR, 29 July 2010), para 132 (emphasis added). See also *Al-Skeini and Others v UK* App no 55721/07 (ECtHR, 7 July 2011), para 166; *Ramsahai and Others v The Netherlands* App no 52391/99 (ECtHR, 15 May 2007), para 324; and *Mikheyev v Russia* App no 77617/01 (ECtHR, 26 January 2006), para 107. See also e.g. *Velásquez Rodríguez v Honduras* Series C no 4 (IACtHR, 29 July 1988), para 177.

[395] *Öneryıldız v Turkey* App no 48939/99 (ECtHR, 30 November 2004), para 96. See also *Rizvanović and Rizvanović v Bosnia and Herzegovina* Comm no 1997/2010 (HRC, 21 March 2014), para 9.5: 'The Committee recalls its jurisprudence according to which the obligation to investigate allegations of enforced disappearances and to bring the culprits to justice is not an obligation of result, but of means...'

[396] See e.g. *Osman v UK* App no 23452/94 (ECtHR, 28 October 1998), para 116.

[397] Seibert-Fohr 2009, 203. While acknowledging that the 'quest for justice may be frustrated if the evidence is not sufficient and the accused is subsequently acquitted' she argues that 'justice and the integrity of the legal system are better served in the long run if a criminal system abides by its own rules. Seibert-Fohr 2009, 225.

[398] Shelton 2005, 397. See also Ochoa-Sanchez 2013, 61.

reason for a criminal court to respond to pre-trial procedural violations by staying the proceedings, excluding the evidence obtained thereby, or by reducing the sentence. The salient question, then, is *when* respect for due process may reasonably be said to require such a response, which is inevitably tied up with the particular rationale or rationales adopted by the court in question when ruling on unlawfulness on the part of the police or the public prosecutor. These rationales are explored in the following two chapters, Chaps. 3 and 4, on national law and practice.

One the one hand, then, measures such as the duty to investigate, including the duty to conduct a criminal investigation, and the duty to prosecute are obligations of means, not result; on the other hand, however, the bodies charged with supervising the compliance with, and implementation of, the comprehensive human rights treaties are increasingly looking to the punishment, i.e. criminal sanction, imposed in determining whether the state in question has discharged its positive obligations, and, in particular, its duty to prosecute, under the relevant human rights treaty. Criminal punishment, it seems, is 'increasingly regarded as a necessary element of human rights protection'.[399] It is worth recalling here that 'classic' responses to procedural violations committed in the pre-trial phase of criminal proceedings may prevent the imposition of punishment; thus, a stay of proceedings prevents the case from proceeding to a verdict on the merits, and the exclusion of (unlawfully obtained) evidence may lead to an acquittal if any remaining evidence is insufficient to found a conviction. And sentence reduction entails the reduction of punishment. Accordingly, the question arises as to whether the duty to prosecute (serious human rights violations) entails a duty to punish.

In order to answer this question, it is important to consider how measures in the criminal law (enforcement) sphere may protect human rights, i.e. allow a state's subjects to exercise their human rights effectively, which goes to the question of how such measures may be rationalized under human rights law. Various legal rationales have been advanced in this regard by the bodies charged with supervising the compliance with, and implementation of, the comprehensive human rights treaties, ranging from the prevention of future human rights violations[400] to avoiding retroactive complicity[401] to ensuring adherence to the rule of law[402] to

---

[399] Seibert-Fohr 2009, 281.

[400] See e.g. *Öneryıldız v Turkey* App no 48939/99 (ECtHR, 30 November 2004), para 96 (where the Court refers to the 'deterrent effect of the judicial system' and the judicial system's 'role ... in preventing violations of the right to life'); and 'Comments of the Human Rights Committee: Sri Lanka' (27 July 1995) UN Doc CCPR/C/79/Add.56, para 15.

[401] See e.g. HRC, 'Summary record of the 1519th meeting: Peru' (1 November 1996) UN Doc CCPR/C/SR.1519, para 44.

[402] See e.g. *Öneryıldız v Turkey* App no 48939/99 (ECtHR, 30 November 2004), para 96 (where the Court states that 'the national courts should not under any circumstances be prepared to allow life-endangering offences to go unpunished' because this 'is essential for maintaining public confidence and ensuring adherence to the rule of law').

providing the victim with redress or satisfaction.[403] Generally speaking, though, the (call for the) prosecution of human rights violations may be rationalized in two main ways: to protect human rights in general (in the interests of society as a whole), whereby the *preventive* function of punishment is emphasized, or to protect the individual victim, whereby the *remedial* function of punishment is emphasized.[404] Regarding the latter rationalization, Seibert-Fohr observes that this is sometimes based on 'the assumption that punishment serves retrospective protection of the infringed right' and sometimes on remedial rights such as the right to an effective remedy.[405] The first rationalization, then, sees prosecution as a means of preventing the commission of serious human rights violations[406] *in the future*, whereas the second sees it as a means of protecting the individual victim. Nevertheless, the distinction is not always easy to draw, as the notions are often mixed: '... prosecution is deemed necessary to deter future violations; while at the same time ... prosecution serves the interest in the individual.' Conversely, 'the award of pecuniary damages may not only serve the interest of the victim but also deter further violations in general and re-establish the validity of the affected right'.[407] Regarding such rationalizations, it is important to note that, whereas the first rationalization of prosecution is relatively uncontroversial, the second is (more) controversial, in practice (in the sense that there is no consensus among the supervisory bodies that such a duty exists for this purpose), in theory (in the sense that it is difficult to reconcile the notion of punishment (understood as retribution or retaliation) with human rights remedial theory),[408] and in the literature (in the sense that there is no consensus that such a duty exists for this purpose).[409]

---

[403] See e.g. *Nikolova and Velichkova v Bulgaria* App no 7888/03 (ECtHR, 20 December 2007), para 64 (where the Court found that the criminal measures taken by the authorities (including the imposition of criminal punishment) 'failed to provide appropriate redress to the applicants'); and HRC, 'General Comment no 31. The Nature of the General Legal Obligation Imposed on States Parties to the Covenant' (26 May 2004) UN Doc CCPR/C/21/Rev.1/Add. 13, para 16 (where the HRC notes that 'bringing to justice the perpetrators of human rights violations' can be a form of reparation within the meaning of the right to an effective remedy provided for in Article 2(3) ICCPR).

[404] Seibert-Fohr 2009, 190.

[405] Ibid., 190. In the context of the ACHR, it has also been based on the right to a fair trial, which has been read by the IACtHR to include a right of the victim to have criminal proceedings instituted against perpetrators of serious human rights violations. See ibid., 59–64.

[406] In other words, only in case of *serious* human rights violations does it require *criminal* punishment. See e.g. Seibert-Fohr 2009, 224; Shelton 2005, 395; and Ochoa-Sanchez 2013, 1–97.

[407] See Seibert-Fohr 2009, 282. See also Shelton 2005, 396 and 465.

[408] See in this regard Seibert-Fohr 2009, 207–211.

[409] According to Seibert-Fohr, there is a 'duty to punish serious human rights violations if it is necessary for the protection of human rights in general. But there is not a necessary element of reparation for the victim.' See Seibert-Fohr 2009, 223. However, Shelton appears to see prosecution of serious human rights violations not only as a preventive measure but also as a personal remedy. Shelton 2005, 396. Similarly, in setting out the legal basis for states' obligations (general human rights protection and protection of the individual) under the ICCPR, Ochoa-Sanchez does not appear to distinguish between investigation (which is widely acknowledged to be required in

How, then, has the duty to prosecute serious human rights violations been rationalized in practice? Traditionally when the HRC has required criminal *prosecution* (in respect of serious human rights violations), whereby it should be recalled that in principle, the duty to prosecute (serious human rights violations) is an obligations of means, not of result in the sense that it does not entail 'an absolute obligation for all prosecutions to result in conviction, or indeed in a particular sentence',[410] it has done so as a matter of general human rights protection, i.e. as a matter of *prevention*,[411] while repeatedly denying an individual right to demand prosecution on the basis of the right to an effective remedy.[412] Thus, the HRC recognises no comprehensive duty to prosecute (even serious) human rights violations *in the interests of the individual*.[413] Similarly, when the ECtHR has required

---

(Footnote 409 continued)

order to provide the individual victim with a remedy) and prosecution (which is not) and also argues (on the basis of the case law) that the right to an effective remedy requires not only a criminal investigation, but also the prosecution, trial and punishment of those responsible. In relation to the ECHR, he argues that the ECtHR's case law is unclear in this regard. Ochoa-Sanchez 2013, 40–42 and 46–48.

[410] See n 393–395 and accompanying text.

[411] This is apparent from the fact that the duty to prosecute those responsible for serious human rights violations is 'most prominently' based on the first two paragraphs of Article 2 ICCPR, rather than the third paragraph. See in this regard Seibert-Fohr 2009, 15–17.

According to Seibert-Fohr prevention should be construed broadly to include not only deterrence but also the 're-establishment of trust in the rule of law'. Ibid., 224.

[412] See e.g. *HCMA v Netherlands* Comm no 213/1986 (HRC, 30 March 1989), para 11.6; *RAVN and Others v Argentina* Comm nos 43, 344 and 345/1988 (HRC, 26 March 1990), para 5.5; *SE v Argentina* Comm no 275/1988 (HRC, 26 March 1990), para 7.3; *MS v Netherlands* Comm no 396/1990 (HRC, 22 July 1992), para 6.2; *Kulomin v Hungary* Comm no 521/1992 (HRC, 16 March 1994), para 6.3; *Rodríguez v Uruguay* Comm no 322/1988 (HRC, 19 July 1994), para 6.4; and *Horvath v Australia* Comm no 1885/2009 (HRC, 27 March 2014), para 8.2. In a number of cases the HRC has rejected such an individual right, while simultaneously holding that the state is under a duty 'to prosecute criminally, try and punish those held responsible' for serious human rights violations. See e.g. *Bautista de Arellana v Colombia* Comm no 563/1993 (HRC, 27 October 1995), para 8.6; *Vicente and others v Colombia* Comm no 612/1995 (HRC, 29 July 1997), para 8.8; and *Rajapakse v Sri Lanka* Comm no 1250/2004 (HRC, 14 July 2006), para 9.3. According to Seibert-Fohr, such decisions should be read as recognising a duty to prosecute *despite* the absence of a corresponding individual right (thereby confirming that prosecution serves purposes other than providing redress to the victim). Seibert-Fohr 2009, 24. This is confirmed by a number of decisions in which the HRC appears to distinguish between what is required for the right to an effective remedy (Article 2(3) ICCPR), including an investigation and compensation, and the duty to prosecute serious human rights violations. See e.g. *Zheikov v Russian Federation* Comm no 889/1999 (HRC, 17 March 2006), para 9; *Boucherf v Algeria* Comm no 1196/2003 (HRC, 30 March 2006), para 11; *Njaru v Cameroon* Comm no 1353/2005 (HRC, 19 March 2007), para 8; *Grioua v Algeria* Comm no 1327/2004 (HRC, 10 July 2007), para 9; and *El Alwani v Libya* App no 1295/2004 (HRC, 11 July 2007), para 8.

[413] HRC, 'General Comment no 31. The Nature of the General Legal Obligation Imposed on States Parties to the Covenant' (26 May 2004) UN Doc CCPR/C/21/Rev.1/Add. 13, para 8.

prosecution it has done so as a matter of prevention,[414] while consistently rejecting the claim that there exists an individual right to demand the prosecution and punishment for serious human rights violations.[415] While the IACtHR has also underscored the importance of prosecution for general human rights protection, i.e. for the prevention of future human rights violations,[416] unlike the HRC and ECtHR it unequivocally recognises that prosecution and (criminal) punishment may (also) be in the interests of the individual victim, i.e. that they have a remedial function, for example on the basis of the right to a fair trial (provided for Article 8 of the ACHR)[417] and of the right to an effective remedy (Article 25 of the ACHR).[418] It is important to note that while the HRC and ECtHR have consistently denied an individual right to demand prosecution, a 'new trend' may be emerging in the HRC's interpretation of the ICCPR at least, whereby 'criminal punishment is increasingly regarded also as a remedy for serious human rights violations'.[419] Such

---

[414] See e.g. *Öneryıldız v Turkey* App no 48939/99 (ECtHR, 30 November 2004), para 96 (where the Court refers to the 'deterrent effect of the judicial system' and the judicial system's 'role … in preventing violations of the right to life').

[415] See e.g. *Öneryıldız v Turkey* App no 48939/99 (ECtHR, 30 November 2004), para 96. See for more recent cases *Kolyadenko and Others v Russia* App nos 17423/05, 20534/05, 20678/05, 23263/05, 24283/05 and 35673/05 (ECtHR, 28 February 2012), para 192; and *Budayeva and Others v Russia* App nos 15339/02, 21166/02, 20058/02, 11673/02 and 15343/02 (ECtHR, 20 March 2008), para 144. According to Seibert-Fohr: 'When the Court requests an investigation capable of leading to the punishment of those responsible it has been cautious not to proclaim an individual right of the victim for the criminal punishment of the perpetrator… The Court has not accepted that *punishment* is required in the interest of a particular victim.' Seibert-Fohr 2009, 148 −149 (footnotes in original omitted). However, the ECtHR has looked to the sentence imposed in criminal proceedings in the context of general human rights protection, i.e. prevention. Thus, in *Nikolova and Velichkova v Bulgaria* the Court looked to the sentences imposed in order to determine whether the authorities had discharged their positive obligations under Article 2 ECHR: 'The Court's task here consists in reviewing whether and to what extent the national courts may be deemed to have submitted the case to the careful scrutiny required by Article 2, so that the *deterrent* effect of the judicial system in place and the significance of the role it is required to play in *preventing* violations of the right to life are not undermined.' See *Nikolova and Velichkova v Bulgaria* App no 7888/03 (ECtHR, 20 December 2007), paras 60−62 (emphasis added). According to Seibert-Fohr, the Court is thus increasingly seeking 'to ensure that those responsible for serious human rights violations serve an adequate sentence as a matter of general human rights protection', although with this development, 'the assertion that the conduct of criminal proceedings is not an obligation of result, is losing ground'. Ibid., 138.

[416] See e.g. *Velásquez Rodríguez v Honduras* Series C no 4 (IACtHR, 29 July 1988), para 175.

[417] See e.g. *Blake v Guatemala* Series C no 36 (IACtHR, 24 January 1998), paras 96−97. Seibert-Fohr is critical in this regard. Seibert-Fohr 2009, 62−64.

[418] See e.g. *Castillo-Páez v Peru* Series C no 34 (IACtHR, 3 November 1997), paras 106−107.

[419] Seibert-Fohr 2009 e.g. 22−23 and 25−27. According to her, this is best illustrated by HRC, 'General Comment no 31. The Nature of the General Legal Obligation Imposed on States Parties to the Covenant' (26 May 2004) UN Doc CCPR/C/21/Rev.1/Add. 13, para 16, because here the HRC notes that 'bringing to justice the perpetrators of human rights violations' (which appears to refer to the prosecution of human rights violations which are 'recognized as criminal under either domestic or international law', i.e. to the criminal prosecution of human rights violations (see para

a trend is also visible in the ECtHR's interpretation of the ECHR.[420] In *Nikolova and Velichkova v Bulgaria*, the Applicants had alleged that their husband and father had died as a result of ill-treatment by two police officers, and that the ensuing criminal proceedings, in which the police officers had been convicted of 'wilfully inflicting grievous bodily harm negligently resulting in death', and received (suspended) sentences of three years' imprisonment, had failed to provide an effective remedy.[421] For the ECtHR, the question was 'whether the suspended sentences imposed on the officers at the close of excessively lengthy criminal proceedings were sufficient to discharge the authorities' positive obligations under Article 2 of the Convention'.[422] It held that: 'By punishing the officers with suspended terms of imprisonment, more than seven years after their wrongful act, and never disciplining them, the State in effect fostered the law-enforcement officers' "sense of impunity" and their "hope that all [would] be covered up"'.[423] The ECtHR concluded that the measures taken by the authorities 'failed to *provide appropriate redress to the applicants*'.[424] Therefore, in this case at least, the ECtHR seemed to treat the duty to prosecute as an obligation of result (by looking to the sentence imposed), and also as a remedial measure for the victim.[425] Nevertheless, the fact

---

(Footnote 419 continued)

18) is a form of 'reparation' within the meaning of the right to an effective remedy provided for in Article 2(3) ICCPR).

[420] See *Nikolova and Velichkova v Bulgaria* App no 7888/03 (ECtHR, 20 December 2007), para 64.

[421] *Nikolova and Velichkova v Bulgaria* App no 7888/03 (ECtHR, 20 December 2007), para 3.

[422] See n 393 and accompanying text.

[423] *Nikolova and Velichkova v Bulgaria* App no 7888/03 (ECtHR, 20 December 2007), para 63.

[424] Ibid., para 64 (emphasis added). According to Seibert-Fohr: 'The difference with previous cases is as follows: while the court had so far dealt with criminal prosecution as a matter of general human rights protection in *Nikolova and Velichkova v Bulgaria* it was called upon to decide whether the failure to resort to criminal measures (not simply to investigation) affected the individual victim. By considering criminal proceedings and enforcement as remedial measures for the victim, the Court went beyond its earlier jurisprudence which required only investigation as a necessary remedy. Previously, accountability had been considered only as a matter of general human rights protection, not as a remedy for the victim.' Seibert-Fohr 2009, 150.

[425] See also *Atalay v Turkey* App no 1249/03 (ECtHR, 18 September 2008), para 46 (where the Court refers to both preventive and remedial aspects of punishment); *Enukidze and Girgvliani v Georgia* App no 25091/07 (ECtHR, 26 April 2011), para 275 (where the Court held that the 'unreasonable leniency' of the sentences imposed 'deprived the criminal prosecution of the four officers of any *remedial* effect under Article 2 of the Convention' (emphasis added)); and *Uğur v Turkey* App no 37308/05 (ECtHR, 13 January 2015), para 102 (where the Court said that 'whether the national authorities did all that could be expected of them in order to examine the applicants' allegations of ill-treatment and prosecute the defendants in a timely fashion ... [would] ... enable ... [it] to determine whether or not the national authorities did all they could to provide the applicants with adequate redress by prosecuting and punishing the persons responsible for their ill-treatment', although the violation of Article 3 in that case was based not on the failure to *prosecute* or *punish*, but to carry out an effective *investigation* (see para 110)).

that the HRC has acknowledged the remedial aspects of punishment does not mean that it has 'accepted an individual right to demand punishment for serious human rights violations'.[426] The same may be argued in respect of the ECtHR. In numerous cases since *Nikolova and Velichkova* in which the Court has looked to the criminal punishment imposed by the domestic court, the Court has focused on the preventive function of punishment.[427] By contrast, the duty to *investigate has* been required as a matter of individual redress. Thus, while the victim of a serious human rights violation does not appear to have an *individual right* to demand the prosecution and punishment thereof, he or she does have a right to an *investigation*.[428] There is thus a duty to *investigate* serious human rights violations, as recognised by the HRC, IACtHR and the ECtHR,[429] whereby such duty serves to protect both society as a whole and the individual victim (and is, accordingly, both preventive and remedial in nature).

Prosecution, then, may be called for as a matter of general human rights protection, rather than of individual redress for the victim,[430] whereby it should be

---

[426] Seibert-Fohr 2009, 223 and 282. See, moreover, the recent case of *Horvath v Australia* Comm no 1885/2009 (HRC, 27 March 2014), para 8.2.

[427] See in this regard the following cases in which the court, in considering the (enforcement of the) criminal punishment imposed by the domestic court (whether for the purpose of determining whether the Applicant possessed victim status or the respondent state's compliance with substantive rights), cited the preventive (rather than the remedial) function of punishment: *Kasap and Others v Turkey* App no 8656/10 (ECtHR, 14 January 2014), paras 60–61; *Külah and Koyuncu v Turkey* App no 24827/05 (ECtHR, 23 April 2013), paras 42–43; *Austrianu v Romania* App no 16117/02 (ECtHR, 12 February 2013), para 74; *Shishkin v Russia* App no 18280/04 (ECtHR, 7 July 2011), para 103; *Kopylov v Russia* App no 3933/04 (ECtHR, 29 July 2010), para 141 (interestingly, in *Shishkin* and *Kopylov* the Court refers to the relevant findings in *Nikolova and Velichkova*, but not the paragraph in which the Court finds that the criminal measures adopted, including the punishment imposed, failed to provide the Applicants with appropriate redress); *Gäfgen v Germany* App no 22978/05 (ECtHR, 1 June 2010), paras 121 and 124; *Fadime and Turan Karabulut v Turkey* App no 23872/04 (ECtHR, 27 May 2010), paras 47–48; and *Bektaş and Özalp v Turkey* App no 10036/03 (ECtHR, 20 April 2010), paras 52–53. In *Beganović v Croatia* no criminal punishment was imposed (because the facts of the case were never established by a competent court of law), but the Court nevertheless emphasized the preventive function of criminal punishment, both in terms of special and general deterrence: *Beganović v Croatia* App no 46423/06 (ECtHR, 25 June 2009), para 85.

[428] In this regard Seibert-Fohr observes that: 'Apart from seeking out offenders and holding them accountable, States parties are also obliged to take additional measures to deal adequately with human rights violations. Regardless of whether there is a duty to prosecute, the Committee recognizes a duty to investigate and compensate victims' and that while an investigation 'is usually part of criminal proceedings', the duty to investigate 'exists independently'. Seibert-Fohr 2009, 34 n 129.

[429] See e.g. *Horvath v Australia* Comm no 1885/2009 (HRC, 27 March 2014), para 8.2; *Kaya v Turkey* App no 22729/93 (ECtHR, 19 February 1998), para 107; and *Velásquez Rodríguez v Honduras* Series C no 4 (IACtHR, 29 July 1988), para 174.

[430] Drawing such a conclusion would seem to require distancing from the approach taken by the Inter-American human rights institutions, for which there are good reasons. See in this regard Seibert-Fohr 2009, 108–109: 'The Inter-American human rights institutions have been very ambitious and strict in their jurisprudence on prosecution and punishment. This not only concerns

recalled that the lack of *punishment*, i.e. where no criminal sanction has been imposed, may, depending on the circumstances, amount to a failure to discharge the duty to *prosecute*;[431] the next question is whether it matters that this is the case. After all, it may be argued that since prosecution may well have the *effect* of providing redress to an individual,[432] it matters not that its primary purpose is general human rights protection. In this regard it may be observed that different considerations are likely to apply under each rationale. General human rights protection is concerned with prevention; when criminal prosecution is construed as general human rights protection, its purpose is to prevent similar human rights violations in the future. In light of this, it seems that a relevant (or, even, pertinent) consideration under the rationale of general human rights protection is whether the abuse in question forms part of a wider pattern of abuse, as well as whether the criminal law enforcement machinery already in place is sufficient to prevent, by way of deterrence, similar human rights violations in the future. Similarly, Seibert-Fohr argues that:

> *Especially* where there is a climate of impunity which gives rise to further serious human rights violations, there is undoubtedly a duty to punish grave human rights abuses. This duty derives from the duty to ensure the enjoyment of fundamental human rights. The pronouncements of the international human rights bodies should be understood in this sense since these usually concern systematic failures to prosecute serious human rights abuses. A culture of impunity is contrary to human rights law regardless of whether the abuses are committed by State officials or private individuals.[433]

By contrast, the existence of a wider pattern of abuse is not likely to be a relevant (let alone pertinent) consideration under the rationale of individual redress for the victim; what matters under that rationale is the harm suffered by the victim. Accordingly, it *does* matter that prosecution may be called for as a matter of general

---

(Footnote 430 continued)

the right to justice but also the ban on amnesties. It is, however, doubtful whether these standards should also be adopted by other human rights bodies. It is submitted that they are context-specific and need to be recognized as a result of the particular regional situation. They evolved in the context of gross and systematic human rights violations. The Court and the Commission developed their doctrine on the basis of experience gained over decades in Latin America. Serious shortcomings of the criminal justice system in several Latin-American States had led to an escalation of crimes. There are still grave systemic deficits in the criminal justice system. Large-scale impunity prevails in several OAS Member States. Therefore, the Inter-American human rights mechanism is regarded as the only means of remedy. In this situation it comes as no surprise that the Inter-American Court assumes a leading role in protecting the rule of law. Its uncompromised call for criminal prosecution seeks to combat a general situation which is detrimental to the enjoyment of human rights. Neither the Court nor the Commission is in favour of a margin of appreciation for the States parties. Otherwise their fight against the phenomenon of *impunidad* could be weakened.' See in this regard also Shelton 2005, 154.

[431] Accordingly, insofar as punishment is required to discharge the duty to prosecute, its rationale is general rights protection, rather than the provision of individual redress for the victim.

[432] See n 407 and accompanying text.

[433] Seibert-Fohr 2009, 202 (emphasis added).

human rights protection, rather than of individual redress for the victim; under the former rationale, whether the abuse forms part of a wider pattern of abuse is likely to be a pertinent consideration, and this has the potential to limit the number of cases in which prosecution may be said to be required in order to allow persons to exercise their human rights effectively. By extension, it has the potential to limit the number of cases in which punishment may be said to be required in order to do so.

The question that now needs to be answered is what this all means for a judge in criminal proceedings, seized with a case whereby the crime charged involves a serious human rights violation (for example, murder),[434] such that there is a duty to prosecute, and being called upon to provide relief in respect of procedural violations committed in the pre-trial phase of criminal proceedings. First, it should be recalled, that, in principle, the duty to prosecute is an obligation of means, not result. In other words, the obligation to *prosecute* serious human rights violations does not entail 'an absolute obligation for all prosecutions to result in conviction, or indeed in a particular sentence'.[435] Nevertheless, in some cases, the fact that punishment, i.e. a criminal sanction, has not been imposed *will* mean a failure to discharge the duty to prosecute.[436] The rationale of the duty to prosecute is general human rights protection, i.e. prevention of future human rights violations; accordingly, in those cases in which the fact that a criminal sanction has not been imposed would amount to a failure to discharge the duty to prosecute, punishment is being required as a means of general human rights protection. In light of the fact that punishment is 'only' required as a matter of general human rights protection, the judge in criminal proceedings, seized with a case whereby the crime charged involves a serious human rights violation such that there is a duty to prosecute, and being called upon to provide relief in respect of pre-trial procedural violations, is (at most) required to make an assessment of whether, in not being able to punish the accused as a result of staying the proceedings or excluding unlawfully obtained evidence (where any remaining evidence is insufficient to found a conviction), or in imposing a lesser sentence, the deterrent value of the system would be undermined, whereby relevant considerations are whether the abuse in question forms part of a wider pattern of abuse, as well as whether the criminal law enforcement machinery already in place is sufficient to prevent similar human rights violations in the future. In other words, the fact that a murder prosecution has not resulted in the imposition of a criminal sanction will not necessarily amount to a failure to discharge the duty to prosecute serious human rights violations; it will not automatically undermine the deterrent value of the system already in place. Put differently again, the fact that a murder prosecution has not resulted in punishment does not necessarily mean that the criminal law system in question is not being implemented effectively, and, by

---

[434] See n 384 and 392 and accompanying text.

[435] See n 393–395 and accompanying text.

[436] See n 399 and accompanying text.

extension, not providing for effective deterrence.[437] It depends on the particular criminal law (enforcement) system in question, whereby what matters is 'the coherence and effectiveness within … [that] system'.[438] In short, there is no 'absolute obligation to *punish* every serious human rights abuse'.[439]

2.3.2   Applicability of States' Duty to Prosecute to International Criminal Tribunals

Having provided an overview of the obligations that human rights law imposes on states on how to address (serious) human rights violations occurring within their jurisdiction, it is time now to turn to the matter of applicability of such obligations to the ICTs. Whether the ICTs are bound by states' duty pursuant to human rights law to prosecute (and in some cases, punish) serious human rights violations is a question that does not lend itself to easy answer. It was argued above[440] that while the ICTs are not states, they are, as international organizations, bound by human rights standards that form part of general international law (which covers the unwritten sources of international law, including customary international law and general principles of law), although the precise 'mechanism' by which they are (considered to be) bound differs per international criminal tribunal.[441] Thus, it is uncontroversial to state that the ICTs are bound by human rights standards that are aimed at protecting the suspect or accused to the extent that they form part of general international law.[442] Nevertheless, the fact that the ICTs are not states may have implications for the scope of the human rights protection afforded by such tribunals to the suspect and accused. Zeegers argues that the 'fundamental factual differences' between states on the one hand and international criminal tribunals on the other mean that the tribunals 'simply cannot be bound by certain human rights standards' and that other standards 'must be interpreted 'contextually'' in order for the tribunals to be able to apply them.[443] The differences between states on the one hand and international criminal tribunals on the other may also be relevant to the question of whether such tribunals are bound by the duty imposed on states to prosecute the most serious crimes, whether pursuant to human rights law,

---

[437] See in this regard Seibert-Fohr 2009, 202: 'There is a general duty on States to establish an effective criminal law system. It goes without saying, that a criminal law system provides for effective deterrence only if it is implemented.'

[438] Seibert-Fohr 2009, 202.

[439] Ibid., 202 (emphasis added).

[440] At the beginning of this chapter, where the applicability of human rights to the ICTs is addressed.

[441] Zeegers 2013, 366–381.

[442] However, according to Zappalà, the 'extension of the notion of fair trial to international criminal proceedings' is 'more a *policy* issue than a legal question'. See Zappalà 2003, 5–7.

[443] Zeegers 2013, 392.

international humanitarian law or other international law. In this regard it is important to note that while the ICTs are bound by human rights standards (to the extent that they form part of general international law), they are *not* bound by the general and specific human rights treaties themselves. As Jacobs points out in relation to the argument made by some that the 'international criminal tribunals are under the same duty to prosecute as States … that arises from treaty and customary law *in the case of each particular [international] crime*',[444] it is important to 'distinguish the *substantial and procedural content of the norms* we are concerned with'.[445] Thus, '[t]he fact that international criminal tribunals will be to a large extent dependent on the *substantial content of a crime in international law*, especially as they are aimed at individuals, in no way implies that they are bound by the *implementation mechanisms* imposed on the signatories of the treaties, or the recipients of the customary norms.'[446] Accordingly, Jacobs argues that 'the international criminal court, as an international institution is not bound by a duty to prosecute that arises in relation to States'.[447] The same may be argued in respect of the duty to prosecute the most serious human rights violations that flows from human rights law (as set out above). Moreover, specifically in relation to human rights law Jacobs observes that, 'the duty to prosecute in human rights covers acts that only partially overlap with international criminal law',[448] while according to Seibert-Fohr, 'the purpose for which punishment is sought in international human rights is not identical to that in international criminal law',[449] thereby calling into question the applicability of the duty to prosecute derived from human rights law to international criminal law. If the ICTs are indeed *not* bound by the duty to prosecute imposed on states pursuant to human rights law (and it is certainly arguable that they are not),[450] international humanitarian law or other international law, the question arises as to whether they are under any other duty to prosecute that might bear upon the question of how to address procedural violations committed in the pre-trial phase of criminal proceedings.[451] In this regard it may be noted that the mandate of the ICTs to prosecute those alleged to be responsible for committing the crimes that fall within their jurisdiction might be construed as a 'duty to prosecute'. Thus, Jacobs speaks of a 'statutory duty to prosecute' for the international criminal tribunals.[452] This statutory duty to prosecute, it should be noted, is subject to the

---

[444] Jacobs 2012, 337.

[445] Jacobs 2012, 337–338 (emphasis added).

[446] Ibid., 338 (emphasis added).

[447] Ibid., 337.

[448] Ibid., 338. See also Seibert-Fohr 2009, 289.

[449] Seibert-Fohr 2009, 290.

[450] Accordingly, the duty under human rights law to prosecute serious human rights violations will receive no further attention in this book.

[451] See n 12 and accompanying text.

[452] Jacobs 2012, 31–32.

principle of 'primacy' at the ad hoc Tribunals[453] and that of 'complementarity' at the ICC.[454] Like states' duty to prosecute pursuant to human rights law, the international criminal tribunals' 'duty' is subject to the condition that due process guarantees be observed, including the presumption of innocence.[455] Like their 'duty to prosecute', the obligation to observe such guarantees is derived from the ICTs' Statutes.

Both the duty of states pursuant to human rights law to prosecute serious human rights violations and the international criminal tribunals' (statutory) 'duty to prosecute' are obligations of means, not result, in the sense that, in prosecuting an alleged perpetrator (of a serious human rights violation or an international crime, respectively), due process or fair trial guarantees must be observed. Again, it may be noted that respect for such guarantees may be a reason for a criminal court to respond to pre-trial procedural violations by staying the proceedings, excluding the evidence obtained thereby, or by reducing the sentence. And the salient question, then, is when respect for due process or fair trial may be said to require such a response. This question is addressed below, in Chap. 7.

2.4 Conclusion

The purpose of this chapter was to set out the human rights framework with respect to the question of how to address pre-trial procedural violations. In this section, the main features of that framework and main points of analysis are summarized.

Several rights enshrined in the ICCPR and the ECHR are relevant to the question of how judges at the ICTs should respond to procedural violations committed in the pre-trial phase of the proceedings. The right to a fair trial, provided for in Articles 14 and 6 of the ICCPR and ECHR, respectively, is an obvious starting point for addressing the aforementioned question; it sheds light on the question of when it is necessary to address pre-trial procedural violations *within the criminal trial*. Other rights are also relevant to the question of how judges at the ICTs should address

---

[453] 'Under [the principle of] 'primacy', the international tribunal takes precedence over national courts, and need not demonstrate, as a question of admissibility for the case, that the national justice system is failing to investigate or prosecute.' See Schabas 2010, 52, referring to Articles 9 (2) ICTY Statute and 8(2) ICTR Statute.

[454] In the ICC case of *Lubanga*, the Pre-Trial Chamber said that: 'The principle of complementarity … provides that the Court shall only exercise jurisdiction over the crimes provided for in the Statute if the States concerned are not taking, or have not taken, action with regard to the said crimes, or are unwilling or unable to carry out their own national proceedings. The principle of complementarity of the Court vis-a-vis national jurisdictions is based on the premise that the investigation and prosecution of the crimes provided for in the Statute lies primarily with national jurisdictions.' See *Prosecutor v Lubanga* (Decision on the Practices of Witness Familiarisation and Witness Proofing) ICC-01/04-01/06, T Ch (8 November 2006) para 34 n 38.

[455] See Articles 21 ICTY Statute, 20 ICTR Statute and 55, 66 and 67 ICC Statute.

procedural violations committed in the pre-trial phase of the proceedings, although they do not require a response within the criminal trial (they may be provided within that context, though).

Turning first the ECtHR's case law with respect to the right to a fair trial provided for in Article 6 of the ECHR,[456] it was seen that in cases in which unlawfulness on the part of public authorities in the pre-trial phase of criminal proceedings is alleged to engage Article 6(1) of the ECHR, the ECtHR attaches significant importance to the use of the evidence so obtained. Put differently, it is *the use of evidence* obtained unlawfully that triggers the protection of Article 6 of the ECHR; on its own, unlawfulness on the part of public authorities in the pre-trial phase, even in case of torture, is not sufficient to do so. While the ECtHR recognizes that an accused person may, on account of such unlawfulness, be deprived of a fair trial 'right from the outset', it has only done so in the context of entrapment, where evidence will by definition have been used.

While the use of evidence obtained unlawfully triggers the protection of Article 6, it does not automatically result in a violation of Article 6 of the ECHR. Accordingly, under the ECHR, there is no automatic exclusion for evidence obtained by violation of the suspect's or accused's Convention rights, let alone for evidence obtained by pre-trial procedural violations more generally. Nevertheless, the ECtHR does recognize an automatic, or near automatic exclusionary rule for some rights violations. Thus, it recognizes an automatic exclusionary rule for evidence obtained by torture within the meaning of Article 3 of the ECHR, and a near automatic exclusionary rule for evidence obtained in violation of the right of access to a lawyer at the time of questioning under Article 6(3)(c). However, for other Convention violations committed in the pre-trial phase of criminal proceedings the impact of the use of evidence obtained thereby on the fairness of the proceedings depends on such factors as whether the rights of the defence were observed, *how* it was used and the public interest in the investigation and prosecution of crime. The ECtHR's practice of taking into account such factors is often referred to in the literature as 'balancing'. In respect of evidence obtained by torture within the meaning of Article 3 of the ECHR, then, the ECtHR will not engage in balancing in order to determine whether its use amounted to a violation of Article 6 of the ECHR; the use of evidence obtained by torture will always do so. In respect of evidence obtained in violation of the right not to incriminate oneself, the ECtHR will similarly refrain from embarking on a balancing exercise for the purposes of the aforementioned determination, although it is important to note that in order to determine whether the right has been violated in the first place, the ECtHR may have regard to such factors as the use to which the material obtained was put and the public interest in the investigation and punishment of crime. In respect of evidence obtained by violation of the right of access to a lawyer at the time of questioning, it will do so only exceptionally, it seems. In respect of the prohibition

---

[456] For the reasons provided in Sect. 2.2.1.1, the analysis of the right to a fair trial focussed on the ECHR and corresponding case law of the ECtHR.

of inhuman and degrading treatment within the meaning of Article 3 of the ECHR, the question of whether the use of evidence obtained thereby constitutes a violation of Article 6 depends firstly on whether the evidence obtained was confessional or real evidence, and, insofar as it concerns the latter, on whether the rights of the defence were observed—in particular, whether the defence could challenge the use of the evidence—and *how* it was used. Finally, in respect of violations of the right to privacy within the meaning of Article 8 of the ECHR, the ECtHR will also engage in balancing in order to determine whether the use of evidence obtained thereby amounted to a violation of Article 6; in this context, the ECtHR also expressly looks to, and attaches significant importance to, the probative value (or the 'quality') of the evidence. Accordingly, for the purposes of the balancing exercise to be undertaken, i.e. the factors to be taken into account, in the determination of Article 6 of the ECHR (where such determination has been triggered by (alleged) unlawfulness in the pre-trial phase of criminal proceedings), the ECtHR distinguishes between different forms of unlawfulness; the factors that may be taken into account and/or the extent to which importance may be attached to them differs as between Convention violations.

While on its own, unlawfulness on the part of public authorities in the pre-trial phase is not sufficient to trigger the protection of Article 6 of the ECHR, under the ECHR (and under the ICCPR) the victim of such unlawfulness nevertheless has remedies to pursue in this regard. Articles 2(3)(a) and 13 of the ICCPR and ECHR, respectively, provide for the right to an effective remedy, and Articles 9(5) and 5(5) of the ICCPR and ECHR, respectively, provide for the right to compensation in case of unlawful arrest or detention, whereby the latter right may be viewed as a specific manifestation of the former. While the latter right requires a remedy before a court, the former does not.

Regarding procedural violations committed by public authorities in an international context, while the ECnHR and the ECtHR recognise that the way in which evidence was gathered abroad may render the subsequent trial in the requesting state unfair, it seems that only flagrant rights violations are capable of doing so, where evidence obtained thereby is used at trial. This would include, most obviously, evidence obtained abroad by torture. As to what else might constitute a 'flagrant rights violation': a trial may be rendered unfair by the use (at trial) of evidence obtained abroad if the evidence was obtained in such a way as to disrespect the defence rights guaranteed in the Convention. This is likely to include a violation of the right of access to counsel in the investigative phase. In delay cases, the international dimension of the case, even when this is unrelated to the underlying offence, appears to be a factor militating against founding a violation of Article 6(1) of the ECHR. This, and the ECtHR's application of a 'qualified' rule of non-enquiry in cases concerning the use of evidence obtained abroad[457] may well warrant the conclusion that the ECtHR attaches more importance to international cooperation than to the protection of individual rights.

---

[457] See n 371 and accompanying text.

References

Ambos K (2009) The Transnational Use of Torture Evidence. Is LR 42:362 et seq.

Ashworth AJ (1977) Excluding Evidence as Protecting Rights. Crim LR 723 et seq.

Ashworth A (2012) The Exclusion of Evidence Obtained by violating a Fundamental Right: Pragmatism Before Principle in Strasbourg Jurisprudence. In: Roberts P, Hunter J (eds) Criminal Evidence and Human Rights: Reimagining Common Law Procedural Traditions. Hart Publishing, Oxford, pp 145–161

Ashworth A (2014) A decade of human rights in criminal justice. Crim LR 325 et seq.

Bachmaier Winter L (2013) Transnational Criminal Proceedings, Witness Evidence and Confrontation: Lessons from the ECtHR's Case Law. Utrecht LR 9:127 et seq.

Chedraui AMT (2010) An analysis of the exclusion of evidence obtained in violation of human rights in light of the jurisprudence of the European Court of Human Rights. Tilburg LR 15:205 et seq.

Choo AL-T (2012) 'Give us what you have'- Information, Compulsion and the Privilege Against Self-Incrimination as a Human Right. In: Roberts P, Hunter J (eds) Criminal Evidence and Human Rights: Reimagining Common Law Procedural Traditions. Hart Publishing, Oxford, pp 239–258

Choo AL-T (2013) The Privilege Against Self-Incrimination and Criminal Justice. Hart Publishing, Oxford

Clapham A (2006) Human Rights Obligations of Non-State Actors. Oxford University Press, Oxford

Currie RJ (2000) Human Rights and International Mutual Legal Assistance: Resolving the Tension. Crim LF 11:143 et seq.

Duff A et al. (2007) The Trial on Trial. Volume Three. Hart Publishing, Oxford

Friedman D (2002) From due deference to due process: Human rights litigation in the criminal law. EHRLR 2:216 et seq.

Goss R (2014) Criminal Fair Trial Rights. Article 6 of the European Convention on Human Rights. Hart Publishing, Oxford

Gradoni L (2006) International Criminal Courts and Tribunals: Bound by Human Rights Norms … or Tied Down? LJIL 19:847 ct seq.

Gradoni L (2013) The Human Rights Dimension of International Criminal Procedure. In: Sluiter G et al. (eds) International Criminal Procedure. Principles and Rules. Oxford University Press, Oxford, pp 74–95

Harris DJ et al. (2009) Harris, O'Boyle & Warbrick. Law of the European Convention on Human Rights, 2nd edn. Oxford University Press, Oxford

Harris DJ et al. (2014) Harris, O'Boyle & Warbrick. Law of the European Convention on Human Rights, 3rd edn. Oxford University Press, Oxford

Hodgson JS (2011) Safeguarding Suspects' Rights in Europe: A Comparative Perspective. New Crim L Rev 14:611 et seq.

Hoyano L (2014) What is balanced on the scales of justice? In search of the essence of the right to a fair trial. Crim LR 4 et seq.

Jackson J (2012) Human Rights, Constitutional Law and Exclusionary Safeguards in Ireland. In: Roberts P, Hunter J (eds) Criminal Evidence and Human Rights: Reimagining Common Law Procedural Traditions. Hart Publishing, Oxford, pp 119–143

Jackson JD, Summers SJ (2012) The Internationalisation of Criminal Evidence. Beyond the Common Law and Civil Law Traditions. Cambridge University Press, Cambridge

Jacobs D (2012) Puzzling over Amnesties: Defragmenting the Debate for International Criminal Tribunals. In: Van den Herik L, Stahn C (eds) The Diversification and Fragmentation of International Criminal Law. Martinus Nijhoff Publishers, Leiden/Boston, pp 305–345

Klip A (2012) European Criminal Law: An Integrative Approach, 2nd edn. Intersentia, Antwerp

Kuiper R (2014) Vormfouten. Juridische Consequenties van Vormverzuimen in Strafzaken. Kluwer, Deventer

Macovei M (2002) Human rights handbooks, No. 5. The right to liberty and security of the person. A guide to the implementation of Article 5 of the European Convention on Human Rights. Council of Europe, Strasbourg

Mowbray AR (2004) The Development of Positive Obligations under the European Convention on Human Rights by the European Court of Human Rights. Hart Publishing, Oxford

Nowak M (2005) U.N. Convention on Civil and Political Rights: CCPR Commentary, 2nd edn. NP Engel Verlag, Kehl

Ochoa-Sanchez JC (2013) The Rights of Victims in Criminal Justice Proceedings for Serious Human Rights Violations. Martinus Nijhoff Publishers, Leiden/Boston

Ölçer FP (2008) Eerlijk Proces en Bijzondere Opsporing. Wolf Legal Publishers, Nijmegen

Ölçer FP (2013) The European Court of Human Rights: The Fair Trial Analysis Under Article 6 of the European Convention of Human Rights. In: Thaman SC (ed) Exclusionary Rules in Comparative Law. Springer, Dordrecht/Heidelberg/New York/London, pp 371–399

Orie AMM (1983) De Verdachte Tussen Wal en Schip Òf de Systeem-breuk in de Kleine Rechtshulp. In: De la Porte EA et al. (eds) Bij Deze Stand van Zaken. Bundel opstellen aangeboden aan A.L. Melai. Gouda Quint, Arnhem, pp 351–361

Ormerod D (2003) ECHR and the exclusion of evidence: trial remedies for Article 8 breaches? Crim LR 61 et seq.

Pattenden R (2006) Admissibility in criminal proceedings of third party and real evidence obtained by methods prohibited by UNCAT. E&P 10:1 et seq.

Rainey B, Wicks E, Ovey C (2014) Jacobs, White & Ovey: The European Convention on Human Rights, 6th edn. Oxford University Press, Oxford

Roberts P (2012) Normative Evolution in evidentiary Exclusion: Coercion, Deception and the Right to a Fair Trial. In: Roberts P, Hunter J (eds) Criminal Evidence and Human Rights: Reimagining Common Law Procedural Traditions. Hart Publishing, Oxford, pp 163–193

Safferling CJM (2003) Towards an International Criminal Procedure. Oxford University Press, Oxford

Schabas WA (2010) The International Criminal Court: A Commentary on the Rome Statute. Oxford University Press, Oxford

Schleker C (2009) Reparations. In: Forsythe DP (ed) Encyclopedia of Human Rights, Vol. 4. Oxford University Press, Oxford, pp 330–341

Seibert-Fohr A (2009) Prosecuting Serious Human Rights Violations. Oxford University Press, Oxford

Shelton D (2005) Remedies in International Human Rights Law, 2nd edn. Oxford University Press, Oxford

Sluiter G (2002) International Criminal Adjudication and the Collection of Evidence: Obligations of States. Intersentia, Antwerp

Starr SB (2008) Rethinking "Effective Remedies": Remedial Deterrence in International Courts. NYU L Rev 83:693 et seq.

Strasser W (1988) The relationship between substantive rights and procedural rights guaranteed by the European Convention on Human Rights. In: Matscher F, Petzold H (eds) Protecting Human Rights: The European Dimension. Carl Heymanns Verlag KG, Cologne, pp 595–604

Thienel T (2006) The Admissibility of Evidence Obtained by Torture under International Law. EJIL 17:349 et seq.

Trechsel S (2006) Human Rights in Criminal Proceedings. Oxford University Press, Oxford

Van de Westelaken R (2010) 'Het EVRM als Wapen tegen Straffeloosheid: Over het Recht van Slachtoffers van Ernstige Mensenrechtenschendingen op een Effectieve Strafrechtelijke Aanpak van de Dader'. NTM/NJCM-Bull 2010, afl 2, p 135–152

Van Hoek AAF, Luchtman MJJP (2005) Transnational Cooperation in Criminal Matters and the Safeguarding of Human Rights. Utrecht LR 1:1 et seq.

Vellinga-Schootstra F, Vellinga WH (2008) 'Positive Obligations' en het Nederlandse Straf (proces)recht. Kluwer, Deventer

Vogler R (2013) Transnational Inquiries and the Protection of Human Rights in the Case-Law of the European Court of Human Rights. In: Ruggeri S (ed) Transnational Inquiries and the

Protection of Fundamental Rights in Criminal Proceedings. Springer-Verlag, Berlin/ Heidelberg, pp 27–40

Zappalà S (2003) Human Rights in International Criminal Proceedings. Oxford University Press, Oxford

Zeegers KJ (2013) De invloed van mensenrechten op het internationaal strafprocesrecht. In: Abels D et al. (eds) Dialectiek van nationaal en internationaal strafrecht. Boom Juridische uitgevers, The Hague, pp 353–400

Zeegers KJ (2016) International Criminal Tribunals and Human Rights Law. Adherence and Contextualization. TMC Asser Press, The Hague

Chapter 3
Judicial Responses to Pre-Trial Procedural Violations in the Netherlands

Abstract This chapter sets out the law and practice with respect to the question of how to address procedural violations committed in the pre-trial phase of criminal proceedings in the Netherlands. It does so by means of an overview of the consequences that the judge may attach to such procedural violations. Consideration is given to the extent to which the determination of whether to attach legal consequences to established procedural violations entails the exercise of judgement, whereby the judge has due regard to the particular circumstances of the case, i.e. the extent to which it should be discretionary in nature (which may be contrasted to an approach whereby the judicial response is more or less automatic), and also to how courts respond to procedural violations committed in an international context. The examination in this chapter is not limited to a description of the relevant law and practice, however; it also includes a description of the (possible) theoretical accounts thereof, as well as an evaluation of the law and practice in light of such accounts.

Keywords (upholding the) rule of law · reparation argument · prevention argument · demonstration argument · protection of the subjective rights of the accused · primacy of crime control · truth-finding · individual legal protection · Schutz-norm · Article 359a CCP · inadmissibility of the prosecution · exclusion of evidence · sentence reduction · declaration without further consequences · discretion · balancing · positive obligations

Contents

© T.M.C. ASSER PRESS and the author 2018
K. Pitcher, *Judicial Responses to Pre-Trial Procedural Violations in International Criminal Proceedings*, International Criminal Justice Series 16,
https://doi.org/10.1007/978-94-6265-219-4_3

3.1   Introduction

The purpose of this chapter is to set out the Dutch theory, law and practice with respect to the question of how to address procedural violations committed in the pre-trial phase of criminal proceedings, as relevant to the central research question of this book: how should judges at the ICTs respond to procedural violations committed in the pre-trial phase of the proceedings? First, an overview will be provided of the aspects of the Dutch legal system that are relevant to the judicial response within the criminal trial to pre-trial procedural violations, in order to facilitate an understanding of this response (Sect. 3.2). Second, the theory on the question of how to address such violations, will be set out, i.e. the possible points of departure and rationales in this regard, including their interrelationship and, where instructive, how they relate to broader objectives of criminal procedure (Sect. 3.3). Then, the legal framework governing the judicial response to such violations will be set out,[1] both as regards procedural violations committed in a purely national context, and as regards those committed in an international context (Sect. 3.4). In setting out the legal framework attention will be paid to the question of the extent to which the Dutch judicial response to pre-trial procedural violations can be said to be discretionary in nature, and/or the extent to which it entails a balancing approach (whereby it may be recalled that in Chap. 1, such questions were said to lie at the heart of the present study). Ultimately, an attempt will be made to 'make sense' of this framework, in terms of the points of departure, rationales and criminal procedure objectives identified in the foregoing section, in order to provide a more complete picture of the Dutch judicial response to procedural violations committed in the pre-trial phase of criminal proceedings, and a solid basis for the comparison to be undertaken in Chap. 7 (Sect. 3.5). Finally, this chapter will conclude with a brief summary of the main features of the legal framework and the main points of the analysis (Sect. 3.6).

---

[1] Of course, the answer to the question of how to address pre-trial procedural violations encompasses more than just the judicial response *within the criminal trial* to such violations. After all, the question implies that such violations could be addressed outside of the criminal trial. It is beyond the scope of this book to explore in any meaningful way other (possible) mechanisms for addressing such violations, and the choice to limit the legal framework to the judicial response to pre-trial procedural violations may be justified on the basis that that response will invariably shed light on the broader question of how to address procedural violations committed in the pre-trial phase of criminal proceedings. Thus, a restrictive response within the criminal trial suggests that such violations should be dealt with elsewhere than in the criminal trial, i.e. through other mechanisms.

In setting out the relevant Dutch theory, law and practice here it has been necessary to translate relevant Dutch legal terms, expressions, findings and (even) entire (legal) provisions into English. In doing so, an attempt has been made to stay as close to the Dutch wording as possible. Where necessary (to avoid misunderstanding) the exact Dutch wording has been provided between parentheses, and where instructive, the (more) common English translation has (also) been provided. Otherwise, all translations are the author's own.

3.2 Relevant Aspects of the Dutch Legal System

In the Netherlands, the police and prosecutorial functions in criminal proceedings (among others) are governed by the principle of legality. Pursuant to Article 1 of the Dutch Code of Criminal Procedure (*Wetboek van Strafvordering*; hereafter: CCP), which enshrines the principle of legality for criminal procedure,[2] the criminal investigation and the prosecution of persons accused of having committed an offence, as well as the enforcement of sentences, i.e. 'the entire procedure in criminal cases',[3] may take place only in accordance with the law, that is, statutory law established by Act of Parliament. Such law can, in the first place be found in the Dutch Code of Criminal Procedure; it can also be found in such 'special laws' as the Opium Act (*Opiumwet*) and the Weapons and Ammunition Act (*Wet wapens en munitie*). Moreover, such functions must be exercised in accordance with principles of proper administration of justice (*beginselen van een behoorlijke procesorde*), i.e. the unwritten principles that operate 'within the law' to further define and limit the provisions contained in the CCP, for example, the principle of proportionality.[4] In addition, the police and prosecutorial functions in criminal proceedings must be exercised in accordance with the human rights treaties to which the Netherlands is a signatory, most notably the ECHR and ICCPR. In other words, in order for conduct on the part of public authorities charged with the investigation and prosecution of crime to be considered lawful, it must accord with a range of different standards, such that 'unlawful conduct' (on the part of such authorities) may be defined broadly. As to the character of the Dutch Code of Criminal Procedure, it should be noted that the CCP does not expressly lay down any individual rights for the suspect; rather it confers on the public authorities powers in order to arrest and

---

[2] Article 1 of the Dutch Criminal Code enshrines the principle of legality for substantive criminal law.

[3] See WvSv, AL Melai/MS Groenhuijsen ea, Article 1 Sv, aant 8 (online, last updated 1 June 2000).

[4] See Cleiren, in T&C Strafvordering 2015, Article 1 Sv, aant 11 (online, last updated 1 July 2015).

detain suspects, and to investigate and prosecute crime, thereby stipulating the conditions under which such powers may be exercised, from which both the notion of rights protection more generally and specific rights for the suspect may be inferred. While there is a written constitution (*Grondwet*), which, it may be noted, does not expressly provide for the right to a fair trial,[5] there is no constitutional court. In the Netherlands, all courts, including the Supreme Court of the Netherlands (*Hoge Raad der Nederlanden*), the highest court of the Netherlands, are prohibited from ruling on the constitutionality of statutory law established by Act of Parliament.[6] They may, however, rule on their compatibility with the human rights treaties to which the Netherlands is a signatory, most notably the ECHR and ICCPR.[7] Such treaties are directly applicable in the Netherlands.

In the Netherlands the public prosecutor (*officier van justitie*) is in charge of, and responsible for, the criminal investigation, which itself is carried out by the police authorities. Criminal justice is administered by professional judges,[8] i.e. there is no jury system in the Netherlands. Criminal cases are adjudicated at three levels: cases are first heard by the district court (*rechtbank*), following which either party may appeal to the court of appeal (*gerechtshof*), following which either party may appeal in cassation to the Supreme Court. On appeal from the district court the appeal will be focused on the grounds of appeal, although the court of appeal is entitled to conduct a full review of both the legal aspects and the facts of the case. On appeal in cassation the Supreme Court reviews whether the law has been applied correctly and whether all formalities have been observed; it does not make any determinations of fact. Lower courts are not obligated to follow the case law of appellate courts (*gerechtshoven*); nor are appellate courts obligated to follow the Supreme Court (save in concrete cases, where the Supreme Court has referred a matter back to an appellate court in in order that it be resolved).[9] Moreover, neither the appellate courts nor the Supreme Court are bound by their own precedents.[10] In rendering a final judgment, judges in criminal proceedings (that is, judges of the district court and the court of appeal) are bound by the 'procedural' and 'substantive' questions of Articles 348 and 350 of the CCP, respectively. Pursuant to Article 348 of the CCP, the judge must answer the following questions, in the following order: (1) is the summons (containing the indictment) valid;[11] (2) is the court competent to try

---

[5] Calls have been made to incorporate the right to a fair trial into the Dutch Constitution. See e.g. Leeuw 2013.

[6] See Article 120 Dutch Constitution.

[7] See Article 94 Dutch Constitution.

[8] In the Netherlands, lawyers, legal scholars and other persons who hold a law degree and have (specialist) knowledge and/or experience of the criminal justice system may be appointed as 'deputy judges' (*rechter-plaatsvervangers*).

[9] Haazen 2007, 6 and 9.

[10] Ibid., 9.

[11] The procedural consequence of an invalid summons is nullity. A summons may be declared null and void if it has not been served properly or if the indictment contained therein is not sufficiently clear.

the case;[12] (3) is the prosecution admissible;[13] and (4) are there any reasons to suspend the proceedings?[14] Pursuant to Article 350 of the CCP, the judge must answer the following questions, in the following order: (1) has it been proven that the accused committed the act set out in the indictment?;[15] (2) does such act constitute a statutory criminal offence?;[16] (3) is the accused him- or herself criminally liable (i.e. culpable or blameworthy)?;[17] and (4) what sanction or measure should be imposed? The fact that judges in criminal proceedings are bound by the aforementioned questions necessarily limits the legal consequences that can be attached to pre-trial procedural violations (within the criminal trial); such consequences must 'fit' within the existing framework.[18] This explains the limitation in Article 359a of the CCP, the central provision for responding to pre-trial procedural violations within the criminal trial, of such consequences to sentence reduction, the exclusion of evidence and a declaration that the prosecution is inadmissible (a procedural consequence akin to a stay of proceedings). Further, the fact that in the Netherlands justice, including criminal justice, is administered by professional judges only, whereby the professional judge is both trier of fact and trier of law, means that the judge excluding (unlawfully obtained) evidence will be aware of its contents.[19]

---

[12] The court is not competent to try the case when the case falls within the jurisdiction of another court's jurisdiction.

[13] The prosecution may be declared inadmissible due to, for example, lapse of time (see Articles 70–73 of the Dutch Criminal Code), the principle of *ne bis in idem* (see Article 68 of the Dutch Criminal Code) or the death of the accused.

[14] The proceedings may be suspended on account of an accused's mental disorder. See Article 16 CCP.

[15] If not, the court must acquit the accused pursuant to Article 352(1) CCP.

[16] An act does not constitute a statutory criminal offence if it cannot be qualified, i.e. it does not fall within the definition of the alleged criminal offence, or if the act, despite falling within the definition of the alleged criminal offence, is not wrongful on account of a successful claim of justification. If the act does not constitute a statutory criminal offence, the court must discharge the accused of further prosecution (*ontslaan van alle rechtsvervolging*) pursuant to Article 352(2) CCP. Only where 'unlawfulness' (*wederrechtelijkheid*) is a constitutive part of the offence (*bestanddeel*) will a successful claim of 'justification' lead to an acquittal.

[17] An accused is not criminally liable if he or she can successfully claim 'excuse'. If the accused is not criminally liable, the court must discharge the accused of further prosecution pursuant to Article 352(2) CCP. Only where 'culpability' (*verwijtbaarheid*) is a constitutive part of the offence will a successful claim of 'excuse' lead to an acquittal.

[18] See e.g. Mevis 1995, 253.

[19] In the literature this has been advanced as an argument against the exclusion of evidence. See in this regard Embregts 2003, 110–111.

3.3   Theoretical Framework: Possible Points of Departure and Specific Rationales

The Dutch literature identifies four points of departure with respect to the question of how to address procedural violations committed in the pre-trial phase of criminal proceedings: the notion inherent to the concept of the rule of law that the authorities must *also* abide by the law (*de rechtsstaatgedachte*),[20] the '(protection of the) subjective rights of the accused' (*(bescherming van) de subjectieve rechten van de verdachte*),[21] 'ensuring the accused's right to a fair trial' (*verzekering van verdachtes recht op een eerlijk proces*)[22] and the 'primacy of crime control' (*het primaat van de criminaliteitsbestrijding*).[23] Each of these points of departure is examined below, as well as how they relate to one another. It is important to note at the outset that it was not until recently that the Dutch Supreme Court, in a leading decision (its second on this topic), addressed (or rather identified what it considers to be the proper) rationales for addressing pre-trial procedural violations pursuant to Article 359a of the CCP (specifically, for excluding evidence on account of the manner in which was obtained).[24] That decision and the statements of principle contained therein are referred to below in setting out the aforementioned points of departure, while later on in this chapter an attempt will be made to 'make sense' of the legal framework governing the judicial response within the criminal trial to procedural violations committed in the pre-trial phase of criminal proceedings, particularly the system of Article 359a of the CCP, in terms of those points of departure and rationales, and with reference to broader objectives of criminal procedure. In order to do so it is of course necessary to first set out that legal framework, while in order to make sense of that framework, it will be necessary to look beyond explicit statements of principle and 'read between the lines'. Before going on to examine the points of departure identified above, it is important to note that Article 359a of the CCP is in principle not concerned with the issue of reliability, in that, if an item of evidence is deemed unreliable, it should be set aside for that reason alone, regardless of how it was obtained.[25]

---

[20] See e.g. Koopmans 2001; Van Woensel 2004, 146–147; Y Buruma in his annotation to HR 30 March 2004, ECLI:NL:HR:2004:AM2533, *NJ* 2004/376; Blom 2008, 2011; Keulen and Knigge 2010, 523; Borgers 2012; and Corstens and Borgers 2014, 817 (Corstens and Borgers refer to both the *rechtsstaatgedachte* and the constitutional perspective to reflect this notion).

[21] See e.g. Koopmans 2001, 887; Y Buruma in his annotation to HR 30 March 2004, ECLI:NL: HR:2004:AM2533, *NJ* 2004/376; Blom 2008, 124; 2011, 14; and Borgers 2012, 260.

[22] See Kuiper 2014, 73–82.

[23] See Borgers 2012, 260–262.

[24] See HR 19 February 2013, ECLI:NL:HR:2013:BY5322, *NJ* 2013/308 m.nt. BF Keulen. This did not go unnoticed in the literature: see e.g. BF Keulen in his annotation to HR 19 February 2013, ECLI:NL:HR:2013:BY5322, *NJ* 2013/308; and Schalken 2013.

[25] See HR 30 March 2004, ECLI:NL:HR:2004:AM2533, r.o. 3.6.4, *NJ* 2004/376 m.nt. Y Buruma. For a discussion of the distinction between unreliable and unlawfully obtained evidence (and of the fact that this distinction has proven difficult to draw in practice), see Dubelaar 2009, 101–114.

3.3.1   The Concept of the Rule of Law

The first point of departure with respect to the question of how to address pre-trial procedural violations is the notion inherent to the concept of the rule of law that the authorities must also abide by the law (*de rechtsstaatgedachte*). On the basis of this notion, a number of authors argue that the appropriate response to procedural violations committed in the pre-trial phase of criminal proceedings is the exclusion of the evidence thereby obtained.[26] Different authors draw on different grounds in making this argument, ranging from the basic structure of the Dutch Code of Criminal Procedure to unwritten principles of law to international treaties.[27] A number of authors draw on Article 1 of the CCP.[28] Cleiren and Mevis construct the argument as follows. The statutory regulation of the powers to be exercised in criminal proceedings reflects, on the one hand, the desire of the legislator to create and to confer on public authorities powers in order to investigate and prosecute crime, and, on the other hand, the desire to *regulate* the exercise of such powers, with a view to safeguarding the rights and interests of citizens (and, in particular, the citizen suspected of having committed an offence).[29] The 'double-sided' character of the statutory regulation of powers is grounded in the *public nature* of the exercise of powers in criminal proceedings (such powers are exercised by public authorities in respect of citizens), and the notion of the rule of law: in a state governed by the rule of law, the public authorities must act, i.e. exercise their powers, within the parameters set by the law *for them, in their capacity as investigative and prosecutorial authorities.*[30] Accordingly, when in the course of criminal proceedings public authorities violate the norms that govern the exercise of powers, which, as stated, are directed at them,[31] i.e. when they act unlawfully, they violate their own rules (the norms directed at them) and, more importantly, they fail in their duty to observe the rules that bind them. Thus, the 'nature of unlawfulness' (i.e. the nature of the violation of procedural norms by public authorities in the course of criminal proceedings) should be sought in the failure on the part of the public authorities to fulfil their own obligation to observe the norms directed at them in their capacity as investigative and prosecutorial authorities,[32] rather than in

---

[26] See e.g. Mevis 1995; Cleiren and Mevis 1996; and Blom 2002.

[27] See Baaijens-van Geloven (2004, 355), referring to, among others, Krikke 1983; De Jong 1985; Groenhuijsen 1996; and Blom 2002.

[28] See n 12 and accompanying text.

[29] Cleiren and Mevis 1996, 189. See also Schalken 1989, 7–9.

[30] Cleiren and Mevis 1996, 189. This requirement, they argue, is emphasized in Article 1 CCP. See also Schalken 1989, 7–9.

[31] Those norms are not limited to those explicitly provided for by statute but also include unwritten norms, i.e. the norms that dictate how the powers provided for by statute should properly be exercised, such as the principles of proportionality and subsidiarity. See Cleiren and Mevis 1996, 189.

[32] Cleiren and Mevis 1996, 190. See also Mevis 1995, 257–258.

the violation of fundamental rights. While it may seem natural or obvious to seek the nature of unlawfulness in the violation of rights,[33] Cleiren and Mevis point to what they consider to be the danger inherent in doing so: that conduct on the part of public authorities will only be deemed unlawful if the rights of the particular accused on trial, i.e. if *this particular accused's* rights, have been violated.[34] In their view, such an approach (whereby only if the subjective rights of the individual accused have been violated will the authorities' conduct be deemed unlawful) fails to recognise the public nature of the norms that govern the exercise of powers, which are, by virtue of this fact, directed at them.[35] Due to this danger, the nature of unlawfulness should, in their view, not be sought in the violation of rights.[36] This is not to say that they are unconcerned with the position of the citizen: the public nature of the exercise of power in criminal proceedings implies, by definition, that the citizen as such and without more, i.e. not as the carrier of subjective rights (but the citizen as *rechtsburger*), has an interest in the observance by public authorities of the norms that bind them.[37] This interest is best understood as a collective interest or right held by *all* citizens, i.e. a public interest, rather than as an individual interest or right. In a manner of speaking, therefore, the nature of unlawfulness can also be sought in the violation of *a* right.[38] However, whether subjective rights have been violated (and, in particular, whether the rights of this particular accused have been violated) is irrelevant to the question of whether the authorities have acted

---

[33] Although it should be noted here that the CCP does not provide for any rights as such; rather it expressly confers on the public authorities powers in order to investigate and prosecute crime, thereby also stipulating the conditions under which such powers may be exercised, from which individual rights may be inferred.

[34] Cleiren and Mevis 1996, 190–192. See also Baaijens-van Geloven 2004, 358 n 68.

Thus, they point to the danger that the question of whether the public authorities have acted unlawfully will not solely be dependent on the violation of objective law.

[35] Cleiren and Mevis 1996, 192. Accordingly, Cleiren and Mevis are, as a matter of principle, opposed to the application of the Schutz-norm (in particular, the second component thereof), which is discussed in more detail below (see in particular n 93, 94 and 103–107 and accompanying text). See also Schalken 1989, 8–11. Similarly, Buruma and Blom observe that the (strict) application of the Schutz-norm in an approach based on the notion that the authorities must also abide by the law is illogical. See Y Buruma in his annotation to HR 30 March 2004, ECLI:NL: HR:2004:AM2533, *NJ* 2004/376, and Blom 2008, 125. See also Borgers 2012, 265; and Kuiper 2014, 269 and 284–285, in this regard.

By contrast, Cleiren and Mevis do not take issue with the practice of courts of refraining from attaching legal consequences to unlawfulness on the part of the police or the public prosecutor in the pre-trial phase of criminal proceedings on the basis that, in the circumstances, the accused has not suffered (actual) prejudice. In their view, such application is not inconsistent with what they argue to be the nature of unlawfulness.

[36] Embregts argues that courts *should*, when addressing unlawfulness on the part of the police or the public prosecutor in the pre-trial phase of criminal proceedings, emphasize the failure of the authorities to observe fundamental rights (see Embregts 2003, 320–331). See, similarly, Van Woensel 2004, 147, 156–160 and 171. For a discussion of this approach, see n 98–108 and accompanying text.

[37] Cleiren and Mevis 1996, 191.

[38] Ibid., 191.

unlawfully.[39] Not only does the citizen (again, as such and without more, i.e. not as the carrier of subjective rights) have an interest therein, he or she is *entitled* to such observance, meaning that he or she is entitled to have the lawfulness of an action, i.e. the exercise of power, performed by the public authorities reviewed and addressed.[40] This entitlement can only be realised by ensuring that the lawfulness of that action is reviewed and addressed by a third, independent authority: a judicial authority.[41] Accordingly, the approach to the question of how to address pre-trial procedural violations based on the (rule of law) notion that the authorities must also abide by the law is closely connected to the notion of 'individual legal protection' (*individuele rechtsbescherming*),[42] i.e. the protection of the citizen to have been drawn into the criminal process from improper interference by the public authorities charged with the investigation and prosecution of crime. Individual legal protection, it should be noted, constitutes an important constraint on the truth-finding endeavour, under the central aim of Dutch criminal procedure: 'the correct application of substantive criminal law'.[43,44] At the same time, however, this approach necessarily recognises and accommodates the truth-finding endeavour: after all, such authorities may exercise (coercive) powers in order to investigate and prosecute crime and thereby search for, and discover the truth within the parameters set by statute, treaty and unwritten principles of proper administration of justice.

According to Cleiren and Mevis, the combination of the nature of unlawfulness, the double-sided character of the statutory regulation of powers and the entitlement of citizens to observance by public authorities of the norms that bind them, points to

---

[39] Ibid., 191. Thus, both Buruma and Blom note that, from the rule of law perspective, the imposition of sanctions for procedural violations is a way to respond to improper conduct on the part public authorities 'as such' (*als zodanig*), i.e. on its own and without more. See Y Buruma in his annotation to HR 30 March 2004, ECLI:NL:HR:2004:AM2533, *NJ* 2004/376; Blom 2008, 124; and 2011, 14. See also Mevis 1995, 255–256.

[40] Cleiren and Mevis 1996, 193–194 and 204. See also Van Leijen 1994, 236–241.

[41] Cleiren and Mevis 1996, 194 and 199. See also Blom 2008, 125.

[42] 'Individual' here is used to denote the distinction between the legal protection of the citizen to have been drawn into the criminal process from improper interference by the public authorities charged with the investigation and prosecution of crime and that of the general public from crime. See in this regard Van der Meij 2008, 61–62; and 2010, 21.

[43] See e.g. Groenhuijsen and Knigge 2001, 15–16; Crijns and Van der Meij 2005, 51–57; Van der Meij 2008, 61; 2010, 20–21; and Keulen and Knigge 2010, 2. However, Brants, Mevis, Prakken and Reijntjes take issue with this description of the aim of criminal procedure. In their view, it opens the door to instrumentalism. See Brants et al. 2003, 26. It should not, however, be assumed that all those to adopt this description of the aim of criminal procedure advocate instrumentalism.

[44] For a comprehensive breakdown of the central aim of Dutch criminal procedure, see Crijns and Van der Meij 2005, 51–55. See also Van der Meij 2010, 20–21. According to Crijns and Van der Meij (Ibid., 55–56), both the central aim and two further aims flow from the passage in the explanatory memorandum (*memorie van toelichting*) to the 1926 Code of Criminal Procedure to identify the aim(s) of criminal procedure: the conviction of the guilty and the protection of the innocent from wrongful prosecution and conviction.

a particular response to procedural violations committed in the pre-trial phase of criminal proceedings: the 'non-use' of the evidence thereby obtained.[45] In particularly serious cases, i.e. where the procedural violation is particularly serious (for example, when the authorities have acted in bad faith),[46] a declaration that the prosecution is inadmissible may be called for.[47] According to Cleiren and Mevis, such responses both allow for the aforementioned entitlement to be realised *and* provide the best fit for the nature of unlawfulness set out above. They go to the heart of what from a rule of law perspective is considered to be the problem (the failure of the public authorities to fulfil their own duty to observe the norms that bind them, rather than the violation of an individual's rights), removing the 'legal effect' of the 'product' of the procedural violation.[48] In this regard, Mevis speaks of a response that is 'inherent to the nature of unlawfulness',[49] and one that is directed at the authorities, rather than at the accused.[50] Van Leijen also speaks of an 'inherent' response in this regard. She points to the fact that the provisions in, for example, the CCP reflect the conditions under which power may be exercised in the investigation and prosecution of crime, whereby such conditions may be seen as expressing what the legislator has (already) decided is the proper balance between the goals of truth-finding and individual legal protection and from which it is apparent that truth-finding is not to be pursued at all costs; individual legal protection constitutes an important constraint on that endeavour.[51] This, she argues, implies that any judicial response to the failure of public authorities to observe these conditions must be 'functionally related' to such failure: that response should nullify or invalidate the action and therefore also the results obtained thereby.[52] Viewed as an inherent response, the nullification or invalidation of the unlawful action and its results is not a matter of *discretion* for the judge; it does not entail the

---

[45] Cleiren and Mevis 1996, 195.

[46] See e.g. Mevis et al. 2001, 47.

[47] Cleiren and Mevis 1996, 197.

[48] Ibid., 95–197. See, similarly, Blom 2002, 1054–1055; and Peters 1973, 249. Peters argues that where the authorities have failed to observe the 'rules of the game', the most effective way to deal with such failure is to respond within the 'game'. Thus, Peters rejects what in the English literature has been termed the 'separation thesis'. The 'separation thesis' is addressed in Chap. 4.

[49] Mevis 1995, 258.

[50] Ibid., 255.

[51] If in the course of the criminal investigation the public authorities violate a statutory procedural norm that governs the exercise of (coercive) power, it might be said that they disrupt the balance envisaged by the legislator; that the exercise of power becomes unbalanced on account of the individual legal protection envisaged by the legislator not being accorded due weight. The exclusion of evidence, then, might redress that imbalance, by now allowing the goal of individual legal protection to prevail (rather than the goal of truth-finding, which may be assumed to have prevailed when the public authorities failed to observe the norms that (also) exist in order protect the citizen to have been drawn into the criminal process from improper interference by the public authorities charged with the investigation and prosecution of crime). See Peters 1973, 248; and Van Leijen 1994, 234. See also Schalken 1989, 8.

[52] Van Leijen 1994, 236, in particular.

exercise of judgement.[53] This suggests that the approach to the question of how to address pre-trial procedural violations based on the rule of law notion is best served by an exclusionary *rule* entailing automatic exclusion (if courts were permitted to make ad hoc exceptions in individual cases, this would undermine the system of individual legal protection); nevertheless, even the most staunch supporters of such an approach would appear to recognise that there may be (exceptional) circumstances in which exclusion would be unreasonable.[54] Due to its disconnectedness to the nature of unlawfulness, Cleiren and Mevis argue that sentence reduction is not an appropriate response to procedural violations committed in the pre-trial phase of criminal proceedings, assuming that the violation in questions amounts to unlawfulness; where the conduct of the authorities is 'merely' undesirable (but falls short of unlawfulness), sentence reduction may well be an appropriate response.[55] Finally, they argue that the fact that the trial judge in criminal proceedings is necessarily, by virtue of the system in place (which only allows the citizen accused of having committed a criminal offence *and* put on trial to have the lawfulness of executive action reviewed and addressed by the trial judge, whereby such a review (and manner in which any unlawfulness may be addressed) is limited by the questions that the trial judge must answer pursuant to Articles 348 and 350 of the CCP in rendering a final judgment),[56] limited in his or her ability pronounce on the (un)lawfulness of public authorities' conduct is not a valid reason to deprive the judge of the options that he or she *does* have at his or her disposal to make such a pronouncement and thereby help to preserve the integrity of the investigation.[57]

Cleiren and Mevis' argument is methodically constructed;[58] most literature to put forward or otherwise address the argument based on the (rule of law) notion that the authorities must also abide by the law that the appropriate response to pre-trial procedural violations is the exclusion of the evidence thereby obtained simply refers to a series of more specific arguments to argue[59] or otherwise illustrate the point:[60] the 'reparation argument' (*het reparatieargument*), the 'demonstration

---

[53] Ibid., 236, in particular. See also Mevis 1995, 252, n 2. This issue is addressed further below, in Sect. 3.5. Similarly, proponents of the vindicatory rationale in respect of the US exclusionary rule argue that that rule is 'part and parcel' of the Fourth Amendment, rather than a judicially created remedy that is subject to judicial limitation. See e.g. Baldiga 1983; and Bloom and Dewey 2011, 38–51.

Ashworth and Redmayne make a similar argument in respect of (violations of) the English rules on the destruction on DNA profiles. See Ashworth and Redmayne 2010, 359–360.

[54] See e.g. Van Leijen 1994, 241; Mevis 1995, 256; Cleiren and Mevis 1996, 191–192; and Blom 2002, 1055.

[55] Cleiren and Mevis 1996, 196. See also Blom 2002, 1055.

[56] See n 11–17 and accompanying text.

[57] Cleiren and Mevis 1996, 200–201 and 205.

[58] See also Van Leijen 1994, for a methodical construction of the argument *for* exclusion.

[59] See e.g. Peters 1973, 236–253; Embregts 2003, 188–189; and Blom 2008, 124–125.

[60] See e.g. Y Buruma in his annotation to HR 30 March 2004, ECLI:NL:HR:2004:AM2533, *NJ* 2004/376; Baaijens-van Geloven 2004, 354–356; Blom 2008, 124–125; 2011, 14; Corstens and Borgers 2014, 817–818; and Borgers 2012, 260.

argument' (*het demonstratieargument*), the 'prevention argument' (*het preven-tieargument*)[61] and the 'integrity argument' (*het integriteitsargument*).[62] These arguments can also be construed as 'goals' which, when invoked to argue that the exclusion of evidence is the appropriate response to procedural violations com-mitted in the pre-trial phase of criminal proceedings, reflect what is achieved by excluding evidence.[63] Pursuant to the reparation argument, the authorities should not 'profit' from (their) unlawful conduct; any advantage gained by such unlaw-fulness should therefore be taken away.[64] By taking away any advantage gained by the authorities, they are put back into the position they would have been in had they not acted unlawfully. From this perspective, it is easy to understand why the exclusion of evidence is sometimes likened to the procedural consequence of nullity (*nietigheid*): the application of the exclusionary rule leads to the (results of the) norm violation being nullified.[65] If when evidence obtained unlawfully is excluded (in order to secure the entitlement of all citizens to observance by the authorities of the norms that bind them) there is sufficient evidence (lawfully obtained) to convict the accused, the reparation goal will still have been fulfilled.[66] Moreover, if when evidence obtained unlawfully is excluded (again, in order to secure the entitlement of all citizens to observance by the authorities of the norms that bind them) any violation of the individual accused's subjective rights caused by the unlawfulness remains 'unrepaired', the reparation goal will still have been fulfilled. The violation of the individual accused's subjective rights is likely to remain 'unrepaired' notwithstanding exclusion when the right to have been violated is a substantive right, such as the right to privacy.[67] Such a violation can only be 'repaired' by *compensation* (it being an impossibility to restore the situation before the violation (of the right to privacy) occurred, i.e. to provide restitution). While compensation is

---

[61] The prevention argument is also known as the 'effectivity argument' (*het effectiviteitsargument*). See Embregts 2003, 105; and Kuiper 2014, 44. Blom and Borgers both use this term (effectivity), rather than prevention: Blom 2002, 1053; and Borgers 2012, 260.

[62] This last argument is frequently omitted from the list. See e.g. Blom 2002, 1053; Keulen and Knigge 2010, 523–524 (although they do note the importance of preserving the credibility of the criminal justice system in a more general sense); Blom 2011, 14; Borgers 2012, 260; BF Keulen in his annotation to HR 19 February 2013, ECLI:NL:HR:2013:BY5322, *NJ* 2013/308; and Corstens and Borgers 2014, 817–818. See also n 72 and 73 and accompanying text.

[63] See e.g. Embregts 2003, 104–107, 189.

[64] Blom 2002, 1053.

[65] See e.g. Krikke 1983, 276. See similarly Peters 1973, 249, where he refers to 'sanctions that turn unlawful action into invalid action'. See also n 52 and accompanying text.

[66] Embregts 2003, 106.

[67] By contrast, if the right to have been impinged on is the right to a fair trial, the exclusion of evidence (pursuant to the entitlement of all citizens to observance by the authorities of the norms that bind them) may well coincide with that which is necessary in order to repair the violation of such right.

a form of reparation,[68] it is not what is envisaged under the reparation argument. Pursuant to the demonstration argument, it must be demonstrated to the general public that public authorities are also bound by the law.[69] This calls for a clear, public response to unlawful conduct on the part of public authorities.[70] The prevention argument calls for a response to unlawful conduct on the part of public authorities that will deter the same or similar conduct in the future. While this argument is typically depicted in terms of 'policing the police', whereby the focus is on the relationship between the judge and the police, Schalken argues that the focus should rather be on the relationship between the judge and the public prosecutor, whereby the judge demarcates, in a general sense, the boundaries of acceptable conduct in the context of a criminal investigation but refrains from trying to police the police, since he or she lacks the expertise and apparatus to do so. Rather, this is a task for the public prosecutor, who, it should be recalled, leads the investigation and who, above all, should lead by example.[71] Finally, pursuant to the integrity argument, the judiciary is required to distance itself from unlawfulness on the part of the executive in order to preserve the integrity of the criminal process.[72] The notion that the judiciary must distance itself from executive unlawfulness in order to preserve the integrity of the judiciary and the criminal process more generally appears to be a necessary implication of the *rechtsstaatgedachte*, i.e. the notion that the authorities charged with the investigation and prosecution of suspected crime must also abide by the law: when in the course of a criminal investigation powers are exceeded or abused, such excess and/or abuse not only corrupts the official(s) involved, but also the third party to make use thereof.[73]

Blom constructs the central argument (that the appropriate response to pre-trial procedural violations is the exclusion of the evidence thereby obtained) as follows. At the heart of the concept of the rule of law lies the notion that the authorities must also abide by the rules. If the authorities do not abide by the rules, a sanction must follow, otherwise such rules are devalued.[74] The exclusion of evidence is the most fitting response to procedural violations committed in the pre-trial phase of criminal proceedings because it best serves the reparation argument, the demonstration

---

[68] See in this regard Chap. 2, n 291–295 and accompanying text.

[69] See e.g. Blom 2002, 1053; and Corstens and Borgers 2014, 817.

[70] Corstens and Borgers 2014, 817.

[71] T Schalken in his annotation to HR 9 September 2014, ECLI:NL:HR:2014:2650, *NJ* 2014/420.

[72] Embregts deals with this argument under the demonstration argument. See Embregts 2003, 106.

[73] Jörg 1989, 658. See, similarly, Schalken 1981, 80 and T Schalken in his annotation to HR 9 September 2014, ECLI:NL:HR:2014:2650, *NJ* 2014/420. See, however, Kuiper 2014, 45 and 75, where the author argues that the integrity argument lacks force on account of the fact that the integrity of the criminal justice system is just as dependent on that system's ability to convict an accused on the basis of reliable evidence.

[74] Blom 2002, 1053. Similarly Embregts argues that in the Dutch 'constitutional state' (*de rechtsstaat*) the principle of legality demands that unlawful conduct on the part of public authorities be sanctioned. See Embregts 2003, 156.

argument and the prevention argument.[75] Thus, while such arguments or goals appear to have a broader application, i.e. they appear to apply to responses to procedural violations within the criminal trial more generally (not just to the exclusion of evidence),[76] those in favour of the exclusion of evidence argue that those arguments are best served, or those goals best achieved, by the exclusion of evidence.[77] In other words, this response arguably provides the best fit for those arguments or goals. In this regard it is worth noting that at the heart of these arguments or goals appears to lie an understanding of the nature of unlawfulness that coincides with that put forward by Cleiren and Mevis: the failure on the part of the public authorities to fulfil their own duty to observe the norms directed at them in their capacity as investigative and prosecutorial authorities. Conversely, Cleiren and Mevis' argument appears to reflect the reparation argument; they argue for the removal of the legal effect of the unlawfulness, which entails restoring the status quo ante.[78] Moreover, any response required by these arguments is clearly directed at the authorities, rather than the accused. Finally, according to Jörg, the *function* of (rather than the *foundation* of and *arguments* for) the exclusionary rule (when applied pursuant to the arguments set out above) is the clarification of the boundaries of executive power, or,[79] put differently, the regulation (*normering*) of the criminal investigation.[80]

It was stated above that the Dutch Supreme Court recently identified what it considers to be the proper rationales for excluding evidence on account of the manner in which was obtained.[81] The relevant judgment and its 'theoretical' implications are considered more carefully below but for now it may be noted that in identifying such rationales, the Supreme Court more or less explicitly referred to the prevention argument and its 'rule of law' dimension in two of the three sets of circumstances in which unlawfully obtained evidence may, according to the Court, be excluded.[82] It did not, however, refer to any of the other arguments (reparation, demonstration or integrity), a fact that did not go unnoticed and is not without criticism in the literature.[83]

---

[75] Blom 2002, 1053. See also Blom 2008, 124–125.

[76] See e.g. Baaijens-van Geloven 2004, 356; and Corstens and Borgers 2014, 817–818.

[77] See e.g. Embregts 2003, 156 and 183; and Van Woensel 2004, 147.

[78] There are many similarities between Cleiren and Mevis' argument for exclusion and Ashworth's protective principle, set out in Chap. 4.

[79] Jörg 1989, 659. By contrast Baaijens-van Geloven and Van Woensel identify this as an *argument*. See Baaijens-van Geloven 2004, 355; and Van Woensel 2004, 149.

[80] Embregts 2003, 108–109. Similarly, Schalken argues that when the authorities do not abide by the norms that bind them, such norms become blurred. See Schalken 1981, 79.

[81] See HR 19 February 2013, ECLI:NL:HR:2013:BY5322, *NJ* 2013/308 m.nt. BF Keulen.

[82] HR 19 February 2013, ECLI:NL:HR:2013:BY5322, r.o. 2.4.5 and 2.4.6, *NJ* 2013/308 m.nt. BF Keulen.

[83] See e.g. BF Keulen in his annotation to HR 19 February 2013, ECLI:NL:HR:2013:BY5322, *NJ* 2013/308 and T Schalken in his annotation to HR 9 September 2014, ECLI:NL:HR:2014:2650, *NJ* 2014/420.

3.3.2   The (Protection of the) Subjective Rights of the Accused

The second point of departure identified in the literature with respect to the question of how to address pre-trial procedural violations is the '(protection of the) subjective rights of the accused'. The primary function of an approach whereby this is the point of departure is the reparation of actual prejudice suffered by the accused.[84] In this regard a distinction is drawn between fair trial rights (the rights enumerated in or otherwise flowing from Article 6 of the ECHR, insofar as applicable to the investigative stage of criminal proceedings) and other rights, such as the right to privacy.[85] While in case of violation of the first set of rights it might well be possible to restore the situation before the violation occurred, i.e. to provide restitution,[86] in case of the second set of rights (assuming they are substantive rights) it will not. The violation of such rights can, however, be compensated.[87] Thus, an approach in which the point of departure is the need to protect the subjective rights of the accused envisages, in principle, a range of judicial responses procedural violations committed in the pre-trial phase of criminal proceedings depending on the right to have been violated: a declaration that the prosecution is inadmissible, the exclusion of evidence thereby obtained, sentence reduction, or a declaration that a violation has occurred.[88] It is worth emphasizing that, insofar as this approach is genuinely and primarily concerned with the protection of rights (and this is questionable, as will be demonstrated below), it combines two distinct ideas or arguments, the first being that *it is a reason* for the trial judge in criminal proceedings to attach legal consequences to pre-trial procedural violations that a fundamental right of the accused has (thereby) been violated, and the second being that the relief to be provided in case of violation of a fundamental right depends on the particular right to have been violated (a notion that arguably underlies the right to an effective remedy). Regarding the second argument, therefore, it does not envisage a particular judicial response to the violation of a fundamental right of the accused that seeks to vindicate the rights of the accused in a general sense.

Given that the aforementioned responses are capable of providing restitution or compensation in respect of the accused's violated rights, it is (perhaps)

---

[84] Borgers 2012, 260. See also Corstens and Borgers 2014, 820.

[85] See Kuiper 2009, 38. See also Borgers 2012, 265.

[86] Perhaps this is what Borgers means when he refers to *herstel*, as opposed to compensation: Borgers 2012, 260). In this regard see also Corstens and Borgers 2014, 820.

[87] Borgers 2012, 260. See also Corstens and Borgers 2014, 820.

[88] See Corstens and Borgers 2014, 817. See also Kuiper 2014, 45, referring to the 'compensation argument' (*het compensatieargument*) in this regard. Accordingly, this approach should be distinguished from an approach to the question of how to address unlawfulness on the part of the police or the public prosecutor in the pre-trial phase of criminal proceedings based on what has been called the 'protective principle', in which the exclusion of evidence is the primary remedy. See e.g. Ashworth 1977. The protective principle is addressed in Chap. 4. Similarly, it should be distinguished from the approach advocated by Embregts. See n 98–108 and accompanying text.

understandable that the judicial response that does, in fact, address the violation of the subjective rights of the accused is often explained in terms of the *protection of such rights*.[89] Thus, for example, Buruma explains that response in terms of the right to an effective remedy within the meaning of Article 13 of the ECHR and, more generally, in terms of the positive obligations resting on states to take measures to prevent human rights violations and to adequately address such violations when they occur.[90] It is questionable, however, whether this account of the judicial response that addresses the violation of the subjective rights of the accused is accurate. To begin with, the approach whereby the violation of the subjective rights of the accused is addressed may be no more than a reflection of the (broad and/or strict) application of the Schutz-norm,[91] a doctrine that originated in private law (more specifically, the law of tort), and has since found application in, among other areas, the law of criminal procedure.[92] The Schutz-norm, as applied in the criminal procedure context, consists of two components: (i) the norm to have been violated must be aimed at protecting accused persons *in general*; and (ii) the violation of that norm must have affected *this particular accused*.[93] There is significant overlap between the content of this norm and the second point of departure identified in the literature with respect to the question of how to address pre-trial procedural violations: the '(protection of) the subjective rights of the accused'. This point of departure assumes that the norm to have been violated was aimed at protecting accused persons *in general* and further that *this particular accused* was affected by the violation of that norm. Given that the Schutz-norm was introduced in order to *temper* the (strict) application of the exclusionary rule,[94] and that the approach whereby the violation of the subjective rights of the accused is addressed may be no more than a reflection of the application of that norm, the explanation of the judicial response that addresses the violation of the subjective rights of the accused in terms of the *protection of* such rights is, on a conceptual level, misleading: the fact that that response may have the (fortuitous) *effect* of providing an effective remedy or of discharging the State's positive obligations does not make such protection of the accused's subjective rights its primary aim. This has implications for how this point of departure is to be understood in terms of broader objectives of Dutch criminal procedure.[95] The desire

---

[89] See e.g. Borgers 2012, 260; and Corstens and Borgers 2014, 820.

[90] See Y Buruma in his annotation to HR 30 March 2004, ECLI:NL:HR:2004:AM2533, *NJ* 2004/376. See also Blom 2008, 125.

[91] In any case, a number of authors have observed that the application of the Schutz-norm in an approach to unlawfulness on the part of the police or the public prosecutor in the pre-trial phase of criminal proceedings that seeks to safeguard the rights of the accused, i.e. protect his or her subjective rights, is logical: see e.g. Y Buruma in his annotation to HR 30 March 2004, ECLI:NL:HR:2004:AM2533, *NJ* 2004/376; Blom 2008, 125 and 133; and Kuiper 2014, 269.

[92] See Doorenbos 1990.

[93] See e.g. Embregts 2003, 124–132. The second component of the Schutz-norm is comparable to the standing requirement in the US. See Embregts, ibid., and Kuiper 2014, 270–274.

[94] See Doorenbos 1990.

[95] For such objectives, see n 42–44 and accompanying text.

to temper the (strict) application of the exclusionary rule must be understood as being motivated by the goal of truth-finding (and, by extension, the crime control objective), given that the exclusion of evidence can, where there is insufficient other evidence to convict, frustrate the realisation of this goal. Accordingly, insofar as the approach whereby the violation of the subjective rights of the accused is addressed is merely a reflection of the application of the Schutz-norm, the judicial response within that approach appears to be inspired primarily by the objective of truth-finding (and other associated goals), rather than by the objective of individual legal protection. Insofar as that judicial response *can* be described in terms of individual legal protection, the scope of such protection seems narrower than that envisaged under the approach to the question of how to address procedural violations committed in the pre-trial phase of criminal proceedings based on the (rule of law) notion that the authorities must also abide by the law, under which it is irrelevant whether the accused was personally affected by the interference in question.

In addition to the conceptual difficulties with construing the judicial response that addresses the violation of the subjective rights of the accused in terms of the *protection of* such rights is, on a practical level it is questionable whether the judicial response within the criminal trial to procedural violations committed in the pre-trial phase of criminal proceedings always has this effect. While a declaration that the prosecution is inadmissible or the exclusion of evidence may well have this effect in respect of (potential) violations of the right to a fair trial, it is questionable whether sentence reduction or a declaration that a violation has occurred will have this effect in respect of the violation of substantive rights, such as the right to privacy. In this regard it should be recalled that the right to an effective remedy consists of a procedural and a substantive component, whereby pursuant to the former, the competent national authority must be able to deal with the substance of the complaint, including—when the right to privacy is alleged to have been violated—the assessment of any 'side-effects concerning private or family life' that the procedural violation had. In other words, it is not sufficient to simply provide substantive relief (moreover, in the absence of a procedural remedy that allows the national authority to deal with the *substance* of the complaint, it is questionable whether any consequence to be attached to a rights violation can properly be considered to constitute *substantive* relief). Given what is required in order to provide an effective remedy, it is, as also observed above,[96] questionable how appropriate a place the criminal trial is to 'remedy', within the meaning of the right to an effective remedy, violations of substantive rights.[97] For this reason also it may be misleading to explain the judicial response within the criminal trial to pre-trial procedural violations that addresses the violation of the subjective rights of the accused in terms of the *protection of* those rights.

---

[96] In Chap. 2.

[97] This is not to say that it is inappropriate for judges in criminal proceedings to attach legal consequences to such violations; however, it is questionable whether it should do so *on the basis of the right to an effective remedy.*

The approach that addresses the violation of the subjective rights of the accused should be distinguished from the approach to pre-trial procedural violations advocated by Embregts, whereby the nature of unlawfulness is sought in the violation of fundamental rights, on the understanding that the statutory regulation of the powers to be exercised in criminal proceedings reflects not only the desire of the legislator to create and to confer on public authorities powers in order to investigate and prosecute crime, but also the desire to *regulate* the exercise of such powers, with a view to protecting the rights and interests of citizens (and, in particular, the citizen suspected of having committed an offence).[98] Rather than emphasizing the failure of the authorities to observe the procedural (written and unwritten) norms that govern the exercise of power,[99] it focuses on the failure of the authorities to observe fundamental rights.[100] In case of the violation of fundamental rights, Embregts envisages a judicial response that is capable of achieving the reparation, prevention and demonstration goals,[101] and therefore one that is directed at the authorities rather than at the accused: the exclusion of evidence.[102] Rather than seeking to provide an effective remedy tailored to the particular right to have been violated, this approach seeks to vindicate rights in a more general sense. Embregts is not, in principle, and perhaps unsurprisingly in view of her rights-focus, opposed to the application of the Schutz-norm, except for when the rights of third persons are deliberately violated in order to obtain evidence against the accused.[103] In her view, the application of the Schutz-norm is a way of *tempering* the (strict) application of the exclusionary rule, which she argues contributes to its social acceptance.[104] Nevertheless, she argues that Schutz-norm 'is not there' to deprive the rule of its 'right of existence'.[105] In this regard it may be observed that it is one thing to not exclude evidence when in the particular circumstances of the case exclusion would not likely serve any purpose (in which case the Schutz-norm provides a useful tool to temper the strict application of the exclusionary rule); it is quite

---

[98] Embregts 2003, 320–331. See, similarly, Van Woensel 2004, 147 and 156–160.

[99] See e.g. Cleiren and Mevis 1996.

[100] Embregts 2003, 322–333.

[101] Ibid., 188–189. These goals are set out above: see n 6172 and accompanying text.

[102] Embregts 2003, 183–184, 188–189.

[103] Ibid., 124–132, 155–156, 189 and 343. See however Cleiren and Mevis 1996, 191–192. See also n 35 and accompanying text.

[104] Embregts 2003, 155–156. Van Woensel also advocates an approach to unlawfulness on the part of the police or the public prosecutor in the pre-trial phase of criminal proceedings whereby the nature of unlawfulness is sought in the violation of fundamental rights. However, unlike Embregts she explicitly argues against a strict application of the Schutz-norm, ultimately arguing for a 'shift in emphasis' from the Schutz-norm to a 'fundamental rights' perspective. See Van Woensel 2004, 158–160 and 171.

[105] Embregts 2003, 155.

another to require *as a rule* that the Schutz-norm criteria be fulfilled.[106] Presumably (given that she is a strong proponent of the exclusionary rule)[107] it is the former application of the Schutz-norm that Embregts has in mind.[108]

What, if anything, does the Dutch Supreme Court say about the second point of departure identified in the literature with respect to the question of how to address procedural violations committed in the pre-trial phase of criminal proceedings? Given that the judicial response that addresses the violation of the subjective rights of the accused may not be a matter of principle at all (at least, not insofar as the underlying principle is the protection of the subjective rights of the accused),[109] in order to answer this question it is necessary to look beyond the Supreme Court's statements of principle in its recent leading decision. In this regard it may be observed that the Supreme Court gives a central role to the Schutz-norm within the system of Article 359a of the CCP.[110] As a rule, the court need not attach any of the consequences listed in the first paragraph of Article 359a to pre-trial procedural violations when the Schutz-norm criteria are not fulfilled. While this falls short of a requirement, it is clear that the Supreme Court envisages a broad application of the norm. Thus, while the court is not required to apply the Schutz-norm, it is 'cordially invited' to do so.[111] Pursuant to what was observed above,[112] it may be noted that the fact that the Supreme Court envisages a broad application of the Schutz-norm does not necessarily mean that the primary aim of Article 359a of the CCP is the protection of the subjective rights of the accused. As to what the primary aim of Article 359a is, then, this question is discussed below.[113]

---

[106] See similarly Schalken 1989, 9; and Mevis et al. 2001, 49.

Here it is worth recalling Cleiren and Mevis' objection to an approach to unlawfulness on the part of the police or the public prosecutor in the pre-trial phase of criminal proceedings that seeks the nature of unlawfulness in the violation of fundamental rights: the danger that conduct on the part of public authorities will only be deemed unlawful if *this particular accused's* rights have been violated. See n 34–36 and accompanying text.

[107] Embregts 2003, 344.

[108] Presumably, at least, it is not the latter (strict) application that she has in mind.

[109] See n 91–95 and accompanying text.

[110] It first did so in its leading decision of 30 March 2004. See HR 30 March 2004, ECLI:NL: HR:2004:AM2533, r.o. 3.5, *NJ* 2004/376 m.nt. Y Buruma. The Court confirmed this line of case law in its second leading decision on Article 359a of the CCP (specifically, on the exclusion of evidence on account of the manner in which was obtained) of 19 February 2013. See HR 19 February 2013, ECLI:NL:HR:2013:BY5322, r.o. 2.4.1, *NJ* 2013/308 m.nt. BF Keulen.

[111] See Y Buruma in his annotation to HR 30 March 2004, ECLI:NL:HR:2004:AM2533, *NJ* 2004/ 376.

[112] See n 91–94 and accompanying text.

[113] See Sect. 3.5.

3.3.3 The Need to Ensure the Accused's Right to a Fair Trial

Turning to the third point of departure, it should be recalled that, in the literature addressing the second point of departure (as set out above), a distinction is drawn between fair trial rights and other rights.[114] In more recent literature, however, the need to ensure the accused's right to a fair trial is recognised as a separate point of departure with respect to the question of how to address pre-trial procedural violations.[115] In this regard it is worth noting that, in identifying the proper rationales for excluding evidence on account of the manner in which it was obtained in its second leading decision on the topic, the Supreme Court explicitly referred to the need to ensure the accused's right to a fair trial within the meaning of Article 6 of the ECHR and as interpreted by the ECtHR.[116] Kuiper observes that the judicial response to pre-trial procedural violations that ensures the accused's right to a fair trial also serves the 'important' public interest in the proper administration of criminal justice.[117] The judicial response to pre-trial procedural violations to ensure the accused's right to a fair trial within the meaning of Article 6 of the ECHR potentially serves both objectives of Dutch criminal procedure: the discovery of the truth and individual legal protection. In this regard it is important to note that, as apparent from the ECtHR's case law, Article 6 of the ECHR, that is, the overarching right to a fair trial and the fair trial rights enumerated in or otherwise flowing from this provision, is concerned with both epistemic and non-epistemic considerations.[118] It has been implied in the Dutch literature that when the need to ensure the accused's right to a fair trial within the meaning of Article 6 of the ECHR is the *only* point of departure with respect to the question of how to address procedural violations committed in the pre-trial phase of criminal proceedings, this may indicate the primacy given by a legal system to efficient crime control.[119] In this regard it is worth recalling that according to the ECtHR, not every instance of unlawfulness to arise, or violation of a Convention right to occur in the course of a criminal investigation renders the trial unfair contrary to Article 6 of the ECHR.[120]

---

[114] See n 85 and accompanying text.

[115] See in particular Kuiper 2014, 73–82.

[116] HR 19 February 2013, ECLI:NL:HR:2013:BY5322, r.o. 2.4.4, *NJ* 2013/308 m.nt. BF Keulen. In doing so it did not, however, point to the need to protect (retrospectively) other rights. However, this is not surprising. In this case, the Supreme Court identified the proper rationales for excluding properly obtained evidence. It has not yet done the same for e.g. sentence reduction, which is arguably the most obvious choice for the (retrospective) protection of substantive rights such as the right to privacy, while bearing in mind that it is questionable how appropriate a place the criminal trial is to remedy violations of substantive rights.

[117] Kuiper 2014, 77.

[118] For Dutch literature in this regard, see Ölçer 2008, in particular 32–36.

[119] See Kuiper 2014, 73.

[120] See in this regard Chap. 2.

3.3.4 The Primacy of Crime Control

The fourth point of departure with respect to the question of how to address pre-trial procedural violations is the 'primacy of crime control'. Whereas the first three points of departure at least[121] assume that it may be necessary or, at least, appropriate for the court to attach a consequence to pre-trial procedural violations, the fourth point of departure assumes the opposite;[122] it assumes that it is inappropriate to do so, ultimately due to the ability of such consequences to prevent the establishment of criminal responsibility (in the case of a declaration that the prosecution is inadmissible or, where there is insufficient other evidence to convict, the exclusion of evidence) or to prevent the imposition of punishment commensurate with the criminal responsibility established (in the case of sentence reduction). Thus, while the first three points of departure are, or purport to be, arguments in favour of responding to pre-trial procedural violations within the criminal trial, the fourth point of departure is a counter-argument in this regard.[123] Such an approach, i.e. an approach in which this is the point of the departure, places the interests of victims and of the general public in law enforcement at the forefront,[124] and envisages a response to pre-trial procedural violations that does not interfere with this interest: a declaration that a violation has occurred.[125] An approach to such violations in which the primacy of crime control is the point of departure is closely connected to the goal of truth-finding. As stated, such an approach regards the judicial response within the criminal trial to procedural violations committed in the pre-trial phase of criminal proceedings as inappropriate insofar as it prevents the establishment of criminal responsibility, which is necessary in order to protect society from crime. In order to establish criminal responsibility, it is necessary to 'discover' the truth. Accordingly, where public authorities have acted unlawfully in the course of a criminal investigation, advocates of the aforementioned approach argue that the goal of truth-finding should prevail over that of individual legal protection, i.e. the judicial response that ensures such protection.

In its latest leading decision on Article 359a of the CCP, in which it identified what it considers to be the proper rationales for excluding evidence on account of how it was obtained, the Supreme Court makes explicit reference to the interests of victims and of the general public in law enforcement. In two of the three categories of exclusion, the court is either permitted or required[126] to weigh the (deterrent) benefits of exclusion against the negative effects that such exclusion may be expected to have on such 'heavily weighted interests' as truth-finding (*waarheidsvinding*), the need to punish perpetrators of ('possibly very serious') crime and

---

[121] See in this regard n 91–94 and accompanying text.

[122] See Borgers 2012, 260; and Corstens and Borgers 2014, 820.

[123] Borgers 2012, 260 n 14.

[124] See Borgers 2012, 261; and Corstens and Borgers 2014, 820.

[125] Ibid.

[126] See n 228 and 234–235 and accompanying text.

'the rights of victims and next-of-kin (in light also of the positive obligations flowing from the ECHR of effective punishment)'.[127]

3.4 Legal Framework

Having set out the Dutch theory with respect to the question of how to address procedural violations committed in the pre-trial phase of criminal proceedings, it is time to turn to the legal framework, i.e. the law and practice, in the Netherlands in respect thereof. The purpose of this section, then, is to set out the Dutch legal framework governing the judicial response within the criminal trial to pre-trial procedural violations. That framework consists of several components. First of all, the aforementioned judicial response is governed by Article 359a of the Dutch Code of Criminal Procedure and the interpretation of that provision by the Dutch Supreme Court. Second, in cases in which that provision does not, strictly speaking, apply (it may be noted at the outset that Article 359a's scope of application is relatively narrow),[128] there is room (albeit limited) to attach legal consequences to unlawful conduct. Finally, the Dutch Supreme Court has recognised that procedural violations committed in the context of inter-state cooperation in criminal matters may also require a judicial response within the (Dutch) criminal trial. Each of these components of the legal framework is set out below. Ultimately, an attempt will be made to 'make sense' of, or assess, this framework, in terms of the theory set out in the foregoing section.[129]

3.4.1 Procedural Violations in the National Context

3.4.1.1 Article 359a of the CCP

Legislative History

Before setting out the system of Article 359a of the CCP, and the case law in respect thereof, it is instructive to consider the legislative history of that provision. Article 359a of the CCP came about amid concerns regarding 'the way in which procedural violations were being addressed in criminal proceedings', including (but not limited to) the judicial response to procedural violations committed in the

---

[127] HR 19 February 2013, ECLI:NL:HR:2013:BY5322, r.o. 2.4.5 and 2.4.6, *NJ* 2013/308 m.nt. BF Keulen.

[128] See n 151–157 and accompanying text.

[129] In Sect. 3.5.

course of a criminal investigation.[130] Specifically, the concern was that too much was being done to address such violations, rather than too little, with all that this entails.[131] The bill proposing the incorporation of Article 359a into the Code of Criminal Procedure was based on the conclusions/recommendations of the 'Moons-Commission', a commission comprised of leading academics and practitioners acting at the Dutch Government's request, regarding, among other things, the desirability of the codification of the specific judicial responses to such violations developed in the case law, and the division of labour between the legislator and the judge in criminal proceedings as regards the determination of the consequences of such violations.[132] According to the Moons-Commission (and the Dutch Government eventually proposing the incorporation of Article 359a into the CCP), the specific judicial responses introduced and developed in the case law—the exclusion of evidence,[133] a declaration that the prosecution is inadmissible[134] and sentence reduction[135]—required a basis in statute, i.e. needed to be codified, in light of the principle of legality. In principle, the Code of Criminal Procedure is a closed system of procedural provisions in which the legal consequences of the failure to observe such provisions, for example the 'formal' procedural nullities (*formele nietigheden*) and the inadmissibility of the prosecution, are also provided for therein.[136] The attachment of legal consequences to such failure *not* envisaged by

[130] This was cited by the 'Moons-Commission' (see in this regard n 132 and accompanying text) as the reason for conducting research into the way in which violations are addressed in criminal proceedings. See Corstens 1993 (incorporating the Moons-Commission's findings), 9 and 12.

[131] See Corstens 1993, e.g. 12 and 24, and *Kamerstukken II* 1993/94, 23075, 3, pp. 1 and 5 (explanatory memorandum).

[132] In other words, the Moons-Commission's conclusions regarding the way in which procedural violations should be addressed in criminal proceedings were adopted by the Dutch Government (see *Kamerstukken II* 1993/94, 23075, 3, p. 5 (explanatory memorandum), save in a number of respects. First, unlike the Moons-Commission, the Dutch Government limited the scope of application of Article 359a CCP to the procedural violations committed in the investigative phase. Second, unlike the Moons-Commission, the Dutch Government was of the view that the judicial responses enumerated in the first paragraph of that provision could only be applied by the court of its own motion and not upon request of the defence or upon application of the public prosecutor. See *Kamerstukken II* 1993/94, 23075, 3, p. 24 (explanatory memorandum).

[133] This legal consequence was first recognized by the Supreme Court in HR 26 June 1962, *NJ* 1962/470 m.nt. W Pompe. It took another 16 years for the Supreme Court to affirm its earlier decision (in HR 18 April 1978, ECLI:NL:HR:1978:AC6236, *NJ* 1978/365 m.nt. ThW van Veen.

[134] The Supreme Court first recognized that a declaration that the prosecution is inadmissible could be an appropriate response to unlawfulness in the investigative phase of criminal proceedings in HR 12 December 1978, ECLI:NL:HR:1978:AC2751, *NJ* 1979/142 m.nt. GE Mulder. Later it was (also) applied in respect of violations of the right to trial within a reasonable time within the meaning of Article 6 ECHR. See e.g. HR 23 September 1980, ECLI:NL:HR:1980:AC6987, *NJ* 1981/116 m.nt. GE Mulder.

[135] This response was introduced as an alternative to a declaration that the prosecution is inadmissible in respect of violations of the right to trial within a reasonable time. See HR 7 April 1987, ECLI:NL:HR:1987:AB9733, *NJ* 1987/587 m.nt. ThW van Veen.

[136] Corstens 1993, 23–24; *Kamerstukken II* 1993/94, 23075, 3, p. 45 (explanatory memorandum).

statute is inconsistent with the notion of a closed system of procedural provisions.[137] Moreover, according to the Moons-Commission and the Dutch Government, such a basis serves to legitimize the judge's decision to attach legal consequences to procedural violations committed in the course of a criminal investigation. Underlying Article 359a of the CCP is the notion that it is for the legislator to establish rules of criminal procedure, and for the trial judge in criminal proceedings to determine the consequences of the violation thereof.[138] According to the Moons-Commission and the Dutch Government, it is the judge, not the legislator, who is best positioned to determine the consequences of failure by the public authorities to observe procedural rules; this is because the circumstances under which such a failure may come about vary widely, such that the consequences thereof should also vary.[139] In addressing procedural violations committed in the course of a criminal investigation, the judge is required to be mindful of such varying consequences.[140] Factors 'such as' the interest that the violated provision purports to protect, the seriousness of the violation and the prejudice caused by it, 'play a role' in this regard.[141] Accordingly, underlying Article 359a of the CCP is the notion that procedural violations committed in the course of a criminal investigation should not invariably lead to a particular response; the judge should therefore look beyond the fact of the procedural violation to the individual circumstances of the case (and, in any case, to the interest that the violated provision purports to protect, the seriousness of the violation and the prejudice caused by it) in determining the appropriate response. In providing a statutory basis for the judicial response within the criminal trial to procedural violations committed in the course of a criminal investigation, the purpose was not for the legislator to assume the task of the judge in this regard and determine what, in the circumstances of the case, the response should be; rather it was to create a framework within which the judge could make such a determination.[142] To this end, Article 359a sets forth the possible legal consequences that may be attached to procedural violations committed in the course of a criminal investigation, thereby reflecting a certain level of 'structure and hierarchy', while at the same time affording the judge the 'freedom' to determine the appropriate response in the concrete circumstances of the case.[143] Moreover, according to the Moons-Commission and the Dutch Government, before it does anything else, the court is required, where possible, to 'repair' the violation, i.e. to bring about (late) compliance of the provision in question, despite initial non-compliance.[144] While Article 359a explicitly lists the possible consequences of

---

[137] Ibid., 23–24; p. 5.

[138] Ibid., 24; pp. 5 and 25. The possible implications of this position are discussed below, in Sect. 3.5.

[139] Ibid., 17, 24 and 53; p. 25.

[140] Ibid., 53; p. 25.

[141] Ibid., 53; p. 25.

[142] Ibid., 53; p. 25.

[143] Ibid., 24 and 53; p. 25.

[144] Ibid., 53; p. 25.

procedural violations committed in the course of a criminal investigation, it does not provide for detailed criteria in this regard. Nor does it (purport to) identify a specific rationale for attaching consequences to such procedural violations.[145] Article 359a of the CCP entered into force on 2 November 1996.[146] It provides as follows:

(1) The court may, if it becomes apparent that during the preliminary investigation procedural violations have occurred that can no longer be repaired and the legal consequences of which are not determined by statute, determine that:

   (a) the sentence shall be reduced in proportion to the seriousness of the violation, provided that the prejudice caused by the violation can be compensated in this way;
   (b) the results of the investigation obtained by the violation may not be used as proof of the crime charged;
   (c) the prosecution is inadmissible if as a result of the violation it is not possible to try the case in a manner consistent with principles of proper administration of justice.

(2) In applying the first paragraph, the court shall take into account the interest that the violated provision purports to protect, the seriousness of the violation and the prejudice caused by it.

(3) The judgment shall set forth the decisions provided for in the first paragraph. These shall be supported by reasons.[147]

General System

The system of Article 359a of the CCP is determined, firstly, by the text of that provision, and, secondly, by the interpretation thereof by the Dutch Supreme Court (and two leading decisions of that Court in particular). The first paragraph of Article 359a of the CCP lists the consequences that the court may attach to procedural violations committed in the course of the criminal investigation: sentence reduction, the exclusion of evidence, a declaration that the prosecution inadmissible. In addition, the court may simply issue a declaration that a violation has occurred without attaching any legal consequences to it.[148] The second paragraph of that provision lists the factors that the court is required to take into account when determining whether to attach consequences to procedural violations committed in the course of a criminal investigation, and, if so, which. These are: the interest that the violated provision purports to protect, the seriousness of the violation and the prejudice caused by it. In its leading decision of March 2004,[149] the Supreme Court

---

[145] The Moons-Commission did not consider it to be the task of the legislator to do so. See Corstens 1993, 54–55.

[146] *Stb.* 1996, 522.

[147] Author's own translation.

[148] HR 30 March 2004, ECLI:NL:HR:2004:AM2533, r.o. 3.6.1, *NJ* 2004/376 m.nt. Y Buruma. This also follows from the wording of Article 359a CCP.

[149] Ibid.

set out a more detailed framework for determining the consequences to be attached to procedural violations committed in the course of a criminal investigation pursuant to Article 359a of the CCP, including tests for each consequence, which it affirmed in its leading decision of February 2013.[150]

First, the court is required to determine whether the procedural violation in question falls within the scope of Article 359a, i.e. whether the procedural violation constitutes a violation within the meaning of that provision. In order to do so, the violation must, first of all, have been committed in the course of the preliminary investigation (*voorbereidend onderzoek*) within the meaning of Article 132 of the CCP. Accordingly, Article 359a of the CCP does not apply to violations committed in the trial phase of criminal proceedings. More specifically, the violation must have been committed in the preliminary investigation *against the accused regarding the offence for which he or she now stands trial*. Accordingly, Article 359a of the CCP is not applicable to violations committed in the course of a preliminary investigation against another person, or of the preliminary investigation against the accused regarding another offence.[151] Nor is Article 359a applicable to violations *not* committed in the exercise of criminal investigation powers. The Supreme Court has held that an extradition request by a public prosecutor does not fall within the scope of the criminal investigation, since such a request does not involve the exercise of criminal investigation powers.[152] Accordingly, unlawfulness in the extradition process does not fall within the scope of Article 359a. In addition, the Supreme Court has held that Article 359a does not apply to unlawful conduct on the part of public authorities for which the public prosecutor is not responsible, for example, the penitentiary authorities.[153] Nor does unlawful conduct on the part of the General Intelligence and Security Service (*Algemene Inlichtingen- en Veiligheidsdienst*) fall within the scope of Article 359a of the CCP.[154] Seemingly in line with this line of case law,[155] the Court of Appeal of The Hague has held that conduct on the part of the Dutch naval authorities in the context of an operation to prevent illicit maritime activity—piracy—off the coast of Somalia does not involve the exercise of criminal investigation powers, with all that this entails.[156] Nor does unlawful conduct on the

---

[150] HR 19 February 2013, ECLI:NL:HR:2013:BY5322, r.o. 2.4.1, *NJ* 2013/308 m.nt. BF Keulen.

[151] HR 30 March 2004, ECLI:NL:HR:2004:AM2533, r.o. 3.4.2, *NJ* 2004/376 m.nt. Y Buruma. Regarding the general requirement that the violation be committed in the course of the preliminary investigation see also the text of Article 359a of the CCP.

[152] HR 8 July 2008, ECLI:NL:HR:2008:BC5973, *NJ* 2009/440 m.nt. Y Buruma.

[153] HR 27 September 2011, ECLI:NL:HR:2011:BQ3765, *NJ* 2011/557 m.nt. TM Schalken.

[154] HR 5 September 2006, ECLI:NL:HR:2006:AV4122, *NJ* 2007/336, m.nt. TM Schalken.

[155] This line of case law has been criticized in the literature. See e.g. Buruma and Schalken in their annotations to HR 8 July 2008, ECLI:NL:HR:2008:BC5973, *NJ* 2009/440 and HR 27 September 2011, ECLI:NL:HR:2011:BQ3765, *NJ* 2011/557, respectively.

[156] Hof Den Haag 21 March 2014. http://uitspraken.rechtspraak.nl/inziendocument?id=ECLI:NL:GHDHA:2014:1007. Accessed 1 March 2017.

part of private individuals fall within the scope of Article 359a of the CCP.[157] Second, Article 359a is in principle not applicable to procedural violations that can be raised before the investigating judge (*rechter-commissaris*), who is charged with supervising the application and ongoing exercise of coercive powers that deprive the accused of his or her liberty at the initial stages, and who may attach consequences to such violations.[158] Third, Article 359a is not applicable to procedural violations that are 'reparable', in the sense that, despite initial non-compliance, the rule in question *can* still be complied with, whereby the underlying norm—most often, a fundamental right of the accused—is not violated.[159] In most cases this—compliance with a rule such that violation of the underlying fundamental right is avoided—is not possible.[160] An example of when it is possible, is where the procedural violations consists of the failure to add an item to the case file (*dossier*): that procedural violation can be repaired by the (late) addition of the item case file.[161] Fourth and finally, Article 359a of the CCP is not applicable to procedural violations in respect of which statute (already) determines the consequence. Statutory provisions that determine the consequence of failure to observe the rule are, however, scarce.[162]

If the procedural violation in question does fall within the scope of Article 359a of the CCP,[163] the next step for the court is to determine which consequence, if any, to attach to the violation, thereby taking into account the factors set out in the second paragraph of Article 359a of the CCP.[164] Thus, in each case, the court is required to identify the interest that the violated provision purports to protect, the seriousness of the violation and the prejudice caused by it. Moreover, according to the Supreme Court, if the norm to have been violated was not aimed at protecting

---

[157] See e.g. HR 18 March 2003, r.o. 3.5.1, ECLI:NL:HR:2003:AF4321, *NJ* 2003/527.

[158] HR 30 March 2004, ECLI:NL:HR:2004:AM2533, r.o. 3.4.2, *NJ* 2004/376 m.nt. Y Buruma. This rule, the purpose of which is to ensure that the closed system of legal remedies (*gesloten stelsel van rechtsmiddelen*) provided for in the CCP is not interfered with, has been criticized in the literature. See e.g. AH Klip in his annotation to HR 13 June 2006, ECLI:NL:HR:2006:AV6195, *NJ* 2006/623, PAM Mevis in his annotation to HR 21 November 2006, ECLI:NL:HR:2006:AY9673, *NJ* 2007/233 and TM Schalken in his annotation to HR 24 April 2007, ECLI:NL:HR:2007:AZ8411, *NJ* 2008/145.

[159] HR 30 March 2004, ECLI:NL:HR:2004:AM2533, r.o. 3.4.3, *NJ* 2004/376 m.nt. Y Buruma.
Kuiper observes that the procedural violation need not actually be repaired; the fact that the violation is reparable may suffice. See Kuiper 2014, 208.
Schalken laments that the concept of reparation has been unduly expanded. See TM Schalken in his annotation to HR 6 January 2015, ECLI:NL:HR:2015:4, *NJ* 2015/109.

[160] See e.g. Keulen and Knigge 2010, 522; Kuiper 2014, 210, and TM Schalken in his annotation to HR 6 January 2015, ECLI:NL:HR:2015:4, *NJ* 2015/109.

[161] See e.g. HR 1 July 2003, ECLI:NL:HR:2003:AF9417, *NJ* 2003/695 m.nt. PAM Mevis.

[162] An example is Article 268 CCP.

[163] It will be seen below that even when it does not, it may nevertheless lead to one of the consequences enumerated in Article 359a(1) CCP.

[164] HR 30 March 2004, ECLI:NL:HR:2004:AM2533, r.o. 3.5, *NJ* 2004/376 m.nt. Y Buruma.

accused persons in general or if the violation of that norm did not affect this particular accused (in other words, if either of the Schutz-norm criteria are not fulfilled), as a rule, the court need not attach any of the consequences enumerated in the first paragraph of Article 359a to the violation.[165] While the court need not attach a consequence to the procedural violation in question where the Schutz-norm criteria have not (both) been fulfilled, the Supreme Court has exceptionally departed from this principle. The most notable exception is a case in which the Amsterdam Court of Appeal used privileged conversations between the co-accused and his lawyer to convict the accused. According to the Supreme Court, it should not have done so, in view of the interest served by the protection of legal professional privilege.[166] Turning back to the factors set out in the second paragraph of Article 359a of the CCP (which are set out in more detail below),[167] it should be noted that the process of identification in an individual case of the interest that the violated provision purports to protect, the seriousness of the violation and the prejudice caused by it, and of taking into account all of the particular circumstances of the case,[168] may lead the court to conclude that a declaration that an irreparable violation has occurred is sufficient (on account of there being minimal or no actual prejudice, for example). If not, however (or rather: *only* when it is not),[169] the court is required to determine which consequence to attach to the violation, by first considering whether sentence reduction is appropriate and, only when it is not, moving on to the exclusion of evidence and, if this is not appropriate, to declare the prosecution inadmissible. The court is required to do so by determining whether the 'test' formulated by the Supreme Court for each consequence has been met, whereby the constituent elements of each test appear to reflect the factors set out in the second paragraph of Article 359a of the CCP. In its leading decision of February 2013,[170] the Supreme Court added to the framework by specifying the circumstances in which evidence may be excluded. The tests for each consequence are set out in the following section.

The requirement that the court take into account such factors as the interest that the violated provision purports to protect, the seriousness of the violation and the prejudice caused by it in the determination of the consequence, if any, to be

---

[165] Some authors read the Schutz-norm into the first factor of Article 359a(2) CCP, i.e. the interest that the violated provision purports to protect (see e.g. Borgers 2012, 270, and Corstens and Borgers 2014, 826). Indeed, there does appear to be overlap between the first component of the Schutz-norm and 'the interest that the violated provision purports to protect'. For a discussion of the relationship between the Schutz-norm and this factor, see Kuiper 2014, 327–328.

[166] HR 12 January 1999, ECLI:NL:HR:1999:ZD1402, *NJ* 1999/290.

[167] Under "Discretion and Balancing".

[168] HR 30 March 2004, ECLI:NL:HR:2004:AM2533, r.o. 3.6.2, *NJ* 2004/376 m.nt. Y Buruma, and HR 19 February 2013, ECLI:NL:HR:2013:BY5322, r.o. 2.4.1, *NJ* 2013/308 m.nt. BF Keulen. This opens the door to *other* facts and circumstances than those explicitly provided for in Article 359a(2) CCP being taken into account.

[169] HR 30 March 2004, ECLI:NL:HR:2004:AM2533, r.o. 3.6.2, *NJ* 2004/376 m.nt. Y Buruma.

[170] HR 19 February 2013, ECLI:NL:HR:2013:BY5322, *NJ* 2013/308 m.nt. BF Keulen.

attached to procedural violations committed in the course of a criminal investigation entails a requirement to look beyond the fact of the procedural violation to the individual circumstances of the case, whereby a 'rigid, knee-jerk response to breaches of procedural rules' is prevented.[171] Not only is the court required to do this; the court must also be *seen* to do so. In other words, the Supreme Court requires a reasoned decision in this regard, whereby the court explicitly takes into account the factors set out in the second paragraph of Article 359a of the CCP.[172] The Supreme Court strictly monitors adherence to this requirement.[173] In addition, the Supreme Court requires the defence to motivate its applications pursuant to Article 359a according to (all) such factors and, in particular, how such factors warrant the relief sought. Only where the application is properly motivated is the court required to rule on it.[174] Moreover, according to the Supreme Court, failure to do so means that the court may refuse to grant the relief sought or simply declare that an irreparable procedural violation has occurred (i.e. it may refuse to take, in a general sense, *responsibility* for procedural violations) without otherwise *enquiring* into the factual circumstances that, according to the defence, warrant such relief.[175]

Judicial Responses

A. Declaration Without Further Consequences

As stated above, the process of identification in an individual case of the interest that the violated provision purports to protect, the seriousness of the violation and the prejudice caused by it pursuant to the second paragraph of Article 359a of the CCP may well lead the court to conclude that a declaration that an irreparable violation has occurred is sufficient. Both the text of Article 359a (according to which the court *may* attach one of the consequences provided for in the first paragraph of that provision to procedural violations committed in the course of a criminal investigation) and the Supreme Court's interpretation of that provision allow for such a response. In its first leading decision on Article 359a, the Supreme Court observed that the text of Article 359a confers on the court a *power* to attach

---

[171] Kuiper 2014, 605. See also 53–54.

[172] See HR 30 March 2004, ECLI:NL:HR:2004:AM2533, r.o. 3.7, *NJ* 2004/376 m.nt. Y Buruma; HR 19 February 2013, ECLI:NL:HR:2013:BY5322, r.o. 2.4.1, *NJ* 2013/308 m.nt. BF Keulen; and HR 22 September 2015, ECLI:NL:HR:2015:2775, r.o. 2.5, NJB 2015/1741. For an example of a case in which the lower court's ruling was overturned by the Supreme Court on account of it not having been properly reasoned, see HR 9 April 2013, ECLI:NL:HR:2013:BX4439, NJ 2013/309 m.nt. BF Keulen.

[173] See Kuiper 2014, 306 and 324–325.

[174] HR 30 March 2004, ECLI:NL:HR:2004:AM2533, r.o. 3.7, *NJ* 2004/376 m.nt. Y Buruma. For an example of a case in which the application was not properly motivated, see HR 6 January 2015, ECLI:NL:HR:2015:4, *NJ* 2015/109 m.nt. TM Schalken.

[175] HR 30 March 2004, ECLI:NL:HR:2004:AM2533, r.o. 3.7, *NJ* 2004/376 m.nt. Y Buruma. Ölçer is highly critical in this regard. See Ölçer 2008, 517–518.

consequences to procedural violations committed in the course of a criminal investigation, not a *duty*. Moreover, according to the Supreme Court the tenor of Article 359a is not that a procedural violation should always lead to benefit for the accused.[176]

Where, for instance, no or minimal 'actual' prejudice is found, the court is likely to find that such a declaration suffices. In a case in which an appellate court had found that the accused had suffered no actual prejudice as a result of a cupboard being opened unlawfully (that is, without authorization) in the accused's personal living quarters on a barge, which led to an empty space, which in turn led to another space below deck where a cannabis farm was set up, the Supreme Court upheld the appellate court's finding that a declaration that a violation had occurred was sufficient.[177] While the appellate court expressly acknowledged the interest served by the protection of the right to privacy (in reference to the first factor under the second paragraph of Article 359a of the CCP), since the space directly behind the door to have been opened unlawfully was empty, that is, did not contain any items of significance from the perspective of the right to privacy, the accused had not suffered any prejudice.[178]

Currently the most common response to procedural violations committed in the course of a criminal investigation is a declaration that an irreparable violation, i.e. a violation within the meaning of Article 359a of the CCP, has occurred,[179] rather than the exclusion of the evidence thereby obtained or sentence reduction.[180] In this regard it should be noted that, according to the Supreme Court, *only* where a declaration that an irreparable violation has occurred would be insufficient in light of the factors set out in the second paragraph of Article 359a of the CCP may the court consider the responses enumerated in the first paragraph of that provision.[181]

---

[176] HR 30 March 2004, ECLI:NL:HR:2004:AM2533, r.o. 3.6.1, *NJ* 2004/376 m.nt. Y Buruma.

[177] HR 4 January 2011, ECLI:NL:HR:2011:BM6673, r.o. 3.5, *NJ* 2012/145 m.nt. MJ Borgers.

[178] In addition, the appellate court's decision to simply issue a declaration that a procedural violation had occurred appears to have been justified on the basis of the second statutory factor, i.e. the seriousness of the violation. In other words, it seemed to argue that the violation was not particularly serious, also on the basis the space directly behind the door to have been opened unlawfully was empty, that is, did not contain any items of significance from the perspective of the right to privacy, so that the privacy violation 'did not go beyond opening the cupboard'. See HR 4 January 2011, ECLI:NL:HR:2011:BM6673, r.o. 2.3, *NJ* 2012/145 m.nt. MJ Borgers, where the appellate court's findings are set out.

[179] See e.g. Buruma 2008; Kuiper 2009, 47; Borgers 2012, 265; and Blom 2015.

[180] In this regard, the concern voiced by a number of commentators at the time of the introduction of Article 359a CCP (see e.g. Van Leijen 1994, 239–240; and Mevis 1995, 259–260) and since its enactment (see e.g. Blom 2002, 1054–1055; and Embregts 2003, 183–184) that sentence reduction would be granted instead of excluding the evidence obtained improperly has not manifested. Nevertheless, the concern that the exclusion of evidence would no longer be the inevitable response to unlawfulness on the part of the police or the public prosecutor in the pre-trial phase of criminal proceedings clearly *has*.

[181] HR 30 March 2004, ECLI:NL:HR:2004:AM2533, r.o. 3.6.2, *NJ* 2004/376 m.nt. Y Buruma. See also n 169 and accompanying text. See in this regard also Kuiper 2014, 324.

B. Sentence Reduction

According to the text of Article 359a of the CCP, the court may (upon conviction of the accused) reduce the sentence 'in proportion to the seriousness of the violation', provided that 'the prejudice caused by the violation can be compensated in this way'.[182] In its first leading decision on Article 359a, the Supreme Court determined that sentence reduction may only be granted if (a) the accused has suffered actual prejudice; (b) this prejudice was caused by the procedural violation; (c) this prejudice lends itself to compensation by way of sentence reduction; and (d) it is justified also in light of the interest that the violated provision purports to protect and the seriousness of the violation.[183] Regarding the first requirement it has been observed in the literature that whereas in earlier cases the Supreme Court interpreted the term 'prejudice' in the first paragraph of Article 359a of the CCP broadly, in later cases (in particular, the Supreme Court's first leading decision) it interpreted it more strictly, to entail only actual prejudice for the individual accused.[184] Given the broad application prescribed by the Supreme Court of the Schutz-norm, both components of which need, as a rule, to be fulfilled before any of the consequences enumerated in the first paragraph of Article 359a can be applied,[185] the restriction of the notion of prejudice in the context of sentence reduction to that suffered by the individual accused may not be surprising. The question, then, is what actual prejudice for the individual accused entails in this context. To answer this question, it is first necessary to look to the third requirement of sentence reduction, i.e. that the prejudice for the accused caused by the violation must lend itself to compensation by way of sentence reduction. Prejudice to the accused's defence (or fair trial) rights, such as the right to counsel, typically does not lend itself to such compensation.[186] Accordingly, actual prejudice for the individual accused does not include actual prejudice to the accused's fair trial rights. What it does appear to include is

---

[182] See Article 359a(1)(a) CCP.

[183] HR 30 March 2004, ECLI:NL:HR:2004:AM2533, r.o. 3.6.3, *NJ* 2004/376 m.nt. Y Buruma.

[184] Kuiper 2009, 46 and 53; and Kuiper 2014, 568–569 and 573. See also MJ Borgers in his annotation to HR 30 March 2010, ECLI:NL:HR:2010:BK4173, *NJ* 2011/603 and Borgers 2012, 264.

[185] See n 165 and accompanying text.

[186] See *Kamerstukken II* 1993/94, 23075, 3, p. 25 (explanatory memorandum). In HR 16 December 2003, ECLI:NL:HR:2003:AN7635, the Supreme Court determined at para 3.4 that prejudice to defence rights does not constitute prejudice within the meaning of Article 359a(1)(a). For literature in this regard, see Kuiper 2009, 55; and 2014, 574–575.

Nevertheless, in a recent ruling the Supreme Court held that sentence reduction would be an appropriate response to a violation of the right to legal assistance during questioning, where the accused's right to legal assistance prior to questioning has been observed. See HR 22 December 2015, ECLI:NL:HR:2015:3608, r.o. 6.4.2, *NJ* 2016/52 m.nt. AH Klip.

actual prejudice to the accused's other rights, such as the right to privacy,[187] whereby the *actual* prejudice consists of non-material damage suffered by the accused as a result of the privacy-violation.[188] This does not include damage to the accused's interest 'not to be caught'.[189] Moving on to the second requirement, the requirement of causal connection between the procedural violation and the prejudice for the accused rarely raises any significant issues.[190] Finally, the fourth requirement explicitly refers to two of the factors set out in the second paragraph of Article 359a of the CCP: the interest that the violated provision purports to protect and the seriousness of the violation. This requirement appears to demarcate, in principle, the boundary between a declaration that an irreparable procedural violation has occurred and sentence reduction.[191] Minimal actual prejudice for the accused can lead to either response, however, sentence reduction may be justified in light of (one of) the other two factors. In addition to the aforementioned 'substantive' requirements, the Supreme Court prescribes requirements of a more procedural nature for sentence reduction: the court granting sentence reduction must explicitly state *that* it is doing so, and must also explain *why* it is doing so. Moreover, the court is required to state in how far it is reducing the sentence in connection with the procedural violation.[192]

While the Supreme Court has not (yet) addressed sentence reduction in the comprehensive way that it has addressed the exclusion of evidence, a number of observations may be made regarding this response's scope of application, as supported by the Supreme Court's case law. First, in view, in particular, of the fact that the Schutz-norm criteria need to be fulfilled before any of the consequences in the first paragraph of Article 359a of the CCP can be applied, and in view of the various components of the test for sentence reduction, it is clear that sentence reduction is not a residual category, whereby procedural violations that do not lead to the exclusion of evidence thereby (because, for example, the Schutz-norm criteria have not been fulfilled or the test for exclusion not met) automatically lead to sentence reduction.[193] This is moreover apparent from the practice of lower courts (in view, presumably, of the preference expressed by the Supreme Court for such a response) of merely declaring that an irreparable procedural violation has occurred. Secondly,

---

[187] See e.g. Kuiper 2009, 56; and 2014, 575. See also Borgers 2012, 265. See e.g. HR 25 June 2002, ECLI:NL:HR:2002:AD9204, *NJ* 2002/625 m.nt. TM Schalken, in which the Supreme Court upheld the Court of Appeal's decision to grant sentence reduction on account of an unlawful search of the suspect's clothing. See also HR 21 March 2000, r.o. 3.6. http://uitspraken. rechtspraak.nl/inziendocument?id=ECLI:NL:HR:2000:AA5254. Accessed 1 March 2017.

[188] See e.g. Kuiper 2009, 54–56; and 2014, 573–576.

[189] See n 276 and accompanying text.

[190] Unlike the requirement of causal connection in the context of the exclusion of evidence, which does potentially raise difficult questions.

[191] See Ter Haar and Meijer 2011, 62. In practice, however, this line may be difficult to draw.

[192] HR 30 March 2004, ECLI:NL:HR:2004:AM2533, r.o. 3.6.3, *NJ* 2004/376 m.nt. Y Buruma.

[193] See similarly Borgers 2012, 264, and Borgers in his annotation to HR 30 March 2010, ECLI: NL:HR:2010:BK4173, *NJ* 2011/603.

also in view of the fact that the Schutz-norm criteria need to be fulfilled for sentence reduction and given that, pursuant to the first and third components of the test, actual prejudice for the accused that lends itself to compensation by way of sentence reduction is required, it appears that the rationale for sentence reduction is the compensation of violations of the individual accused's subjective rights, *other* than his or her fair trial rights.[194] According to Kuiper, its purpose is not to ensure observance by public authorities of the norms that bind them, which he argues is apparent from the requirement set out in the first leading decision of the Supreme Court on Article 359a of the CCP of actual prejudice for the accused. Moreover, sentence reduction can hardly be expected to have a deterrent effect.[195]

C. Exclusion of Evidence

According to the text of Article 359a of the CCP, the court may determine that the results of the investigation obtained by procedural violation may not be used as proof of the offence charged.[196] In its leading decision of March 2004, the Supreme Court determined that the test for excluding evidence pursuant to Article 359a of the CCP is as follows: an important provision or principle (of criminal procedure) must have been seriously breached and the evidence must have been obtained by the breach.[197] In the same breath, the Supreme Court made clear that the exclusion of evidence thereby obtained is not the inevitable consequence of procedural violations committed in the course of a criminal investigation, by reiterating that Article 359a confers on the court a *power* to attach consequences to such violations, including the exclusion of evidence, not a *duty*, whereby the exercise of such power is dependent on the factors set out in the second paragraph of Article 359a and on the particular circumstances of the case.[198] Further, it observed that Article 359a of the CCP is not relevant to procedural violations committed in the course of a criminal investigation as a result of which the reliability of the evidence thereby obtained is significantly affected. Such evidence should be set aside by the court for that reason alone.[199]

Turning first to the requirement of causal connection between the procedural violation and the evidence sought for exclusion, the Supreme Court's position in this regard is best explained in terms of the 'fruits of the poisonous tree' metaphor,[200] a metaphor sometimes used to depict an exclusionary rule prescribing

---

[194] See Kuiper 2009, 53–57; and 2014, 575–576.

[195] Ibid., 573; 53–54. See also Borgers in his annotation to HR 30 March 2010, ECLI:NL:HR:2010:BK4173, *NJ* 2011/603.

[196] See Article 359a(1)(b) CCP.

[197] HR 30 March 2004, ECLI:NL:HR:2004:AM2533, r.o. 3.6.4, *NJ* 2004/376 m.nt. Y Buruma. This is repeated in HR 19 February 2013, ECLI:NL:HR:2013:BY5322, r.o. 2.4.2, *NJ* 2013/308 m.nt. BF Keulen.

[198] Ibid., r.o. 3.6.4; r.o. 2.4.2.

[199] HR 30 March 2004, ECLI:NL:HR:2004:AM2533, r.o. 3.6.4, *NJ* 2004/376 m.nt. Y Buruma.

[200] See also Kuiper in this regard. Kuiper 2014, 501–520.

exclusion in respect of evidence obtained with the assistance of illegally obtained information as the 'fruit of the poisonous tree'. It is worth noting that the legislator seems to have had a restrictive application of the requirement of causal connection in mind. In the explanatory memorandum to Article 359a of the CCP, the Minister of Justice emphasizes the need for a 'direct causal relationship' between the procedural violation in question and the evidence in respect of which exclusion is sought. According to the Minister, 'derivative' evidence need not be excluded when it is likely that other factors contributed to it being obtained.[201] That the Supreme Court might also favour a restrictive application of the 'fruits-rule' is apparent from its formulation of the degree of causal connection required between the violation and the evidence. Recently, it has framed that requirement in terms of evidence to have been obtained 'solely and directly' (*uitsluitend en rechtstreeks*) by the violation.[202] In other cases it has simply framed the requirement in terms of evidence to have been obtained 'directly' by the violation.[203] Since the Supreme Court's case law in this regard appears to be highly casuistic, it is difficult to say with any certainty when evidence may be said to have been obtained 'solely and directly', or simply 'directly', by the violation.[204] Certainly the Supreme Court purports to favour a restrictive application of the 'fruits-rule' (as apparent from its formulation of the degree of causal connection required),[205] which, as Kuiper observes, appears to allow significant leeway for the recognition of exceptions to the exclusionary rule connected to causation, for example, 'attenuation' or 'inevitable discovery'.[206]

As to the requirement that an important provision or principle (of criminal procedure) be seriously breached, in its second leading decision on Article 359a of the CCP, the Supreme Court, drawing on and consolidating its earlier case law, explained how this requirement should be construed. First, it repeated its position[207] that a violation of the right to privacy, as protected by Article 8 of the ECHR, does not necessarily infringe on the right to a fair trial, as protected by Article 6 of the ECHR, and, moreover, that an unjustified infringement of the first paragraph of Article 8 of the ECHR need not lead to legal consequences in the criminal

---

[201] *Kamerstukken II* 1993/94, 23075, 3, p. 25–26 (explanatory memorandum).

[202] HR 16 September 2014, ECLI:NL:HR:2014:2670, r.o. 4.4, *NJ* 2014/461 m.nt. TM Schalken, and HR 16 September 2014, ECLI:NL:HR:2014:2749, r.o. 2.5.1, *NJ* 2014/462 m.nt. TM Schalken.

[203] HR 17 September 2013, ECLI:NL:HR:2013:BZ9992, r.o. 3.3, *NJ* 2014/91 m.nt. TM Schalken; HR 13 November 2012, ECLI:NL:HR:2012:BW9338, r.o. 2.7.7, *NJ* 2013/413 m.nt. MJ Borgers; and HR 30 June 2009, ECLI:NL:HR:2009:BH3079, r.o. 2.7.3, *NJ* 2009/349 m.nt. TM Schalken.

[204] Kuiper 2014, 519.

[205] Or, as Schalken puts it, the Supreme Court 'only likes freshly picked fruit, not fruit that is already lying on the ground'. See Schalken in his annotation to HR 16 September 2014, ECLI:NL:HR:2014:2670, *NJ* 2014/461 and HR 16 September 2014, ECLI:NL:HR:2014:2749, *NJ* 2014/462.

[206] Kuiper 2014, 519.

[207] See e.g. HR 7 July 2009, ECLI:NL:HR:2009:BH8889, r.o. 4.5, *NJ* 2009/399, and HR 5 October 2010, ECLI:NL:HR:2010:BL5629, r.o. 4.4.1, *NJ* 2011/169 m.nt. TM Schalken.

proceedings against the accused, provided the accused's right to a fair trial within the meaning of the first paragraph of Article 6 of the ECHR is protected.[208] Second, the Supreme Court identified, seemingly exhaustively, three categories of procedural violation that require or may require the exclusion of evidence, whereby the underlying rationales for exclusion are also addressed.

First, exclusion may be necessary to secure the accused's right to a fair trial within the meaning of Article 6 of the ECHR, as also interpreted by the ECtHR.[209,210] By way of example, the Supreme Court points to its case law on the right to legal assistance at the time of questioning purporting to implement the ECtHR *Salduz*-case law,[211] and its case law on the use of statements made by a suspect to an undercover agent pretending to be a fellow detainee,[212] which draws on the ECtHR's judgment in *Allan v. United Kingdom*.[213] This category probably also includes cases in which evidence has been obtained in violation of Article 3 of the ECHR, cases in which an incriminating statement has been obtained from the suspect by improper compulsion and cases in which the authorities have failed to caution the suspect (among other cases).[214] Once a violation of this nature has been established, there is (very) limited room for the court to nevertheless decide not to exclude the evidence on account of the factors set out in the second paragraph of Article 359a of the CCP. In this regard it may be observed that the case law cited by the Supreme Court is based on, or otherwise draws on, case law of the ECtHR that adopts a principled, 'interventionist' approach to the admissibility (or use) of (unlawfully obtained) evidence.[215]

Second, where the accused's right to a fair trial is not (directly) at stake but another important provision or principle (of criminal procedure) has been seriously breached, the exclusion of evidence may be necessary in order to prevent

---

[208] HR 19 February 2013, ECLI:NL:HR:2013:BY5322, r.o. 2.4.2, *NJ* 2013/308 m.nt. BF Keulen.

[209] Ibid., r.o. 2.4.4.
According to Kuiper, the scope of this exclusionary rule is, to a large extent, 'in the hands of the ECtHR' as the highest authority to interpret this provision. See Kuiper 2014, 521.

[210] It is worth noting here that Article 6 ECHR has direct effect in the Dutch legal order, so that it is questionable whether allegations that the procedural violation in question threatens to undermine the right to a fair trial would be (and certainly whether they should be) subject to the regime of Article 359a CCP in its entirety, i.e. whether the procedural violation in question would need to be considered one within the meaning of Article 359a CCP. See in this regard n 151–162 and accompanying text, and also the text accompanying n 316–328.

[211] HR 30 June 2009, ECLI:NL:HR:2009:BH3079, *NJ* 2009/349 m.nt. TM Schalken. See also *Salduz v Turkey* App no 36391/02 (ECtHR, 27 November 2008). However, in a recent ruling the Supreme Court held that *sentence reduction* would be an appropriate response to a violation of the right to legal assistance *during* questioning, where the accused's right to legal assistance prior to questioning has otherwise been observed. See HR 22 December 2015, ECLI:NL:HR:2015:3608, r.o. 6.4.2, *NJ* 2016/52 m.nt. AH Klip.

[212] HR 28 March 2006, ECLI:NL:HR:2006:AU5471, *NJ* 2007/38 m.nt. TM Schalken.

[213] *Allan v UK* App no 48539/99 (ECtHR, 5 November 2002).

[214] Kuiper 2014, 522.

[215] See in this regard Chap. 2, n 36, 77 and 129 and accompanying text.

comparable violations in the future and to provide a strong incentive for public authorities to abide by the rules. In the words of the Supreme Court, exclusion may be necessary as a means of upholding the rule of law and of preventing the public authorities charged with the investigation and prosecution of crime from acting unlawfully.[216] Thus, the Supreme Court cites the prevention argument (or deterrence rationale) as the rationale for this category of exclusion.[217] It refers to two types of situations that are likely to fall into this category: a 'very intrusive' breach of a fundamental right of the accused and cases in which the use of the evidence obtained 'fundamentally devalues' the interest served by the protection of legal and other types of professional privilege. Regarding the first type of violation, the Supreme Court cites, by way of example, a case in which evidence had been obtained by means of an unlawful vaginal cavity search of the accused; the Supreme Court in that case upheld an appellate court's decision to exclude the evidence pursuant to Article 359a of the CCP.[218] Thus, very intrusive breaches violations of the right to bodily integrity fall under this second of category of exclusion. A very intrusive breach of the right to respect for the home might also require the evidence obtained thereby to be excluded pursuant to this category.[219] Regarding the second type of violation, the Supreme Court cites by way of example two cases. The first concerns legal professional privilege: the Court of Appeal had used to convict the accused conversations between the co-accused and his lawyer. According to the Supreme Court, the appellate court should not have done so, in view of the interest served by the protection of legal professional privilege.[220] The second concerns medical professional privilege: the appellate court had used to convict the accused (of the import into the Netherlands of prohibited drugs) a police report of an interview conducted with the accused from which it was apparent that the accused had been confronted with the conversations he had had with a medical professional, and from which his reaction to the confrontation (admission of the presence of cocaine-filled balloons in his body) was also apparent; according to the Supreme Court, the appellate court should not have done so, on account of the applicable medical professional privilege.[221]

Regarding the first type of situation referred to by the Supreme Court (a very intrusive breach of a fundamental right of the accused), whether such a violation, once established, requires the exclusion of the evidence thereby obtained depends on the factors set out in the second paragraph of Article 359a of the CCP and the individual circumstances of the case. Moreover, the court *may* consider whether the

---

[216] HR 19 February 2013, ECLI:NL:HR:2013:BY5322, r.o. 2.4.5, *NJ* 2013/308 m.nt. BF Keulen.

[217] See also BF Keulen in his annotation to HR 19 February 2013, ECLI:NL:HR:2013:BY5322, *NJ* 2013/308 and T Schalken in his annotation to HR 9 September 2014, ECLI:NL:HR:2014:2650, *NJ* 2014/420.

[218] See HR 29 May 2007, ECLI:NL:HR:2007:AZ8795, *NJ* 2008/14 m.nt. JM Reijntjes.

[219] Kuiper 2014, 537–540.

[220] HR 12 January 1999, ECLI:NL:HR:1999:ZD1402, *NJ* 1999/290.

[221] HR 2 October 2007, ECLI:NL:HR:2007:BA5632, *NJ* 2008/374 m.nt. J Legemaate.

(presumably, preventive or deterrent) benefits of exclusion outweigh the negative effects that it may be expected to have on such 'heavily weighted interests' as truth-finding, the need to punish perpetrators of ('possibly very serious') crime and the rights of victims and next of kin (in light also of the positive obligations flowing from the ECHR of effective punishment).[222] While it appears that a consideration of the factors set out in the second paragraph of Article 359a of the CCP *after* the court has found that the procedural violation amounts to a very intrusive breach of a fundamental right of the accused is unlikely to lead the court to conclude that the evidence obtained thereby should not be excluded (since it appears that such a finding necessarily implies the violation of an interest of *significant weight or importance*, a *serious* violation and *prejudice* for the accused, such that the deterrent benefits of exclusion may be presumed to outweigh its social costs),[223] the consideration of whether the preventive or deterrent value of exclusion outweighs its societal costs (again, after the court has found that the procedural violation amounts to a very intrusive breach of a fundamental right of the accused), would appear create significant scope for the court to do so.[224] Such 'additional' balancing[225] allows the court to consider facts and circumstances that might diminish the presumed deterrent value of excluding evidence obtained by a very intrusive breach of a fundamental right of the accused, as well as those that might increase its societal costs. Facts and circumstances that might *diminish* the deterrent benefits of the exclusion include, according to Kuiper (who draws on the case law of the US Supreme Court on the admissibility of evidence obtained by Fourth Amendment violations in this regard), the existence of other mechanisms to ensure observance by the public authorities of the rights in question, the existence of other remedies to address violations when they occur and the fact that the official in question acted in good faith.[226] Facts and circumstances that might *increase* the societal costs of exclusion include the seriousness of the offence in question. While, according to the Dutch Supreme Court, the court *may*, after it has made this finding, undertake such additional balancing,[227] Kuiper is of the view that the court *must* do so, since the interest in truth-finding is always at stake, and victims' interests are often so.[228] He nevertheless observes that the room in this category to, on the basis of the additional balancing exercise identified above, *not* exclude the evidence obtained, is dependent on what is held in practice to constitute 'a very intrusive breach of a fundamental right of the accused'. The stricter the interpretation, the less room there is for

---

[222] HR 19 February 2013, ECLI:NL:HR:2013:BY5322, r.o. 2.4.5, *NJ* 2013/308 m.nt. BF Keulen.

[223] Kuiper 2014, 543 and 545.

[224] Ibid., 544–545.

[225] It may be considered to constitute 'additional' balancing because it goes beyond that which may be presumed to underlie a finding that the unlawfulness in question amounts to a very intrusive breach of a fundamental right of the accused.

[226] See Kuiper 2014, 546.

[227] HR 19 February 2013, ECLI:NL:HR:2013:BY5322, r.o. 2.4.5, *NJ* 2013/308 m.nt. BF Keulen.

[228] Kuiper 2014, 545.

additional balancing and, in his view, the greater the worth of a clear signal to the authorities that such a breach should not be repeated.[229] More will be said about the issue of 'balancing' below, in the following section.

Turning to the third category of procedural violation that may require the exclusion of evidence, the exclusion of evidence is not 'ruled out' in all circumstances in the 'highly exceptional' situation in which the procedural violation in question forms part of a wider pattern (as apparent from objective facts and circumstances), such that its structural nature is evident, and whereby the responsible authorities have, from the moment that they must have become aware of the structural nature of this violation, failed to make sufficient efforts to prevent breaches of the provision in question.[230] According to the Supreme Court, it is up to the defence to demonstrate, on the basis of existing data, that the violation is structural in nature, while it is up to the public prosecutor to provide data on the basis of which it can be ascertained whether the responsible authorities are doing enough to prevent violation on a structural basis of the provision in question.[231] Moreover, according to the Supreme Court, only if it is likely that it would actually deter such structural violation in the future should the evidence thereby obtained be excluded, whereby the court may take account the cause of the violation and what measures are already being undertaken by the relevant authorities to prevent violation of the provision in question.[232] However, even where this—the actual deterrence of such structural violation—is to be expected, the court is *required*[233] to undertake the same cost-benefit analysis that the court *may* (and perhaps, must) undertake in the context of the second category of exclusion.[234] Thus, in the third category of exclusion, the court is required to take into account facts and circumstances that might diminish the expected deterrent value of exclusion (for example, the fact that the official in question acted in good faith), as well as those that might increase its societal costs (for example, the seriousness of the offence). Finally, if the court does decide to exclude evidence pursuant to the third category, it must provide further reasoning in this regard.[235] Kuiper has said of the third category that, 'if all goes well', this third rule of exclusion will never lead to exclusion; rather its purpose is to stimulate research into the structural nature of certain procedural violations and to bring about action on the part of the authorities primarily responsible for preventing such violations.[236] In a recent decision, the Amsterdam Court of Appeal established such a 'structural' procedural violation—the widespread utilization by the Dutch police of roadside checks, as provided for under the

---

[229] Ibid., 546–547.

[230] HR 19 February 2013, ECLI:NL:HR:2013:BY5322, r.o. 2.4.6, *NJ* 2013/308 m.nt. BF Keulen.

[231] Ibid., r.o. 2.4.6.

[232] Ibid., r.o. 2.4.6.

[233] Ibid., r.o. 2.4.6.

[234] See n 222 and accompanying text.

[235] HR 19 February 2013, ECLI:NL:HR:2013:BY5322, r.o. 2.4.6, *NJ* 2013/308 m.nt. BF Keulen.

[236] Kuiper 2014, 548 and 551.

Road Traffic Act 1994, for purposes other than those for which they were intended (i.e. in order to come into contact with (potential) offenders and to obtain information), in violation of the prohibition of *détournement de pouvoir*—and excluded the evidence obtained thereby pursuant to Article 359a of the CCP.[237] On appeal in cassation, however, the Supreme Court ruled that the utilization of roadside checks for such purposes is not per se unlawful, provided the power under the Road Traffic Act 1994 is not solely utilized for criminal investigative purposes;[238] in light of this finding, the issue of exclusion was not considered.

D. Declaring the Prosecution Inadmissible

According to the text of Article 359a of the CCP, the prosecution may be declared inadmissible if, as a result of the violation, it is not possible to try the case in a manner consistent with principles of proper administration of justice (*beginselen van een behoorlijke procesorde*). As stated above, this procedural consequence is akin to a stay of proceedings (and is sometimes referred to as 'barring the prosecution'). The violation must be so grave that, for example, the exclusion of evidence or sentence reduction does not suffice.[239] A declaration that the prosecution is inadmissible results in a final judgment on the formal questions of Article 348 of the CCP.[240] In its leading decision of March 2004, the Supreme Court determined that the test for a declaration that the prosecution is inadmissible is as follows: the public authorities must have committed serious violations of principles of proper administration of justice, either intentionally or by gross negligence, as a result of which the suspect is prevented from receiving a fair trial.[241] This test is known as the *Zwolsman*-criterion.[242] In addition, the Supreme Court emphasized that such a declaration is only warranted in exceptional circumstances.

Before examining the *Zwolsman*-criterion, it is important to note that the Supreme Court has in the past approved other grounds for declaring the prosecution inadmissible on account of improper conduct on the part of the public authorities.[243] In the *Karman*-case, which was decided after the *Zwolsman*-case, the Supreme Court affirmed the decision of an appellate court declaring the prosecution inadmissible on the grounds that the prosecutor had made promises to the accused,

---

[237] Hof Amsterdam 21 December 2015, ECLI:NL:GHAMS:2015:5307.

[238] HR 1 November 2016, ECLI:NL:HR:2016:2454, r.o. 3.4, thereby confirming its earlier judgment in HR 21 November 2006, ECLI:NL:HR:2006:AY9670, *NJ* 2006/653.

[239] *Kamerstukken II* 1993/94, 23075, 3, p. 26 (explanatory memorandum).

[240] That is, it results in a judgment within the meaning of Article 349(1) in conjunction with Article 138 CCP.

[241] HR 30 March 2004, ECLI:NL:HR:2004:AM2533, r.o. 3.6.5, *NJ* 2004/376 m.nt. Y Buruma.

[242] See HR 19 December 1995, ECLI:NL:HR:1995:ZD0328, r.o. 5.2, *NJ* 1996/249 m.nt. TM Schalken.

[243] In addition, the prosecution may be declared inadmissible on grounds wholly unconcerned with the propriety of the investigation. See n 13 and accompanying text.

Karman, that it was not authorised to make, namely that he would not be deprived of his liberty any further in pre-trial detention, and that, if convicted and sentenced, he would not have to sit out his sentence, in exchange for his evidence regarding his own involvement and that of others in the underlying offences. According to the Supreme Court, the appellate court had not erred in declaring the prosecution inadmissible in the case against Karman, in view of the appellate court's finding that the prosecutor's conduct, which violated 'principles of proper prosecution' (*beginselen van een behoorlijke strafvervolging*), 'went to the core of the legal system'. The fact that such conduct did not prejudice concrete defence interests and, by extension, the right to a fair trial, was immaterial, particularly given the 'fundamental character' of the violation.[244] Keulen and Knigge observe that the prosecutor's conduct had put the appellate court in an 'impossible position', since although the promise may have been unlawful, Karman may have been entitled to rely on it. As such, the case against Karman had become a 'farce'.[245] However, in its leading decision of March 2004 the Supreme Court makes no reference to the *Karman*-case in setting out the requirements for a declaration that the prosecution is inadmissible. Nor does it appear to have applied or otherwise endorsed the reasoning in that case in subsequent (Supreme Court) decisions.[246] Moreover, in a recent decision, the Supreme Court rejected an appellate court's reasoning (which bore resemblance to the Supreme Court's reasoning in *Karman*) in declaring the prosecution inadmissible, holding that the violation in question should have been assessed in the light of Article 359a of the CCP,[247] which, it should be recalled, incorporates the *Zwolsman*-criterion. In conclusion, then, it appears that the only possible ground for declaring the prosecution inadmissible on account of improper conduct on the part of the public authorities is the *Zwolsman*-criterion of Article 359a of the CCP.

As to the *Zwolsman*-criterion, or test, its apparent stringency has not gone unnoticed in the literature.[248] The test consists of numerous components, which appear to be cumulative. In particular, the question arises as to whether, if it is found that the procedural violation in question prevents the accused from receiving a fair trial, it *must* also be shown that the relevant public authorities committed such violation (which, moreover, must constitute a serious violation of principles of proper administration of justice) either intentionally or by gross negligence.[249] More generally the question arises as to whether such components are, in fact, cumulative, and whether, rather, the test should be understood as providing for two different grounds for a declaration that the prosecution is inadmissible: the need to

---

[244] HR 1 June 1999, ECLI:NL:HR:1999:ZD1143, r.o. 3.8, *NJ* 1999/567 m.nt. TM Schalken.

[245] Keulen and Knigge 2010, 543.

[246] Kuiper 2014, 389–390.

[247] HR 13 December 2011, ECLI:NL:HR:2011:BT2173, r.o. 4.2, *NJ* 2012/299 m.nt. JM Reijntjes.

[248] See e.g. Knigge 2003; Borgers 2012, 263–264; Corstens and Kuiper 2013, 125; and Kuiper 2014, 367–370.

[249] See e.g. Knigge 2003, 193; Corstens and Kuiper 2013, 133; and Kuiper 2014, 368.

ensure the accused's right to a fair trial, and ensuring observance by the public authorities of the norms that bind them.[250] Regarding the second question, there are strong indications in the Supreme Court's case law that the second ground is, on its own, insufficient to justify a declaration that the prosecution is inadmissible.[251] This brings us (back) to the first question: is the need to ensure the accused's right to a fair trial, on its own and without more, sufficient to justify this response? There are indications in the Supreme Court's case law that if the procedural violation in question clearly prevents the accused from receiving a fair trial, whether the public authorities committed such violation intentionally or by gross negligence is of less importance.[252] Certainly in the literature it has been argued that where this is the case, the question of culpability should be irrelevant.[253] Where, however, the inability of the accused to receive a fair trial is less clear, the culpability of the public authorities may be a reason to nevertheless declare the prosecution inadmissible.[254]

If, indeed, what matters under the Zwolsman-criterion is the (in)ability of the accused to receive a fair trial, the next question to arise is how 'fair trial' is to be construed in this context. It appears that only actual prejudice to defence rights, such as to prevent the accused from receiving a fair trial, i.e. the inability of the accused to mount an effective defence, can warrant a declaration of inadmissibility. An example of such a case is where material which would allow the Defence to challenge the case against the accused is lost or destroyed. In a case in which material had been destroyed before the Defence was able to obtain a sample thereof and seek a second opinion in respect of the results of the investigations carried out by the prosecuting authorities on it, the Supreme Court found that the Court of Appeal had erred in rejecting the Defence's application for a declaration that the

---

[250] Corstens and Kuiper 2013, 133–134; and Kuiper 2014, 370–371. That 'ensuring observance by the public authorities of the norms that bind them' might be a (separate) ground for declaring the prosecution inadmissible is derived from the requirement that the public authorities must have committed serious violations of principles of proper administration of justice, *either intentionally or by gross negligence*.

[251] See e.g. HR 29 June 2010, ECLI:NL:HR:2010:BL0656, r.o. 3.5, *NJ* 2010/442 m.nt. TM Schalken, and HR 7 February 2012, r.o. 2.4, ECLI:NL:HR:2012:BU6784, *NJB* 2012/539. See also TM Schalken in his annotation to that case, Borgers 2012, 263; Corstens and Kuiper 2013, 139; and Kuiper 2014, 405.

[252] See e.g. HR 18 February 1997, ECLI:NL:HR:1997:ZD0643, r.o. 6.3, *NJ* 1997/484 m.nt. JM Reijntjes. In that case the defence had argued on appeal in cassation before the Supreme Court that the Court of Appeal had erred in rejecting the application for a declaration that the prosecution was inadmissible on account of it not having been shown that the public prosecutor had purposely prejudiced the defendant's fair trial rights. The defence argued that 'purpose', i.e. intent need not be shown for such a declaration and that gross negligence suffices. However, the Supreme Court, in finding that the Court of Appeal had indeed erred as regards the rejection of the application, said nothing of the prosecutor's culpability, focusing instead of the Court of Appeal's failure to respond to an important aspect of the defence's argument regarding the prejudice caused to the defendant's fair trial rights. See also Kuiper 2014, 379 and 403.

[253] See e.g. Knigge 2003, 194; and Kuiper 2014, 368.

[254] See Kuiper 2014, 382.

prosecution was inadmissible. While the Court of Appeal had acknowledged that the destruction of the material had deprived the Defence of the opportunity to challenge the results of the investigations carried out by the prosecuting authorities, it had failed to address the plea advanced by the Defence that the destruction of the material had deprived the Defence of its only opportunity to effectively challenge the case against the Accused.[255] However, in another case, in which material had been lost before the Defence was able to conduct its own investigations in respect thereof, the Supreme Court found that the Court of Appeal had not erred in rejecting the Defence's application for a declaration that the prosecution was inadmissible, seemingly because the availability of such material and the ability of the Defence to conduct its own investigations in respect thereof would not have the changed the course of the proceedings in view of the (strength of the) remaining evidence.[256] According to Keulen and Knigge, an accused will be prevented from receiving a fair trial where the inability of the defence to exercise its fair trial rights seriously hampers the court in 'establishing the truth'.[257] This is not the case where excessive force is applied at the time of arrest,[258] or where the accused has, prior to the commencement of trial, been detained in conditions that raise issues under Article 3 of the ECHR.[259] In short, it appears that the notion of fair trial in the context of the test for declaring the prosecution inadmissible is to be construed narrowly, in the sense of being concerned with accurate truth-finding and the protection of the innocent from wrongful conviction.

Discretion and Balancing

This section will address the question of the extent to which the Dutch judicial response to procedural violations committed in the pre-trial phase of criminal proceedings can be said to be discretionary in nature, i.e. the extent to which it entails the exercise of judgement, whereby the judge has regard to the particular circumstances of the case, and/or the extent to which it entails a balancing approach (whereby it may be recalled that in Chap. 1, such questions were said to lie at the heart of the present study).[260]

---

[255] HR 18 February 1997, ECLI:NL:HR:1997:ZD0643, r.o. 6.3, *NJ* 1997/484 m.nt. JM Reijntjes.

[256] HR 20 October 1998, ECLI:NL:HR:1998:ZD1309, *NJ* 1999/122. See also HR 14 January 2003, ECLI:NL:HR:2003:AE9038, *NJ* 2003/288 m.nt. Y Buruma.

[257] See also Keulen and Knigge 2010, 543.

[258] See e.g. HR 12 February 2008, ECLI:NL:HR:2008:BC3496, *NJ* 2008/248 m.nt. TM Schalken and HR 5 January 2016, ECLI:NL:HR:2016:9, *NJ* 2016/153 m.nt. F Vellinga-Schootstra.

[259] HR 8 July 2008, ECLI:NL:HR:2008:BC5973, *NJ* 2009/440 m.nt. Y Buruma.

[260] In Chap. 1, 'balancing' was defined as an approach to the question of how to address pre-trial procedural violations whereby the court (also) takes into account factors that seemingly have nothing to do with that which warranted the court's attention in the first place, and which militate against a (potentially) far-reaching response thereto.

Underlying Article 359a of the CCP is the notion that pre-trial procedural violations should not invariably lead to a particular response; the judge should therefore look beyond the fact of the procedural violation to the individual circumstances of the case (and, in any case, to the factors set out in the second paragraph of Article 359a of the CCP). The judge is required to be mindful of the different consequences that may be attached to such violations.[261] According to the Supreme Court, in introducing Article 359a into the CCP, the legislator sought to enable the court to, within the legal framework, tailor the response to procedural violations to the particular circumstances of the case.[262] On the face of it, therefore, the Dutch judicial response within the criminal trial to pre-trial procedural violations may appear to be a matter of *discretion*, in the sense that the consequence, if any, to be attached to such violations depends on the individual circumstances of the case, and whereby the trial judge is afforded a degree of freedom. Kuiper argues that the purpose of the requirement of having regard to the individual circumstances of the case is to prevent a 'rigid, knee-jerk response to breaches of procedural rules',[263] i.e. to prevent the application of a single, unvarying *rule*. And a 'rigid, knee-jerk response to breaches of procedural rules' may be considered undesirable because it appears to reflect an approach to the question of how to address pre-trial procedural violations whereby a legitimate interest is, at the outset, removed from the equation. This leads us (back) to the topic of 'balancing', because it appears, on the basis of the Supreme Court's case law, that underlying the process of taking into consideration the individual circumstances of the case (at least, as far as the exclusion of evidence is concerned) is a balancing exercise in the form of a cost-benefit analysis, whereby the benefits of a certain course of action, in terms of the rationale pursued, are weighed against its societal costs.[264] This cost-benefit analysis is addressed later on in this section. Insofar as the Dutch judicial response within the criminal trial to procedural violations committed in the pre-trial phase of criminal proceedings *can* be depicted as a balancing discretion, it is important to note that this discretion is confined in at least one noteworthy way. There is little to no room to consider facts and circumstances that might militate against a (certain) response once it is established that the right of the accused to a fair trial, within the meaning of Article 6 of the ECHR and, importantly, as also interpreted by the ECtHR, is at stake. Accordingly, the balancing discretion is 'confined' to those

---

[261] See n 140 and accompanying text.

[262] HR 22 September 1998, ECLI:NL:HR:1998:ZD1277, r.o. 4.4, *NJ* 1999/104 m.nt. J de Hullu. It is worth noting the cautious language of the Supreme Court in this regard; it does not speak of an obligation on the part of the court to do so, but the power or the opportunity to do so. The Dutch text reads as follows: 'De wetgever heeft de rechter aldus uitdrukkelijk in de gelegenheid gesteld binnen het wettelijke kader de sancties op vormverzuimen af te stemmen op de omstandigheden van het geval.'

[263] Kuiper 2014, 605. See also 53–54.

[264] While this may appear natural or logical, it need not be the case; more will be said about this issue in Chap. 7.

cases that do not involve procedural violations that undermine, or threaten to undermine this right.

If indeed the Dutch judicial response within the criminal trial to procedural violations committed in the pre-trial phase of criminal proceedings *can* be depicted as a balancing discretion, a number of questions arise. First, regarding this response's depiction as a *discretion*, the question arises as to just how 'free' the judge in criminal proceedings is in exercising the discretion—exercising judgement—and doing justice according to the needs of the case. Secondly, regarding its depiction as a *balancing* discretion, more specifically, as a cost-benefit analysis, what factors may be taken into account, and why? And what is the impact of the consideration of such factors on the scope of the Dutch judicial response within the criminal trial to such violations? These questions are addressed in the current section, by reference to the factors set out in the second paragraph of Article 359a of the CCP: the interest that the violated provision purports to protect, the seriousness of the violation and the prejudice caused by it. In addition, it appears that the court may take into account the seriousness of the offence in question. Each of these factors is addressed below.

§ Factors

Under the first statutory factor, the interest that the violated provision purports to protect, consideration should be given to the importance of the provision to have been violated. Provisions may be considered to have importance when they protect fundamental rights,[265] although within this category, a distinction may be drawn between rights which, when violated, (potentially) prevent the accused from receiving a fair trial, and rights that do not. The first set of rights may have more weight than the second set, such that the violation thereof warrants a more far-reaching judicial response than the second set would. Kuiper puts this distinction down to the ability of the first set of rights to, when violated, negatively impact on the court's truth-finding endeavour.[266] Further, the right to privacy is broad, and the right to respect for the home and the right to bodily integrity are likely to weigh more heavily than other rights falling under the general right to privacy. The first statutory factor should be distinguished from the Schutz-norm, pursuant to which the violation of the norm aimed at protecting accused persons *in general* must have affected *this particular accused*. In this regard Kuiper notes that this factor requires the court to determine not only the underlying interest that the provision in question purports to protect, but also whose interest it is. This is important in view of the fact that while, according to the Supreme Court, the court need not attach a consequence to the procedural violation in question where the Schutz-norm criteria are not (both) fulfilled, this principle may, exceptionally, be departed from, for example, in case of the infringement of legal professional privilege, regardless of whether the accused

---

[265] See e.g. Schoep, in T&C Strafvordering 2015, Article 359a Sv, aant 3 (online, last updated 1 July 2015).

[266] See Kuiper 2014, 328.

was party to the attorney-client relationship in question.[267] Accordingly, consideration of the first factor ensures that other heavily weighted interests than those of the particular accused on trial are, where they arise, brought to the forefront.

In its first leading decision on Article 359a of the CCP, the Supreme Court held that the determination pursuant to the second statutory factor, the seriousness of the violation, requires a consideration of the circumstances under which the violation occurred, whereby the degree of blameworthiness (*verwijtbaarheid*) may also play a role.[268] Thus, pursuant to this factor, it is relevant to consider whether the violation was the result of good or bad faith on the part of the public authorities.[269] In its second leading decision, the Supreme Court elaborated on this point, on the basis of the particular facts underlying the appeal in that case, which were as follows. A warrant to enter the accused's home had been issued by an authority that was not authorized to do so (the individual in question had not passed the requisite examination to act as 'acting public prosecutor' (*hulpofficier van justitie*), which he knew, such that he was not qualified to issue a warrant pursuant to Article 2 of the General Act on Entry into Dwellings (*Algemene wet op het binnentreden*)), whereupon the police authorities entered said home, without the accused's permission (such that a valid warrant was required), where they found a cannabis farm. According to the Supreme Court, this course of events could not be equated to a situation in which police authorities enter a home without any warrant. In its view, in determining the seriousness of the violation within the meaning of the second paragraph of Article 359a, it is also important to consider whether the relevant police authorities could in good conscience act on this warrant, i.e. whether they could assume that it had been validly issued,[270] even if the issuing authority had acted in bad faith. Furthermore, according to the Supreme Court, it was important to consider whether in the circumstances the warrant could have (and, most likely, would have) been issued by *another* authority that *was* authorized to do so.[271]

---

[267] Ibid., 327–328. Accordingly, Kuiper *distinguishes* between the first statutory factor, the interest that the violated provision purports to protect, and the Schutz-norm. See, by contrast, Borgers 2012, 270; Corstens and Borgers 2014, 826–827; and Schoep, in: T&C Strafvordering 2015, Article 359a Sv, aant 3 (online, last updated 1 July 2015).

[268] HR 30 March 2004, ECLI:NL:HR:2004:AM2533, r.o. 3.5, *NJ* 2004/376 m.nt. Y Buruma.

[269] See e.g. Kuiper 2014, 331–335.

[270] HR 19 February 2013, ECLI:NL:HR:2013:BY5322, r.o. 2.7.4, *NJ* 2013/308 m.nt. BF Keulen. See also Keulen in his annotation to this judgment, referring to HR 19 June 2001, ECLI:NL:HR:2001:AB2202, *NJ* 2001/574 m.nt. JM Reijntjes, in order to demonstrate that the Supreme Court has previously pointed to the good faith of the public authorities as a factor militating against the exclusion of evidence. According to Keulen, that (earlier) case differs from the present one, since in the present case the bad faith of the authority to have issued the warrant was beyond dispute.

[271] HR 19 February 2013, ECLI:NL:HR:2013:BY5322, r.o. 2.7.5, *NJ* 2013/308 m.nt. BF Keulen.
   In addition, Borgers has suggested that in determining the seriousness of the violation the court should, arguably, also take into account any efforts already undertaken to address the violation, e.g. further investigation into the matters, apologies, financial compensation, disciplinary proceedings etc. See Borgers 2012, 270–271.

Regarding the final statutory factor, the prejudice caused by the violation, the explanatory memorandum to Article 359a of the CCP states that such prejudice encompasses 'the damage, if any, suffered by the accused or the victim' (as a result of the violation).[272] Logically, 'victim' here refers to the victim of the procedural violation, not the victim of the crime in question. In this regard it should be recalled that according to the Supreme Court, if the violation of the norm (aimed at protecting accused persons in general) did not affect the particular accused now on trial, as a rule, the court applying Article 359a of the CCP need not attach any of the consequences listed in the first paragraph thereof to the violation. In other words, the court need not respond in this way if the Schutz-norm criteria are not fulfilled. The fact that according to the explanatory memorandum prejudice includes damage suffered by another person than the particular accused on trial suggests that the legislator did not envisage a strict application, i.e. the application in *all* cases, with all that this entails, of the Schutz-norm.[273] Nor, it should be recalled, does the Supreme Court prescribe such an application of the Schutz-norm: exceptionally, the Supreme Court has departed from the principle that, if either or both of the Schutz-norm criteria are not fulfilled, the court need not attach any of the consequences listed in the first paragraph of Article 359a of the CCP to the violation. Nevertheless, *as a rule*, it requires actual, concrete prejudice for the particular accused on trial,[274] whereby the exceptions to this rule correspond to the exceptions recognised by the Supreme Court in respect of the Schutz-norm.[275] Specifically, it requires actual prejudice to the accused's *legitimate* interests, for example, to his or her fundamental rights, such as the right to privacy or defence/fair trial rights. According to the Supreme Court, such prejudice does not include prejudice to the accused's interest 'not to be caught',[276] or not to have incriminating evidence gathered against him or her. In other words, the fact that incriminating evidence has been (illegally or unlawfully) obtained is not necessarily sufficient for the purposes of Article 359a of the CCP.[277] Schalken has observed that while it may be self-evident that the accused's interest not to be caught is not a legitimate interest, it does not necessarily follow that this truism may be invoked as a general and determinative argument to legitimize otherwise unlawful action on the part of the authorities by not attaching consequences to it.[278] Kooijmans similarly notes (and laments) the potentially far-reaching implications of this finding, while simultaneously questioning whether it reflects the Supreme Court's case law regarding the

---

[272] *Kamerstukken II* 1993/94, 23075, 3, p. 26 (explanatory memorandum).

[273] See also Kuiper 2014, 340.

[274] See in this regard Kooijmans 2011, 1102–1103. For sentence reduction the requirement of concrete prejudice for the accused is explicit. For exclusion it is not, but it can be inferred from the case law.

[275] Kuiper 2014, 341.

[276] HR 4 January 2011, ECLI:NL:HR:2011:BM6673, r.o. 3.2.2, *NJ* 2012/145 m.nt. MJ Borgers, and HR 19 February 2013, ECLI:NL:HR:2013:BY5322, r.o. 2.4.1, *NJ* 2013/308 m.nt. BF Keulen.

[277] HR 3 July 2012, ECLI:NL:HR:2012:BV1800, r.o. 2.9, *NJB* 2012/1772.

[278] TM Schalken in his annotation to HR 6 January 2015, ECLI:NL:HR:2015:4, *NJ* 2015/109.

exclusion of evidence in years gone by (wherein the accused's interest not to be caught may well have been considered a legitimate interest, or, at least, wherein the obvious illegitimacy of this interest was not generally considered to be fatal to an application for exclusion).[279]

As to the question of what, then, constitutes (actual) prejudice to the accused's 'legitimate' interests, according to the Supreme Court in its leading decision of 2004, it is important to consider, '*among other things* whether, and, if so, to what extent the accused has been harmed in his or her defence'.[280] More generally, in order to answer this question reference must be had to the criteria of the response in question; such criteria would appear to determine the (actual) prejudice required.[281] In this regard it should be recalled that the criteria for a declaration that the prosecution is inadmissible and for the first category of exclusion of evidence are based on the need to ensure the accused's right to a fair trial. Where a declaration that the prosecution is inadmissible is sought, the prejudice required is the inability of the accused to receive a fair trial, whereby fair trial is, apparently, to be construed narrowly, as primarily concerned with epistemic considerations. Thus, if notwithstanding the violation of the accused's defence rights there is sufficient (other) evidence to convict the accused, such that, had the accused been able to exercise his or her defence rights it would not have made a difference, the accused will not be considered to have suffered *actual* prejudice for the purposes of seeking a declaration that the prosecution is inadmissible.[282] The question, then, is whether *in the circumstances* the underlying fundamental right was violated, which may require the court to make difficult judgements of fact. In terms of the aforementioned statutory factors, the question is whether 'the interest that the provision purports to protect' has been violated; if not, 'the seriousness of the violation' may be said to be diminished and 'actual prejudice' may be said to be absent.[283] Where sentence reduction is sought, the prejudice required depends on the right violated, whereby it bears recalling that prejudice to the accused's defence (or fair trial) rights typically does not lend itself to compensation by way of sentence reduction. While demonstrating actual prejudice to the right to a fair trial or to fair trial rights is not likely to be an easy task,[284] the ability of the violation of (procedural) fair trial rights to harm the accused, with all that this entails, is at least imaginable (and, it is submitted, there may therefore be more cause in cases in which such rights have not been observed to *presume* prejudice); the ability of the violation of other rights,

---

[279] Kooijmans 2011, 1105–1108. Kuiper also points to the (potentially) far-reaching implications of the Supreme Court's finding. See Kuiper 2014, 341 and 575.

[280] HR 30 March 2004, ECLI:NL:HR:2004:AM2533, r.o. 3.5 (emphasis added), *NJ* 2004/376 m.nt. Y Buruma.

[281] See also Kuiper 2014, 341–343.

[282] See e.g. HR 20 October 1998, ECLI:NL:HR:1998:ZD1309, *NJ* 1999/122 and HR 14 January 2003, ECLI:NL:HR:2003:AE9038, *NJ* 2003/288.

[283] Kuiper 2014, 524.

[284] See n 282 and accompanying text.

such as the (substantive) right to bodily integrity or the (substantive) right to privacy, to 'actually' prejudice the accused may be less evident *in the context of the criminal trial*.[285] Here it should be recalled that 'prejudice' within the meaning of the second paragraph of Article 359a does not include prejudice to the accused's interest 'not to be caught'.[286] What it does appear to entail in case of violation of other rights is non-material damage to the accused, for example, physical pain, emotional distress and suffering and/or injury to honour,[287] which will need to be shown. In conclusion then, the prejudice (as meant in the second paragraph of Article 359a of the CCP) required depends on the criteria of the response in question. However, given the criteria for a declaration that the prosecution is inadmissible and for the first category of exclusion, and given the obstacles put in place for the second and third categories of exclusion, it appears that 'prejudice' within the meaning of the second paragraph of Article 359a of the CCP should primarily be understood as encompassing (potential) prejudice to the accused's right to a fair trial within the meaning of Article 6 ECHR.[288]

In addition to the statutory factors set out above, which the court applying Article 359a of the CCP *must* take into account, the court *may* according to the Supreme Court also take into account the seriousness of the offence.[289] It seems that the seriousness of the offence may be invoked as an argument against attaching a particular consequence to unlawful conduct on the part of the authorities. For example, the seriousness of the offence may be a reason to not exclude the evidence obtained, and, rather, to reduce the sentence.[290] According to the Supreme Court, taking into account the seriousness of the offence is warranted in light of the legislative history, which, in its view, allows for other factors than those explicitly provided for in the second paragraph of Article 359a to be considered.[291] Nevertheless, the Supreme Court's finding has been subject to criticism in the literature. First, it is questionable whether the legislative history does in fact allow

---

[285] For the distinction between procedural and substantive rights see Strasser 1988, 595–604.

[286] Nor does it appear to include 'expressive harm', i.e. the harm that is done when government actors disrespect individual rights, whereby such disrespect sends 'demeaning messages about human worth'. Starr 2009, 1534–1535.

[287] See e.g. Kuiper 2014, 573–575.

[288] See e.g. Kuiper 2014, 342–343.

[289] HR 25 June 2002, ECLI:NL:HR:2002:AD9204, *NJ* 2002/625 m.nt. TM Schalken. In its second leading decision on Article 359a CCP the Supreme Court seems to confirm that the seriousness of the offence may be taken into account. See HR 19 February 2013, ECLI:NL:HR:2013:BY5322, r.o. 2.4.5 and 2.4.6, *NJ* 2013/308 m.nt. BF Keulen, and also n 222 and 233–234 and accompanying text. See, however, n 228 and accompanying text.

[290] As was the case in the case underlying the appeal before the Supreme Court in HR 25 June 2002, ECLI:NL:HR:2002:AD9204, *NJ* 2002/625 m.nt. TM Schalken.

[291] See HR 25 June 2002, ECLI:NL:HR:2002:AD9204, r.o. 3.7, *NJ* 2002/625 m.nt. TM Schalken, where the Supreme Court refers to *Kamerstukken II* 1993/94, 23075, 3, p. 25 (explanatory memorandum).

for other factors to be taken into account,[292] and, even if it does, it does not necessarily follow that the seriousness of the offence may be taken into account. In this regard Schalken observes that the Supreme Court's finding implies that, in case of serious offences, the authorities are not obliged to abide by the law,[293] whereas it may be argued that precisely in such cases the authorities should abide by the law.[294] According to Schalken, the response to pre-trial procedural violations should be proportionate to the seriousness of *the violation*, not to the seriousness of *the offence*.[295] In this regard it may be observed that focusing on the seriousness of the violation already provides significant scope to prevent 'rigid, knee-jerk responses' to procedural violations.[296] The same may be argued in respect of the other statutory factors (the interest that the violated provision purports to protect and the prejudice caused by the violation). The question, then, is whether, where the statutory factors do *not* give cause to *not* attach a certain legal consequence to procedural violations committed in the pre-trial phase of criminal proceedings (for example, the exclusion of evidence), i.e. where the procedural violation is such that it warrants a certain consequence being attached to it, the seriousness of the offence could, by itself, justify not doing so. Furthermore, it has been argued that the seriousness of the offence is a difficult criterion to work with, on account of it being difficult to ascertain when an offence is so serious that it warrants a less far-reaching response.[297] In support of the Supreme Court's finding, Kuiper points to the ECtHR's case law explicitly taking into account 'the public interest in the investigation and punishment of the particular offence at issue' in the determination of Article 6 of the ECHR.[298] In addition, he argues that taking into account the seriousness of the offence in the determination of the consequence, if any, to be attached to pre-trial procedural violations is justified in view of the positive obligations arising from the ECHR.[299] In the case referred to above, the Supreme Court upheld an appellate court's decision not to exclude the evidence, in which it had attached importance to the fact that the seriousness of the offence with which the accused had been charged was a serious one.[300] However, the (seriousness of the)

---

[292] See TM Schalken in his annotation to HR 25 June 2002, ECLI:NL:HR:2002:AD9204, *NJ* 2002/625, para 7.

[293] Ibid., para 7.

[294] Van Woensel 2004, 153.

[295] TM Schalken in his annotation to HR 25 June 2002, ECLI:NL:HR:2002:AD9204, *NJ* 2002/625, para 7.

[296] Ibid., para 7.

[297] Van Woensel 2004, 153.

[298] Kuiper 2014, 344, referring to *Jalloh v Germany* App no 54810/00 (ECtHR, 11 July 2006). This case, and the extent to which the public interest in the investigation and prosecution of crime may be taken into account in cases in which unlawfulness in the pre-trial phase is argued to violate Article 6 ECHR, are addressed in Chap. 2.

[299] Kuiper 2014, 346.

[300] See n 289–291 and accompanying text. The appellate court's findings in this regard are reproduced in the Supreme Court's decision at para 3.3.

charges brought against the accused may (also) enter the analysis in another way, than as a 'separate' factor. De Hullu argues that because the seriousness of the procedural violation is dependent on whether the conduct in question can be said to have been consistent with principles of proportionality and subsidiarity, in the determination of whether to declare the prosecution inadmissible, the court may take into account the seriousness of the offence. In other words, he seems to argue that the seriousness of the offence may be taken into account insofar as it bears upon the question of how serious the procedural violation was.[301] Considered in this way, the offence in question does not constitute a 'separate' or 'standalone' factor; rather it provides 'context' for the conduct concerned.

§ Cost-benefit analysis and the freedom of the judge

It was stated at the beginning of this section that underlying the process of taking into consideration the individual circumstances of the case in the determination of the consequences to be attached to procedural violations committed in the pre-trial phase of criminal proceedings appears to be a balancing exercise in the form of a cost-benefit analysis, pursuant to which the benefits of a certain course of action, in terms of the rationale pursued, are to be weighed against its costs. Certainly such an analysis appears to underlie the court's *discretion* to exclude evidence, which, it should be recalled, is confined in at least one noteworthy way: it is 'confined' to those cases that do not involve procedural violations that undermine, or threaten to undermine the right of the accused to a fair trial, within the meaning of Article 6 of the ECHR, as also interpreted by the ECtHR. It was seen above that under the second and third categories of exclusion, which both cite prevention or deterrence as the underlying rationale, the court is explicitly permitted or required (depending on the category) to undertake a cost-benefit analysis for the purpose of determining whether the violation concerned requires the exclusion of the evidence thereby obtained. For the second category, such analysis may be said to constitute *additional* balancing, because it goes beyond the balancing that may be presumed to be inherent in a finding that the procedural violation in question amounts to a very intrusive breach of a fundamental right of the accused, such finding implying as it does the violation of an interest of *significant weight or importance*, a *serious* violation and *prejudice* for the accused, such that the deterrent benefits of exclusion may be presumed to outweigh its social costs. This analysis entails the consideration of facts and circumstances that might diminish the preventive or deterrent value of exclusion, as well as those that might increase its societal costs. Facts and circumstances that might *diminish* the deterrent benefits of exclusion include, according to Kuiper (who draws on the case law of the US Supreme Court on the admissibility of evidence obtained by Fourth Amendment violations in this regard), the existence of other mechanisms to ensure observance by the public authorities of the rights in question, the existence of other remedies to address violations when

---

[301] See De Hullu in his annotation to HR 22 September 1998, ECLI:NL:HR:1998:ZD1277, *NJ* 1999/104. Regarding the requirement of proportionality, see n 4 and accompanying text.

they occur and the fact that the official in question acted in good faith.[302] Facts and circumstances that might *increase* the societal costs of exclusion include the seriousness of the offence in question. Arguably, the more serious the offence, the higher the societal costs of exclusion. Regarding this last factor, the Supreme Court appears to allow, if not encourage its inclusion in the analysis. Indeed, the preventive or deterrent benefits of exclusion are, according to the Supreme Court, to be weighed against the negative effects that it may be expected to have on such 'heavily weighted interests' as truth-finding, the need to punish perpetrators of ('possibly very serious') crime and the rights of victims and next of kin (in light also of the positive obligations flowing from the ECHR of effective punishment). Regarding the 'positive obligations flowing from the ECHR of effective punishment', however, it should recalled that the scope to invoke the state's positive obligations as an argument against the imposition of a stay of proceedings or the exclusion of evidence on account of pre-trial procedural violations appears to be limited.[303]

Returning now to the questions posed at the beginning of this subsection, while on the face of it the Dutch judicial response within the criminal trial to procedural violations committed in the pre-trial phase of criminal proceedings appears to be a matter of discretion, in the sense that the consequence, if any, to be attached to such a violation depends on the individual circumstances of the case, and whereby the trial judge is afforded a degree of freedom, the trial judge's room to manoeuvre in this regard appears to be extremely limited. On the basis of the Supreme Court's case law, it seems that the factors set out in the second paragraph of Article 359a of the CCP are to be treated as cumulative criteria. It is not merely that the court is required to take into account such factors (i.e. to expressly acknowledge them, and their capacity to 'guide' the court), and/or that it must be *seen* to do so. Rather, what is meant here is that the response to a procedural violation committed by the police or prosecution in the context of criminal proceedings must be *justified* by a combination of the factors. Kooijmans refers to the 'cumulative character' of the factors in the second paragraph of Article 359a in this regard.[304] Certainly, the response to such a violation must be justified by the existence of prejudice;[305] in other words, it seems that the absence of prejudice cannot be 'compensated' by either one, or both of the other factors. It is also worth observing that the factors, and, in particular, that of prejudice, are defined precisely, and also narrowly. Here it should be recalled that the fact that incriminating evidence has been obtained is not sufficient for the purposes of showing prejudice within the meaning of the second paragraph of Article 359a of the CCP. This is an important point, because it would seem to be one thing to require that a decision to attach a legal consequence to pre-trial procedural violations be justified by a combination of factors where such factors are

---

[302] See Kuiper 2014, 546.

[303] See Chap. 2, n 434–439 and accompanying text.

[304] Kooijmans 2011, 1102.

[305] See n 274 and accompanying text.

defined broadly or loosely, but quite another to do so when they are defined precisely and narrowly. Always requiring prejudice for the accused, i.e. requiring prejudice for each of the responses enumerated in the first paragraph of Article 359a of the CCP,[306] may be tantamount to importing into the judge's analysis a *rule*; prejudice for the accused is precisely and narrowly defined, and, in principle, its absence means that no consequence need be attached to the procedural violation in question. While there are indications in the legislative history of Article 359a of the CCP that, what the legislator had mind was a more restrictive judicial response within the criminal trial to pre-trial procedural violations,[307] and therefore that a rule that tends to lead to such a (restrictive) response may be thought to be entirely fitting in this regard, the application of rules in the context of that provision sits uneasily with the freedom seemingly conferred on the trial judge to address such violations[308] (although it may well be that what the legislator had in mind in this regard was the freedom of the trial judge to not attach a particular legal consequence to such violations). What such a restrictive approach might signify in terms of the theory underlying the attachment of legal consequences to procedural violations committed in the pre-trial phase of criminal proceedings, and of broader objectives of criminal procedure, is discussed below.

Regarding the court's *balancing* discretion to exclude evidence, the court must, in any case, take into account the factors set out in the second paragraph of Article 359a of the CCP. In the second category, those factors are most relevant to the question of whether a very intrusive breach of a fundamental right of the accused has been committed.[309] In addition, the court may take into account factors relevant to the cost-benefit analysis that the court is, according to the Supreme Court, permitted (in case of the second category of exclusion) and required (in case of the third category) to undertake in determining whether the violation concerned requires the evidence thereby obtained to be excluded. On the benefit side of the analysis, the factors that may be taken into account depend on the underlying rationale for exclusion. In both the second and the third categories of exclusion the Supreme Court cites prevention or deterrence as the underlying rationale. The factors that may be taken into account, then, relate to the ability in the individual circumstances of the case of exclusion to (actually) deter future violations; arguably, these include the existence of other mechanisms to ensure observance by the public authorities of the rights in question (which might render superfluous the exclusion of evidence as a means of deterring the police or the public prosecutor

---

[306] It should be recalled that *all* legal consequences require prejudice for the accused. See n 305 and 274 and accompanying text.

[307] For example, the legislative history refers to the need to reduce the attachment of 'undesirable' consequences to procedural violations within the criminal trial, and to societal discontent in this regard. See *Kamerstukken II* 1993/94, 23075, 3, pp. 1 and 5 (explanatory memorandum). See also *Kamerstukken II* 1993/94, 23075, 6, pp. 3 and 9.

[308] See similarly T Schalken in his annotation to HR 9 September 2014, ECLI:NL:HR:2014:2650, *NJ* 2014/420, para 7; Ölçer 2008, 517; and Brinkhoff 2016.

[309] See n 223 and accompanying text.

from committing procedural violations) and the fact that the official in question acted in good faith. On the cost side of the analysis the factors that may be taken into account are the negative effects that exclusion may be expected to have on the such 'heavily weighted interests' as truth-finding, the need to punish perpetrators of ('possibly very serious') crime and the rights of victims and next-of-kin (in light also of the positive obligations flowing from the ECHR of effective punishment).[310] It is worth emphasizing the point that the cost-benefit analysis envisaged by the Dutch Supreme Court in the second and third categories of exclusion appears to entail the consideration of facts and circumstances relevant to the cost side of the analysis, *as well as* those relevant to the benefit side thereof. While this might appear logical, or obvious, a brief look at the American literature on the use of cost-benefit analysis or balancing in the determination of the admissibility of evidence obtained by Fourth Amendment violations may suggest otherwise. It appears that the cost-benefit analysis envisaged by the Dutch Supreme Court combines two different types of cost-benefit analysis: 'proportionality', whereby proportionality is sought between 'the police error and the "drastic" remedy of exclusion', and 'comparative reprehensibility', whereby proportionality is sought between 'the officer's conduct and the defendant's'.[311] The first type of cost-benefit analysis involves taking into account such factors as the good faith of the officer concerned *on the benefit side of the analysis* (as relevant to the determination of the deterrent value of exclusion in the individual circumstances of the case), while the second type involves taking into account the seriousness of the offence *on the cost side of the analysis* (as relevant to the determination of the societal costs of exclusion in the individual circumstances of the case). Kamisar notes that while the two types of analysis are 'conceptually distinct ... they can be easily confused or lumped together'.[312] Indeed, it appears possible to be a proponent of one type of cost-benefit balancing, but not the other.[313] The lumping together of the two types of cost-benefit analysis need not be inadvertent, however. Thus, in an article published in 1984, Cameron and Lustiger advocated an approach to the issue of admissibility of evidence obtained by violation of the Fourth Amendment that combines *both* types of analysis.[314] The key point is that taking into account facts and circumstances on both sides of the cost-benefit analysis (that involves questioning the assumption on the benefit side of the equation that exclusion (always) has some significant deterrent effect and, on the cost side thereof, that exclusion (always) has the same societal costs: 'freeing the guilty') may create significant scope to *not* exclude evidence obtained unlawfully. Consideration of the benefit side of the equation might lead the court to conclude that the deterrent value of

---

[310] For an overview of the (alleged) costs of exclusion in the American context, see Cameron and Lustiger 1984, 132–142.

[311] Kamisar 1987, 6–11.

[312] Kamisar 1987, 6.

[313] See Kamisar 1987, 9.

[314] See Cameron and Lustiger 1984, 145–147.

exclusion is diminished to such an extent that exclusion is uncalled for. However, if upon consideration of the benefit side of the equation it is concluded that the deterrent value is not diminished to such an extent, the court may nonetheless conclude that exclusion is uncalled for on the basis of the seriousness of the crime. While it is important to note in relation to the second category of exclusion that the cost-benefit analysis that the court is permitted (and perhaps, required) to undertake appears calculated to ensure that the scope of that category is narrowly construed,[315] the Supreme Court's findings are formulated in such a way as to allow the court to *not* exclude the evidence in question pursuant to this exercise, regardless of how the criterion of 'a very intrusive breach of a fundamental right of the accused' is interpreted.

3.4.1.2   Other Standards

It was stated above that in order for the court to be able to attach any of the consequences enumerated in the first paragraph of Article 359a of the CCP to pre-trial procedural violations, it must first be established that the procedural violation in question falls within the scope of Article 359a, i.e. that it constitutes a procedural violation within the meaning of that provision. Nevertheless, in a situation in which the impugned conduct cannot be said to constitute such a violation, the court may, in certain circumstances, attach legal consequences thereto, including the exclusion of evidence thereby obtained.[316] Borgers lists four different types of cases in which the Supreme Court recognises the ability of the court to do so.[317]

First, the Supreme Court has held that unlawful conduct on the part of natural or legal persons (that is, conduct on the part of private individuals or entities that breaches civil law (*burgerlijk recht*) standards, which therefore does not fall within the scope of Article 359a of the CCP) may result in such a violation of principles of

---

[315] See n 229 and accompanying text.

[316] The attachment of legal consequences to unlawful conduct outside of the framework of Article 359a CCP has been criticized in the literature for a variety of reasons. First, it makes it difficult to have a clear view of the circumstances under which the court may attach legal consequences to such conduct (see e.g. Kuiper 2014, 229). Second, it seems to undermine the Supreme Court's restrictive application of Article 359a CCP (see e.g. TM Schalken in his annotation to HR 17 September 2013, ECLI:NL:HR:2013:BZ9992, *NJ* 2014/91, para 3). In this regard Schalken argues that the Supreme Court would do best to attach additional and more specific requirements to the judicial response to unlawful conduct not falling within the scope of Article 359a CCP. More generally Borgers raises the question as to why when the Supreme Court, when ruling on cases involving such conduct, already borrows certain elements from Article 359a CCP, it does not simply refer to that provision and declare the framework thereof applicable thereto. See MJ Borgers in his annotation to HR 11 January 2011, ECLI:NL:HR:2011:BN2297, *NJ* 2012, 297, para 6.

[317] See MJ Borgers in his annotation to HR 29 January 2013, ECLI:NL:HR:2013:BY2814, *NJ* 2013/415, paras 2 and 3.

proper administration of justice (*beginselen van een behoorlijke procesorde*) or undermine the rights of the defence to such an extent that it is necessary to exclude the evidence obtained thereby.[318] Thus, unlawful conduct on the part of private individuals or entities (for which the public authorities are not responsible) may on account of the extreme methods adopted or of the serious frustration of the exercise of defence rights lead to exclusion.[319] Second, the Supreme Court has implied that where unlawful conduct on the part of public authorities for which the Public Prosecution Service (*het Openbaar Ministerie*) is not responsible (and which therefore does not fall within the scope of Article 359a of the CCP) has resulted in such a violation of principles of proper administration of justice or in such disregard for the rights of the defence it may be necessary to declare the prosecution inadmissible or to exclude the evidence thereby obtained.[320] Here it should be recalled that unlawful conduct on the part of, for example, the penitentiary authorities and the Dutch naval authorities, does not fall within the scope of Article 359a.[321] Third, the Supreme Court has held in respect of investigative activities unlawfully carried out outside of the Netherlands under the responsibility of foreign authorities (for which the Public Prosecution Service is not responsible, such that they do not fall within the scope of Article 359a of the CCP) that it is the court's duty to ensure that the way in which the results thereby obtained are used in the case against the accused does not undermine his right to a fair trial within the meaning of Article 6 of the ECHR.[322] These findings are discussed in more detail below, in the following section. Fourth, the Supreme Court has held in respect of conduct on the part of public authorities in the exercise of criminal investigation powers that does not fall within the 'preliminary investigation' for the purposes of Article 359a of the CCP because, for example, it does not fall within the preliminary investigation in respect of the offence for which the accused now stands trial, that if it has resulted in such a violation of the principles of proper administration of justice or in such disregard for the rights of the defence it may be necessary to exclude the evidence thereby obtained.[323] In 2013, the Supreme Court seemingly introduced a new criterion in respect of, at least, the fourth category of conduct falling outside the scope of Article 359a of the CCP. In a case in which the procedural violation in question concerned the unlawful storage in a DNA-database of a DNA-sample obtained from the accused in connection with another case (the (rape-)case was eventually dropped, following which the public prosecutor instructed the relevant authorities to remove the DNA-sample from the database, which they did not, such that the

---

[318] See e.g. HR 18 March 2003, ECLI:NL:HR:2003:AF4321, r.o. 3.5.1, *NJ* 2003/527.

[319] See MJ Borgers in his annotation to HR 29 January 2013, ECLI:NL:HR:2013:BY2814, *NJ* 2013/415, paras 2 and 3.

[320] HR 27 September 2011, ECLI:NL:HR:2011:BQ3765, r.o. 2.5, *NJ* 2011/557 m.nt. TM Schalken. See also HR 5 September 2006, ECLI:NL:HR:2006:AV4122, r.o. 4.7.2, *NJ* 2007/336, m.nt. TM Schalken.

[321] See n 153–156 and accompanying text.

[322] HR 5 October 2010, ECLI:NL:HR:2010:BL5629, r.o. 4.4.1, *NJ* 2011/169 m.nt. TM Schalken.

[323] HR 31 May 2011, ECLI:NL:HR:2011:BP1179, r.o. 3.7, *NJ* 2011/412 m.nt. TM Schalken.

accused's DNA-sample formed part of the reference material when a search was performed in respect of DNA-material found at the scene of a suspected burglary), the Supreme Court held that only in exceptional circumstances will a procedural violation that does not strictly speaking fall within the scope of Article 359a lead to the exclusion of evidence; the procedural violation in question must result in so serious a breach of an important provision or principle of criminal procedure that the exclusion of the evidence obtained thereby is necessary.[324] This criterion is clearly based on the general test for the exclusion of evidence under Article 359a of the CCP,[325] but the threshold for exclusion in respect of procedural violations that do not fall within the scope of that provision appears to be higher than in respect of procedural violations that do (it is not sufficient for the breach to be serious; it must be *so* serious as to require exclusion). This raises the question as to when a serious breach of an important provision or principle of criminal procedure (which is the result of unlawful conduct that does not fall within the scope of Article 359a of the CCP) is 'so serious' as to require exclusion.[326] In addition, the question arises as to whether this criterion is in fact so different to the one prescribed in respect of the fourth (and first and second) categories of cases set out above. Borgers argues that it is not, and that the latter criterion may be used to give substance to the former, since the latter criterion clearly concerns very serious breaches of important provisions or principles of criminal procedure.[327] On the basis of the aforementioned (and other) cases it may be concluded that outside of the scope of Article 359a there is limited room to attach legal consequences to unlawful conduct. In view of the focus in those cases on 'the rights of the defence', the criterion for determining whether conduct that does not fall within the scope of Article 359a of the CCP requires the court to attach a legal consequence to it appears to be the need to ensure the accused's right to a fair trial within the meaning of Article 6 of the ECHR.[328]

3.4.2 Procedural Violations in an International Context

In light of the central research question of this book (how should judges *at the ICTs* respond to procedural violations committed in the pre-trial phase of the proceedings?), it is instructive to consider the Dutch law and practice with respect to the question of how criminal courts should address procedural violations committed in an 'international context'. This term covers a wide range of conduct on the part of public officials that has the potential to raise issues at any ensuing criminal trial, including unlawfulness in bringing a person into the jurisdiction in which he or she

---

[324] HR 29 January 2013, ECLI:NL:HR:2013:BY2814, r.o. 2.3.3, *NJ* 2013/415 m.nt. MJ Borgers.

[325] See n 197 and accompanying text.

[326] See also MJ Borgers in his annotation to HR 29 January 2013, ECLI:NL:HR:2013:BY2814, *NJ* 2013/415, para 5, referring to a 'non-criterion' in this regard.

[327] Ibid., para 6.

[328] Kuiper 2014, 228–238.

is sought for prosecution, and unlawfulness in the evidence-gathering process abroad. Such unlawfulness potentially raises difficult questions for the criminal court trying the case, given that the impugned activities may have been carried out by or with the assistance of foreign authorities. The purpose of this section is, then, to set out the Dutch law and practice with respect to (alleged) irregularities in the context of the two most common forms of international cooperation in criminal matters: extradition and mutual legal assistance.[329]

§ Extradition

It is important to recall that, in order for a procedural violation to be considered a procedural violation within the meaning of Article 359a of the CCP, it must have been committed in the course of the preliminary investigation (*voorbereidend onderzoek*) within the meaning of Article 132 of the CCP. This in turn implies that a procedural violation will fall within the scope of Article 359a where it involves the exercise of criminal investigation powers. As stated above, the Supreme Court has held that an extradition request by a public prosecutor does not fall within the scope of the criminal investigation, since such a request does not involve the exercise of criminal investigation powers.[330] Accordingly, unlawfulness in the execution of a request for extradition does not, strictly speaking, fall within the scope of Article 359a. In the case in question, the Accused had been detained, pursuant to a Dutch extradition request, in Thailand. According to the Defence, the 'abominable' conditions of detention in Thailand warranted a declaration that the prosecution was inadmissible, since, by requesting his extradition—whereby it had been aware of such conditions, such conditions being a fact of common knowledge—the Dutch authorities had violated his right to a fair trial. According to the Supreme Court, the Court of Appeal had not erred in declining to grant such relief, since the public prosecutor's request that the Accused be detained pending extradition did not fall within the scope of Article 359a.[331] In the proceedings before the Court of Appeal, this fact did not stop it from considering whether that request (entailing as it did a period of detention in Thailand) had prevented the accused from receiving a fair trial, which could be attributed to the prosecution (which it should be recalled, is, ultimately, the test for declaring the prosecution inadmissible).[332] And the Supreme Court did not find that the Court of Appeal had erred in nevertheless considering whether a declaration that the prosecution is inadmissible was warranted,[333]

---

[329] Other forms of international cooperation in criminal matters include: transfer of criminal proceedings, execution of foreign sentences, recognition of foreign criminal judgements and collection and exchange of information between intelligence and law enforcement services.

[330] See n 152 and accompanying text.

[331] HR 8 July 2008, ECLI:NL:HR:2008:BC5973, r.o. 3.3, *NJ* 2009/440 m.nt. Y Buruma.

[332] See n 241, 251–259 and accompanying text.

[333] See in this regard Buruma's annotation to this decision, where he argues that the Court of Appeal was right to nevertheless consider whether a declaration that the prosecution is inadmissible was warranted, and the Supreme Court was right not to interfere, in light of the fact that the conditions of detention raised issues under Article 3 ECHR, thereby referring the ECtHR's

seemingly approving of the fact that the Court of Appeal had taken the accused's detention in Thailand into account at the sentencing stage.[334]

§ Mutual legal assistance

It is clear, then, that extradition requests do not entail the exercise of criminal investigation powers. According to Van Sliedregt and Sjöcrona, nor do acts of mutual assistance; rather, they form part of a *sui generis* procedure combining aspects of national law (including the ECHR) and international law.[335] Ultimate responsibility for such acts lies with the Minister of Justice, while the public prosecutor is the central 'mutual assistance authority'.[336] In this regard it should be recalled that the Dutch Supreme Court has held that investigative activities unlawfully carried out *outside of the Netherlands* under the responsibility of *foreign authorities* (for which the Public Prosecution Service is therefore not responsible) do not fall within the scope of Article 359a of the CCP.[337] The case in question is the leading authority with respect to the Dutch judicial response to procedural violations committed by public authorities *outside of the Netherlands*,[338] and it is set out here.

According to the Supreme Court, the nature and scope of the review of Dutch (criminal) courts of the lawfulness of investigative activities to have taken place outside of the Netherlands depends on who was responsible for such activities: the Dutch authorities or foreign authorities.[339] Turning first to investigative activities carried out under the responsibility of the foreign authorities of a state party to the ECHR, according to Supreme Court the duty of the criminal court trying the case is limited to ensuring that the way in which the results obtained by such investigative activities are used in the case against the accused does not undermine his right to a fair trial within the meaning of Article 6 of the ECHR.[340] It is *not* the duty of the court to assess whether the way in which those activities were carried out was in accordance with the law of the country in question.[341] Moreover, according to the Supreme Court, the expectation that the state in question party to the ECHR will respect the Convention's provisions and the fact that the accused, in case of the violation of another Convention right than his or her right to a fair trial within the meaning of Article 6(1) of the ECHR, has the right to an effective remedy within

---

(Footnote 333 continued)

findings in *Jalloh v Germany* App no 54810/00 (ECtHR, 11 July 2006). However, according to Buruma, the current case could be distinguished, on the basis that while in *Jalloh*, evidence obtained by the Article 3 violation had been used at trial, in the current case it had not.

[334] HR 8 July 2008, ECLI:NL:HR:2008:BC5973, r.o. 3.3, *NJ* 2009/440 m.nt. Y Buruma.

[335] Van Sliedregt and Sjöcrona 2008, 22.

[336] Reijntjes et al. 2008, 272–273.

[337] See n 322 and accompanying text.

[338] HR 5 October 2010, ECLI:NL:HR:2010:BL5629, *NJ* 2011/169 m.nt. TM Schalken.

[339] Ibid., r.o. 4.3.

[340] Ibid., r.o. 4.4.1.

[341] Ibid., r.o. 4.4.1.

the meaning of Article 13 of the ECHR before an authority in that state means that the Dutch criminal court is not required to assess whether the investigative activities, which may have infringed on the accused's right to privacy within the meaning of Article 8(1) of the ECHR, had an adequate basis in law in the law of that state, or whether any such infringement can be considered to have been 'necessary' as meant in Article 8(2) of the ECHR.[342] In this connection, the Supreme Court pointed to the ECtHR's judgments in *Khan v United Kingdom* and *PG and JH v United Kingdom*.[343] Accordingly, in respect of investigative activities unlawfully carried out under the responsibility of foreign authorities it may be concluded that the only rationale or ground for attaching legal consequences thereto is to ensure the accused's right to a fair trial within the meaning of Article 6 of the ECHR.[344]

As to investigative activities carried out under the responsibility of the Dutch authorities, according to the Supreme Court the criminal court trying the case is required to assess whether the Dutch law regulating such activities was observed, including Convention rights.[345] In other words, that review is not limited to a determination of Article 6 of the ECHR.[346] According to Supreme Court, the question of whether in carrying out investigative activities outside of the Netherlands the Dutch authorities breached the sovereignty of the state in question is irrelevant in the criminal proceedings against the accused.[347] In other words, the accused cannot successfully invoke a breach of state sovereignty in order to obtain relief within the criminal trial for unlawfulness arising in the context of inter-state cooperation in criminal matters. Moreover, the Supreme Court held that international law does not, as such, rule out inter-state cooperation in criminal matters that is not based on a treaty between the relevant states,[348] such that, presumably, any inter-state cooperation in criminal matters not based on a treaty will not be considered unlawful. In this regard Schalken argues in his annotation to the decision that 'the purpose of treaties and their formalities is not to limit police assistance, but

---

[342] Ibid., r.o. 4.4.1. According to Kuiper, support for this position can be found in the case of *Echeverri Rodriguez v Netherlands* App no 3286/98 (ECtHR, Decision of 27 June 2000). See Kuiper 2014, 291–292. This case is addressed in Chap. 2.

[343] HR 5 October 2010, ECLI:NL:HR:2010:BL5629, r.o. 4.4.1, *NJ* 2011/169 m.nt. TM Schalken, referring to *Khan v UK* App no 35394/97 (ECtHR, 12 May 2000) and *PG and JH v UK* App no 44787/98 (ECtHR, 25 September 2001). These cases are set out in Chap. 2.

[344] See also Kuiper 2014, 299.

[345] HR 5 October 2010, ECLI:NL:HR:2010:BL5629, r.o. 4.4.2, *NJ* 2011/169 m.nt. TM Schalken. In this regard it is important to note that pursuant to Article 539a(1) CCP, the powers conferred on public authorities for the purpose of investigating crime may also be exercised outside of the Netherlands.

[346] See also Kuiper 2014, 301.

[347] HR 5 October 2010, ECLI:NL:HR:2010:BL5629, r.o. 4.4.2, *NJ* 2011/169 m.nt. TM Schalken.

[348] Ibid., r.o. 4.5.

rather to enhance it'.[349] Finally, the Supreme Court declared the framework of Article 359a of the CCP, as set out in its leading decision of 2004, applicable to defence applications regarding the lawfulness of investigative activities carried out outside of the Netherlands (regardless of who was responsible), as regards both the motivation of such applications and the conditions under which legal consequences can be attached to procedural violations.[350] Although the decision currently under consideration was issued before the Supreme Court's leading decision on Article 359a of the CCP of 2013, it is reasonable to assume that the 2013 decision is also applicable to such applications, with all that this entails.

The Supreme Court's leading decision of 2010 does not cover all cases of unlawfulness in the context of international cooperation in criminal matters. In principle, it only determines what the judicial response (of the Dutch criminal court trying the case) to unlawful conduct on the part of public authorities *outside of the Netherlands* should be. Moreover, in respect of investigative activities unlawfully carried out under the responsibility of foreign authorities it only determines what the judicial response should be where such foreign authorities are acting on behalf of a state party to the ECHR. Nevertheless, the decision may serve as a starting point for dealing with other cases of unlawfulness in the context of inter-state cooperation, i.e. cases that do not strictly speaking fall within its scope.[351]

3.5 Synthesis

Having set out the Dutch legal framework governing the judicial response to procedural violations committed in the pre-trial phase of criminal proceedings, the question now is how this framework is to be understood in terms of the theoretical framework also set out above: the points of departure with respect to the question of how to address pre-trial procedural violations, the more specific rationales in this regard and the objectives of criminal procedure.

Starting with Article 359a of the CCP and, specifically, the text of that provision, it was observed above in addressing the first point of departure with respect to the question of how to address procedural violations committed in the pre-trial phase of criminal proceedings, i.e. the notion inherent to the concept of the rule of law that the authorities must also abide by the law, and the argument based on this notion that the appropriate response to such violations is the exclusion of evidence, that the judicial response envisaged (in the first place the exclusion of evidence and, in

---

[349] TM Schalken in his annotation to HR 5 October 2010, ECLI:NL:HR:2010:BL5629, *NJ* 2011/169, para 2.

[350] HR 5 October 2010, ECLI:NL:HR:2010:BL5629, r.o. 4.6, *NJ* 2011/169 m.nt. TM Schalken. Presumably, therefore, the criminal court trying the case is required to undertake the balancing exercise prescribed by Article 359a(2) CCP, to be seen to be doing so and to apply the criteria for each legal response.

[351] Kuiper 2014, 292.

particularly serious cases, a declaration that the prosecution is inadmissible) is considered to be inherent to the 'nature of unlawfulness' (which, pursuant to the aforementioned notion, should be sought in the failure on the part of the public authorities to fulfil their own obligation to observe the norms directed at them in their capacity as investigative authorities)[352] and/or in the legal provisions on the exercise of power themselves.[353] That response nullifies or invalidates the unlawful action on the part of public authorities and therefore also the results obtained thereby. Thus, the judicial response envisaged pursuant to the aforementioned argument is not a matter of discretion for the trial judge; it does not entail the exercise of judgement. The text of Article 359a of the CCP suggests that the judicial response to procedural violations committed in the pre-trial phase of criminal proceedings, including unlawfulness in the investigation, does entail the exercise of judgement, whereby the judge takes into consideration the particular circumstances of the case, i.e. that it *is* a matter of discretion for the judge.[354] And this reflects what the Dutch Government had in mind when incorporating Article 359a into the Code of Criminal Procedure: in its view, it is for the legislator to establish rules of criminal procedure and for the judge to determine the consequences of the violation thereof. In itself, the division of labour between the legislator and the judge inherent to Article 359a may have implications for the question of how the legal framework is to be understood in theoretical terms (or, rather, how it is *not* to be understood).[355] While Article 359a of the CCP provides for the exclusion of evidence and a declaration that the prosecution is inadmissible (and there is, therefore, room for the judge in criminal proceedings to nullify or invalidate unlawful action by public authorities and therefore also its results in order to uphold the rule of law),[356] it also provides for sentence reduction, while the text itself and the explanatory memorandum thereto provide little guidance as to when each response is warranted, thereby allowing for the possibility of sentence reduction being granted instead of excluding evidence or declaring the prosecution inadmissible.[357] The Supreme Court *does* provide such guidance, and the consistency of Article 359a of the CCP with the argument based on the notion that the authorities must also abide by the law that the appropriate response to procedural violations committed by the police

---

[352] See n 48–50 and accompanying text.

[353] See n 52–53 and accompanying text.

[354] This fact has been subject to criticism in the literature. See e.g. Van Leijen 1994, 241; and Mevis 1995, 259.

[355] See n 49–53 and accompanying text.

[356] See Borgers and Kooijmans 2013, 19. They argue that the explanation for the limited scope for responding to unlawfulness on the part of the police or the public prosecutor in the pre-trial phase of criminal proceedings within the criminal trial should not be sought in Article 359a CCP itself, but in the interpretation thereof by the Supreme Court.

[357] See Van Leijen 1994, 239–240. Such an approach whereby sentence reduction is granted instead of excluding the evidence obtained had been advocated in the literature: see e.g. Fokkens 1991. It is (also) worth noting that Article 359a CCP also 'provides' for a (mere) declaration that a procedural violation has occurred.

or the public prosecutor in the course of the criminal investigation is the exclusion of evidence can, therefore, only be properly determined by reference to the Supreme Court's case law in this regard. Accordingly, reference is had to such case law below.

As stated, under Article 359a of the CCP the judge is required to take into account a number of pre-determined factors in the determination of whether to attach a consequence to pre-trial procedural violations, and if so, which: the interest that the violated provision purports to protect, the seriousness of the violation and the prejudice caused by it.[358] According to Kuiper, the purpose of this requirement is to prevent a 'rigid, knee-jerk response to breaches of procedural rules',[359] whereby such a reaction is, in his view presumably, undesirable. However, Van Leijen argues that a requirement for the judge to take into account such factors is inconsistent with the notion that the provisions in, for example, the CCP reflect the conditions under which according to the legislator power may be exercised, implying as it does a judicial response to the failure to observe these conditions that is functionally related to such unlawfulness: the nullification or invalidation of the unlawful action and therefore its results (which corresponds to the exclusion of evidence or a declaration that the prosecution is inadmissible). On this basis she argues that there is *no room* for the exercise of judgement, i.e. for judicial dis-cretion, when addressing unlawful conduct on the part of public authorities.[360] While the incorporation into the text of Article 359a of the CCP of a judicial (balancing) discretion appears, at first glance, to be inconsistent with the argument based on the notion that the authorities are also bound by the law that the appro-priate response is the exclusion of evidence, it is important to emphasize that the text of Article 359a envisages the exercise of judgement only as regards the question of whether to attach a consequence to a procedural violation and, if so, which; it does not prescribe such discretion as regards the question of whether the authorities acted unlawfully.[361] Accordingly, an approach whereby the judge is required to take into the individual circumstances of the case to determine the consequence, if any, to be attached to procedural violations committed in the pre-trial phase of criminal proceedings, does not necessarily deny the 'nature of unlawfulness' (the failure on the part of the public authorities to fulfil their own obligation to observe the norms directed at them in their capacity as investigative authorities) or, more generally, the notion inherent to the concept of the rule of law that the authorities must also abide by the law (or indeed the entitlement of citizens to the observance by the public authorities of the norms directed at them); by restricting the (balancing) discretion to the determination of the consequence, if any, to be attached to procedural violations, the court is (in principle at least)

---

[358] See Article 359a(2) CCP.

[359] Kuiper 2014, 605. See also 53–54.

[360] Van Leijen 1994, 241.

[361] See e.g. Baaijens-van Geloven 2004, 358.

prevented from 're-defining' unlawfulness according to, for example, the serious-ness of the violation or the seriousness of the offence. What it does deny, however, is the *argument based on* the nature of unlawfulness and/or the notion that the authorities must also abide by the law that the exclusion of evidence (or a decla-ration that the prosecution is inadmissible), i.e. a (certain) judicial response within the criminal trial, is the *necessary* consequence of a failure by the authorities to abide by the law. In view of the fact that Article 359a of the CCP confers a discretionary power on the court to determine the consequence of procedural vio-lations committed in the pre-trial phase of criminal proceedings and, in particular, of the fact that the text of this provision does not preclude the possibility of sentence reduction being granted instead of excluding evidence (whereby it is assumed that the purpose of such sentence reduction is not necessarily to secure observance by public authorities of the norms that bind them, on account of its inability, and in any case its limited ability, to do so), and that it requires judges to take into account the individual circumstances of the case when making the aforementioned determina-tion, the incorporation of Article 359a into the CCP may in itself be an acknowl-edgement that observance by the public authorities charged with investigating and prosecuting crime of the norms that bind them can be ensured in other ways than within the criminal trial.[362] Certainly the Supreme Court's case law on this pro-vision and on the judicial response within the criminal trial to pre-trial procedural violations more generally[363] suggests as much, by prescribing a restrictive appli-cation thereof.

Before describing how the Supreme Court prescribes a restrictive application of Article 359a of the CCP and of the judicial response within the criminal trial to pre-trial procedural violations more generally (and in order to substantiate the statement made above that the Supreme Court's case law suggests that observance by public authorities of the norms that bind them can be ensured elsewhere than in the criminal trial), it is important to first note that, like the text of Article 359a of the CCP, the Supreme Court in its interpretation of that provision does not, in principle, deny the 'nature of unlawfulness' and/or the notion inherent to the concept of the rule of law that the authorities must also abide by the law (or indeed the entitlement of citizens to the observance by the public authorities of the norms directed at them). After all, it restricts the balancing exercise prescribed by the second paragraph of Article 359a to the question of whether to attach a conse-quence to procedural violations committed in the pre-trial phase of criminal

---

[362] The 'location' of Article 359a within the CCP may also be an acknowledgement that that observance by the public authorities charged with investigating and prosecuting crime of the norms that bind them can be ensured in other ways than through, that is, within, the criminal trial. See in this regard Ölçer 2008, 208.

[363] In this regard it should be recalled that the Supreme Court recognizes that unlawfulness on the part of public authorities that does not, strictly speaking, constitute a procedural violation within the meaning of Article 359a of the CCP (including procedural violations committed abroad in the context of international cooperation in criminal matters) may still warrant one of the responses enumerated in the first paragraph of that provision.

proceedings, and, if so, which.[364] It also restricts the application of the Schutz-norm to that question.[365] In other words, according to the Supreme Court, neither the factors set out in the second paragraph of Article 359a nor the Schutz-norm are relevant to the question of whether the authorities acted unlawfully. Accordingly, it may be assumed that if the Supreme Court is not of the view that the best or only way to ensure observance by the authorities of the norms that bind them is to exclude evidence or declare the prosecution inadmissible (or, in other words, to address unlawfulness on the part of the authorities within the criminal trial), it must be of the view that this can, in principle, be done elsewhere.[366] By extension it may be argued that a restrictive application of Article 359a of the CCP is justified only insofar as the 'other' mechanisms that may be used for the purpose of securing the observance by public authorities of the norms that bind them are effective in this regard.[367] For those of the view that the exclusion of evidence (or a declaration that the prosecution is inadmissible) represents the 'flipside' of unlawful conduct on the part of public authorities in the course of a criminal investigation,[368] such 'other' mechanisms are never likely to be as effective as a response that nullifies or invalidates such conduct and its results.[369] Rather than seeking to compensate a restrictive judicial response within the criminal trial to pre-trial procedural violations elsewhere, they argue for the adoption of an expansive response in this regard. For those who argue otherwise, the effectiveness of 'other' mechanisms depends on, for example, the existence of an appropriate legal framework[370] and/or the likelihood that such a framework will actually be enforced.

The restrictive application of Article 359a of the CCP and of the judicial response within the criminal trial to procedural violations committed in the pre-trial phase of criminal proceedings more generally,[371] as referred to above, is apparent from the following. First, only violations *within the meaning of Article 359a* are eligible for one of the responses enumerated in the first paragraph of that provision

---

[364] See HR 30 March 2004, ECLI:NL:HR:2004:AM2533, r.o. 3.5, *NJ* 2004/376 m.nt. Y Buruma; HR 19 February 2013, ECLI:NL:HR:2013:BY5322, r.o. 2.4.1, *NJ* 2013/308 m.nt. BF Keulen. See TM Schalken in his annotation to HR 17 September 2013, ECLI:NL:HR:2013: BZ9992, *NJ* 2014/91, para 5 and T Schalken in his annotation to HR 9 September 2014, ECLI:NL: HR:2014:2650, *NJ* 2014/420, para 6.

[365] See HR 30 March 2004, ECLI:NL:HR:2004:AM2533, r.o. 3.5, *NJ* 2004/376 m.nt. Y Buruma; HR 19 February 2013, ECLI:NL:HR:2013:BY5322, r.o. 2.4.1, *NJ* 2013/308 m.nt. BF Keulen.

[366] See also Kuiper 2014, 580.

[367] See e.g. Borgers and Kooijmans 2013, 35.

[368] See n 49–53 and accompanying text.

[369] According to Borgers and Kooijmans, this is how Embregts' scepticism regarding alternatives to the exclusionary rule outside of the criminal trial is to be understood. See Borgers and Kooijmans 2013, 26 n 24, referring to Embregts 2003, 115–122.

[370] See e.g. Buruma 2013b, 14.

[371] It should be recalled here that outside of the framework of Article 359a CCP there is room (albeit limited room) to attach legal consequences to unlawful conduct.

and even then a declaration may suffice, on account of, for example, no or minimal prejudice having being caused. It is true that the Supreme Court recognises that a procedural violation committed by the police or prosecution in the context of criminal proceedings that does not, strictly speaking, constitute a procedural violation within the meaning of Article 359a of the CCP may still warrant one of the responses enumerated in the first paragraph of that provision; however, the room to do so seems to be (very) limited. Second, while the manner in which the Schutz-norm should, according to the Supreme Court, be applied falls short of a requirement in this regard (the court is not required but 'cordially invited' to apply the norm, with all that it entails), it is clear that the Supreme Court envisages a broad application of the norm. In principle, where the norm to have been violated does not protect accused persons in general and/or the violation of that norm did not affect the particular accused on trial, the court need not attach *any* of the consequences enumerated in the first paragraph of Article 359a of the CCP to the violation. Therefore, in principle, violations of a co-accused's or another third party's rights, while unlawful, are not eligible for any such response in the accused's trial. There are noteworthy exceptions to this rule, but these are rare. Third, the court is required, after it has established that the procedural violation constitutes a violation within the meaning of Article 359a of the CCP and the Schutz-norm criteria have been fulfilled, before it does anything else, to expressly identify the circumstances set out in the second paragraph of Article 359a of the CCP, i.e. to look beyond the fact of the procedural violation to circumstances that may militate against attaching a (certain) consequence to the violation, and to adhere to the 'upward sliding-scale' approach prescribed by the Supreme Court. Thus, the court is required to first consider whether a (mere) declaration suffices, before it considers responses that in most cases will have more far-reaching consequences. Fourth, in principle, only where there is actual prejudice for the accused (that is not negligible, such that a declaration that a violation has occurred does not suffice) is the court required to consider the applicability of the responses provided for the first paragraph of Article 359a of the CCP. Given the broad application prescribed by the Supreme Court of the Schutz-norm, the restriction (in principle) of the notion of prejudice to that suffered by the accused may not be surprising. That prejudice does not include prejudice to the interest of the accused 'not to be caught'. Moreover, the focus (as regards the judicial response within the criminal trial generally, i.e. not just the judicial response based on Article 359a) appears to be on a certain type of prejudice (to the accused's legitimate interests): prejudice to the accused's fair trial rights, such that it jeopardizes his or her right to a fair trial within the meaning of Article 6 of the ECHR.[372] Regarding the requirement of *actual* prejudice, it may be noted that whereas in respect of the violation of (*procedural*) fair trial rights the harm to the accused is, at least, imaginable, in respect of the accused's other rights and, in

---

[372] See e.g. the test for declaring the prosecution inadmissible and, regarding the exclusion of evidence, see HR 30 March 2004, ECLI:NL:HR:2004:AM2533, r.o. 3.5, *NJ* 2004/376 m.nt. Y Buruma, and HR 19 February 2013, ECLI:NL:HR:2013:BY5322, r.o. 2.4.1 and 2.4.4, *NJ* 2013/308 m.nt. BF Keulen.

particular, the accused's *substantive* rights (such as the right to privacy), this may be less so. While there are exceptions to the rule that only where there is actual prejudice for the accused is the court required to determine whether any of the consequences enumerated in first paragraph of Article 359a of the CCP should be attached, as these exceptions are, in turn, based on the exceptions to rule formulated by the Schutz-norm, such exceptions are rare. Fifth and finally, the criteria for each of the responses are strict. Thus, regarding the declaration that the prosecution inadmissible, the public authorities must have committed serious violations of principles of proper administration of justice, either intentionally or by gross negligence, as a result of which the suspect is prevented from receiving a fair trial. Regarding the exclusion of evidence, the enumeration of categories of exclusion in the Supreme Court's leading decision of 2013 is exhaustive, while the categories themselves are restrictive and a balancing exercise in the form of a cost-benefit analysis is prescribed for the second and third categories of exclusion. Finally, sentence reduction may, according to the Supreme Court, be granted only if the accused has suffered actual prejudice, this prejudice was caused by the procedural violation and lends itself to compensation by way of sentence reduction, and if sentence reduction is justified also in light of the interest that the violated provision purports to protect and the seriousness of the violation. As stated above, this last component of the test for sentence reduction appears to reflect the preference given by the Supreme Court to a declaration that a violation has occurred. In respect of procedural violations to arise in the context of inter-state cooperation in criminal matters it should be recalled that the Supreme Court has declared Article 359a of the CCP applicable to defence applications regarding the lawfulness of investigative activities carried out outside of the Netherlands (regardless of who was responsible: the Dutch authorities or foreign authorities), as regards both the motivation of such applications and the conditions under which legal consequences can be attached to pre-trial procedural violations. Presumably, therefore, the criminal court trying the case is required to take into account the factors set out in the second paragraph of Article 359a and to apply the criteria for each legal consequence, including the cost-benefit analysis falling under the second and third categories if exclusion. Accordingly, it may be concluded that the Supreme Court also takes a restrictive approach to the judicial response within the criminal trial to procedural violations to arise in the context of inter-state cooperation. Moreover, in respect of investigative activities unlawfully carried out outside of the Netherlands under the responsibility of foreign authorities, the criminal court trying the accused is required only to ensure that the way in which the results obtained by such investigative activities are used in the case against the accused does not undermine his right to a fair trial within the meaning of Article 6 of the ECHR.

Before going on to discuss the Supreme Court's restrictive approach to Article 359a of the CCP and to the judicial response within the criminal trial to procedural violations committed in the pre-trial phase of criminal proceedings more generally in terms of broader objectives of criminal procedure, and before saying something about the Supreme Court's apparent view (apparent, that is, from the fact that it does not deny the nature of unlawfulness, coupled with its restrictive approach to the judicial response within the criminal trial to such violations) that observance by the public authorities charged with investigating and prosecuting crime of the norms that bind them can be ensured in other ways than within the criminal trial, it is worth first trying to make sense of this approach, aside from such objectives and in terms of the points of departure and more specific rationales identified above. That restrictive approach was consolidated by the Supreme Court in its two leading decisions, and it is instructive to consider the 'theoretical' implications of each decision here, separately. According to the literature, the Supreme Court's first leading decision (of 2004) is to be understood primarily in terms of the second point of departure with respect to the question of how to address pre-trial procedural violations: the subjective rights of the accused.[373] This is due to the primacy accorded by the Supreme Court to 'reparability' (herstelbaarheid), i.e. the ability of the rule in question to nevertheless be complied with (such that violation of the underlying norm is avoided), the central role given by the Supreme Court in that decision to the Schutz-norm in the system of Article 359a of the CCP and to the weight accorded by it to the existence of actual prejudice for the accused.[374] Also on the basis of the role given to the Schutz-norm and the weight accorded to the existence of actual prejudice for the accused, it may be concluded that ensuring observance by public authorities of the norms that bind them is *not* the primary focus of Article 359a.[375] That ensuring such observance is not, according to the Supreme Court, the primary focus of Article 359a of the CCP[376] is (it is hereby submitted) also apparent from the fact that before it considers any of the responses enumerated in the first paragraph of that provision (and therefore also the exclusion of evidence), the court in criminal proceedings is required to consider whether a declaration that a violation has occurred suffices. Not only should the Supreme Court's first leading decision (and its subsequent case law affirming that decision) be understood in terms of the second point of departure; it should moreover be understood as being primarily concerned with the fair trial rights of the individual accused and/or the individual accused's right to a fair trial more generally,[377] in view of the tests for declaring the prosecution inadmissible and for excluding

---

[373] See e.g. Kuiper 2009, 52–53; and 2014, 572.

[374] Borgers 2012, 265. It should be noted that Borgers speaks of the *protection* of the subjective rights of the accused in this article. For the reasons cited above (see n 94–96 and accompanying text), this is undesirable. Interestingly, he and Kooijmans do not do so in a later piece. See Borgers and Kooijmans 2013, 20.

[375] Borgers 2012, 265–266. See also Blom 2011, 16; and Borgers and Kooijmans 2013, 20–21.

According to Kuiper 2014, 209, the primacy accorded by the Supreme Court to 'repair' (*herstel*), whereby the rule in question is nevertheless complied with (and violation of the underlying norm is thereby avoided) also demonstrates that ensuring such observance is not, according to the Supreme Court, the primary focus of Article 359a CCP. After all, such repair does not 'undo' the impugned action, it merely prevents the possible (negative) consequences.

[376] See in this regard also e.g. Y Buruma in his annotation to HR 30 March 2004, ECLI:NL:HR:2004:AM2533, *NJ* 2004/376 and TM Schalken in his annotation to HR 3 July 2001, ECLI:NL:HR:2001:AB2732, *NJ* 2002/8.

[377] Borgers 2012, 266. See also Borgers and Kooijmans 2013, 20–21.

evidence.[378] Sentence reduction *can* be understood in the more general terms of the subjective rights of the accused; although the Supreme Court has not explicitly addressed the issue, the rationale for sentence reduction appears to be the compensation of violations of the individual accused's *substantive* rights. According to Borgers and Kooijmans, it is this aspect of the Supreme Court's case law on Article 359a of the CCP—the focus on the need ensure the accused's right to a fair trial within the meaning of Article 6 of the ECHR—that warrants the conclusion that the Supreme Court envisages a restrictive application of that provision.[379] In this regard they observe that the fourth point of departure identified above with respect to the question of how to address procedural violations committed in the pre-trial phase of criminal proceedings, the primacy of crime control, can also be read into the case law of the Supreme Court.[380]

Turning now to the Supreme Court's second leading decision (of 2013), it should be recalled that that decision left intact the general framework set out in the first leading decision, but built on the test for excluding evidence. It identified three categories of cases in which the exclusion of evidence is warranted. The first category is concerned with the need to ensure the accused's right to a fair trial within the meaning of Article 6 of the ECHR (and as interpreted by the ECtHR), while the second and third categories are concerned with the need to ensure observance by the public authorities charged with the investigation and prosecution of crime of the norms that bind them, in particular by deterring such authorities from acting unlawfully in the future. Thus, the Supreme Court cites the prevention argument (or deterrence) as the rationale for the second and third categories of exclusion. At first glance, therefore, the Supreme Court's second leading decision on Article 359a of the CCP would appear to prescribe a less restrictive application of the judicial response within the criminal trial to pre-trial procedural violations, by expanding the grounds on which evidence may be excluded.[381] It is, however, (highly) questionable whether this—a less restrictive application of the judicial response within the criminal trial to such violations—is what the Supreme Court had in mind when citing the prevention (or deterrence) argument as a rationale for the exclusion of evidence.[382] Supreme Court Judge Buruma's observations in the wake of the Court's second leading decision on Article 359a of the CCP are elucidating in this respect; he observes that this decision, among others issued

---

[378] Borgers 2012, 265. Regarding the latter, presumably Borgers is referring not only to the general test for exclusion, but also to subsequent case law in which the Supreme Court determined that evidence obtained in violation of Article 8 ECHR need not be excluded so long as the trial as a whole is fair, thereby implying that the yardstick for exclusion is Article 6 ECHR.

[379] Borgers and Kooijmans 2013, 19–21.

[380] Ibid., 21. See also Borgers 2012, 265–266, and n 119 and accompanying text.

[381] See in this regard Schalken 2013, 1391 and 1393.

[382] In the USA the adoption of the deterrence rationale in respect of the exclusionary rule seems to have gone hand in hand with a *more* restrictive judicial response within the criminal trial to unlawfulness in the course of a criminal investigation amounting to a violation of the Fourth Amendment. See e.g. Baldiga 1983, 165–166; and Bloom and Dewey 2011, 38–51.

around that time, demonstrates 'once again' that the assumption that the exclusion of evidence is the logical consequence of unlawfulness on the part of public authorities is largely wrong and that exclusion is only warranted in certain 'very precisely defined' circumstances.[383] Moreover, as regards the (already narrowly formulated) second and third categories of the exclusion of evidence, even when the procedural violation constitutes a very intrusive breach of a fundamental right of the accused, or when it forms part of a wider pattern of misconduct such that its structural nature is established, the court in criminal proceedings is, depending on the category, permitted or required to undertake a balancing exercise in the form of a cost-benefit analysis to determine whether exclusion is warranted. Given the obstacles put in place for the second and third categories (which, it should be recalled, cite as the rationale for exclusion the prevention argument) it seems that the Supreme Court's second leading decision is also to be understood primarily in terms of the need to ensure the accused's right to a fair trial within the meaning of Article 6 of the ECHR. That also appears to be the primary (if not sole) concern of the judicial response within the criminal trial to procedural violations committed in the pre-trial phase of criminal proceedings outside of the framework of Article 359a of the CCP.

The specific rationales for responding to procedural violations committed by the police or public prosecutor in the course of the criminal investigation (whether inside or outside the framework of Article 359a of the CCP), then, are: ensuring the accused's right to a fair trial (in the case of a declaration that the prosecution is inadmissible and of the exclusion of evidence), preventing public authorities from acting unlawfully in the future (in the case of the exclusion of evidence) and compensating violations of the individual accused's substantive rights (in the case of sentence reduction). However, to describe the Dutch judicial response within the criminal trial to pre-trial procedural violations solely in those terms, i.e. in terms of arguments that *justify* such a response, would obscure its true nature. The fact that the Supreme Court does not deny the notion inherent to the concept of the rule of law that the authorities must also abide by the law, but at the same time prescribes a restrictive application of the judicial response within the criminal trial to such violations suggests that it is of the view that ensuring the observance by public authorities of the norms that bind them can and indeed should be achieved elsewhere than in the criminal trial. Accordingly, it can be concluded in respect of the Supreme Court's approach to the judicial response *within the criminal trial* to pre-trial procedural violations that the goal of truth-finding (*waarheidsvinding*) outweighs the goal of individual legal protection (*individuele rechtsbescherming*), save in certain 'very precisely defined' and, probably, exceptional circumstances.[384] Further, given that the need to ensure the right to a fair trial continues to be the primary focus of the judicial response within the criminal trial to such violations, it

---

[383] Buruma 2013a. See also Kuiper 2014, 323–324.

[384] See similarly e.g. Röttgering 2013, 427; and T Schalken in his annotation to HR 9 September 2014, ECLI:NL:HR:2014:2650, *NJ* 2014/420.

is worth recalling that when the need to ensure the accused's right to a fair trial is the only point of departure with respect to the question of how to address procedural violations committed in the pre-trial phase of criminal proceedings, this may be indicative of the primacy afforded in a given legal system to efficient crime control (in this particular context, at least).[385] Whether this is the case then depends on how the right to a fair trial is construed. As regards the exclusion of evidence at least, the Supreme Court has, in the past, drawn (heavily) on the ECtHR's interpretation of Article 6 of the ECHR in this respect, i.e. as regards the issue of unlawfulness in the investigative stage of criminal proceedings, and, in particular, the ECtHR's position that reliance on evidence obtained through a violation of Article 8 of the ECHR does not necessarily render the trial unfair under Article 6, and has made clear its intention to continue to do so in the future.[386]

Finally, it is worth saying something about the Supreme Court's apparent view that ensuring the observance by public authorities of the norms that bind them can be achieved elsewhere than in the criminal trial. In the wake of the Supreme Court's first leading decision, but prior to its second, Borgers and Kooijmans concluded, on the basis of the restrictive application of Article 359a of the CCP prescribed by the Supreme Court (which, in turn, is based on the focus on the need to ensure the accused's right to a fair trial), that Article 359a of the CCP is insufficient to ensure observance by the public authorities of the norms that bind them. In view of the obstacles (put) in place for the second and third categories of exclusion, which, it should be recalled, see exclusion as a means of ensuring observance by the public authorities of the norms that bind them, the Supreme Court's second leading decision does not warrant a reconsideration of that conclusion. The insufficiency of Article 359a of the CCP (and of the judicial response within the criminal trial more generally) to ensure such observance has, in turn, has led to renewed interest in the literature[387] and beyond[388] in the possible alternatives to the exclusion of evidence in case of pre-trial procedural violations (and to the judicial response within the criminal trial more generally), whereby such alternatives are supposed to compensate such insufficiency. For example, some authors envisage a more central role for the (Dutch) National Ombudsman to monitor and, where necessary or desirable, to respond to procedural violations committed in the course of a criminal investigation.[389] It has, understandably, also led to concerns being voiced as to the ability

---

[385] See n 119 and accompanying text.

[386] Schalken is critical in this regard. He argues that simply because the ECtHR has 'severed' the relationship between Article 8 and Article 6 of the ECHR, national courts need not do so; moreover, there are good reasons for not doing so. See T Schalken in his annotation to HR 9 September 2014, ECLI:NL:HR:2014:2650, *NJ* 2014/420.

[387] See e.g. Borgers 2012, 267–270; Borgers and Kooijmans 2013; and Kuiper 2014, 596–601.

[388] See the outline policy document (*contourennota*) for the 'Modernisation of the Code of Criminal Procedure' project currently being carried out in the Netherlands: *Kamerstukken II* 2015/16, 29279, 278, pp. 102–104.

[389] See e.g. Borgers 2012, 269; and Borgers and Kooijmans 2013, 25–29. See however Cleiren and Mevis 1995.

of the current 'other' mechanisms to ensure such observance and to provide individual legal protection more generally.[390]

3.6 Conclusion

The purpose of this chapter was to set out the Dutch theory, law and practice with respect to the question of how to address pre-trial procedural violations. In the penultimate section of the chapter the legal framework governing the Dutch judicial response within the criminal trial was 'assessed' in light of the possible points of departure and rationales for such a response. In this section the main features of the legal framework and the main points of the analysis are summarised.

On the face of it, the Dutch judicial response within the criminal trial to procedural violations committed by the police or public prosecutor in the course of the criminal investigation appears to be a matter of judicial discretion, in the sense that the consequence, if any, to be attached to such violations depends on the individual circumstances of the case, and whereby the trial judge is afforded a degree of freedom. Nevertheless, the judge's room to manoeuvre in this regard is extremely limited. It is not merely that the court is required to take into account the factors set out in the second paragraph of Article 359a of the CCP (i.e. to expressly acknowledge them, and their capacity to 'guide' the court), and/or that it must be *seen* to do so (as it must). Rather, what is meant is that the response to a procedural violation committed by the police or public prosecutor in the course of the criminal investigation must be justified by a combination of the factors. Certainly, the response to such violations must be justified by the existence of prejudice, whereby prejudice is defined precisely and narrowly, and does not encompass damage to the accused's ('illegitimate') interest 'not to be caught' or not to have incriminating evidence gathered against him or her. This raises questions as to the extent to which the Dutch judicial response within the criminal trial to procedural violations committed in the course of the criminal investigation can, accurately, be depicted as discretionary in nature. Indeed, the discretionary power conferred on judges by Article 359a of the CCP appears to be structured in such a way that the trial judge is strongly directed towards a certain response (*not* attaching a legal consequence to the procedural violation). Arguably, the requirement of prejudice for the accused does just that, and this may sit uneasily with the freedom seemingly conferred by the legislator on the trial judge to address procedural violations committed by the police or public prosecutor in the course of the criminal investigation in the context of Article 359a of the CCP (although, again, this may depend on what the legislator had in mind when it did so).

Moreover, underlying the process of taking into consideration the individual circumstances of the case appears to be a balancing exercise, requiring the

---

[390] See e.g. Samadi 2016.

consideration of facts and circumstances that might militate against attaching a (certain) consequence to the procedural violation. This is expressly recognised in the context of the exclusion of evidence: under the second and third categories of exclusion, which both cite prevention or deterrence as the underlying rationale, the court is explicitly permitted or required (depending on the category) to undertake a cost-benefit analysis for the purpose of determining whether the violation concerned requires the exclusion of the evidence thereby obtained. Nevertheless, insofar as the Dutch judicial response within the criminal trial to procedural violations committed by the police or public prosecutor in the course of the criminal investigation can be depicted as a balancing discretion, it is important to note that this discretion is confined in at least one noteworthy way. There is little to no room to consider facts and circumstances that might militate against a (certain) response once it is established that the right of the accused to a fair trial, within the meaning of Article 6 of the ECHR and, importantly, as interpreted by the ECtHR, is at stake. Regarding the court's *balancing* discretion to exclude evidence on the basis of a cost-benefit analysis, it appears that the analysis envisaged by the Dutch Supreme Court entails the consideration of facts and circumstances relevant to the benefit side of the equation, as well as those relevant to the cost side thereof (that involve questioning the assumption on the benefit side of the equation that exclusion (always) has some significant deterrent effect and, on the cost side thereof, that exclusion (always) has the same societal costs: 'freeing the guilty'), which appears to significantly widen the scope to not exclude unlawfully obtained evidence. Accordingly, the Dutch judicial response to procedural violations committed by the police or public prosecutor in the course of the criminal investigation may be said to be sensitive to public interest considerations related to the investigation and prosecution of (serious) crime. In terms of broader goals of criminal procedure, in light also of the overall restrictive application of the judicial response within the criminal trial to procedural violations committed by the police or public prosecutor in the course of the criminal investigation (as discussed above), it appears to give precedence to the goal of truth-finding, and, by extension, the crime control-objective, over that of individual legal protection, save in exceptional circumstances. At first glance such a conclusion may be surprising given that the aforementioned response is expressly underpinned by the need to ensure the accused's right to a fair trial within the meaning of Article 6 of the ECHR. In this regard it should be recalled that in invoking this right as a (or rather: *the main*) rationale for responding to procedural violations committed by the police or public prosecutor in the course of the criminal investigation within the criminal trial, the Supreme Court draws heavily on the relevant case law of the ECtHR. In particular, it expressly relies on the ECtHR's position that reliance on evidence obtained through a violation of Article 8 of the ECHR does not necessarily render the trial unfair under Article 6. Just as the depiction of the Dutch judicial response to procedural violations committed by the police or public prosecutor in the course of the criminal investigation in terms of the 'protection of the subjective rights of the accused' may be misleading (in view of the mechanism by which such protection is achieved: the application of the Schutz-norm), so too does the depiction of that response in terms of individual legal protection on account of the emphasis placed by the Supreme Court on the need to ensure the accused's right to a fair trial misrepresent its true nature.

In the Netherlands, the defence is required to motivate its applications pursuant to Article 359a according to (all three of) the factors set out in the second paragraph of Article 359a of the CCP and, in particular, how such factors warrant the relief sought. Only where the application is properly motivated is the court required to rule on it. Failure to do so means that the court may refuse to grant the relief sought or simply declare that an irreparable procedural violation has occurred without otherwise enquiring into the factual circumstances that, according to the defence, warrant such relief. This onerous substantiation requirement also applies to defence applications for relief in respect of alleged unlawful investigative activity carried out by public authorities outside of the Netherlands in the context of inter-state cooperation in criminal matters (whereby the Netherlands is the requesting/receiving state), regardless of who was responsible: the Dutch authorities or the foreign authorities. Unlawful investigative activity carried out by foreign public authorities outside of the Netherlands, for which the public prosecutor is not responsible, does not fall within the scope of Article 359a of the CCP. While this does not mean that Dutch criminal courts may never attach legal consequences to such violations, the room to do so is (extremely) limited.

It is fair to say, therefore, that the Dutch Supreme Court prescribes a restrictive application of Article 359a of the CCP and of the judicial response within the criminal trial to procedural violations committed by the police or public prosecutor in the course of the criminal investigation more generally.

References

Ashworth AJ (1977) Excluding Evidence as Protecting Rights. Crim LR 723 et seq.
Ashworth A, Redmayne M (2010) The Criminal Process, 4th edn. Oxford University Press, Oxford
Baaijens-Van Geloven YGM (2004) De rechtsgevolgen (sanctionering) van onrechtmatigheden in het opsporingsonderzoek. In: Groenhuijsen MS, Knigge G (eds) Afronding en Verantwoording. Eindrapport onderzoeksproject Strafvordering 2001. Kluwer, Deventer, pp 341–420
Baldiga WR (1983) Excluding Evidence to Protect Rights: Principles Underlying the Exclusionary Rule in England and the United States. BC Int'l & Comp L Rev 6:133 et seq.
Blom T (2002) De meest passende sanctie: de Hoge Raad en onrechtmatig verkregen bewijs. DD 2002/32, afl 9, pp 1049–1055
Blom T (2008) Vormverzuimen. In: Cleiren CPM et al. (eds) Jurisprudentie Strafrecht Select, 3rd edn. Sdu Uitgevers, The Hague, pp 113–133
Blom T (2011) Vormen verzuimd bij het politieverhoor. Vossiuspers UvA, Amsterdam
Blom T (2015) R. Kuiper, Vormfouten. Juridische consequenties van vormverzuimen in strafzaken, thesis. RM Themis 2015, afl 3, pp 116–120
Bloom RM, Dewey E (2011) When rights become empty promises: Promoting an exclusionary rule that vindicates personal rights. IJ 46:38 et seq.

Borgers MJ (2012) De toekomst van artikel 359a Sv. DD 2012/25, afl 4, pp 257–273

Borgers MJ, Kooijmans T (2013) Alternatieven voor rechterlijke controle op vormverzuimen. In: Groenhuijsen MS et al. (eds) Roosachtig strafrecht: Liber amicorum Theo de Roos. Kluwer, Deventer, pp 17–36

Brants CH et al. (2003) Op zoek naar grondslagen. In: Brants CH et al. (eds) Op zoek naar grondslagen. Strafvordering 2001 ter discussie. Boom Juridische uitgevers, The Hague, pp 1–27

Brinkhoff S (2016) De toepassing van artikel 359a Sv anno 2016. Een pleidooi voor herstel van balans en de terugkeer naar echte rechterlijke vrijheid. DD 2016/8, afl 2, pp 101–116

Buruma Y (2008) Onprofessioneel politie optreden. DD 2008/8, afl 1, pp 87–104

Buruma Y (2013) Als de politie zich niet aan de wet houdt… NJB 2013/494, afl 10, p 595

Buruma Y (2013) Strafrechtelijke rechtsvorming. Strafblad 2013/3, afl 1, pp 6–14

Cameron JD, Lustiger R (1984) The Exclusionary Rule: A Cost-Benefit Analysis. FRD 101:109 et seq.

Cleiren CPM (2015) Art 1 Sv, aant 11 (online, last updated 1 July 2015). Tekst & Commentaar Strafvordering, Kluwer, Deventer

Cleiren CPM, Mevis PAM (1995) Beoordeling van strafvorderlijk overheidsoptreden. DD 1995/25, afl 7, pp 700–713

Cleiren CPM, Mevis PAM (1996) Het dubbelzijdig karakter van onrechtmatig strafvorderlijk overheidsoptreden. In Cleiren CPM et al. (eds) Voor risico van de overheid? Vooruitzichten van de aansprakelijkheid van de overheid in bestuurs-, straf- en civielrechtelijk perspectief. Gouda Quint, Deventer, pp 187–205

Corstens GJM (ed) (1993) Rapporten herijking strafvordering 1993. Gouda Quint, Arnhem

Corstens GJM (2014) In: Borgers MJ (ed) Het Nederlands strafprocesrecht, 8th edn. Kluwer, Deventer

Corstens G, Kuiper R (2013) Niet-ontvankelijkverklaring van het openbaar ministerie als reactie op een vormverzuim. In: Groenhuijsen MS et al. (eds) Roosachtig strafrecht: Liber amicorum Theo de Roos. Kluwer, Deventer, pp 125–140

Crijns JH, Van der Meij PPJ (2005) Over de grenzen van de materiële waarheidsvinding. In: Haveman RH, Wiersinga HC (eds) Langs de randen van het strafrecht. Wolf Legal Publishers, Nijmegen, pp 45–69

De Jong DH (1985) Bewijsuitsluiting kent meer dan één rechtsgrond. In: Balkema JP et al. (eds) Liber Amicorum Th.W. van Veen. Opstellen aangeboden aan Th.W. van Veen ter gelegenheid van zijn vijfenzestigste verjaardag. Gouda Quint, Arnhem, pp 97–111

Doorenbos DR (1990) Een absolute relativiteitstheorie? DD 1990/20, afl 1, pp 21–34

Dubelaar MJ (2009) Betrouwbaarheid versus rechtmatigheid in strafzaken. RM Themis 2009, afl 3, pp 101–114

Embregts MCD (2003) Uitsluitsel over bewijsuitsluiting. Een onderzoek naar de toelaatbaarheid van onrechtmatig verkregen bewijs in het strafrecht, het civiele recht en het bestuursrecht. Kluwer, Deventer

Fokkens JW (1991) Enkele gedachten over de sanctie op onrechtmatige bewijsgaring. In: Corstens GJM et al. (eds) Met hoofd en hart: Opstellen aangeboden aan prof. mr. J.C.M. Leijten ter gelegenheid van zijn afscheid als hoogleraar aan de Katholieke Universiteit Nijmegen. Tjeenk Willink, Zwolle, pp 227–234

Groenhuijsen MS (1996) Het niet realiseren van gegronde materieelrechtelijke aanspraken in het strafprocesrecht. In: Van de Griend ESGNAI, De Waard BWN (eds) Rechtsvinding. Gedachtenwisseling over het nieuwe Algemeen Deel** van de Asser-serie. Tjeenk Willink, Zwolle, pp 9–20

Groenhuijsen MS, Knigge G (2001) Algemeen deel. In: Groenhuijsen MS, Knigge G (eds) Het onderzoek ter zitting. Eerste interimrapport onderzoeksproject Strafvordering 2001. Gouda Quint, Deventer, pp 1–55

Haazen OA (2007) Precedent in the Netherlands. EJCL 11. http://www.ejcl.org/111/art111-12.pdf. Accessed 2 April 2016

Jörg N (1989) De exclusionary rule als drijfveer achter normering van bevoegdheden. DD 1989/ 19, afl 7, pp 654–670

Kamisar Y (1987) "Comparative Reprehensibility" and the Fourth Amendment Exclusionary Rule. Mich L Rev 86:1 et seq.

Keulen BF, Knigge G (2010) Strafprocesrecht, 12th edn. Kluwer, Deventer

Knigge G (2003) Het Zwolsman-criterium op de helling. RM Themis 2003, afl 4, pp 193–195

Kooijmans T (2011) Elk nadeel heb z'n voordeel? Artikel 359a Sv en de ontdekking van het strafbare feit. DD 2011/78, afl 9, pp 1091–1108

Koopmans FAJ (2001) Art. 359a. In: Cleiren CPM, Nijboer JF (eds) Tekst & Commentaar Strafvordering. Kluwer, Deventer, pp 886–888

Krikke A (1983) De rechtsgrond van de bewijsuitsluiting in strafzaken. In: De la Porte EA et al. (eds) Bij deze stand van zaken. Bundel opstellen aangeboden aan A.L. Melai. Gouda Quint, Arnhem, pp 273–294

Kuiper R (2009) Strafvermindering als reactie op vormverzuimen. Van Via della Conciliazione tot Afvoerpijp en verder. In: Duker MJA et al. (eds) Welberaden. Beschouwingen over de rechtsontwikkeling in de rechtspraak van de Hoge Raad der Nederlanden. Wolf Legal Publishers, Nijmegen, pp 35–59

Kuiper R (2014) Vormfouten. Juridische Consequenties van Vormverzuimen in Strafzaken. Kluwer, Deventer

Leeuw BJG (2013) Grondwet en eerlijk proces. Een onderzoek naar de eventuele meerwaarde van het opnemen van het recht op een eerlijk proces in de Nederlandse Grondwet. Wolf Legal Publishers, Oisterwijk

Mevis PAM (1995) De rechtsgevolgen van onrechtmatigheden in het vooronderzoek. In: Balkema JP et al. (eds) Dynamisch strafrecht. Opstellen ter gelegenheid van het afscheid van Prof.mr. G.J.M. Corstens van de Katholieke Universiteit van Nijmegen. Gouda Quint, Arnhem, pp 251–268

Mevis PAM et al. (2001) Rechtmatigheidstoetsing in het nieuwe millennium. In: Brants CH et al. (eds) Legitieme Strafvordering. Rechten van de mens in de 21ste eeuw. Intersentia, Antwerpen/ Groningen, pp 37–55

Ölçer FP (2008) Eerlijk Proces en Bijzondere Opsporing. Wolf Legal Publishers, Nijmegen

Peters AAG (1973) Illegale radiozender 'de Marconist'. AA 1973, afl 5, pp 236–253

Reijntjes JM et al. (2008) Wederzijdze rechtshulp. In: Van Sliedregt E et al. (eds) Handboek Internationaal Strafrecht. Kluwer, Deventer, pp 245–301

Röttgering AEM (2013) Cassatie in strafzaken. Een rechtsbeschermend perspectief. Sdu uitgevers, The Hague

Samadi M (2016) Policing the police: het toezicht op de opsporing. DD 2016/37, afl 6, pp 406–418

Schalken TM (1981) Zelfkant van de rechtshandhaving. Over onrechtmatig verkregen bewijs in strafzaken. Gouda Quint, Arnhem

Schalken TM (1989) Schending van wettelijke voorschriften en het redelijke belang van de verdachte: een redelijk criterium? Enkele inleidende opmerkingen. In: Schalken TM, Hofstee EJ (eds) In zijn verdediging geschaad. Over vormverzuimen en het belang van de verdachte. Gouda Quint, Arnhem, pp 3–15

Schalken T (2013) Een renaissance van vormverzuimen in het strafrecht?. NJB 2013/1301, afl 21, pp 1391–1394

Schoep GK (2015) Art 359a Sv, aant 3 (online, last updated 1 July 2015). Tekst & Commentaar Strafvordering, Kluwer, Deventer

Starr SB (2009) Sentence Reduction as a Remedy for Prosecutorial Misconduct. Geo LJ 97:1509 et seq.

Strasser W (1988) The relationship between substantive rights and procedural rights guaranteed by the European Convention on Human Rights. In: Matscher F, Petzold H (eds) Protecting Human Rights: The European Dimension. Carl Heymanns Verlag KG, Cologne, pp 595–604

Ter Haar R, Meijer GH (2011) Vormverzuimen. Kluwer, Deventer

Van der Meij PPJ (2008) De raadsman bij het politieverhoor en de audiovisuele registratie. De verdedigingsrol bij de materiële waarheidsvinding in het strafrechtelijk vooronderzoek. In: Crijns JH et al. (eds) De waarde van waarheid. Opstellen over waarheidsvinding in het strafrecht. Boom Juridische uitgevers, The Hague, pp 57–93

Van der Meij PPJ (2010) De driehoeksverhouding in het strafrechtelijk vooronderzoek. Een onverminderde zoektocht naar evenwicht in de rolverdeling tussen rechter-commissaris, de officier van justitie en de verdediging. Kluwer, Deventer

Van Leijen G (1994) Sanctionering van normverzuimen en de betekenis van vormvoorschriften in het strafproces. Recht en kritiek 1994/20, afl 3, pp 227−247

Van Sliedregt E, Sjöcrona JM (2008) Algemene inleiding. In: Van Sliedregt E et al. (eds) Handboek Internationaal Strafrecht. Kluwer, Deventer, pp 1–27

Van Woensel AM (2004) Sanctionering van onrechtmatig verkregen bewijsmateriaal. Preadvies voor de Vereniging voor de vergelijkende studie van het recht van België en Nederland. DD 2004/10, afl 2, pp 119–171

Chapter 4
Judicial Responses to Pre-Trial Procedural Violations in England and Wales

Abstract This chapter sets out the law and practice with respect to the question of how to address procedural violations committed in the pre-trial phase of criminal proceedings in England and Wales. It does so by means of an overview of the consequences that the judge may attach to such procedural violations. Consideration is given to the extent to which the determination of whether to attach legal consequences to established procedural violations entails the exercise of judgement, whereby the judge has due regard to the particular circumstances of the case, i.e. the extent to which it should be discretionary in nature (which may be contrasted to an approach whereby the judicial response is more or less automatic), and also to how courts respond to procedural violations committed in an international context. The examination in this chapter is not limited to a description of the relevant law and practice, however; it also includes a description of the (possible) theoretical accounts thereof, as well as an evaluation of the law and practice in light of such accounts.

Keywords reliability rationale · deterrence rationale · protective rationale · integrity rationale · public attitude integrity · court-centred integrity · abuse of process doctrine · stay of proceedings · impossibility of a fair trial · epistemic considerations · need to protect the integrity of the proceedings · non-epistemic considerations · exclusionary rule · exclusionary discretion · common law exclusionary rule · common law exclusionary discretion · Section 76(2) PACE · Section 78(1) PACE · discretion · balancing · sentence reduction · judicial condemnation

Contents

K. Pitcher, *Judicial Responses to Pre-Trial Procedural Violations in International Criminal Proceedings*, International Criminal Justice Series 16,
https://doi.org/10.1007/978-94-6265-219-4_4

4.1 Introduction

The purpose of this chapter is to set out the English theory, law and practice with respect to the question of how to address procedural violations committed in the pre-trial phase of criminal proceedings, as relevant to the central research question of this book: how should judges at the ICTs respond to procedural violations committed in the pre-trial phase of the proceedings? First, an overview will be provided of the (general) aspects of English legal system that are relevant to the judicial response within the criminal trial to pre-trial procedural violations (committed by the police or public prosecutor),[1] in order to facilitate an understanding of that response (Sect. 4.2). Second, the theory on the question of how to address procedural violations committed in the pre-trial phase of criminal proceedings will be set out, i.e. the possible rationales in this regard, including their interrelationship and, where instructive, how they relate to broader objectives of criminal justice (Sect. 4.3). Then the legal framework governing the judicial response to such violations will be set out,[2] both as regards procedural violations committed in a purely national context, and as regards those committed in an international context (Sect. 4.4). In setting out the legal framework attention will be paid to the question of the extent to which the English judicial response to pre-trial procedural violations can be said to be discretionary in nature, and/or the extent to which it entails a

---

[1] As stated in Chap. 1, in this book the term 'procedural violations committed in the pre-trial phase of international criminal proceedings' encompasses those procedural violations that at the national level would be described as *police* illegality or unlawfulness. However, at the international level, this term—'police illegality' or 'unlawfulness'—is apt to mislead, since the ICTs do not have their own enforcement agencies, i.e. police forces (and are reliant on state cooperation for such activities as the apprehension of persons suspected or accused of crimes falling within their jurisdiction and for the carrying out of investigations). It also encompasses the violation by the *prosecution* of its pre-trial obligations.

[2] Of course, the answer to the question of how to address pre-trial procedural violations encompasses more than just the judicial response *within the criminal trial* to such violations. After all, the question implies that such violations could be addressed outside of the criminal trial. It is beyond the scope of this book to explore in any meaningful way other (possible) mechanisms for addressing such violations, and the choice to limit the legal framework to the judicial response to pre-trial procedural violations may be justified on the basis that that response will invariably shed light on the broader question of how to address procedural violations committed in the pre-trial phase of criminal proceedings. Thus, a restrictive response within the criminal trial suggests that such violations should be dealt with elsewhere than in the criminal trial, i.e. through other mechanisms.

balancing approach (whereby it may be recalled that in Chap. 1, such questions were said to lie at the heart of the present study). Ultimately, an attempt will be made to 'make sense' of this framework, in terms of the rationales and criminal justice objectives identified in the foregoing section, in order to provide a more complete picture of the English judicial response to procedural violations committed in the pre-trial phase of criminal proceedings, and a solid basis for the comparison to be undertaken in Chap. 7 (Sect. 4.5). Finally, this chapter will conclude with a brief summary of the main features of the legal framework and the main points of the analysis (Sect. 4.6).

4.2 Relevant Aspects of the English Legal System

In England and Wales, the criminal investigation is (now) largely regulated by statute, although there is no comprehensive code in this regard. Standards for the conduct of criminal investigation can be found in several statutes, including the Police and Criminal Evidence Act 1984 (hereafter: PACE), which deals with powers to stop and search, powers of entry, search and seizure, arrest and detention, and questioning and treatment of persons by the police, including searches of detained persons, intimate searches and access to legal advice (and is supplemented by a number of codes of practice, which further regulate the aforementioned areas), the Road Traffic Act 1988, which regulates the administration of breath, blood and urine tests in road traffic cases, and the Regulation of Investigatory Powers Act 2000, which regulates the interception of communications. England does not have a comprehensive written, i.e. codified, constitution; it is governed by an unwritten, or, rather, an uncodified constitution, formed of Acts of Parliament, court judgments and 'conventions' (i.e. 'political customs' or 'unwritten rules of constitutional practice').[3] One of the Acts of Parliament to make up the uncodified constitution is the Human Rights Act 1998. Pursuant to Section 3 of the Act, public authorities, including the police, the Crown Prosecution Service, and 'courts and tribunals', are required to act in a way which is compatible with the ECHR rights.[4] Section 2 of the Act requires courts to take into account decisions of the European Court of Human Rights, while Section 3 requires courts to 'read and give effect' to legislation 'in a way which is compatible with the Convention rights'.

In England and Wales, the police are responsible for the criminal investigation, i.e. the collection of evidence, and for charging (in the majority of cases), while the Crown Prosecution Service, the principal prosecuting authority for England and Wales, is responsible for deciding which cases should be prosecuted, for charging in the more serious and complex cases, and for prosecuting. There are two modes of

---

[3] See Blackburn R, 'Britain's unwritten constitution', https://www.bl.uk/magna-carta/articles/britains-unwritten-constitution Accessed 1 March 2017.

[4] See s 6(1) HRA.

criminal trial: summary trial by a magistrates' court or trial by jury on indictment in the Crown Court. Whereas the first mode of criminal trial is intended for less serious criminal offences, the second is intended for the most serious ones. Under the first mode, the case is tried by lay magistrates or a judge sitting alone,[5] while under the latter, a professional judge sits with a jury,[6] although in cases of serious and complex fraud the trial on indictment may be held without a jury.[7] Trial on indictment in the Crown Court involves a division of responsibility between the judge and jury: 'Generally speaking, questions of law are for the judge and questions of fact are for the jury.'[8] For present purposes, it is important to note that questions of law include the question of whether certain evidence should be admitted or excluded, while questions of fact include the question of how much weight is to be accorded to evidence that has been admitted. As to the moment at which a determination of whether evidence should be excluded may be made, Choo notes that:

> In criminal cases, the traditional procedure involves determinations of whether evidence should be excluded being made at the point of the trial at which it is sought to adduce the evidence; it is only if the evidence is so crucial that the prosecution cannot even open its case without referring to it that a determination of whether it should be excluded may take place immediately after the jury has been sworn. However, this traditional procedure now stands alongside the provision made by the Criminal Procedure and Investigations Act 1996 for pre-trial hearings. Such hearings, which may be used to make determinations of whether evidence should be excluded, take place before the jury is sworn.[9]

In addition to ruling on questions of law, judges 'play a role in guarding against false conviction by ensuring that a weak case does not go to the jury', and, in cases that do go to the jury, the judge will, at the end of the trial, 'sum up on the facts'.[10] Moreover, in many cases the judge will give some direction to the jury on fact-finding, for example, a warning about suspect evidence.[11]

Appeals against conviction or sentence by a magistrates' court are heard by the Crown Court,[12] while appeals against conviction by the Crown Court (as a court of first instance) are heard by the Criminal Division of the Court of Appeal of England and Wales.[13] A defendant is able to appeal his or her conviction by the Crown Court on grounds of either fact or law.[14] Appeals from the Criminal Division of the Court of Appeal are, in turn, heard by the Supreme Court of the United Kingdom, the highest appellate court in the United Kingdom. Appeals to the Supreme Court are limited to

---

[5] Ashworth and Redmayne 2010, 323.

[6] Ibid., 323.

[7] s 43 Criminal Justice Act 2003.

[8] Ashworth and Redmayne 2010, 339.

[9] Choo 2015, 11.

[10] Ashworth and Redmayne 2010, 339.

[11] Ibid., 339.

[12] s 108 Magistrates' Courts Act 1980.

[13] s 1 Criminal Appeal Act 1968.

[14] Ashworth and Redmayne 2010, 371.

cases raising questions of law of general public importance.[15] Unlike the Criminal Division of the Court of Appeal, the Supreme Court, like its predecessor, the Appellate Committee of the House of Lords,[16] does not speak with one voice;[17] a written judgment of the Supreme Court consists of several individual judgments (of each Justice hearing the case), whereby one judgment can usually be singled out as the lead or majority judgment. The Court's decision may be reached either by unanimity or by a simple majority, and 'dissenters' are permitted to write a dissenting opinion. Judgments of the Supreme Court are binding on the Court of Appeal and on the lower courts; lower courts are also bound by the judgments of the Court of Appeal.

4.3 Theoretical Framework: Possible Rationales

The English literature identifies a number of rationales or principles with respect to the question of how to address procedural violations committed in the pre-trial phase of criminal proceedings: the 'reliability' rationale, the 'disciplinary' rationale, the 'protective' (or 'remedial') rationale, and the 'integrity' rationale(s). In particular, such rationales or principles have been used to rationalize the exclusion of unlawfully obtained evidence,[18] although they may also be used to explain the judicial stay of criminal proceedings on account of pre-trial police and/or prosecutorial misconduct.[19] Each of these rationales is examined below, as well as how they relate to one another, while later on in this chapter an attempt will be made to 'make sense' of the legal framework governing the judicial response within the criminal trial to pre-trial procedural violations in terms of those rationales, with reference also to broader objectives of criminal justice. It should be noted at the outset that it is rare for English courts to identify a particular rationale as underlying the exclusion of evidence,[20] while, at first glance, they appear to be more forthcoming as regards the rationale(s) for staying the proceedings on the basis of the abuse of process doctrine. Certainly calls have been made for courts to be more explicit about the rationales that they are advancing, and to be more principled in their approach, given that 'the way in which the exclusionary discretion is exercised

---

[15] s 33 Criminal Appeal Act 1968.

[16] The Supreme Court was established by the Constitutional Reform Act 2005 to assume the judicial functions of the House of Lords. It commenced work on 1 October 2009.

[17] See s 59 Senior Courts Act 1981.

[18] See e.g. Ashworth 1977; Zuckerman 1987; Dennis 1989, 28; Zuckerman 1989, 343–360; Mirfield 1997, 6–33; Duff 2004; Ormerod and Birch 2004, 778–784; Ashworth and Redmayne 2010, 344–348 and 357–362; Roberts 2012a; Dennis 2013; Keane and McKeown 2014, 56–57; and Choo 2015, 171–172 and 185–191.

[19] See e.g. Choo 2008, 106–113; and Martin 2005, 158.

[20] See e.g. Grevling 1997, 676; Mirfield 1997, 23; Ormerod and Birch 2004, 778; Ashworth and Redmayne 2010, 357; Roberts 2012a, 172, 183–184.

inevitably depends upon certain preferences of principle'.[21] Nevertheless, it is important to bear in mind that to apply one rationale or principle may well be to give effect to another.[22]

4.3.1 The Reliability Rationale

Pursuant to the reliability rationale, 'determining the truth of the criminal charges is the sole purpose of the criminal trial, and evidence should be admitted or excluded solely on that basis'.[23] Thus, pursuant to the reliability rationale, if evidence is rendered unreliable by the (unlawful) manner in which it was obtained, it should be excluded;[24] if, however, the reliability of the evidence is not in question, it should *not* be excluded, i.e. it should be admitted. While the first implication of the reliability rationale is relatively uncontroversial (although the question of how unreliable an item of evidence must be in order for it to be subject to exclusion does not lend itself to easy answer), the second is less so.

Closely connected to the (second implication of the) reliability rationale is the 'external' approach, which holds that the exclusion of evidence is never appropriate, since '[s]o long as the relevant evidence is reliable … the court should use it in its primary task of fact finding'.[25] Perhaps not surprisingly, therefore, it has been said of the reliability principle that it is 'not so much a genuine 'principle' as a hard-headed pragmatic preference for receiving relevant information bearing on the issues at trial, almost irrespective of its provenance'.[26] While advocates of an external approach do not condone the non-observance of standards for the conduct of criminal investigation (nor 'deny the need to have and enforce standards for the conduct of criminal investigations',[27] or argue that such non-observance be overlooked), they argue that it should be dealt with elsewhere than within the criminal trial, i.e. 'in a venue *external* to the present trial'.[28] Therefore, what is advocated under an external approach is 'a clear *separation* of functions between the criminal court, whose purpose it is to determine the truth of the charges against the accused, and other agencies such as police disciplinary tribunals, which deal with improprieties by law enforcement officers'.[29] Herein lies a common objection to an

---

[21] Ashworth 1977, 723. See also Duff 2004, 159.

[22] See e.g. Keane and McKeown 2014, 57.

[23] Ashworth 1977, 723.

[24] As a principle *for* exclusion, the reliability principle would better be described as the 'unreliability principle'. See e.g. Keane and McKeown 2014, 56.

[25] Ashworth and Redmayne 2010, 347.

[26] Roberts 2012a, 172.

[27] Ashworth 1977, 725.

[28] Ashworth and Redmayne 2010, 347 (emphasis added).

[29] See Ashworth 1977, 724 (emphasis added). See also Roberts 2012a, 172: 'For reliabilists, impropriety in criminal investigations (no matter how serious) is one thing and the admissibility of reliable evidence at trial is quite another.'

external approach: it assumes that the 'other' mechanisms for addressing pre-trial procedural violations are effective, whereas this is (highly) questionable.[30] The external approach is a manifestation of what Ashworth has called the 'separation thesis',[31] which posits that because the courts are independent of law enforcement agencies, 'any violation of fundamental rights is an entirely separate matter from the admissibility of evidence in a criminal trial and also … that the actions of the police are entirely separate from those of the judiciary'.[32] In short, it posits that 'there is no real connection between the actions of the police in investigating the crime and the court's verdict'.[33] Perhaps the most compelling counter-arguments in this regard are those from 'coherence', for example, the argument that the different stages of the criminal process cannot, or in any case should not, be treated in isolation in view of the *purpose* of (many of) the pre-trial activities of police and prosecutors, which is 'to obtain evidence, or 'leads' that may produce evidence, with a view to constructing a case against a suspect … that will either yield sufficient evidence for a prosecution or lead the defendant to plead guilty'.[34] The separation thesis and its counter-arguments are addressed in the penultimate chapter of this thesis. Suffice to say for now that the separation thesis poses particular problems for the integrity rationale (discussed below),[35] and that the thesis appears to be at its strongest where (pre-trial) procedural violations are committed by an agent of a foreign state.[36]

Other objections to an approach to the question of how to address procedural violations committed in the pre-trial phase of criminal proceedings in which accuracy of decision-making or 'rectitude of decision' (or, in terms of broader objectives of criminal justice: the conviction of the guilty and, correspondingly, the acquittal of the innocent) is the exclusive concern, tend to correspond to the arguments supporting the other rationales (discussed below). Thus, from the point of view of the disciplinary rationale the concern might be that, in the absence of an incentive to do so, the police may be disinclined to observe the boundaries for lawful investigation in the future, whereas from the point of view of the protective rationale, such an approach fails to take 'declared standards for the conduct of criminal investigation', and the rights they serve, seriously.[37] From the point of view of the integrity rationale, such an approach fails to take into account the 'public interest in the quality of the proceedings'.[38]

---

[30] See e.g. Ashworth and Redmayne 2010, 347. See also Mirfield 1997, 22–23; and Ormerod 2003.

[31] Ashworth 2003, 112–115.

[32] Ibid., 112–113. See also Ashworth and Redmayne 2010, 361.

[33] Redmayne 2009, 305.

[34] Ashworth 2003, 113–114.

[35] See Ashworth 2003; and Redmayne 2009, 305–310.

[36] Ashworth and Redmayne 2010, 362.

[37] Ashworth 1977, 729.

[38] Dennis 1989, 30. See also Ormerod and Birch 2004, 782.

4.3.2   The Disciplinary Rationale

Another approach to the question of how to address procedural violations committed in the pre-trial phase of criminal proceedings is that based on the disciplinary rationale. Pursuant to the disciplinary approach, the court should attach a legal consequence to such violations in order to deter future misconduct by the police, i.e. to deter such violations in future proceedings. There are two ways in which a judicial response within the criminal trial could deter future misconduct by the police. First, such a response might deter the individual police officer(s) responsible for the misconduct. A police officer might 'feel aggrieved if his or her efforts were to be thwarted by a stay [of proceedings]' or, it is submitted, by the exclusion of unlawfully obtained evidence, which might 'induce him or her to take greater care in the future'.[39] Secondly, a judicial response within the criminal trial might deter police misconduct in a more general sense, since a judicial policy of excluding unlawfully obtained evidence and/or staying the proceedings might 'result, inter alia, in the formulation of education programmes and administrative directives for the police, leading, in the long term, to some improvement in police practices'.[40] Accordingly, under an approach based on the disciplinary rationale, the judicial response within the criminal trial to pre-trial procedural violations appears to be a didactic tool: its purpose is to 'teach the police a lesson',[41] 'to educate police officers to respect the boundaries of proper conduct'.[42] However, the disciplinary rationale may also cover a slightly different justification for excluding evidence: 'to *punish* an errant law enforcement officer'.[43] It seems that the disciplinary rationale is best served by an exclusionary *rule* entailing automatic exclusion of unlawfully obtained evidence, to send

> an unequivocal message to law enforcement officers that violating or 'bending' the rules to procure evidence is futile, and might even result in the loss of crucial information that could have been obtained through lawful means. Regrettably, some criminals must be allowed to go free when the constable misbehaves or 'blunders', because the deterrent effect of evidentiary exclusion would be jeopardised if the courts started making ad hoc exceptions in individual cases.[44]

Both of the aforementioned justifications for excluding evidence on the basis of the disciplinary rationale have been subject to criticism in the literature. Regarding the first justification, an objection often raised is that the criminal trial is not the appropriate place to discipline or 'educate' the police, since 'the discipline of

---

[39] Choo 2008, 107. Regarding the exclusion of unlawfully obtained evidence, see Mirfield 1997, 20.

[40] Ibid., 107. Regarding the exclusion of unlawfully obtained evidence, see Mirfield 1997, 20.

[41] Ashworth and Redmayne 2010, 344.

[42] Mirfield 1997, 20.

[43] Ashworth 1977, 723 n 2 (emphasis added).

[44] Roberts 2012b, 172.

officers who act improperly is not a proper function of the trial court'.[45] Another objection often raised is more pragmatic in nature; it concerns the ability of the judicial response within the criminal trial (and, in particular, the exclusion of evidence and the stay of proceedings) to actually deter. According to Mirfield, there are three particularly important factors that are likely to affect that judicial response's ability to (actually) deter:

> First, where the substantive rules with which the officer is to be encouraged to comply are vague or complex, or both, the potential for success is thereby reduced. ... Secondly, the judge must make it clear what rule has been broken and that he has excluded the evidence because of that breach. If his reasoning is shrouded in uncertainty, the officer will find it difficult to work out how he meant to react. ... [Thirdly,] [t]he direct recipients of the message, if the evidence is excluded, will be solely the officers involved in the case, while, if a judge's decision not to exclude is overturned on appeal, even they may not receive it. Presumably, more dissemination is required, and this will have to entail some internal police procedure designed to achieve that purpose.[46]

To this list may be added the fact that the gathering of evidence for use it trial may *not* be what is motivating police conduct (rather, it may be 'order maintenance'),[47] and the existence of countervailing influences on police behaviour, such as peer expectations and public pressure.[48] Regarding the second justification for excluding evidence on the basis of the disciplinary rationale—the punishment of an errant law enforcement officer—Roberts has argued, seemingly by way of objection thereto, that it is 'patently dubious', since '[p]olice officers are 'punished' by excluding improperly obtained evidence only in a highly attenuated sense'.[49]

4.3.3 The Protective (or Remedial) Rationale

Yet another approach to the question of how to address procedural violations committed in the pre-trial phase of criminal proceedings is that based on the protective (or remedial) rationale, which sees the judicial response within the criminal trial as (a way of) protecting rights. In advancing this rationale as a novel rationale for excluding unlawfully obtained evidence,[50] Ashworth, writing in 1977, constructed the argument as follows:

---

[45] See e.g. Ashworth 1977, 725: 'Advocates of the reliability principle ... are surely right in their assertion that the discipline of officers who act improperly is not a proper function of the trial court and should be treated as a separate matter for separate prosecution.' See also Mirfield 1997, 22–23.

[46] Mirfield 1997, 21–22.

[47] Ashworth and Redmayne 2010, 344.

[48] See Zuckerman 1987, 59; Dennis 1989, 29.

[49] Roberts 2012a, 173.

[50] Roberts 2012a, 171.

If a legal system declares certain standards for the conduct of criminal investigation—whether they are enshrined in a constitution, detailed in a comprehensive code or scattered in various statutes and judicial precedents—then it can be argued that citizens have corresponding rights to be accorded certain facilities and not be treated in certain ways. If the legal system is to respect those rights, then it is arguable that a suspect whose rights have been infringed should not thereby be placed at any disadvantage: by "disadvantage" is meant ... that evidence obtained by the investigators as a result of the infringement should not be used against the suspect. And the appropriate way of ensuring that the suspect does not suffer this disadvantage is for the court of trial to have the power to exclude evidence obtained by improper methods. The presentation of evidence in court may in this context be viewed as the natural conclusion of a criminal investigation, and it is therefore fitting that the court should protect the defendant from disadvantages resulting from any infringement of his rights during that investigation.[51]

For Ashworth, the primary question was 'whether we are willing to recognise rights in suspects and accused persons and to protect them',[52] and the rationale for excluding unlawfully obtained evidence lies in the need to protect *recognised* rights of the suspect and accused (i.e. the rights underlying *declared* standards for the conduct of criminal investigation). In other words, it lies in the need to 'take rights seriously'.[53] Ashworth's argument appears to be based on the assumption that the declaration by a legal system of standards for the conduct of criminal investigation, 'whether they are enshrined in a constitution, detailed in a comprehensive code or scattered in various statutes and judicial precedents',[54] reflects the desire to *regulate* the exercise of criminal investigation powers (and not merely create and confer on public authorities powers in order to investigate and prosecute crime), with a view

---

[51] Ashworth 1977, 725. See also 733: 'A legal system must reach a decision on an acceptable demarcation between permissible and impermissible methods ... once agreement has been reached the rights which flow from it should be respected and protected. An essential part of taking such an agreement seriously is to protect suspects and accused persons from any disadvantage which results from an infringement of the rights declared or implied. ... where a legal system lays down certain standards or procedures for criminal investigation, it is both appropriate and desirable to protect defendants from any disadvantage resulting from the breach of a declared standard or procedure by excluding the evidence obtained as a result of that breach.' Ashworth continues to favour the protective rationale: see e.g. Ashworth 2003; and Ashworth and Redmayne 2010.

Zuckerman summarizes the argument based on the protective rationale (which he refers to as the 'vindication or remedial theory)' as follows: 'A person has a right not to have his person and premises illegally searched, not to have his possessions illegally seized and not to be unlawfully arrested. It is suggested that by imposing these restrictions the state has staked out the boundaries for lawful access to evidence and has indicated that beyond these limits it is *willing* to forego evidence of crime in *defence* to individual freedom. Consequently, it is said, exclusion of evidence secured through illegal search, seizure and arrest puts the prosecution back in the position where the constitution, or the legislature, meant to put it when it imposed those restrictions: without the evidence.' See Zuckerman 1987, 57.

[52] Ashworth 1977, 735.

[53] Ibid., 731. Ashworth refers to 'the need for a protective principle if a legal system accepts that suspects have rights and that those rights should be taken seriously'.

[54] Ibid., 725.

to safeguarding the rights and interests of individuals. Accordingly, non-observance of *declared* standards for the conduct of criminal investigation 'subverts the values which the standards and procedures for investigation promote'.[55] Nevertheless, Ashworth recognises that not 'every procedure laid down for criminal investigation is intended to protect the liberty of the subject' (individual liberty being, presumably, a value that declared standards for the conduct of criminal investigation promote) and, furthermore, that not 'every breach of a procedure which *is* intended to safeguard liberty in fact does infringe that liberty'.[56] Accordingly, he argues that the 'most appropriate criterion' for the admissibility of unlawfully obtained evidence is a '*qualified* protective principle', whereby 'evidence obtained by means of a departure from a declared standard or procedure *should be liable to exclusion, unless* the court is satisfied that the accused in fact suffered no disadvantage as a result of the breach'.[57] At the beginning of his article, Ashworth defines disadvantage as 'the use of evidence obtained by the investigators as a result of the infringement against the suspect'.[58] What he is likely to have had in mind here is '*forensic* disadvantage', meaning that an accused will not be considered to have suffered any disadvantage as a result of the rights violation if the admission of the evidence obtained thereby did not (materially) increase the chances of conviction.[59] Depending on how this question is approached,[60] an example of a situation in which it may be said that 'the violation of the accused's rights had no material bearing on the conduct or outcome of the proceedings', i.e. the accused did not in fact suffer any disadvantage as a result of the rights violation, is 'where the accused is a hardened professional criminal who does not need custodial advice'.[61] Ashworth and Redmayne cite the example of a suspect who was denied access to

---

[55] Ibid., 729.

[56] Ibid., 729. See also 731: 'On a protective principle ... [t]he triviality or seriousness of the breach is measured according to its consequences for the accused, and the reason behind the particular procedure must be examined. If the procedure was intended not to safeguard individual liberty but rather to ensure the accuracy of the evidence collected, the protective principle does not require the exclusion of evidence obtained in contravention of the procedure: its admissibility should depend purely on its reliability.').

[57] Ibid., 729 (emphasis added). See also 725: 'The protective principle does not necessarily lead to the view that all improperly obtained evidence should be peremptorily excluded.'). See also Ashworth and Redmayne 2010, 347: 'Under the protective rationale the courts will have considerable leeway in deciding whether the evidence in question was obtained as a result of police wrongdoing'.

[58] Ibid., 725: 'by "disadvantage" is meant, here and throughout the article, that evidence obtained by the investigators as a result of the infringement should not be used against the suspect'.

[59] See Roberts 2012a, 179. Giannoulopoulos speaks of the 'evidentiary impact of the rights violation' in this regard. See Giannoulopoulos 2007, 206.

[60] See n 68 and accompanying text.

[61] Roberts 2012a, 179. Other examples are where the evidence fails to withstand cross-examination, where other evidence reliably proves the same point, or where the case as a whole against the accused is overwhelming. Thanks to Professor Paul Roberts for his clarification of this point.

legal advice, but who would have confessed anyway.[62] Another situation in which, in Ashworth's view, the violation of the accused's rights need not lead to the exclusion of the evidence thereby obtained is where the evidence was seized (unlawfully) in order to prevent it from being destroyed. In such circumstances, the 'court might hold that the urgency justified the infringement of the individual's liberty'.[63,64] In conclusion, then, Ashworth advocates an exclusionary discretion based on a qualified protective principle, rather than an exclusionary rule entailing automatic exclusion.[65]

As to the objections to an approach to unlawfully obtained evidence based on the protective principle (some of which clearly correspond to the arguments supporting the other rationales), it has been pointed out that the protective rationale presents problems of definition and width of exclusion. For instance, what rights do 'declared legal standards for the conduct of criminal investigation' purport to protect and do all (such) rights count as 'rights' under the protective rationale?[66] Does the protective principle apply only to criminal process rights, or does it also apply to substantive rights? Ashworth himself recognises the challenges of extending the protective rationale to breaches of (certain) substantive rights: 'It is one thing to say that deprivation of one of the 'fair trial' safeguards in Article 6 [of the ECHR] should usually have a chilling effect on the trial. It is quite another to argue that a breach of Article 8 [of the ECHR]—which declares a general right to respect for private life, not necessarily related to subsequent criminal trials—ought to be accorded the same effect.'[67] A further objection to the 'qualified protective principle' advocated by Ashworth concerns the definition of 'disadvantage'; how is it to be established? As Roberts observes this question can be approached in two ways: by assessing whether the admission of the evidence obtained by the rights violation (materially) increased the chances of conviction *in this particular case*, or by making 'generalized predictions of forensic disadvantage in particular scenarios, e.g. where interrogators employed tactics known to produce false confessions

---

[62] Ashworth and Redmayne 2010, 345. However, see Choo 2015, 103–104, who warns that such reasoning may open the door to 'post hoc rationalization of events'. See also Giannoulopoulos 2007, 206.

[63] Ashworth 1977, 732. However, courts should not 'readily' apply the concept of urgency, since 'the declared rights would stand for less and less'.

[64] Later on in the article Ashworth cites both the concepts of 'no disadvantage/prejudice' and 'urgency' as reasons not to exercise the exclusionary discretion based on the protective principle. See Ashworth 1977, 733.

[65] Ashworth 1977, 733.

[66] See e.g. Dennis 1989, 30. See also Roberts 2012a, critically reflecting on the definition of 'rights' under Ashworth's protective principle.

In England and Wales this appears to be complicated by the fact that Britain does not have a constitutional or codified declaration of individual rights or of standards for the conduct of criminal investigation. See Ashworth 1977, 726; Roberts 2012a, 184.

[67] Ashworth 2003, n 84. At the very least, the protective rationale applies to breaches of criminal process rights and, in particular, those provided for under PACE. See Ashworth and Redmayne 2010, 360. See also Redmayne 2009, 309–310.

(irrespective of the truth of the accused's admissions in the instant case)'. Only the first approach is susceptible to 'harmless error analysis'[68] and herein lies the objection: it allows for the 'post hoc rationalization of events'.[69] Further, Dennis finds it 'hard to see how the law of evidence can be said to be protecting rights, when the mechanism of protection is an exclusionary discretion'.[70] He argues that what is needed in order to protect rights are 'compensatory or punitive remedies which are … available in all cases', and that even if scepticism regarding the effectiveness of such remedies is justified, 'it does not follow that the law of evidence should be asked to do a job for which it is not appropriate'.[71] Finally, advocates of the integrity rationale (more specifically, the 'public attitude' variation thereof) have objected to an approach based on the protective rationale in view of the difficulty inherent in such an approach of 'maintaining a satisfactory balance between illegality and its remedy'. Zuckerman points out that the exclusion of evidence is capable of resulting in the collapse of the case against the accused and his or her acquittal, whereby '[i]t is by no means self-evident that acquittal of the guilty is an appropriate response to earlier police transgressions.'[72]

4.3.4 The Integrity Rationale

Finally, some authors advocate an approach to the question of how to address pre-trial procedural violations based on the integrity rationale. There are a number of variations of this rationale, but the general idea is that the integrity of the administration of justice might be compromised by the admission of unlawfully obtained evidence (or, in the context of the abuse of process doctrine, by allowing the proceedings to continue). Mirfield distinguishes the following variations of the integrity rationale: 'court-centred integrity', 'public conduct integrity' and 'public attitude integrity', whereby the last two constitute the 'public reaction' variations thereof.[73] The basis of the court-centred variation of the rationale lies in 'the moral scruple of the court'[74] and an approach to pre-trial procedural violations based on this variation involves the court taking a moral stance on such conduct and applying its *own* standards of propriety and decency in this regard. In other words, under this conception of the integrity rationale, the judge acts for moral reasons stemming from his or her *own* conscience,[75] whereby the validity of those reasons is

---

[68] See Roberts 2012a, 180.

[69] See Giannoulopoulos, 206, referring to Choo 2006, 44. See also Choo 2015, 104.

[70] Dennis 1989, 30.

[71] Ibid., 30 and 39. See also Dennis 2013, 204–205.

[72] Zuckerman 1987, 58. See also Dennis 1989, 30.

[73] Mirfield 1997, 24–25.

[74] Ibid., 24.

[75] Ibid., 27.

independent of (predicted) public reaction.[76] Those reasons may be based on considerations related to the system of criminal justice as a whole, or on considerations related solely to the court.[77]

The public *conduct* variation of the rationale is based on the assumption that unlawful conduct on the part of public authorities may encourage members of the general public to (also) break the law. Pursuant to this variation, the 'judge should ask himself the question whether exclusion in the particular case would be more likely to increase than decrease lawbreaking'.[78] Finally, pursuant to the public *attitude* variation of the integrity rationale, the court, when deciding whether to exclude unlawfully obtained evidence, 'must seek to gauge how the public will respond in its attitude to the criminal legal system', i.e. it must predict whether exclusion 'would be more likely to enhance rather than reduce the reputation of the administration of justice'.[79] Reputation, it should be noted, cuts two ways: 'disrepute can flow no less from the guilty escaping conviction than from the judiciary putting up with or condoning the unlawful action of law enforcement agencies'.[80] This variation of the integrity rationale, then, requires the court to perform a balancing exercise involving competing public interests, in which a variety of factors may be taken into account (that, as will be seen below, are *not* limited to that which made the use of the evidence problematic in the first place). In response to criticism that this variation of the integrity rationale in particular lacks clarity, Zuckerman has argued that:

> The social need to balance two conflicting constitutional requirements is in itself a powerful engine. Indeed, it is important that the courts should be seen to exercise a balancing jurisdiction, for this will inform the public of the difficulty of choosing between admissibility and inadmissibility [of evidence] and will secure support even from those who might have preferred a different result in an individual case.[81]

More will be said about 'balancing' below.

If the public attitude variation of the integrity rationale involves the court predicting how the public will respond in its attitude to the criminal law system, the question that necessarily arises is *how* courts ought to make such a prediction.[82] In this regard it has been suggested that rather than basing themselves on the attitude

---

[76] Ibid., 24. Mirfield himself seems to favour this variation of the integrity rationale over the others. See ibid., 369–370.

[77] See in this regard Ashworth 2003, 108, where the author refers to 'two varieties of the integrity principle'.

[78] Mirfield 1997, 25.

[79] Ibid., 25.

[80] Ibid., 27.

Ashworth and Redmayne argue that, accordingly, the public attitude variation of the integrity rationale takes 'comparative reprehensibility' as its central element. See Ashworth and Redmayne 2010, 345–346) referring to Kamisar 1987.

[81] Zuckerman 1987, 59. Indeed, as Mirfield points out, Zuckerman appears to favour the public attitude variation of the integrity rationale, as does Dennis. See Mirfield 1997, 27–28.

[82] See generally Mirfield 1997, 33, 368–370.

of the general public itself (for example, by reference to opinion polls), courts should take as their point of departure the 'views of the hypothetical, reasonable, well-informed and dispassionate person in the community'.[83] Dennis freely admits that this person's views are 'a construction of the judiciary themselves',[84] while Mirfield is sceptical in this regard: 'it would seem strange to regard the disrepute in which the administration of justice would be held as properly to be assessed by those who themselves administer it; one's reputation is a reflection of what others think of one'.[85] Choo notes that although it is understandable that references to the 'moral integrity' rationale 'sometimes implicate in some way considerations of the reaction of the public' (given that, 'after all, the criminal law, and its administration, is meant to serve the public interest, and [that] the politics of criminal justice appear to demand that the public be seen to view the system in a good light'),[86] it is important to appreciate the potential dangers of such an approach: losing sight of the 'fundamental point … that it may be inappropriate for a court, whose duty it is to uphold the law, effectively to turn a blind eye to misconduct in the course of enforcing it'.[87] In response to criticism that the integrity rationale does not take rights (sufficiently) seriously, Choo argues that, properly applied, this rationale 'requires important rights to be taken as seriously as would a remedial principle'.[88] In the context of the abuse of process doctrine, he argues that 'there is much to be said for recognizing a rule that, where there is reasonable likelihood that the prosecution would not have been possible but for the breach, in relation to the defendant, of an article of the European Convention on Human Rights that is … directly enforceable in domestic law, the proceedings should be automatically stayed'.[89] In his view, to turn a blind eye to a Convention violation in respect of the defendant that was causal for the proceedings 'must necessarily impugn the moral integrity of the criminal justice system'.[90] Moreover, unlike the remedial principle or protective rationale, the integrity rationale (whichever variation thereof) would

---

[83] Dennis 2013, 108. Similarly Zuckerman argues that in relation to 'considerations such as the likely effect of admissibility or inadmissibility on public sentiment … the courts will have to make a judgment that combines social and moral considerations. They will have to consider what, in a society with high moral standards, should be the public reaction to institutional violations. In other words, decisions will be taken by reference to a normative model as well as a factual one.' See Zuckerman 1987, 64. However, see Ashworth 2003, 110–111; Ashworth and Redmayne 2010, 346.

[84] Dennis 2013, 108.

[85] Mirfield 1997, 369.

[86] Choo 2008, 111.

[87] Ibid., 113.

[88] Choo 2008, 190. Ashworth himself appears to accept that the court-centred variation of the integrity rationale allows for rights to be taken sufficiently seriously. See Ashworth 2003 and also Ashworth and Redmayne 2010, 358. Nevertheless, he favours the protective principle, 'because it chimes better with the notion of human rights'.

[89] Choo 2008, 190. Choo makes a similar argument in the context of the exclusionary discretion under s 78(1) PACE. See Choo 2015, 189–190.

[90] Choo 2008, 190.

appear to apply to the violation of a third party's rights, and to wrongdoing to the defendant on the part of non-state agents.[91]

Under the court-centred variation of the integrity rationale, then, the court acts for reasons that are independent of (predicted) public reaction, whereas under the public reaction variations thereof, it does not. However, if under the public attitude variation of the integrity rationale the likely public reaction is determined by reference to the 'views of the hypothetical, reasonable, well-informed and dispassionate person in the community', which are 'a construction of the judiciary themselves', there may not be much between that variation of the rationale and the court-centred variation thereof. The three variations of the integrity rationale may be (further) distinguished by reference to factors that courts have cited as relevant to decisions on the admission of unlawfully obtained evidence. For example, whereas under the court-centred variation of the integrity rationale the 'cogency of the evidence' should not inform the decision on whether to exclude the (unlawfully obtained) evidence in question,[92] under the public attitude variation it arguably should (or at least *may*). Mirfield explains as follows:

> In the court-centred version, the essence of the objection is to the court joining hands, so to speak, with the officer who conducted himself as he did. It follows that the key time, at which the principle bites, is the time of the unlawful or improper investigative step. With either public reaction version, by contrast, the reaction which the courts have in mind is to the decision made at trial whether or not to exclude the evidence. It will quickly be apparent that cogency is properly a matter which informs a judicial decision predicated upon public reaction, for the spectacle of the guilty going free (because cogent evidence is excluded) is quite capable of having a negative effect upon their perception of the criminal justice system. It seems to be clearly otherwise with court-centred integrity. The acceptability of conduct cannot be changed merely by chance consequences...[93]

Similarly, whereas under the court-centred variation of the integrity rationale the 'seriousness of the offence' should not inform the decision on whether to exclude the (unlawfully obtained) evidence in question,[94] under the public attitude variation it should (or, at least, may) do, although under this variation this factor appears to cut two ways, as Zuckerman observes: 'On the one hand, the more serious the offence, the more difficult it is to justify exclusion and thereby risk acquittal of a guilty and possibly dangerous person. On the other hand, the more serious the consequences of conviction the higher should be the moral rectitude of the means by which it is achieved.'[95] As to the 'seriousness of the breach', this factor may properly inform the decision on whether to exclude the (unlawfully obtained) evidence in question in either approach. As Mirfield explains:

---

[91] Ibid., 110–111. Regarding the breach of a third party's rights, see Ashworth and Redmayne 2010, 347; Redmayne 2009, 310. See also Roberts 2012a, 185.

[92] It is in fact more complicated than this (see Mirfield 1997, 29)

[93] Mirfield 1997, 29.

[94] It is in fact more complicated this (see Mirfield 1997, 32–33).

[95] Zuckerman 1987, 62–63.

> There is a clear moral distinction between the mistaken or ignorant officer and the one who deliberately flouts the law ... This applies no less where the principle is concerned with public reaction than where it is court-centred, for the public is surely able to draw that distinction and will find it relevant to what it thinks of action taken by the court. It would seem no less plain that the seriousness of the breach will be a factor tending towards exclusion, for it must be worse to condone more serious or significant breaches than to condone other breaches.[96]

Taking into account the seriousness of the breach is likely to entail consideration of a wide range of facts and circumstances, such that, any approach to the question of how to address procedural violations committed in the pre-trial phase of criminal proceedings in which this factor is the focus might properly be said to entail the exercise of discretion, if not the performance of a balancing exercise. More will be said about 'discretion' and 'balancing' below.

4.4 Legal Framework

The purpose of this section is to set out the English legal framework governing the judicial response within the criminal trial to procedural violations committed in the pre-trial phase of criminal proceedings. That framework will be set out according to the consequences that the judge may attach to such violations—a stay of proceedings, the exclusion of evidence, sentence reduction and judicial condemnation—as it applies in a purely national context, as well as in an international context. Ultimately, in Sect. 4.5, an attempt will be made to 'make sense' of, or assess, this framework, in terms of the theory set out in the foregoing section.

4.4.1 Procedural Violations in the National Context

4.4.1.1 Judicial Responses

Stay of Proceedings

A judicial stay of criminal proceedings is a procedural remedy by which a prosecution 'which has passed successfully through the relevant filters and actually been brought'[97] is halted by the court, i.e. prevented from proceeding, on the ground that it—the prosecution—amounts to an abuse of process of that court. The power of a

---

[96] Mirfield 1997, 31.
[97] Choo 2008, 11.

court to stay criminal proceedings on such ground is known as the 'abuse of process doctrine' or the 'abuse of process discretion',[98] and it derives from the general responsibility of the court to regulate proceedings.[99] Choo observes that in the determination of whether to stay the proceedings on the basis of the abuse of process doctrine, the court is 'effectively reviewing the exercise of prosecutorial discretion by the executive'.[100] While the notion of the courts reviewing the exercise by the executive of prosecutorial discretion is not uncontroversial, it seems to be established that it is 'well within the province of a court to determine in appropriate circumstances that a prosecution should not have been brought, and to stay the proceedings accordingly'.[101] The question, then, is what those circumstances are. In *R v Horseferry Road Magistrates' Court, Ex parte Bennett*, the leading case on the application of the abuse of process doctrine, Lord Lowry identified two categories of case in which a court has a discretion to stay the proceedings on the ground that to try those proceedings will amount to an abuse of its own process: 'either (1) because it will be impossible (usually by reason of delay) to give the accused a fair trial or (2) because it offends the court's sense of justice and propriety to be asked to try the accused in the circumstances of a particular case'.[102] In that case, the defendant, a citizen of New Zealand, had been arrested in South Africa and forcibly returned to England under the pretext of deporting him to New Zealand via Heathrow, where he was arrested for offences of dishonesty. This was done in (deliberate) disregard of available extradition process, in breach of international law and of the law of the state where the defendant had been found. In that case the majority held that in such circumstances courts should refuse to try the defendant. Lord Lowry put it as follows: 'If British officialdom at any level has participated in or encouraged the kidnapping, it seems to represent a grave contravention of international law, the comity of nations and the rule of law generally if our courts allow themselves to be used by the executive to try an offence which the courts would not be dealing with if the rule of law had prevailed.'[103]

That the abuse of process discretion may be exercised in two broad categories of case has been confirmed in the case law.[104] A stay of proceedings that falls within

---

[98] See Choo 2008, 1. The question of what it means to say that the abuse of process involves the exercise of judicial *discretion* is addressed below, in Sect. 4.4.1.2.

[99] See e.g. Choo 2008, 12. In *Beckford*, the Court of Appeal said that: 'The constitutional principle which underlies the jurisdiction to stay proceedings is that the courts have the power and the duty to protect the law by protecting its own purposes and functions.' *R v Beckford* [1996] 1 Cr App R 94, 100.

[100] Choo 2008, 9.

[101] Ibid., 11.

[102] *R v Horseferry Road Magistrates' Court, Ex parte Bennett* [1994] 1 AC 42, 74.

[103] Ibid., 76 (Lord Lowry).

[104] See e.g. *R v Beckford* [1996] 1 Cr App R 94, 101; *R v Latif; R v Shahzad* [1996] 1 WLR 104, 113 (Lord Steyn); *R (Ebrahim) v Feltham Magistrates' Court* [2001] 1 WLR 1293 [18]–[24]; *R v Maxwell* [2011] 1 WLR 1837 [13] (Lord Dyson), [91] (Lord Brown). It is also widely recognised in the literature. See e.g. Choo 2008; and Rogers 2008.

the first category of case in which a court has the discretion to stay the proceedings seeks to 'ensure that the defendant does not in some way suffer from forensic prejudice or disadvantage at trial with the result that he or she may be unable to defend him- or herself properly, leading to the danger of a factually inaccurate verdict of guilty ensuing',[105] and is accordingly concerned with 'considerations of intrinsic policy',[106] or *epistemic* considerations. In terms of broader objectives of criminal justice, a stay imposed under the first limb of the abuse of process doctrine seeks to protect the accused from wrongful conviction.[107] By contrast, a stay that falls within the second category of case seeks to protect the integrity of the adjudicative process.[108] The need to protect the integrity of the adjudicative process by staying the proceedings may arise in a variety of situations, including cases of serious police and/or prosecutorial impropriety at the investigative stage. The question in such cases is not whether the *impropriety* constituted an 'abuse of process', but rather whether any ensuing *trial* would, in light of the impropriety, amount to an abuse of process.[109] A stay of proceedings imposed under the second limb of the abuse of process doctrine is concerned with 'considerations of extrinsic policy'[110] or of 'public policy', or, *non-epistemic* considerations, and, in terms of broader objectives of criminal justice, it seeks to protect the moral integrity of the criminal justice system generally.[111]

---

[105] Choo 2008, 18. See also Dennis 2003, 227, 230–233: the author describes the first category of case under the abuse of process doctrine as being concerned with 'the equities of the adversarial relationship between prosecution and defendant', 'prejudice to the defence', 'hampering the defendant in the conduct of the defence' and 'prejudice to the defendants in the conduct of their defence'.

[106] Choo 2008, 18.

[107] According to Rogers, it is unfortunate that the first category has been labelled a subspecies of 'abuse of process': 'Sometimes the laws of evidence cannot provide an adequate protection against some prejudice which affects the accused. For example, crucial evidence which defendant A could have used in her defence might have vanished, or defendant B might no longer be able to effectively cross-examine the key witnesses against him, or there might have been such adverse publicity that the defendant cannot get a fair trial anytime or anywhere in the country. The jurisdiction to stay such cases appeals to the values that underpin our broader commitment to factual accuracy, equality of arms in the criminal trial, and to the appearances that a case has been heard by an impartial tribunal. We will always want to recognize this jurisdiction, if not through respect for the importance of fair trials, then at least for the pragmatic reason that stopping the trial before it inevitably leads to an unsafe conviction spares the expense of the trial and appeal process. But it would seem better to conceptualize this as a separate 'jurisdiction to prevent an unsafe conviction'. Then we would more readily recognize it as being nothing more than the weapon of last resort available to all judges and magistrates at all stages of the trial when no lesser means of ensuring a fair trial is sufficient.' See Rogers 2008, 290–291.

[108] Choo 2008, 16 and 109. See also Zuckerman 1989, 344.

[109] See O'Connor 2012, 674. See also Choo 2008, 186: 'courts are not … consistent in their use of the term 'abuse of process'. While it is typically used as a label for *proceedings* which should be stayed, courts have on occasion used it as a label for *particular pre-trial actions* of the executive which should lead to stay'.

[110] Choo 2008, 18.

[111] Ibid., 16 and 109.

Focusing for the moment on the second category of case, it is often pointed out that only in exceptional circumstances will a stay of proceedings be necessary in order to protect the integrity of the proceedings. For example, in *R v Horseferry Magistrates' Court, Ex parte Bennett* Lord Lowry said that, 'prima facie it is the duty of a court to try a person who is charged before it with an offence over which the court has power to try and therefore that the jurisdiction to stay must be exercised carefully and sparingly and only for very compelling reasons'.[112] Indeed, cases that fall into the second category under the abuse of process doctrine appear to be relatively 'uncommon'.[113] According to Lord Lowry, '[t]he discretion to stay the proceedings is not a disciplinary jurisdiction and ought not to be exercised in order to express the court's disapproval of official conduct.'[114] However, such statements should not be taken to mean that 'marking disapproval and discouraging repetition by the grant of stay, are wholly irrelevant'.[115] Rather, they should be taken to mean that a stay should not be granted *purely* for such reasons; indeed, the deterrent potential of a stay may be a 'welcome collateral benefit'.[116] That the disciplinary rationale might be thought to be at the forefront of the appellate courts thinking as regards the second category of case under the abuse of process doctrine is understandable; as Dennis observes, bad faith on the part of the authorities may be a defining characteristic of this category of case.[117] Regarding the overriding criterion for the second type of stay of proceedings, O'Connor observes that this criterion has been formulated in several different ways.[118] In *R v Horseferry Road Magistrates' Court, Ex parte Bennett*, the central criterion was whether 'it offends the *court's* sense of justice and propriety to be asked to try the accused in the circumstances of a particular case',[119] whereas in *Latif; Shahzad* it was 'whether there has been an abuse of process, which amounts to an affront to the *public* conscience'.[120] In *Looseley*, Lord Nicholls said that: 'Ultimately the overall consideration is always whether the conduct of the police or other law enforcement agency was so seriously improper *as to bring the administration of justice into disrepute.*'[121] The implications of these different formulations are discussed below.[122] Finally, it seems that

---

[112] *R v Horseferry Road Magistrates' Court, Ex parte Bennett* [1994] 1 AC 42 at 74.

[113] Dennis 2013, 229.

[114] *R v Horseferry Road Magistrates' Court, Ex parte Bennett* [1994] 1 AC 42 at 74. See also *R v Looseley* [2001] 1 WLR 2060 [17] (Lord Nicholls).

[115] O'Connor 2012, 674.

[116] See e.g. *R v Mullen* [2000] QB 520 at 535–536. See also Choo 2008, 109: 'deterrence is not to be regarded as the rationale, or at least the primary rationale, for a stay'. See also Lord Dyson's comments in *Warren and Others v Attorney General for Jersey* [2012] 1 AC 22 [37].

[117] Dennis 2013, 227, 229–230.

[118] See O'Connor 2012, 673.

[119] *R v Horseferry Road Magistrates' Court, Ex parte Bennett* [1994] 1 AC 42 at 74 (emphasis added).

[120] *R v Latif; R v Shahzad* [1996] 1 WLR 104 at 112 (emphasis added).

[121] *R v Looseley* [2001] 1 WLR 2060 at 25 (emphasis added).

[122] In Sect. 4.4.1.2 and in Sect. 4.5.

until relatively recently, evidential prejudice was not always considered to be a prerequisite for a stay of proceedings under the second limb of the abuse of process doctrine. In *Grant*[123] the defendant had been charged with conspiracy to murder. Before the trial commenced an application was made for the proceedings to be stayed on the basis of the abuse of process doctrine; it was alleged that the police had deliberately eavesdropped upon and recorded privileged conversation between the defendant and his solicitor in the exercise yard of the police station following the defendant's arrest and in parallel with the interview process. However, those recordings had not given rise to evidence to be relied on by the prosecution. The Court of Appeal held as follows:

> We are quite clear that the deliberate interference with a detained suspect's right to the confidence of privileged communications with his solicitor, such as we have found was done here, seriously undermines the rule of law and justifies a stay on grounds of abuse of process, notwithstanding the absence of prejudice consisting in evidence gathered by the Crown as the fruit of police officers' unlawful conduct. ... As for prejudice, it is a particular vice of the police conduct in such circumstances as these ... that the court cannot know whether the police misconduct has in fact yielded fruit in the form of evidence, whether directly or indirectly, without enquiry as to what the covert surveillance revealed; but that would further violate the suspect's right of legal professional privilege.[124]

In doing so, it 'had well in mind' the seriousness of the offence in question. In this case, it could not be said that, but for the serious misconduct the trial would not have taken place (since the recordings had not given rise to evidence to be relied upon by the prosecution), and even still the Court of Appeal was of the view that the proceedings should have been stayed. In earlier cases, however, 'but for' causation appears to have been the central consideration.[125] In *Mullen*, for example, in which the British authorities had 'initiated and subsequently assisted in and procured the deportation of the defendant, by unlawful means, in circumstances in which there were specific extradition facilities', and had, in so doing, acted 'in breach of public international law', the Court of Appeal had held that the proceedings had to be stayed, 'on the basis that, *but for* the unlawful manner of his deportation, he would not have been in this country to be prosecuted when he was, and there was a real prospect that he would never have been brought to this country at all'.[126] In that case also, the Court had 'had well in mind' the seriousness of the offence in question, namely conspiracy to cause explosions likely to endanger life or cause serious injury to property.[127] In cases of entrapment, 'but for' causation

---

[123] *R v Grant* [2006] QB 60. See the following works discussing this (fascinating) case: Choo 2008, 127–129; O'Connor 2012, 674; and Dennis 2013, 344–346.

[124] *R v Grant* [2006] QB 60 [57].

[125] See *Warren and others v Attorney General for Jersey* [2012] 1 AC 22 [27], where Lord Dyson refers to Lord Brown's judgment in *Panday v Virgil (Senior Superintendent of Police)* [2008] AC 1386.

[126] *R v Mullen* [2000] QB 520 at 536 (emphasis added).

[127] Ibid., 535.

lies at the heart of the objection to such conduct: the incitement of the accused to commit an offence *that he or she might not otherwise have committed*. In *Warren and others v Attorney General for Jersey*,[128] a Privy Council case,[129] the Board (the panel of judges hearing the case) expressly distanced itself from the decision in *Grant*,[130] on the basis that it—*Grant*—was not a 'but for' case: the misconduct had caused no prejudice for the accused, it had had no influence on the proceedings at all.[131] However, this should not be taken to mean that the Board was endorsing an approach to the determination of whether the proceedings should be stayed in order to protect the integrity of the adjudicative process whereby 'but for' causation *is* the central consideration. Earlier on in the judgment, the Board said that it did 'not consider that the "but for" test will always or even in most cases necessarily determine whether a stay should be granted on the grounds of abuse of process.'[132] *Warren* itself was a 'but for' case, something that the prosecution in that case had acknowledged all along. In that case it *could* be said that, but for the misconduct of the Jersey Police, which consisted of the use of an audio device, fitted to the hire car of one of the defendants, without the consent of the French and Dutch authorities (which was necessary, because the recordings were going to made of the suspect's conversations on his way to and from the Netherlands, where the Jersey Police thought he was going to pick up a large quantity of drugs to import into Jersey), and deceiving the French authorities when fitting the car with the audio device (telling them that it was a back-up for the tracking device, the use of which the French authorities had not objected to), 'the prosecution in this case could not have succeeded and there would have been no trial unless the police were able to obtain the necessary evidence by other (lawful) means'.[133] Thus, in the Board's view, even in cases in which there can be said to be 'but for' causation, as in *Warren* itself, other factors may well require the court to allow the prosecution to proceed to trial.[134] The Board did not expressly comment on the use of the 'but for' test in cases such as *Mullen* or the entrapment cases, i.e. having held that the 'but for' test was not central to the determination of whether or not to stay the proceedings on the basis of the abuse of process doctrine, it did not then expressly distance itself from such cases. Nor, however, did it endorse it. Rather, it was said that 'in abduction and

---

[128] *Warren and others v Attorney General for Jersey* [2012] 1 AC 22.

[129] The Judicial Committee of the Privy Council (JCPC) is the highest court of appeal for many current and former Commonwealth countries, as well as the United Kingdom's overseas territories, crown dependencies (including Jersey), and military sovereign base areas. See https://www.jcpc. uk/about/role-of-the-jcpc.html. Accessed 1 March 2017. Judgments of the JCPC are not generally binding on courts in England, although they do have significant persuasive authority. See Ward and Akhtar 2011, 79.

[130] *R v Grant* [2006] QB 60. Lord Dyson had already done so in *R v Maxwell* [2011] 1 WLR 1837 [28].

[131] *Warren and others v Attorney General for Jersey* [2012] 1 AC 22 [36] (Lord Dyson).

[132] Ibid., [30] (Lord Dyson).

[133] Ibid., [30], [46] (Lord Dyson).

[134] Rogers is critical in this regard. See Rogers 2011, 7–8.

entrapment cases, the court will generally conclude that the balance favours a stay'.[135]

It is sometimes said that the second category of case in which a court has the discretion to stay the proceedings is concerned with 'fairness to try'.[136] In *Beckford* the Court of Appeal held that proceedings can be stayed on the basis of the abuse of process doctrine in cases where it is impossible to give the accused a fair trial, *and* in cases 'where the court concludes that it would be *unfair* for the defendant *to be tried'*.[137] Insofar as the second category may be said to be concerned with 'fairness to try',[138] the question is whether it would be fair to try someone *at all*, even if they can be given a fair trial. It is this reference to the concept of fairness in both categories of case that 'invites comparison' with the reference to the concept of fairness in Section 78(1) of PACE.[139] More generally the question may arise as to how the power to stay the proceedings relates to the power to exclude evidence under Section 78(1). In the context of entrapment, the House of Lords has held that, as a matter of principle, a stay of proceedings rather than the exclusion of evidence is the appropriate response.[140] However, according to Dennis, outside of this context 'the relationship between the power to exclude evidence and the power to stay the proceedings is somewhat obscure'.[141] There certainly seems to be potential for overlap,[142] although it should be noted that not all cases in which a stay of proceedings is sought raise issues about 'the proper admissibility and use of evidence at trial'.[143] In such cases, the abuse of process discretion will have no competition from the exclusionary discretion under Section 78(1) of PACE. In

---

[135] *Warren and others v Attorney General for Jersey* [2012] 1 AC 22 [26], [36] (Lord Dyson).

[136] See Choo 2008, 18.

[137] *R v Beckford* [1996] 1 Cr App R 94 at 100–101. See also *R (Ebrahim) v Feltham Magistrates' Court* [2001] 1 WLR 1293 [20].

[138] The 'fairness to try' terminology has been subject to criticism. See in this regard Choo 2008, 187): 'It is confusing, to say the least, to use the term 'unfair trial' to connote a trial that has the potential to result in a factually incorrect guilty verdict, and to say that it would be 'unfair to try' a defendant in circumstances where, even if a 'fair trial' can be held, it will nevertheless be inappropriate to try the defendant because of considerations of moral integrity. To make matters even more confusing, the courts sometimes display lack of care in their use of these terms.' In *Warren*, Lord Dyson was similarly critical: 'It is unhelpful and confusing to say that this category [the second category of case under the abuse of process doctrine] is founded on the imperative of avoiding unfairness to the accused. It is unhelpful because it focuses attention on what is fair to the accused, rather than on whether the court's sense of justice and propriety is offended or public confidence in the criminal justice system would be undermined by the trial. It is confusing because fairness to the accused should be the focus of the first category of case.' See *Warren and others v Attorney General for Jersey* [2012] 1 AC 22 [35].

[139] Dennis 2013, 341.

[140] See n 322–323 and accompanying text.

[141] Dennis 2013, 341–342. See also Ormerod and Birch 2004, 782–784.

[142] See e.g. *R v Maxwell* [2011] 1 WLR 1837 [11] (Lord Dyson). See also Mirfield 1997, 152.

[143] See Dennis 2013, 341, referring to *R v Horseferry Road Magistrates' Court, Ex parte Bennett* [1994] 1 AC 42.

cases in which the impropriety in question does raise such issues, where there is little or no other evidence than the evidence obtained improperly, however, the exclusion of such evidence pursuant to Section 78(1) will have the same practical effect as would a stay of proceedings.

Whereas delay[144] and non-disclosure[145] typically raise issues under the first limb of the abuse of process doctrine, disguised extradition[146] and entrapment[147] typically raise issues under the second.[148] However, the two categories are not mutually exclusive, i.e. they may overlap,[149] and a given set of circumstances may warrant consideration under both limbs of the abuse of process discretion. In such cases it is important that the court remains alert to the fact that different considerations apply in each category. Specifically, it is important that it remains alert to the fact that while in the second category of case in which a court has the discretion to stay the proceedings a 'balancing exercise' may be appropriate, in the first it is not.[150] In *Latif; Shahzad*, a conjoined appeal before the House of Lords involving allegations of entrapment, Lord Steyn explained it as follows:

> If the court concludes that a fair trial is not possible, it *will* stay the proceedings. That is not what the present case is concerned with. It is plain that a fair trial was possible and that such a trial took place. In this case the issue is whether, despite the fact that a fair trial was possible, the judge ought to have stayed the criminal proceedings on broader considerations of the integrity of the criminal justice system. ... *Weighing countervailing considerations of policy and justice*, it is for the judge in the exercise of his discretion to decide whether there has been an abuse of process, which amounts to an affront to the public conscience and requires the criminal proceedings to be stayed ... General guidance as to how the discretion should be exercised in particular circumstances will not be useful. But it is possible to say that in a case such as the present the judge must *weigh in the balance* the public interest in ensuring that those that are charged with grave crimes should be tried and the competing public interest in not conveying the impression that the court will adopt the approach that the end justifies any means.[151]

In other words, if the court concludes that a fair trial is not possible, the proceedings must automatically, i.e. without further consideration or 'balancing', stayed. This is

---

[144] See e.g. *R v F* [2011] 2 Cr App R 13, in which it was held that the delay in question meant that a fair trial had not been possible. See further Choo 2008, 90–91. Nevertheless, it is important to note that delay may also raise issues under the second limb. See Choo, ibid., 93.

[145] See e.g. *R v Davis, Rowe and Johnson* [2001] 1 Cr App R 8.

[146] See e.g. *R v Horseferry Road Magistrates' Court, Ex parte Bennett* [1994] 1 AC 42 and *R v Mullen* [2000] QB 520. See further Choo 2008, 113–123.

[147] *R v Looseley* [2001] 1 WLR 2060 [41] (Lord Hoffmann). See also *R v Latif; R v Shahzad* [1996] 1 WLR 104, 112 (Lord Steyn).

[148] This list is not intended to be exhaustive. For an overview of the situations that may give rise to the need to stay the proceedings on the grounds of abuse of process, see e.g. Choo 2008.

[149] See e.g. *R v Beckford* [1996] 1 Cr App R 94 at 101 and *R (Ebrahim) v Feltham Magistrates' Court* [2001] 1 WLR 1293 [18].

[150] On the practice of 'mixing' the considerations applicable under each category in the context of lost and destroyed evidence, see Martin 2005.

[151] *R v Latif; R v Shahzad* [1996] 1 WLR 104, 112–113 (Lord Steyn) (emphasis added).

a reference to the first limb of the abuse of process doctrine, i.e. the ability of the trial to determine the guilt or innocence of the accused properly.[152] Whether the 'forensic' prejudice suffered (i.e. the inability of the trial to determine the guilt or innocence of the accused properly) was caused by a violation of a Convention right, or the conduct that caused the prejudice was deliberate, i.e. whether there was bad faith, is immaterial. However, if the court concludes that it is possible to hold a fair trial, it must then consider whether to stay the proceedings on account of 'broader considerations of the integrity of the criminal justice system', which is often said to involve a balancing exercise.[153] The issue of balancing is addressed in more detail below,[154] but for now it may be noted that this exercise involves taking into account various factors, as relevant to one or both of the competing interests underlying it. Thus, the seriousness of the offence is relevant to the 'public interest in ensuring that those that are charged with grave crimes should be tried', and the seriousness of the conduct of the police or prosecution, including whether one or the other or both have acted in bad faith, is relevant to the 'public interest in not conveying the impression that the court will adopt the approach that the end justifies any means'.[155] While a balancing exercise is not appropriate in the first category of the abuse of process discretion, what *is* appropriate to take into account is whether a 'lesser remedy' suffices, such as the exclusion of certain evidence on which the prosecution proposes to rely.[156] The Administrative Court's comments in *R (Ebrahim) v Feltham Magistrates' Court* are worth noting in this regard:

> The circumstances in which any court will be able to conclude, with sufficient reasons, that a trial of a defendant will inevitably be unfair are likely to be few and far between. The power of a court to regulate the admissibility of evidence by the use of its powers under section 78 of the Police and Criminal Evidence Act 1984 is one example of the inherent strength of the trial process itself to prevent unfairness.[157]

Section 78 of PACE is dealt with below.

Exclusion of Evidence

The legal framework governing the exclusion of unlawfully obtained evidence in England and Wales is complex and, in order to set it out, it is necessary to first explain some general features of the (English) law of evidence. In England and Wales, evidence must be 'sufficiently relevant to be admissible, but sufficiently

---

[152] Choo 2008, 140.

[153] See e.g. *R v Mullen* [2000] QB 520 and *Warren and others v Attorney General for Jersey* [2012] 1 AC 22 [25]–[26]. See also *R v Maxwell* [2011] 1 WLR 1837. The balancing approach for entrapment was refined in *R v Looseley* [2001] 1 WLR 2060. See also Choo 2008, 140–141.

[154] In Sect. 4.4.1.2.

[155] See also O'Connor 2012, 673.

[156] Choo 2008, 186–187, 188–189.

[157] *R (Ebrahim) v Feltham Magistrates' Court* [2001] 1 WLR 1293 [26].

relevant evidence is only admissible insofar as it is not excluded by any rule of the law of evidence or by the exercise of judicial discretion'.[158] In other words, evidence that is not sufficiently relevant is inadmissible, and evidence that *is*, is prima facie admissible.[159] Sufficiently relevant evidence may, however, be made inadmissible on the basis of an exclusionary *rule*. And sufficiently relevant evidence that is admissible (that is, not subject to an exclusionary rule), may be excluded pursuant to an exclusionary *discretion*. However, discretionary exclusion does not render the evidence in question 'inadmissible'.[160] Both exclusionary rules and exclusionary discretions can be found in the common law and in statute. The distinction between rules and discretions is examined below;[161] for now it may be noted that an exclusionary rule represents 'a judgment that the "costs" of the type of evidence in question are sufficiently great to justify a general rule of restriction, rather than an ad hoc decision on the facts of each case'.[162]

In light of the foregoing, the legal framework governing the exclusion of unlawfully obtained evidence in England and Wales can be sketched as follows. English law makes no general provision for the exclusion of relevant evidence on the grounds that it was obtained unlawfully.[163] In other words, as a matter of law, unlawfully obtained evidence that is relevant is prima facie admissible; that is the general rule of law, the point of departure, with respect to unlawfully obtained evidence. According to Keane and McKeown, this general rule of law can be accurately expressed in the terms adopted by Crompton J in *Leatham*: 'It matters not how you get it; if you steal it even, it would be admissible in evidence.'[164] There are, however, (important) exceptions to this principle, in the form of exclusionary *rules* that make prima facie admissible evidence *in*admissible.[165] An example of such a rule is contained in Section 76(2) of PACE, pursuant to which a confession made by an accused that was or may have been obtained by oppression, or in consequence of anything said or done which was likely, in the circumstances existing at the time, to render unreliable any confession which might be made by

---

[158] Keane and McKeown 2014, 28. See also Choo 2015, 2 and 13.

[159] See e.g. Dennis 2013, 64.

[160] See e.g. Mirfield 1997, 122; and Choo 2015, 13.

[161] In Sect. 4.4.1.2.

[162] See Dennis 2013, 88. See also *A v Secretary of State for the Home Department (No 2)* [2005] 3 WLR 1249 [15] (Lord Bingham). Speaking of the common law exclusionary *rule* in respect of confessions, His Lordship said that: '[I]t is in my opinion of significance that the common law has refused to accept that oppression or inducement should go to weight rather than the admissibility of confession. The common law has insisted on an exclusionary rule.'

[163] See e.g. Keane and McKeown 2014, 57; Dennis 2013, 304; and Mirfield 1997, 109.

[164] See Keane and McKeown 2014, 57–58, referring to *R v Leatham* [1861] Cox CC 498 at 501. See also Dennis 2013, 304.

[165] See e.g. Keane and McKeown 2014, 58–59; and Dennis 2013, 307–309.

him in consequence thereof, is inadmissible.[166] In addition, evidence obtained by torture is inadmissible; it falls to be excluded at common law and in accordance with the ECHR.[167] Moreover, unlawfully obtained evidence that is admissible (that is, sufficiently relevant and not subject to any exclusionary *rule*) may nevertheless be excluded pursuant to an exclusionary *discretion*. The exercise of such an exclusionary discretion, then, entails the judge overriding the relevant rules of admission of evidence.[168] Exclusionary discretions can be found in the common law, and in statute. For example, there is a common law discretion to exclude evidence on the basis that its prejudicial effect on the minds of the jury outweighs its probative value,[169] or on the basis of 'unfairness' (or, rather, in fairness to the accused).[170] The common law exclusionary discretion is examined below; for now it may be noted that certain types of evidence, for example, confession evidence and identification evidence, may raise issues under both heads of the discretion. In addition, Section 78(1) of PACE provides for a discretion to exclude evidence if its admission 'would have such an adverse effect on the fairness of the proceedings that the court ought not to admit it'. Section 78 does not (purport to) render obsolete the aforementioned exclusionary *rules*, or the common law exclusionary *discretion*; pursuant to Section 78(2) of PACE, Section 78 operates without prejudice to 'any rule of law requiring a court to exclude evidence', and pursuant to Section 82(3) of PACE, Section 78(1) operates without prejudice to 'any power of a court to exclude evidence … at its discretion. The relationship between Section 78(1) of PACE and the common law exclusionary discretion is examined below, in setting out in more detail the exclusionary rules and discretions referred to above. Those rules and discretions will be set out in the order in which they were brought up, in 'sketching'

---

[166] s 76(2) PACE enacts, in a general sense, a rule established at common law, which was set out as follows in the Judges' Rules, [1964] 1 WLR 152 at 153: 'it is a fundamental condition of the admissibility in evidence against any person, equally of an oral answer given by that person to a question put by a police officer and of any statement made by that person, that it shall have been voluntary, in the sense that it has not been obtained from here by fear of prejudice or hope of advantage, exercised or held out by a person in authority, or by oppression.' Mirfield describes the relationship between s 76(2) and the (old) common law exclusionary rule as follows: 'Briefly put, the oppression head of the common law rule remains, though … its substantive content may have changed. But there has ceased to be any magic in the fear of prejudice or the hope of advantage. That threat or promise element of the old rule is replaced by an unreliability head which requires the court to look directly to the issue of whether or not any confession which the accused might have made in the prevailing circumstances was likely to be rendered unreliable.' See Mirfield 1997, 77.

[167] See *A v Secretary of State for the Home Department (No 2)* [2005] 3 WLR 1249 [51]–[52] (Lord Bingham).

[168] See Tapper 2010, 191.

[169] This 'head' of the common law exclusionary discretion has been recognised since at least the case of R v *Christie* [1914] AC 545. See also Mirfield 1997, 112) and Dennis 2013, 90–91 and 310.

[170] It appears that this head of the exclusionary discretion was first recognized in *Kuruma v R* [1955] AC 197. See in this regard Mirfield 1997, 112; and Dennis 2013, 90–91 and 310–311. See also Keane and McKeown 2014, 60 n 30.

the legal framework governing the exclusion of unlawfully obtained evidence in England and Wales.

A. Section 76(2) of PACE

Section 76(2) of PACE constitutes a statutory *rule* to exclude certain evidence. It provides as follows:

> If, in any proceedings where the prosecution proposes to give in evidence a confession made by an accused person, it is represented to the court that the confession was or may have been obtained—
>
> (a) by oppression of the person who made it; or
> (b) in consequence of anything said or done which was likely, in the circumstances existing at the time, to render unreliable any confession which might be made by him in consequence thereof,
>
> the court shall not allow the confession to be given in evidence against him except in so far as the prosecution proves to the court beyond reasonable doubt that the confession (notwithstanding that it may be true) was not obtained as aforesaid.

Each head of the exclusionary rule—the 'oppression head' and the 'unreliability head', is addressed below. It is important to note that if the matter is not raised by the defence, the court may '*of its own motion*' do so and 'require the prosecution, as a condition of allowing it to [give in evidence a confession made by an accused person], to prove that the confession was not obtained as mentioned in subsection (2)'.[171] In other words, the trial judge may be required to adopt a proactive stance in relation to Section 76(2).[172] It is also important to note, at the outset, that if a confession cannot be excluded pursuant to the exclusionary rule in Section 76(2) of PACE, it may still be possible for it to be excluded in the exercise of discretion, for example, the discretion under Section 78(1) of PACE.[173] Indeed, Section 78(1) also applies to confession evidence, notwithstanding that the admissibility in law of such evidence is governed by another provision. Section 78(1) of PACE is addressed below.

Turning first to the oppression head, it may be noted at the outset that 'oppression' in Section 76(2)(a) is given a restrictive meaning,[174] such that that provision is rarely applied.[175] Section 76(8) of PACE provides that '"oppression" includes torture, inhuman or degrading treatment, and the use or threat of violence (whether or not amounting to torture)'. As this provision provides a partial definition of 'oppression' (after all, it provides that 'oppression' *includes* certain conduct),[176]

---

[171] s 76(3) PACE.

[172] See e.g. Choo 2015, 110.

[173] See e.g. Choo 2015, 100.

[174] See e.g. Choo 2015, 109; and Mirfield 1997, 81.

[175] See e.g. Ashworth and Redmayne 2010, n 164.

[176] See e.g. Dennis 2013, 229; and Tapper 2010, 630.

the question arises as to what other cases might fall within Section 76(2)(a).[177] *Fulling* is the leading case on the oppression head of Section 76(2), and in that case the Court of Appeal held that 'oppression' in Section 76(2)(a) 'should be given its ordinary dictionary meaning', namely '"exercise of authority or power in a burdensome, harsh or wrongful manner; unjust or cruel treatment of subjects, inferiors, etc., or the imposition of unreasonable or unjust burdens"'.[178] In addition, the Court of Appeal drew attention to one of the quotations given in the *Oxford English Dictionary*: '"There is not a word in our language which expresses more detestable wickedness than oppression"'.[179] It added that it would 'find it hard to envisage any circumstances in which such oppression would not entail some impropriety on the part of the interrogator'.[180] On the facts of the case, there had been no oppression within the meaning of Section 76(2)(a): a police officer had told the appellant, who had been charged with obtaining property by deception and who, during persistent questioning, had exercised her right to silence, that her lover was having an affair with another woman, who was in the next cell, whereupon the appellant confessed to the charge, as she thought it was the only way she might be released from custody. While it may be difficult to imagine a situation in which there was oppression without police impropriety, there may be 'oppression without unlawfulness', whereby unlawfulness denotes a breach with a rule, for example, a provision of PACE or a code of practice dealing with the detention, treatment and questioning of suspects by police officers. In this regard Mirfield notes that the police 'are nowhere told that they must not question in a hostile and intimidating way, or solely in order to persuade the bullied suspect to mouth formal acceptance of the police view of the facts'.[181] Accordingly, insofar as oppression entails impropriety, impropriety should not be construed as encompassing only 'unlawfulness'. Conversely, unlawfulness, for example, a breach of PACE or a code of conduct, 'does not, of itself, entail oppression'.[182] It seems that oppression will almost certainly entail bad faith,[183] such that breach of a provision of PACE or a code of practice made in good faith is

---

[177] Dennis 2013, 229.

[178] *R v Fulling* (1987) 85 Cr App R 136 at 142.

[179] Ibid., 142.

[180] Ibid., 142. Nevertheless, questions remain as to how this definition of 'oppression' relates to the partial definition provided for in s 76(8), especially because the Court of Appeal in *Fulling* made no reference whatsoever to the partial definition provided for in s 76(8), a fact that has not gone unnoticed in the literature: see e.g. Keane and McKeown 2014, 386; Dennis 2013, 231; Tapper 2010, 639; and Mirfield 1997, 78.

[181] Mirfield 1997, 82–83. See also Dennis 2013, 232.

[182] Mirfield 1997, 83. Thus the word 'wrongful' in the Oxford Dictionary definition (see n 178 and accompanying text) 'should be understood in the context of the rest of the definition, particularly the words "burdensome" and "harsh" which preceded it and "unjust or cruel treatment" which followed. Otherwise, any breaches of the Code, which might be said to be wrongful, could be said to amount to oppression, which clearly was not so.' See *R v Parker* [1995] Crim LR 1995 233. See also Dennis 2013, 232.

[183] See e.g. Choo 2015, 97; Keane and McKeown 2014, 387; and Dennis 2013, 232.

unlikely to amount to oppression.[184] However, deliberate impropriety will not necessarily amount to oppression within the meaning of Section 76(2)(a). In *Emmerson*, one of the police officers conducting the interview at which the appellant made an admission spoke in a raised voice and swore at the appellant, thereby giving the impression of impatience and irritation, but this did not amount to oppression.[185] The Court of Appeal agreed with the trial judge that to exclude the evidence of the admission 'would be to give oppression a completely false meaning'.[186] By contrast, in *Paris*[187] the conduct in question did amount to oppression. The defendant Miller had been 'bullied and hectored. The officers ... were not questioning him so much as shouting at him what they wanted him to say. Short of physical violence, it is hard to conceive of a more hostile and intimidating approach by officers to a suspect. It is impossible to convey on the printed page the pace, force and menace of the officer's delivery'.[188] In addition, the Court of Appeal attached significance to the length of the interviews: Miller had been interviewed for some 13 hours, spread over five days.[189] Finally, it seems that under Section 76(2)(a), regard should be had to the personal characteristics of the suspect, which may be of 'critical importance' in deciding not only whether there was a causal link between the conduct and the confession (i.e. whether the 'confession was or may have been *obtained ... by* oppression of the person who made it'), but also whether the conduct in question amounted to oppression in the first place.[190]

Turning now to the unreliability head of the exclusionary rule in respect of confessions, pursuant to Section 76(2)(b), the court is required to determine whether 'the confession was or may have been obtained ... in consequence of anything said or done, which was likely, in the circumstances existing at the time, to render unreliable any confession which might be made by him in consequence thereof'. Regarding the phrase 'anything said or done',[191] the Court of Appeal has held that this is limited to something *external* to the person making the confession'.[192] In other words, it does not cover anything said or done *by the person making the confession*. In *Goldenberg*,[193] the appellant had himself asked for an interview, five days after being arrested on a charge of conspiracy to supply diamorphine, seemingly because he wished to obtain bail. It was submitted at trial that the evidence of

---

[184] Dennis 2013, 232.

[185] *R v Emmerson* (1991) 92 Cr App R 284.

[186] Ibid., 287.

[187] *R v Paris* (1993) 97 Cr App R 99.

[188] Ibid., 103.

[189] Accordingly, the 'physical and temporal' circumstances may also come into it. See in this regard Mirfield 1997, 84−85.

[190] See Keane and McKeown 2014, 387; and also Mirfield 1997, 85, referring to *R v Paris* (1993) 97 Cr App R 99 and *R v Seelig* [1992] 1 WLR 148.

[191] Interestingly, while Choo says that it has been interpreted strictly (see Choo 2015, 98, 109), Keane and McKeown say that it has been interpreted widely (see Keane and McKeown 2014, 389).

[192] *R v Goldenberg* (1989) 88 Cr App R 285 at 290 (emphasis added).

[193] *R v Goldenberg* (1989) 88 Cr App R 285.

the interview should be excluded pursuant to Section 76(2)(b) since the confession might have been made in consequence of what the appellant had himself said or done and his words or actions might indicate that his confession was or might be unreliable. In other words, no reliance was placed (by defence counsel at trial) on anything said or done by the interviewing officer. That argument was rejected and on appeal it was held that the trial judge's ruling in this regard had been correct.[194] In *Crampton*, the Court of Appeal expressed doubt as to whether 'the mere holding of an interview at a time when the appellant is withdrawing from the symptoms of heroin addiction is something which is done within the meaning of Section 76(2)', since 'the words of the subsection seem to postulate some words spoken by the police or acts done by them which were likely to induce unreliable confessions'.[195] Nevertheless, it appears that the phrase 'anything said or done' is not limited to things said or done by a police officer or persons in authority more generally.[196] Moreover, while the phrase certainly appears to cover inducements, it covers more besides. Thus, a breach of a provision of PACE or its codes of practice, for example, the unlawful denial of access to legal advice, may amount to something 'said or done' for the purposes of Section 76(2)(b),[197] although impropriety is by no means a requirement in this regard.[198] Nor is *deliberate* impropriety, i.e. a breach made in bad faith, required.[199] Nevertheless, as Mirfield observes, breaches of PACE and/or its codes of practice 'will be present in the vast majority of cases where Section 76(2)(b) is relied upon, precisely because very many of their provisions are designed to ensure reliability'.[200] Moving on to the requirement of a causal link between what was 'said or done' and the confession, there are indications in the case law that, in order for it to be able to be said that there exists such a link, whatever was 'said or done' need not be the dominant, let alone sole, reason for the decision to confess.[201] In other words, if other factors than the thing 'said or done' by the police have contributed to the decision to confess, for example, the accused's own desire and belief, it may still be possible to speak of a causal link between 'that thing' and the confession, particularly if 'that thing' involves mention of the prospect of bail.[202] However, if the motive of the accused to confess was

---

[194] Mirfield is critical in this regard, although he concedes that *Goldenberg* does 'establish the proposition that self-induced confessions are not caught by Section 76(2)(b)'. See Mirfield 1997, 90.

[195] *R v Crampton* (1991) 92 Cr App R 369 at 372.

[196] See e.g. Mirfield 1997, 88; Dennis 2013, 238; and Keane and McKeown 2014, 389.

[197] See *R v McGovern* (1991) 92 Cr App R 228.

[198] See e.g. *R v Fulling* (1987) 85 Cr App R 136 at 142: 'What however it abundantly clear is that a confession may be invalidated under Section 76(2)(b) where there is no suspicion of impropriety'. See also Mirfield 1997, 91–93; Keane and McKeown 2014, 393; and Dennis 2013, 236.

[199] See e.g. Dennis 2013, 236.

[200] Mirfield 1997, 91. See however Dennis 2013, 238–239.

[201] See e.g. Mirfield 1997, 105.

[202] See *R v Barry* [1992] 95 Cr App R 384. See also Mirfield 1997, 105, where the author discusses this case, and see also Ashworth and Redmayne 2010, 110–111.

prompted *wholly* by self-generated hope of release (or a lighter sentence), it will not be possible to speak of such a link.[203] Further, Section 76(2)(b) requires the trial court to have regard to 'the circumstances existing at the time' in determining whether what was said or done was likely to render unreliable any resulting confession. This includes the defendant's personal characteristics, for example, his or physical condition and emotional state.[204] Finally, the Court of Appeal has held that an unreliable confession within the meaning of Section 76(2)(b) is one which 'cannot be *relied upon* as being the truth'.[205] In other words, for the purposes of Section 76(2)(b), an unreliable confession is not one which is in fact unreliable. This is apparent from the words 'notwithstanding that it may be true' in Section 76 (2). Pursuant to that provision, the question that the court should ask itself is whether *any* confession that the accused might have made at the point at which the actual confession was made was likely to be unreliable as a result something said or done.[206] Accordingly, Section 76(2)(b) is concerned with *hypothetical* unreliability, rather than *actual* unreliability.[207] According to Dennis, it follows that 'because the court is dealing only with the hypothetical issue at the particular moment in the interview, the prosecution cannot overcome problems about the reliability of a confession by using extrinsic evidence that is likely to be true'.[208]

Two final issues require consideration: the question of admissibility of 'subsequent confessions', i.e. of a properly obtained confession, which repeats an unlawfully obtained confession that is inadmissible pursuant to Section 76(2) of PACE, and the question of admissibility of real evidence discovered as a result of a confession that is inadmissible pursuant to Section 76(2). As to the first issue, the Court of Appeal does *not* recognise a rule that confessions rendered inadmissible by oppression within the meaning of Section 76(2)(a) 'must inevitably be a continuing blight on any subsequent confessions'.[209] In other words, whether the oppressive conduct that rendered an earlier confession inadmissible 'taints' any subsequent confession made by the accused such as to require its exclusion depends on the

---

[203] Such reasoning appears to underlie the decision in *R v Crampton* (1991) 92 Cr App R 369. See also Mirfield 1997, 104.

[204] See e.g. *R v McGovern* (1991) 92 Cr App R 228. See also Mirfield 1997, 93–95; Keane and McKeown 2014, 392–393; and Choo 2015, 99.

[205] *R v Crampton* (1991) 92 Cr App R 369 at 372 (emphasis added).

[206] See e.g. Dennis 2013, 234. The Court of Appeal has clarified this in a number of cases. See e.g. *R v Barry* [1992] 95 Cr App R 384 at 389.

[207] Ashworth and Redmayne 2010, 109.

[208] Dennis 2013, 234–235. See also Ashworth and Redmayne 2010, 109–110, where the authors suggest that the reason for being concerned with hypothetical unreliability 'is presumably that the provision is intended to sanction bad questioning practices, even if they produce a confession which can proven to be reliable, for example, by evidence corroborating it or even a further admission by the defendant'.

[209] *R v Glaves* [1993] Crim LR 685 at 686.

particular facts of the case.[210] As to the unreliability head of the exclusionary rule for confessions, in *McGovern*[211] the Court of Appeal held that the circumstances under which the earlier confession had been made (the absence of a solicitor during the interview in breach of PACE) were not only such that they required exclusion of *that* confession under the unreliability head of Section 76(2); the 'more coherent' confession made by the accused the following day in the presence of her solicitor also required exclusion under that head.[212,213] It is important to note that even if a 'subsequent confession' cannot be excluded under Section 76(2), it may still be possible for it to be excluded under Section 78(1) of PACE.[214] The exclusionary discretion under Section 78(1) is examined below, including the question of whether the exclusion of the initial confession pursuant to Section 78(1) leads to the exclusion of the subsequent confession.

As to the second issue, the admissibility of real evidence discovered as a result of an inadmissible confession, Section 76 provides in relevant part that:

(4) The fact that a confession is wholly or partly excluded in pursuance of this section shall not affect the admissibility in evidence—

(a) of any facts discovered as a result of the confession; ...

[...]

(5) Evidence that a fact to which this subsection applies was discovered as a result of a statement made by an accused person shall not be admissible unless evidence of how it was discovered is given by him or on his behalf.

Thus, pursuant to Section 76(4)(a), derivative evidence constitutes admissible evidence; facts discovered as a result of the inadmissible confession are prima facie admissible at law. As Dennis points out, there is thus no 'fruit of the poisonous tree' doctrine in English law.[215] However, pursuant to Section 76(5), the prosecution is forbidden from introducing evidence that such facts were discovered as a result of the inadmissible confession.[216] And this prohibition has the ability to impact on the relevance of the derivative evidence in question, which goes to the admissibility thereof.[217] As Dennis explains:

... the facts in question [i.e. the facts discovered as a result of the inadmissible confession] must satisfy the normal rules of admissibility, including of course the requirement of relevance. In order to be relevant to the issue of the accused's guilt, the facts must tend to incriminate the accused. If they cannot do this without reference to the inadmissible

---

[210] See also Dennis 2013, 227: The decision in *Glaves* suggests that it will be 'a question of fact in each case whether earlier oppression continues to operate on the defendant's mind'.

[211] *R v McGovern* (1991) 92 Cr App R 228.

[212] Ibid., 234.

[213] For a discussion of *Glaves* and *McGovern*, see Mirfield 1997, 106–107.

[214] See e.g. *R v Ismail* [1990] Crim LR 109. See in this regard Mirfield 1997, 107–108.

[215] Dennis 2013, 250.

[216] The defence may, though.

[217] See n 158 and accompanying text.

confession, they cannot affect the issue one way or the other and will be inadmissible as part of the prosecution case.[218]

In view of the fact that the prosecution may not introduce evidence that the facts in question were discovered as a result of the inadmissible confession, 'derivative evidence will in many cases be of little or no use to the prosecution'.[219] In cases in which it *is* of use to the prosecution, it should be noted that it may still be possible for the evidence of facts discovered as a result of the confession to be excluded pursuant to Section 78(1) of PACE.[220]

B. Exclusion of evidence obtained by torture

Another exclusionary rule in the context of unlawfully obtained evidence concerns evidence obtained by torture. In *A v Secretary of State for the Home Department (No 2)* the House of Lords held that 'evidence obtained by torturing another human being may [not] lawfully be admitted against a party to proceedings in a British court, irrespective of where, or by whom, or on whose authority the torture was inflicted'.[221] In other words, evidence obtained by torture is inadmissible in judicial proceedings in England and Wales. Lord Bingham, with whom the other six Lords agreed (on the point of admissibility of evidence obtained by torture, at least),[222] said that:

> The principles of the common law, standing alone, in my opinion compel the exclusion of third party torture evidence as unreliable, unfair, offensive to ordinary standards of humanity and decency and incompatible with the principles which should animate a tribunal seeking to administer justice. But the principles of the common law do not stand alone. Effect must be given to the European Convention, which itself takes account of the all but universal consensus embodied in the Torture Convention. The answer to the central question posed at the outset of this opinion is to be found not in a governmental policy, which may change, but in law.[223]

---

[218] Dennis 2013, 250. This was the principle established in *R v Warickshall* (1783) 1 Leach CC 263. Regarding *Warickshall* and the position at common law with respect to facts discovered in consequence of an inadmissible confession, see also Keane and McKeown 2014, 420; and Choo 2015, 114.

[219] Choo 2015, 115–116. See also Keane and McKeown 2014, 421: 'proof that the stolen goods were hidden in a particular place, without reference to the confession, will do little or nothing to advance the prosecution case unless, as it happens, there is some link between the accused and the goods, because, for example, they were found at a place frequented by him, such as his house or place of work, or bore his fingerprints'.

[220] See Choo 2015, 116; and Mirfield 1997, 225.

[221] *A v Secretary of State for the Home Department (No 2)* [2005] 3 WLR 1249 [51] (Lord Bingham). For a detailed discussion of the case, see e.g. Roberts 2012b, 169–177.

[222] However, their Lordships were divided on the issue of the burden of proof that should apply in proceedings before the Special Immigration Appeals Commission.

[223] *A v Secretary of State for the Home Department (No 2)* [2005] 3 WLR 1249 [52].

In concluding that evidence obtained by torture is inadmissible, the House of Lords relied primarily on the common law.[224]

Lord Bingham's speech refers to 'evidence obtained by torturing another human being' and 'torture evidence' (and elsewhere reference is made to the 'fruits of torture'), which raises the question of whether the exclusionary rule extends to real evidence obtained by torture. For example, the accused or a third party may have been tortured into revealing the whereabouts of real evidence that incriminates the accused, which the prosecution then seeks to rely on. However, *A v Secretary of State for the Home Department (No 2)* does not provide an unequivocal answer to this question.[225] While both Lord Bingham and Lord Hoffmann cite the case of *Warickshall*[226] as establishing the principle that 'while an involuntary statement is inadmissible real evidence which comes to light as a result of such statement is not',[227] as Dennis observes, that case did not involve torture.[228] Lord Hoffmann himself appears to have had doubts about the applicability of that principle to cases in which real evidence has been obtained in consequence of a statement made under torture,[229] although he said that 'even when the evidence has been obtained by torture … that evidence may be so compelling and so independent that it does not carry enough of the smell of the torture chamber to require its exclusion'.[230]

Regarding evidence obtained by inhuman or degrading treatment, Lord Bingham said that:

> Ill-treatment falling short of torture may invite exclusion of evidence as adversely affecting the fairness of a proceeding under section 78 of the 1984 Act, where that section applies. But I do not think the authorities on the Torture Convention justify the assimilation of these two kinds of abusive conduct. Special rules have always been thought to apply to torture, and for the present at least must continue to do so. It would, on the other hand, be wrong to regard as immutable the standard of what amounts to torture.[231]

In other words, the exclusionary rule recognised in *A v Secretary of State for the Home Department (No 2)* does not extend to evidence obtained by inhuman or degrading treatment.

---

[224] Ibid., [52] (Lord Bingham).

[225] According to Lord Hoffmann, that was not the question in this case: 'We are concerned with the admissibility of the raw product of interrogation under torture.' *A v Secretary of State for the Home Department (No 2)* [2005] 3 WLR 1249 [88].

[226] *Warickshall* (1783) 1 Leach 263.

[227] *A v Secretary of State for the Home Department (No 2)* [2005] 3 WLR 1249, [16], [87]–[88].

[228] See also Dennis 2013, 308–309. See however Loof 2011, 52.

[229] *A v Secretary of State for the Home Department (No 2)* [2005] 3 WLR 1249 [87].

[230] Ibid., [88].

[231] Ibid., [53]. See also [97] (Lord Hoffmann).

C. Common Law Exclusionary Discretion

As stated above, there is a common law discretion to exclude evidence on the basis that its prejudicial effect (on the minds of the jury) outweighs its probative value, or on the basis of 'unfairness'. Regarding the first head, Dennis explains that evidence is unduly prejudicial 'if its use at trial would tend to leave the factfinder to convict the accused for reasons other than the proper probative value of the evidence'.[232] According to Keane and McKeown, this head of the exclusionary discretion should be exercised in those cases in which there is 'a serious risk that the jury will attach undue weight to an item of evidence which is, in reality, of dubious reliability or of no more than trifling or minimal probative value'.[233] In *Sang*, this head of the common law exclusionary discretion, which was unanimously affirmed by the House of Lords in that case, was founded on the duty of the trial judge to ensure that the accused receives a fair trial, by ensuring the fair use of evidence at trial.[234] This head, then, is concerned with the preservation of the fairness of the trial itself,[235] rather than the fairness of the pre-trial phase, suggesting that it has limited application in the context of unlawfully obtained evidence[236] (here it should be recalled that the fact that evidence has been obtained unlawfully, won't necessarily cast doubt on its reliability; indeed, in many cases the quality of the evidence concerned will be unaffected by the manner of its obtaining). As Dennis observes, a more appropriate head of discretion to consider in such cases, is based on fairness to the accused.[237] Some early cases support the existence of such a head; the dicta contained therein refer to the fair treatment of the accused in the evidence-gathering process.[238] Regarding the 'unfairness' head of the common law exclusionary discretion, Lord Diplock, in answering the certified question before the House of Lords in *Sang* (namely: 'Does a trial judge have a discretion to refuse to allow evidence—being evidence other than evidence of admission—to be given in any circumstances in which such evidence is relevant and of more than minimal probative value?'),[239] said that: 'Save with regard to admissions and confessions and generally with regard to evidence obtained from the accused after commission of the offence, [the trial judge] has no discretion to refuse to admit relevant admissible evidence on the

---

[232] Dennis 2013, 91.

[233] Keane and McKeown 2014, 48.

[234] *R v Sang* [1980] AC 402 HL, 436–437 (Lord Diplock). See also Dennis 2013, 90 and 312.

[235] See e.g. Mirfield 1997, 131; and Dennis 2013, 90–92.

[236] It also suggests that the discretion at common law to exclude evidence is not restricted in its scope of application to *unlawfully obtained* evidence. See in this regard Dennis 2013, 90–91.

[237] Dennis 2013, 310. In fact, this head is 'almost exclusively concerned with evidence obtained by illegal or unfair means'. See ibid., 91.

That the common law exclusionary discretion has two 'heads' is widely recognized. See (also) Mirfield 1997, 111–114; Ormerod and Birch 2004, 770; Tapper 2010, 196–198; and Keane and McKeown 2014, 395.

[238] See n 170 and accompanying text.

[239] *R v Sang* [1980] AC 402, 424.

ground that it was obtained by improper or unfair means.'[240] While this view of the unfairness head is widely acknowledged to be restrictive,[241] on account of the types of evidence identified by Lord Diplock as falling under the unfairness head of the exclusionary discretion and of the rationale identified by his Lordship for the exclusion of unlawfully obtained evidence, namely, that of the privilege against self-incrimination,[242] which effectively meant that the discretion would be unavailable in respect of a wide range of impropriety (including entrapment and unlawful searches),[243] according to Dennis it also constituted the

> ... first clear acknowledgement at the highest judicial level in England that the common law ought to have concerns that go further than the quality of the evidence adduced at trial, and how the evidence might be used or misused by the factfinder. Although the general stance was maintained that the courts were not concerned with the means of obtaining evidence, the exception allowed that this could not be absolute.[244]

Nevertheless, as stated above, this view of unfairness is widely regarded as being restrictive, and *Sang* has been subject to robust criticism in the literature for its lack of clarity and guidance, especially as regards the unfairness head of the common law exclusionary discretion.[245]

It was stated above that PACE expressly preserves the common law exclusionary discretion, by virtue of Section 82(3) of the Act. This raises the question of how the exclusionary discretion under Section 78(1) of the Act relates to that under the common law. To begin with, it should be noted that the terms of Section 78(1) appear wide enough to cover both heads of the common law exclusionary discretion: unreliability and unfairness.[246] Further, it has been observed in the literature that 'since PACE came into force, there has been very little reference to s. 82(3),

---

[240] Ibid., 437 (Lord Diplock). Two points should be made here. First, although all members of the House approved of this formulation, 'the actual speeches of their Lordships added significant glosses thereto which are inconsistent with each other'. See Mirfield 1997, 116. Second, this formulation is, strictly speaking, obiter dictum. Nevertheless, 'it has had a very powerfully persuasive effect'. See Tapper 2010, 196.

[241] See e.g. Grevling 1997, 668; Ormerod and Birch 2004, 771–772; Tapper 2010, 202; Dennis 2013, 91–92 and 317; and Choo 2015, 101.

[242] *R v Sang* [1980] AC 402, 435 and 436 (Lord Diplock).

[243] Indeed, Lord Diplock expressly linked the unavailability of the discretion in cases involving evidence obtained by an unlawful search to what in his view was the underlying rationale for exclusion on the grounds of unfairness: that of the privilege against self-incrimination. See *R v Sang* [1980] AC 402, 436.

[244] Dennis 2013, 92.

[245] The relevant parts of their Lordships' opinions are not easy to reconcile and subsequent cases did not clarify the ruling on the unfairness head. See e.g. Grevling 1997, 668–669; Mirfield 1997, 116–120; Ormerod and Birch 2004, 771–772; Tapper 2010, 202; and Dennis 2013, 92 and 311–316. According to Mirfield, '[o]n balance, it seems right to conclude that the unfairness discretion at common law is reasoned in the way suggested by Lord Diplock in *Sang*', who, it should be recalled, identified as the underlying rationale of the unfairness discretion that of the privilege against self-incrimination. See Mirfield, Ibid., 119.

[246] See e.g. Keane and McKeown 2014, 51 and 65; and Mirfield 1997, 120 n 68 and 121.

and no attempt at all to clarify more precisely the scope and limits of the discretion at common law to exclude evidence'.[247] It seems, therefore, that the common law exclusionary discretion, or at least the unfairness head thereof, has been absorbed by Section 78(1).[248] The question, then, is whether Section 78(1) is merely a restatement of the position adopted in *Sang* in relation to the unfairness head of the common law exclusionary discretion, or, rather, an enlargement thereof.[249] This issue is examined below.

D. *Section 78(1) of PACE*

Section 78(1) of PACE provides as follows:

> In any proceedings the court may refuse to allow evidence on which the prosecution proposes to rely to be given if it appears to the court that, having regard to all the circumstances, including the circumstances in which the evidence was obtained, the admission of the evidence would have such an adverse effect on the fairness of the proceedings that the court ought not to admit it.

In order to address the question raised above, i.e. whether the exclusionary discretion under Section 78(1) is a restatement or an enlargement of that under the common law (as set out in *Sang*), it is necessary to examine the case law on Section 78(1), as regards the question of when pre-trial procedural violations will be considered to have such an adverse affect on the fairness of the proceedings that the evidence obtained thereby ought to be excluded. Before doing so, however, some issues of a more practical nature need to be addressed. To begin with, it should be noted that, like the common law exclusionary discretion,[250] Section 78 (1) is not limited in its application to *unlawfully obtained* evidence;[251] its scope of application is wider than that. For example, it also applies to otherwise admissible

---

[247] See e.g. Dennis 2013, 93 and 316. See also Mirfield 1997, 120 n 68; and Choo 2015, 101.

[248] According to Dennis, it is 'unclear after PACE whether this head of the discretion [the unreliability head, pursuant to which evidence should be excluded if its probative value is outweighed by its prejudicial effect on the minds of the jury] has been absorbed by the general discretion under s. 78, or whether it has been preserved as a separate head of discretion by s. 82 (3)'. By contrast, it seems 'to have been generally assumed that the discretion discussed in *Sang*, founded on fairness to the accused, has been absorbed into the discretion under s. 78 to safeguard the fairness of the proceedings.' See Dennis 2013, 73, 100 n 163 and 316; and Keane and McKeown 2014, 402.

[249] See e.g. Dennis 2013, 316. See also Ormerod and Birch 2004, 775.

[250] See n 236 and accompanying text.

[251] This is confirmed in the case law: see e.g. *R v Samuel* [1988] QB 615 at 630: 'It is undesirable to attempt any general guidance as to the way in which a judge's discretion under Section 78 or his inherent powers should be exercised. Circumstances vary infinitely. … Mr. Jones has made the extreme submission that, in the absence of impropriety, the discretion should never be exercised to exclude admissible evidence. We have no hesitation in rejecting that submission, although the propriety or otherwise of the way in which the evidence was obtained is something which a court is, in terms, enjoined by the section to take into account.' See also Dennis 2013, 89, 98–99; and Keane and McKeown 2014, 51 and 402.

hearsay evidence.[252] Moreover, it is not restricted in its application to evidence whose admissibility is not governed by any other provision.[253] Accordingly, it also applies to confession evidence, whose admissibility *in law* is governed by Section 76(2) of PACE.[254] Section 78(1) only applies to evidence on which the *prosecution* proposes to rely; thus, it does not apply to evidence tendered by the defence.[255] The question of exclusion may be raised by the accused, while the judge is under no duty to raise the issue if the defence, for whatever reason, does not.[256] It is unclear where the burden of proof lies in the context of Section 78(1), if it lies anywhere at all, given that the terms of that provision are 'wide enough for its exercise on the court's own motion'.[257] Accordingly, it appears that the provision is neutral as between the parties.[258] Finally, the fact that Section 78(1) confers on the trial judge a *discretion* to not admit evidence on which the prosecution proposes to rely, means that the Court of Appeal will only interfere with the trial judge's decision in this regard in limited circumstances, according to *Wednesbury* principles, i.e. where the decision is one which no reasonable court could have come to.[259] The issue of discretion in the context of Section 78(1) is addressed in more detail below;[260] suffice to say for now that the reluctance of the appellate courts to interfere with the trial judge's exercise of discretion under Section 78(1) should be borne in mind when attempting to 'make sense' of the appellate case law in terms of the rationales for excluding evidence, and of broader objectives of criminal justice more generally.

Given that Section 78(1) may be used to exclude unlawfully obtained evidence, the question arises as to *when* unlawfulness will be considered to have such an adverse effect on the fairness of the proceedings that the evidence obtained thereby ought to be excluded. It was stated above that the powers of the police in England and Wales to investigate crime are now to a large extent regulated by statute. For example, the Police and Criminal Evidence Act 1984 deals with powers to stop and search, powers of entry, search and seizure, arrest and detention, and questioning and treatment of persons by the police, including searches of detained persons, intimate searches and access to legal advice. This statute is supplemented by a number of codes of practice, which further regulate the aforementioned areas. In addition, by virtue of the Human Rights Act 1998, public authorities, including the police, the

---

[252] See e.g. *R v Horncastle* [2009] UKSC 14 [28]. See also Dennis 2013, 98–99; and Keane and McKeown 2014, 64.

[253] See e.g. Dennis 2013, 318.

[254] See e.g. *R v Keenan* [1990] 2 QB 54 at 62. See also Mirfield 1997, 121, referring to the earlier cases of *R v Mason* [1988] 1 WLR 139 and *R v Samuel* [1988] QB 615.

[255] See e.g. Dennis 2013, 103, 318; and Keane and McKeown 2014, 64.

[256] See e.g. Keane and McKeown 2014, 63. See also Dennis 2013, 103 and 318.

[257] *R (Saifi) v Governor of Brixton Prison* [2001] 1 WLR 1134 [52].

[258] Ibid., [52]. See also Dennis 2013, 318.

[259] See Dennis 2013, 103–104, 318. See also Keane and McKeown 2014, 65; and Mirfield 1997, 123–124.

[260] In Sect. 4.4.1.2.

Crown Prosecution Service and 'courts and tribunals', in England and Wales are required to act in a way which is compatible with the ECHR rights.[261] The question that naturally arises is whether a breach of the provisions of PACE or of its codes of practice, or of a provision of the ECHR will be considered to have such an adverse effect on the fairness of the proceedings that any evidence thereby obtained ought to be excluded. Turning first to breaches of PACE and/or its codes of practice, the short answer is that such a breach will *not* always result in the exclusion of the evidence obtained thereby. In other words, exclusion is not automatic in respect of evidence obtained by breach of a provision of PACE and/or its codes of practice.[262] A preliminary question is often whether the breach is 'significant and substantial'; only if the breach can be qualified as such will it be likely to have such an adverse effect on the fairness of the proceedings that the evidence obtained thereby ought to be excluded.[263] It seems that a breach of the right of access to legal advice, as provided for in Section 58 of PACE, will be considered to qualify as 'significant and substantial'.[264] In *Absolam*, the failure to inform the suspect of his right to consult a solicitor 'and the initiation of a course of very pertinent questioning at a time when he had not had the opportunity of obtaining that advice' was held to amount to a 'significant and substantial' breach of Code C (the Code of Practice for the Detention, Treatment and Questioning of Persons by Police Officers).[265] In addition, the breach of the 'anti-verballing' provisions, i.e. the requirements pertaining the duty of the police to make an accurate record of each interview with a suspect, for example, of the requirement of making a contemporaneous record of the interview, of recording the reason for not doing so, and/or of giving the defendant the opportunity to read the record and comment on its accuracy, may amount to a 'significant and substantial' breach of Code C.[266] The failure to caution the suspect prior to questioning may, in the circumstances, also amount to a significant and substantial breach of Code C.[267] However, not every breach of Code C, which

---

[261] See s 6(1) HRA

[262] See e.g. *R v Delaney* (1989) 88 Cr App R 338 at 341, and also *R v Parris* (1989) 89 Cr App R 68 at 72: 'A breach of the Act or Codes does not mean that any statement made by a defendant after such a breach will necessarily be ruled out. Every case has to be determined on its own merits.' See also *R v Stewart* [1995] Crim LR 499 and *R v Gill* [2004] 1 WLR 469 [41]. See also Ashworth and Redmayne 2010, 348; and Dennis 2013, 320.

[263] See in particular *R v Keenan* [1990] 2 QB 54 and *R v Gill* [2004] 1 WLR 469 [41]. See also e.g. Ashworth and Redmayne 2010, 348; Dennis 2013, 240–241, 320; and Choo 2015, 101 and 173.

[264] See e.g. *R v Walsh* [1990] 91 Cr App R 161. See also *R v Samuel* [1988] QB 615 at 630, where the Court of Appeal emphasizes the fundamental nature of the right, although it does not adopt the significant and substantial terminology. And see *Parris*, in which the Court of Appeal ruled that in the circumstances, the breach of the right of access to legal advice had such an adverse effect on the fairness of the proceedings that the interview obtained thereby should have been excluded. See *R v Parris* (1989) 89 Cr App R 68 at 73.

[265] *R v Absolam* (1989) 88 Cr App R 332.

[266] See e.g. *R v Keenan* [1990] 2 QB 54 and *R v Canale* (1990) 91 Cr App R 1.

[267] See e.g. *R v Nelson* [1998] 2 Cr App R 399 and *R v Kirk* [2000] 1 WLR 567. See also Dennis 2013, 248; and Keane and McKeown 2014, 69.

regulates the detention, treatment and questioning of persons by the police, will be regarded as significant and substantial. For example, in *Blackwell*, the exclusion of a series of police interviews with one of the defendants was sought on account of a number of breaches of Code C, including that the defendant had had breakfast and a light lunch, but not been offered a main meal; this breach was described as 'technical'.[268] Moreover, as suggested above, not every breach that qualifies as significant and substantial will result in the exclusion of the evidence obtained thereby; in other words, exclusion is not automatic for such breaches. Prima facie such breaches have an adverse effect on the fairness of the proceedings, but this is not sufficient for exclusion under Section 78(1) of PACE: 'The task of the court is not merely to consider whether there would be an adverse effect on the fairness of the proceedings, but *such* an adverse effect that justice requires the evidence to be excluded.'[269] In other words, Section 78(1) 'still requires the judge to make a judgment of degree'.[270] An important consideration appears to be whether the police acted in bad faith (although this should not be taken to mean that 'disciplining the police' or 'punishing police officers' is seen as part of the judicial function; in numerous cases the Court of Appeal has said that it is not).[271] For example, in *Alladice*, the Court of Appeal said that, '[i]f the police have acted in bad faith, the court would have little difficulty in ruling the confession inadmissible'.[272] Bad faith 'may make substantial or significant that which might not be otherwise', however, breaches of PACE or its codes of practice that are, themselves, significant and substantial are not rendered otherwise by *good* faith on the part of the police officers involved.[273] Nevertheless, the good faith of the officers involved (or, at least, the absence of bad faith on their part) does seem to warrant an enquiry into the question of whether the defendant was prejudiced, or disadvantaged, by the breach; indeed, in such cases, it may be that prejudice for the accused is a requirement for exclusion of the evidence obtained by the breach.[274] In *Samuel*, the defendant had suffered prejudice as a result of the breach because, had he been able to exercise his right of access to legal advice, he would, in all probability, not have made any incriminating statements during further questioning,[275] whereas in *Alladice*, the defendant had not been disadvantaged. In that case, in which the defendant had been denied access to legal advice, the

---

[268] *R v Blackwell* [1995] 2 Cr App R 625 at 641.

[269] *R v Walsh* [1990] 91 Cr App R 161 at 163 (emphasis added).

[270] Dennis 2013, 242. See also Choo 2015, 103.

[271] See e.g. *R v Mason* [1988] 1 WLR 139 at 144 and *R v Hughes* [1994] 1 WLR 876 at 879.

[272] *R v Alladice* (1988) 87 Cr App R 380 at 386. See also *R v Delaney* (1989) 88 Cr App R 338 at 342 −343 where the Court of Appeal refers to bad faith in the context of s 76 PACE but later on states that these principles also apply to S. 78. at 343. See also *R v Canale* (1990) 91 Cr App R 1 at 6.

[273] *R v Walsh* [1990] 91 Cr App R 161 at 163. See also Choo 2015, 102 and 173.

[274] See e.g. *R v Alladice* (1988) 87 Cr App R 380 at 386. See also Dennis 2013, 241−243, 279 −282, 320; and Choo 2015, 102. Where there is bad faith, the court may also enquire into how far the defendant was prejudiced by the breach; while prejudice is not a requirement in such cases, '[a] n element of prejudice will provide further support for exclusion.' See ibid., 242−243.

[275] *R v Samuel* [1988] QB 615 at 630.

appellant himself had said that he was well able to cope with the interviews, had been cautioned, had understood the caution and was aware of his rights. The Court of Appeal concluded that: 'Had the solicitor been present, his advice would have added nothing to the knowledge of his rights which the appellant already had. The police ... had acted with propriety at the interviews and therefore the solicitor's presence would not have improved the appellant's case in that respect.'[276] Accordingly, it appears that there has to be a causal link between the breach and the prejudice suffered by the accused, i.e. the obtaining of the evidence.[277]

A similar approach has been taken to cases in which the breach relates to Code D of PACE, which governs the exercise by police of statutory powers to identify persons. Not every breach of this code (which may entail the failure to observe the provisions of the code in carrying out a pre-trial identification, thereby giving rise to the risk of 'contamination', or the failure to carry out an identification at all in circumstances in which such a procedure was called for)[278] will result in the exclusion of evidence.[279] As with breaches of Code C, an important consideration in cases concerning breaches of Code D is whether there was bad faith on the part of the officers involved, in the sense that it is likely to result in exclusion of the evidence obtained as a result of an unlawfully carried out identification, or, as the case may be, of 'other, less satisfactory, identification evidence'.[280] For example, in *Nagah*, in which the police had failed to hold an identification parade where it clearly should have, and had (instead) orchestrated a street identification, the Court of Appeal qualified the conduct of the police officers involved as a 'complete flouting of the Code', and concluded that in those circumstances the trial judge should have excluded the street identification evidence.[281] Conversely, the absence

---

[276] *R v Alladice* (1988) 87 Cr App R 380 at 386–387.

Causing the accused to produce incriminating evidence is one form of prejudice (see in this regard also Grevling 1997, 677–678; another is where the effect of the breach is to make it more difficult for the accused to challenge incriminating evidence. See Dennis 2013, 320. Regarding the latter form of prejudice, see e.g. *R v Keenan* [1990] 2 QB 54 at 70. See further Mirfield 1997, 133 –135; and Grevling 1997, 678–679.

[277] See also Dennis 2013, 320; and Choo 2015, 103–104: 'Only if the breach could have 'made a difference' in the case would exclusion appear to be justified'. Choo notes that this is problematic: 'The notion that a confession will not be excluded from evidence under Section 78(1) if it is determined that the presence of a legal advisor would have 'made no difference', since the defendant would have made the confession in any event, is a problematic one. It is clear that such a determination can involve courts in a certain amount of post hoc rationalization of events. The desirability of this may be questioned.' Dennis is similarly critical; see ibid., 243.

[278] See in this regard Mirfield 1997, 189–199.

[279] Dennis observes that in such cases the 'significant and substantial' formula is not always adopted. See Dennis 2013, 279.

[280] Mirfield 1997, 189.

[281] *R v Nagah* (1991) 92 Cr App R 344. See also *R v Finley* [1993] Crim LR 50. Other deliberate breaches of Code D than the failure to hold an identification parade are also likely to result in the exclusion of evidence.

of bad faith is a factor weighing in favour of admission,[282] although ultimately the question of whether the trial judge properly exercised the discretion under Section 78(1) to admit the evidence is likely to depend on whether the accused can be said to have suffered prejudice as a result of the breach. In *Ryan*, it was held that the breach of Code D (contrary to the Code, officers involved in the investigation of the case had taken part in the identification procedure, thereby raising the risk of contamination) had not caused prejudice to the accused, since the accused's solicitor had been present and had taken certain precautions.[283] On the other hand, in *Preddie*, in which there was a breach of the Code in deciding to carry out a street identification, and further breaches in carrying it out, neither the evidence of the street identification, nor the evidence of a video identification later on that day (which was rendered valueless by the street identification)[284] could be safely or properly adduced.[285] In other words, it (the aforementioned identification evidence) could not safely be left to the jury to assess its weight.

Other breaches of PACE and/or its codes of practice may also result in the exclusion of the evidence thereby obtained, though, again, not automatically. In *Nathaniel*,[286] the retention of DNA samples taken from the defendant in connection with a rape committed in 1991, despite the defendant having been acquitted thereof, was found to constitute a breach of PACE.[287] Those samples had led to a positive DNA identification of the defendant in connection with another rape, committed in 1989. According to the Court of Appeal, the trial judge (in the case concerning the rape committed in 1989) should have exercised the discretion under Section 78(1) to exclude the DNA identification evidence.[288] In so finding, the Court of Appeal attached importance not only to the breach of PACE, but also to the fact that the defendant 'had in effect been misled in consenting to give the blood sample by statements and promises which were not honoured'.[289] On the other hand, in

---

[282] See e.g. *R v Tiplady* [1995] Crim LR 65.

[283] *R v Ryan* [1992] Crim LR 187. See also *H v DPP* [2007] EWHC 2192 (Admin) [16]. Mirfield observes that whereas in *Ryan* the Court of Appeal had focused on actual prejudice, i.e. actual contamination, in other cases concerning identification evidence, the 'appearance of unfairness' has sufficed for exclusion (see e.g. *R v Gall* [1990] 90 Cr App R 64). Mirfield 1997, 195.

[284] This was because the witness had seen the two suspects being arrested from quite close up and there was therefore a substantial chance that during the video procedure the witness would simply pick out the two suspects who he had seen being arrested.

[285] *R v Preddie* [2011] EWCA Crim 312 [30]–[53].

[286] *R v Nathaniel* [1995] 2 Cr App R 565.

[287] Specifically, it constituted a breach of s 64(1) PACE, as it read then.

[288] *R v Nathaniel* [1995] 2 Cr App R 565 at 571. See Dennis 2013, 322.

[289] *R v Nathaniel* [1995] 2 Cr App R 565 at 571. See Mirfield 1997, 136; and Ashworth and Redmayne 2010, 353, where the authors remark that this may have been crucial to the decision to exclude. According to Keane and McKeown, this constituted bad faith on the part of police. See Keane and McKeown 2014, 66. However, according to Dennis, the Court of Appeal's decision can be explained by the fact that the accused had suffered prejudice as a result of the breach. See Dennis 2013, 319–320.

Cooke,[290] which also concerned a charge of rape and where the Court of Appeal was prepared to accept for the sake of argument that the hair from which the DNA profile had been composed had been obtained unlawfully, i.e. in breach of Sections 63 and 65 of PACE, the trial judge had properly admitted the DNA evidence. The manner in which it was obtained, even if it was unlawful, 'did not in any way cast doubt upon the accuracy or strength of the evidence'.[291] As to the breach of the provisions of PACE and codes of practice concerning the power to stop and search (Code A), and to search premises and seize evidence (Code B), respectively, it appears that only rarely will such breaches result in the exclusion of the evidence thereby obtained.[292] Here it should be recalled that in cases involving an unlawful search, the evidence obtained is likely to be highly probative.[293] In *Stewart*,[294] in which the appellant had been convicted of abstracting electricity and stealing gas, the entry into the defendant's home, where mechanical apparatus to divert both the gas and electricity supply so as to bypass the meters recording consumption was found, was alleged to involve a number of breaches of Code B. On appeal, it was held that the admission of the evidence 'did not have any effect at all' on the fairness of the proceedings, seemingly because there was no causal link between the breach and the obtaining of the evidence; the evidence 'was there for all to see whether the entry was effected properly or not. Its existence was such that no possible injustice to [the defendant] could have been occasioned, even if the Code should have been complied with.'[295] In a number of cases the Court of Appeal focussed on the absence of bad faith (or the presence of good faith) on the part of the officers concerned, and/or the lack of prejudice (or rather the lack of a causal link between the breach and the obtaining of the evidence) in finding that the

---

[290] *R v Cooke* [1995] 1 Cr App R 318.

[291] Ibid., 328–329.

[292] For one such case, see *R v Fennelly* [1989] Crim LR 142.

[293] However, this need not to be the case. As Mirfield explains, referring to *Kuruma v R* [1955] AC 197: 'The tendency is to assume that, particularly in the case of real evidence, the mode of acquisition is irrelevant to its reliability. Superficially, this assumption is true; it is what it says it is. However, we often depend upon oral evidence for details of its provenance. Thus a person illegally searched may say that nothing was found in his possession and that the police are simply lying when they say that they found upon him the drugs which they now produce in court. Usually, this will come down to a question of who is believed by the trier of fact, a difficulty which may equally be faced where the search itself was utterly lawful. Sometimes, though, as in *Kuruma* itself, there may be a connection between the illegality and the allegation that evidence had been 'planted'. The relevant regulation, under Kenyan emergency legislation, allowed the police to exercise stop and search powers, but only if the officer involved was of a rank of assistant inspector or above. Kuruma had been searched by officers below that rank. They claimed that they had found ammunition in his possession, but he flatly denied that allegation. It seems highly likely that the requirement of rank was designed to ensure that the officer would not 'plant' evidence. Hence, there would seem to have been a strong argument for exclusion of the ammunition evidence even in terms of unreliability.' Mirfield 1997, 109–110.

[294] See *R v Stewart* [1995] Crim LR 499.

[295] See *R v Stewart* [1995] Crim LR 499 at 500.

admission of the evidence in question was appropriate.[296] In *Sanghera* there was no causal link between the breach and the obtaining of the evidence, since, according to the Court of Appeal, if the defendant had been asked for his written consent to search the premises, it is likely that he would have provided it. In other words, the evidence would have been obtained anyway.[297]

Police impropriety has also raised issues under the ECHR, for example, Article 8 of the ECHR, which protects the right to respect for private and family life, home and correspondence.[298] Breaches of this right have been alleged in cases involving the covert recording of communications of persons suspected of having committed a criminal offence. In *Khan*,[299] the police had installed an electronic listening device on the outside of house of a third party suspected of supplying heroine on a large scale. It was installed without that person's knowledge or consent, but in accordance with Home Office guidelines (although the installation of the device had involved civil trespass to the outside of a private building and the infliction on the building of some damage). Tape recordings were made of a conversation between the defendant and others from which it was apparent that the defendant had been involved in the importation of a large amount of heroine. The trial judge declined to exclude the recorded conversation, which was the only evidence against the defendant, and the defendant pleaded guilty. On appeal before the House of Lords, Lord Nolan, with whom the other Lords agreed, rejected the argument that evidence obtained by breach of Article 8 of the ECHR was inadmissible as a matter of law.[300] While he was of the view that a (probable) breach of the ECHR 'is a consideration which may be taken into account' in the exercise of the discretion under Section 78(1), the significance of behaviour by the police that amounts to such a breach 'will normally be determined not so much by its apparent unlawfulness or irregularity as upon its effect, taken as a whole, upon the fairness or unfairness of the proceedings'.[301] Moreover, in the determination of the effect of the police behaviour on the fairness of the proceeding, the fact that it constitutes a breach of the ECHR 'can plainly be of no greater significance per se than if it constituted a breach of English law'.[302] On the facts of the case, the trial judge had, according to Lord Nolan, been 'fully entitled' to admit the recorded conversation, even if it was obtained in breach

---

[296] See e.g. *R v McCarthy* [1996] Crim LR 818, *R v Wright* [1994] Crim LR 55 and *R v Sanghera* [2001] 1 Cr App R 20.

[297] *R v Sanghera* [2001] 1 Cr App R 20 [16].

[298] This was particularly so prior to the enactment of the Regulation of Investigatory Powers Act 2000 and the Police Act 1997. Prior to this, interferences with privacy could not be said to be in accordance with the law, as required under Article 8(2) ECHR.

[299] *R v Khan* [1997] AC 558.

[300] Ibid., 577–578. This was the first issue that needed to be resolved. According to Lord Nolan '[t]he evidence of the taped conversation was clearly admissible as a matter of law.'

[301] Ibid., 582.

[302] Ibid., 582.

of Article 8 of the ECHR.[303] In *Hardy*,[304] in which it was argued that tape recordings of telephone conversations between one of the appellants and two undercover police officers had been obtained unlawfully and should not have been admitted, the Court of Appeal held that 'although surveillance may in some circumstances be a breach of Article 8 of the Convention, if not conducted according to law, that breach, even if established, does not necessarily import a further breach of Article 6, provided that the Court has power to regulate admission of evidence in such a way as to ensure that the trial is fair',[305] thereby suggesting that, in criminal proceedings, 'giving consideration to the possibility of excluding the evidence under Section 78 of the Police and Criminal Evidence Act 1984 is ... sufficient to secure compliance with Article 6 of the [ECHR]'.[306]

In a number of cases involving the covert recording of communications of suspects in police custody the Court of Appeal has declined to interfere with the trial judge's decision under Section 78(1) to admit evidence obtained by breach of Article 8 of the ECHR. In *Mason*,[307] the police had been having difficulty in obtaining evidence against those they thought responsible for a series of burglaries and armed robberies, and sought authority to carry out a covert operation which involved the arrest, interview and charging of the appellants in respect of different robberies, and detaining them in the custody suite of a police station in which covert audio equipment would be installed so that the conversation of the appellants could be recorded. The conversations were recorded and played a fundamental role in the prosecution case; the appellants were convicted. However, on appeal, the Court of Appeal declined to interfere with the trial judge's decision to admit the recorded conversations; while the covert surveillance constituted a breach of Article 8 of the ECHR (on account of there having been no statutory authorisation for such surveillance, such that it could not have been conducted in according with the law),[308] and while such a breach is a matter that the trial judge was required to take into account when exercising the discretion under Section 78(1) of PACE,[309] this did not mean that the recordings could not be relied upon as evidence.[310] The ruling in *Mason* is in line with an earlier case, *Bailey and Smith*,[311] in which the police had 'acted out a charade' with the custody officer to trick the appellants into believing that the police did not want them to share a cell; the appellants were in fact put in a cell together, which had earlier been fitted with listening equipment, where they made damaging admissions in conversation. The appellants were convicted of

---

[303] Ibid., 582.

[304] *R v Hardy* [2003] 1 Cr App R 30.

[305] *R v Hardy* [2003] 1 Cr App R 30 [19]. See also [18]: 'the Court's powers to regulate the admission of evidence, pursuant inter alia to s. 78 and its inherent jurisdiction, represent means of ensuring that Article 6 is not infringed'.

[306] Choo 2015, 182 and 203.

[307] *R v Mason* [2002] 2 Cr App R 38.

[308] Ibid., [73].

[309] Ibid., [75].

[310] Ibid., [74]. See also *R v Loveridge* [2001] 2 Cr App R 29 [33].

[311] *R v Bailey* [1993] 97 Cr App R 365.

robbery and, on appeal, the Court of Appeal declined to interfere with the trial judge's decision to admit the recordings, seemingly because the trickery employed was not prohibited by the legislative regime of PACE and its codes of practice, and because they had not been oppressively obtained and were not unreliable.[312] In *Chalkley*[313] the police had also employed deceptive methods (beyond the deception inherent in the covert interception and recording of communications). The defendants were suspected of planning serious robberies, and in order to obtain evidence the police reopened an investigation into a credit card fraud concerning one of the defendants to enable them to arrest him and install a listening device in his home during his absence. The trial judge ruled that the recordings had not been unlawfully obtained and that they ought not to be excluded under Section 78(1). The Court of Appeal declined to interfere with the trial judge's decision. Regarding the evidence of the recordings, it said that,

> there was no dispute as to its authenticity, content or effect; it was relevant, highly probative of the defendants' involvement in the conspiracy and otherwise admissible; it did not result from incitement, entrapment or inducement or any other conduct of that sort; and none of the unlawful conduct of the police or other of their conduct of which complaint is made affects the quality of the evidence.[314]

However in (a different) *Mason*,[315] the method adopted by the police in questioning —falsely informing the suspect, and subsequently his solicitor, that his fingerprint had been found on a fragment of glass at the scene of the crime—meant that the evidence obtained thereby—a confession—should not have been admitted. The trial judge, who had admitted the evidence, had not exercised his discretion under Section 78(1) properly; he had 'omitted a vital factor from his consideration, namely, the deceit practiced upon the appellant's solicitor'.[316] In *Christou*, the Court of Appeal regarded the method adopted in *Mason* as distinguishable from the facts before it: the carrying out of an undercover operation involving the setting up of a shop to buy and sell jewellery commercially, staffed solely by undercover officers purporting to be shady jewellers willing to buy stolen property, and fitted with cameras and sound equipment to record all that occurred over the counter. In *Mason*, the defendant had been in police custody. Moreover, Mason had suffered prejudice as a result of the deception: after advice from his solicitor, who had also been lied to, the defendant made admissions. By contrast, in *Christou*, the appellants had 'voluntarily applied themselves to the trick'.[317] Accordingly, the trial judge had not erred in exercising the discretion under Section 78(1) to admit the evidence resulting from the undercover operation. Nevertheless, the Court of Appeal said that it 'would be wrong for police officers to adopt or use an undercover pose or disguise to enable themselves to ask questions about an offence

---

[312] Ibid., 375.

[313] *R v Chalkley* [1998] QB 848.

[314] Ibid., 876.

[315] *R v Mason* [1988] 1 WLR 139.

[316] Ibid., 144.

[317] *R v Christou* [1992] QB 979.

uninhibited by the requirements of the Code [C on the detention, treatment and questioning of persons by police officers] and with the effect of circumventing it'.[318] In *Smurthwaite*, the Court of Appeal listed a number of factors which the trial judge may take into account in exercising his or her discretion whether to admit the evidence of an undercover officer:

> Was the officer acting as an *agent provocateur* in the sense that he was enticing the defendant to commit an offence he would not otherwise have committed? What was the nature of any entrapment? Does the evidence consist of admissions to a completed offence, or does it consist of the actual commission of an offence? How active or passive was the officer's role in obtaining the evidence? Is there an unassailable record of what occurred, or is it strongly corroborated? ... a further consideration for the judge in deciding whether to admit an undercover officer's evidence, is whether he has abused his role to ask questions which ought properly to have been asked as a police officer and in accordance with the Codes.[319]

The first factor suggests that the exclusionary discretion under Section 78(1) is available in cases of entrapment, i.e. in cases involving the use of an *agent provocateur*.[320] This was confirmed in the case of *Looseley*,[321] although in that case it was held that, as a matter of principle, a stay of proceedings 'should normally be regarded as the appropriate response in a case of entrapment'. Lord Nicholls explained as follows:

> Exclusion of evidence from the trial will often have the same result in practice as an order staying the proceedings. Without, for instance, the evidence of the undercover police officers the prosecution will often be unable to proceed. But this is not necessarily so. There may be real evidence, or evidence of other witnesses. Exclusion of all the prosecution evidence would, of course, dispose of any anomaly in this regard. But a direction to this effect would really be a stay of the proceedings under another name. Quite apart from these practical considerations, as a matter of principle a stay of the proceedings, or of the relevant charges, is the more appropriate form of remedy. A prosecution founded on entrapment would be an abuse of the court's process. The court will not permit the prosecutorial arm of the state to behave in this way.[322]

Thus, a stay of proceedings is the appropriate remedy because entrapment 'goes to the propriety of there being a prosecution at all for the relevant offence, having regard to the state's involvement in the circumstance in which it was committed'.[323] Logically, then, the question of whether the proceedings should be stayed on the grounds of entrapment should be decided before the proceedings have begun. However, as Lord Hoffmann observed, 'sometimes proceedings are not conducted entirely logically' and an application to exclude evidence under Section 78(1) may in substance be an application for a belated stay; if so, the application for exclusion should be treated as

---

[318] Ibid., 991. In *Bryce*, the officers had done just that: [1992] 95 Cr App R 320.

[319] *R v Smurthwaite* (1994) 98 Cr App R 437 at 440-441.

[320] See e.g. Mirfield 1997, 201; Keane and McKeown 2014, 77; and Choo 2015, 197.

[321] *R v Looseley* [2001] 1 WLR 2060.

[322] Ibid., [16]. See also [36], [42] (Lord Hoffmann).

[323] Ibid., [17] (Lord Nicholls).

an application for a stay 'and decided according to the principles appropriate to the grant of stay'.[324] If a stay is not ordered (whether, presumably, it was applied for before the proceedings began, or once the trial was under way), the participation of state agents in the commission of the offence may still be relevant to the exercise of discretion under Section 78(1), whereby the question is whether the admission of the evidence obtained by the participation of the state agents would have such an adverse effect on the fairness of the proceedings that it ought to be excluded.[325]

Two final issues require consideration: the question of admissibility of 'subsequent confessions', i.e. of a properly obtained confession, which repeats an unlawfully obtained confession which has been excluded pursuant to the discretion under Section 78(1) of PACE, and the question of admissibility of real evidence discovered as a result of a confession that has been excluded pursuant to that discretion. Regarding the first issue, in *Neil* the Court of Appeal held that:

> Where there is a series of two or more interviews and the court excludes one on the grounds of unfairness, the question whether a later interview which is itself unobjectionable should also be excluded is a matter of fact and degree... It is likely to depend on a consideration of whether the objections leading to the exclusion of the first interview were of a fundamental and continuing nature, and, if so, if the arrangements for the subsequent interview gave the accused a sufficient opportunity to exercise an informed and independent choice as to whether he should repeat or retract what he said in the excluded interview or say nothing.[326]

Regarding the second issue, it should be noted that the prohibition under Section 76 (5) of PACE only applies in respect of a confession made by the accused that is inadmissible pursuant to Section 76(2) of PACE.[327] In other words, where the confession that led to the discovery of real evidence has been excluded *not* pursuant to Section 76(2) but in the exercise of the discretion under Section 78(1), i.e. on grounds of unfairness, there is no express prohibition of the introduction by the prosecution of evidence that the fact that was discovered, was discovered as a result of the statement of the accused.[328]

---

[324] Ibid., [44].

[325] Ibid., [43], where Lord Hoffmann refers to *R v Shannon* [2001] 1 WLR 51. In referring to *Shannon*, Lord Hoffmann (and Lord Hutton) appear to understand s 78 as being concerned with reliability. See Choo 2015, 203.

[326] *R v Neil* [1994] Crim LR 441. In the circumstances, it was held that the judge should have exercised his discretion to exclude the evidence, since the accused 'would have considered himself bound to the admissions in the first statement', and because '[t]he circumstances of the second interview were insufficient to provide him with a safe and confident opportunity of withdrawing the admissions.' See, for a critical discussion of the case law on this point, Mirfield 1997, 146–148.

[327] See n 216 and accompanying text.

[328] This has not gone unnoticed in the literature. According to Choo: 'Surely consistency requires ... that an analogous principle to that in Section 76(5) should apply in relation to confessions excluded from evidence in the exercise of discretion under Section 78(1). This result can be achieved by using Section 78(1) itself to exclude evidence that the fact which was discovered was discovered as a result of the statement already excluded from evidence under Section 78(1).' See Choo 2015, 116.

Returning now to the question raised above, i.e. whether Section 78(1) is merely a restatement of the position adopted in *Sang* in relation to the unfairness head of the common law exclusionary discretion, or, rather, an enlargement thereof, it is worth briefly recalling what that position entails before looking to the case law on Section 78(1). Pursuant to *Sang*, confessions and evidence obtained *from the accused, after commission of the offence* may be excluded on grounds of unfairness, whereby the rationale for exclusion is that of the privilege against self-incrimination. On the face of it, therefore, the unfairness head of the discretion, as set out in the case of *Sang*, does not cover evidence obtained by entrapment, i.e. the use of an *agent provocateur* (the discretion being restricted to confessions and evidence obtained from the accused *after* commission of the offence), or evidence obtained by an unlawful search (the discretion being restricted to confessions and evidence obtained *from the accused*, and the rationale for exclusion being that of the privilege against self-incrimination).[329] Certainly the legislative history of Section 78(1) suggests that the exclusionary discretion under that provision is (intended to be) wider than that under the common law, as set out in *Sang*; after all, the common law exclusionary discretion was preserved by PACE, while Section 78(1) was added only later, seemingly in order to 'respond to strongly felt political opposition to the perceived limitations of the common law in dealing with improperly obtained evidence'.[330] Furthermore, it has been argued that the text of Section 78(1) itself suggests that the discretion provided for therein is wider than that set out in *Sang*, as regards the unfairness head of the common law discretion. For example, the inclusion of the words 'the circumstances in which the evidence was obtained' in Section 78(1) appears to '[contrast] with the rejection in Sang of the idea that the court should be concerned with how evidence is obtained'.[331] As to the case law, there is certainly case law to support the contention that the discretion under Section 78(1) is wider than that under the common law.[332] In the first place, *Smurthwaite* confirms that the exclusionary discretion under Section 78(1) is available in cases of entrapment,[333] i.e. the use of *agents provocateurs*, something

---

[329] See e.g. Mirfield 1997, 143, 209. However, even if it is accepted that the rationale for exclusion under the unfairness head of the common law exclusionary discretion is that of the privilege against self-incrimination, Mirfield argues that it is 'not at all clear' why the accused's will should 'have been engaged any the less where the evidence was eventually obtained from his surroundings or his house, rather than from his person' (ibid., 143).

[330] Dennis 2013, 95. See also Zander 1985, 115–116.

[331] Dennis 2013, 95, 101 and 317. See also Choo 2015, 173.

[332] See *R v Cooke* [1995] 1 Cr App R 318 at 328: the Court of Appeal said that 'it is now clear that Section 78 has given the courts a substantially wider discretion to refuse to admit evidence improperly obtained' immediately after observing that, prior to PACE entering into force, the discretion to exclude improperly obtained evidence that was relevant and admissible was strictly circumscribed (thereby referring to House of Lords' decision in *R v Sang* [1980] AC 402).

[333] See n 319 and accompanying text.

that was ruled out in *Sang*. Moreover, there is appellate authority to suggest that the discretion under Section 78(1) is available in respect of evidence obtained by an unlawful search,[334] something that also appears to have been ruled out in *Sang*. In view of the availability of the Section 78(1) discretion in case of entrapment or of an unlawful search, and also in view of its availability in case of a breach of the PACE code of practice regulating identification evidence, it seems clear that 'the boundaries of the unfairness element of the discretion ... are not set by the self-incrimination rationale',[335] which it should be recalled, was the rationale identified by Lord Diplock in *Sang* as underlying the unfairness head of the common law exclusionary discretion.[336]

However, there is also case law to suggest otherwise, i.e. that the discretion under Section 78(1) does not alter, and merely entails a restatement of, the position in *Sang*,[337] or even that the discretion under that provision is narrower than that set out in *Sang*. In *Chalkley*, the Court of Appeal said that the law prior to the coming into force of PACE was not that the trial judge 'could, even if it considered that the intrinsic nature of the evidence was not unfair to the accused, exclude it as a mark of disapproval of the way in which it had been obtained'.[338] In other words, in the Court's view, the law prior to PACE was *not* that evidence could be excluded even if its quality was unaffected by the manner in which was obtained. It formulated the rule in *Sang* as follows: 'save in the case of admissions and confessions and generally as to evidence obtained from the accused after the commission of the offence, there is no discretion to exclude evidence *unless its quality was or might have been affected by the way in which it was obtained*'.[339] In doing so, it appears to have narrowed 'even further what was already a narrow discretion'; after all, in *Sang*, Lord Diplock 'did not refer to impropriety affecting the *quality* of the evidence, he referred to the discretion being available to exclude evidence "which the accused has been induced to produce voluntarily if the method of inducement is unfair"'.[340] Thus, whereas as in *Sang* itself the availability of the exclusionary discretion in respect of unlawfully obtained confessions and 'evidence obtained from the accused after commission of the offence' was rationalized in terms of the privilege against self-incrimination, in *Chalkley*, the unfairness head of the common law of the exclusionary discretion, and, by extension, the exclusionary discretion under Section 78(1),[341] appears to have been rationalized in terms of (potential)

---

[334] See e.g. *R v Khan, Sakkaravej and Pamarapa* [1997] Crim LR 508; *R v Stewart* [1995] Crim LR 499; *R v McCarthy* [1996] Crim LR 818; and *R v Wright* [1994] Crim LR 55.

[335] In other words, self-incrimination is no longer 'the key'. See Mirfield 1997, 143–144.

[336] See n 242 and accompanying text.

[337] See e.g. *R v Mason* [1988] 1 WLR 139 at 144. See also Dennis 2013, 99–103.

[338] *R v Chalkley* [1998] QB 848, 874–875.

[339] Ibid., 875.

[340] Dennis 2013, 101 n 167.

[341] In *Chalkley*, the Court of Appeal was called to rule on s 78(1); in its view, s 78(1) does not widen the common law exclusionary discretion, such that its considerations in relation to the common law discretion also apply to s 78(1).

unreliability.[342] It is curious, then, that the Court of Appeal suggested, impliedly, that the discretion was available in cases of 'incitement, entrapment of inducement or any other conduct of that sort',[343] since evidence obtained thereby may be perfectly reliable (it is curious also on account of the fact that, in *Sang*, which it cited with approval, such cases were excluded from the scope of the exclusionary discretion). *Chalkley*, then, suggested that Section 78(1) does no more than restate the position at common law, as set out in *Sang*. Moreover, it suggested that the exclusionary discretion under Section 78(1) was unavailable in cases in which the procedural violation in question did not affect the quality of the evidence obtained thereby.[344] However, the decision in *Chalkley* has been subject to robust criticism in the literature, on both counts,[345] whereby various authors have suggested that that (aspect of the) decision is wrong and/or best disregarded as a matter of law.[346] If that is so, then it may be concluded that the exclusionary discretion under Section 78(1) is wider in its scope of application than that under the common law (as set out in *Sang*),[347] in the sense that it is available in a wider variety of cases of impropriety than was the exclusionary discretion under the common law. Nevertheless, the question of *availability* of the exclusionary discretion under Section 78(1) of PACE in the first place should be distinguished from the question of its 'proper exercise', i.e. of what the appellate courts consider to constitute its proper exercise.[348] This point is explored further below.[349]

Other Responses

Having set out the English law and practice with respect to the abuse of process discretion and the exclusion of evidence as judicial responses to pre-trial procedural violations, the question arises as to whether any other, perhaps 'lesser', trial remedies are available in respect of such conduct. It is instructive to examine the case law with respect to entrapment in this regard. Prior to *Looseley*, in which, it should be recalled, it was held that the appropriate response in case of entrapment is a stay of proceedings rather than the exclusion of evidence,[350] it seems that

---

[342] This is certainly how the Court of Appeal's decision in *Chalkley* has been interpreted in the literature. See e.g. Choo 2015, 177 and 186; Dennis 2013, 102 and 343; and Ashworth and Redmayne 2010, 351.

[343] *R v Chalkley* [1998] QB 848 at 876.

[344] See also *R v Shannon* [2001] 1 WLR 51. For a (critical) discussion of this case, see Choo 2015, 196–197. See also Dennis 2013, 102.

[345] See e.g. Dennis 2013, 101–103, 343; and Choo 2015, 177 and 186.

[346] Ashworth and Redmayne 2010, 351. Presumably the same would apply to the decision in *Shannon*. See n 344 and accompanying text.

[347] See e.g. Dennis 2013, 102; and Keane and McKeown 2014, 64.

[348] See Mirfield 1997, 213.

[349] In Sect. 4.5.

[350] See n 322–323 and accompanying text.

entrapment was no more than a mitigating factor.[351] In other words, prior to the House of Lords' decision in that case, sentence reduction appears to have been considered the appropriate response to entrapment, where (strong) judicial condemnation did not suffice.[352] While a stay of proceedings is now considered the appropriate response in case of entrapment, in borderline cases, i.e. in cases in which the conduct in question does not quite amount to entrapment, sentence reduction may still have a role to play.[353]

In case of undue delay, the trial judge has a variety of remedies at his or her disposal, as apparent from the case *A-G's Reference (No 2 of 2001)*.[354] In that case the Court of Appeal held that a stay of proceedings is not the necessary consequence of a contravention of the reasonable time requirement in Article 6 of the ECHR, and that 'there are many other actions which the court can take which avoid the need for such action':

> In particular ... the court can *mark the fact* that the way the prosecution has been conducted does contravene the reasonable time requirement in article 6(1) and acknowledge the rights of the defendant by so doing. In many cases the court will come to the conclusion that that is not a sufficient recognition of the defendant's rights. If that be so, then the court can take other action. It can, for example, *take account of the failure to proceed with the case with due expedition in the sentence which the court imposes.*[355]

In cases involving pre-trial procedural violations it has also been suggested that 'judicial condemnation' may suffice as a response thereto.[356]

4.4.1.2 Discretion and Balancing

This section will address the question of the extent to which the English judicial response to procedural violations committed in the pre-trial phase of criminal proceedings can be said to be discretionary in nature, and/or the extent to which it

---

[351] See in this regard *R v Looseley* [2001] 1 WLR 2060 [7]–[9] (Lord Nicholls). See also Ashworth 1999 and Ashworth 2002.

[352] For an example of a case in which the Court of Appeal held that the entrapment should have been taken into account in imposing the sentence, see *R v Tonnessen* [1998] 2 Cr App R (S) 328.

[353] See Ashworth 2002, 164.

In academic discussions also, it has been acknowledged that sentence reduction may be an appropriate response to procedural violations committed in the pre-trial phase of criminal proceedings, although often it is argued that such a response is only appropriate when a more far-reaching response is, for one reason or another, not called for. See e.g. Ashworth 1977, 725 −726; Ormerod 2003, 69; and Choo 2008, 186−187.

[354] *A-G's Reference (No 2 of 2001)* [2001] 1 WLR 1869.

[355] Ibid., [20].

[356] See e.g. *R v Mason* [2002] 2 Cr App R 38 [75]. While in *Warren and others v Attorney General for Jersey* [2012] 1 AC 22 the Board does not explicitly say this, according to O'Connor, it 'relied heavily upon verbal condemnations of the misconduct and warnings for the future, even suggesting that they alone would dispel any "integrity" issue'. See O'Connor 2012, 676.

entails a balancing approach (whereby it may be recalled that in Chap. 1, such questions were said to lie at the heart of the present study).[357]

It was said above that the power of a court to stay criminal proceedings on the ground that it amounts to an abuse of process of that court is known as the 'abuse of process *discretion*', while the legal framework governing the exclusion of unlawfully obtained evidence in England and Wales was sketched in terms of exclusionary *rules*, of which Section 76(2) of PACE is an example, and exclusionary *discretions*, of which Section 78(1) of PACE is an example. Having set out the law and practice with respect to the abuse of process discretion, and with respect to the aforementioned exclusionary rules and discretions, the question that now needs to be addressed is what it means to say that the power to stay the proceedings on the basis of the abuse of process doctrine, or that Section 78(1) involves the exercise of judicial *discretion*. And, further, what does it mean to say that Section 76(2) of PACE provides for an exclusionary *rule*, rather than an exclusionary *discretion*?

In the context of the abuse of process doctrine, Choo states that there are two possible interpretations of the concept of judicial discretion. The first 'treats judicial discretion as signifying totally unfettered power on the part of the trial judge', whereby a judge would be 'at liberty to reach conclusion B even though an application of the relevant test or standard requires that conclusion A be reached'.[358] The second interpretation of the concept of judicial discretion 'relates to the open-texturedness of the test or standard to be applied in reaching a conclusion'.[359] In the context of the law of evidence, and, more particularly, of exclusionary discretions (which, it should be noted, are available not only in the context of unlawfully obtained evidence), the same distinction may be drawn. Noting that '"discretion" is a term that is used with more than one meaning in the law of evidence, as in the law generally', Dennis explains that:

> In its first, weaker, sense, "discretion" refers to a legal standard, cast in broad and flexible terms, which gives the judge a good deal of latitude in its application to a given set of facts. However, once the judge concludes that the standard is satisfied on the facts before him, it is his duty to apply the standard. He is not then free to disregard it. "Discretion" in the second, stronger, sense refers to a power of the judge to act in any way that he thinks fit on the facts before him.[360]

Choo argues that, under the abuse of process doctrine, it is the interpretation of the concept of judicial discretion that relates to the open-texturedness of the test or

---

[357] In Chap. 1, 'balancing' was defined as an approach to the question of how to address pre-trial procedural violations whereby the court (also) takes into account factors that seemingly have nothing to do with that which warranted the court's attention in the first place, and which militate against a (potentially) far-reaching response thereto.

[358] Choo 2008, 156.

[359] Ibid., 156–157. For these two interpretations, Choo draws on Dworkin's *Taking Rights Seriously*, in which a distinction is drawn between 'discretion' in a weak sense and 'discretion' in a strong sense. See Dworkin 1977, 31–32.

[360] Dennis 2013, 89. Dennis also draws on Dworkin's *Taking Rights Seriously*. See in this regard n 359. See also Tapper 2010, 191–196; and Choo 2015, 14.

standard to be applied, i.e. discretion in its weaker sense, that is envisaged.[361] The same may be said of the exclusionary discretion under Section 78(1) of PACE.[362] In other words, Section 78(1) does not provide for discretion in its stronger sense; indeed, once it is established that the admission of the evidence in question would have such an adverse effect on the fairness of the proceedings that it ought not to be admitted, the judge must exclude the evidence.[363] Having established what is means to say that the abuse of process doctrine and Section 78(1) of PACE involve the exercise of judicial discretion, we may now turn to second question: what does it mean to say that a provision provides for an exclusionary *rule*? Choo explains that whereas exclusionary discretions (including that provided for by Section 78(1)) accord 'a degree of latitude' to the trial judge in deciding whether to exclude of evidence, 'exclusionary rules are traditionally more rigid, often prescribing that, where certain conditions are satisfied, a particular consequence will automatically follow'.[364] As stated above, Section 76(2) of PACE provides for an exclusionary rule, in respect of confessions obtained 'by oppression of the person who made it' and confessions obtained 'in consequence of anything said or done which was likely, in the circumstances existing at the time, to render unreliable any confession which might be made by him in consequence thereof'. As regards the first limb (or the oppression head), the trial judge is required to reach a judgment on whether or not the confession was obtained by oppression of the person who made it; if it was, the trial judge must exclude it. Of course, under Section 78(1) of PACE the trial judge is also required to reach a judgment on whether or not the overriding criterion has been fulfilled; as stated above, if it has, it *must* be excluded. However, the standard in Section 78(1)—whether 'admission ... would have *such an* adverse effect on the *fairness of the proceedings*'—is cast in broader and more flexible terms[365] than the standard in, for example, Section 76(2)(a). Moreover, under Section 78, the trial judge is expressly allowed to take into account *all* relevant factors.[366] And while the standard in Section 76(2)(a)—whether 'the confession was or may have been obtained by oppression of the person who made it'—requires careful consideration of the facts and circumstances of the particular case, it would be erroneous to, on this basis, describe the decision to be made in this context as 'a

---

[361] Choo 2008, 157.

[362] See generally Dennis 2013, 89−90.

[363] See e.g. *R v Chalkley* [1998] QB 848, 874, where the Court of Appeal said that if the court is of the view that the admission of the evidence would have such an adverse effect on the fairness of the proceedings that it ought not to be admitted 'it cannot logically "exercise a discretion" to admit the evidence, despite the use of the permissive formula in the opening words of the provision that it "may refuse" to admit the evidence in that event'. See also e.g. Keane and McKeown 2014, 51 and 63; Dennis 2013, 89−90; Ormerod and Birch 2004, 780 n 101; and Mirfield 1997, 122−123.

[364] Choo 2015, 14−15. See also Choo 2008, 156−157, drawing on Pound's *Jurisprudence*. Pound defines a rule as 'a legal precept attaching a definite detailed legal consequence to a definite detailed state of fact'. Pound 1959, 124.

[365] See n 360 and accompanying text.

[366] See also Ormerod and Birch 2004, 780.

matter of discretion'. Perhaps the most important difference between exclusionary rules and exclusionary discretions concerns the way in which appellate courts review their application.[367] Choo explains as follows:

> If, on applying an exclusionary rule, a trial judge in a Crown Court concludes that the evidence should not be excluded, the Court of Appeal will not hesitate to substitute its own conclusion if it disagrees with that reached by the trial judge. It is immaterial that the trial judge may have, in reaching his or her conclusion, taken all relevant factors into account and left irrelevant factors out of consideration. However, where a decision is reached pursuant to judicial discretion and the decision is subject to appeal, the appellate court will interfere with the decision only in limited circumstances.[368]

The appellate court will only interfere with the trial judge's exercise of discretion according to *Wednesbury* principles, i.e. where the decision is one which no reasonable court could have come to.[369] This means that, upon review of the exercise of an exclusionary discretion, 'it is entirely coherent for the higher court to say that it *would* regard the admission in evidence of the material in question as rendering the proceedings unfair and *would* itself have excluded that material, yet at the same time, for it to uphold the judge's discretion'.[370]

Both the abuse of process doctrine and Section 78(1) of PACE, then, entail the exercise of judicial discretion. The question that now arises is: what facts and circumstances are considered to be relevant to the exercise of discretion under each? Before addressing this question, it is worth noting that in both contexts calls have been made for a more 'structured' approach to the exercise of judicial discretion, 'through the recognition of guidelines', which 'ensure more open and rational decision-making'.[371] For example, regarding the exercise of the abuse of process discretion in the context of pre-trial impropriety (which implicates the second limb of the doctrine), Choo argues that it might involve consideration of such 'factors' as 'the seriousness of any violation of the defendant's (or even a third party's) rights; whether the police have acted in bad faith or maliciously, or with an improper motive; whether the misconduct was committed in circumstances of urgency, emergency or necessity; the availability or otherwise of a direct sanction against the person(s) responsible for the misconduct; and the seriousness of the offence with which the defendant is charged'.[372] In addition, he argues for the discretion under the second limb of the abuse of process doctrine to be *confined* to situations where the police and/or prosecutorial misconduct that has made the trial possible does not

---

[367] Choo 2015, 14.

[368] Ibid., 14.

[369] See e.g. Dennis 2013, 103–104, 318; Mirfield 1997, 123–124; and Keane and McKeown 2014, 65.

[370] Mirfield 1997, 123.

[371] Choo 2008, 163.

[372] Ibid., 164–165. O'Connor also calls for a more structured approach in context of the abuse of process doctrine. See O'Connor 2012, 685.

constitute a breach of an ECHR right.[373] Put differently, he argues for the recognition of 'a rule that, where there is a reasonable likelihood that the prosecution would not have been possible but for the breach, in relation to the defendant, of an article of the European Convention on Human Rights … the proceedings should automatically be stayed.' Regarding Section 78, Ormerod and Birch observe that while it 'exemplifies one of the great virtues of discretion—it allows the courts to respond to the needs of the individual case and to achieve "justice" in individual circumstances', it is not sufficiently clear or transparent as regards 'the standard to which the judge must be satisfied' or 'the factual issues on which he must be satisfied to apply the discretion'.[374] They argue for a more structured approach to the decision to be made under Section 78, which would 'identify more clearly the purpose of the discretion … [and] the interests to be served'.[375] This would involve making the criteria for decision-making more explicit, i.e. identifying the 'significant factors' to which the trial judge should attach importance in exercising his or her discretion.[376] In the context of Section 78 also, calls have been made for the discretion to be confined to situations where the procedural violation concerned does not constitute the breach of a Convention right.[377] Which factors may be taken into account in a structured approach to the exercise of discretion will depend on the particular rationale pursued, such that ensuring a more structured approach to the decision to be made under Section 78 would necessarily entail identification of the rationale for exclusion. While advocating a more structured approach to the exercise of the discretion under Section 78, Ormerod and Birch emphasize the need to steer clear of 'spurious "balancing" exercises':

> … discretions should avoid enticing the judge "into the shadowy and metaphorical world of balancing, where issues of principle may be presented as 'facts' and where the relative weight of the countervailing factors (and the reasons for assigning that weight) are rarely spelt out." An obvious example of this in s.78 is the "balancing" of the defendant's right to privacy against the need to convict the factually guilty on reliable evidence: the reliable conviction invariably wins.[378]

More will be said about 'balancing' below.

What facts and circumstances, then, are considered to be relevant to the exercise of judicial discretion under the abuse of process doctrine and Section 78(1) of PACE? Turning first to the abuse of process doctrine, it is important to distinguish between the two categories of case under the doctrine when determining what is appropriate for the court to take into account when ruling on applications for the

---

[373] Choo 2008, 190–191. For a discussion of the distinction between structuring and confining in the context of the exercise of judicial discretion, see ibid., 162–165.

[374] Ormerod and Birch 2004, 785.

[375] Ibid., 786.

[376] See e.g. Ormerod and Birch 2004, 786.

[377] See e.g. Choo 2015, 189–191. See also Ormerod 2003.

[378] Ormerod and Birch 2004, 785–786.

proceedings to be stayed. While the first category of case is concerned with 'forensic prejudice', i.e. the ability of the trial to determine the guilt or innocence of the accused properly, Dennis has said that the 'distinguishing characteristic' of the second type of case is 'bad faith on the part of the enforcement authorities', defined as the 'knowing breach of the investigating or prosecuting authority's legal obligations in order to secure some advantage that might not be obtainable by compliance with the law'.[379] Postponing for the moment the explanation of *why* different considerations apply under each category of case, and looking first to the second category of case, more generally this category involves an enquiry into the seriousness of the police misconduct, a factor that has the potential to give rise to a whole host of (further) lines of enquiry,[380] such that (as observed above), any approach to the question of how to address pre-trial procedural violations in which this factor is the focus might properly be said to entail the exercise of discretion, if not the performance of a balancing exercise. However, the enquiry under the second limb is not always limited to this factor. One factor that is often referred to in this context is the seriousness of the offence with which the defendant is charged. This factor appears to enter the analysis by virtue of the balancing exercise that is often said to apply under this limb. In *Latif; Shahzad*, for example, it was said that a balancing exercise applies under the second limb of the abuse of process doctrine, which Lord Steyn, delivering the main speech in the House of Lords, formulated as follows:

> ... in this case the issue is whether ... the judge ought to have stayed the criminal proceedings on broader considerations of the integrity of the criminal justice system. The law is settled. Weighing countervailing considerations of policy and justice, it is for the judge in the exercise of his discretion to decide whether there has been an abuse of process, which amounts to an affront to the public conscience and requires the criminal proceedings to be stayed ... in a case such as the present the judge must weigh in the balance *the public interest in ensuring that those that are charged with grave crimes should be tried* and the competing public interest in not conveying the impression that the court will adopt the approach that the end justifies any means.[381]

The justification for such a balancing exercise relates to the avoidance of 'extreme positions'. Thus, in *Latif; Shahzad* the formulation of the balancing exercise was preceded by the observation that:

> If the court *always* refuses to stay such proceedings, the perception will be that the court condones criminal conduct and malpractice by law enforcement agencies. That would undermine public confidence in the criminal justice system and bring it into disrepute. On the other hand, if the court were *always* to stay proceedings in such cases, it would incur the

---

[379] Dennis 2003, 227.

[380] See in this regard O'Connor 2012, 685.

[381] *R v Latif; R v Shahzad* [1996] 1 WLR 104 at 112–113 (emphasis added). O'Connor is critical of this formulation of the balancing exercise: "'impression" ... can be dispelled by mere words of condemnation. It must be doubted whether Lord Steyn will have intended, or even foreseen, that, by this choice of words, "intervention" by the court could, in future, be reduced to "finger-wagging". See O'Connor 2012, 676.

reproach that it is failing to protect the public from serious crime. The weaknesses of both extreme positions leaves only one principled solution. The court has a discretion: it has to perform a balancing exercise.[382]

In that case, the House of Lords concluded that the trial judge had not erred in declining to stay the proceedings, having taken into consideration 'the relevant considerations placed before him' and having 'performed the balancing exercise'.[383] The conduct of the police in that case was no match for the conduct of appellant; it was 'venial compared to that of Shahzad'.[384] In *Latif; Shahzad* Lord Steyn appears to have had the public attitude variation of the integrity rationale in mind as the rationale for a stay of proceedings under the second limb of the abuse of process doctrine.[385] For Lord Steyn, the ultimate issue is 'whether there has been an abuse of process, which amounts to an affront to the *public* conscience and requires the criminal proceedings to be stayed', whereby a decision on this issue is to be made on the basis of a balancing exercise involving competing public interests. Moreover, it is to be made with reference not only to the seriousness of the police misconduct, but also to the seriousness of the offence with which the defendant is charged.[386] Under the public attitude variation of the integrity rationale, which involves the court undertaking a balancing exercise involving competing public interests, it seems that the seriousness of the offence may (also) be taken into account as an altogether 'separate' (or standalone) factor, separate, that is, from the police misconduct.[387] In other words, under this rationale, the mere fact that the offence with which the defendant has been charged is a serious one, appears to be a relevant consideration. However, the (seriousness of the) charges brought against the accused may (also) enter the analysis in another way. In *Looseley* Lord Nicholls identified a number of factors 'of particular relevance' in cases in which entrapment is alleged and a stay of proceedings is sought: the nature of the offence, the reason for the particular police operation, the nature and extent of police participation in the crime, and the defendant's criminal record.[388] Regarding the nature of the offence he said that: 'The use of pro-active techniques is more needed and, hence, more appropriate, in some circumstances than others. The secrecy and difficulty of detection, and the manner in which the particular criminal activity is carried on, are relevant considerations.'[389] In other words, the (seriousness, or nature of the) offence with which the defendant is charged may be relevant to the determination of the seriousness of the police misconduct (there may be a link between the charges

---

[382] *R v Latif; R v Shahzad* [1996] 1 WLR 104, 112 (Lord Steyn) (emphasis added).

[383] Ibid., 113.

[384] Ibid., 113. See also n 80 and accompanying text.

[385] See also Mirfield 1997, 26–27 and 151–153. Regarding the public attitude variation of the integrity rationale, see n 79–81 and accompanying text.

[386] See in this respect also *R v Mullen* [2000] QB 520.

[387] Rogers 2011, 8.

[388] *R v Looseley* [2001] 1 WLR 2060 [25]–[29].

[389] Ibid., [26].

and the misconduct);[390] it may serve to contextualize the conduct in question. When it is considered in this way, the offence in question does not constitute a separate or standalone factor; rather it is taken into account 'as relevant to the justification of police tactics'.[391] In *Warren and others v Attorney General for Jersey*, the seriousness of the offence appears to have entered the analysis (specifically, Lord Dyson's analysis) in both ways: as a standalone factor,[392] and as relevant to the determination of the seriousness of the misconduct,[393] or, as Rogers puts it, 'in order to get a more accurate picture of exactly how far the police misconduct ought to be condemned'.[394] Taking into account the seriousness of the offence on both 'sides' of the equation—the competing public interests to which Lord Steyn referred in *Latif; Shahzad*—may create significant scope for a trial judge to decide not to stay the proceedings.

Whereas Lord Steyn's words in *Latif; Shahzad* suggest that the more specific rationale in the second category of cases under the abuse of process doctrine is the public attitude variation of the integrity rationale,[395] Lord Lowry's words in *R v Horseferry Road Magistrates' Court, Ex parte Bennett* are more reminiscent of the court-centred variation thereof.[396] It should be recalled that, under this (latter) variation of the integrity rationale, it is not appropriate to take into account the seriousness of the offence with which the defendant is charged.[397] It may, therefore, be that, when it is argued in the literature that the seriousness of the offence should not inform the trial judge's decision on whether or not to stay the proceedings under the second limb of the abuse of process doctrine,[398] what is being argued is that the specific rationale in this regard is the court-centred variation of the integrity rationale (rather than the public attitude variation thereof).

Turning back now to the first category of case in which a court has a discretion to stay the proceedings on the ground that to try those proceedings will amount to an abuse of its own process, under this limb it is neither appropriate to take into account the seriousness of any impropriety on the part of the police, nor the seriousness of the offence with which the defendant is charged. Once the court concludes that the accused cannot receive a fair trial, i.e. where the court is unable to properly determine the guilt or innocence of the accused properly (whereby to try

---

[390] Rogers 2011, 8. Mirfield is also mindful of the different ways in which the 'seriousness of the offence' may enter the analysis under the integrity rationale. See Mirfield 1997, 32–33.

[391] O'Connor 2012, 683.

[392] *Warren and others v Attorney General for Jersey* [2012] 1 AC 22 [47] (Lord Dyson). See also Rogers 2011, 8.

[393] *Warren and others v Attorney General for Jersey* [2012] 1 AC 22 [50] (Lord Dyson).

[394] Rogers 2011, 8.

[395] See n 120 and 385 and accompanying text.

[396] See n 119 and accompanying text.

[397] See n 94 and accompanying text.

[398] See e.g. Rogers 2011, 8. While of the view that the seriousness of the offence should not be taken into account as a standalone factor under the second limb of the abuse of process doctrine, Rogers takes a different view in the context of s 78 PACE. See ibid., 9.

the accused would be to subject him to an unacceptable risk of wrongful conviction), the proceedings must automatically, i.e. without further consideration or 'balancing', be stayed. As stated above, whether the prejudice suffered (i.e. the inability of the trial to determine the guilt or innocence of the accused properly) was caused by a violation of a (Convention) right, or the conduct that caused the prejudice was deliberate, or the offence with which the accused is charged is a particularly serious one, is immaterial. In *R (Ebrahim) v Feltham Magistrates' Court*,[399] the Administrative Court appears to have recognized the inappropriateness of taking into account any bad faith on the part of the police or prosecution in cases involving the first limb of the abuse of process doctrine; in setting out the situations in which proceedings can be stayed pursuant to the abuse of process doctrine, it only referred to bad faith in the context of the second limb.[400] Choo also recognizes the distinction between the first and second limbs as regards the considerations that may properly inform the trial judge's decision:

> In determining whether a stay of proceedings is warranted in the interests of the protection of the innocent from wrongful conviction ('first limb' abuse of process), it is important to appreciate what criteria it would not be relevant to consider, or at least would be relevant to consider only to the extent that they bear on the question whether the continuation of the proceedings might result in a factually erroneous conviction. These criteria include: whether there has been some serious violation of the defendant's rights by the police or prosecution (was there, for example, a breach of a Convention right?); whether the police or prosecution acted in bad faith or maliciously, or with an improper motive; and the seriousness of the offence with which the defendant is charged... Logically, given that the question is whether protection against the risk of a factually erroneous conviction requires a stay, it *is* relevant to consider whether some lesser remedy, such as the exclusion of certain prosecution evidence, or a direction to the jury, would suffice to provide such protection.[401]

The reason *why*, under the first limb, it is inappropriate to take account of such criteria as bad faith on the part of the law enforcement authorities is that under this limb 'it is the *effects* of the conduct of the police with which the court should be primarily concerned',[402] i.e. whether the defence has been prejudiced. By contrast, under the second limb of the abuse of process doctrine 'it is the *nature* of this conduct which should be the focus'.[403] Under the second limb, therefore, it is appropriate to consider such criteria as 'whether the police or prosecution acted in bad faith or maliciously'. What would not be relevant to consider under the second limb is whether the defendant suffered forensic prejudice, i.e. prejudice at trial, in the sense that the absence of such prejudice cannot be a reason not to stay the proceedings under this limb. Thus, Dennis observes that: 'If the prosecution should not have taken place because of the state authorities' bad faith, then it is immaterial

---

[399] *R (Ebrahim) v Feltham Magistrates' Court* [2001] 1 WLR 1293.

[400] Ibid., [19], [23]. See also Martin 2005, 158).

[401] Choo 2008, 189–190 (emphasis added). See also 94–95, 102 and 132. Nevertheless, courts do not always get it right. See in this regard Martin 2005.

[402] Martin 2005, 181 (emphasis in original).

[403] Ibid., 181 (emphasis in original).

whether there was unfairness in the subsequent trial process. The focus is on the nature of the authorities' conduct, not on its effect on the trial'.[404]

As to Section 78(1) of PACE, the overriding criterion of whether 'admission of the evidence would have *such* an adverse effect on the fairness of the proceedings that it ought not to be admitted' clearly allows the court a great deal of latitude in deciding whether or not to exclude the evidence. Indeed, it was seen above that even breaches of PACE and/or its codes of practice do not automatically lead to exclusion under Section 78(1). A preliminary question in cases involving such breaches is often whether the breach was 'significant and substantial', and even if it can be qualified as such, it will not automatically be excluded. An important consideration in this regard is whether the police acted in bad faith; bad faith on the part of the police has the capacity to render 'significant and substantial' that which may not be otherwise. However, it seems that courts may also take into account other factors, such as the seriousness of the offence with which the defendant is charged.[405] In *A-G's Reference (No 3 of 1999)*,[406] for example, in which the appellant had been convicted on the basis of evidence of a link between the a DNA profile obtained from the defendant and that obtained from a swab taken from a rape victim, whereby the former had been obtained from the appellant only after the National DNA Database had revealed a match between the swab and an unlawfully retained DNA profile (obtained from the accused in connection with another offence of which he had been acquitted), Lord Hutton suggested that in light of the seriousness of the offence with which the appellant had been charged (rape), and in light of the need to take into account the interests of the victim and the public, he would not have excluded the evidence of the link.[407] In *Plunkett*, the Court of Appeal said that the 'immense seriousness of the crime [a violent burglary] and the need to protect the ... [victims]' rendered 'minor' any breach of the Regulation of Investigatory Powers Act and PACE.[408] In that case, upon being arrested, the defendants were deliberately left alone in the back of a police, where incriminating conversations between them were recorded; the trial judge had declined to exercise the discretion under Section 78 to exclude the recordings thereof. The Court of

---

[404] Dennis 2003, 228.

[405] Yet another factor appears to be the 'state of the other evidence'. See Dennis 2013, 249, in this regard.

[406] *A-G's Reference (No 3 of 1999)* [2001] 2 AC 91.

[407] Ibid., 124−125 (Lord Hutton). See also Dennis 2013, 323; and Ashworth and Redmayne 2010, 353−354, where the authors discuss this case. Ashworth remarks, regretfully, that consideration of whether the offence charged is a serious one is a 'judicial favourite'. See Ashworth 2003, 120. For other cases that suggest that courts may, in the context of s 78 PACE, take into the seriousness of the offence, see e.g. *R v Bailey* [1993] 97 Cr App R 365, 375; *R v Khan* [1997] AC 558, 582 (Lord Nolan: 'I confess that I have reached this conclusion not only quite firmly as a matter of law, but also with relief. It would be a strange reflection on our law if a man who has admitted his participation in the illegal importation of a large quantity of heroin should have his conviction set aside on the grounds that his privacy has been invaded.'); *R v McLeod* [2002] EWCA Crim 989, [31]; and *R v Plunkett* [2013] 1 WLR 3121, [58].

[408] *R v Plunkett* [2013] 1 WLR 3121 [58].

Appeal held that, not only was it within the ambit of the trial judge's discretion to admit the recordings, he was also correct in doing so.[409] In this regard it may be noted that 'fairness of the proceedings' has been held by the appellate courts to mean fairness to both sides, i.e. to the prosecution as well as to the defence.[410] Insofar as the notion that 'fairness of the proceedings' means fairness to both sides has been taken to mean that such factors as the seriousness of the offence and the probative value of the evidence concerned may inform the decision to be made under Section 78(1) of PACE,[411] it has been subject to robust criticism in the literature. According to Grevling, such factors, which are 'sometimes associated with fairness to the prosecution or public',[412] 'distort' the exercise of the discretion under Section 78: 'As soon as the gravity of the crime is taken into account, it must signify a tendency towards, if not complete acceptance of, "ends justifies the means" reasoning.'[413] More generally, Ormerod and Birch have criticized the overriding criterion of Section 78(1) on the basis that it invites the court to take into account *all* relevant factors, which 'renders it easier for the courts to admit reliable evidence even if it was unfairly obtained', whereby '[a]rguments of justice can all too readily become assimilated with arguments for accuracy of verdict.'[414] However, insofar as the notion that 'fairness of the proceedings' means fairness to both sides simply means that courts should ensure that a 'balanced picture' of the circumstances, including those in which the evidence was obtained, emerges,[415] or that 'reliable prosecution evidence should not be excluded without good reason',[416] it is relatively uncontroversial. In light of the fact that 'fairness of the proceedings' has been held to mean fairness to both sides, the Court of Appeal's findings in *Chalkley* regarding the use of balancing exercises in the context of Section 78 are somewhat surprising. It effectively held that while it may be appropriate to undertake a balancing exercise under the second limb of the abuse of process doctrine, under Section 78(1) it is not.[417] In so holding, the Court of Appeal appeared to reject the notion that reliable prosecution evidence could be excluded for public policy reasons. As stated above, *Chalkley* had been subject to robust criticism in the literature, precisely because of its apparent rejection of the notion

---

[409] *R v Plunkett* [2013] 1 WLR 3121 [60].

[410] See e.g. *R v Cooke* [1995] 1 Cr App R 318, 328 and *R v Sanghera* [2001] 1 Cr App R 20 [17]. See in this regard e.g. Mirfield 1997, 141; Grevling 1997, 680; Ormerod and Birch 2004, 784; and Dennis 2013, 318.

[411] Rogers argues that, unlike in the context of the second limb of the abuse of process doctrine, in the context of the exclusionary discretion under s 78 PACE, the seriousness of the offence should be an independent factor. See Rogers 2011, 9.

[412] See also Mirfield 1997, 141, explaining how the prosecution may come to represent 'an element of the public interest'.

[413] Grevling 1997, 681.

[414] Ormerod and Birch 2004, 780.

[415] Grevling 1997, 681.

[416] Ashworth and Redmayne 2010, 354.

[417] *R v Chalkley* [1998] QB 848, 874–876.

that unlawfully obtained evidence might be excluded even if its reliability is not in question. While it may well be that this case is best disregarded in this respect, it is surely right in suggesting that, insofar as Section 78(1) allows for the exclusion of unreliable evidence,[418] and in cases in which exclusion is sought on this basis, it would be inappropriate for the court to undertake a balancing exercise. As has been succinctly put: 'There can be no public interest in adducing unreliable evidence against the accused which has more potential for prejudice than for proof'.[419]

4.4.2 Procedural Violations in an International Context

In light of the central research question of this book (how should judges at the ICTs respond to procedural violations committed in the pre-trial phase of the proceedings?), it is instructive to consider the English law and practice with respect to the question of how criminal courts should address procedural violations committed in an 'international context'. This term covers a wide range of conduct on the part of public officials that has the potential to raise issues at any ensuing criminal trial, including unlawfulness in bringing a person into the jurisdiction in which he or she is sought for prosecution, and unlawfulness in the evidence-gathering process abroad. Such conduct potentially raises difficult questions for the criminal court trying the case, given that the impugned activities may have been carried out by or with assistance of foreign authorities, with all that this entails.

Turning first to unlawfulness in bringing a person into the jurisdiction in which he or she is sought for prosecution, it should be recalled that serious police misconduct may warrant the granting of a stay of proceedings on the basis of the abuse of process doctrine. In *R v Horseferry Road Magistrates' Court, Ex parte Bennett*,[420] the defendant, a citizen of New Zealand, had been arrested in South Africa and forcibly returned to England in order to have him face trial for offences of dishonesty. This was done under the pretext of deporting him to New Zealand via Heathrow; he was in fact arrested at Heathrow in connection with those offences. The English police denied that they were in any way involved with the South African police in returning the defendant to England, but for the purpose of the appeal before the House of Lords it was assumed that 'the English police took a deliberate decision not to pursue extradition procedures but to persuade the South African police to arrest and forcibly return the appellant to [England]' and that 'the Crown Prosecution Service were consulted and approved of the behaviour of the police'.[421] The way in which the defendant had been brought to England had been

---

[418] See n 248, 251–252 and accompanying text.

[419] See Mirfield 1997, 141.

[420] *R v Horseferry Road Magistrates' Court, Ex parte Bennett* [1994] 1 AC 42.

[421] *R v Horseferry Road Magistrates' Court, Ex parte Bennett* [1994] 1 AC 42, 52 (Lord Griffiths), delivering the main speech in the House of Lords.

in disregard of available extradition process, in breach of international law and of the law of the state where the defendant had been found. According to the majority, courts should refuse to try the defendant in such circumstances. This is not because it would be impossible in such circumstances to give the defendant a fair trial; rather it is in order to uphold the rule of law.[422] In *Mullen*[423] there was evidence to show that the British authorities had colluded with their Zimbabwean counterparts in order to procure the deportation of the defendant from Zimbabwe to England, in order to arrest him and have him face trial. Significantly, they had done so in circumstances in which there were specific extradition facilities. Moreover, the 'vital element in the operation, the insulation of the defendant from any legal advice following his detention' in Zimbabwe, as a result of which he was effectively prevented from requesting that he be deported to Ireland or some other jurisdiction, was 'in breach of specific provisions of the law of Zimbabwe, or, at the least, was contrary to the defendant's entitlement as a matter of human rights'.[424] The Court of Appeal held that the proceedings had to be stayed on the basis that, but for the unlawful conduct, it is unlikely that the defendant would have been in the country—England—to be prosecuted.[425]

Turning now to unlawfulness in the evidence-gathering process, in *Quinn*[426] it was alleged that the way in which an identification had been carried out in Ireland (in which the appellant had, unbeknownst to him, been positively identified as the murderer of a policeman), was not in accordance with established procedures in England, such that the trial judge had wrongly admitted the evidence thereof in the English trial proceedings against him. In rejecting this argument, the Court of Appeal attached importance to the fact that the identification had come about 'as a result of arrangements made by a foreign police force' and that the British authorities were not responsible for departures from said procedures. It held that: 'Where identification evidence has come into existence abroad as a result of arrangements made by a foreign police force, it is important to appreciate that for the purposes of Section 78 the critical factor is the fairness of the subsequent English criminal proceedings.'[427] It further held that:

> English courts cannot expect English procedural requirements to be complied with by police forces operating aboard, even if, as in the present case, they have similar procedural requirements. The fact that identification was carried out in a way which did not conform with [established procedures in England] cannot be disregarded if and insofar as it affects the intrinsic fairness of the identification procedure adopted.[428]

---

[422] *R v Horseferry Road Magistrates' Court, Ex parte Bennett* [1994] 1 AC 42, 61−62 (Lord Griffiths).

[423] *R v Mullen* [2000] QB 520.

[424] Ibid., 535. The insulation of the defendant from any legal advice was a vital element in the operation because it meant that he was effectively prevented from requesting that he be deported to Ireland or to some other jurisdiction.

[425] Ibid., 536.

[426] *R v Quinn* [1990] Crim LR 581.

[427] Ibid., 582.

[428] Ibid., 582.

Apparently the trial judge did not consider the conduct in question to be intrinsically unfair. In *Konscol*[429] the defendant had been interviewed by Belgian custom officials after the vehicle in which he was travelling was stopped and searched, in which was found a large quantity of amphetamines and LSD. On trial in England for conspiracy to import drugs into the United Kingdom, it was argued that the evidence of the interviews with the Belgian custom officials should be excluded under Section 78 of PACE. It was alleged that the interview had been conducted in breach of PACE; the defendant had not been cautioned and he had not been told that he could have a legal representative at the interview. In rejecting the argument, the Court of Appeal held that: 'This court does not propose to lay down any guidelines as to when a court should or should not admit a statement taken in a foreign country according to their rules which may not coincide with the procedure established under the Police and Criminal Evidence Act.'[430] In the circumstances the trial judge had exercised his discretion properly in admitting the interview.[431] *Quinn* and *Konscol* establish that evidence obtained abroad in accordance with local requirements, but in a manner inconsistent with English statutory requirements, is not inadmissible in English criminal proceedings, subject to the discretion under Section 78 of PACE. This approach appears to have been followed in *Lane*.[432] In that case, it was argued that the trial judge had wrongly declined to exclude a statement obtained in Scotland, in a manner incompatible with English statutory requirements. The appellant had been cautioned, but denied access to a solicitor. In rejecting this argument, the Court of Appeal attached importance to the fact that the interview had been conducted in accordance with Scottish procedure, and that there had been no bad faith on the part of the Scottish police. In *P*,[433] the appellants, who had each been charged with assisting in the United Kingdom in the commission of drug offences in two European countries, argued that the trial judge had wrongly declined to exclude the recordings of a number of intercepted telephone conversations between them and a third party in one of those countries. Lord Hobhouse, with whom the other Lords agreed, said that: 'The law of country A under which these intercepts were made does not treat secrecy as paramount; it permits, subject to judicial supervision, the use of intercepts in evidence. There is no basis for the argument that there is a rule of English public policy which makes this evidence, which is admissible in country A, inadmissible in England.'[434]

While it certainly seems that, as regards the question of whether evidence obtained abroad may be used in English criminal proceedings, 'the starting principle for the English courts is *locus regit actum*, i.e. the law applicable is that of the

---

[429] *R v Konscol* 1993 WL 965659.

[430] Ibid.

[431] It is worth noting that this case was decided prior to the Grand Chamber's leading decision in *Salduz v Turkey* (App no 36391/02 (ECtHR, 27 November 2008)).

[432] *R v McNab and Others* [2002] 1 Cr App R (S.) 72.

[433] *R v P* [2002] 1 AC 146.

[434] Ibid., 165.

geographic location of the subject-matter',[435] this should not be taken to mean that where the evidence concerned has been obtained in breach of local laws, it will be excluded.[436] In *Redmond* it was argued that the trial judge had wrongly refused the defendant's application for the proceedings to be stayed on the basis that the covert recordings of conversations between the defendant and two undercover police officers in Spain and Ireland had been obtained in breach of local laws. In rejecting this argument, the Court of Appeal held as follows:

> *Irrespective of whether the judge fell into error in concluding that there would be no breach of Spanish law in the way the evidence was obtained,* unless the conduct of the British police involved knowingly riding roughshod over the Spanish and Irish rules ... the judge's conclusion that he could properly permit the prosecution to proceed is not one that was outside the lawful ambit of his discretion.[437]

In other words, for the Court of Appeal the crucial issue was whether the British police had acted in bad faith, i.e. whether the prosecuting authorities had 'knowingly abused their executive powers.'[438] While this decision concerns the abuse of process discretion, it may be relevant to the exercise of the exclusionary discretion under Section 78 of PACE in cases involving evidence obtained abroad.

Finally, it worth briefly recalling the case of *A v Secretary of State for the Home Department (No 2)* here, in which the House of Lords held that evidence obtained by torture is inadmissible in judicial proceedings in England and Wales, 'irrespective of where, or by whom, or on whose authority the torture was inflicted'.[439]

4.5 Synthesis

Having set out the English legal framework governing the judicial response to procedural violations committed in the pre-trial phase of criminal proceedings, the question now is how this framework is to be understood in terms of the theoretical framework also set out above: the rationales with respect to the question of procedural violations, and broader objectives of criminal justice.

Turning first to the abuse of process doctrine, it was stated above that the discretion may be exercised in two broad categories of case. A stay of proceedings that falls within the first category seeks to ensure that the defendant does not receive an unfair trial, i.e. a trial that exposes the defendant to an unacceptable risk of wrongful conviction, and is concerned with epistemic considerations. By contrast, a stay of proceedings that falls within the second category of case in which a court

---

[435] Loof 2011, 54.

[436] Ibid., 54.

[437] *R v Redmond* [2009] 1 Cr App R 25, 342 (emphasis added).

[438] Ibid., 342.

[439] *A v Secretary of State for the Home Department (No 2)* [2005] 3 WLR 1249 [51] (Lord Bingham).

has the discretion to stay the proceedings is concerned with non-epistemic considerations. As to the more specific rationale for a stay of proceedings under the
second limb of the abuse of process doctrine, it should be recalled that in a number
of cases, the appellate court seems to have rejected the notion that the proceedings
may be stayed solely or primarily in order to discipline the police or prosecution, or
to deter them from acting in a similar way in the future.[440] The more specific
rationale for a stay of proceedings under the second limb appears to be the integrity
rationale, which reflects the notion that the integrity of the administration of justice
might be compromised if the trial was allowed to take place. It was stated above
that there are a number of variations of this rationale (the court-centred variation,
the public *conduct* variation and the public *attitude* variation);[441] here it may be
recalled that the test for staying the proceedings under the second limb of the abuse
of process doctrine has been formulated in several different ways.[442] It was
observed above that whereas in *R v Horseferry Road Magistrates' Court, Ex parte
Bennett* Lord Lowry seemed to have the court-centred variation of the integrity
rationale in mind, in *Latif; Shahzad* Lord Steyn seemed to embrace the public
attitude variation thereof.[443] In the recent case of *Warren and others v Attorney
General for Jersey*, Lord Dyson, delivering the main speech, adopted Lord Steyn's
words in *Latif; Shahzad*, and by extension, it seems, an approach based on the
public attitude variation of the integrity rationale.[444] In that case, Lord Dyson
argued that in *Ex parte Bennett* no mention had been made of the need for a
balancing exercise simply because the House of Lords in that case had 'considered
that the balance obviously came down in favour of a stay on the facts of that
case',[445] but this interpretation is questionable, as it fails to take into account the
fact that the omission of any such reference is consistent with the court-centred
variation of the integrity rationale (which does not seem to involve a balancing
exercise at all). In any case, it may be that the public attitude variation thereof is
now at the forefront of the appellate courts' thinking as regards the second limb of
the abuse of process discretion. As stated, this rationale involves the court undertaking a balancing exercise, involving competing public interests, in order to
determine whether the proceedings should be stayed. Under this rationale, various
factors may be taken into account, as relevant to each of the public interests
involved. Notably, the seriousness of the offence may be a relevant consideration
under the exercise.[446] Rogers is critical in this regard, as well as of the suggestion

---

[440] See n 114–116 and accompanying text.

[441] See n 73–96 and accompanying text.

[442] See n 118 and accompanying text.

[443] See n 395–396 and accompanying text.

[444] *Warren and others v Attorney General for Jersey* [2012] 1 AC 22 [26]. This was a Privy
Council case. It should be recalled that while judgements of the Judicial Committee of the Privy
Council are not generally binding on courts in England, they do have significant persuasive
authority. See in this regard n 129 and accompanying text.

[445] Ibid., [26].

[446] See n 95 and accompanying text.

that the second limb of the abuse of process doctrine requires the court perform a balancing exercise more generally:

> At the theoretical level, abuse of process arises in cases of executive misconduct where the irregularity enables and infects the subsequent proceedings, such that the court would be perpetuating the wrong by entertaining the trial. If the irregularity is of such seriousness that the court thinks it should not do this, it is not clear why the gravity of ... [the defendant's] own conduct should be relevant. Moreover it is incongruous to balance the gravity of the various wrongs. There is no simple answer to the question whether a minor crime by an official in the purported exercise of his duty is comparable to a more serious one committed by a private citizen who claims no such authorisation. Notably, it is never made clear by those who would attempt such a test whether the conduct of the official should have to be almost as bad as, or equally as bad as, or worse than, the conduct of the accused in order to justify a stay. This equivocation is hardly a sign that this balancing test is soundly based.[447]

He argues that the judge's discretion to stay the proceedings under the second limb should be 'one-sided, directed at deciding how offensive the official misconduct should be regarded'.[448] Be that as it may, so long as the public attitude variation of the integrity rationale is the applicable rationale under this limb of the abuse of process doctrine, the seriousness of the offence will be a relevant consideration, and may be taken into account as both a standalone factor, and as relevant to the seriousness of the police misconduct in question.[449] As a standalone factor, the seriousness of the offence may be (and has been) employed as an argument *not* to grant a stay or proceedings, and thereby 'do justice' to the 'the public interest in ensuring that those that are charged with grave crimes should be tried'.

Turning now to the exclusion of unlawfully obtained evidence, and to Section 78(1) of PACE in particular, on a very general level it may be observed that the appellate courts have in different cases focussed on different factors, which in turn suggests that the appellate case law can be explained by reference to more than one rationale, or, put differently, that it cannot be explained by reference to one rationale alone. In cases involving breaches of PACE, the language and reasoning adopted by the Court of Appeal is reminiscent of the protective principle or remedial rationale (although, as Ashworth and Redmayne observe, it could also be explained in terms of 'some version' of the integrity rationale, 'especially one which emphasizes respect for rights').[450] For example, in *Samuel* the Court of Appeal referred to the right under Section 58 of PACE as 'one of the most important and fundamental rights of a citizen', and that had the trial judge found, as he should have, that the defendant had been wrongly denied this right, 'he might well have concluded that the refusal of access and consequent unlawful interview compelled him to find that the admission of evidence as to the final interview would have "such an adverse

---

[447] Rogers 2011, 8.

[448] Ibid., 8. This suggests that Rogers favours an approach to the second limb of the abuse of process doctrine based on the court-centred variation of the integrity rationale.

[449] See n 387–394 and accompanying text.

[450] See e.g. Ashworth and Redmayne 2010, 357; and also Keane and McKeown 2014, 67.

effect on the fairness of the proceedings" that he ought not to admit it'.[451] Moreover, the enquiry into whether the defendant was prejudiced by the breach of PACE or its codes of practice, while raising 'a difficult question of fact',[452] is not *inconsistent* with the remedial rationale.[453] However, what is inconsistent with the remedial rationale is the importance that the Court of Appeal has in a number of cases involving a breach of PACE and/or its codes of practice attached to the question of whether the authorities acted in bad faith.[454,455] What matters under the protective principle is whether the defendant was disadvantaged by the breach of a right; whether the violation was committed in bad faith is immaterial.[456] At first glance, the focus in cases involving a breach of PACE and/or its codes of practice on the question of whether the authorities acted in bad faith might suggest that the rationale being advanced by the appellate courts is a disciplinary one. After all, it may be argued that precisely in cases in which the public authorities have deliberately flouted the law, a reaction that is likely to deter them from acting in a similar way in the future is called for. However, the Court of Appeal has on numerous occasions said that 'disciplining the police' or 'punishing police officers' is *not* part of the judicial function.[457] Accordingly, while it may be that exclusion has such an effect, and that courts have this effect well in mind when excluding unlawfully obtained evidence, the disciplinary rationale does not seem to be at the forefront of the appellate courts' thinking. Of course, bad faith is also a relevant consideration under the integrity rationale (regardless of the variation thereof), such that consideration of this factor may arguably represent a move 'towards a *sub silentio* adoption of the integrity principle'.[458] However, in *Chalkley*[459] the Court of Appeal held that Section 78(1) does *not* involve a balancing exercise, which, it should be recalled, is key to one of the variations—the public attitude variation—of the integrity rationale. Of course, *Chalkley* itself has been subject to robust criticism in the literature for implying that the exclusionary discretion under Section 78(1) is only available in cases in which the procedural violation in question has affected the quality of the evidence obtained thereby. However, this criticism should not be taken to mean that the provision does, or should involve a balancing exercise. The court-centred variation of the integrity rationale, it should be recalled, does not involve a balancing

---

[451] *R v Samuel* [1988] QB 615 at 630.

[452] See Ashworth and Redmayne 2010, 357.

[453] See n 57–62 and accompanying text.

[454] See Ashworth and Redmayne 2010, 358.

[455] Nevertheless, according to Ashworth and Redmayne, 'although several cases make this point, it may be less significant when it comes to actual decisions made by the courts. We are not aware of any decision under s 78 where evidence is obtained in breach of a PACE right but is admitted owing to the absence of bad faith.' See Ashworth and Redmayne 2010, 358.

[456] See e.g. Mirfield 1997, 32: 'One's rights are no less damnified by the blundering police officer than by the malevolent one.'

[457] See e.g. *R v Mason* [1988] 1 WLR 139 and *R v Hughes* [1994] 1 WLR 876.

[458] Choo 2015, 187.

[459] *R v Chalkley* [1998] QB 848.

exercise at all. On the other hand, consideration of the seriousness of the offence (as a separate, standalone factor) *is* consistent with the public attitude variation of the integrity rationale, but inconsistent with the court-centred variation thereof, as well as with the protective principle and the disciplinary rationale. In conclusion, then, it seems that the appellate case law cannot be explained by reference to one rationale alone. However, that is not the whole story here, and, in order to come to more representative conclusions as regards the theory or ideas underlying the practice with respect to the admissibility and use of unlawfully obtained evidence, it is necessary to investigate further. To begin with, it is necessary to return to a point raised above, regarding the availability of the discretion under Section 78(1) of PACE, and its proper exercise.[460] For this purpose it is instructive to recall what the position in England and Wales has traditionally been with respect to unlawfully obtained evidence: provided it is relevant, unlawfully obtained evidence is prima facie admissible; that is the point of departure with respect to such evidence. By way of exception, the common law recognised an exclusionary *rule* for confessions obtained by threats, promises or oppression. In other words, such confessions were treated as inadmissible at law. Therefore, according to Mirfield, '[i]n *effect*, the common law regarded as paramount the reliability principle, so far as non-confession was concerned ...'.[461] Certainly, it appears to have envisaged a restrictive application of the judicial response within the criminal trial to pre-trial procedural violations. In *Sang*, which was decided shortly before PACE entered into force, the House of Lords certainly appears to have had a restrictive application of that response in mind. In that case, a (very) narrow discretion to exclude evidence on grounds of unfairness was recognised; according to Lord Diplock, the discretion to exclude evidence on such grounds was restricted to confessions and 'evidence obtained from the accused after the commission of the offence', whereby the more specific rationale in this regard was that of the privilege against self-incrimination.[462] In other words, the discretion at common law to exclude evidence on grounds of unfairness was *available* in only a narrow set of circumstances.

It was stated above that the exclusionary discretion under Section 78(1) of PACE is *available* in a wider variety of cases than was the exclusionary discretion under the common law (based on what was held in relation to the unfairness head of the common law exclusionary discretion in *Sang*). For example, unlike the common law exclusionary discretion, the discretion under Section 78 is available in cases involving entrapment, i.e. the use of an *agent provocateur*. However, as also stated above, the question of availability of the exclusionary discretion under Section 78 (1) of PACE should be distinguished from the question of its 'proper exercise', i.e.

---

[460] See n 348 and accompanying text.

[461] Mirfield 1997, 109 (emphasis added).

[462] In *Chalkley* the Court of Appeal interpreted the relevant passage of Lord Diplock's judgment in *Sang* as saying that the rationale underlying the unfairness head of the common law exclusionary discretion is that of reliability, but this reading of the passage is questionable. See n 339–340 and accompanying text.

of what the appellate courts consider to constitute its proper exercise. Put differently, it is one thing to say that courts *would not* exclude certain unlawfully obtained evidence (which goes to the question of the proper exercise of the discretion), but quite another to say that courts *could not* do so (which goes to the question of availability).[463] Nash and Choo helpfully distinguish two cases concerning covertly recorded incriminating conversations (both of which are addressed above) on this basis:

> A possible difference between *Khan* and *Chalkley* lies in the fact that the House of Lords in the former case appeared to acknowledge that such evidence *could* be excluded in the exercise of discretion, albeit probably only in very limited circumstances, while the Court of Appeal in the latter case appeared to suggest that such evidence *could not* be excluded in the exercise of discretion.[464]

Indeed, in a number of cases concerning unlawfully obtained non-confession evidence, where no issue of unreliability has arisen, the appellate court appears to have entertained the possibility of exclusion, i.e. accepted that the discretion was, in principle, available, only to conclude that the trial judge did not err in declining to exclude it. *Khan*[465] is a notable example of such reasoning, although, as Nash and Choo observe, Lord Nolan does not explain *why* exactly the trial judge did not err in this regard.[466] In *Cooke*,[467] *McCarthy*,[468] *Khan, Sakkaravej and Pamarapa*[469] and *Sanghera*[470] also, such reasoning appears to have been adopted (implicitly, at least). In each of these (four) cases, the Court of Appeal attached importance to the fact that the (alleged) procedural violation had had no effect on the *quality* of the (real) evidence concerned, to evidence of this sort being highly *probative*, there being no issue as to reliability of the evidence and/or the 'consequence' of not admitting the evidence: 'interference with the achievement of justice'. Accordingly, it seems that in cases concerning unlawfully obtained *non-confession* evidence, in which issues of reliability are unlikely to arise,[471] exclusion will be rare.[472] The question, then, is whether it matters that considerations that once went to the question of the availability of the discretion, now go to the question of its proper exercise. According to Dennis, the fact that in cases concerning unlawfully obtained non-confession evidence exclusion will be rare 'does not detract from the significance of recognising

---

[463] See Choo 2015, 177. See also Nash and Choo 1999, 936.

[464] See Nash and Choo 1999, 936.

[465] *R v Khan* [1997] AC 558.

[466] See Nash and Choo 1999, 936.

[467] *R v Cooke* [1995] 1 Cr App R 318.

[468] *R v McCarthy* [1996] Crim LR 818.

[469] *R v Khan, Sakkaravej and Pamarapa* [1997] Crim LR 508.

[470] *R v Sanghera* [2001] 1 Cr App R 20.

[471] See however n 293 and accompanying text.

[472] See e.g. Dennis 2013, 97. See also Mirfield 1997, 110: 'That the rule of inclusion for non-confession evidence has survived the enactment of the Police and Criminal Evidence Act 1984 … has been categorically confirmed by Lord Nolan in *Khan*.'

that s. 78 confers a discretion to exclude such evidence',[473] while Nash and Choo are more sceptical in this regard. In observing that *Khan* and *Chalkley* may be distinguished on the basis that, while the former recognises that the discretion is available in cases involving covert recordings of incriminating conversations, the latter seems to rule this out, they nevertheless conclude that 'the commitment to a reliability principle in both cases seems abundantly clear'.[474] More generally, they lament the move from the focus in the earlier years on the *nature of the breach*, to a focus on the *nature of the evidence*.[475] Indeed, despite the discretion being available in a wide array of cases, the fact remains that in cases in which the reliability, or 'quality of the evidence', is not in question, courts have demonstrated an unwillingness to exclude it. *Cooke* concerned DNA evidence, which the Court of Appeal was prepared to accept had been obtained unlawfully; however, the trial judge had not erred in admitting it since the manner of its obtaining in no way 'cast doubt upon the accuracy or strength of the evidence'.[476] *Sanghera* concerned real evidence obtained by an unlawful search, but the trial judge had not erred in admitting it, since, among other things, there was 'no issue as to the reliability of the evidence'.[477] *Khan* concerned covert recordings of incriminating conversations to which the appellant was a party, and while in finding that the trial judge had not erred in declining to exclude the evidence Lord Nolan did not explicitly refer to considerations of reliability or quality of evidence, this case is widely recognised as, at least in effect, regarding the reliability rationale as paramount.[478]

Indeed, it is not uncommon to encounter in the literature statements to the effect that it is the reliability rationale that is (and/or remains) at the forefront of the appellate courts' thinking with respect to Section 78(1) of PACE.[479] Lord Nicholls' statement in *Looseley* is considered by a number of commentators to be representative of the appellate courts' thinking in this regard: 'The phrase "fairness of the proceedings" in Section 78 is directed primarily at matters going to fairness in the actual conduct of the trial; for instance, the reliability of the evidence and the defendant's ability to test its reliability.'[480] In this case, then (as in others), the reference in Section 78(1) to 'the fairness of the proceedings' is interpreted as meaning *trial* fairness. *Chalkley* is another case in which the reliability of the evidence concerned weighed heavily for the Court of Appeal; in concluding that there was no basis to exclude the evidence pursuant to Section 78 of PACE, it

---

[473] Dennis 2013, 97.

[474] Nash and Choo 1999, 936.

[475] Ibid., 933. See also Choo 2015, 175.

[476] *R v Cooke* [1995] 1 Cr App R 318, 328–329.

[477] *R v Sanghera* [2001] 1 Cr App R 20 [15]. See also *R v Khan, Sakkaravej and Pamarapa* [1997] Crim LR 508; and *R v McCarthy* [1996] Crim LR 818.

[478] See e.g. Mirfield 1997, 109–110; and Nash and Choo 1999, 936.

[479] See e.g. Choo 2015, 186; Nash and Choo 1999, 935, 936 and 937; Ormerod and Birch 2004; and Keane and McKeown 2014, 65–66.

[480] *R v Looseley* [2001] 1 WLR 2060 [12]. As to the commentators, see e.g. Keane and McKeown 2014, 66) and Ormerod and Birch 2004, 779–780.

attached significant importance to the fact that the manner of its obtaining had had no effect on the quality of the evidence. Moreover, it was suggested in that case that the discretion under Section 78 was unavailable in cases in which the reliability of the evidence is not in question. Even if this aspect of the decision is best disregarded as a matter of law, it may still be indicative of the Court of Appeal's thinking as regards unlawfully obtained non-confession evidence, particularly in light of the fact that it has been cited with approval in other cases.[481]

In addition to the fact that courts have, in determining whether the trial judge properly exercised the discretion under Section 78, attached importance to considerations of reliability or quality of evidence, a further indicator that the reliability rationale may be at the forefront of the appellate courts' thinking, may be that even in case of 'significant and substantial' breaches of PACE and/or its codes of practice exclusion is not automatic. Indeed, according to Ormerod and Birch, the fact that Section 78(1) entails making a judgement of degree, whereby the court may take into account *all* relevant factors may make it easier for courts to 'admit reliable evidence even if it was unfairly obtained'.[482] Moreover, they suggest that the fact that the appellate courts' have sought to draw an analogy between the application of Section 78 of PACE and the way in which the ECtHR determines Article 6 of the ECHR[483] should not be taken to mean that they are seeking to adopt an approach to exclusion based on the protective principle. They observe, regretfully, that 'the opportunity to take account of *all* factors in securing 'fairness' has enabled the courts to claim that s. 78 guarantees Article 6 compliance, without adopting an explicitly rights-based approach to exclusion'.[484] Indeed, in some cases in which the analogy has been drawn, the appellate court has appeared keen to emphasize that a breach of Article 8 need not render the trial unfair, within the meaning of Article 6 of the ECHR.[485] Finally, it was stated above that the language and reasoning adopted by the Court of Appeal in the 'significant and substantial' cases is reminiscent of the protective principle or remedial rationale, while the significance attached in some of those cases to the question of whether the authorities acted in bad faith is inconsistent with this principle. Two points may be made in this regard. First, it may be observed in respect of the cases involving 'significant and substantial' breaches of the provisions of PACE and/or its Codes of Practice regulating the questioning of persons by the police and the powers of the

---

[481] See e.g. *R v Shannon* [2001] 1 WLR 51; and see Choo 2015, 196–197; and Dennis 2013, 102, where this case is discussed.

[482] Ormerod and Birch 2004, 780.

[483] See e.g. *R v Hardy* [2003] 1 Cr App R 30 [18]–[19].

[484] Ormerod and Birch 2004, 780.

[485] See e.g. *R v Hardy* [2003] 1 Cr App R 30 [19]. See also *R v Rosenberg* [2006] Crim LR 540.

police to identify persons, that such breaches have the potential to affect the reliability of the evidence obtained thereby. While this is certainly not to suggest that such cases can (let alone should) be explained in terms of the reliability principle,[486] it does shed light on the appellate courts' tendency to *not* interfere with a trial judge's discretion to *admit* unlawfully obtained *non-confession* evidence (other than identification evidence), for example, unlawfully obtained real evidence; the exclusion of such evidence is clearly more controversial than the exclusion of evidence whose reliability or quality may well have been compromised by the manner in which it was obtained (as is the case for confession evidence, and for identification evidence).[487] The second point concerns the appellate courts' tendency to attach significance to the question of whether the authorities acted in bad faith. It was suggested above that, while this question is irrelevant under the protective principle, it *is* a relevant consideration under other rationales, specifically, the disciplinary and integrity rationales. However, in seeking to explain the tendency of the appellate courts to take the question of bad faith into account in terms of such rationales, and, in particular, of the disciplinary rationale, caution may be warranted. Ormerod and Birch observe that while basing a decision to exclude evidence on the bad faith of the authorities might indicate that the court is excluding the evidence in order to discipline the police, 'when examined more closely, its effect is quite the opposite':

> The courts approach to bad faith as a measure of admissibility has resulted in exclusion only in extreme cases where the police can be shown to have deliberately flouted the regulation. The more commonly occurring negligent or sloppy policing which breaches the pre-trial safeguards thus remain admissible and undisciplined. The effect of this use of s.78 might even be to encourage the police to be sloppy in their investigations since if an officer is unaware of the regulation he cannot be said to have acted in bad faith by deliberately flouting it![488]

In attempting to 'make sense' of the appellate case law regarding Section 78(1) of PACE in terms of the theory, i.e. the rationales for excluding evidence, it is important to be mindful of the standard of review applied by the Court of Appeal, and of the fact that most appeals brought before the Court of Appeal of England and Wales are *defence* appeals.[489] It is fair to say then, that, in the majority of appellate cases in which issue has been taken with the trial judge's exercise of discretion under Section 78 of PACE (which, it should be recalled, is restricted in its application to evidence on which the *prosecution* proposes to rely), the issue on which a ruling will have been sought is whether the trial judge could reasonably have exercised the discretion under Section 78 to *admit* certain evidence. Regarding the

---

[486] In this regard it should be noted that the Court of Appeal's attempts to do so (see e.g. *R v Chalkley* [1998] QB 848) have been subject to robust criticism in the literature. See e.g. Choo 2015, 186.

[487] See also e.g. Ormerod and Birch 2004, 775–776.

[488] Ormerod and Birch 2004, 781.

[489] Thanks to Professor Andrew Choo for drawing my attention to this point.

standard of review, it should be recalled here that the Court of Appeal will only interfere with the trial judge's exercise of discretion under this provision in limited circumstances, i.e. where the decision is one which no reasonable court could have come to. To say that a decision pursuant to Section 78(1) of PACE is one which the trial judge could reasonably have come to is not necessarily to say that it was the 'right' decision. Indeed, it is entirely possible for an appellate court to say that it would itself have excluded the evidence in question, while at the same time for it to uphold the trial judge's decision to admit it.[490] This may have consequences for how the appellate case law regarding Section 78 is to be interpreted in terms of the rationales for exclusion; insofar as the appellate courts have merely ruled on the reasonableness of the trial judge's decision, it would seem to call for caution in seeking to argue that such courts are adopting or applying a particular rationale. Accordingly, in respect of cases in which the Court of Appeal has declined to interfere with the trial judge's discretion to *admit* unlawfully obtained but reliable evidence it may be more accurate to say that such cases have *the effect* of placing reliability considerations at the forefront. However, in many of the cases examined above (and in many other relevant cases) concerning unlawfully obtained but seemingly reliable evidence, the appellate court appears to go beyond ruling on the reasonableness of the trial judge's decision, to say that the trial judge's decision to admit the unlawfully obtained but reliable evidence was 'right'. In *Mason*, for example, the Court of Appeal not only said that the trial judge's decision to admit the evidence obtained by covert audio surveillance in breach of Article 8 of the ECHR was a reasonable one, but also that it would have come to the same conclusion itself.[491] In *Cooke* the Court of Appeal 'wholly agreed' with the trial judge's decision to admit the DNA evidence, even if it had been obtained unlawfully.[492] In *Sanghera*, which concerned unlawfully obtained real evidence, the Court of Appeal said that it thought that the trial judge had come to the 'right decision' in admitting it.[493] In each of these cases, the Court of Appeal explicitly noted that the reliability of the evidence was not in question.

In conclusion, the tendency of appellate courts not to interfere with trial judges' decisions pursuant to Section 78(1) of PACE to admit unlawfully obtained but reliable evidence at the very least *gives effect to* the reliability principle. Moreover, there are indications in the appellate case law regarding Section 78—the (questionable) reasoning adopted by the Court of Appeal in cases such as *Chalkley*, and the statements of the appellate courts expressing agreement with the trial judge's decision to admit unlawfully obtained but reliable evidence—that the appellate courts regard the reliability principle as paramount. It is worth noting here that reliability may not be the sole or even primary rationale as regards the exclusionary *rules* set out above. Regarding Section 76(2), Dennis observes that, the fact that the subsection provides that if either para (a) or (b) is satisfied, the confession is inadmissible 'notwithstanding that it may be true' suggests that 'presumed unreliability

---

[490] See n 370 and accompanying text.

[491] *R v Mason* [2002] 2 Cr App R 38 [83].

[492] *R v Cooke* [1995] 1 Cr App R 318, 328–329.

[493] *R v Sanghera* [2001] 1 Cr App R 20 [17].

of the actual confession is not the rationale for exclusion'.[494] Regarding the exclusionary rule at common law for evidence obtained by torture, it seems that none of their Lordships in *A v Secretary of State for the Home Department (No 2)*[495] regarded 'presumed unreliability' to be the primary let alone sole rationale for the exclusion of such evidence. Lord Rodger put it as follows: 'the torturer is abhorred as a *hostis humani generis* not because the information he produces may be unreliable but because of the barbaric means he uses to extract it'.[496]

The focus on reliability, be it 'merely' an (unfortunate) effect of the reluctance of the appellate courts to interfere with the trial judge's exercise of judicial discretion under Section 78(1) of PACE coupled with the fact that most appeals brought before the Court of Appeal are *defence* appeals, or (rather) a matter of principle for the Court of Appeal, has been roundly criticized in the literature.[497] Such a focus is said to be problematic, because 'the trial is not merely about reliably convicting the guilty and ensuring the innocent are protected from wrongful conviction'; indeed, it is by now widely recognised that 'there is an important judicial responsibility to maintain the moral integrity of the process'.[498] Here it may be observed that insofar as the appellate courts attach importance to the seriousness of the offence, and the interests of victims and their families, in the context of the determination of whether it was within the trial judge's discretion to admit unlawfully obtained evidence, this may also have the effect of placing the objective of convicting the guilty (and, correspondingly, ensuring that the innocent are protected from wrongful conviction), or 'epistemic' considerations at the forefront. Indeed, the practice of taking these factors into account has been sharply criticized on this basis. According to Ormerod and Birch, an approach to exclusion in which these are considered to be relevant factors 'renders s. 78 even more susceptible to reliability based decision-making, factoring in society's and victims' interests in convicting the "factually guilty" against whom there is reliable evidence however obtained, since the exclusion of reliable evidence can endanger the community'.[499]

4.6 Conclusion

The purpose of this chapter was to set out the English theory, law and practice with respect to the question of how to address pre-trial procedural violations. In the penultimate section of the chapter the legal framework governing the English judicial response within the criminal trial was 'assessed' in light of the possible

---

[494] Dennis 2013, 227 n 87. See also Choo 2015, 186.

[495] *A v Secretary of State for the Home Department (No 2)* [2005] 3 WLR 1249.

[496] *A v Secretary of State for the Home Department (No 2)* [2005] 3 WLR 1249 at 130. See also Roberts 2012b, 172.

[497] See e.g. Nash and Choo 1999; Ormerod and Birch 2004; and Choo 2015, 186.

[498] Ormerod and Birch 2004, 782.

[499] Ibid., 785.

rationales for such a response. In this section the main features of the legal framework and the main points of the analysis are summarised.

In England and Wales, there are a number of ways in which pre-trial procedural violations may be addressed within the criminal trial. The trial judge may stay the proceedings, exclude evidence obtained by the violation, take the violation into account at the sentencing stage or simply condemn the conduct in question. A court's power to stay the proceedings and to exclude evidence on grounds of unfairness entails the exercise of judicial *discretion*, which means, among other things, that the standard to be applied is 'open-textured', i.e. 'cast in broad and flexible terms', thereby allowing the court applying it to 'do justice' according to the individual needs of the case. Discretions should be distinguished from rules, which also feature in the English judicial response within the criminal trial to pre-trial procedural violations. For example, Section 76(2) of PACE provides for an exclusionary rule in respect of confessions. As to the discretions, under the first limb of the abuse of process doctrine, the trial judge is afforded a degree of latitude in determining whether the prejudice caused, in terms of the ability of the court to determine the guilt or innocence of the accused accurately, is such that the proceedings ought to be stayed, on account of it exposing the accused to an unacceptable risk of wrongful conviction. However, once the court decides that the prejudice is such that it does so, the proceedings must automatically, i.e. without further consideration or 'balancing', be stayed. Under the second limb, the overriding criterion is whether, if the proceedings were allowed to continue, the integrity of the adjudicative process, and, by extension, of the criminal justice system as a whole, would be undermined, a standard that is clearly open-textured in nature. The more specific rationale under this limb appears to be the public attitude variation of the integrity rationale, pursuant to which the court must undertake a balancing exercise involving competing public interests (the public interest in the conviction of the 'factually guilty' against whom there is reliable evidence and the public interest in the judiciary not condoning the unlawful action of law enforcement agencies). Under this rationale, the court may take into account a variety of factors, as relevant to one or both of the competing public interests, including the seriousness of the police misconduct and the seriousness of the offence. This balancing exercise may create significant scope for a court *not* to stay the proceedings. In light of the conceptual difficulties involved in performing such a balancing exercise (and, essentially, 'comparing reprehensibility'),[500] it is not surprising that calls have been made for more structured decision-making in the context of the second limb of the abuse of process doctrine, whereby the factors to which courts should attach importance are clearly identified and/or the discretion is confined.

Section 78(1) of PACE, pursuant to which a court has the power to exclude (prosecution) evidence on grounds of unfairness, also involves the exercise of judicial discretion. The overriding criterion of whether 'admission of the evidence

---

[500] See n 80 and accompanying text.

would have *such* an adverse effect on the fairness of the proceedings that it ought not to be admitted' clearly allows the court a great deal of latitude in deciding whether or not to exclude the evidence. The trial judge exercising the discretion under Section 78 is required to make a judgement of degree; in other words, for unlawfully obtained evidence, the fact of the unlawfulness is not, in itself, sufficient to justify its exclusion. Even 'significant and substantial' breaches of PACE and/or its codes of practice do not lead to the automatic exclusion of evidence obtained thereby. In cases involving such a breach, the Court of Appeal has looked to whether the officials involved had acted in bad faith, and/or whether the accused had been prejudiced by the conduct concerned; such factors weigh in favour of exclusion. In cases concerning unlawfully obtained non-confession evidence (other than identification evidence), the appellate courts have attached importance to the fact that the (improper) manner in which the evidence was obtained will not have had an effect on its reliability or quality. This factor weighs against exclusion. The fact that the reliability of the evidence is considered to be a relevant factor (and apparently one to which significant weight may be attached) means that, in practice, exclusion of certain types of evidence is likely to be rare. Moreover, in a number of cases, the appellate courts have sanctioned consideration of the seriousness of the offence as a standalone factor. Together with the reliability of the (unlawfully obtained) evidence in question, the seriousness of the offence has in some cases made for a compelling case against exclusion.[501] This factor, it seems, has been allowed to enter the analysis on the basis that, under Section 78, fairness is owed to 'both sides': the defence *and* prosecution. The appellate courts, then, have taken a variety of factors into account in the determination of whether the discretion under Section 78 was properly exercised. The wording of Section 78 would seem to support such an approach, and the appellate courts have sought to draw an analogy with the ECtHR's approach to the determination of Article 6 of the ECHR on this basis. However, this should not be taken to mean that they are seeking to adopt a rights-based approach to exclusion. In this regard it should be recalled that the appellate courts have consistently emphasized that a breach of Article 8 need not render the trial unfair, within the meaning of Article 6 of the ECHR. Further, in light of the fact that the appellate courts have not been consistent in their selection of the factors that they consider to be relevant under Section 78(1) of PACE, in this context also, calls have been made for a more structured approach to decision-making, whereby the factors to which the trial judge should attach importance are clearly identified, and for the discretion to be confined.

---

[501] See e.g. *R v Plunkett* [2013] 1 WLR 3121 [58]–[60].

References

Ashworth AJ (1977) Excluding Evidence as Protecting Rights. Crim LR 723 et seq.

Ashworth A (1999) Defending the entrapped. Arch. News 5 et seq.

Ashworth A (2003) Exploring the Integrity Principle in Evidence and Procedure. In: Mirfield P, Smith R (eds) Essays for Colin Tapper. LexisNexis UK, London/Edinburgh, pp 107–125

Ashworth A, Redmayne M (2010) The Criminal Process, 4th edn. Oxford University Press, Oxford

Choo AL-T (2006) Evidence. Oxford University Press, Oxford

Choo AL-T (2008) Abuse of Process and Judicial Stays of Criminal Proceedings, 2nd edn. Oxford University Press, Oxford

Choo AL-T (2015) Evidence, 4th edn. Oxford University Press, Oxford

Dennis IH (1989) Reconstructing the Law of Criminal Evidence. CLP 42:21 et seq.

Dennis I (2003) Fair Trials and Safe Convictions. CLP 56:211 et seq.

Dennis IH (2013) The Law of Evidence, 5th edn. Sweet & Maxwell, London

Duff P (2004) Admissibility of Improperly Obtained Physical Evidence in the Scottish Criminal Trial: The Search for Principle. Edin LR 8:152 et seq.

Dworkin R (1977) Taking Rights Seriously. Duckworth, London

Giannoulopoulos D (2007) The Exclusion of Improperly Obtained Evidence in Greece: Putting Constitutional Rights First. E&P 11:181 et seq.

Grevling K (1997) Fairness and the exclusion of evidence under section 78(1) of the Police and Criminal Evidence Act. LQR 667 et seq.

Kamisar Y (1987) "Comparative Reprehensibility" and the Fourth Amendment Exclusionary Rule. Mich L Rev 86:1 et seq.

Keane A, McKeown P (2014) The Modern Law of Evidence, 10th edn. Oxford University Press, Oxford

Loof R (2011) Obtaining, adducing and contesting evidence from abroad: A defence perspective on cross-border evidence. Crim LR 40 et seq.

Martin S (2005) Lost and destroyed evidence: The search for a principled approach to abuse of process. 9 E&P 158 et seq.

Mirfield P (1997) Silence, Confessions and Improperly Obtained Evidence. Oxford University Press, Oxford

Nash S, Choo AL-T (1999) What's the matter with Section 78? Crim LR 929 et seq.

O'Connor P (2012) "Abuse of process" after Warren and Maxwell. Crim LR 672 et seq.

Ormerod D (2003) ECHR and the exclusion of evidence: Trial remedies for Article 8 breaches? Crim LR 61 et seq.

Ormerod D, Birch D (2004) The evolution of the discretionary exclusion of evidence. Crim LR 767 et seq.

Pound R (1959) Jurisprudence (Vol II). West Publishing Co, St Paul, Minn

Redmayne M (2009) Theorizing the Criminal Trial. New Crim L Rev 12:287 et seq.

Roberts P (2012) Excluding Evidence as Protecting Constitutional or Human Rights? In: Zedner L, Roberts JV (eds) Principles and Values in Criminal Law and Criminal Justice: Essays in Honour of Andrew Ashworth. Oxford University Press, Oxford, pp 171–190

Roberts P (2012) Normative Evolution in evidentiary Exclusion: Coercion, Deception and the Right to a Fair Trial. In: Roberts P, Hunter J (eds) Criminal Evidence and Human Rights: Reimagining Common Law Procedural Traditions. Hart Publishing, Oxford, pp 163–193

Rogers J (2008) The Boundaries of Abuse of Process in Criminal Trials. CLP 61:289 et seq.

Rogers J (2011) Abuse of process reconsidered. Arch Rev 6 et seq.

Tapper C (2010) Cross & Tapper on Evidence, 12th edn. Oxford University Press, Oxford

Ward R, Akhtar A (2011) Walker & Walker's English Legal System, 11th edn. Oxford University Press, Oxford

Zander M (1985) The Police and Criminal Evidence Act 1984. Sweet & Maxwell, London

Zuckerman AAS (1987) Illegally-Obtained Evidence—Discretion as a Guardian of Legitimacy. CLP 55 et seq.

Zuckerman AAS (1989) The Principles of Criminal Evidence. Clarendon Press, Oxford

Chapter 5
Law and Practice of the International Criminal Tribunals—General Overview

Abstract In this chapter the law and practice of the international criminal tribunals with respect to the question of how to address procedural violations committed in the pre-trial phase of the proceedings is set out by means of an overview of the consequences that the judge may attach to such procedural violations which (potentially) have general application, i.e. are applicable in respect of a wider range of pre-trial procedural violations, including their general features. Those consequences are: a stay of proceedings, the exclusion of evidence, financial compensation, sentence reduction and express acknowledgement of the violation. It also compares the law and practice of the ad hoc Tribunals to that of the ICC, and concludes that the approaches of the ad hoc Tribunals and of the ICC to the question of how to address procedural violations committed in the pre-trial phase of international criminal proceedings are broadly similar, with a few notable differences.

Keywords features of international criminal procedure · fragmentation of the investigation · reliance on state-cooperation · nature of regulation of the investigative phase · abuse of process doctrine · stay of proceedings · exclusion of evidence · Rule 95 RPE · Article 69(7) ICC Statute · discretion · balancing · financial compensation · sentence reduction · express acknowledgement

Contents

© T.M.C. ASSER PRESS and the author 2018

K. Pitcher, *Judicial Responses to Pre-Trial Procedural Violations in International Criminal Proceedings*, International Criminal Justice Series 16, https://doi.org/10.1007/978-94-6265-219-4_5

5.1   Introduction

The purpose of this chapter is to set out the law and practice of the international criminal tribunals with respect to the question of how to address procedural violations committed in the pre-trial phase of the proceedings.[1] This will be done by means of an overview of the consequences that the judge may attach to such procedural violations which (potentially) have *general* application, i.e. are applicable in respect of a wider range of pre-trial procedural violations, including their general features. Those consequences are: a stay of proceedings, the exclusion of evidence, financial compensation, sentence reduction and 'express acknowledgement' of the violation. In Chap. 6, the law and practice of the ICTs with respect to the aforementioned question will be addressed in two specific contexts, namely, arrest and detention, and disclosure. This more 'contextual' chapter provides an opportunity to bring to light important issues which (potentially) have general application, that are not appropriately dealt with in the present chapter, because their significance goes beyond a particular response to procedural violations (committed in the pre-trial phase of international criminal proceedings) or, more generally, because the analysis required in order to tease out such issues is not in keeping with the general nature of the overview provided in this chapter. The purpose of the contextual chapter, then, is to complement the overview provided in the present chapter, and thereby provide a fuller picture of the law and practice of the ICTs with respect to the question of how to address procedural violations committed in the pre-trial phase of the proceedings. Ultimately, such law and practice will be evaluated in light of the human rights standards set out in Chap. 2, and compared to the national law and practice set out in Chaps. 3 and 4. This will be done in Chap. 7. The present chapter, then, does not

---

[1] Parts of this chapter are based on earlier work by the same author. See in this regard De Meester et al. 2013. Due to a mistake on the part of the publisher, this chapter was presented as a co-authored chapter. However, part 5 of this chapter ('Remedies') is to be attributed to the present author. This will be corrected in the next edition. See also Pitcher 2013.

seek to argue what the law and practice at the ICTs with respect of the question of how to address procedural violations committed in the pre-trial phase of international criminal proceedings *should* be. Nevertheless, where instructive in order to clarify what the law and practice *is*, note has been made of the criticism on the law and practice, also with a view to putting the reader on notice as to the issues that will be addressed in Chap. 7.

As to the structure of this chapter, in Sect. 5.3 the relevant law and practice at the ad hoc Tribunals, i.e. the consequences that a judge may attach to procedural violations committed in the pre-trial phase of the proceedings which (potentially) have *general* application, will be set out, while in Sect. 5.4 the relevant law and practice at the ICC will be set out. Before setting out such law and practice, however, it is worth considering (on a very general level) some distinctive features of international criminal procedure that have the potential to lead to a more restrained or restrictive approach at the ICTs to the question of how to address pre-trial procedural violations or, otherwise, to complicate the determination by the ICTs of the consequences, if any, to be attached to such procedural violations (vis-à-vis that to be made in a purely national context); such features, which were alluded to in the introduction to this book, will be set out in Sect. 5.2. In the penultimate section of this chapter, Sect. 5.5, the law and practice at the ad hoc Tribunals and that at the ICC will be compared, which will be followed by a conclusion, in Sect. 5.6.

5.2 Features of International Criminal Procedure

As stated above, several distinctive features of international criminal procedure have the potential to lead to a more restrained or restrictive approach by the ICTs to the question of how to address procedural violations committed in the context of international criminal proceedings, or, otherwise, to complicate the determination by the ICTs of the consequences, if any, to be attached to procedural violations committed in the context of international criminal proceedings (as compared to that made in a purely national context). Such features, which are interrelated, are: the nature of the regulation of the investigation in international criminal procedure (i.e. the broad attribution of powers and absence of detailed rules in respect of the investigation), the lack of an own enforcement agency to execute investigative measures (and the resulting reliance on state-cooperation) and the fragmentation of the investigation over several jurisdictions. The purpose of this section is to briefly set out such features, as well as to provide other, background, information of a more general nature regarding the procedure applicable at the ICTs, in order to assist the reader in understanding the law and practice set out in this chapter. Whether the aforementioned features have, in fact, led to a restrained or restrictive approach to to the question of how to address procedural violations committed in the context of international criminal proceedings (and whether they *should* do so) is addressed later on the book, in Chap. 7.

At the ICTs, 'procedure' is regulated, in the first place, by the ICTs' *own* Statutes and RPEs. Typical 'pre-trial activities' in any system of criminal justice include the arrest and detention of persons suspected or accused of committing crimes and the collection of evidence; in this regard it should be recalled that neither the ad hoc Tribunals nor the ICC have their own enforcement agencies, as a result of which they are (largely) reliant on state-cooperation for the apprehension of a suspect or an accused, and for the collection of evidence.[2] For this reason, ICTs have been likened to 'giant[s] without arms and legs', in need of 'artificial limbs to walk'.[3] The lack of an own enforcement agency goes some way to explaining the nature of the regulation of such activities in the respective Statutes and RPEs of the ICTs; such documents confer on the ICTs broad coercive powers (of both a custodial and non-custodial nature), but, in general, they say little about the actual execution of coercive measures. For example, while at the ad hoc Tribunals, the Prosecutor may, 'in case of urgency', request a state to arrest a suspect or accused 'provisionally', whereby the state concerned is obliged to comply with such a request,[4] neither the Statutes nor the RPEs provide for a procedure for national authorities implementing a request for provisional arrest and detention pursuant to Rule 40 of the RPE. Nor do they provide for a procedure for national authorities implementing an arrest warrant issued by the relevant ad hoc Tribunal.[5] As for the other pre-trial activities referred to above, De Meester speaks of the 'broad attribution of powers and the absence of detailed rules on the collection of evidence' in this regard, which he argues should be 'understood in light of the need for state cooperation'.[6] It is worth pointing out here that in a number of early ICTR decisions, trial chambers have declined to exercise jurisdiction over the circumstances of an arrest carried out by national authorities at the request of the ICTR Prosecutor *because* the Statute and RPE are silent on how a request for provisional arrest is to be effected. More will be said about this issue in Chap. 6, where the law and practice of the ICTs with respect to the question of how to address procedural violations committed in the context of arrest and detention will be considered in detail, and in Chap. 7, where the adequacy of the judicial response at the ad hoc Tribunals and that at the ICC to procedural violations committed in the context of international criminal proceedings will be assessed.

Related to the nature of the regulation of pre-trial activities in the respective Statutes and RPEs of the ICTs, is the notion of 'fragmentation'. Indeed, the 'fragmentation of the investigation' may be said to be a feature of investigations by ICTs. This is because such investigations are inevitably spread over more than one

---

[2] ICTs may also seek the assistance of *international organizations*. See Rule 39(iii) ICTY RPE; Rule 39(iii) ICTR RPE; Article 87(6) ICC Statute.

[3] Cassese 1998, 9.

[4] See Rule 40 ICTY RPE and Rule 40 ICTR RPE.

[5] By contrast, such a procedure is provided for at the ICC. See Article 59 ICC Statute. More will be said about this issue in Chap. 6.

[6] De Meester 2014, 114.

procedural regime; in this regard it should be recalled that the actual execution of investigative measures, is not regulated by the ICTs' procedural regimes. It may be assumed that, when requested to cooperate by an international criminal tribunal, states, acting through their law enforcement authorities, will execute the measure in question according to their own (domestic) laws.[7] And when they do so, 'this leads to fragmentation of the investigation over several jurisdictions', and may give rise to 'complicated situations ... causing tensions and conflicts between different procedural regimes'.[8] Moreover, it may lead to diminished legal protection for the suspect or accused,[9] including the ability of such a person to obtain relief for the violation of his or her rights. More will be said about this issue in Chap. 6, but for now it may be noted that in several early ICTR decisions concerning defence motions for relief in respect of alleged illegality or unlawfulness on the part of national authorities in the execution of a request for cooperation (in particular, the arrest and detention of the suspect) by the ICTR Prosecutor (including applications for the exclusion of evidence obtained thereby), it was held that the suspect or accused would be able to seek a remedy in the state concerned, i.e. in the state whose authorities executed the request.

While it is clear that the ICTs are reliant on state cooperation for, among other things, the carrying out of investigations,[10] it is important to note that the Statutes and RPE of such tribunals also seem to envisage the Prosecutor's *own* staff carrying out investigations on the territory of a state.[11] However, the ability of the Prosecutor's staff to do so varies from tribunal to tribunal,[12] which can be attributed to differences in the 'model of cooperation' (between the institution in question and states) applicable at each. While the model of cooperation at the ad hoc Tribunals may be described as 'vertical' in nature,[13] the model of cooperation at the ICC has been described as being 'mixed' in nature, i.e. as reflecting both the 'horizontal' and 'vertical' models.[14] The 'vertical' and 'horizontal' terminology is derived from the literature on international law, specifically, the law on extradition and judicial assistance.[15] Whereas 'vertical cooperation' is associated with 'superiority' and

---

[7] De Meester 2014, 134–138.

[8] Ibid., 134.

[9] See e.g. De Meester 2014, 134–138. See also Orie 1983, where the point is made in the context of inter-state cooperation in criminal matters.

[10] As apparent from the many references in the governing documents of the ICTs to state cooperation; see e.g. Article 29 ICTY Statute; Article 29 ICTR Statute; Article 54(3)(c) and (d); and Part 9 ICC Statute.

[11] As regards the ICTY, see Article 18(2) ICTY Statute and Rule 39(i) ICTY RPE. As regards the ICTR, see Article 17(2) ICTR Statute and Rule 39(i) ICTR RPE. As regards the ICC, see Article 54(2).

[12] See Alamuddin 2010, 242.

[13] See *Prosecutor v Blaškić* (Judgement on the Request of the Republic of Croatia For Review of the Decision of Trial Chamber II of 18 July 1997) IT-95-14, A Ch (29 October 1997) para 47.

[14] See e.g. Swart 2002, 1594.

[15] For an explanation of the terms, see generally Sluiter 2002, 81–89.

'authority'[16] and depicts a hierarchical relationship in matters of cooperation, 'horizontal cooperation' is associated with 'sovereignty', 'equality' and 'voluntarism',[17] and depicts the 'voluntary cooperation relationship that exists between states (inter-state cooperation in criminal matters) and which respects the requested state's sovereignty'.[18] As stated above, the model of cooperation at the ad hoc Tribunals is *vertical* in nature; the respective Statutes of the ad hoc Tribunals impose on states a general duty to cooperate with them.[19] By contrast, at the ICC, only states parties are obliged to cooperate, and these obligations 'have been listed exhaustively'.[20] Turning back to the ability of Prosecutor to carry out investigations (through his or her own staff) on the territory of a state, it seems that under a vertical 'model' of cooperation, there is *more* room for the Prosecutor to do so. As Alamuddin observes:

> [The] horizontal model is based on sovereign equality—the requested state decides what measures it is prepared to take to assist the requesting state and will generally carry out these measures *itself*. The other model puts the international prosecutor above the state in a 'vertical' hierarchical relationship that not only allows the prosecutor to request cooperation, but also allows the court's judges to order it. The vertical model may also allow the international prosecutor to collect evidence within a state *without the consent or participation of that state's authorities*.[21]

At the ad hoc Tribunals, then, there appears to be more room for the Prosecutor's own staff to carry out investigations on the territory of a state, including the carrying out of search and seizure operations.[22] Regarding such operations, Alamuddin obseat odds with the depiction of an internationalrves that the 'image of an *ad hoc* Tribunal prosecutor breaking down a door to search a facility is somewhat tribunal as a 'giant without arms or legs'', but an 'often-ignored exception to the ubiquitous phrase … [in the literature] that the tribunals lack police powers and must rely on national authorities to conduct any coercive enforcement measure on the territory of states'.[23] In this regard she observes that there is a distinction to be drawn between conducting 'on-site investigations' and collecting evidence[24] on the one hand, and effecting arrests on the other.[25] At the ICC, chambers have expressly acknowledged the limited ability of the ICC's own (prosecution) staff to collect evidence on the

---

[16] Mégret 2008, 5.

[17] Mégret 2008, 5.

[18] De Meester 2014, 119.

[19] See Article 29 ICTY RPE and Article 28 ICTR RPE.

[20] De Meester 2014, 121.

[21] Alamuddin 2010, 242 (emphasis added).

[22] See in this regard *Prosecutor v Kordić and Čerkez* (Decision Stating Reasons for Trial Chamber's Ruling of 1 June 1999 Rejecting Defence Motion to Suppress Evidence) IT-95-14/2-T, T Ch III (25 June 1999).

[23] Alamuddin 2010, 255–256.

[24] See Article 18(2) ICTY Statute and Article 17(2) ICTR Statute.

[25] Alamuddin 2010, 256.

territory of a state, or at least, that any such operations are likely to be exceptional. In *Lubanga*, an investigator of the prosecution had been present at a search and seizure operation carried out by national authorities in the Democratic Republic of Congo. The Trial Chamber said that:

> it 'may turn out to be the case that this kind of evidence-gathering exercise is not normally carried out by investigators of the prosecution, particularly since the [International Criminal] Court is said to be "a giant without arms and legs". It has not been endowed with an enforcement apparatus enabling it readily to obtain evidence in this way, but instead it must rely on the assistance of sovereign States.'[26]

It is worth pointing out here that, at both the ad hoc Tribunals and the ICC, the lack of involvement of an organ of the international criminal tribunal in question in the procedural violation has been invoked by the judges ruling on applications for relief in this regard as a reason *not* to attach consequences to it. More will be said about this below, as well as in Chaps. 6 and 7.

At the ICTs, investigations and prosecutions are not governed by Statutes and RPEs alone. They are also governed by relevant human rights standards; indeed, the ICTs are required to observe human rights standards pertaining to the position of the suspect or accused. While this might appear obvious, it is important to note that there has been much discussion in the literature as to the basis for such an obligation.[27] It appears that the most convincing argument for such an obligation is that the ICTs are international organizations and therefore bound by human rights standards that form part of general international law (i.e. customary international law and general principles of law).[28] Through this law, the ICTs, as international organizations, are bound by norms 'similar or identical in content' to those provided for in the human rights instruments.[29] ICTs may, moreover (and perhaps more importantly), be said to be bound by 'internationally recognised' human rights on account of their own law and practice. For example, pursuant to Article 21(3) of the ICC Statute, the ICC is required to apply and interpret the law applicable to it (as set forth in Article 21(1) and (2) of the ICC Statute) in a manner consistent with 'internationally recognized human rights'.[30] At first glance, the function of the relevant human rights standards may appear to be to fill in lacunae in the regulation of the investigation and prosecution in the respective Statutes and RPEs of the

---

[26] *Prosecutor v Lubanga* (Decision on the admission of material from the "bar table") ICC-01/04-01/06, T Ch I (24 June 2009) para 45.

[27] See, most recently, Zeegers 2016.

In this regard it should be noted that the ICTs are not party to the universal and/or regional instruments that 'provide the basic legal materials out of which human rights obligations are usually fashioned'. Gradoni 2013, 81.

[28] See e.g. Gradoni 2013, 81.

[29] Ibid., 81.

[30] While the source of obligation differs for the ad hoc Tribunals, according to Gradoni, this has 'no bearing on the status of human rights norms within the legal systems of ICTs'. See Gradoni 2013, 83.

ICTs; however, as a recent study shows, the relationship between the ICTs' own governing documents and international human rights standards in regulating the (international) criminal process is complex.[31]

At the ICTs, it is the Prosecutor who is in charge of the investigation and prosecution, and, as stated above, since the ICTs lack their own enforcement agencies, he or she is (largely) reliant on state cooperation for the apprehension of persons suspected or accused of crimes falling within such tribunals' jurisdiction, and for the collection of evidence. Criminal justice is administered by professional judges only, i.e. there is no jury system in place at the ICTs. At the ICTs, criminal cases are adjudicated at two levels: cases are first heard by a trial chamber,[32] following which either party may appeal to the Appeals Chamber. At the ad hoc Tribunals, parties may appeal on grounds of either error of fact or error of law,[33] while at the ICC, parties may appeal on grounds of procedural error, error of fact or error or law.[34] Moreover, at both the ad hoc Tribunals and the ICC parties to the proceedings may, under certain circumstances, bring an appeal against a trial chamber's ruling in the course of the trial; this is known as an 'interlocutory appeal'. At the ad hoc Tribunals, the Appeals Chamber has held that 'a proper construction of the [ICTY] Statute requires that the ratio decidendi of … [the Appeals Chamber's] decisions is binding on Trial Chambers', although 'decisions of Trial Chambers … have no binding force on each other'.[35] As for the ICC, Article 21(2) of the ICC Statute provides that: 'The Court *may* apply principles and rules of law as interpreted in its previous decisions.'[36] According to Ambos, this provision 'emphasizes the importance of previous decisions taken by the ICC, however, without providing for a binding effect in terms of the stare-decisis doctrine'.[37]

In the next section, the relevant law and practice at the ad hoc Tribunals, i.e. the consequences that a judge may attach to procedural violations committed in the pre-trial phase of the proceedings which (potentially) have *general* application, will be set out, starting with the stay of proceedings. The other judicial responses under examination in this chapter are: the exclusion of evidence, financial compensation, sentence reduction and express acknowledgement of the procedural violation.

---

[31] Zeegers 2016. It is beyond the scope of this book to provide a comprehensive analysis in this regard.

[32] As regards the ICTY, see Articles 20, 23–24 ICTY Statute. As regards the ICTR, see Articles 19, 22–23 ICTR Statute. As regards the ICC, see Part 6 ICC Statute.

[33] Article 25 ICTY Statute and Article 24 ICTR Statute.

[34] Moreover, at the ICC an additional ground of appeal is provided for, for a 'convicted person': 'Any other ground that affects the fairness of reliability of the proceedings or decision.' See Article 81(1)(b)(iv) ICC Statute.

[35] *Prosecutor v Aleksovski* (Judgement) IT-95-14/1-A, A Ch (24 March 2000) paras 113–114.

[36] Article 21(2) ICC Statute (emphasis added).

[37] Ambos 2013, 79.

5.3 Ad Hoc Tribunals

5.3.1 Stay of Proceedings

A stay of proceedings at the ad hoc Tribunals (otherwise known as 'setting aside jurisdiction' or 'declining to exercise jurisdiction')[38] is a judicial ruling by which the proceedings are brought to a halt due to serious impropriety in the process of exercising jurisdiction over a suspect or in the conduct of the investigation, or due the impossibility of a fair trial, whereby a distinction may be drawn between 'permanent' and 'non-permanent' stays.[39] Neither is explicitly provided for in the governing documents of the ad hoc Tribunals. While a permanent stay of proceedings bars prosecution for the same charges at a later date, a non-permanent stay does not, at least, not initially. Both types of stay may be imposed on grounds of unfairness (and, as will be seen below, the permanent stay of proceedings may *also* be imposed on other grounds). Unlike a permanent stay, however, the non-permanent stay presupposes that a fair trial is still possible, i.e. that the 'problem' that necessitated the imposition of the stay in the first place is resolvable. Both types of stay are examined below.

5.3.1.1 Permanent Stay of Proceedings

To impose a permanent stay of proceedings at the ad hoc Tribunals is to decline to exercise jurisdiction over the accused. It entails the dismissal of the case, i.e. of the charges against the accused, and bars prosecution for the same charges at a later date.[40] The basis for a permanent stay of proceedings at the ad hoc Tribunals is the abuse of process doctrine,[41] which, according to the Appeals Chamber, may be invoked as 'a matter of discretion'.[42] In invoking the abuse of process doctrine, the Appeals Chamber in *Barayagwiza* observed that, under the doctrine, courts have an *inherent* power to stay the proceedings; moreover, in its view, the doctrine is closely related to the 'notion of supervisory powers', i.e. the notion that 'courts have supervisory powers that may be utilized in the interests of justice'.[43] While it is generally accepted at the ad hoc Tribunals that the *basis* for a stay of proceedings

---

[38] For an explanation of such terminology, see n 44–49 and accompanying text.

[39] In a trial decision in the ICTY case of *Karadžić*, the Trial Chamber rather referred to 'indefinite' and 'temporary' stays. See *Prosecutor v Karadžić* (Decision on Motion for Stay of Proceedings) IT-95-5/18-T, T Ch III (8 April 2010) para 3.

[40] See *Prosecutor v Barayagwiza* (Decision) ICTR-97-19-AR72, A Ch (3 November 1999) paras 108–110.

[41] See e.g. *Prosecutor v Barayagwiza* (Decision) ICTR-97-19-AR72, A Ch (3 November 1999); *Prosecutor v Nikolić* (Decision on Defence Motion Challenging the Exercise of Jurisdiction by the Tribunal) IT-94-2-PT, T Ch II (9 October 2002); and *Prosecutor v Nikolić* (Decision on Interlocutory Appeal Concerning Legality of Arrest) IT-94-2-AR73, A Ch (5 June 2003).

[42] *Prosecutor v Barayagwiza* (Decision) ICTR-97-19-AR72, A Ch (3 November 1999) para 74.

[43] Ibid., paras 75–76.

is the abuse of process doctrine, views have differed as to the basis for *applications* for a permanent stay of proceedings, i.e. challenges to the exercise jurisdiction. In a number of decisions, such challenges have been based on Rule 72(D) of the ICTY and ICTR RPEs,[44] often linked directly to the issue of personal jurisdiction.[45] In others, however, Rule 72(D) has been construed narrowly such that challenges that do not, strictly speaking, challenge the indictment on the grounds set out in Rule 72 (D) of the ICTY and the ICTR RPEs, i.e. the personal, territorial, temporal or subject-matter jurisdiction, do not fall within its purview.[46] This includes challenges alleging unlawful arrest and/or detention,[47] which instead go to the issue of jurisdiction 'in a wide sense',[48] i.e. to the discretion of the court to take cognizance of the case against the accused, that is, to exercise jurisdiction in the matter at hand.[49] As a result, such challenges have been based on Rule 73 of the RPE,[50]

---

[44] *Prosecutor v Brđanin* (Decision on Petition for a Writ of Habeas Corpus on Behalf of Radoslav Brđanin) IT-99-36-PT, T Ch II (8 December 1999) para 6; *Prosecutor v Kanyabashi* (Decision on the Defence Extremely Urgent Motion on Habeas Corpus and for Stoppage of Proceedings) ICTR-96-15-I, T Ch II (23 May 2000) paras 28–30; and *Prosecutor v Barayagwiza* (Decision) ICTR-97-19-AR72, A Ch (3 November 1999) para 71.

[45] See e.g. *Prosecutor v Semanza* (Decision) ICTR-97-23-A, A Ch (31 May 2000) para 70; *Prosecutor v Nikolić* (Decision on Interlocutory Appeal Concerning Legality of Arrest) IT-94-2-AR73, A Ch (5 June 2003) para 19. In the latter decision, however, the challenge to jurisdiction appears—somewhat confusingly—not to have been based on Rule 72 ICTY RPE, but Rule 73 (see paras 1 and 4).

[46] See e.g. *Prosecutor v Rwamakuba and others* (Decision on the Defence Motion Concerning the Illegal Arrest and Illegal Detention of the Accused) ICTR-98-44-T, T Ch II (12 December 2000) paras 12–14; *Prosecutor v Nikolić* (Decision on Notice of Appeal) IT-94-2-AR72, A Ch (9 January 2003) 3; *Prosecutor v Nzirorera* (Decision Pursuant to Rule 72(E) of the Rules of Procedure and Evidence on Validity of Appeal of Joseph Nzirorera Regarding Chapter VII of the Charter of the United Nations) ICTR-98-44-AR72, A Ch (10 June 2004) para 8; *Prosecutor v Boškoski and Tarčulovski* (Decision on Ljube Boškoski's Appeal on Jurisdiction) IT-04-82-AR72.2, A Ch (9 January 2007) para 5; *Prosecutor v Tolimir* (Decision on Zdravko Tolimir's Appeal Against the Decision on Submissions of the Accused Concerning Legality of Arrest) IT-05-88/2-AR72.2, A Ch (12 March 2009) paras 11–12; and *Prosecutor v Karadžić* (Decision on the Accused's Holbrooke Agreement Motion) IT-95-5/18-PT, T Ch III (8 July 2009) paras 41–43. See also Judge Shahabuddeen separate opinion to *Prosecutor v Barayagwiza* (Decision) ICTR-97-19-AR72, A Ch (3 November 1999), under 'If there was abuse of process, this did not lead to a lack of jurisdiction on the part of the Tribunal'.

[47] See e.g. *Prosecutor v Nikolić* (Decision on Notice of Appeal) IT-94-2-AR72, A Ch (9 January 2003) and *Prosecutor v Tolimir* (Decision on Zdravko Tolimir's Appeal Against the Decision on Submissions of the Accused Concerning Legality of Arrest) IT-05-88/2-AR72.2, A Ch (12 March 2009) paras 11–12.

[48] Khan and Dixon 2013, 111.

[49] See e.g. *Prosecutor v Milošević* (Decision on Preliminary Motions) IT-02-54, T Ch III (8 November 2001) para 48.

[50] See e.g. *Prosecutor v Rwamakuba and others* (Decision on the Defence Motion Concerning the Illegal Arrest and Illegal Detention of the Accused) ICTR-98-44-T, T Ch II (12 December 2000) paras 12–14; *Prosecutor v Nikolić* (Decision on Notice of Appeal) IT-94-2-AR72, A Ch (9 January 2003) 3; and *Prosecutor v Tolimir* (Decision on Zdravko Tolimir's Appeal Against the Decision on Submissions of the Accused Concerning Legality of Arrest) IT-05-88/2-AR72.2, A Ch (12 March 2009) para 13.

which governs motions other than those challenging jurisdiction within the meaning of Rule 72(D) of the ICTY and ICTR RPEs.

As to the circumstances under which a permanent stay may be granted, in the ICTR case of *Barayagwiza*, the Appeals Chamber held that 'the abuse of process doctrine may be relied on in two *distinct* situations: (1) where delay has made a fair trial for the accused impossible; and (2) where in the circumstances of a particular case, proceeding with the trial of the accused would contravene the court's sense of justice, due to pre-trial impropriety or misconduct'.[51] In formulating this 'test', the Appeals Chamber appears to have drawn heavily on Lord Lowry's formulation of the categories of case in which a court in England has a discretion to stay the proceedings as an abuse of process in the (English) case of *R v Horseferry Road Magistrates' Court, Ex parte Bennett*,[52] which it had earlier set out.[53] Both the first and second limbs of the abuse of process doctrine, as set out in *Barayagwiza*, would appear to afford a chamber ruling on an abuse of process application a good deal of latitude in the determination of an application for the proceedings to be stayed. Regarding the first limb, although the Appeals Chamber only refers to 'delay', the ultimate question is whether a fair trial has become impossible, whereby it is clear that a fair trial may become impossible for other reasons also, for example, the non-disclosure of evidence to the defence (where there are no other means by which to secure a fair trial). In the context of the second limb also, the standard that needs to be met would seem to afford a good deal of latitude to a chamber ruling on an application in this regard. The Appeals Chamber has emphasized that proceedings may be stayed as 'a matter of discretion'.[54] While it does not explain what it means to say this, it is seems likely that what it meant here is that, clear-cut cases aside, minds may well differ as to whether a stay of proceedings is necessary in order to ensure a fair trial, or, as the case may be, in order to protect the integrity of the proceedings.

It seems that it was the second limb that was at stake in *Barayagwiza*,[55] and in order for proceedings to be stayed on this basis, the 'pre-trial impropriety or

---

[51] *Prosecutor v Barayagwiza* (Decision) ICTR-97-19-AR72, A Ch (3 November 1999) para 77 (emphasis added). See also *Prosecutor v Karadžić* (Decision on Karadžić's Appeal of Trial Chamber's Decision on Alleged Holbrooke Agreement) IT-95-5/18-AR73.4, A Ch (12 October 2009) para 45.

[52] *R v Horseferry Road Magistrates' Court, ex parte Bennett* [1994] 1 AC 42.

[53] *Prosecutor v Barayagwiza* (Decision) ICTR-97-19-AR72, A Ch (3 November 1999) para 75: '[A] court has a discretion to stay any criminal proceedings on the ground that to try those proceedings will amount to an abuse of its own process either (1) because it will be impossible (usually by reason of delay) to give the accused a fair trial or (2) because it offends the court's sense of justice and propriety to be asked to try the accused in the circumstances of a particular case.'

[54] Ibid., para 74. See also *Prosecutor v Karadžić* (Decision on Karadžić's Appeal of Trial Chamber's Decision on Alleged Holbrooke Agreement) IT-95-5/18-AR73.4, A Ch (12 October 2009) para 45.

[55] *Prosecutor v Barayagwiza* (Decision) ICTR-97-19-AR72, A Ch (3 November 1999) para 77. Nevertheless, it should be noted that the Appeals Chamber's decision is not a model of clarity as regards the rationales for staying the proceedings or the rationale that it was pursuing. More will be said about this in Chap. 7.

misconduct' would have to entail 'serious and egregious violations of the accused's rights'.[56] This was indeed the case according to the Appeals Chamber. According to the Chamber, the cumulative effect of the violations of the ICTR Statute, the ICTR RPE and internationally recognized human rights relating to the right to personal liberty,[57] coupled with the ICTR Prosecutor's failure to act with due diligence to ensure the protection of Jean-Bosco Barayagwiza's rights, warranted the application of the abuse of process doctrine and, by extension, the imposition of a permanent stay of proceedings.[58] It reasoned that, 'to proceed with the Appellant's trial when such violations have been committed, would cause irreparable damage to the integrity of the judicial process', and, moreover, that a permanent stay was 'the only effective remedy for the cumulative breaches of the [A]ccused's rights' and that it 'may very well deter the commission of such serious violations in the future'.[59] Finally, the Appeals Chamber was of the view that under the abuse of process doctrine it is 'irrelevant which entity or entities were responsible for the alleged violations …'[60] Nevertheless, it should be noted that most of the violations established by the Appeals Chamber in *Barayagwiza* were attributable to the ICTR and, more specifically, to the Prosecutor (by virtue of the Prosecutor's failure to act with due diligence to ensure the protection of Barayagwiza's rights, having initiated a case against him).[61] Upon review (at the ICTR Prosecutor's request), however, the Appeals Chamber considered that, although the Appellant's rights had been violated, the 'new facts' submitted by the Prosecution 'diminish[ed] the role played by the failings of the Prosecutor as well as the intensity of the violation of the rights of the Appellant'.[62] Therefore, a permanent stay of proceedings was no longer justified. Nevertheless, since 'all

---

[56] Ibid., paras 73–75. See also the ICTY case of *Karadžić*, in which the Appeals Chamber confirmed that there are two limbs to the abuse of process doctrine (fair trial and integrity) and that the Appeals Chamber's finding in *Barayagwiza* that, invoking the abuse of process doctrine as a matter of discretion 'is a process by which Judges may decline to exercise the court's jurisdiction in cases where to exercise that jurisdiction in light of serious and egregious violations of the accused's rights would prove detrimental to the court's integrity', refers to the second limb. See *Prosecutor v Karadžić* (Decision on Karadžić's Appeal of Trial Chamber's Decision on Alleged Holbrooke Agreement) IT-95-5/18-AR73.4, A Ch (12 October 2009) para 51.

[57] The precise nature of the violations are set in Chap. 6.

[58] *Prosecutor v Barayagwiza* (Decision) ICTR-97-19-AR72, A Ch (3 November 1999) para 73.

[59] Ibid., para 108. See also para 76.

[60] Ibid., paras 73–77.

[61] More will be said about this issue in Chap. 6.

[62] *Prosecutor v Barayagwiza* (Decision (Prosecutor's Request for Review or Reconsideration)) ICTR-97-19-AR72, A Ch (31 March 2000) para 71. See also para 74. While the role played by the Prosecution's failings was diminished, the new facts did not negate it altogether.

violations demand a remedy',[63] the Appeals Chamber found that the Appellant was entitled either to financial compensation upon acquittal, or sentence reduction upon conviction.[64] Upon conviction, Barayagwiza's sentence was reduced from one of life imprisonment to thirty-two years.[65]

Although the stay of proceedings imposed in *Barayagwiza* was eventually reversed, the test formulated by the Appeals Chamber in that case for a permanent stay of proceedings has been endorsed in numerous cases before the ad hoc Tribunals.[66] In the ICTY case of *Nikolić*, the Accused, Dragan Nikolić, had been captured by unknown individuals in the Federal Republic of Yugoslavia, before being handed over to the NATO-led Stabilisation Force (SFOR) in Bosnia and Herzegovina and ultimately to the ICTY.[67] In considering whether the remedy sought (the setting aside of jurisdiction and release of the Accused)[68] was warranted, the Trial Chamber cited with approval the Appeals Chamber's finding in *Barayagwiza* that 'the abuse of process doctrine may be relied on if "in the circumstances of a particular case, proceeding with the trial of the accused would contravene the court's sense of justice"', thereby stressing that, in order to invoke the doctrine, 'it needs to be clear that the rights of the [a]ccused have been egregiously violated'.[69] In other words, it was the second limb of the abuse of process

---

[63] Ibid., para 74.

[64] Ibid., para 75.

[65] *Prosecutor v Nahimana, Barayagwiza and Ngeze* (Judgement and Sentence) ICTR-99-52-T, T Ch I (3 December 2003) para 1107; *Prosecutor v Nahimana, Barayagwiza and Ngeze* (Judgement) ICTR-99-52-A, A Ch (28 November 2007) para 1097.

[66] *Prosecutor v Karadžić* (Decision on Motion to Dismiss for Abuse of Process) IT-95-5/18-PT, T Ch III (12 May 2009) para 8; *Prosecutor v Karadžić* (Decision on the Accused's Holbrooke Agreement Motion) IT-95-5/18-PT, T Ch III (8 July 2009) para 80; *Prosecutor v Karadžić* (Decision on Karadžić's Appeal of Trial Chamber's Decision on Alleged Holbrooke Agreement) IT-95-5/18-AR73.4, A Ch (12 October 2009) para 45 (citing Lord Lowry's test in *R v Horseferry Road Magistrates' Court, ex parte Bennett* [1994] 1 AC 42 (see n 53), rather than the Appeals Chamber's own formulation of the test (see n 51 and accompanying text)) and 51; and *Prosecutor v Šešelj* (Decision on Oral Request of the Accused for Abuse of Process) IT-03-67-T, T Ch III (10 February 2010) para 21 (again, citing Lord Lowry's test).

[67] The Defence and Prosecution agreed on these facts. See *Prosecutor v Nikolić* (Decision on Defence Motion Challenging the Exercise of Jurisdiction by the Tribunal) IT-94-2-PT, T Ch II (9 October 2002) para 21.

[68] The Defence's submissions are set out in more detail in Chap. 6.

[69] *Prosecutor v Nikolić* (Decision on Defence Motion Challenging the Exercise of Jurisdiction by the Tribunal) IT-94-2-PT, T Ch II (9 October 2002) para 111, referring to *Prosecutor v Barayagwiza* (Decision) ICTR-97-19-AR72, A Ch (3 November 1999) paras 77 and 73. The Defence had also argued that a stay was warranted on the basis of a violation state sovereignty. More will be said about this in Chap. 6.

doctrine, as it applies at the ad hoc Tribunals, that was at stake in this case.[70] As to what constitutes an egregious violation, the Trial Chamber held that 'in a situation where an accused is very seriously mistreated, maybe even subjected to inhuman, cruel or degrading treatment, or torture, before being handed over to the [ICTY], this may constitute a legal impediment to the exercise of jurisdiction over such an accused' and that even without the involvement of the Prosecution or SFOR, the Trial Chamber would find it 'extremely difficult to justify the exercise of jurisdiction over a person … after having been seriously mistreated'.[71] The Appeals Chamber has since confirmed that the remedy of setting aside jurisdiction is not limited to cases of serious mistreatment and that 'other egregious violation[s]' are imaginable.[72] In addition, the *Nikolić* Trial Chamber endorsed the Appeals Chamber's finding in *Barayagwiza* that, 'in cases of *egregious* violations of the rights of the [a]ccused', it is 'irrelevant' which entity was involved.[73] Therefore, it is not only in cases of serious mistreatment that it is irrelevant which entity was involved. Rather, that finding applies to *all* 'egregious' violations of the rights of the accused, of which serious mistreatment may be said to be an example.[74] Further, in finding that the serious mistreatment of an accused prior to being surrendered to the ICTY might impede the exercise of jurisdiction over such an accused, the *Nikolić* Trial Chamber noted that this would '*certainly* be the case if the Tribunal was somehow involved'.[75] In other words, the collusion by (an organ of) the ad hoc Tribunals in the violation of the accused's rights is a factor weighing in favour of setting aside of jurisdiction, due to its capacity to elevate serious violations of the

---

[70] See also *Prosecutor v Nikolić* (Decision on Interlocutory Appeal Concerning Legality of Arrest) IT-94-2-AR73, A Ch (5 June 2003) paras 29–30.

[71] *Prosecutor v Nikolić* (Decision on Defence Motion Challenging the Exercise of Jurisdiction by the Tribunal) IT-94-2-PT, T Ch II (9 October 2002) para 114.

[72] See *Prosecutor v Karadžić* (Decision on Karadžić's Appeal of Trial Chamber's Decision on Alleged Holbrooke Agreement) IT-95-5/18-AR73.4, A Ch (12 October 2009) para 47. See also *Prosecutor v Kajelijeli* (Judgement) ICTR-98-44A-A, A Ch (23 May 2005) para 206 and *Prosecutor v Karemera, Ngirumpatse and Nzirorera* (Decision on Édouard Karemera's Motion Relating to his Right to be Tried without Undue Delay) ICTR-98-44-T, T Ch III (23 June 2009) para 6.

[73] *Prosecutor v Nikolić* (Decision on Defence Motion Challenging the Exercise of Jurisdiction by the Tribunal) IT-94-2-PT, T Ch II (9 October 2002) para 114 (emphasis added). In *Karadžić*, the Trial Chamber sought to 'downplay' this finding by stressing that it was strictly obiter. See *Prosecutor v Karadžić* (Decision on the Accused's Holbrooke Agreement Motion) IT-95-5/18-PT, T Ch III (8 July 2009) para 85.

[74] *Prosecutor v Karadžić* (Decision on Karadžić's Appeal of Trial Chamber's Decision on Alleged Holbrooke Agreement) IT-95-5/18-AR73.4, A Ch (12 October 2009) para 47.

[75] *Prosecutor v Nikolić* (Decision on Defence Motion Challenging the Exercise of Jurisdiction by the Tribunal) IT-94-2-PT, T Ch II (9 October 2002) para 114 (emphasis added). See also paras 106 and 113, where the involvement of the prosecuting forum is identified as a factor weighing in favour of finding that a human rights violation has occurred.

accused's rights, to egregious ones.[76,77] In the end, the Trial Chamber in *Nikolić* found that the treatment of the Accused by the unknown individuals at the time of arrest was not of such an egregious nature as to impede the exercise of jurisdiction. The Appeals Chamber came to the same conclusion on interlocutory appeal.[78] It found that: 'Although the assessment of the seriousness of the human rights violation depends on the circumstances of each case and cannot be made *in abstracto*, certain human rights violations are of such a serious nature that they require that the exercise of jurisdiction be declined' and that, apart from such exceptional cases, the remedy of setting aside jurisdiction 'will … usually be disproportionate'.[79] The restriction of cases in which a permanent stay of proceedings may be ordered to those involving an 'egregious' violation of the accused's rights (i.e. to 'exceptional' cases) ensures that a 'correct balance' is maintained between 'the fundamental rights of the accused and essential interests of the international community in the prosecution of persons charged with serious violations of international humanitarian law'.[80] Earlier on in the decision the Appeals Chamber seemed to suggest that the determination of whether to stay the proceedings entails the performance of a balancing exercise, which in that particular case entailed weighing the 'legitimate expectation that those accused of … ['crimes such as genocide, crimes against humanity and war crimes which are universally recognized and condemned as such'] will be brought to justice swiftly' against 'the principle of State sovereignty and the fundamental human rights of the accused'.[81] In finding that the evidence did not show 'that the rights of the accused were *egregiously* violated in the process of

---

[76] It is noteworthy that while the Appeals Chamber in *Barayagwiza* refers to 'serious and egregious' violations of the Accused's rights (*Prosecutor v Barayagwiza* (Decision) ICTR-97-19-AR72, A Ch (3 November 1999) para 74), in *Nikolić* (*Prosecutor v Nikolić* (Decision on Defence Motion Challenging the Exercise of Jurisdiction by the Tribunal) IT-94-2-PT, T Ch II (9 October 2002) para 114; *Prosecutor v Nikolić* (Decision on Interlocutory Appeal Concerning Legality of Arrest) IT-94-2-AR73, A Ch (5 June 2003) para 32) and in *Karadžić* (*Prosecutor v Karadžić* (Decision on the Accused's Holbrooke Agreement Motion) IT-95-5/18-PT, T Ch III (8 July 2009) para 85; *Prosecutor v Karadžić* (Decision on Karadžić's Appeal of Trial Chamber's Decision on Alleged Holbrooke Agreement) IT-95-5/18-AR73.4, A Ch (12 October 2009) para 47) the Trial Chamber and Appeals Chamber referred to 'egregious' violations.

[77] Another factor weighing in favour of the setting aside of jurisdiction may be the 'intensity' of the violation of the rights of the accused. *Prosecutor v Barayagwiza* (Decision (Prosecutor's Request for Review or Reconsideration)) ICTR-97-19-AR72, A Ch (31 March 2000) para 71.

[78] In fairness to the Accused, the Appeals Chamber reviewed all of the facts of the case proprio motu. *Prosecutor v Nikolić* (Decision on Interlocutory Appeal Concerning Legality of Arrest) IT-94-2-AR73, A Ch (5 June 2003) para 31.

[79] *Prosecutor v Nikolić* (Decision on Interlocutory Appeal Concerning Legality of Arrest) IT-94-2-AR73, A Ch (5 June 2003) para 30. See also *Prosecutor v Kajelijeli* (Judgement) ICTR-98-44A-A, A Ch (23 May 2005) para 206.

[80] Ibid., para 206.

[81] *Prosecutor v Nikolić* (Decision on Interlocutory Appeal Concerning Legality of Arrest) IT-94-2-AR73, A Ch (5 June 2003) paras 24–26. See also *Prosecutor v Tolimir* (Decision on Preliminary Motions on the Indictment pursuant to Rule 72 of the Rules) IT-05-88/2-PT, T Ch II (14 December 2007) paras 19 and 25. More will be said about the principle of state sovereignty in Chap. 6.

his arrest',[82] and in concluding that there was 'no basis upon which jurisdiction should not be exercised',[83] the Appeals Chamber made no further reference to the balancing exercise it had set out earlier on in the decision. It seems, therefore, that this balancing exercise is *inherent* in the determination of whether there has been an egregious violation of the accused's rights. More will be said about this, and the issue of balancing more generally, in Chap. 7.

As stated above, the test formulated in *Barayagwiza* for a permanent stay of proceedings has been endorsed in numerous cases before the ad hoc Tribunals. In setting out that test, it should be recalled, the Appeals Chamber stated that there were two 'distinct' categories of case in which the proceedings may be stayed as an abuse of process: '(1) where delay has made a fair trial for the accused impossible; and (2) where in the circumstances of a particular case, proceeding with the trial of the accused would contravene the court's sense of justice, due to pre-trial impropriety or misconduct'.[84] In *Stanišić and Župljanin*, the Appeals Chamber said that the main purposes of the 'discretionary power of a court to stay or terminate proceedings by reason of abuse of process ... are to *prevent wrongful convictions* and *preserve the integrity, of the judicial system*'.[85] In saying so, the Appeals Chamber confirmed that the first limb under the abuse of process doctrine, as it applies at the ad hoc Tribunals, is concerned with a chamber's 'epistemic' endeavour, i.e. to protect the accused from wrongful conviction. By contrast, the second limb may be said to be concerned with 'non-epistemic' considerations. While some chambers seem to have had the distinction between the categories well in mind when considering an application for the proceedings to be stayed as an abuse of process (or otherwise ruling on the doctrine), others have not. An example of a case in which the chamber has had the distinction between the categories well in mind in this regard is the appeals decision regarding Radovan Karadžić's application for a stay of proceedings on the basis that, in mid-1996, he had been promised immunity from prosecution before the ICTY by representatives of the Government of the United States of America, in exchange for his withdrawal from public life. Having earlier set out the test for a permanent stay of proceedings as referred to in *Barayagwiza*,[86] and applying it now to the facts of the case, the Appeals Chamber explained as follows:

> The Appeals Chamber observes at the outset that none of the Appellant's allegations qualify as a situation making a fair trial impossible, pursuant to the first prong of the test set out in the *Barayagwiza* Decision. The Appellant's allegations point instead to the second prong of

---

[82] *Prosecutor v Nikolić* (Decision on Interlocutory Appeal Concerning Legality of Arrest) IT-94-2-AR73, A Ch (5 June 2003) para 32 (emphasis added).

[83] Ibid., para 33.

[84] *Prosecutor v Barayagwiza* (Decision) ICTR-97-19-AR72, A Ch (3 November 1999) para 77.

[85] *Prosecutor v Stanišić and Župljanin* (Decision on Mićo Stanišić's Motion Requesting a Declaration of Mistrial and Stojan Zupljanin's Motion to Vacate Trial Judgement) IT-08-91-A, A Ch (2 April 2014) para 35.

[86] The Appeals Chamber referred to Lord Lowry's test in *R v Horseferry Road Magistrates' Court, ex parte Bennett* [1994] 1 AC 42 (see n 53), rather than the Appeals Chamber's own formulation of the test in *Barayagwiza* (see n 51 and accompanying text).

the test set out in the *Barayagwiza* Decision. In other words, the question before the Appeals Chamber is whether, assuming that the Appellant's factual submissions are accepted, proceeding with the trial of the Appellant would contravene to the Tribunal's sense of justice or would be detrimental to the Tribunal's integrity, due to pre-trial impropriety or misconduct amounting to serious and egregious violations of the Appellant's rights.[87]

In that decision, the Appeals Chamber seemed to imply that the abuse of process doctrine entails the performance of a balancing exercise in which 'the public interest in the prosecution of an individual accused of … [genocide, crimes against humanity and war crimes], [which are] universally condemned' is weighed against the interests of the accused.[88] In light of its findings that only the second limb of the doctrine was in issue in that case, it is reasonable to assume that it was endorsing the performance of a balancing exercise in the context of this limb only. In rejecting the application for a stay of proceedings, the Appeals Chamber held that the Accused's expectation of immunity from prosecution was not a legitimate interest for the purposes of the aforementioned balancing exercise.[89] More will be said about the issue of balancing in Chap. 7.

In another (trial) decision in the same case, the Trial Chamber seemed to 'mix' the two categories:

> It is undoubtedly the case that a Chamber has the power to stay the proceedings in a case where the circumstances are such that a fair trial for the accused is impossible. The right to a fair trial is a fundamental one and it is the duty of the Trial Chamber to ensure that it is protected. However, the Prosecution correctly observes that the jurisprudence on indefinite stays of proceedings is that there must be found to have been a serious violation of human rights justifying such an extreme measure. The Trial Chamber would therefore need to be satisfied that (1) its decisions on judicial notice of adjudicated facts and on the admission of certain evidence pursuant to Rule 92 *bis* together result in a violation of the Accused's right to a fair trial, and (2) that this violation is of such an egregious nature that the Chamber should stay the proceedings.[90]

In finding that 'the jurisprudence on indefinite stays of proceedings is that there must be found to have been a serious violation of human rights justifying such an extreme measure', the Trial Chamber relied on the Appeals Chamber's decisions on

---

[87] *Prosecutor v Karadžić* (Decision on Karadžić's Appeal of Trial Chamber's Decision on Alleged Holbrooke Agreement) IT-95-5/18-AR73.4, A Ch (12 October 2009) para 51.

[88] Ibid., para 49. See also *Prosecutor v Nikolić* (Decision on Interlocutory Appeal Concerning Legality of Arrest) IT-94-2-AR73, A Ch (5 June 2003) paras 25–26, and 30.

[89] *Prosecutor v Karadžić* (Decision on Karadžić's Appeal of Trial Chamber's Decision on Alleged Holbrooke Agreement) IT-95-5/18-AR73.4, A Ch (12 October 2009) para 52.

[90] *Prosecutor v Karadžić* (Decision on Motion for Stay of Proceedings) IT-95-5/18-T, T Ch III (8 April 2010) para 4. See also *Prosecutor v Kanyarukiga* (Judgement) ICTR-02-78-A, A Ch (8 May 2012) paras 16–18.

The Trial Chamber's formulation is unfortunate also in that it suggests that the right to a fair trial is not absolute and may be balanced against countervailing interests.

the abuse of process doctrine in *Nikolić* and *Karadžić*.[91] In the latter case, it should be noted, the Appeals Chamber clarified that the question of whether 'serious and egregious violations of the accused's rights' have been committed pertains to the second, 'integrity' limb of the abuse of process doctrine. Under the first limb, it seems, the impossibility of a fair trial is sufficient to justify the imposition of a stay of proceedings. Of course, the impossibility of a fair trial may, in a general sense, be denoted as 'an egregious violation of the accused's rights'; after all, the impossibility of a fair trial may be taken to mean the violation of the accused's right to a fair trial. The point is that the violation of the accused's right to a fair trial need not be *egregious* in order to justify a stay of proceedings.

The Appeals Chamber's judgment in the ICTR case of *Akayesu* is another example of a decision that does not clearly distinguish between the two categories of case in which a chamber may stay the proceedings as an abuse of process. In the judgment, the Appeals Chamber held that in order for an application for the proceedings to be stayed to succeed, the accused must 'show that he had suffered prejudice';[92] in doing so, it did not refer to the two 'distinct' categories set out in the *Barayagwiza* case (although it did refer to the relevant decision). As a result, it implied that *all* abuse of process applications require a showing of prejudice, i.e. regardless of the ground on which a stay is sought. In support of its assertion, the Appeals Chamber referred to an English case, *DPP v Hussain*, in which it was held by the Divisional Court that 'an order staying the proceedings on the ground of abuse of process [...] should never be made where there were other ways of achieving a fair hearing of the case, still less where there was no evidence of prejudice to the defendant'.[93] In that case, the prosecution had failed to disclose certain documents to the defendant; non-disclosure, it should be recalled, typically raises issues under the first limb of the abuse of process doctrine, as it applies in England and Wales.[94] A stay of proceedings imposed on the basis of the first limb of that doctrine, it should further be recalled, seeks to 'ensure that the defendant does not in some way suffer from forensic prejudice or disadvantage at trial with the result that he or she may be unable to defend him- or herself properly, leading to the danger of a factually inaccurate verdict of guilty ensuing'.[95] In light of the concern under the first limb, i.e. protection of an accused from wrongful conviction, it is logical under this limb to consider whether any forensic prejudice caused to the

---

[91] The Trial Chamber referred to *Prosecutor v Karadžić* (Decision on Karadžić's Appeal of Trial Chamber's Decision on Alleged Holbrooke Agreement) IT-95-5/18-AR73.4, A Ch (12 October 2009) paras 45–47 and *Prosecutor v Nikolić* (Decision on Interlocutory Appeal Concerning Legality of Arrest) IT-94-2-AR73, A Ch (5 June 2003) paras 28–33.

[92] *Prosecutor v Akayesu* (Judgment) ICTR-96-4-A, A Ch (1 June 2001) para 340. See also *Prosecutor v Karemera, Ngirumpatse and Nzirorera* (Decision on Joseph Nzirorera's Motion to Dismiss for Abuse of Process: Payments to Prosecution Witnesses and "Requete de Mathieu Ngirumpatse en Retrait de L'Acte D'Accusation") ICTR-98-44-T, T Ch III (27 October 2008) para 3 and *Prosecutor v Kanyarukiga* (Judgement) ICTR-02-78-A, A Ch (8 May 2012) para 19.

[93] *DPP v Hussain, The Times* 1 June 1994.

[94] See Chap. 4, n 145 and accompanying text.

[95] Choo 2008, 18.

defendant can be (or has been) 'remedied' in the course of the trial. By contrast, it is not at all obvious that this is a *pertinent* consideration under the second limb of the abuse of process doctrine, which is concerned with protecting the integrity of the court.

Turning now to some practical matters, in the ICTR case of *Akayesu*, the Appeals Chamber held that 'the burden of showing that there has been an abuse of process rests with the accused'.[96] Further, depending on the type of stay imposed, the accused is entitled to release from custody. Where a non-permanent stay is imposed, the 'consequences of such a stay upon the continued detention of the accused would depend upon the circumstances of the particular case'.[97] In other words, a non-permanent stay will not necessarily result in the release of the accused. By contrast, where the proceedings are stayed permanently, the accused must be released from custody.[98]

5.3.1.2 Non-Permanent Stay of Proceedings

A non-permanent stay of proceedings at the ad hoc Tribunals does not involve the setting aside of jurisdiction, at least, not initially.[99] Like permanent stays, a non-permanent stay may be imposed on grounds of unfairness. Unlike a permanent stay, however, the non-permanent stay presupposes that a fair trial is still possible, by virtue of the fact that the underlying procedural violation, and its effect on the fairness of the proceedings, is reparable. For example, in the ICTY case of *Brđanin and Talić*, the Pre-Trial Judge held that, 'if the Trial Chamber is satisfied that the absence of [the resources necessary to ensure a fair trial] will result in a miscarriage of justice, it has the inherent power and the obligation to stay the proceedings *until* the necessary resources are provided, in order to prevent the abuse of process involved in such a trial'.[100] In another ICTY case, the Appeals Chamber held that:

> The only inherent power that a Trial Chamber has is to ensure that the trial of an accused is fair; it cannot appropriate for itself a power which is conferred elsewhere. As such, the only option open to Trial Chamber, where the Registrar has refused the assignment of new Counsel, and an accused appeals to [the Trial Chamber], is to stay the trial *until* the President has reviewed the decision of the Registrar.[101]

In the ICTR case of *Nahimana, Barayagwiza and Ngeze*, the Pre-Appeal Judge found that 'in order to preserve the fairness and efficiency of the proceedings', it

---

[96] *Prosecutor v Akayesu* (Judgment) ICTR-96-4-A, A Ch (1 June 2001) para 340.

[97] *Prosecutor v Brđanin and Talić* (Decision on Second Motion by Brđanin to Dismiss the Indictment) IT-99-36-PT, T Ch II (16 May 2001) para 5.

[98] See *Prosecutor v Barayagwiza* (Decision) ICTR-97-19-AR72, A Ch (3 November 1999) paras 106–113.

[99] It is reasonable to assume that if, as time goes on, the non-permanent stay violates the accused's right to trial within a reasonable time, it may be converted into a permanent stay.

[100] *Prosecutor v Brđanin and Talić* (Decision on Second Motion by Brđanin to Dismiss the Indictment) IT-99-36-PT, T Ch II (16 May 2001) para 5 (emphasis added).

[101] *Prosecutor v Blagojević* (Public and Redacted Reasons for Decision on Appeal by Vidoje Blagojevic to Replace his Defense Team) IT-02-60-AR73.4, A Ch (7 November 2003) para 7.

was 'necessary to stay the proceedings … *until* a new lead counsel has been assigned to represent [the Appellant]'.[102]

It is important to note that not all procedural violations committed in the pre-trial phase of international criminal proceedings (and their effect on the fairness of the proceedings) are reparable. As such, a non-permanent stay will not always be an appropriate judicial response in case of procedural violations. For example, violations of rules governing arrest and/or pre-trial detention, and their effect on certain fundamental values, are typically irreparable. To impose a non-permanent stay for egregious violations of such rules would achieve nothing; in such cases the damage will have already been done.[103]

5.3.2 *Exclusion of Evidence*

Both the ICTY and ICTR RPEs explicitly provide for the exclusion of unlawfully obtained evidence[104] in certain circumstances. Under Rule 95 of both the ICTY and ICTR RPEs,[105] evidence may be excluded 'because of how it was obtained'.[106] In addition, unlawfully obtained evidence may be 'caught' by the exclusionary mechanism in Rule 89(D) of the ICTY RPE or its jurisprudential counterpart at the ICTR. Pursuant to Rule 89(D) of the ICTY RPE, '[a] Chamber may exclude evidence if its probative value is substantially outweighed by the need to ensure a fair trial', and according to ICTR case law, chambers at the ICTR have 'an inherent power to exclude evidence if its probative value is substantially outweighed by its prejudicial effect or otherwise by the need to ensure a fair trial.'[107] This mechanism,

---

[102] *Prosecutor v Nahimana, Barayagwiza and Ngeze* (Decision on Ngeze's Motion for a Stay of Proceedings) ICTR-99-52-A (4 August 2004) 2 (emphasis added). See also *Prosecutor v Blagojević* (Public and Redacted Reasons for Decision on Appeal by Vidoje Blagojevic to Replace his Defense Team) IT-02-60-AR73.4, A Ch (7 November 2003).

[103] Violations of rules governing arrest and/or pre-trial detention will not usually affect the fairness of the trial itself, but may (if sufficiently serious) undermine the integrity of the proceedings.

[104] In this book, the term 'unlawfully obtained evidence' denotes evidence which has been obtained illegally, unlawfully or otherwise unfairly.

[105] The wording of the rule under Rule 95 ICTR RPE is identical to that under Rule 95 ICTY RPE.

[106] ICTY, 'Second Annual Report of the International Tribunal for the Prosecution of Persons Responsible for Serious Violations of International Humanitarian Law Committed in the Territory of the Former Yugoslavia Since 1991' (23 August 1995) UN Doc A/50/365–S/1995/728, 45. At the ICTR, the title of this rule reads as follows: 'Exclusion of Evidence on the Grounds of the Means by Which It was Obtained'.

[107] *Prosecutor v Karemera, Ngirumpatse and Nzirorera* (Decision on the Prosecutor's Motion for Admission of Certain Exhibits into Evidence) ICTR-98-44-T, T Ch III (25 January 2008) para 9. See also *Prosecutor v Karemera, Ngirumpatse and Nzirorera* (Decision on the Prosecution Motion for Admission into Evidence of Post-Arrest Interviews with Joseph Nzirorera and Mathieu Ngirumpatse) ICTR-98-44-T, T Ch III (2 November 2007) para 3; *Prosecutor v Karemera, Ngirumpatse and Nzirorera* (Decision on Defence Oral Motions for Exclusion of XBM's Testimony, for Sanctions Against the Prosecution and for Exclusion of Evidence Outside the Scope of the Indictment) ICTR-98-44-T, T Ch III (19 October 2006) para 20; *Prosecutor v Karemera, Ngirumpatse and Nzirorera* (Decision on the Prosecution Motion for

then, is concerned with the need to ensure a fair trial; specifically, it appears to be linked to a chamber's truth-finding task, i.e. the ability of a chamber to determine the guilt or innocence of accused accurately, or otherwise to '*trial* fairness'.[108] As will

---

(Footnote 107 continued)

Admission Into Evidence of Certain Exhibits from Other Trials) ICTR-98-44-T, T Ch III (30 October 2007) para 11; *Prosecutor v Muvunyi* (Decision on the Prosecutor's Motion Pursuant to Trial Chamber's Directives of 7 December 2005 for the Verification of the Authenticity of Evidence Obtained Out of Court Pursuant to Rules 89(C) and (D)) ICTR-2000-55A-T, T Ch II (26 April 2006) para 15; and *Prosecutor v Bagosora, Kabiligi, Ntabakuze and Nsengiyumva* (Decision on Prosecutor's Interlocutory Appeals Regarding Exclusion of Evidence) ICTR-98-41-AR93 & ICTR-98-41-AR93.2, A Ch (19 December 2003) paras 16–17.

See further Gosnell 2010, 378 ('The ICTR Rules contain no such express provision, but the same principle is applied as a matter of jurisprudence.'), and Nerenberg and Timmermann 2010, 477.

[108] In *Kordić and Čerkez*, the Trial Chamber excluded certain material pursuant to Rule 89(D) ICTY RPE (reports 'based on based on anonymous sources or hearsay statements'), in light of the fact that the late stage of the proceedings at which admission of the material was sought meant that 'the Defence would have no opportunity … of cross-examining any witness about the reports, which are based on a variety of sources (sometimes anonymous)'. The lack of opportunity for the Defence to test the evidence meant that the probative value of the material was 'substantially outweighed by the need to ensure a fair trial'; in other words, to admit the material at that stage would, according to the Trial Chamber, have violated the accused's right to a fair trial. See *Prosecutor v Kordić and Čerkez* (Decision on Prosecutor's Submissions Concerning "Zagreb Exhibits" and Presidential Transcripts) IT-95-14/2-T, T Ch III (1 December 2000) para 40. The inability of the defence to test the evidence also lay at the heart of the Trial Chamber's decision in *Milutinović and others* to exclude the testimony of General Wesley Clark pursuant to Rule 89(D) ICTY RPE; the restrictions imposed by the information provider—in this case, the United States Government—meant that the defence would be prevented from 'challenging the honesty and reliability of the witness by looking at inconsistencies on what he may have said on matters outwith the territory of the examination', and from 'cross-examining on relevant matters favourable to the Defence case that are excluded by the restriction'. See *Prosecutor v Milutinović, Sainović, Ojdanić, Pavković, Lazarević and Lukić* (Second Decision on Prosecution Motion for Leave to Amend its Rule 65 *ter* Witness List to Add Wesley Clark) IT-05-87-T, T Ch III (16 February 2007) para 27. In *Kvočka and others*, the Trial Chamber excluded, pursuant to Rule 89(D) ICTY RPE, an extract from a newspaper article about the Omarska camp (one of the camps featuring in the indictment against the accused), on the basis that its probative value was low, 'as it contains unsupported allegations about the camp', and that the 'inflammatory nature' of those allegations was 'so prejudicial to the Defence that this outweighs any probative value it may have'. See *Prosecutor v Kvočka, Prcać, Kos, Radić and Žigić* (Decision on Zoran Žigić's Motion for Rescinding Confidentiality of Schedules Attached to the Indictment Decision on Exhibits) IT-98-30/1-T, T Ch I (19 July 2001). In the ICTR case of *Bagosora and others*, it was held that if the only purpose for the introduction of the evidence 'is to establish that the accused was capable of committing the offence, is inclined to commit the offence, or on some prior occasion actually did have the intent to commit the criminal offence', it should be excluded. This is because such evidence 'may so severely blacken the reputation of the accused as to make acquittal virtually impossible, even though the direct evidence of the commission of the offence is weak.' Moreover, 'dealing with evidence of past conduct may be unduly distracting and time-consuming, leading to an unfocused trial that undermines the truth-finding function.' In short, 'the damning effect' of such evidence 'tends to outweigh its true probative value and to obscure more direct evidence of the crime alleged'. See *Prosecutor v Bagosora, Kabiligi, Ntabakuze and Nsengiyumva* (Decision on Admissibility of Proposed Testimony of Witness DBY) ICTR-98-41-T, T Ch (18 September 2003) paras 12 and 17.

be seen below, the (improper) manner in which evidence is obtained is capable of impacting on the ability of the accused to mount an effective defence, i.e. to exercise his or her fair trial rights, for example, the right to effectively challenge that evidence. To this extent, the mechanism in Rule 89(D) of the ICTY RPE, and its jurisprudential counterpart at the ICTR, may be said to provide for the exclusion of unlawfully obtained evidence. However, it is clear that the improper manner in which evidence is obtained is not the primary concern under that mechanism; accordingly, only those cases involving the mechanism in Rule 89(D) or its jurisprudential counterpart at the ICTR, in which the evidence concerned was *unlawfully obtained* will be addressed here. Such cases are clearly relevant to the aforementioned research question. It is instructive to address that mechanism for another reason, also; that mechanism and the literature that it has inspired, may shed light on another question of importance for this book: to what extent can the judicial response to procedural violations committed in the pre-trial phase of international criminal proceedings at the ICTs be said to be discretionary in nature, and/or to entail a 'balancing' approach? In this regard, it may be noted that while the mechanism in Rule 89(D) of the ICTY RPE and its jurisprudential counterpart at the ICTR are widely acknowledged to provide for an exclusionary discretion, Rule 95 of the ICTY and ICTR RPEs is often described (in the case law as well as in the literature) as 'mandatory' in nature.[109] In order to gain a better understanding of the nature of the mechanism in Rule 95, it is instructive to consider the nature of the former one. Nevertheless, for the reason given above, the primary focus of the current section is the exclusionary mechanism in Rule 95 of the ICTY and ICTR RPEs. To the extent that they bear upon the central research question of this book and the question of the extent to which the judicial response to procedural violations committed in the pre-trial phase of the proceedings at the ICTs can be said to be discretionary in nature, and/or to entail a balancing approach, the mechanism in Rule 89(D) of the ICTY RPE and its jurisprudential counterpart at the ICTR are also examined here. It is instructive to examine the latter mechanisms first.

Turning first to the characterization of the mechanism in Rule 89(D) of the ICTY RPE and its jurisprudential counterpart at the ICTR as 'discretionary' in nature, although Rule 89(D) may appear to have been drafted in such a way that even when the evidence's probative value is substantially outweighed by the need to ensure a fair trial the chamber may nevertheless admit the evidence, it is reasonable to assume that, once a chamber has determined that the probative value of the evidence is substantially outweighed by its prejudicial effect, it *must* exclude the evidence.[110] The same may be said of that provision's jurisprudential counterpart at

---

[109] As to the case law, see e.g.: *Prosecutor v Karemera, Ngirumpatse and Nzirorera* (Decision on the Prosecution Motion for Admission into Evidence of Post-Arrest Interviews with Joseph Nzirorera and Mathieu Ngirumpatse) ICTR-98-44-T, T Ch III (2 November 2007) para 4.

As to the literature, see e.g. Alamuddin 2010, 284; Combs 2010, 328; and Zahar and Sluiter 2008, 380.

[110] But cf Gosnell 2010, 421; and Zahar and Sluiter 2008, 382–383.

the ICTR. And there is authority to support this assumption.[111] In the context of the exclusionary mechanism in Rule 89(D) of the ICTY RPE and its jurisprudential counterpart at the ICTR, then, the descriptor 'discretionary' would appear to denote something else than the power of a chamber at the ad hoc Tribunals to rule in any way it sees fit; what it appears to denote is the latitude afforded to a chamber in determining an application for the exclusion of evidence, which seems to be inherent in the standard that must be met in order to be able to justify exclusion: the need to ensure a *fair* trial. In this regard it may be observed that while there are likely to be some clear categories of cases in which the need to ensure a fair trial will (substantially) outweigh the probative value of the evidence sought for admission,[112] the circumstances in which the fairness of the proceedings will be imperilled by the admission of evidence (that is otherwise relevant and probative) are impossible to define exhaustively. This proposition is supported by the relevant case law at the ICTY and ICTR, in which the availability of the exclusionary mechanism has been considered in a wide range of circumstances and in respect of different types of evidence.[113] That trial chambers are afforded a degree of latitude under the mechanism currently under discussion is further apparent from the fact that, at the ICTY at least, the question that a trial chamber should ask itself is not whether the probative value of the evidence sought for admission is outweighed by the need to ensure a fair trial, but whether it is *substantially* outweighed thereby. In other words, under Rule 89(D) of the ICTY RPE, a trial chamber is required to make a judgement of degree.[114] On the basis of the test provided for thereunder,

---

[111] According to the Trial Chamber in *Kvočka and others*, the probative value of the evidence in question was low, and the inflammatory nature of the allegations contained therein 'so prejudicial' that this outweighed 'any probative value it may have [had], *so that it should be excluded in the interests of a fair trial pursuant to Rule 89(D) of [the ICTY RPE]*'. See *Prosecutor v Kvočka, Kos, Radić, Žigić and Prcać* (Decision on Zoran Zigić's Motion for Rescinding Confidentiality of Schedules Attached to the Indictment Decision on Exhibits) IT-98-30/1-T, T Ch I (19 July 2001). In the ICTR case of *Muvunyi*, the Trial Chamber said that '[w]here, in the Chambers' assessment, the prejudicial effect of the proposed evidence is likely to outweigh its probative value, they would generally exercise their discretion against admitting such evidence.' See *Prosecutor v Muvunyi* (Decision on the Prosecutor's Motion Pursuant to Trial Chamber's Directives of 7 December 2005 for the Verification of the Authenticity of Evidence Obtained Out of Court Pursuant to Rules 89(C) and (D)) ICTR-2000-55A-T, T Ch II (26 April 2006) para 15.

[112] See in this regard Gosnell 2010, 422, where the author observes that the determination of 'prejudicial effect' 'necessarily incorporates a weighing exercise that includes considering the *essential* elements of fairness, and whether any infringement on fairness also undermines the reliability of the evidence.'

[113] See in this regard n 108 and accompanying text.

[114] It seems that, at the ICTR, a trial chamber is also required to make a judgement of degree. See the following decisions, which state that the probative value of the evidence in question must be substantially outweighed by its prejudicial effect or by the need to ensure a fair trial: *Karemera, Ngirumpatse and Nzirorera* (Decision on the Prosecutor's Motion for Admission of Certain Exhibits into Evidence) ICTR-98-44-T, T Ch III (25 January 2008) para 9; *Prosecutor v Karemera, Ngirumpatse and Nzirorera* (Decision on the Prosecution Motion for Admission into Evidence of Post-Arrest Interviews with Joseph Nzirorera and Mathieu Ngirumpatse) ICTR-98-44-T, T Ch III (2 November 2007) para 3; *Prosecutor v Karemera, Ngirumpatse and*

then, it may indeed be said that Rule 89(D) of the ICTY RPE and its jurisprudential counterpart at the ICTR provide for an *exclusionary discretion*.

As to the relevant case law on the mechanism in Rule 89(D) of the ICTY RPE and its jurisprudential counterpart at the ICTR, i.e. cases in which the evidence concerned was unlawfully obtained, in the ICTY case of *Halilović*, the Defence had sought to have a statement of the accused, based on interviews conducted with the Prosecution, excluded pursuant to Rule 89(D) of the ICTY RPE. The Prosecution had not kept notes of the interviews in its records and the interviews were not audio- or video recorded,[115] in violation of Rule 43 of the ICTY RPE.[116] According to the Trial Chamber, Rule 43 'aims at ensuring the integrity of the proceedings, *inter alia*, by providing for an instrument to ascertain the voluntariness of a statement and the adherence to other relevant safeguards as provided for in Rule 42 and Rule 95', and 'is a safeguard for a full and accurate reflection of the questions and answers during the interview and thus enables the parties and the Trial Chamber to verify the exact wording of what was said during the interview'.[117] Applying these principles to the case, it found that the inability of the Defence to verify the accuracy of the statement (there having been no audio- or video recording available), which it had every reason to want to do in light of the fact that it was 'more probable than not that not every detail or nuance of the interview was included in the [s]tatement', thereby affecting the statement's reliability, and that the Accused had not chosen to waive his right to remain silent at trial, meant that

---

(Footnote 114 continued)

Nzirorera (Decision on Defence Oral Motions for Exclusion of XBM's Testimony, for Sanctions Against the Prosecution and for Exclusion of Evidence Outside the Scope of the Indictment) ICTR-98-44-T, T Ch III (19 October 2006) para 20; and *Prosecutor v Karemera, Ngirumpatse and Nzirorera* (Decision on the Prosecution Motion for Admission Into Evidence of Certain Exhibits from Other Trials) ICTR-98-44-T, T Ch III (30 October 2007) para 11. See, however, *Prosecutor v Muvunyi* (Decision on the Prosecutor's Motion Pursuant to Trial Chamber's Directives of 7 December 2005 for the Verification of the Authenticity of Evidence Obtained Out of Court Pursuant to Rules 89(C) and (D)) ICTR-2000-55A-T, T Ch II (26 April 2006) para 15: 'Where, in the Chambers' assessment, the prejudicial effect of the proposed evidence is likely to outweigh its probative value, they would generally exercise their discretion against admitting such evidence.'

[115] *Prosecutor v Halilović* (Decision on Motion for Exclusion of Statement of Accused) IT-01-48-T, T Ch I (8 July 2005) para 2.

[116] The Prosecution argued that it was not obliged to do so, since, at the time of questioning, Halilović was not a suspect; rather, he was interviewed as a witness. According the Trial Chamber, however, this mattered not: 'in order to protect the right of the Accused to a fair trial, in accordance with Article 21 of the [ICTY] Statute, it should be taken into account whether the safeguards of Rules 42, 43 and 63 of the … [ICTY RPE] have been fully respected when deciding on the admission of any former statement of an accused irrespective of the status of the accused at the time of taking the statement.' *Prosecutor v Halilović* (Decision on Motion for Exclusion of Statement of Accused) IT-01-48-T, T Ch I (8 July 2005) para 21.

[117] *Prosecutor v Halilović* (Decision on Motion for Exclusion of Statement of Accused) IT-01-48-T, T Ch I (8 July 2005) para 24.

the statement had to be excluded (pursuant to Rule 89(D)).[118] To admit the statement would have been to infringe upon the Accused's right to a fair trial.[119]

Pursuant to Rule 95 of both the ICTY and ICTR RPEs, '[n]o evidence shall be admissible if obtained by methods which cast substantial doubt on its reliability or if its admission is antithetical to, and would seriously damage, the integrity of the proceedings.' At first glance, the characterization of the exclusionary mechanism under Rule 95 as 'mandatory' in nature[120] would appear to be warranted by the use of the word 'shall', whereas pursuant to Rule 89(D), the chamber 'may' exclude evidence. However, if the question of whether a given exclusionary mechanism may properly be characterized as 'mandatory' in nature were to turn on whether, once certain conditions have been satisfied, the evidence in question *must* be excluded, then the exclusionary mechanism under Rule 89(D) would also have to be described as mandatory in nature (it being fair to assume that once it has been determined that the probative value of the evidence in question is substantially outweighed by the need to ensure a fair trial, such evidence *must* be excluded), whereas it is widely recognised, and is argued here, that that provision provides for an exclusionary *discretion*. It seems, then, that an explanation for the characterization of the exclusionary mechanism under Rule 95 as 'mandatory' is to be sought elsewhere. Zahar and Sluiter seem to employ the term 'mandatory' in this context to denote an exclusionary mechanism that entails the *automatic* exclusion of certain evidence.[121] They seem to argue that initially, at least, Rule 95 was meant to provide for the automatic exclusion of evidence obtained by breach of an internationally recognised human right.[122] In this regard, they refer to the original title of that provision, which for the ICTY they observe was 'Evidence Obtained by Means Contrary to Internationally Protected Human Rights'.[123] However, this interpretation is questionable. Initially, and until its amendment in January 1995, Rule 95 of the ICTY RPE read as follows: 'Evidence obtained directly or indirectly by means which constitute a serious violation of internationally protected human rights shall not be admissible.' The use of the word 'serious' here suggests that the drafters of the ICTY RPE did *not* envisage automatic exclusion for evidence obtained by a (i.e.

---

[118] Ibid., para 25.

[119] Ibid., paras 26–27. The Trial Chamber's decision was upheld on appeal. According to the Appeals Chamber: 'It is clear that the Trial Chamber instead excluded the Statement because, in accordance with Rule 89(D) of the Rules, it did not deem the statement reliable enough, so that it could have threatened the fairness of the proceedings.' See *Prosecutor v Halilović* (Judgement) IT-01-48-A, A Ch (16 October 2007) para 38.

[120] See n 109 and accompanying text.

[121] See also Zappalà 2003, 80, 149–152.

[122] Zahar and Sluiter 2008, 381–382. See also Zappalà 2003, 80–81 (criticizing the similar, but not identical, exclusionary rule adopted for the ICC), and Safferling 2003, 295 ('every human rights violation must … hamper the integrity of the proceedings. Evidence obtained in violation of human rights must therefore be declared inadmissible').

[123] Rule 95 ICTY RPE, IT/32, 14 March 1994. At the ICTR, the title of this rule has *always* read as follows: 'Exclusion of Evidence on the Grounds of the Means by Which It was Obtained'.

for *any*) breach of an internationally recognized human right,[124] even though the title of the rule (as it read then: 'Evidence Obtained by Means Contrary to Internationally Protected Human Rights') might have suggested otherwise. After its amendment in January 1995, Rule 95 of the ICTY RPE read as it currently does ('No evidence shall be admissible if obtained by methods which cast substantial doubt on its reliability or if its admission is antithetical to, and would seriously damage, the integrity of the proceedings'), although the title remained the same ('Evidence Obtained by Means Contrary to Internationally Protected Human Rights') and was amended only later, in November 1997, to 'Exclusion of Certain Evidence'. It seems that the title was amended in order to 'expand the rule's scope of application'.[125] The current wording of Rule 95 (of both the ICTY and ICTR RPEs) reflects the tenor of the original wording thereof, namely that not *every* breach of an internationally recognized human right should lead to the exclusion of the evidence obtained thereby; the requirement that the method of obtaining the evidence must cast *substantial* doubt on its reliability, or that it must *seriously* damage the integrity of the proceedings suggests that Rule 95 requires the trial chamber to make a judgement of degree. And given that Rule 95 is no longer limited in its scope of application to violations of internationally recognized human rights (as apparent from its (amended and current) title, and from the fact that the rule itself no longer stipulates the nature of the norm that needs to be violated), it is reasonable to assume that the trial chamber is required to make the same judgement of degree with respect to all other procedural violations. Based on a textual analysis of Rule 95 of both the ICTY and ICTR RPEs, and of the overriding criteria for exclusion, it seems that the trial chamber is afforded a good degree of latitude in the determination of an application for the exclusion of evidence on account of the manner in which it was obtained, which calls into question the suitability of the descriptor 'mandatory' in the context of Rule 95.[126] The question that now needs to be answered is how the exclusionary mechanism under Rule 95 has been construed in the case law: have judges at the ICTY and ICTR embraced the discretionary approach to the question of exclusion seemingly prescribed by that provision?

Another question that arises upon reading the text of Rule 95 and consulting its drafting history concerns the first limb of the exclusionary mechanism under Rule 95: the 'unreliability' limb. When the content of Rule 95 was amended in January 1995 to how it currently reads, the ICTY said that the amendment was made to

---

[124] Similarly, Fairlie observes that: 'Admittedly, the original version of the Rule [95] was not entirely in line with the theory that 'the admission of evidence obtained through the violation of human rights should be per se considered damaging to the integrity of the proceedings'. Fairlie 2004, 286–287.

[125] Zahar and Sluiter 2008, 381. See also Fairlie 2004, 287.

[126] See, similarly, Fairlie, who argues that describing Rule 95 ICTY/ICTR RPE, and Article 69(7) ICC Statute as 'mandatory exclusionary rules' is 'unhelpful if not misleading, as exclusion is "mandatory" only in the wake of a Chamber's *discretionary* analysis regarding the reliability of the evidence at issue and/or the manner in which its admission would affect the integrity of the proceedings'. See Fairlie 2013, 30 n 177.

'[put] parties on notice that although a Trial Chamber is not bound by national rules of evidence, it will refuse to admit evidence—no matter how probative—if it was obtained by improper methods'.[127] At first glance, the inclusion of an unreliability head under Rule 95 appears to be at odds with the proposition that the text of Rule 95 reflects the willingness to exclude unlawfully obtained evidence, 'no matter how probative'.[128] However, whether this is indeed the case depends on how 'unreliability' is interpreted in practice. In particular it would appear to depend on whether unreliability is understood as *actual* unreliability, or, rather, as *hypothetical* unreliability, whereby the latter would require a chamber to ask itself whether *any* evidence (of the same type as the impugned evidence) that might have been obtained at the point at which the impugned evidence was in fact obtained, was likely to be unreliable as a result of the manner of obtaining. In other words, hypothetical unreliability involves making generalized predications of unreliability in particular sets of circumstances. If *hypothetical* unreliability is indeed what the drafters had in mind, the phrase 'no matter how probative' in the quote above may be read as 'notwithstanding that the evidence is *actually* reliable'. Certainly, the wording of Rule 95 itself suggests that this is what the drafters had in mind; it is sufficient that the manner in which the evidence was obtained *casts doubt* on its reliability. If hypothetical unreliability is indeed what the concern ought to be under the first limb of Rule 95, it would be inappropriate for a chamber to take into account information already admitted into evidence for the purposes of the determination to be made under that limb (namely, whether the evidence was obtained by methods which cast substantial doubt on its reliability). How judges at the ICTY and ICTR have approached the unreliability head of Rule 95 of the ICTY RPE and ICTR RPE, respectively, is examined below.

As observed above, Rule 95 of the ICTY and ICTR RPEs does not stipulate the nature of the norm that needs to be violated in order to trigger the exclusionary mechanism provided for thereunder. Nevertheless, it is clear from the case law that some norms are, when violated, more capable of meeting the standard for exclusion under Rule 95 than others. Turning first to the norms that, when violated, are less likely to meet that standard, it seems that, by itself, a violation of state sovereignty will not lead to the exclusion of any evidence obtained thereby. In *Naletilić and Martinović*, the Accused Mladen Naletilić had sought the exclusion of material obtained by a search, which he argued had been carried out in violation of customary international law provisions on state sovereignty; in executing the search warrant (validly) issued by the Tribunal, the Prosecution had not sought the cooperation of the Bosnian authorities, which the Accused argued it should have done. The Appeals Chamber held that for the Accused to successfully challenge the admissibility of the evidence concerned on such grounds, he would have had to

---

[127] See ICTY 'Second Annual Report of the International Tribunal for the Prosecution of Persons Responsible for Serious Violations of International Humanitarian Law Committed in the Territory of the Former Yugoslavia Since 1991' (23 August 1995) UN Doc A/50/365–S/1995/728, 45.

[128] See in this regard Fairlie 2004, 267: 'Ironically, the revised language of the Rule creates the opposite effect by linking exclusion in the first instance with a lack of reliability.'

have shown 'not only … that the Prosecution was under the obligation to seek the cooperation of the local authorities, but also that the failure to so "cast[s] substantial doubt" on the reliability of the evidence in question or that its admission "is antithetical to, and would seriously damage, the integrity of the proceedings."'[129] The Accused had not shown this to be the case.

Nor, it seems, will a violation of national law, by itself, lead to exclusion of any evidence obtained thereby under Rule 95. Before considering the relevant case law in this regard, it is worth pointing out that in several early ICTR decisions concerning defence motions for relief in respect of alleged illegality or unlawfulness on the part of national authorities in the execution of a request for cooperation (including the arrest and detention of the suspect) from the ICTR Prosecutor (including applications for the exclusion of evidence obtained thereby), it was held that the suspect or accused would be able to seek a remedy *in the state concerned*. In *Ngirumpatse*, the Trial Chamber held that: 'It is a sovereign State that executes the request, controls the authorities executing the request, *and against whom the person arrested may seek a remedy against the arrest, custody, search, and seizure under the laws of the requested State*. The Tribunal is not competent to supervise the legality of arrest, custody, search, and seizure executed by the requested State.'[130] In subsequent ICTR decisions, and in several cases at the ICTY, however, chambers have entertained applications for the exclusion of evidence obtained (allegedly improperly) *by national authorities*. Nevertheless, it is clear from such cases that, by itself, a violation of national law will not lead to exclusion of any evidence obtained thereby under Rule 95. It may be noted at the outset that most of the cases set out below (which demonstrate that a violation of national law will not lead to exclusion of any evidence obtained thereby under Rule 95) concern facts which raise issues under the internationally recognized human right to privacy; however, as will be seen below, chambers have tended not to address this issue.[131] In addition, they have not always examined the relevant national law for the purpose of establishing whether manner in which the evidence was obtained was

---

[129] *Prosecutor v Naletilić and Martinović* (Judgement) IT-98-34-A, A Ch (3 May 2006) para 238.

[130] *Prosecutor v Ngirumpatse* (Decision on the Defence Motion Challenging the Lawfulness of the Arrest and Detention and Seeking Return or Inspection of Seized Items) ICTR-97-44-I, T Ch II (10 December 1999) para 56. See also *Prosecutor v Nyiramasuhuko* (Decision on the Defence Motion for Exclusion of Evidence and Restitution of Property Seized) ICTR-97-21-T, T Ch II, 12 October 2000, para 26; *Prosecutor v Karemera* (Decision on the Defence Motion for the Restitution of Documents and other Personal or Family Belongings Seized (Rule 40(C) of the Rules of Procedure and Evidence), and the Exclusion of such Evidence which may be Used by the Prosecutor in Preparing an Indictment against the Applicant) ICTR-98-44-I, T Ch II (10 December 1999) para 4.2; *Prosecutor v Nzirorera* (Decision on the Defence Motion Challenging the Legality of the Arrest and Detention of the Accused and Requesting the Return of Personal Items Seized) ICTR-98-44-T, T Ch II (7 September 2000) para 27; and *Prosecutor v Kajelijeli* (Decision on the Defence Motion Concerning the Arbitrary Arrest and Illegal Detention of the Accused and on the Defence Notice of Urgent Motion to Expand and Supplement the Record of 8 December 1999 Hearing) ICTR-98-44-I, T Ch II (8 May 2000) 34–35.

[131] See in this regard Zeegers 2016, 165–166.

illegal. In one ICTR case, the chamber held (relying on an early ICTY decision) that it was for the Defence to 'show that the search and seizure as a result of which the documents were obtained were tainted with illegality either under the Tribunal's Rules or at international law'.[132] Turning now to the case law which demonstrate that a violation of national law will not lead to exclusion of any evidence obtained thereby under Rule 95, in *Mucić and others*, the Defence (for all four Accused) had objected to the admission of certain exhibits 'on grounds of non-compliance with the procedural laws of Austria in the carrying out of the search [by which they were obtained]'.[133] The Trial Chamber seemed to accept that 'mistakes did occur' in the execution of the search warrant issued by the Austrian judge,[134] but opined that it seemed 'to be consistent with the ... [ICTY RPE] that where evidence is relevant and has probative value, it is *immaterial* how it has been obtained', subject to the exclusionary discretion under Rule 95.[135] Moreover, it was of the view that 'it would constitute a dangerous obstacle to the administration of justice if evidence which is relevant and of probative value could not be admitted merely because of a minor breach of procedural rules which the Trial Chamber is not bound to apply'.[136] It did not consider the relevant Austrian law, however (seemingly because it had determined that it was not bound by national laws of evidence); nor did it consider whether the search and seizure violated the internationally

---

[132] *Prosecutor v Muvunyi* (Decision on the Prosecutor's Motion Pursuant to Trial Chamber's Directives of 7 December 2005 for the Verification of the Authenticity of Evidence Obtained Out of Court Pursuant to Rules 89(C) and (D)) ICTR-2000-55A-T, T Ch II (26 April 2006) para 23, referring to *Prosecutor v Stakić* (Decision) IT-97-24-AR73.5, A Ch (10 October 2002).

[133] *Prosecutor v Delalić, Mucić, Delić and Landžo* (Decision on the Tendering of Prosecution Exhibits 104–108) IT-96-21-T, T Ch II (9 February 1998) para 18.

[134] Ibid., para 8.

[135] Ibid., para 19. See also *Prosecutor v Brđanin* (Decision on the Defence "Objection to Intercept Evidence") IT-99-36-T, T Ch II (3 October 2003) para 21 (emphasis added).

[136] *Prosecutor v Delalić, Mucić, Delić and Landžo* (Decision on the Tendering of Prosecution Exhibits 104–108) IT-96-21-T, T Ch II (9 February 1998) para 20, as referred to in *Prosecutor v Brđanin* (Decision on the Defence "Objection to Intercept Evidence") IT-99-36-T, T Ch II (3 October 2003) para 63. See also *Prosecutor v Karadžić* (Decision on the Accused's Motion to Exclude Intercepted Conversations) IT-95-5/18-T, T Ch III (30 September 2010) para 10 ('Rule 95 does not serve to exclude evidence based on violations of procedural safeguards set forth in domestic law. [...] In light of the Tribunal's mandate to prosecute persons allegedly responsible for serious violations of international humanitarian law, it would be inappropriate to exclude relevant and probative evidence due to procedural considerations, as long as the fairness of the trial is guaranteed'); *Prosecutor v Stanišić and Župljanin* (Decision Denying the Stanišić Motion for Exclusion of Recorded Intercepts) IT-08-91-T, T Ch II (16 December 2009) para 14 ('The admission of an intercept does not depend, per se, on whether it was obtained legally or illegally under the domestic law in force at the time the intercept was recorded.'); and *Prosecutor v Milošević* (Preliminary Decision on The Admissibility of Intercepted Communications) IT-02-54-T, T Ch III (16 December 2003) 3 ('whether the process of recording the intercepts is in accordance with the domestic law of BiH does not necessarily determine whether the intercepts are admissible; but rather it is the law relating to the admissibility of evidence under the Statute and Rules of this Tribunal and international law which must be applied.').

recognized human right to privacy.[137] In any case the Trial Chamber was not satisfied that the method by which the evidence was obtained amounted to 'such conduct as to induce the exercise of … [the discretion under Rule 95] to exclude it'.[138] In *Brđanin*, where the Defence sought the exclusion of several intercepted telephone conversations on the grounds that such intercepts had been 'obtained illegally because they did not conform with the law of Bosnia and Herzegovina at the time', the Trial Chamber held that,

> admitting illegally obtained intercepts into evidence does not, in and of itself, necessarily amount to seriously damaging the integrity of the proceedings. Rather, in situations of armed conflict, intelligence which may be the result of illegal activity may prove to be essential in uncovering the truth; all the more so when this information is not available from other sources. As stated above, in applying the provisions of Rule 95, this Tribunal considers all the relevant circumstances and will only exclude evidence if the integrity of the proceedings would indeed otherwise be <u>seriously</u> damaged.[139]

Earlier on in the decision, the Trial Chamber had said that:

> It is clear from the review of national laws and international law, and the Rules and practice of this International Tribunal, that before this Tribunal evidence obtained illegally is not, a priori, inadmissible, but rather that the manner and surrounding circumstances in which evidence is obtained, *as well as* its reliability and effect on the integrity of the proceedings, will determine its admissibility. Illegally obtained evidence may, therefore, be admitted under Rule 95 since the jurisprudence of the International Tribunal has never endorsed the exclusionary rule as a matter of principle.[140]

According to the Trial Chamber, several factors militated towards admission of the intercepts: that those who carried out the intercepts were acting in 'good faith'; that the intercepts were carried out in circumstances of urgency, emergency and necessity; the apparent voluntariness with which those whose communications were intercepted spoke; that the intercepted evidence could not have been available through any other source; that the intercepts had been obtained in violation of *national law* and were not, therefore, inadmissible under Tribunal case law; the responsibility of the Tribunal under the ICTY Statute to bring to justice persons allegedly responsible for serious violations of international law and the seriousness of the charges with which the accused was charged (which made it 'utterly inappropriate to exclude relevant evidence due to procedural considerations, as long as the fairness of the trial is guaranteed'); that exclusion would not discourage the use

---

[137] See in this regard *Prosecutor v Delalić, Mucić, Delić and Landžo* (Decision on the Tendering of Prosecution Exhibits 104–108) IT-96-21-T, T Ch II (9 February 1998) para 23. See also *Prosecutor v Muvunyi* (Decision on the Prosecutor's Motion Pursuant to Trial Chamber's Directives of 7 December 2005 for the Verification of the Authenticity of Evidence Obtained Out of Court Pursuant to Rules 89(C) and (D)) ICTR-2000-55A-T, T Ch II (26 April 2006) para 24.

[138] *Prosecutor v Delalić, Mucić, Delić and Landžo* (Decision on the Tendering of Prosecution Exhibits 104–108) IT-96-21-T, T Ch II (9 February 1998) para 20.

[139] *Prosecutor v Brđanin* (Decision on the Defence "Objection to Intercept Evidence") IT-99-36-T, T Ch II (3 October 2003) para 61 (emphasis in original). See also paras 53–54.

[140] Ibid., para 55 (emphasis added).

of interception of communications in times of crisis or in time of armed conflict; and the relevance and importance of the intercepts.[141] Although the Trial Chamber acknowledged that the manner in which the intercepts had been obtained raised issues under the right to privacy,[142] and assessed its legality under national law,[143] it stopped short of assessing whether it had been contrary to the right to privacy. Regarding its point that exclusion would not discourage the use of interception of communications in times of crisis or in time of armed conflict, the Trial Chamber held, more generally, that, at the ICTY at least, evidence should not be excluded for the purpose of deterring national authorities from acting improperly:

> Domestic exclusionary rules are based, in part, on the principle of discouraging and punishing over-reaching law enforcement. The Trial Chamber does not think for a moment that by taking a different approach to the one it is taking, it would in any event discourage the use of interception of communications in times of crisis or in time of armed conflict. By excluding what would appear to be on a prima facie basis relevant and important evidence, it would only be denying itself the possibility of having available evidence which would be otherwise difficult, if not impossible, to obtain. *The function of this Tribunal is not to deter and punish illegal conduct by domestic law enforcement authorities by excluding illegally obtained evidence.*[144]

In the ICTR case of *Renzaho*, in which the Defence had sought the exclusion of certain intercepted communications, the Trial Chamber cited with approval the Trial Chamber's decision in *Brđanin*, relying on it for the proposition that non-compliance with Rwandan law 'would not in itself lead to exclusion under ... Tribunal case law'.[145] The Trial Chamber did not actually establish whether the intercepts had been obtained in accordance with Rwandan law, since there was 'no information about the Rwandan law that was applicable to interception during the circumstances that prevailed in April 1994, when the recording was made, and hence whether the interception was illegal'.[146] In the circumstances there was no basis to exclude the evidence under Rule 95. In an earlier decision, the Trial Chamber (in a different case) had held that: 'Violation of national law might be a consideration in determining whether evidence should be excluded under Rule 95'.[147]

---

[141] Ibid., para 63.

[142] Ibid., para 31.

[143] Ibid., para 60.

[144] Ibid., para 63.

[145] *Prosecutor v Renzaho* (Decision on Exclusion of Testimony and Admission of Exhibit) ICTR-97-31-T, T Ch I (20 March 2007) paras 15–16. See also *Prosecutor v Muvunyi* (Decision on the Prosecutor's Motion Pursuant to Trial Chamber's Directives of 7 December 2005 for the Verification of the Authenticity of Evidence Obtained Out of Court Pursuant to Rules 89(C) and (D)) ICTR-2000-55A-T, T Ch II (26 April 2006) para 24.

[146] *Prosecutor v Renzaho* (Decision on Exclusion of Testimony and Admission of Exhibit) ICTR-97-31-T, T Ch I (20 March 2007) para 16.

[147] *Prosecutor v Bagosora, Kabiligi, Ntabakuze and Nsengiyumva* (Decision on Motion to Harmonize and Amend Witness Protection Orders) ICTR-98-41-T, T Ch I (1 June 2005) para 15. See, however, n 130 and accompanying text.

Moving on now to other norms, there are (strong) indications in the case law of the ad hoc Tribunals that the violation of an internationally recognized human right will not always lead to the exclusion of evidence obtained thereby, whether under the discretion to exclude evidence if its probative value is (significantly) outweighed by the need to ensure a fair trial or under Rule 95 of both the ICTY and ICTR RPEs.[148] In *Haraqija and Morina*, a case concerning 'contempt' within the meaning of Rule 77 of the ICTY RPE, the Defence had sought the exclusion of certain intercepted communications between the accused Bajrush Morina and a protected witness in the *Haradinaj, Balaj and Brahimaj* trial, on the basis that the audio surveillance, which was carried out by the 'domestic police in the country where the conversation occurred, in consultation with the Prosecution',[149] had lacked a legal basis in the relevant domestic law and had been carried out without a court order. Citing with approval the Trial Chamber's decision in *Brđanin*,[150] the Trial Chamber declined to exclude the evidence either under Rule 89(D) or Rule 95 of the ICTY RPE, thereby relying on the ECtHR's decisions in the cases of *Khan* and *PG and JH* as establishing that the use of evidence obtained in breach of Article 8 of the ECHR was not inconsistent with the right to a fair trial under Article 6 (thereby implying that the manner in which the evidence was alleged to have been obtained raised issues under the right to privacy, although it did not make a determination in this regard).[151] In declining to exclude the evidence under Rule 89 (D), the Trial Chamber also attached importance to the following facts and circumstances: that the police officers who carried out the surveillance had acted in good faith; that it had been carried out in circumstances of necessity; that the accused had not been entrapped or coerced into participating in the conversations;

---

[148] The case law set out above, concerning the admissibility of evidence obtained by search and seizure, and by covert surveillance, also indicate as much. Such cases clearly raise issues under the internationally recognized human right to privacy, even if chambers have not always acknowledged this, or not established whether the manner in which the evidence was obtained violated that right.

[149] *Prosecutor v Haraqija and Morina* (Judgement) IT-04-84-R77.4-A, A Ch (23 July 2009) para 17.

[150] *Prosecutor v Haraqija and Morina* (Decision on Morina and Haraqija Second Request for a Declaration of Inadmissibility and Exclusion of Evidence) IT-04-84-R77.4, T Ch I (27 November 2008) paras 14–15 and 26.

[151] Ibid., paras 13 and 18, referring to *Khan v UK* App no 35394/97 (ECtHR, 12 May 2000) and *PG and JH v UK* App no 44787/98 (ECtHR, 25 September 2001). See also *Prosecutor v Karadžić* (Decision on the Accused's Motion to Exclude Intercepted Conversations) IT-95-5/18-T, T Ch III (30 September 2010) para 11: 'The Chamber does not consider that admitting intercepts of conversations involving the Accused that may have been obtained in contravention of domestic law would violate the Accused's right to privacy to such an extent that the integrity of these proceedings would be damaged. As acknowledged by the Accused, the fundamental right to privacy is not absolute, and may be derogated from in times of emergency. Likewise, the Chamber does not consider the admission of evidence that may have been obtained illegally to conflict with the need to ensure a fair trial.'

and that the evidence was relevant and probative.[152] These factors also seem to have informed the Trial Chamber's decision (not to exclude the evidence) under (the second, 'damage to integrity', limb of) Rule 95 of the ICTY RPE.[153] In this regard it may be observed that whereas the fact that the authorities acted in good faith is, arguably, a relevant consideration under the second ('integrity') limb of Rule 95, the logic of 'invoking' it in the context of Rule 89(D) of the ICTY RPE, which, it should be recalled, is concerned with the ability of a chamber to determine the guilt or innocence of the accused accurately, or otherwise with trial fairness, is far from obvious. What the Trial Chamber did not take into consideration (under either provision), however, was the fact that the Prosecution *had* been involved, a fact that has not gone unnoticed in the literature.[154] The Trial Chamber's decision not to exclude the evidence was upheld by the Appeals Chamber.[155]

Turning now to a case in which evidence *was* excluded on account of the manner of its obtaining, in the ICTY case of *Mucić and others* the evidence in question concerned an interview conducted by the Austrian police with the Accused Mucić (following his arrest by the Austrian authorities at the ICTY's request),[156] during which he did not have access to counsel; such access was not required (or rather, prohibited, it seems) under Austrian law.[157] While not inconsistent with the relevant Austrian law, the lack of access to counsel during the interview was, according to the Trial Chamber, inconsistent with Article 18 of the ICTY Statute (which, among other things, provides for the right of suspect to legal assistance when questioned) and Rule 42 of the ICTY RPE (which fleshes out that right, and which specifically refers to questioning *by the Prosecutor*);[158] therefore, the interview had to be excluded, although not pursuant to Rule 95. The Trial Chamber's findings in this regard are worth reproducing here:

> The question is whether the interview is one which can pass the test of Article 18 and Rule 42. The allegation of the Defence of inducement to confess did not go beyond reading the rules of the Austrian Police procedure to the suspect. This being the only offensive conduct, the Trial Chamber is not satisfied that this by itself was sufficient. This is because though the [Austrian] rules relating to silence and confession are contradictory to the relevant rules in Rule 42, they do not fall below fundamental fairness and such as to render admission antithetical to or to seriously damage the integrity of the proceedings [such as to warrant

---

[152] *Prosecutor v Haraqija and Morina* (Decision on Morina and Haraqija Second Request for a Declaration of Inadmissibility and Exclusion of Evidence) IT-04-84-R77.4, T Ch I (27 November 2008) 20–23.

[153] Ibid., para 26: 'As found earlier, the circumstances of the audio and video recordings are such as to militate towards the admission of evidence.'

[154] See e.g. Alamuddin 2010, 289; and Zeegers 2016, 164.

[155] *Prosecutor v Haraqija and Morina* (Judgement) IT-04-84-R77.4-A, A Ch (23 July 2009) paras 17–29.

[156] *Prosecutor v Delalić, Mucić, Delić and Landžo* (Judgement) IT-96-21-T, T Ch (16 November 1998) para 30.

[157] *Prosecutor v Delalić, Mucić, Delić and Landžo* (Decision on Zdravko Mucić's Motion for the Exclusion of Evidence) IT-96-21-T, T Ch II (2 September 1997) para 50.

[158] Ibid., paras 50–55.

exclusion pursuant to Rule 95 ICTY RPE]. However violation of Sub-rules 42A(i) and 42 (B) by themselves would be sufficient by virtue of Rule 5 to render the statements before the Austrian Police null and inadmissible in proceedings before us and to be excluded.[159]

It seems clear, therefore, that the statement was excluded pursuant to Rule 5 of the ICTY RPE, which at the time read as follows: 'Any objection by a party to an act of another party on the ground of non-compliance with the Rules or Regulations shall be raised at the earliest opportunity; it shall be upheld, and *the act declared null*, only if the act was inconsistent with the fundamental principles of fairness and has occasioned a miscarriage of justice.'[160] Although the Austrian police interview was not, in fact, excluded pursuant to Rule 95 of the ICTY RPE,[161] the Trial Chamber's observation that, '[i]t seems … extremely difficult for a statement taken in violation of Rule 42 [of the ICTY RPE, which confers on suspects certain rights related to questioning by the ICTY Prosecutor (or rather, through his or her staff)] to fall within Rule 95 [of the ICTY RPE] which protects the integrity of the proceedings by the non-admissibility of evidence obtained by methods which cast substantial doubts on its reliability',[162] has been cited in a number of ICTR decisions as meaning that statements obtained in violation of Rule 42 should be excluded pursuant to Rule 95 of the ICTR RPE.[163] In *Karemera, Ngirumpatse and Nzirorera*, for example, the Trial Chamber, having found that the Prosecutor had 'not established beyond reasonable doubt that Joseph Nzirorera waived his right to be silent and to be assisted by counsel in an express and unequivocal manner',[164] concluded that there was 'substantial doubt as to the reliability of the interview [with Nzirorera]' and that 'its admission into evidence would be antithetical to and seriously damage the integrity of the proceeding[s], wherefore pursuant to Rule 95, the interview is not admissible'.[165] These authorities suggest that statements

---

[159] Ibid., para 55 (emphasis added).

[160] Rule 5 ICTY RPE, IT/32/Rev11, 25 July 1997 (emphasis added).

[161] See Fairlie 2013, for a more detailed analysis of the decision in this regard. She notes that: 'Because the opinion is not a model of clarity, many have mistakenly concluded that the Chamber suppressed Mucić's statements pursuant to Rule 95'. See ibid., 35 n 206. See in this regard e.g. Alamuddin 2010, 280; Nerenberg and Timmermann 2010, 479; and Zahar and Sluiter 2008, 304–305.

[162] *Prosecutor v Delalić, Mucić, Delić and Landžo* (Decision on Zdravko Mucić's Motion for the Exclusion of Evidence) IT-96-21-T, T Ch II (2 September 1997) para 43.

[163] See also Fairlie 2013, 35–36.

[164] *Prosecutor v Karemera, Ngirumpatse and Nzirorera* (Decision on the Prosecution Motion for Admission into Evidence of Post-Arrest Interviews with Joseph Nzirorera and Mathieu Ngirumpatse) ICTR-98-44-T, T Ch III (2 November 2007) para 31.

[165] Ibid., para 32. See also *Prosecutor v Bagosora, Kabiligi, Ntabakuze and Nsengiyumva* (Decision on the Prosecutor's Motion for the Admission of Certain Materials under Rule 89(C)) ICTR-98-41-T, T Ch I (14 October 2004) para 21; *Prosecutor v Zigiranyirazo* (Decision on the Voir Dire Hearing of the Accused's *Curriculum Vitae*) ICTR-2001-73-T, T Ch III (29 November 2006) para 13; and *Prosecutor v Nchamihigo* (Decision on the Prosecutor's Application to Admit into Evidence the Transcript of the Accused's Interview as a Suspect and the Defense's Request to Hold a *Voir Dire*) ICTR-01-63-T, T Ch III (5 February 2007).

obtained in violation of Rule 42 of the ICTY and ICTR RPEs will usually lead to exclusion under Rule 95.[166] In addition, it seems that a violation of the privilege against self-incrimination will normally lead to exclusion. In the ICTY case of *Martić*, for example, the Trial Chamber said that 'statements which are *not voluntary*, but rather are obtained by means including *oppressive conduct*, cannot be admitted pursuant to Rule 95. If there are *prima facie* indicia that there was such oppressive conduct, the burden is on the party seeking to have the evidence admitted to prove that the statement was voluntary and not obtained by oppressive conduct.'[167]

In summary, then, neither a violation of state sovereignty nor a violation of national law will, by itself, lead to the exclusion of evidence obtained thereby under Rule 95 of the ICTY or ICTR RPE. Nor will the violation of an internationally recognized human right automatically lead to exclusion. For violations of national law and certain internationally recognized human rights, at least, the determination of whether to exclude the evidence obtained thereby under Rule 95 entails a consideration of the particular facts and circumstances of the case, including factors that have nothing to do with that which made the evidence problematic in the first place, for example, the fact that the offence(s) with which the accused is charged are very serious. In respect of such violations, chambers of the ad hoc Tribunals have adopted a truly discretionary, or 'balancing' approach. On this basis, the characterization of the exclusionary mechanism under Rule 95 as 'mandatory' in nature may be said to be misleading.[168] However, the term 'mandatory' may not be entirely out of place in the context of Rule 95, on account of the fact that violation of a fair trial right, and, in particular, violation of a provision of the Statute or RPE that purports to protect such a right, will, according to the case law of the ad hoc Tribunals, ordinarily lead to exclusion of the evidence thereby obtained.[169] In other words, exclusion appears to be 'mandatory' or 'automatic' for evidence obtained by such a violation. The question is whether this is because one or both of the prongs under Rule 95 is automatically satisfied in such cases, or because exclusion is already inherent in the rule to have been violated. In other words, the question is whether evidence obtained by such a violation falls within the scope of Rule 95 *at all*, or, put differently again, whether the exclusionary discretion provided for under

---

[166] See also Fairlie 2013, 33–39; Khan and Dixon 2013, 868; Alamuddin 2010, 280–281 and 303; and Gosnell 2010, 422–423.

[167] *Prosecutor v Martić* (Decision Adopting Guidelines on the Standards Governing the Admission of Evidence) IT-95-11-T, T Ch I (19 January 2006) para 9 (emphasis added). The Trial Chamber does not, however, specify which leg—reliability or integrity—is at stake in such circumstances. See also *Prosecutor v Delalić, Mucić, Delić and Landžo* (Decision on Zdravko Mucić's Motion for the Exclusion of Evidence) IT-96-21-T, T Ch II (2 September 1997) para 41. See also *Prosecutor v Brđanin* (Decision on the Defence "Objection to Intercept Evidence") IT-99-36-T, T Ch II (3 October 2003) para 67(2).

[168] See n 126 and accompanying text.

[169] Similarly, Klamberg suggests that, in the context of Rule 95 ICTY/ICTR RPE, a distinction may be drawn between violations of the ad hoc Tribunals' 'own Statutes and Rules or internationally protected human rights' and *other* procedural violations. Klamberg 2013b, 1033.

Rule 95 is confined to evidence obtained by a procedural violation other than the violation of a fair trial right, or, rather, the violation of a provision of the Statute or RPE that purports to protect such a right. Whereas the ICTR cases suggest that evidence obtained by breach of Rule 42 of the RPE falls to be excluded under Rule 95,[170] the decision in the ICTY case of *Mucić and others* seems to suggest otherwise.[171] This issue is as yet unresolved,[172] and, by extension, the extent to which the exclusionary mechanism under Rule 95 can accurately be depicted as mandatory in nature is unclear. Related to this issue is the question raised above of how the first limb of the exclusionary mechanism under Rule 95 of both the ICTY and ICTR RPEs, under which a chamber must ask itself whether the evidence was 'obtained by methods which cast substantial doubts on its reliability', is to be approached; should a chamber making a determination under this limb be concerned with 'hypothetical' unreliability, or, rather, with 'actual' unreliability?[173] The (same) ICTR cases referred to above suggest that under the first limb of Rule 95, a chamber should be concerned with *hypothetical* unreliability. In *Karemera, Ngirumpatse and Nzirorera*, for example, the fact that the statement had been obtained in violation of Rule 42 of the ICTR RPE (which, as at the ICTY, provides for the right of a suspect to legal assistance during questioning) was sufficient to warrant its exclusion under Rule 95; *both* tests under Rule 95 were automatically satisfied upon finding that the statement had been obtained in this way.[174] In other words, according to the Trial Chamber in that case, the violation of Rule 42 *by definition* 'cast substantial doubt on the reliability' of the statement obtained thereby; the (actual) probative value (which, at the admissibility stage, might be determined by looking to evidence already admitted) of the statement was immaterial. In a separate opinion to the *Halilović* appeals judgment, in which the Appeals Chamber upheld the Trial Chamber's decision to exclude a statement of the accused

---

[170] See in this regard *Prosecutor v Karemera, Ngirumpatse and Nzirorera* (Decision on the Prosecution Motion for Admission into Evidence of Post-Arrest Interviews with Joseph Nzirorera and Mathieu Ngirumpatse) ICTR-98-44-T, T Ch III (2 November 2007) paras 25 and 32, and *Prosecutor v Bagosora, Kabiligi, Ntabakuze and Nsengiyumva* (Decision on the Prosecutor's Motion for the Admission of Certain Materials under Rule 89(C)) ICTR-98-41-T, T Ch I (14 October 2004) para 21.

[171] See in this regard *Prosecutor v Delalić, Mucić, Delić and Landžo* (Decision on Zdravko Mucić's Motion for the Exclusion of Evidence) IT-96-21-T, T Ch II (2 September 1997) paras 43–44. See also Gosnell 2010, 422–423. Confusingly, though, the ICTR authorities rely on this decision for the assertion that evidence obtained by a violation of Rule 42 ICTR RPE is subject to exclusion pursuant to Rule 95 ICTR RPE. See n 163–166 and accompanying text.

[172] According to Alamuddin: 'It remains unclear whether the dual test [under Rule 95] always governs exclusion of evidence or whether exclusion is automatic when certain violations occur.' Alamuddin 2010, 303.

[173] See n 127 and accompanying text.

[174] *Prosecutor v Karemera, Ngirumpatse and Nzirorera* (Decision on the Prosecution Motion for Admission into Evidence of Post-Arrest Interviews with Joseph Nzirorera and Mathieu Ngirumpatse) ICTR-98-44-T, T Ch III (2 November 2007) paras 31–32.

obtained in breach of Rule 43 of the ICTY RPE,[175] Judge Meron argued that a statement based on an interview conducted in breach of Rule 43 of the ICTY RPE (which, it should be recalled, provides that questioning of a suspect by the Prosecutor must be audio- or video-recorded) should be excluded because it is per se unreliable. However, in his view, such a statement does not fall to be excluded pursuant to either Rule 95 or Rule 89(D) of the ICTY RPE, seemingly because the discretion provided for under those provisions would allow a chamber to look *beyond* the hypothetical unreliability of a statement obtained in breach of Rule 43 in the determination of whether to exclude it (for example, to other information already admitted into evidence which tends to corroborate the contents of the statement). The relevant parts of the opinion are worth quoting here:

> Rule 43 reflects a substantive judgment that unrecorded statements by the accused are, by definition, insufficiently reliable. *A Trial Chamber normally assesses reliability on a case-by-case basis* under Rule 95 and excludes evidence when there is "substantial doubt" about its reliability. Similarly, it determines probativeness under Rule 89(D). The *discretion* that a Trial Chamber normally exercises pursuant to these rules is inapposite, though, because an unrecorded statement by an accused is per se unreliable under Rule 43. As an unrecorded statement by an accused *is never sufficiently reliable*, the only appropriate remedy is exclusion of that statement.

> My conclusion about the appropriateness of exclusion for violations of Rule 43 is bolstered by the precedents of the Tribunal. The *Čelebići* Appeal Judgement noted that the Appeals Chamber must seek to ensure (1) that procedural safeguards are respected and (2) that the evidence is reliable. The Appeals Chamber there clearly contemplated that, despite scrupulous adherence to all procedural safeguards, some evidence might still be unreliable. It did not indulge the converse (*i.e.*, that despite procedural violations, some evidence might still be sufficiently reliable). A violation of Rule 43 thus incurably taints the evidence.

> In light of the foregoing analysis, the majority's holding fails to appreciate that a Trial Chamber *exercises discretion in assessing probativeness* under Rule 89(D), and *in determining reliability* under Rule 95, only *after* the Trial Chamber has established that the Prosecution respected certain procedural safeguards, including Rule 43. Once it is established that Rule 43 applied, and that it was violated, *there is no room for discretion*—the statement must be excluded.[176]

The question of whether, under the first limb of Rule 95, the concern should be with hypothetical (rather than actual) unreliability, then, is to a large extent tied up with that of whether evidence obtained by violation of a fair trial right, and, in particular, violation of a provision of the Statute or RPE that purports to protect such a right, falls within the scope of Rule 95 at all. As noted above, this question has not been unequivocally answered in the case law of the ad hoc Tribunals.

---

[175] See n 119 and accompanying text.

[176] *Prosecutor v Halilović* (Judgement) IT-01-48-A, A Ch (16 October 2007), Separate Opinion of Judge Meron, paras 6–8 (emphasis added), referring to *Prosecutor v Delalić, Mucić, Delić and Landžo* (Judgement) IT-96-21-A, A Ch (20 February 2001) para 533. See also Judge Schomberg's separate opinion to the *Halilović* appeals judgement, para 7.

5.3.3   Financial Compensation

Neither the Statutes nor RPE of the ICTY or ICTR expressly provide for financial compensation in case of procedural violations committed in the pre-trial phase of international criminal proceedings. Nevertheless, the shared Appeals Chamber of the ad hoc Tribunals has held that such compensation may, under certain circumstances, be claimed.[177] In finding that the violations of the Accused's rights were less extensive than previously thought (and therefore no longer justified the setting aside of jurisdiction), the Appeals Chamber in *Barayagwiza* found that the Accused would be entitled to financial compensation upon acquittal or to sentence reduction upon conviction. Therefore, financial compensation is considered a less far-reaching response than a stay of proceedings. According to the Appeals Chamber, the Accused was entitled to one of these remedies in view of the fact that 'all [rights] violations demand a remedy'.[178] Therefore, the primary purpose of both financial compensation and sentence reduction appears to be the provision of a personal remedy for rights violations. While the Appeals Chamber in *Barayagwiza* did not otherwise consider the authority of the ad hoc Tribunals to make an award of financial compensation, since then, the availability of financial compensation in case of procedural violations in the pre-trial phase (specifically, procedural violations that violate the rights of the suspect or accused) has been confirmed in several cases before the ad hoc Tribunals,[179] but ordered in only one.[180] In *Rwamakuba*, the Appeals Chamber sought the authority to make an award of financial compensation in case of rights violations in 'international law', specifically, the right to an effective remedy as provided for in Article 2(3)(a) of the ICCPR; it observed that

---

[177] In addition, the Appeals Chamber has held that compensation may be claimed in case of a 'grave and manifest miscarriage of justice', in case of acquittal (although an acquittal is not sufficient for claiming compensation on this basis). See generally *Prosecutor v Zigiranyirazo* (Decision on Protais Zigiranyirazo's Motion for Damages) ICTR-2001-01-073, T Ch III (18 June 2012). Errors of fact and/or of law that lead to a defendant being acquitted on appeal may be seen as *judicial* procedural violations, and as such are not discussed in this book. Nevertheless it is worth noting here that an acquittal is likely to be considered an appropriate remedy for such procedural violations. See *Prosecutor v Zigiranyirazo* (Decision on Protais Zigiranyirazo's Request to Appeal Trial Chamber III's Decision of 18 June 2012) ICTR-O1-73-A, A Ch (26 February 2013) para 8.

[178] *Prosecutor v Barayagwiza* (Decision (Prosecutor's Request for Review or Reconsideration)) ICTR-97-19-AR72, A Ch (31 March 2000) para 74. See also *Prosecutor v Semanza* (Decision) ICTR-97-23-A, A Ch (31 May 2000).

[179] See e.g. *Prosecutor v Semanza* (Decision) ICTR-97-23-A, A Ch (31 May 2000) and *Prosecutor v Karadžić* (Decision on the Accused's Motion for Remedy for Violation of Rights in Connection with Arrest) IT-95-5/18-PT, T Ch III (31 August 2009).

[180] *Prosecutor v Rwamakuba* (Decision on Appropriate Remedy) ICTR-98-44C-T, T Ch III (31 January 2007), as confirmed on appeal in *Prosecutor v Rwamakuba* (Decision on Appeal against Decision on Appropriate Remedy) ICTR-98-44C-A, A Ch (13 September 2007).

it had previously found that 'the ICCPR is a persuasive authority in determining the Tribunal's powers under international law'.[181] Moreover, it appears to have been of the view that such authority derived from the Tribunal's 'inherent powers'.[182] Following the Appeals Chamber's decisions in *Barayagwiza* and *Semanza* cases confirming the availability of financial compensation in case of violation of an accused's (or former accused's) rights, the Presidents of the ICTR and ICTY wrote letters to Security Council seeking the amendment of the respective Statutes of the ICTY and ICTR to include a provision on financial compensation as a remedy for violations of the rights of the accused. In particular, they envisaged compensation in three situations: where an individual is unlawfully arrested or detained, where an individual is wrongly prosecuted and where an individual is wrongly convicted.[183] In their view, the absence of a provision allowing for compensation in such situations was a cause for concern, in light of 'internationally recognised norms relating to the rights of suspects and accused persons'. A number of authors have argued that the incorporation of such a provision in the respective Statutes of the ICTY and ICTR would strengthen the ad hoc Tribunals' authority to award financial compensation, by facilitating the creation of a specific budget or, alternatively, the allocation of part of the general budget (as funded by the member states of the United Nations) for this purpose.[184] Conversely, the absence of a provision on financial compensation in the Statutes of the ad hoc Tribunals might make the

---

[181] *Prosecutor v Rwamakuba* (Decision on Appeal against Decision on Appropriate Remedy) ICTR-98-44C-A, A Ch (13 September 2007) para 25, referring to *Prosecutor v Kajelijeli* (Judgement) ICTR-98-44A-A, A Ch (23 May 2005) para 209.

[182] In any case, it found that the Trial Chamber had not erred in finding that it—the Trial Chamber —'had the [inherent] authority in general to award an effective remedy for the violations of Mr. Rwamakuba's rights as an accused person, including financial compensation'. See *Prosecutor v Rwamakuba* (Decision on Appeal against Decision on Appropriate Remedy) ICTR-98-44C-A, A Ch (13 September 2007) para 26.

[183] 'Letter dated 19 September 2000 from the President of the International Criminal Tribunal for the Former Yugoslavia Addressed to the Secretary-General', annexed to 'Letter Dated 26 September 2000 from the Secretary-General Addressed to the President of the Security Council' (26 September 2000) UN Doc S/2000/904 and 'Letter dated 26 September 2000 from the President of the International Criminal Tribunal for Rwanda Addressed to the Secretary-General', annexed to 'Letter dated 28 September 2000 from the Secretary-General Addressed to the President of the Security Council' (6 October 2000) UN Doc S/2000/925.

[184] Zappalà 2002, 1582. See also Beresford in this regard: 'the most striking argument against attributing the necessary competence to the ad hoc Tribunals is that their powers and functions are determined by the terms of their Statutes and these instruments—as currently drafted—do not contain any provisions giving the courts the authority to award compensation. Such authority is a significant power that raises legitimate budgetary considerations, as well as doubts whether the courts, as organs of the United Nations, may unilaterally create financial liability for the Organization as a whole. While their Statutes may be interpreted liberally in many respects, particularly so as to provide the ad hoc Tribunals with the power to carry out their mandates, they contain no language implying that the Security Council intended to allow them to make such awards. Moreover, should they unilaterally decide to award compensation, the courts may be seen by some members of the Security Council as overstepping their authority and violating their Statutes.' Beresford 2002, 641.

allocation of funds for such purposes more difficult and, in this way, undermine the availability of the remedy of financial compensation at those tribunals. To date, the Security Council does not appear to have addressed this issue.[185]

As stated above, the availability of financial compensation in case of procedural violations committed in the pre-trial phase has been confirmed in several cases before the ad hoc Tribunals, but ordered in only one; the ICTR case of *Rwamakuba*. In that case, the Appeals Chamber confirmed[186] the Trial Chamber's decision ordering, pursuant to its '*inherent power* to give effect to an accused's or former accused's *right to an effective remedy*,[187] the Registrar to pay André Rwamakuba financial compensation (US$2,000) on account of his responsibility for the violation of Rwamakuba's right to legal assistance in the initial months of detention (and in doing so confirmed the authority of trial chambers to award financial compensation).[188] Such compensation was to be paid 'for the moral injury sustained as a result of this violation'.[189] However, it took some time for the compensation to be paid,[190] as the Registrar initially indicated that he would not be paying the compensation, on the grounds that 'neither the [S]tatute nor the budget of the ICTR make it possible to carry out financial reparations' and that he would instead be referring the matter 'to his hierarchy' at the United Nations.[191] While it may, therefore, be true that 'internal institutional considerations related to the execution of an order, including budgetary matters, are separate considerations from the Tribunal's authority to award an effective remedy',[192] the lack of an express provision and a specific budget for such purposes certainly has the ability to undermine the availability of financial compensation for violations of the accused's rights at the ad hoc Tribunals.[193]

---

[185] See also Judge Shahabuddeen in his separate opinion to *Prosecutor v Rwamakuba* (Decision on Appeal against Decision on Appropriate Remedy) ICTR-98-44C-A, A Ch (13 September 2007), noting the 'long silence' of the Security Council in this regard.

[186] See *Prosecutor v Rwamakuba* (Decision on Appeal against Decision on Appropriate Remedy) ICTR-98-44C-A, A Ch (13 September 2007).

[187] *Prosecutor v Rwamakuba* (Decision on Appropriate Remedy) ICTR-98-44C-T, T Ch III (31 January 2007) para 58 (emphasis added).

[188] Ibid., the disposition.

[189] Ibid., the disposition.

[190] Reported by Hirondelle News Agency, 'ICTR Compensates Genocide Acquitted Person For Legal Discrepancy', 27 February 2008, at: http://www.hirondellenews.com/ictr-rwanda/363-trials-ended/rwamakuba-andre/21559-en-en-270208-ictrrwamakuba-ictr-compensates-genocide-acquitted-person-for-legal-discrepancy1061010610 Accessed 1 March 2017.

[191] Reported by Hirondelle News Agency, 'The ICTR Registrar Is Unable to Enforce a Judgment of the ICTR', 18 September 2007, at http://www.hirondellenews.com/ictr-rwanda/363-trials-ended/rwamakuba-andre/20846-en-en-180907-ictrrwamakuba-the-ictr-registry-is-unable-to-enforce-a-judgment-of-the-ictr98979897 Accessed 1 March 2017.

[192] *Prosecutor v Rwamakuba* (Decision on Appeal against Decision on Appropriate Remedy) ICTR-98-44C-A, A Ch (13 September 2007) para 30.

[193] That the ad hoc Tribunals and, in particular, the Trial Chamber's have the authority to order financial compensation was confirmed in the ICTY case of *Karadžić*, in which the Trial Chamber

As to whether the attribution of the rights violation to (an organ of) the relevant ad hoc Tribunal is a prerequisite for financial compensation, in both *Barayagwiza* and *Semanza*, the Appeals Chamber held that 'all violations demand a remedy',[194] which has been construed by some authors as suggesting that 'the Tribunal will remedy *any* violations in the context of its case, whether or not the violations could be attributed to the Prosecutor'.[195] However, it is questionable whether such an interpretation is supported by the case law. The relevant case law is set out in detail in Chap. 6,[196] but for now it may be observed that in recent case law, it has been suggested that financial compensation and sentence reduction are only available where a right of the accused has been (gravely) violated *by an organ of the Tribunal*. For example, in the ICTY case of *Karadžić* (in which the Accused had sought remedies for his alleged unlawful arrest and detention in Belgrade, Serbia, in July 2008), the Trial Chamber 'noted' that: 'the major discussions and findings [in the relevant ICTR decisions in *Barayagwiza*, *Semanza* and *Kajelijeli*, as relied upon by Karadžić in support of his argument that attribution of rights violations to the ad hoc Tribunals need not be shown] ultimately revolved around the Prosecution's responsibility for violations, rather than the responsibility of state authorities'.[197] According to the Trial Chamber there was 'substance in the Prosecution's submission that, before being able to obtain the remedy he seeks, the Accused has to be able to attribute the infringement of his rights to one of the organs of the Tribunal or show that at least some responsibility for that infringement lies with the Tribunal'.[198] It is also worth noting that in the one case in which financial compensation was granted for violations of an accused's rights—*Rwamakuba*—the violations in question—of the right to legal assistance and to an initial appearance without delay—were attributable to the ICTR Registrar.[199] Regarding the alleged delay in setting up the initial appearance of the Accused, the Trial Chamber held

---

(Footnote 193 continued)

considered that 'it would be premature for it to award compensation to the Accused at this point in time, as it would have to make this decision on the assumption that he will be acquitted'. *Prosecutor v Karadžić* (Decision on the Accused's Motion for Remedy for Violation of Rights in Connection with Arrest) IT-95-5/18-PT, T Ch III (31 August 2009) para 5 (emphasis added).

[194] *Prosecutor v Barayagwiza* (Decision (Prosecutor's Request for Review or Reconsideration)) ICTR-97-19-AR72, A Ch (31 March 2000) para 74; *Prosecutor v Semanza* (Decision) ICTR-97-23-A, A Ch (31 May 2000) para 125.

[195] Paulussen 2010, 518.

[196] It was in the context of unlawful arrest and detention, one of the subjects of Chap. 6, that the availability of financial compensation and sentence reduction was first considered as a remedy for rights violations.

[197] *Prosecutor v Karadžić* (Decision on the Accused's Motion for Remedy for Violation of Rights in Connection with Arrest) IT-95-5/18-PT, T Ch III (31 August 2009) para 6.

[198] Ibid., para 6. Nevertheless, the Trial Chamber's language appears cautious in this regard: '… the Chamber also notes its view that there is substance in the Prosecution's submission that …'.

[199] See *Prosecutor v Rwamakuba* (Decision on Appropriate Remedy) ICTR-98-44C-T, T Ch III (31 January 2007), and *Prosecutor v Rwamakuba* (Decision on Appeal against Decision on Appropriate Remedy) ICTR-98-44C-A, A Ch (13 September 2007).

that, although the initial appearance had not been scheduled by Court Management 'without delay', as required under Rule 62 of the ICTR RPE, this delay was 'mainly attributable to the difficulties in having Counsel assigned to the Accused'.[200] Although the Registry was not responsible for the delay in assigning counsel to the Accused, the Trial Chamber found that the Registrar had failed 'to act pursuant to Rule 44*bis* so as to appoint a Duty Counsel for the Accused pending assignment of his Counsel pursuant to Rule 45 of the [RPE]'.[201] According to the Trial Chamber, '[t]his omission resulted in the absence of any legal assistance for the Accused over an extended period of time in contradiction with, notably Article 20(4)(c) of the [ICTR] Statute, and, further, in the delay of the Accused's initial appearance.'[202] However, the Trial Chamber did not consider that the 'delay in providing the Accused with legal representation and thus, in the initial appearance' had caused him 'serious and irreparable prejudice'.[203] On interlocutory appeal, the Appeals Chamber held that it would be 'open to the Appellant to invoke the issue of the alleged violation of his fundamental human rights *by the Tribunal* in order to seek reparation as the case may be, at the appropriate time'.[204]

5.3.4 Sentence Reduction

Although sentence reduction beyond time served is not expressly provided for in the Statutes or Rules of the ad hoc Tribunals,[205] the shared Appeals Chamber of the ICTY and ICTR has held that such a step may, under certain circumstances, be warranted. In finding that the violations of the Accused's rights were less extensive than previously thought (and therefore no longer justified the setting aside of jurisdiction), the Appeals Chamber in *Barayagwiza* found that the Accused would be entitled to sentence reduction upon conviction (or to financial compensation upon acquittal).[206]

---

[200] *Prosecutor v Rwamakuba and others* (Decision on the Defence Motion Concerning the Illegal Arrest and Illegal Detention of the Accused) ICTR-98-44-T, T Ch II (12 December 2000) para 36.

[201] Ibid., paras 40 and 43.

[202] Ibid., para 43. According to the Appeals Chamber, Rwamakuba had not been offered the assistance of a duty counsel for a period of four months. See *Prosecutor v Rwamakuba* (Decision on Appeal against Decision on Appropriate Remedy) ICTR-98-44C-A, A Ch (13 September 2007) para 16.

[203] *Prosecutor v Rwamakuba and others* (Decision on the Defence Motion Concerning the Illegal Arrest and Illegal Detention of the Accused) ICTR-98-44-T, T Ch II (12 December 2000) para 44.

[204] *Prosecutor v Rwamakuba* (Decision (Appeal against Dismissal of Motion concerning Illegal Arrest and Detention)) ICTR-98-44-A, A Ch (11 June 2001) 4 (emphasis added).

[205] Remedial sentence reduction should be distinguished from the procedural step envisaged in Rule 101(C) ICTY and ICTR Rules, pursuant to which '[c]redit shall be given to the convicted person for the period, if any, during which the convicted person was detained in custody pending [his] surrender to the Tribunal or pending trial or appeal.'

[206] *Prosecutor v Barayagwiza* (Decision (Prosecutor's Request for Review or Reconsideration)) ICTR-97-19-AR72, A Ch (31 March 2000) paras 74–75.

Like financial compensation, therefore, sentence reduction is considered a less far-reaching response than a stay of proceedings. Upon conviction, Jean-Bosco Barayagwiza's sentence was reduced from one of life imprisonment to thirty-two years.[207] The same approach was adopted in the *Semanza* case.[208] In convicting the Accused, the ICTR Trial Chamber found that 'it was appropriate to reduce the Accused's sentence by a period of six months' in view of the violations committed in the context of his pre-trial detention.[209] In the *Kajelijeli* case, the ICTR Appeals Chamber found that the violations committed in the context of the Accused's pre-trial detention, together with the violation of the Accused's other fundamental rights (such as the right to counsel), warranted the conversion of ICTR Trial Chamber's sentence of two life sentences and fifteen years[210] into a single sentence consisting of a fixed term of imprisonment of forty-five years.[211] Regarding the question of whether the attribution of the rights violation to (an organ of) the relevant ad hoc Tribunal is a prerequisite for sentence reduction, it should be noted that the comments made above on this issue in the context of financial compensation[212] apply equally here. The three ICTR cases referred to above are discussed in detail in Chap. 6, but for now it is worth noting that in another ICTR case, the Trial Chamber found that in each of these cases, the sentences were reduced 'following a finding that a specific right of the accused was gravely violated by an organ of the Tribunal'.[213]

Finally, as to the moment at which an application for remedial sentence reduction may be made, in the ICTY case of *Karadžić*, the Trial Chamber held that because such remedy is '… dependent on the outcome of the trial and is to take effect following the issuing of the judgement' it was 'premature' to impose such a remedy at that point (in the pre-trial stages of the proceedings)[214] and, furthermore, that it would be open to the Accused '… to make arguments relevant to sentencing towards the end of his trial'.[215]

---

[207] *Prosecutor v Nahimana, Barayagwiza and Ngeze* (Judgement and Sentence) ICTR-99-52-T, T Ch I (3 December 2003) para 1107; *Prosecutor v Nahimana, Barayagwiza and Ngeze* (Judgement) ICTR-99-52-A, A Ch (28 November 2007) para 1097.

[208] See *Prosecutor v Semanza* (Decision) ICTR-97-23-A, A Ch (31 May 2000) para 129 and the 'Disposition'.

[209] *Prosecutor v Semanza* (Judgement and Sentence) ICTR-97-20-T, T Ch III (15 May 2003) paras 579–580, as upheld in *Prosecutor v Semanza* (Judgement) ICTR-97-20-A, A Ch (20 May 2005) paras 323–329.

[210] *Prosecutor v Kajelijeli* (Judgement and Sentence) ICTR-98-44A-T, T Ch II (1 December 2003) para 968.

[211] *Prosecutor v Kajelijeli* (Judgement) ICTR-98-44A-A, A Ch (23 May 2005) paras 255 and 320 –324.

[212] See n 194–198 and accompanying text.

[213] *Prosecutor v Zigiranyirazo* (Decision on Protais Zigiranyirazo's Motion for Damages) ICTR-2001-01-073, T Ch III (18 June 2012) para 50.

[214] The trial of Radovan Karadžić commenced on 26 October 2009.

[215] *Prosecutor v Karadžić* (Decision on the Accused's Motion for Remedy for Violation of Rights in Connection with Arrest) IT-95-5/18-PT, T Ch III (31 August 2009) para 5. In so doing, the Trial

5.3.5 Express Acknowledgement

According to the shared Appeals Chamber of the ad hoc Tribunals, '… any violation [of the accused's rights], even if it entails a relative degree of prejudice,
requires a proportionate remedy',[216] and, in practice, such a remedy '… will almost
always take the form of equitable or declaratory relief'.[217] The latter form of relief
appears to be appropriate where the violation of the suspect's or accused's rights
results in minimal to no prejudice. In *Bagosora and others*, the Trial Chamber
distinguished the violation in question (violation of Théoneste Bagosora's right to
be brought before a judge without delay) from those established in the *Rwamakuba*
and *Kajelijeli* cases (in respect of which financial compensation and sentence
reduction had been granted, respectively),[218] on the basis that those two cases
'involved excessive delays before the initial appearance and were coupled with
other serious fair trial rights violations including the right to counsel for extended
periods'.[219] By contrast, the 28 day delay in holding Bagosora's initial appearance
had caused him 'minimal, if any, prejudice', which was apparent from the fact that
counsel for Bagosora had not brought the delay to the Trial Chamber's attention
until the very end of the trial.[220] In the Trial Chamber's view, 'the appropriate
remedy for the violation of the rights of … Bagosora in view of the circumstances
of this case is *formal recognition that they occurred*'.[221]

In the ICTY case of *Karadžić*, declaratory relief has been granted on numerous
occasions for disclosure violations on the part of the Prosecutor, where there has

---

(Footnote 215 continued)

Chamber confirmed the availability of sentence reduction as a remedy at the ICTY for violations of
an accused's rights.

[216] *Prosecutor v Semanza* (Decision) ICTR-97-23-A, A Ch (31 May 2000) para 125. See also
Prosecutor v Rwamakuba (Decision on Appeal against Decision on Appropriate Remedy)
ICTR-98-44C-A, A Ch (13 September 2007) para 24, and *Prosecutor v Bagosora, Kabiligi,
Ntabakuze and Nsengiyumva* (Judgement and Sentence) ICTR-98-41-T, T Ch I (18 December
2008) para 97.

[217] *Prosecutor v Rwamakuba* (Decision on Appeal against Decision on Appropriate Remedy)
ICTR-98-44C-A, A Ch (13 September 2007) para 27 n 102. See also *Prosecutor v Bagosora,
Kabiligi, Ntabakuze and Nsengiyumva* (Judgement and Sentence) ICTR-98-41-T, T Ch I (18
December 2008) para 97.

[218] See n 199–204 and 210–211 and accompanying text.

[219] *Prosecutor v Bagosora, Kabiligi, Ntabakuze and Nsengiyumva* (Judgement and Sentence)
ICTR-98-41-T, T Ch I (18 December 2008) para 97. See also *Prosecutor v Mugenzi and
Mugiraneza* (Judgement) ICTR-99-50-A, A Ch (4 February 2013), Partially Dissenting Opinion of
Judge Patrick Robinson, para 9, where Judge Robinson approved the analysis in *Bagosora,
Kabiligi, Ntabakuze and Nsengiyumva*.

[220] *Prosecutor v Bagosora, Kabiligi, Ntabakuze and Nsengiyumva* (Judgement and Sentence)
ICTR-98-41-T, T Ch I (18 December 2008) para 96.

[221] *Prosecutor v Bagosora, Kabiligi, Ntabakuze and Nsengiyumva* (Judgement and Sentence)
ICTR-98-41-T, T Ch I (18 December 2008) para 97 (emphasis added).

been *no* prejudice to the Accused.[222] In a partially dissenting opinion on the matter, however, Judge Kwon opined that '… when the Accused does not suffer any prejudice resulting from the Prosecution's violation of Rule 68 … it is unnecessary, moot or even frivolous to issue a declaratory finding that the Prosecution has violated Rule 68 of the Rules. It serves no purpose.'[223] He further stated that,

> [t]he jurisprudence clearly states that "if the Defence satisfies the Tribunal that there has been a failure by the Prosecution to comply with Rule 68, the Tribunal … will examine whether or not the Defence has been prejudiced by that failure to comply before considering whether a remedy is appropriate[.]" Accordingly, in the absence of prejudice, the Accused will not be given any remedy, including a declaration that the Prosecution has violated Rule 68.[224]

Nevertheless, the Trial Chamber has continued to grant declaratory relief where the violation has caused no, or minimal prejudice to the suspect of accused.[225] More will be said about the judicial response of express acknowledgement in Chap. 6.

Having set out the relevant law and practice at the ad hoc Tribunals, i.e. the consequences that a judge at the ad hoc Tribunals may attach to procedural violations committed in the pre-trial phase of the proceedings which (potentially) have *general* application, it is time now to turn to the relevant law and practice at the ICC, starting with the stay of proceedings. The other judicial responses under examination in this chapter are: the exclusion of evidence, financial compensation, sentence reduction and express acknowledgement of the procedural violation.

5.4 ICC

5.4.1 *Stay of Proceedings*

At the ICC, a stay of proceedings is a judicial ruling by which the proceedings are brought to a halt, or discontinued, on grounds of unfairness, whereby the notion of 'unfairness' is to be construed broadly. The ICC draws a distinction between permanent and non-permanent—'conditional'—stays of proceedings, depending on whether the damage caused to the fairness of the proceedings is reparable.

---

[222] In other cases also, chambers have responded to such violations by formally recognizing that a violation has occurred. See, generally, Chap. 6.

[223] *Prosecutor v Karadžić* (Decision on Accused's Thirty-Seventh to Forty-Second Disclosure Violation Motions with Partially Dissenting Opinion of Judge Kwon) IT-95-5/18-T, T Ch III (29 March 2011), Partially Dissenting Opinion of Judge Kwon, para 4.

[224] Ibid., para 5.

[225] See e.g. *Prosecutor v Karadžić* (Decision on Accused's Sixtieth, Sixty-First, Sixty-Third, and Sixty-Fourth Disclosure Violation Motions) IT-95-5/18-T, T Ch III (22 November 2011) para 37 n 68.

5.4.1.1 Permanent Stay of Proceedings

In the ICC case of *Lubanga*, the Appeals Chamber considered the availability of a permanent stay of proceedings amid allegations that Thomas Lubanga Dyilo had been illegally detained and ill-treated by the Congolese authorities with the ICC's collusion.[226] The relief sought by the Defence in respect of such alleged impropriety was the setting aside of jurisdiction, but the application was rejected by the Pre-Trial Chamber on the basis that it had not been shown that the Accused had been seriously mistreated by the Congolese authorities; nor was there any evidence to indicate that the Accused's deprivation of liberty prior to the ICC's request for his arrest and detention was the result of any concerted action between the ICC and the Democratic Republic of Congo (hereafter: DRC).[227] On appeal, the Appeals Chamber held that:

> Where fair trial becomes impossible because of breaches of the fundamental rights of the suspect or the accused by his/her accusers, it would be a contradiction in terms to put the person on trial. Justice could not be done. A fair trial is the only means to do justice. If no fair trial can be held, the object of the judicial process is frustrated and the process must be stopped.[228]

Also in the same decision, the Appeals Chamber held that:

> Where the breaches of the rights of the accused are such as to make it impossible for him/her to make his/her defence within the framework of his rights, no fair trial can take place and the proceedings can be stayed. … Unfairness in the treatment of the suspect or the accused may rupture the process to an extent making it impossible to piece together the constituent elements of a fair trial.[229]

According to the Appeals Chamber, in such circumstances, 'the interest of the world community to put persons accused of the most heinous crimes against humanity on trial, great as it is, is outweighed by the need to sustain the efficacy of the judicial process as the potent agent of justice'.[230] In a subsequent decision in the same case, the Appeals Chamber observed that the 'nature of such allegations were such that, if established, the breaches of the rights of the appellant might have led to an objectively irreparable and incurable situation' and that a stay of proceedings imposed on such a basis 'would be absolute and permanent'.[231] As such, a

---

[226] The allegations are set out in detail in Chap. 6.

[227] *Prosecutor v Lubanga* (Decision on the Defence Challenge to the Jurisdiction of the Court pursuant to Article 19(2)(a) of the Statute) ICC-01/04-01/06, P T Ch I (3 October 2006) 10–11.

[228] *Prosecutor v Lubanga* (Judgment on the Appeal of Mr. Thomas Lubanga Dyilo against the Decision on the Defence Challenge to the Jurisdiction of the Court pursuant to Article 19(2)(a) of the Statute of 3 October 2006) ICC-01/04-01/06, A Ch (14 December 2006) para 37.

[229] Ibid., para 39.

[230] Ibid., para 39.

[231] *Prosecutor v Lubanga* (Judgment on the appeal of the Prosecutor against the decision of Trial Chamber I entitled "Decision on the consequences of non-disclosure of exculpatory materials covered by Article 54(3)(e) agreements and the application to stay the prosecution of the accused, together

(permanent) stay of proceedings is a 'drastic' and 'exceptional' remedy, because it 'brings proceedings to a halt, potentially frustrating the objective of the trial of delivering justice in a particular case as well as affecting the broader purposes expressed in the preamble to the Rome Statute'.[232] In yet another decision in the same case, the Appeals Chamber clarified that a permanent stay of proceedings should be distinguished from an acquittal:

> ... a stay of proceedings and an acquittal address two fundamentally different aspects of criminal proceedings. An acquittal is a decision taken on the basis of the merits of the case, that is, it involves a consideration of the evidence presented at trial weighed against the threshold of beyond reasonable doubt for conviction. On the other hand, a permanent stay of proceedings stops proceedings without any such consideration.[233]

As observed by the Appeals Chamber in *Lubanga*, neither the ICC Statute nor ICC RPE provide for a permanent (or a conditional) stay of proceedings.[234] Moreover, 'the [ICC] Statute does not provide for stay of proceedings *for abuse of process* as such'.[235] Nevertheless, according to the Appeals Chamber, the abuse of process doctrine

---

(Footnote 231 continued)

with certain other issues raised at the Status Conference on 10 June 2008") ICC-01/04-01/06 OA 13, A Ch (21 October 2008) para 79. See also *Prosecutor v Kenyatta* (Decision on defence application pursuant to Article 64(4) and related requests) ICC-01/09-02/11, T Ch V (26 April 2013) paras 70 and 74, in which the permanent or 'unconditional' stay of proceedings was equated to a 'termination of proceedings', as referred to in Article 85(3) ICC Statute.

[232] *Prosecutor v Lubanga* (Judgment on the appeal of the Prosecutor against the decision of Trial Chamber I of 8 July 2010 entitled "Decision on the Prosecution's Urgent Request for Variation of the Time-Limit to Disclose the Identity of Intermediary 143 or Alternatively to Stay Proceedings Pending Further Consultations with the VWU") ICC-01/04-01/06 OA 18, A Ch (8 October 2010) para 55. See also *Prosecutor v Lubanga* (Redacted Decision on the "Defence Application Seeking a Permanent Stay of the Proceedings") ICC-01/04-01/06, T Ch I (7 March 2011) para 168; *Prosecutor v Gbagbo* (Decision on the "Corrigendum of the challenge to the jurisdiction of the International Criminal Court on the basis of Articles 12(3), 19(2), 21(3), 55 and 59 of the Rome Statute filed by the Defence for President Gbagbo (ICC-02/11-01/11-129)") ICC-02/11-01/11, P T Ch I (15 August 2012) para 91; and *Prosecutor v Banda and Jerbo* (Decision on the defence request for a temporary stay of proceedings) ICC-02/05-03/09, T Ch IV (26 October 2012) paras 78–80.

[233] *Prosecutor v Lubanga* (Judgment on the appeal of Mr. Thomas Lubanga Dyilo against his conviction) ICC-01/04-01/06, A Ch (1 December 2014) para 149.

[234] *Prosecutor v Lubanga* (Judgment on the Appeal of Mr. Thomas Lubanga Dyilo against the Decision on the Defence Challenge to the Jurisdiction of the Court pursuant to Article 19(2)(a) of the Statute of 3 October 2006) ICC-01/04-01/06, A Ch (14 December 2006) para 35; *Prosecutor v Lubanga* (Judgment on the appeal of the Prosecutor against the decision of Trial Chamber I entitled "Decision on the consequences of non-disclosure of exculpatory materials covered by Article 54(3)(e) agreements and the application to stay the prosecution of the accused, together with certain other issues raised at the Status Conference on 10 June 2008") ICC-01/04-01/06 OA 13, A Ch (21 October 2008) para 77.

[235] *Prosecutor v Lubanga* (Judgment on the Appeal of Mr. Thomas Lubanga Dyilo against the Decision on the Defence Challenge to the Jurisdiction of the Court pursuant to Article 19(2)(a) of the Statute of 3 October 2006) ICC-01/04-01/06, A Ch (14 December 2006) para 35 (emphasis added).

had *ab initio* a human rights dimension in that the causes for which the power of the Court to stay or discontinue proceedings were largely associated with breaches of the rights of the litigant, the accused in the criminal process, such as delay, illegal or deceitful conduct on the part of the prosecution and violations in the process of bringing him/her to justice.[236]

'More importantly', though, Article 21(3) of the ICC Statute requires the ICC to exercise its power to exercise jurisdiction 'in accordance with internationally recognized human rights norms'.[237] According to the Appeals Chamber, the obligation to abide by human rights standards when exercising jurisdiction, 'first and foremost … the right to a fair trial', confers on chambers of the ICC the power to stay the proceedings (i.e. to *not* (continue to) exercise jurisdiction). Therefore, while the Appeals Chamber has rejected the abuse of process doctrine insofar as it suggests that the power to stay proceedings is 'an indispensable power of a court of law, an inseverable attribute of the judicial power',[238] it certainly does not appear to have rejected the 'contextual and policy considerations'[239] underlying it.[240] The following passage from a decision in the *Banda and Jerbo* case sheds light on why such a suggestion is problematic in the context of the ICC:

> … inherent powers or incidental jurisdiction may only be invoked in a restrictive manner in the context of the ICC. This caveat is important for the reason, among others, that its proceedings are governed by an extensive legal framework of instruments in which the States Parties have spelt out the powers of the Court to a great degree of detail. This restrictive approach should particularly be adopted when considering a procedural step such as stay of proceedings. Not only is this procedural step not contemplated in the Rome Statute or its procedural instruments, as recognised by the Appeals Chamber, but it might appear contradictory to the object and purpose of the Court, as it may frustrate the possibility of administering justice in a case.[241]

Regarding the basis for an application for a permanent stay of proceedings, the ICC Appeals Chamber has held that such applications do not constitute challenges to jurisdiction within the meaning of Article 19(2) of the ICC Statute, but rather argue that the ICC 'should refrain from exercising its jurisdiction in the matter in hand'. According to the Appeals Chamber, the true characterisation of such applications is that of a '*sui generis* application, an atypical motion, seeking a stay of proceedings', whereby the term '*sui generis*' in this context conveys

---

[236] Ibid., para 36.

[237] Ibid., para 36. See also *Prosecutor v Mbarushimana* (Decision on the "Defence request for a permanent stay of proceedings") ICC-01/04-01/10, P T Ch I (1 July 2011) 4.

[238] *Prosecutor v Lubanga* (Judgment on the Appeal of Mr. Thomas Lubanga Dyilo against the Decision on the Defence Challenge to the Jurisdiction of the Court pursuant to Article 19(2)(a) of the Statute of 3 October 2006) ICC-01/04-01/06, A Ch (14 December 2006) para 35.

[239] Naqvi 2010, 332.

[240] For such considerations, see Chap. 4, Sect. 4.4.1.1 under 'Stay of Proceedings'.

[241] *Prosecutor v Banda and Jerbo* (Decision on the defence request for a temporary stay of proceedings) ICC-02/05-03/09, T Ch IV (26 October 2012) para 78.

... the notion of a procedural step not envisaged by the Rules of Procedure and Evidence or the Regulations of the Court invoking a power possessed by the Court to remedy breaches of the process in the interest of justice. The application could only survive, if the Court was vested with jurisdiction under the Statute or endowed with inherent power to stop judicial proceedings where it is just to do so.[242]

In *Banda and Jerbo*, the Trial Chamber preferred to construe the power of ICC chambers to stay proceedings in terms of 'incidental' jurisdiction, rather than in terms of 'inherent' powers or jurisdiction, for which it found support in a decision of the STL: 'With regard to the Tribunal, by 'inherent jurisdiction' we mean the power of a Chamber of the Tribunal to determine incidental legal issues which arise as a direct consequence of the procedures of which the Tribunal is seized by reason of the matter falling under its primary jurisdiction'.[243]

Turning back now to the statements set out above regarding the circumstances in which a stay of proceedings may be imposed at the ICC,[244] in subsequent decisions the Appeals Chamber has referred to such statements as the test for imposing a stay of proceedings.[245] As to the scope of the test, it appears that the references to 'fair

---

[242] *Prosecutor v Lubanga* (Judgment on the Appeal of Mr. Thomas Lubanga Dyilo against the Decision on the Defence Challenge to the Jurisdiction of the Court pursuant to Article 19(2)(a) of the Statute of 3 October 2006) ICC-01/04-01/06, A Ch (14 December 2006) para 24. See also *Prosecutor v Katanga and Ngudjolo* (Public redacted version of the "Decision on the Motion of the Defence for Germain Katanga for a Declaration on Unlawful Detention and Stay of Proceedings" of 20 November 2009 (ICC-01/04-01/07-1666-Conf-Exp)) ICC-01/04-01/07, T Ch II (3 December 2009) para 36; and *Prosecutor v Gbagbo* (Judgment on the appeal of Mr. Laurent Koudou Gbagbo against the decision of Pre-Trial Chamber I on jurisdiction and stay of the proceedings) ICC-02/11-01/11 OA 2 (12 December 2012) paras 100–101.

[243] *Prosecutor v Banda and Jerbo* (Decision on the defence request for a temporary stay of proceedings) ICC-02/05-03/09, T Ch IV (26 October 2012) paras 75–77, referring to: *In the Matter of El Sayed* (Decision on Appeal of Pre-Trial Judge's Order regarding Jurisdiction and Standing) CH/AC/2010/02, A Ch (10 November 2010) para 45.

[244] See n 228–229 and accompanying text.

[245] See *Prosecutor v Lubanga* (Judgment on the appeal of Mr. Thomas Lubanga Dyilo against his conviction) ICC-01/04-01/06, A Ch (1 December 2014) para 147; *Prosecutor v Lubanga* (Judgment on the appeal of the Prosecutor against the decision of Trial Chamber I entitled "Decision on the consequences of non-disclosure of exculpatory materials covered by Article 54 (3)(e) agreements and the application to stay the prosecution of the accused, together with certain other issues raised at the Status Conference on 10 June 2008") ICC-01/04-01/06 OA 13, A Ch (21 October 2008) paras 77–79; *Prosecutor v Lubanga* (Judgment on the appeal of the Prosecutor against the decision of Trial Chamber I of 8 July 2010 entitled "Decision on the Prosecution's Urgent Request for Variation of the Time-Limit to Disclose the Identity of Intermediary 143 or Alternatively to Stay Proceedings Pending Further Consultations with the VWU") ICC-01/04-01/ 06 OA 18, A Ch (8 October 2010) para 55; and *Prosecutor v Katanga and Ngudjolo* (Judgment on the Appeal of Mr. Katanga Against the Decision of Trial Chamber II of 20 November 2009 Entitled "Decision on the Motion of the Defence for Germain Katanga for a Declaration on Unlawful Detention and Stay of Proceedings") ICC-01/04-01/07 OA 10, A Ch (12 July 2010) para 48 n 95. See also the following decisions, which refer to one or both of the statements in *Lubanga* as the test for imposing a stay of proceedings: *Prosecutor v Bemba* (Decision on the Admissibility and Abuse of Process Challenges) ICC-01/05-01/08, T Ch III (24 June 2010) para 252; *Prosecutor*

trial' in at least the first of the statements are to be 'perceived and applied' broadly, to '[embrace] the judicial process in its entirety'.[246] Such references appear to denote something more than just 'trial fairness', i.e. the ability of the accused to defend him- or herself properly (which, it should be noted, may be compromised by the failure to respect the accused's fair trial rights in the pre-trial phase of proceedings).[247,248] Accordingly, it seems that a fair trial may become impossible due to the violation of *other* rights (than fair trial rights), such as 'violations of the rights of the accused in the process of bringing him/her to justice', i.e. in the process of exercising jurisdiction over the accused,[249] even if such violations do not affect the ability of the accused to mount an effective defence and, by extension, the ability of the judges to determine guilt accurately. In other words, in such cases the question is not whether the suspect or accused can receive a fair trial in the narrow sense of the term, but whether in the circumstances it would be fair to *put them on trial at all*. The Appeals Chamber's reference to the ECtHR case of *Teixeira de Castro v Portugal* is telling in this regard;[250] in that case the tactics employed by the Portuguese police, which amounted to entrapment, and the use of the evidence obtained thereby in criminal proceedings 'meant that, *right from the outset*, the applicant was *definitively* deprived of a fair trial', in violation of Article 6(1) of the

---

(Footnote 245 continued)

v Lubanga (Redacted Decision on the "Defence Application Seeking a Permanent Stay of the Proceedings") ICC-01/04-01/06, T Ch I (7 March 2011) paras 164–164; *Prosecutor v Mbarushimana* (Decision on the "Defence request for a permanent stay of proceedings") ICC-01/04-01/10, P T Ch I (1 July 2011) 4–5; *Prosecutor v Gbagbo* (Decision on the "Corrigendum of the challenge to the jurisdiction of the International Criminal Court on the basis of Articles 12(3), 19(2), 21(3), 55 and 59 of the Rome Statute filed by the Defence for President Gbagbo (ICC-02/11-01/11-129)") ICC-02/11-01/11, P T Ch I (15 August 2012) paras 89 and 92; *Prosecutor v Banda and Jerbo* (Decision on the defence request for a temporary stay of proceedings) ICC-02/05-03/09, T Ch IV (26 October 2012) paras 81–83; *Prosecutor v Kenyatta* (Decision on defence application pursuant to Article 64(4) and related requests) ICC-01/09-02/11, T Ch V (26 April 2013) para 75; and *Prosecutor v Bemba* (Decision on "Defence Request for Relief for Abuse of Process") ICC-01/05-01/08, T Ch III (17 June 2015) para 9.

[246] *Prosecutor v Lubanga* (Judgment on the Appeal of Mr. Thomas Lubanga Dyilo against the Decision on the Defence Challenge to the Jurisdiction of the Court pursuant to Article 19(2)(a) of the Statute of 3 October 2006) ICC-01/04-01/06, A Ch (14 December 2006) para 37. See also *Prosecutor v Lubanga* (Judgment on the appeal of Mr. Thomas Lubanga Dyilo against his conviction) ICC-01/04-01/06, A Ch (1 December 2014) para 147.

[247] For a discussion of the applicability of fair trial rights in the pre-trial phase of proceedings, see Summers 2007, 163–168; and Jackson and Summers 2012.

[248] The second statement in *Lubanga* (see n 229 and accompanying text) does, however, appear to refer to trial fairness.

[249] *Prosecutor v Lubanga* (Judgment on the Appeal of Mr. Thomas Lubanga Dyilo against the Decision on the Defence Challenge to the Jurisdiction of the Court pursuant to Article 19(2)(a) of the Statute of 3 October 2006) ICC-01/04-01/06, A Ch (14 December 2006) para 36.

[250] Ibid., para 38, referring to *Teixeira de Castro v Portugal* App no 25829/94 (ECtHR, 9 June 1998).

ECHR.[251] As has been observed, in that case, the ECtHR found a violation of Article 6 of the ECHR 'on account of considerations ... which were in no way related to any potential impairment of the ability to determine guilt accurately'.[252]

Indeed, the test formulated by the Appeals Chamber for imposing a permanent stay of proceedings[253] has, in subsequent case law, been interpreted as providing for two separate bases on which to stay the proceedings. According to Trial Chamber in *Lubanga*, the Appeals Chamber's test made it necessary to ask two questions: '**first**, would it be "odious" or "repugnant" to the administration of justice to allow the proceedings to continue, or **second** have the accused's rights been breached to the extent that a fair trial has been rendered impossible.'[254] These questions translate to the following two grounds for staying the proceedings: (1) where it would be 'odious' or 'repugnant' to the administration of justice to allow the proceedings to continue, or (2) where the accused's rights have been breached to the extent that a fair trial has been rendered impossible. Regarding the first, "odious' or 'repugnant' to the administration of justice', 'limb' of the test for imposing a permanent stay of proceedings, the Trial Chamber said that: 'this is a matter of judgment, an exercise of discretion involving judicial assessment'.[255] Later on in the decision, it clarified *what it means* to say that the first limb is a 'matter of judgment', that entails the 'exercise of discretion':

> Not *every example* of suggested prosecutorial misconduct will lead to a permanent stay of the proceedings; instead, this is a matter of *fact and degree*, given that the Chamber has to decide whether it would be "repugnant" or "odious" to the administration of justice to allow the case to continue. For instance, a stay of proceedings may well be the appropriate remedy if actions by the Prosecutor threaten basic human rights, the foundations of a fair trial or the rule of law. Clear examples of situations where a stay may be necessary include the material mistreatment of the accused in order to obtain evidence (e.g. by use of torture) or the non-disclosure of significant exculpatory evidence. *Furthermore*, the Chamber must weigh the nature of the alleged abuse of process against the fact that only the most serious crimes of concern for the international community as a whole fall under the jurisdiction of the Court.[256]

Regarding the second, 'impossibility of a fair trial', limb, the Trial Chamber expressly linked the 'impossibility' of a fair trial to the inability of the accused to properly defend him- or herself.[257] On the face of it, then, the questions formulated by the Trial Chamber in *Lubanga* represent two *distinct* bases for staying the

---

[251] *Teixeira de Castro v Portugal* App no 25829/94 (ECtHR, 9 June 1998), para 39 (emphasis added).

[252] Choo 2008, 188.

[253] See n 228–229 and accompanying text.

[254] *Prosecutor v Lubanga* (Redacted Decision on the "Defence Application Seeking a Permanent Stay of the Proceedings") ICC-01/04-01/06, T Ch I (7 March 2011) paras 165–166 (emphasis added).

[255] Ibid., para 189.

[256] Ibid., para 195 (emphasis added).

[257] Ibid., para 188.

proceedings, whereby it is only in the context of the first "odious' or 'repugnant' to the administration of justice' limb that a 'balancing exercise' envisaged. The Trial Chamber's interpretation of the test formulated by the Appeals Chamber has been cited in other decisions as the test for a stay of proceedings.[258] However, chambers have not always treated the two grounds as distinct. In *Bemba*, for example, the Trial Chamber said that the 'impossibility of a fair trial' and "odious' or 'repugnant' to the administration of justice' formulations 'clearly reflect one [an]other'; therefore, the Trial Chamber was 'unpersuaded that there is any meaningful distinction to be drawn between applying them cumulatively or alternatively'.[259] While the *Lubanga* decision itself, at times, suggests that the two grounds are separate and distinct, in the application of the grounds to the particular facts of the case, there seemed to be not much between them at all.[260]

In the determination of whether to stay the proceedings, ICC chambers have attached importance to a variety of facts and circumstances. For example, chambers have looked to the ability of the trial process to remedy any prejudice caused to the accused. The ability of the trial process to remedy prejudice is an argument weighing *against* the imposition of a stay of proceedings. As the Trial Chamber explained in the case of *Banda and Jerbo*, in which the Defence had sought a stay of proceedings on the basis of the difficulties it was experiencing in conducting (defence) investigations in the Sudan,

> to conceive of a stay of proceedings as a remedy in every case in which a claim of frustration of access to information or facilities needed for trial preparation has been made, would run contrary to the responsibility of trial judges to relieve unfairness as part of the trial process. As the Appeals Chamber has noted, the stay of the proceedings is the necessary remedy only if (i) the "essential preconditions of a fair trial are missing", and (ii) there is "no sufficient indication that this will be resolved during the trial process".[261]

---

[258] See e.g. *Prosecutor v Bemba* (Decision on "Defence Request for Relief for Abuse of Process") ICC-01/05-01/08, T Ch III (17 June 2015) para 30; *Prosecutor v Kenyatta* (Decision on Defence application for a permanent stay of the proceedings due to abuse of process) ICC-01/09-02/11, T Ch V (5 December 2013) para 14; *Prosecutor v Kenyatta* (Decision on defence application pursuant to Article 64(4) and related requests) ICC-01/09-02/11, T Ch V (26 April 2013) para 110. Moreover, the Appeals Chamber does not appear to disapprove of this interpretation; see *Prosecutor v Lubanga* (Judgment on the appeal of Mr. Thomas Lubanga Dyilo against his conviction) ICC-01/04-01/06, A Ch (1 December 2014) paras 154, 156 and 168.

[259] *Prosecutor v Bemba* (Decision on "Defence Request for Leave to Appeal the 'Decision on Defence Request for Relief for Abuse of Process'") ICC-01/05-01/08, T Ch III (24 July 2015) para 12. See also *Prosecutor v Bemba* (Decision on "Defence Request for Relief for Abuse of Process") ICC-01/05-01/08, T Ch III (17 June 2015) para 11 (where the trial chamber seemed to treat the two limbs as one and the same standard).

[260] *Prosecutor v Lubanga* (Redacted Decision on the "Defence Application Seeking a Permanent Stay of the Proceedings") ICC-01/04-01/06, T Ch I (7 March 2011), see e.g. paras 204, 212 and 217. In this regard it is worth noting that it is not unthinkable for a given set of circumstances to raise issues under both limbs (although this will not always be the case).

[261] *Prosecutor v Banda and Jerbo* (Decision on the defence request for a temporary stay of proceedings) ICC-02/05-03/09, T Ch IV (26 October 2012) para 79, referring to *Prosecutor v Lubanga* (Judgment on the appeal of the Prosecutor against the decision of Trial Chamber I

This factor, then, appears to be of particular relevance to the second, 'impossibility of a fair trial' limb of the test for staying the proceedings. And it may be that the ability of the trial process to remedy any prejudice to the accused is what the Appeals Chamber had in mind when it held that '[w]here the breaches of the rights of the accused are such as to make it impossible for him/her to make his/her defence within the framework of his rights, no fair trial can take place and the proceedings *can* be stayed.'[262]

Another factor to which ICC chambers have had reference when ruling on applications for the proceedings to be stayed is the gravity of the violation of the rights of the suspect or accused. In *Gbagbo*, for example, in which the accused had sought a stay of proceedings on the basis of his (alleged) unlawful arrest and detention in Côte d'Ivoire, the Pre-Trial Chamber opined that: 'a permanent stay of proceedings is a remedy of an exceptional nature and not every infraction of the law or breach of the rights of the suspect will give rise to a finding of abuse of process: "the illegal conduct must be such as to make it otiose, repugnant to the rule of law to put the accused on trial"'.[263] This factor, then, would appear to be of particular relevance to the first, 'integrity' (or "odious' and 'repugnant' to the administration of justice') limb of the test for staying the proceedings. Of course, the impossibility of a fair trial (the concern under the second limb of the test for staying the proceedings at the ICC)[264] may, in a general sense, be denoted as 'a grave violation of the accused's rights'; after all, the impossibility of a fair trial may be taken to mean the violation of the accused's right to a fair trial. This might explain why, in some cases, chambers have emphasized the need for grave violations of the suspect's or accused's rights in the context of applications for the proceedings to be stayed *more generally*. Building on the 'fair trial' test formulated by the Appeals Chamber in

---

(Footnote 261 continued)

entitled "Decision on the consequences of non-disclosure of exculpatory materials covered by Article 54(3)(e) agreements and the application to stay the prosecution of the accused, together with certain other issues raised at the Status Conference on 10 June 2008") ICC-01/04-01/06 OA 13, A Ch (21 October 2008) para 76. See also ibid., para 121. In other cases also, the ability of the trial process to remedy prejudice weighed against the imposition of a stay of proceedings: see e.g. *Prosecutor v Kenyatta* (Decision on defence application pursuant to Article 64(4) and related requests) ICC-01/09-02/11, T Ch V (26 April 2013) paras 96 and 110 and *Prosecutor v Kenyatta* (Decision on Defence application for a permanent stay of the proceedings due to abuse of process) ICC-01/09-02/11, T Ch V (5 December 2013) paras 14, 53, 80 and 101.

[262] See n 229. Presumably, if there is no such ability, the proceedings *must* be stayed. Nevertheless, the language of the Appeals Chamber is unfortunate in this regard.

[263] *Prosecutor v Gbagbo* (Decision on the "Corrigendum of the challenge to the jurisdiction of the International Criminal Court on the basis of Articles 12(3), 19(2), 21(3), 55 and 59 of the Rome Statute filed by the Defence for President Gbagbo (ICC-02/11-01/11-129)") ICC-02/11-01/11, P T Ch I (15 August 2012) para 91, referring to *Prosecutor v Lubanga* (Judgment on the Appeal of Mr. Thomas Lubanga Dyilo against the Decision on the Defence Challenge to the Jurisdiction of the Court pursuant to Article 19(2)(a) of the Statute of 3 October 2006) ICC-01/04-01/06, A Ch (14 December 2006).

[264] See n 254 and accompanying text.

Lubanga,[265] the Pre-Trial Chamber in *Mbarushimana* held that 'not each and every breach of the rights of the suspect and/or the accused [entails] the need to stay the relevant proceedings' and that 'only gross violations of those rights, such as to make it impossible for the accused "to make his/her defence within the framework of his rights", justify that the course of justice be halted'.[266]

Another line of enquiry pursued by ICC chambers in the determination of whether to stay the proceedings is that of 'involvement of (an organ or agents of) the ICC'. It is worth recalling the wording of the test originally set forth by the Appeals Chamber in the *Lubanga* case: 'Where fair trial becomes impossible because of breaches of the fundamental rights of the suspect or the accused *by his/ her accusers*, it would be a contradiction in terms to put the person on trial. Justice could not be done.'[267] This suggests that, in order for breaches of the accused's rights to lead to a stay of proceedings, (an organ of) the ICC must have been involved in the violation. In an early decision in the *Lubanga* case, the Pre-Trial Chamber said that, where the violations have been committed by national authorities or unknown third parties, 'concerted action' between such authorities or individuals and the ICC (as the 'accuser') must be shown.[268] Regarding the requirement of concerted action, the ICC Appeals Chamber held, on appeal from the Pre-Trial Chamber's decision, that: 'Mere knowledge on the part of the Prosecutor of the investigations carried out by the Congolese authorities is no proof of involvement on his part in the way they were conducted or the means including detention used for the purpose.'[269] What is unclear, however, is whether, in case of torture or serious mistreatment of a suspect or an accused by national authorities or

---

[265] See n 228–229 and accompanying text.

[266] *Prosecutor v Mbarushimana* (Decision on the "Defence request for a permanent stay of proceedings") ICC-01/04-01/10, P T Ch I (1 July 2011) 4–5. See also *Prosecutor v Kenyatta* (Decision on defence application pursuant to Article 64(4) and related requests) ICC-01/09-02/11, T Ch V (26 April 2013) para 78.

[267] See n 229.

[268] *Prosecutor v Lubanga* (Decision on the Defence Challenge to the Jurisdiction of the Court pursuant to Article 19(2)(a) of the Statute) ICC-01/04-01/06, P T Ch I (3 October 2006) 9–11; *Prosecutor v Lubanga* (Judgment on the Appeal of Mr. Thomas Lubanga Dyilo against the Decision on the Defence Challenge to the Jurisdiction of the Court pursuant to Article 19(2)(a) of the Statute of 3 October 2006) ICC-01/04-01/06, A Ch (14 December 2006) para 42. Paulussen notes that this requirement only appears to apply to violations committed prior to the transmission of an official request for arrest and surrender pursuant to Article 89 ICC Statute. Once such a request has been transmitted, no such concerted action need be shown. In this regard, Paulussen relies on *Lubanga*, ibid., 9–11, where the Pre-Trial Chamber held that concerted action would only have to be shown after 14 March 2006, the date on which the official request for cooperation was transmitted to the Congolese national authorities, and n 30, where the Pre-Trial Chamber observed that the ICTR '... has repeatedly stated that the Tribunal is not responsible for the illegal arrest and detention of the accused in the custodial State if the arrest and detention was not carried out at the behest of the [ICTR]'. See Paulussen 2010, 87.

[269] *Prosecutor v Lubanga* (Judgment on the Appeal of Mr. Thomas Lubanga Dyilo against the Decision on the Defence Challenge to the Jurisdiction of the Court pursuant to Article 19(2)(a) of the Statute of 3 October 2006) ICC-01/04-01/06, A Ch (14 December 2006) para 42.

unknown individuals, it is necessary to establish concerted action between such authorities or individuals and the ICC in order to justify a stay of proceedings.[270] While a number of authors have interpreted the Appeals Chamber's findings to mean that the ICC would decline to exercise jurisdiction in such cases *regardless* of the entity or entities involved (in line with the ICTY's approach in *Nikolić*),[271] others have not ruled out the possibility that such cases will be subject to the test formulated by the Appeals Chamber in its entirety (pursuant to which jurisdiction may be set aside upon violation of the rights of the accused 'by his/her accusers').[272] There is certainly case law to suggest that attribution to an organ of the ICC must always be shown for a stay of proceedings, regardless of the nature of the right to have been violated. Thus, according to the Pre-Trial Chamber in *Gbagbo*, in which the Defence had sought a stay of proceedings in connection with Gbagbo's arrest and detention in Côte d'Ivoire,

> violations of fundamental rights, however serious, can have the requisite impact on the proceedings to constitute an abuse of process *only insofar as they can be attributed to the Court*. Attribution in this sense means that the act of violation of fundamental rights is: (i) either directly perpetrated by persons associated with the Court; or (ii) perpetrated by third persons in collusion with the Court. Conversely, when a violation of the suspect's fundamental rights, however grave, is established, but demonstrates no such link with the Court, the exceptional remedy of staying the proceedings is not available.[273]

In so holding, the Pre-Trial Chamber suggested that, as far as permanent stays of proceedings are concerned, the gravity of the violation(s) cannot make up for a lack

---

[270] On appeal, the *Lubanga* Pre-Trial Chamber's finding that no concerted action had taken place between the Congolese authorities and the ICC was confirmed. In addition, the Appeals Chamber confirmed the Pre-Trial Chamber's findings 'respecting the absence of torture or serious mistreatment'. See *Prosecutor v Lubanga* (Judgment on the Appeal of Mr. Thomas Lubanga Dyilo against the Decision on the Defence Challenge to the Jurisdiction of the Court pursuant to Article 19(2)(a) of the Statute of 3 October 2006) ICC-01/04-01/06, A Ch (14 December 2006) paras 42–43.

[271] See e.g. Sluiter 2009, 471; and Ryngaert 2008, 735–736. Indeed, the Pre-Trial Chamber said that, where there is no concerted action, the torture or serious mistreatment of a suspect may lead to a stay of proceedings. See *Prosecutor v Lubanga* (Decision on the Defence Challenge to the Jurisdiction of the Court pursuant to Article 19(2)(a) of the Statute) ICC-01/04-01/06, P T Ch I (3 October 2006) 10. However, the test set out by the Appeals Chamber for staying the proceedings is as follows: 'Where fair trial becomes impossible because of breaches of the fundamental rights of the suspect or the accused *by his/her accusers*, it would be a contradiction in terms to put the person on trial. Justice could not be done.' See n 267 and accompanying text.

[272] See Paulussen 2010, 897–900.

[273] *Prosecutor v Gbagbo* (Decision on the "Corrigendum of the challenge to the jurisdiction of the International Criminal Court on the basis of Articles 12(3), 19(2), 21(3), 55 and 59 of the Rome Statute filed by the Defence for President Gbagbo (ICC-02/11-01/11-129)") ICC-02/11-01/11, P T Ch I (15 August 2012) para 92. The Pre-Trial Chamber's decision was upheld on appeal, and while this was not an issue on appeal, the Appeals Chamber did not distance itself from the Pre-Trial Chamber's finding on attribution. See *Prosecutor v Gbagbo* (Judgment on the appeal of Mr. Laurent Koudou Gbagbo against the decision of Pre-Trial Chamber I on jurisdiction and stay of the proceedings) ICC-02/11-01/11 OA 2 (12 December 2012).

of involvement of the ICC or otherwise for the inability to attribute the violation to the ICC. Equally, being able to attribute the rights violation in question to the ICC is not sufficient for a stay of proceedings; the violation(s) must be *grave*.[274] The following passage from a decision handed down by the Trial Chamber in the *Lubanga* case also suggests that attribution to an organ of the ICC must be shown for a stay of proceedings, even in case of torture:

> ... a stay of proceedings may well be the appropriate remedy if actions *by the Prosecutor* threaten basic human rights, the foundations of a fair trial or the rule of law. Clear examples of situations where a stay may be necessary include the material mistreatment of the accused in order to obtain evidence (e.g. by use of *torture*) or the non-disclosure of significant exculpatory evidence.[275]

Nevertheless, regarding the suggestion that attribution to an organ of the ICC must always be shown for a stay of proceedings, it is worth noting that in *Gbagbo*, the Pre-Trial Chamber appears to have considered the allegations of the Defence to raise issues under the 'integrity' (or "odious' and 'repugnant' to the administration of justice') limb of the test for staying the proceedings only,[276] while the Trial Chamber's comments in *Lubanga* pertained to the same limb.[277] In *Banda and Jerbo* the Defence argued that the difficulties that it was experiencing in conducting investigations in the Sudan meant that it would be unable to mount an effective defence and that *a fair trial was therefore impossible*.[278] Such difficulties had not been caused by the Prosecution; indeed, it was acknowledged that the Prosecution was also experiencing difficulties in conducting investigations in the Sudan (although the Defence argued that the Prosecution was not doing enough to 'offset' the difficulties experienced by it). In ruling on the Defence application for the proceedings to be stayed (conditionally), the Trial Chamber expressly refrained from answering the question of whether 'prosecutorial fault' was necessary in order to stay the proceedings, focusing instead on the question of whether the accused was prejudiced by such difficulties.[279] In the end, the Trial Chamber concluded that

---

[274] *Prosecutor v Gbagbo* (Decision on the "Corrigendum of the challenge to the jurisdiction of the International Criminal Court on the basis of Articles 12(3), 19(2), 21(3), 55 and 59 of the Rome Statute filed by the Defence for President Gbagbo (ICC-02/11-01/11-129)") ICC-02/11-01/11, P T Ch I (15 August 2012) para 93.

[275] *Prosecutor v Lubanga* (Redacted Decision on the "Defence Application Seeking a Permanent Stay of the Proceedings") ICC-01/04-01/06, T Ch I (7 March 2011) para 195 (emphasis added).

[276] See *Prosecutor v Gbagbo* (Decision on the "Corrigendum of the challenge to the jurisdiction of the International Criminal Court on the basis of Articles 12(3), 19(2), 21(3), 55 and 59 of the Rome Statute filed by the Defence for President Gbagbo (ICC-02/11-01/11-129)") ICC-02/11-01/11, P T Ch I (15 August 2012) paras 89 and 91. However, the Pre-Trial Chamber did not expressly acknowledge this fact and in this regard, the decision is not a model of clarity.

[277] See n 256 and accompanying text.

[278] *Prosecutor v Banda and Jerbo* (Decision on the defence request for a temporary stay of proceedings) ICC-02/05-03/09, T Ch IV (26 October 2012) para 13.

[279] Ibid., para 89.

the Defence had not shown any prejudice that could not be remedied in the course of trial.[280] Nevertheless, this case suggests that under the 'impossibility of a fair trial' limb of the test for staying the proceedings at least, attribution to an organ of the ICC will not always be necessary.

There is authority to suggest that *mala fides*, i.e. 'bad faith' on the part of those responsible, need not be shown in order to justify the imposition of a stay of proceedings. In *Kenyatta*, for example, the Trial Chamber observed that in staying the proceedings in the *Lubanga* case in 2008 for non-disclosure to the defence of a large amount of potentially exculpatory material, the Trial Chamber expressly held that in order stay the proceedings, it was not necessary to establish bad faith on the part of the prosecution.[281] In that case, i.e. *Lubanga*, the Trial Chamber had held that it is sufficient to show that 'the essential preconditions of a fair trial are missing' and that 'there is no sufficient indication that this will be resolved during the trial process'; in such circumstances 'it is necessary—indeed, inevitable—that the proceedings should be stayed'.[282] The findings in *Kenyatta* and *Lubanga* regarding 'bad faith' were endorsed by the Trial Chamber in *Bemba*; it implied that a finding of bad faith was unnecessary regardless of the basis on which the stay is sought: the "odious' or 'repugnant' to the administration of justice' ground, or the 'impossibility of a fair trial' ground.[283] In that decision, the Trial Chamber seemed, at times, to treat the two grounds as interchangeable.[284]

Finally, on a more practical note, the Appeals Chamber has held in relation to the timing of applications for a stay of proceedings on the grounds of unlawful arrest and detention that: 'It is consistent with the role of the Pre-Trial Chamber and the purpose of the confirmation proceedings that, in the absence of any provision to the contrary, motions alleging unlawful pre-surrender arrest and detention and seeking a stay of proceedings should be brought during the pre-trial phase of the

---

[280] Ibid., e.g. paras 155 and 159.

[281] *Prosecutor v Kenyatta* (Decision on defence application pursuant to Article 64(4) and related requests) ICC-01/09-02/11, T Ch V (26 April 2013) para 76, referring to *Prosecutor v Lubanga* (Decision on the consequences of non-disclosure of exculpatory materials covered by Article 54(3) (e) agreements and the application to stay the prosecution of the accused, together with certain other issues raised at the Status Conference on 10 June 2008) ICC-01/04-01/06, T Ch I (13 June 2008) para 90: 'It is not a necessary precondition ... for the exercise of this jurisdiction that the prosecution is found to have acted mala fides.' See also *Prosecutor v Kenyatta* (Decision on Defence application for a permanent stay of the proceedings due to abuse of process) ICC-01/09-02/11, T Ch V (5 December 2013) para 14(ii).

[282] *Prosecutor v Lubanga* (Decision on the consequences of non-disclosure of exculpatory materials covered by Article 54(3)(e) agreements and the application to stay the prosecution of the accused, together with certain other issues raised at the Status Conference on 10 June 2008) ICC-01/04-01/06, T Ch I (13 June 2008) para 91.

[283] *Prosecutor v Bemba* (Decision on "Defence Request for Relief for Abuse of Process") ICC-01/05-01/08, T Ch III (17 June 2015) para 11.

[284] Ibid., paras 10 and 18.

proceedings.'[285] Only in exceptional circumstances will the accused be permitted to raise his or her alleged unlawful arrest, surrender or pre-trial detention at the trial stage.[286] In relation to the timing of applications for the proceedings to be stayed in connection with alleged violations of the accused's fair trial rights, it has held that: 'Article 21(3) of the Statute applies to all aspects of the Statute and to all stages of the proceedings. Thus, an accused should be able to raise a claim that his or her fair trial rights have been violated at any stage of the proceedings.'[287] Further, various (trial) chambers have held that applications for the proceedings to be stayed must be 'properly substantiated'.[288] In *Lubanga*, the Trial Chamber rejected the prosecution's proposition that such an application 'should only be granted on "clear and convincing evidence"'. It said that '[s]o long as the facts supporting the abuse application are properly substantiated, it is unnecessary to impose further restrictions on the Chamber's exercise of its judicial discretion, particularly in the way suggested.'[289] Regarding this substantiation requirement, the Trial Chamber in *Bemba* held that it is not sufficient to demonstrate 'that there has been an infraction of the law or a violation of the Accused's rights': 'What must be demonstrated ... is that it is "impossible to piece together the constituent elements of a fair trial" and that it would be "'repugnant' or 'odious' to the administration of justice to allow the case to continue".'[290] Regarding the 'impossibility of a fair trial' limb, at least, the Defence must 'identify and substantiate the existence of prejudice to the fairness of the trial, whether actual or potential', and while the defence 'need not prove prejudice, it is insufficient to merely state that prejudice to ... [an accused's] right to a fair trial ... or a risk thereof exists'.[291] According to the Trial Chamber, [t]his is

---

[285] *Prosecutor v Katanga and Ngudjolo* (Judgment on the Appeal of Mr. Katanga Against the Decision of Trial Chamber II of 20 November 2009 Entitled "Decision on the Motion of the Defence for Germain Katanga for a Declaration on Unlawful Detention and Stay of Proceedings") ICC-01/04-01/07 OA 10, A Ch (12 July 2010) para 41.

[286] Ibid., para 48.

[287] *Prosecutor v Lubanga* (Judgment on the appeal of Mr. Thomas Lubanga Dyilo against his conviction) ICC-01/04-01/06, A Ch (1 December 2014) para 148.

[288] *Prosecutor v Lubanga* (Redacted Decision on the "Defence Application Seeking a Permanent Stay of the Proceedings") ICC-01/04-01/06, T Ch I (7 March 2011) para 169; *Prosecutor v Banda and Jerbo* (Decision on the defence request for a temporary stay of proceedings) ICC-02/05-03/09, T Ch IV (26 October 2012) para 90; and *Prosecutor v Bemba* (Decision on "Defence Request for Relief for Abuse of Process") ICC-01/05-01/08, T Ch III (17 June 2015) para 30.

[289] *Prosecutor v Lubanga* (Redacted Decision on the "Defence Application Seeking a Permanent Stay of the Proceedings") ICC-01/04-01/06, T Ch I (7 March 2011) para 169.

[290] *Prosecutor v Bemba* (Decision on "Defence Request for Relief for Abuse of Process") ICC-01/05-01/08, T Ch III (17 June 2015) para 30, referring to *Prosecutor v Lubanga* (Judgment on the Appeal of Mr. Thomas Lubanga Dyilo against the Decision on the Defence Challenge to the Jurisdiction of the Court pursuant to Article 19(2)(a) of the Statute of 3 October 2006) ICC-01/04-01/06, A Ch (14 December 2006) para 39, and *Prosecutor v Lubanga* (Redacted Decision on the "Defence Application Seeking a Permanent Stay of the Proceedings") ICC-01/04-01/06, T Ch I (7 March 2011) para 195, among other decisions.

[291] *Prosecutor v Bemba* (Decision on "Defence Request for Relief for Abuse of Process") ICC-01/05-01/08, T Ch III (17 June 2015) para 125.

particularly so where such prejudice, irrespective of any illegality of impropriety, is not self-evident'.[292] A chamber ordering a stay of proceedings 'enjoys a margin of appreciation, based on its intimate understanding of the process thus far, as to whether and when the threshold meriting a stay of proceedings has been reached'.[293] Therefore, the 'Appeals Chamber should not substitute its judgment for that of the Trial Chamber but rather should review whether the Trial Chamber went beyond its margin of appreciation in determining that the threshold was met'.[294] Regarding the issue of release, the Appeals Chamber has held that '… if a permanent and irreversible stay of the proceedings is imposed the accused person will have to be released because continued detention would not be in connection with the exercise of criminal jurisdiction by the [ICC]'.[295]

5.4.1.2 Conditional Stay of Proceedings

At the ICC, the availability of the non-permanent, or 'conditional', stay of proceedings was first confirmed in the *Lubanga* case, although in a different context to that in which the availability of the permanent stay of proceedings was considered. Prior to the commencement of trial in that case, the Prosecution indicated that it had 'Article 54(3)(e) material' in its possession, i.e. 'documents or information' obtained by the Prosecutor 'on the condition of confidentiality and solely for the purpose of

---

[292] Ibid., para 125.

[293] *Prosecutor v Lubanga* (Judgment on the appeal of the Prosecutor against the decision of Trial Chamber I entitled "Decision on the consequences of non-disclosure of exculpatory materials covered by Article 54(3)(e) agreements and the application to stay the prosecution of the accused, together with certain other issues raised at the Status Conference on 10 June 2008") ICC-01/04-01/ 06 OA 13, A Ch (21 October 2008) para 84. See also *Prosecutor v Bemba* (Decision on "Defence Request for Relief for Abuse of Process") ICC-01/05-01/08, T Ch III (17 June 2015) para 11; *Prosecutor v Lubanga* (Judgment on the appeal of Mr. Thomas Lubanga Dyilo against his conviction) ICC-01/04-01/06, A Ch (1 December 2014) para 155; *Prosecutor v Lubanga* (Redacted Decision on the "Defence Application Seeking a Permanent Stay of the Proceedings") ICC-01/ 04-01/06, T Ch I (7 March 2011) para 167; and *Prosecutor v Lubanga* (Judgment on the appeal of the Prosecutor against the decision of Trial Chamber I of 8 July 2010 entitled "Decision on the Prosecution's Urgent Request for Variation of the Time-Limit to Disclose the Identity of Intermediary 143 or Alternatively to Stay Proceedings Pending Further Consultations with the VWU") ICC-01/04-01/06 OA 18, A Ch (8 October 2010) para 56.

[294] *Prosecutor v Lubanga* (Judgment on the appeal of the Prosecutor against the decision of Trial Chamber I of 8 July 2010 entitled "Decision on the Prosecution's Urgent Request for Variation of the Time-Limit to Disclose the Identity of Intermediary 143 or Alternatively to Stay Proceedings Pending Further Consultations with the VWU") ICC-01/04-01/06 OA 18, A Ch (8 October 2010) para 56.

[295] *Prosecutor v Lubanga* (Judgment on the appeal of the Prosecutor against the decision of Trial Chamber I entitled "Decision on the release of Thomas Lubanga Dyilo") ICC-01/04-01/06 OA 12, A Ch (21 October 2008) para 36.

generating new evidence',[296] which it had identified as potentially exculpatory or otherwise material to the Defence. After various (fruitless) attempts to obtain consent from the Article 54(3)(e) information providers to lift the confidentiality agreements so as to be able to disclose the material, the Prosecution proposed various 'counter-balancing' measures, including the provision of 'similar material' to that which it was withholding, which, in its view, would allow the Defence to prepare for trial. Upon ordering the Prosecution to provide to the Trial Chamber the undisclosed materials, in order for it to be able to review the material and determine whether the non-disclosure constituted a breach of the accused's right to a fair trial, the Prosecution indicated that it would be unable to comply (due to lack of consent on the part of the information providers).[297] The Trial Chamber then directed the Prosecution to provide it with *descriptions* of the undisclosed material; however, the Prosecution indicated that it was also unable to comply with this order,[298] where-upon the Trial Chamber stayed the proceedings.[299] According to the Trial Chamber, the failure to disclose a 'significant body' of potentially exculpatory evidence to the accused, which 'improperly ... [inhibited] the opportunities for the accused to prepare his defence', coupled with the inability of the Trial Chamber to review the evidence in order to determine whether the non-disclosure constituted a breach of the accused's right to a fair trial, meant that 'the trial process has been ruptured to such a degree that it is now impossible to piece together the constituent elements of a fair trial'.[300] *After* concluding that a stay of proceedings was warranted, it said that:

> Although the Chamber has no doubt that this stay of proceedings is necessary, it has nonetheless imposed it with great reluctance, not least because it means the Court will not make a decision on issues which are of significance to the international community, the peoples of the Democratic Republic of the Congo, the victims and the accused himself. When crimes, particularly of a grave nature, are alleged it is necessary for justice that, whenever possible, a final determination is made as to the guilt or innocence of the accused. The judicial process is seriously undermined if a court is prevented from reaching a verdict on the charges brought against an individual. One consequence is that the victims will be denied an opportunity to participate in a public forum, in which their views and concerns were to have been presented and their right to receive reparations will be affected. The judges are acutely aware that by staying these proceedings the victims have, in this sense, been excluded from justice.[301]

---

[296] Article 54(3)(e) ICC Statute provides as follows: 'The Prosecutor may ... [a]gree not to disclose, at any stage of the proceedings, documents or information that the Prosecutor obtains on the condition of confidentiality and solely for the purpose of generating new evidence, unless the provider of the information consents'.

[297] *Prosecutor v Lubanga* (Decision on the consequences of non-disclosure of exculpatory materials covered by Article 54(3)(e) agreements and the application to stay the prosecution of the accused, together with certain other issues raised at the Status Conference on 10 June 2008) ICC-01/04-01/06, T Ch I (13 June 2008) para 44.

[298] Ibid., para 44.

[299] Ibid., para 44. The facts leading up to the stay are set out in more detail in Chap. 6.

[300] Ibid., paras 92–93.

[301] Ibid., para 95.

The stay imposed by the Trial Chamber was upheld on appeal, with the Appeals Chamber confirming that the stay imposed by the Trial Chamber was not permanent, but rather halted the proceedings indefinitely. More specifically, the stay imposed by the Trial Chamber could, according to the Appeals Chamber, be characterized as 'conditional'.[302] In other words, the stay was subject to the condition that the obstacles that led to the imposition of the stay *in the first place* remain in place, whereby such obstacles were, from the outset, understood to be of such a nature that a fair trial might become possible at a later stage. In characterizing the stay imposed by the Trial Chamber as 'conditional', the Appeals Chamber does not appear to have envisaged a different response to that envisaged by the Trial Chamber. Indeed, according to the Appeals Chamber it was clear that the Trial Chamber intended to impose a stay that was conditional and therefore potentially only temporary, referring to the Trial Chamber's explicit acknowledgment that the stay might be lifted.[303] Moreover, according to the Appeals Chamber, the stay imposed by the Trial Chamber was not inconsistent with its—the Appeals Chamber's—earlier decision setting out the test for imposing a (permanent) stay of proceedings.[304] According to the Appeals Chamber, the earlier decision did not rule out the imposition of a conditional stay in suitable circumstances.[305] Indeed, both permanent and conditional stays may be imposed on grounds of unfairness. Unlike the permanent stay of proceedings, however, the conditional stay presupposes that a fair trial is, theoretically at least, still possible. Thus, a conditional stay of proceedings may be lifted where the 'obstacles' that led to the imposition of such a stay fall away.[306] Nevertheless, a conditional stay may need to be converted to a permanent stay where, 'in particular because of the time that has elapsed', a fair trial has become 'permanently and incurably impossible'.[307] Finally, while the

---

[302] *Prosecutor v Lubanga* (Judgment on the appeal of the Prosecutor against the decision of Trial Chamber I entitled "Decision on the consequences of non-disclosure of exculpatory materials covered by Article 54(3)(e) agreements and the application to stay the prosecution of the accused, together with certain other issues raised at the Status Conference on 10 June 2008") ICC-01/04-01/06 OA 13, A Ch (21 October 2008) paras 4, 75 and 80.

[303] Ibid., para 75.

[304] See n 228–229 and accompanying text.

[305] *Prosecutor v Lubanga* (Judgment on the appeal of the Prosecutor against the decision of Trial Chamber I entitled "Decision on the consequences of non-disclosure of exculpatory materials covered by Article 54(3)(e) agreements and the application to stay the prosecution of the accused, together with certain other issues raised at the Status Conference on 10 June 2008") ICC-01/04-01/06 OA 13, A Ch (21 October 2008) para 80. The availability of this response has been confirmed in a number of subsequent decisions, e.g. *Prosecutor v Banda and Jerbo* (Decision on the defence request for a temporary stay of proceedings) ICC-02/05-03/09, T Ch IV (26 October 2012) paras 84–85.

[306] *Prosecutor v Lubanga* (Judgment on the appeal of the Prosecutor against the decision of Trial Chamber I entitled "Decision on the consequences of non-disclosure of exculpatory materials covered by Article 54(3)(e) agreements and the application to stay the prosecution of the accused, together with certain other issues raised at the Status Conference on 10 June 2008") ICC-01/04-01/06 OA 13, A Ch (21 October 2008) para 80.

[307] Ibid., para 81.

imposition of a permanent stay of proceedings requires the accused to be released,[308] the unconditional release of the person concerned is not the inevitable consequence of a conditional stay.[309]

5.4.2 Exclusion of Evidence

Before considering the law and practice at the ICC with respect to the exclusion of unlawfully obtained evidence, it is important to note that, at the ICC, the question of whether such evidence should be excluded may arise in the context of the confirmation of charges procedure under Article 61 of the ICC Statute,[310] as well as at trial, and that different 'thresholds' may apply in this regard at each stage (in light of the different nature and function of confirmation proceedings vis-à-vis the trial: whereas the purpose of the confirmation hearing is to 'ensure that no case proceeds to trial without sufficient evidence to establish substantial grounds to believe that the person committed the crime or crimes with which he has been charged',[311] the function of the trial is to determine the guilt or innocence of the suspect). In this regard it is worth noting that it has been held that the admission by the pre-trial chamber of (unlawfully obtained) evidence at the confirmation stage is without prejudice to the trial chamber's exercise of its functions and powers to make a final determination as to the admissibility and probative value of any evidence.[312]

Turning now to the law and practice at the ICC with respect to the exclusion of unlawfully obtained evidence, at the ICC, express provision is made for such exclusion[313] under Article 69(7) of the ICC Statute. In addition, evidence which has

---

[308] See n 295 and accompanying text.

[309] *Prosecutor v Lubanga* (Judgment on the appeal of the Prosecutor against the decision of Trial Chamber I entitled "Decision on the release of Thomas Lubanga Dyilo") ICC-01/04-01/06 OA 12, A Ch (21 October 2008) paras 1 and 37. Thus, the Appeals Chamber had to overturn the Trial Chamber's decision to release the Accused (*Prosecutor v Lubanga* (Decision on the release of Thomas Lubanga Dyilo) ICC-01/04-01/06, T Ch I (2 July 2008) following its decision to stay the proceedings (*Prosecutor v Lubanga* (Decision on the consequences of non-disclosure of exculpatory materials covered by Article 54(3)(e) agreements and the application to stay the prosecution of the accused, together with certain other issues raised at the Status Conference on 10 June 2008) ICC-01/04-01/06, T Ch I (13 June 2008)).

[310] Unlike at the ad hoc Tribunals, at the ICC, confirmation proceedings take place *after* the issuance of an arrest warrant or summons to appear, and 'as a general rule', the suspect is before the chamber and can 'participate actively in the proceedings', by, inter alia, presenting his or her own evidence (see Article 61(6)(c) ICC Statute) and challenging the evidence relied on by the prosecution for the purposes of such proceedings (Article 61(6)(b) ICC Statute).

[311] *Prosecutor v Katanga and Ngudjolo* (Decision on the confirmation of charges) ICC-01/04-01/07, P T Ch I (30 September 2008) para 63.

[312] See e.g. *Prosecutor v Lubanga* (Decision on Confirmation of Charges) ICC-01/04-01/06, P T Ch I (29 January 2007) para 90; and *Prosecutor v Katanga and Ngudjolo* (Decision on the admissibility for the confirmation hearing of the transcripts of interview of deceased Witness 12) ICC-01/04-01/07, P T Ch I (18 April 2008) 5.

[313] See n 104 and accompanying text.

been obtained improperly may be 'caught' by Article 69(4) of the ICC Statute, pursuant to which '[t]he Court may rule on the relevance or admissibility of any evidence, taking into account, *inter alia*, the probative value of the evidence and any prejudice that such evidence may cause to a fair trial or to a fair evaluation of the testimony of a witness, in accordance with the Rules of Procedure and Evidence.' While not expressed as an exclusionary rule or discretion as such, 'by inserting fair trial considerations into the Trial Chamber's decision on admissibility', this provision appears to allow for the exclusion of evidence on the grounds that its probative value is (substantially) outweighed by the need to ensure a fair trial. The availability of such an exclusionary mechanism has been confirmed in the case law. In setting out its general approach to the admissibility of documents in the *Lubanga* case, the Trial Chamber stated that: 'First, the Chamber must ensure that the evidence is *prima facie* relevant to the trial ... Second, the Chamber must assess whether the evidence has, on a *prima facie* basis, probative value ... Third, the Chamber must, where relevant, weigh the probative value of the evidence against its prejudicial effect.'[314] Regarding the third prong of the 'test', the Trial Chamber said that it 'must be careful to ensure that it is not unfair to admit the disputed material, for instance because evidence of slight or minimal probative value has the capacity to prejudice the Chamber's fair assessment of the issues in the case'.[315] According to the Trial Chamber, 'this will always be a fact-sensitive decision, and the court is free to assess any evidence that is relevant to, and probative of, the issues in the case, so long as it is fair for the evidence to be introduced'.[316] The approach of the Trial Chamber in *Lubanga* was followed in *Katanga and Ngudjolo*. Regarding the test set out in *Lubanga*, the Trial Chamber in the latter case said that 'although the applicable admissibility test allows the Chamber wide discretion, the Chamber has no discretion in whether or not to apply the test. Before admitting any item of evidence, the Chamber *must* be satisfied that the admissibility criteria have been met.'[317] Later on in the decision it said that: 'Once the probative value of a particular item of evidence has been determined, the Chamber *must* weigh this against the potential prejudice, if any, that its admission might cause.'[318] Nevertheless, it remains unclear *in how far* the probative value of the evidence must be outweighed by its prejudicial effect on the fairness of the proceedings in order to

---

[314] *Prosecutor v Lubanga* (Decision on the admissibility of four documents) ICC-01/04-01/06, T Ch I (13 June 2008) paras 27–31. This approach was followed in *Prosecutor v Katanga and Ngudjolo* (Decision on the Prosecutor's Bar Table Motions) ICC-01/04-01/07, T Ch II (17 December 2010) paras 16–36.

[315] *Prosecutor v Lubanga* (Decision on the admissibility of four documents) ICC-01/04-01/06, T Ch I (13 June 2008) para 31.

[316] Ibid., para 32.

[317] *Prosecutor v Katanga and Ngudjolo* (Decision on the Prosecutor's Bar Table Motions) ICC-01/04-01/07, T Ch II (17 December 2010) para 15 (footnotes in original omitted, emphasis added).

[318] *Prosecutor v Lubanga* (Decision on the admissibility of four documents) ICC-01/04-01/06, T Ch I (13 June 2008) para 37.

justify exclusion.[319] The manner in which the evidence was obtained may well impact on the ability of the accused to exercise his or her fair trial rights, such that the discretion under Article 69(4) may also be exercised in respect of unlawfully obtained evidence. However, it is clear that the improper manner in which evidence is obtained is not the primary concern under the exclusionary mechanism provided for in Article 69(4). It appears that, to date, no chamber has excluded *unlawfully obtained* evidence pursuant to Article 69(4). The primary focus of the current section, then, is the exclusionary mechanism in Article 69(7) of the ICC Statute.

Pursuant to Article 69(7), '[e]vidence obtained by means of a violation of this Statute or internationally recognized human rights shall not be admissible if: (a) The violation casts substantial doubt on the reliability of the evidence; or (b) The admission of the evidence would be antithetical to and would seriously damage the integrity of the proceedings.' Before analysing the text of this provision and its interpretation in the case law, it is instructive to consider the relationship between this provision and Article 69(4) of the ICC Statute. Regarding this relationship, one commentator has said that:

> Clearly, violations of rights that are specifically enumerated in the Statute or recognized internationally find their remedy regarding admissibility in paragraph 7 [of Article 69]. Therefore, in situations where paragraphs 4 and 7 [of Article 69] overlap, paragraph 4 is either a statement of principle to which paragraph provides specific rules in the situations therein outlined, or is a residual means of non-admissibility or exclusion where paragraph 7 does not apply but the fairness of the trial may nonetheless be prejudiced by the admission of the evidence.[320]

In the *Lubanga* case, the Trial Chamber explained that Article 69(7) 'is *lex specialis*, when compared with the general admissibility provisions set out elsewhere in the Statute.'[321] This includes, most obviously, Article 69(4) of the ICC Statute.[322] According to the Trial Chamber, the '*lex specialis* nature of Article 69(7) vis-à-vis the general admissibility provisions set out in the [ICC] Statute' has implications for the factors that may be taken into account in making a determination under Article 69(7).[323] The Trial Chamber's findings in this regard are set out below, but for now it may be noted that while the 'probative value' of the evidence is a relevant consideration under the exclusionary mechanism provided for under Article 69(4), under Article 69(7) it is not.

Under Article 69(7), evidence may be excluded on account of how it was obtained; specifically, it may be excluded if it was obtained by means of a violation of a provision of the ICC Statute or of an internationally recognized human right.

---

[319] See in this regard Piragoff 2008, 1324.

[320] Piragoff 2008, 1326.

[321] *Prosecutor v Lubanga* (Decision on the admission of material from the "bar table") ICC-01/04-01/06, T Ch I (24 June 2009) para 33.

[322] See n 314 and accompanying text.

[323] *Prosecutor v Lubanga* (Decision on the admission of material from the "bar table") ICC-01/04-01/06, T Ch I (24 June 2009) para 43.

Article 69(7), then, defines the nature of the norm that needs to be violated in order to trigger the exclusionary mechanism provided for therein, i.e. to warrant consideration under one (or both) of the prongs of the test provided for therein.[324] A question that immediately arises in this regard is whether violation of a provision of the ICC RPE is capable of triggering the exclusionary mechanism; on the face of it, it seems that it is not.[325] Moreover, on the face of it, it would seem that a violation of national law is incapable of triggering the mechanism under Article 69(7). This is not to say that illegality of unlawfulness in the collection of evidence by national authorities may never lead to exclusion under Article 69(7); however, it seems that in order for it to be able to do so more will be required than a showing that a provision of national law was violated in obtaining the evidence now sought for exclusion. Support for this proposition can be found in Article 69(8) of the ICC Statute, which provides that: 'When deciding on the relevance or admissibility of evidence collected by a State, the Court shall not rule on the application of the State's national law.' It seems that this provision was included in the Statute in order to ensure that the ICC remains focused on applying its *own* law (i.e. the law by which it is bound) in ruling on the admissibility of evidence, thereby avoiding the appearance of interference by the Court with the sovereignty of a state that might arise if the Court were to rule on the application of a state's national law.[326] However, this should not be taken to mean that chambers of the ICC may not have regard *to* the relevant national law and/or its application in the case at hand in ruling on the admissibility on evidence.[327] Indeed, the consideration of such facts and circumstances may assist the court in making the determinations that it is required to make under Article 69(7). Regarding the second set of norms set out in the chapeau of Article 69(7)—'internationally recognized human rights'—it seems that it need not be the accused's rights that were violated in order to trigger the exclusionary mechanism provided for in that provision in the first place. In *Lubanga*, it was not the accused's right to privacy that had been breached, but that of the individual in whose home the documents in question had been seized; this did not stop the Pre-Trial Chamber (ruling on the application for the exclusion of evidence obtained thereby in the context of the conformation of charges), and later the Trial Chamber (ruling on the application for the exclusion of evidence obtained thereby at trial), from considering whether the standards provided for in Article 69(7) had been satisfied.[328] The Pre-Trial Chamber's and Trial Chamber's decisions also demonstrate that, for the purposes of Article 69(7), 'internationally recognized

---

[324] Vanderpuye speaks of a 'threshold standard' in this regard. See Vanderpuye 2005, 129.

[325] See also Piragoff 2008, 1332–1333; and Alamuddin 2010, 281.

[326] Piragoff 2008, 1311.

[327] Ibid., 1311.

[328] See *Prosecutor v Lubanga* (Decision on the admission of material from the "bar table") ICC-01/04-01/06, T Ch I (24 June 2009) paras 37 and 47.

human rights' are not restricted to those specifically mentioned in the ICC Statute;[329] the right (of the suspect or accused) to privacy, it should be noted, does not feature in the ICC Statute or RPE.[330] However, the right in question must be 'internationally recognized'; violation of national standards on human rights does not automatically trigger the application of Article 69(7) of the ICC Statute.[331]

The fact that evidence has been obtained by means of a violation of a provision of the ICC Statute or of an internationally recognized human right is not sufficient to warrant its exclusion; the violation in question must either cast substantial doubt on the reliability of the evidence obtained thereby, or be such that the admission of the evidence obtained thereby would be antithetical to and would seriously damage the integrity of the proceedings. According to one commentary on the ICC Statute, a question at the preparatory stages of the Statute was 'whether the basis of the rule should be *the manner by which the evidence was collected*' (for example, by means of a violation of the ICC Statute or of a human right) or '*the effects of such collection* on other values such as the reliability of the evidence or the integrity of the proceedings'.[332] In the end, an approach which incorporates both bases was settled on; after all, Article 69(7) stipulates both the manner by which the evidence must have been collected and the effects that the collection of the evidence must have. The fact that Article 69(7) also stipulates the effects that the collection of evidence must have suggests that the drafters did not envisage automatic or 'mandatory' exclusion for evidence obtained by means of a violation of either of the types of norm specified in the chapeau.[333] In other words, it appears that what the drafters had in mind was an exclusionary *discretion*, rather than an exclusionary *rule*. Nevertheless, the term 'mandatory' has sometimes been used to describe the exclusionary mechanism under Article 69(7). Piragoff, for example, distinguishes the exclusionary mechanism under para 4 of Article 69 of the ICC Statute from that under para 7 thereof on the basis that while the former provides for a discretion, the latter provides for a mandatory rule of exclusion: 'Paragraph 4 creates a flexible balance in which various factors can be weighed against the probative value of the evidence. Paragraph 7, on the other hand, specifically stipulates specific predicate events regarding the manner of collection of the evidence and detrimental effects on

---

[329] See also Piragoff 2008, 1333.

[330] See most recently, Zeegers 2016, 146. Zeegers observes that the only references to the right to privacy in the ICC Statute relates to victims and witnesses (see Articles 57(3)(c) and 68(1) ICC Statute). See also Alamuddin 2010, 236.

[331] See *Prosecutor v Lubanga* (Decision on the admission of material from the "bar table") ICC-01/04-01/06, T Ch I (24 June 2009) para 36. See also *Prosecutor v Katanga and Ngudjolo* (Decision on the Prosecutor's Bar Table Motions) ICC-01/04-01/07, T Ch II (17 December 2010) para 58.

[332] Piragoff 2008, 1309.

[333] Zahar and Sluiter have criticized the formulation of this provision on the grounds that it appears to imply that not all violations of internationally recognized human rights will seriously damage the integrity of the proceedings. They argue that such an interpretation 'makes a mockery of human rights law as an indivisible set of minimum legal standards'. Zahar and Sluiter 2008, 382. See also Zappalà 2003, 80–81 and 151–152.

the trial process which, if they are found to exist, justify exclusion.'[334] Nevertheless, he also notes that 'the determination of the existence of those predicate events or effects necessitates the exercise of evaluation and, thereby, discretion by the Court'.[335] In light, in particular, of the 'evaluation' required in order to establish whether the collection of evidence has had the *effect* specified (particularly as regards the 'serious damage to integrity' limb of the test), the descriptor 'discretionary' seems more apt in respect of the exclusionary mechanism provided for in Article 69(7).[336] Not only is the standard for exclusion under the second limb ('damage' to 'the integrity of the proceedings') of the test cast in broad and flexible terms (thereby seemingly affording a chamber a good deal of latitude in the determination of an application for the exclusion of evidence); under this limb the chamber is required to make a judgement of degree (admission of the evidence concerned would have to *seriously* damage the integrity of the proceedings). Under the first limb of the test also, a chamber is required to make a judgement of degree (the violation of the ICC Statute or internationally recognized human right would have to cast *substantial* doubt on the reliability of the evidence obtained thereby).

Regarding the first limb more generally, it may be observed that, the fact that what matters is whether the violation of a provision of the Statute or an internationally recognized human right *casts doubt* on the reliability of evidence, suggests that what the first limb is concerned with, is *hypothetical* unreliability, rather than *actual* unreliability.[337] This would require ICC chambers to make generalized predictions of unreliability in particular sets of circumstances; logically, it would also require them to have reference to the purpose of the provision of the ICC Statute, or the rationale underlying the right, (alleged) to have been violated, i.e. whether it is to ensure, or is otherwise concerned with, the reliability of evidence. The room for a discretionary approach under the first limb of the exclusionary mechanism under Article 69(7), then, may be tied up with the norm (alleged) to have been violated; the clearer it is that that norm seeks to ensure the reliability of evidence, the less room there would appear to be for a discretionary approach under the first limb. By contrast, the less clear this is, the more room there would appear to be for a discretionary approach in this regard. Based on the drafting history and the text itself, then, it seems that Article 69(7) is best understood as providing for an exclusionary *discretion*. The question that now needs

---

[334] Piragoff 2008, 1333. Alamuddin also refers to the exclusionary mechanism under Article 69(7) ICC Statute as 'mandatory' (Alamuddin 2010, 239), as does Klamberg. See Klamberg 2013a, 406.

[335] Piragoff 2008, 1333.

[336] Similarly, see Fairlie 2013, 30 n 177; and Vanderpuye 2005, 129. See also Schabas 2010, 848.

However, that the determination of whether a predicate event 'exists' also involves an evaluation is apparent from e.g. *Prosecutor v Bemba, Kilolo, Mangenda, Babala and Arido* (Decision on Kilolo Defence Motion for Inadmissibility of Material) ICC-01/05-01/13, T Ch VII (16 September 2015). See also *Prosecutor v Bemba, Kilolo, Mangenda, Babala and Arido* (Decision on Request to declare telephone intercepts inadmissible) ICC-01/05-01/13, T Ch VII (24 September 2015).

[337] As Piragoff explains: 'This basis of exclusion reflects the concern that the manner by which the evidence is obtained ... can adversely affect the reliability of the evidence. Some forms of illegality or violations of human rights create the danger that the evidence ... may not be truthful or reliable ...'. Piragoff 2008, 1334.

to be answered is how the exclusionary mechanism under Article 69(7) has been construed in the case law: have chambers embraced the discretionary approach to the question of exclusion seemingly prescribed by that provision?

In an early decision on the matter in the *Lubanga* case, it was 'observed' by the Pre-Trial Chamber that 'Article 69(7) … rejects the notion that evidence procured in violation of internationally recognized human rights should be automatically excluded' and that '[c]onsequently … judges have the discretion to seek an appropriate balance between the Statute's fundamental values in each concrete case'.[338] Indeed, the limited case law available on the matter seems to confirm the proposition that not *every* breach of an internationally recognized human right should lead to exclusion under Article 69(7); such case law suggests that some internationally recognized human rights are, when violated, more likely to lead to exclusion under Article 69(7) than others. In *Lubanga*, the Defence sought the exclusion of evidence obtained by seizure during the search of the home of a third party in the Democratic Republic of Congo.[339] While both the Pre-Trial Chamber at the confirmation of charges stage,[340] and the Trial Chamber at the trial stage of the proceedings, found that the search and seizure had violated internationally recognized human rights—in this case the right to privacy (and, more specifically, the principle of proportionality)[341]—neither found that exclusion was warranted.[342] Both stressed that a violation of domestic law alone cannot lead to the exclusion of evidence so obtained, referring to Article 69(8) of the ICC Statute.[343] And both rejected the notion that breach of an

---

[338] *Prosecutor v Lubanga* (Decision on Confirmation of Charges) ICC-01/04-01/06, P T Ch I (29 January 2007) para 84.

[339] It is not entirely clear who initiated the search and seizure operation: the domestic, Congolese, authorities or the ICC Prosecutor. The Pre-Trial Chamber seems to have accepted that it was the former. See *Prosecutor v Lubanga* (Decision on Confirmation of Charges) ICC-01/04-01/06, P T Ch I (29 January 2007) paras 71, 76 and 80.

[340] See n 310–312 and accompanying text.

[341] *Prosecutor v Lubanga* (Decision on Confirmation of Charges) ICC-01/04-01/06, P T Ch I (29 January 2007) paras 81–82; *Prosecutor v Lubanga* (Decision on the admission of material from the "bar table") ICC-01/04-01/06, T Ch I (24 June 2009) para 38.

In *Lubanga*, then, both the Pre-Trial Chamber and the Trial Chamber were prepared to enquire into the circumstances surrounding the search and seizure operation carried out by national authorities. This approach may be contrasted with that in the case of *Mbarushimana*. In that case, the Pre-Trial Chamber held, in the context of the confirmation hearing (see in this regard n 310–312 and accompanying text), that: 'At the outset, the Chamber notes that it may be presumed that the investigative activities carried out by national judicial and executive authorities in pursuance of domestic investigations or further to a request for co-operation by the Court have been carried out in accordance with the legal provisions applicable in that State.' According to the Pre-Trial Chamber, it was for the Defence to show that the domestic procedures had been carried out illegally. See *Prosecutor v Mbarushimana* (Decision on the Confirmation of Charges) ICC-01/04-01/10, P T Ch I (16 December 2011) paras 58 and 60.

[342] *Prosecutor v Lubanga* (Decision on Confirmation of Charges) ICC-01/04-01/06, P T Ch I (29 January 2007) para 90; *Prosecutor v Lubanga* (Decision on the admission of material from the "bar table") ICC-01/04-01/06, T Ch I (24 June 2009) para 48.

[343] *Prosecutor v Lubanga* (Decision on Confirmation of Charges) ICC-01/04-01/06, P T Ch I (29 January 2007) para 69; *Prosecutor v Lubanga* (Decision on the admission of material from the

internationally recognized human should automatically lead to exclusion of the evidence obtained thereby. According to the Trial Chamber,

> [t]he argument that any violation of internationally recognized human rights will necessarily damage the integrity of the proceedings before the ICC does not take into account the fact that the Statute provides for a "dual test", which is to be applied following a finding that there has been a violation. Therefore, should the Chamber conclude that the evidence has been obtained in violation of the [ICC] Statute or internationally recognized human rights, under Article 69(7) it is always necessary for it to consider the criteria in a) and b), because the evidence is not automatically inadmissible.[344]

Both the Pre-Trial Chamber and the Trial Chamber were of the view that the violation of the principle of proportionality did not affect the reliability of the evidence; therefore, the evidence did not require exclusion under Article 69(7)(a).[345] As regards the second limb, i.e. Article 69(7)(b), the Pre-Trial Chamber implied that while constituting a breach of an internationally recognized human right, the breach of the principle of proportionality did not constitute a '*serious* human rights violation', such that it did not require exclusion; for the proposition that only serious breaches require evidence obtained thereby to be excluded, it relied on the 'human rights and ICTY jurisprudence which focuses on the balance to be achieved between the seriousness of the violation and the fairness of the trial as a whole'.[346] The Trial Chamber was also of the view that the evidence in question did not require exclusion under Article 69(7)(b).[347] In arriving at this conclusion, it argued that 'the violation was not of a particularly grave kind',[348] that 'the impact of the violation on the integrity of the proceedings is lessened because the right violated related to someone other than the accused',[349] and that 'the illegal acts were committed by the Congolese authorities, albeit in the presence of an investigator from the prosecution'.[350] Regarding the last point, it had earlier found that 'the search was the sole responsibility of the Congolese authorities', and that they had carried it out, whereas 'the

---

(Footnote 343 continued)

"bar table") ICC-01/04-01/06, T Ch I (24 June 2009) para 36. See also Klamberg 2013b, 1034–1035.

[344] *Prosecutor v Lubanga* (Decision on the admission of material from the "bar table") ICC-01/04-01/06, T Ch I (24 June 2009) para 41 (footnote in original omitted).

[345] *Prosecutor v Lubanga* (Decision on Confirmation of Charges) ICC-01/04-01/06, P T Ch I (29 January 2007) para 85; *Prosecutor v Lubanga* (Decision on the admission of material from the "bar table") ICC-01/04-01/06, T Ch I (24 June 2009) paras 40 and 48.

[346] *Prosecutor v Lubanga* (Decision on Confirmation of Charges) ICC-01/04-01/06, P T Ch I (29 January 2007) para 89.

[347] *Prosecutor v Lubanga* (Decision on the admission of material from the "bar table") ICC-01/04-01/06, T Ch I (24 June 2009) para 48.

[348] Ibid., para 47.

[349] Ibid., para 47.

[350] Ibid., para 47.

prosecution's investigator was only "permitted to assist".[351] According to the Trial Chamber, there were 'no indicators that the investigator controlled or could have avoided the disproportionate gathering of evidence, or that he acted in bad faith'.[352] In other words, the prosecution's investigator had not been in control of the process, which meant that, in this case at least, the exclusionary mechanism under Article 69 (7) could not be employed as a means of disciplining the prosecution, or of deterring similar conduct in the future, since, in the Trial Chamber's view: 'Deterrence and discipline, if they are to be given any sustainable meaning and purpose within the framework of exclusionary rules, should be directed *at those in authority*—the individuals who control the process or who have the power, at least, to prevent improper or illegal activity'.[353] Earlier on in the decision, the Trial Chamber had cited, seemingly with approval, the Trial Chamber's comments in the ICTY case of *Brđanin*, regarding the applicability of the deterrence rationale where evidence sought for exclusion has been obtained improperly by national authorities.[354]

In making the determination under Article 69(7)(b) of the ICC Statute, the Trial Chamber also identified two factors that (in its view) could *not* appropriately be taken into account for this purpose. First, it argued that the probative value of the evidence 'cannot inform' the decision to be made under Article 69(7).[355] This conclusion, the Trial Chamber said,

> results, in part, from the aforementioned *lex specialis* nature of Article 69(7) vis-à-vis the general admissibility provisions set out in the Statute. For instance, Article 69(4) enables the "probative value of the evidence" to be weighed along with other considerations, such as the fair evaluation of a witness's testimony and, more broadly, any prejudice the evidence may cause to the fairness of the trial.[356]

The fact that probative value may not inform the decision to be made under Article 69(7) supports the suggestion made above that Article 69(7)(a) is concerned with *hypothetical* unreliability, rather than *actual* unreliability. The most obvious way of determining the *actual* (un)reliability of an item of evidence is to look to information already admitted into evidence, which may or may not corroborate that item

---

[351] Ibid., para 46.

[352] Ibid., para 46.

[353] Ibid., para 46.

[354] Ibid., para 45, where the Trial Chamber refers to *Prosecutor v Brđanin* (Decision on the Defence "Objection to Intercept Evidence") IT-99-36-T, T Ch II (3 October 2003) para 63. See n 144 and accompanying text.

[355] *Prosecutor v Lubanga* (Decision on the admission of material from the "bar table") ICC-01/04-01/06, T Ch I (24 June 2009) para 43, as endorsed in *Prosecutor v Katanga and Ngudjolo* (Decision on the Prosecutor's Bar Table Motions) ICC-01/04-01/07, T Ch II (17 December 2010) para 64.

[356] *Prosecutor v Lubanga* (Decision on the admission of material from the "bar table") ICC-01/04-01/06, T Ch I (24 June 2009) para 43. In saying that this results 'in part' from the lex specialis nature of Article 69(7) vis-à-vis the general admissibility provisions set out in the ICC Statute suggests that the contention that probative value may not inform the decision to be made under Article 69(7) is also inspired by other reasons. This point is elaborated on in Chap. 7.

of evidence; however, such an enquiry seems to be precluded under Article 69(7) of the ICC Statute, by virtue of the fact that the probative value of the evidence may not inform the decision to made thereunder.[357] Second, it argued that the seriousness of the offence(s) with which the accused is charged cannot inform the decision to be made under that provision:

> ... the seriousness of the alleged crimes committed by the accused is not a factor relevant to the admissibility of evidence under Article 69(7). As set out in the Preamble and Article 1 of the [ICC] Statute, the Court has jurisdiction over the most serious crimes of international concern. Article 17(1)(d) of the [ICC] Statute renders cases inadmissible that do not possess sufficient gravity to justify further action by the Court. Therefore, the core crimes and the cases which justify "further action" by the Court will always be of high seriousness, *but the public interest in their prosecution and punishment cannot influence a decision on admissibility under this statutory provision.* Indeed, there is no basis with the Rome Statute framework generally for an approach that would allow the seriousness of the crimes to inform decisions as to the admissibility of evidence.[358]

The Trial Chamber's findings regarding the 'probative value of the evidence' and the 'seriousness of the alleged crimes committed by the accused' were (immediately) preceded by the following passage:

> When deciding whether there has been serious damage to the "integrity of the proceedings" as provided in Article 69(7) (b), *it has been stressed that* "the respect for the integrity of the proceedings is necessarily made up of respect for the core values which run through the Rome Statute'". *It has been suggested that* applying this provision involves balancing a number of concerns and values found in the Statute, including "respect for the sovereignty of States, respect for the rights of the person, the protection of victims and witnesses and the effective punishment of those guilty of grave crimes". In respect of the latter, the effective punishment of serious crimes *has been said to* render it "utterly inappropriate to exclude relevant evidence due to procedural considerations, as long as the fairness of the trial is guaranteed".[359]

Insofar as they would require such factors as the probative value of the evidence and the seriousness of the offence(s) with which the accused is charged to inform the decision to be made under Article 69(7), the Trial Chamber seems to have rejected the propositions that 'respect for the integrity of the proceedings [within the meaning of Article 69(7)(b) of the ICC statute] is necessarily made up of respect for the core values which run through the Rome Statute' and that 'applying this provision [i.e. Article 69(7)(b)] involves balancing a number of concerns and values

---

[357] In order for an item of evidence to be admissible, it must possess probative value. At the admissibility stage it is sufficient that there are 'indicia of reliability' in respect of that item of evidence; if there are such indicia, the item of evidence will be considered to possess (sufficient) probative value. Where the content of an item of evidence is corroborated by information already admitted into evidence, there may be said to be sufficient indicia of reliability. See Gosnell 2010, 387.

[358] *Prosecutor v Lubanga* (Decision on the admission of material from the "bar table") ICC-01/04-01/06, T Ch I (24 June 2009) para 44 (emphasis added).

[359] Ibid., para 42 (footnotes in original omitted; emphasis added).

found in the Statute, including "respect for the sovereignty of States, respect for the rights of the person, the protection of victims and witnesses and the effective punishment of those guilty of grave crimes'. At the very least, it is clear from the manner in which those propositions are set out (whereby the Trial Chamber made sure to make clear that such propositions emanated from *other* sources) that the Trial Chamber was not necessarily agreeing with them. In sum, in determining whether the evidence obtained by search and seizure had to be excluded pursuant to Article 69(7)(b), the Trial Chamber focussed on the seriousness of the *violation*.

In *Lubanga*, the conduct in question did not lead to exclusion under Article 69 (7), 'notwithstanding the breach of the fundamental right to privacy'.[360] In *Katanga and Ngudjolo*, the conduct in question did. In that case, defence counsel for the accused Germain Katanga had sought the exclusion of a statement taken by the Congolese authorities, on the basis that the accused had not been told that he was entitled to have a lawyer present during questioning. The Defence acknowledged that the authorities had not been acting on behalf of the ICC Prosecutor.[361] While the right to counsel provided for in Article 55(2)(d) of the ICC Statute did not apply in such circumstances,[362] the Trial Chamber found that the right to counsel, as recognized by the ECtHR in the case of *Salduz v Turkey*, did.[363] Observing that 'the main importance of the right to counsel in the context of pre-trial interrogations is to protect the essence of the accused's right, which is to be presumed innocent, to remain silent and not to be forced to self-incriminate', the Trial Chamber looked to the facts and circumstances of the case to assess whether the privilege against self-incrimination had been breached. It noted that while it had not been alleged that the accused was coerced into making the statements concerned, and that (by the accused's own account) he had already had the assistance of counsel at that time, 'as this was the accused's first interview after he was detained and as he was unaware of the reasons for his detention, it is highly improbable that he would have obtained adequate legal advice from his lawyer prior to the interrogation' and that 'even if he had been able to consult with his lawyer shortly before the interrogation, this advice would necessarily have been based on incomplete information'.[364] Accordingly, there were 'serious concerns' that the self-incriminating statements 'were obtained from the accused in violation of his right to remain silent and of the

---

[360] Ibid., para 48.

[361] *Prosecutor v Katanga and Ngudjolo* (Decision on the Prosecutor's Bar Table Motions) ICC-01/04-01/07, T Ch II (17 December 2010) para 57.

[362] Ibid., para 59. Article 55(2) ICC Statute is only applicable in the context of an ICC request for cooperation within the meaning of Part 9 of the ICC Statute.

[363] *Prosecutor v Katanga and Ngudjolo* (Decision on the Prosecutor's Bar Table Motions) ICC-01/04-01/07, T Ch II (17 December 2010) paras 60–63, referring to *Salduz v Turkey* App no 36391/02 (ECtHR, 27 November 2008).

[364] *Prosecutor v Katanga and Ngudjolo* (Decision on the Prosecutor's Bar Table Motions) ICC-01/04-01/07, T Ch II (17 December 2010) para 63.

privilege against self-incrimination'.[365] Therefore, the statement had to be excluded.[366] In excluding the evidence, the Trial Chamber expressly endorsed the Trial Chamber's assertion in *Lubanga* that the probative value of the evidence in question cannot inform the decision to be made under Article 69(7).[367] It did not, however, specify which of the two limbs the statement fell under: reliability or integrity. In any case, there does not seem to have been much at all between the finding that the privilege against self-incrimination had been violated and the conclusion that the statement had to be excluded.

5.4.3 *Financial Compensation*

Article 85 of the ICC Statute provides for (financial) compensation 'to an arrested or convicted person' in three different scenarios.[368] First, where a person has been unlawfully arrested or detained, that person is entitled to financial compensation (para 1). Second, where a person has been convicted and punished, and the conviction is later overturned on the basis of newly discovered facts, that person is entitled to compensation to the extent that he or she has undergone punishment (para 2). Third, where a person has been acquitted or the proceedings terminated, compensation may be available to a person who has been detained, but only in exceptional circumstances i.e. upon showing that there has been a 'grave and manifest miscarriage of justice' (para 3). In light of the subject matter of this book, only the first category of case will be addressed here.

Turning first to the text of Article 85(1), that provision reads as follows: 'Anyone who has been the victim of unlawful arrest or detention shall have an enforceable right to compensation.' As Staker observes, Article 85(1) adopts verbatim the wording of Article 9(5) of the ICCPR.[369] What is unclear from the text, however, is *when* an arrest or detention will be considered to be unlawful. Non-compliance with relevant provisions of the ICC Statute—most obviously, Article 55(1)(d) thereof[370]—would certainly seem to render an arrest or detention unlawful for the

---

[365] Ibid., para 63.

[366] Ibid., para 65. It should be noted that the statement in question *was* admitted for the purposes of the confirmation hearing. See *Prosecutor v Katanga and Ngudjolo* (Decision on the confirmation of charges) ICC-01/04-01/07, P T Ch I (30 September 2008) paras 79–99.

[367] *Prosecutor v Katanga and Ngudjolo* (Decision on the Prosecutor's Bar Table Motions) ICC-01/04-01/07, T Ch II (17 December 2010) para 64.

[368] See Rule 175 ICC RPE, which speaks of 'amount of compensation', thereby implying financial compensation.

[369] Staker 2008, 1500.

[370] Article 55(1)(d) ICC Statute provides that: 'In respect of an investigation under this Statute, a person […] [s]hall not be subjected to arbitrary arrest or detention, and shall not be deprived of his or her liberty except on such grounds and in accordance with such procedures as are established in this Statute.'

purposes of Article 85(1), as would non-compliance with internationally recognized human rights.[371] What is unclear is whether non-compliance with relevant provisions of the ICC RPE, or with national law, is sufficient to render an arrest or detention unlawful for the purposes of Article 85(1). According to Staker, Article 85(1) 'could arguably apply also to arrests or detentions by State authorities *in connection with proceedings before the Court*, which are unlawful under the national law of that State',[372] although he concedes that the provision is 'ambiguous' in this regard: 'it does not specify whether it is limited to unlawful conduct by Court officials, or whether it also extends to unlawful arrest and detentions by State authorities and other persons in connection with proceedings before the Court'.[373] In any case, it seems clear that, in order for an individual to be able to obtain financial compensation in respect thereof, the arrest or detention must be attributable to the ICC in some way. Also worth noting in relation to the text of Article 85(1) is that, unlike the other two situations in which financial compensation is envisaged under Article 85 (as set out in the second and third paragraphs thereof), the right to compensation in the first paragraph is not dependent on a particular outcome of the proceedings. It would seem, therefore, that compensation for unlawful arrest or detention (as provided for in Article 85(1) of the ICC Statute) is available upon conviction *and* acquittal, but also if the person concerned is never brought to trial.[374]

Turning now to the case law, in *Muthaura and Kenyatta*, the Trial Chamber held, in relation to an application for compensation under Article 85 of the ICC Statute on the part of an individual who alleged that he had been unlawfully arrested by Kenyan authorities on suspicion of the intimidation of prosecution witnesses in two ICC cases, that 'in order for the Chamber to make a finding of unlawful arrest pursuant to Article 85(1) of the Statute, a domestic arrest must breach *a provision of the Court's statutory framework and be attributable in some way to the Court.*'[375] In its view,

---

[371] According to Staker, an arrest or detention will be considered by the ICC to be unlawful 'where a person is arrested or detained in violation of specific provisions of the [ICC] Statute (in particular, Article 55, para 1(d) of the Rules), and presumably, where the arrest or detention was unlawful under other applicable rules of international law'. Staker 2008, 1500. See also Brady and Jennings 2001, 303 ('[d]elegations agreed a person who has been the subject of an unlawful arrest or detention, in violation of either the Statute or internationally recognised human rights law, shall have a right to compensation from the Court. This is reflected in Article 85(1).').

[372] Staker 2008, 1501 (emphasis added).

[373] Ibid., 1502.

[374] Schabas 2010, 966. See also Bitti 2001, 628: '… the relevant decision whereby the court declares the arrest or detention unlawful could be made only when the question of guilt is decided upon after trial, but also long before the commencement of the trial'.

[375] *Prosecutor v Muthaura and Kenyatta* (Decision on the application for a ruling on the legality of the arrest of Mr. Dennis Ole Itumbi) ICC-01/09-02/11, T Ch V (19 November 2012) para 6.

[a]lthough Article 85(1) is broadly framed ... its meaning and application must be interpreted in light of other relevant provisions of the [ICC] Statute. In particular ... Article 85 (1) must in this case be read together with Article 55(1)(d) of the Statute, which protects persons from arbitrary arrest or detention "in respect of an investigation under this Statute". Furthermore, the Chamber considers that the right guaranteed under Article 55(l)(d) does not extend to every arrest or detention that related in any way to an investigation by the Court. Rather, in the view of the Chamber, in order for an arrest or detention to be "in respect of an investigation" within the meaning of Article 55(l)(d), it would need to be demonstrated, at minimum, that there is concerted action between the Court and national authorities.[376]

Regarding the last point, it ruled that 'in order to obtain a finding under Article 85 (1) of the Statute it is insufficient to establish that a person's arrest is merely "connected with Court proceedings" in the absence of concerted action',[377] whereby '[m]ere knowledge on the part of the Prosecutor of the investigations carried out by the Congolese authorities is no proof of involvement on his part in the way they were conducted or the means including detention used for the purpose.'[378] On the facts, there was no 'concerted action': the Trial Chamber was not satisfied that the arrest and detention by the Kenyan authorities, even assuming that it had taken place as alleged, was '"instigated" or otherwise requested by the prosecution or any other organ of the Court', and while there was evidence that the Applicant was being investigated by Kenyan authorities 'for matters connected with this Court's proceedings', this was insufficient for the purposes of Article 85(1) of the ICC Statute.[379] In other words, the Applicant had not been 'arrested in a manner attributable to the Prosecution or any other organ of the ICC'; accordingly, the application had to be rejected.[380]

As to the procedure for awarding financial compensation, the request for compensation must be based on a decision by the court that the arrest or detention was/ is unlawful (for requests pursuant to the first paragraph of Article 85 of the ICC Statute).[381] Pursuant to Rule 173(1) of the ICC RPE, which applies to all three paragraphs of Article 85, it is a chamber of judges, designated by the presidency especially for that purpose, that considers and decides on the request for

---

[376] Ibid., para 7.

[377] Ibid., para 9.

[378] Ibid., para 8, referring to *Prosecutor v Lubanga* (Judgment on the Appeal of Mr. Thomas Lubanga Dyilo against the Decision on the Defence Challenge to the Jurisdiction of the Court pursuant to Article 19(2)(a) of the Statute of 3 October 2006) ICC-01/04-01/06, A Ch (14 December 2006) para 42.

[379] *Prosecutor v Muthaura and Kenyatta* (Decision on the application for a ruling on the legality of the arrest of Mr. Dennis Ole Itumbi) ICC-01/09-02/11, T Ch V (19 November 2012) para 9.

[380] Ibid., para 10.

[381] Rule 173(2) ICC RPE.

compensation. Those judges '… shall not have participated in any earlier judgement … regarding the person making the request'.[382] As such, the proceedings for awarding compensation are separate from those in which the unlawfulness of the arrest or detention is determined.[383]

Finally, it is important to note that, although financial compensation is expressly provided for in the ICC Statute, no indication is provided as to how such compensation is to be funded.[384] The ICC Statute does not make provision for a specific budget or fund in this regard.[385] While no specific budget exists for such purposes, the incorporation of such a provision in the ICC Statute may, arguably, be construed as implicit consent on the part of the states parties (as bearers of the ICC budget) that any financial compensation ordered is to be paid out of the general budget, as determined by the Assembly of States Parties, which in turn consists of assessed contributions by states parties and funds provided by the UN.[386] It may be that such compensation will be paid out of the 'Contingency Fund' established in 2004 by the Assembly of States Parties.[387] Staker has suggested that, insofar as Article 85(1) also applies to arrest and detention *by state authorities* in connection with ICC proceedings, it may be that that provision 'merely imposes an obligation on States Parties to establish their own machinery for compensating victims of unlawful arrests and detentions by their authorities in connection with ICC proceedings'.[388] Such a suggestion is understandable in light of the wording of Article 85(1), which, as stated above, adopts verbatim that of Article 9(5) of the ICCPR. Zappalà is critical in this regard:

> [W]hile it seems rather obvious that the ICCPR and the ECHR adopt those terms, as they are intended to impose on States the obligation to implement in their own municipal system a mechanism that enables the victim of an unlawful arrest or detention to obtain compensation, it would not have seemed necessary to state that the unlawfully detained should have 'an enforceable right to compensation' in the ICC system. It would have been enough to explicitly provide for such a right.[389]

How the compensation envisaged under Article 85 of the ICC Statute is funded, remains to be seen.

---

[382] Rule 173(1) ICC RPE.

[383] This has been subject to criticism in the literature. See e.g. Zappalà 2002, 1584; and Zappalà 2003, 75.

[384] Staker 2008, 1502.

[385] The trust fund envisaged by Article 79 ICC Statute 'for the benefit of victims of crimes within the jurisdiction of the [ICC], and of the families of such victims' is clearly not intended for such purposes.

[386] See Articles 114–115 ICC Statute.

[387] See ASP, 'Resolution ICC-ASP/3/Res.4. Programme budget for 2005, Contingency Fund, Working Capital Fund for 2005, scale of assessments for the apportionment of expenses of the International Criminal Court and financing of appropriations for the year 2005' (10 September 2004) ICC-ASP/3/Res.4.

[388] Staker 2008, 1502.

[389] Zappalà 2002, 1582.

5.4.4 Sentence Reduction

While neither the ICC Statute nor RPE provide for sentence reduction in case of procedural violations committed in the pre-trial phase of international criminal proceedings (which violate the rights of the suspect or accused),[390] the case law confirms that this 'remedy' is available in such circumstances. While in the *Lubanga* case the Trial Chamber did not consider the alleged prosecutorial conduct (among other things, disclosure violations) to 'merit a reduction in ... sentence', it did not reject sentence reduction as a possible response to rights violations.[391] On appeal from the Trial Chamber's sentencing decision, the Appeals Chamber again confirmed (implicitly) the availability at the ICC of sentence reduction in case of procedural violations committed in the context of international criminal proceedings;[392] its express reference to relevant ICTR case law[393] is telling in this regard:

> The Appeals Chamber notes that the jurisprudence of the ICTR indicates that an effective remedy should automatically be available where there has been a serious violation of a person's fundamental rights. Examples of such violations have been found to include a person not being promptly informed of the nature of the charges against him for a significant period of time and a person being held in provisional detention for more than three years. In the present case, the Appeals Chamber notes that Mr Lubanga's allegations [regarding the consequences to be attached to the violations of his rights] have already been addressed and dismissed ... and that neither the Appeals Chamber ... nor the Trial Chamber ... found that a serious violation of Mr Lubanga's fundamental rights had occurred. In the Appeals Chamber's view, these allegations were dealt with as part of the trial proceedings and finds that the jurisprudence referred to by Mr Lubanga is not applicable to the circumstances of this case.[394]

In *Katanga*, the Trial Chamber also drew on ICTR case law (namely, the relevant decisions in *Semanza, Barayagwiza* and *Kajelijeli*)[395] in finding that, in the event of

---

[390] This ground for sentence reduction is not reflected in Article 110(4) ICC Statute. See *Prosecutor v Lubanga* (Decision on the review concerning reduction of sentence of Mr. Thomas Lubanga Dyilo) ICC-01/04/01/06 (22 September 2015) para 74.

[391] *Prosecutor v Lubanga* (Decision on Sentence pursuant to Article 76 of the Statute) ICC-01/04-01/06, T Ch I (10 July 2012) para 90.

[392] *Prosecutor v Lubanga* (Judgment on the appeals of the Prosecutor and Mr. Thomas Lubanga Dyilo against the "Decision on Sentence pursuant to Article 76 of the Statute") ICC-01/04-01/06 A 4 A 6, A Ch (1 December 2014) paras 109–110, in particular.

[393] It refers to *Prosecutor v Kajelijeli* (Judgement) ICTR-98-44A-A, A Ch (23 May 2005); *Prosecutor v Barayagwiza* (Decision) ICTR-97-19-AR72, A Ch (3 November 1999); *Prosecutor v Semanza* (Decision) ICTR-97-23-A, A Ch (31 May 2000). These cases are set out above.

[394] *Prosecutor v Lubanga* (Judgment on the appeals of the Prosecutor and Mr. Thomas Lubanga Dyilo against the "Decision on Sentence pursuant to Article 76 of the Statute") ICC-01/04-01/06 A 4 A 6, A Ch (1 December 2014) para 109 (footnotes in original omitted).

[395] See n 393 and accompanying text.

it being established that a convicted person's fundamental rights were violated in the context of his or her pre-trial detention, 'it would indeed be appropriate to take that into account in mitigation of the sentence to be imposed on him.'[396]

5.4.5 Express Acknowledgement

ICC trial chambers have in several cases resorted to judicial condemnation in case of procedural violations committed by the prosecution or otherwise by members of the Office of the Prosecutor in the course of international criminal proceedings. In *Kenyatta*, for example, it was held by the Trial Chamber that 'the authority to issue a reprimand and warning for failure to identify and disclosure of materials which may affect the credibility of Prosecution evidence, whilst not expressly provided for in the statutory framework of the Court, falls squarely within the Chamber's broad discretionary powers set out in Articles 64(2) and 64(6)(f)'.[397] In its view, Article 71 of the ICC Statute, which confers upon ICC chambers the power to sanction 'persons *present before it* who commit misconduct', was not applicable in such circumstances.[398] According to the Trial Chamber, it was 'appropriate for a reprimand to be issued, as a form of sanction against the Prosecution, in cases of clear violations of … [the right to a fair trial]', which, 'in appropriate circumstances … could be coupled with additional, more stringent sanctions or remedies for the Defence (for instance, the exclusion of evidence or imposition of fees)'.[399] In that case, a reprimand was sufficient; the materials concerned had eventually been disclosed and the prejudice suffered by the Accused could be rectified at trial. Moreover, there was no evidence to suggest that the Prosecution had acted in bad faith in failing to disclose the document.[400] In *Lubanga* also, judicial condemnation was considered an appropriate response to the out-of-court statements of a member of the Office of the Prosecutor to the press regarding certain aspects of the case. While the Trial Chamber was 'wholly uninfluenced by these misleading and inaccurate remarks' (by which it presumably meant to say that the accused had not been prejudiced by the statements),[401] it made clear its strong disapproval of the conduct concerned:

> The Chamber … deprecates the prosecution's use of a public interview, first, to misrepresent the evidence and to comment on its merits and weight, and including by way of

---

[396] *Prosecutor v Katanga* (Decision on Sentence pursuant to Article 76 of the Statute) ICC-01/04-01/07, T Ch II (23 May 2014) para 136.

[397] *Prosecutor v Kenyatta* (Decision on defence application pursuant to Article 64(4) and related requests) ICC-01/09-02/11, T Ch V (26 April 2013) para 89.

[398] Ibid., para 89 n 176. See also Schabas 2010, 859–860.

[399] Ibid., para 90.

[400] Ibid., para 97, the disposition.

[401] See in this regard *Prosecutor v Lubanga* (Redacted Decision on the "Defence Application Seeking a Permanent Stay of the Proceedings") ICC-01/04-01/06, T Ch I (7 March 2011) para 222.

remarks on the credibility of its own witnesses in the context of a trial where much of the evidence has been heard in closed session with the public excluded; second, to express views on matters that are awaiting resolution by the Chamber, thereby intruding on the latter's role; third, to criticise the accused without foundation; and, finally, to purport to announce how the Chamber will resolve the submissions on the abuse of process application, and, moreover, that the accused will be convicted in due course and sentenced to lengthy imprisonment at the end of the case.[402]

In the circumstances, (strong) judicial condemnation sufficed; however the Trial Chamber made clear its intention to 'take appropriate action against the party responsible', if 'objectionable public statements of this kind' were repeated.[403]

5.5 Comparison

As stated above, the purpose of this chapter is to set out the law and practice of the ICTs with respect to the question of how to address procedural violations committed in the pre-trial phase of the proceedings. Having set out the relevant law and practice at the ad hoc Tribunals, and that at the ICC, *respectively*, the question that now needs to be answered is how the law and practice of the ad hoc Tribunals compares to that of the ICC, and vice versa. The purpose of the present section, then, is to compare the approaches of the ad hoc Tribunals and the ICC to the aforementioned question.

5.5.1 Stay of Proceedings

At both the ad hoc Tribunals and the ICC the proceedings may be stayed in exceptional circumstances. However, neither the ad hoc Tribunals nor the ICC expressly provide for such a procedural step in their governing documents, i.e. their respective statutes and RPEs. At the ad hoc Tribunals, chambers may stay the proceedings by virtue of their inherent powers to supervise the proceedings, while at the ICC chambers may do so by virtue of the fact that Article 21(3) of the ICC Statute requires them to exercise jurisdiction in accordance with internationally human rights norms, in particular, the right to a fair trial. At the ad hoc Tribunals, the basis for a stay of proceedings is the abuse of process doctrine; while the ICC Appeals Chamber has rejected the abuse of process doctrine insofar as it suggests that the power to stay proceedings is 'an indispensable power of a court of law, an inseverable attribute of the judicial power', it has not rejected the contextual and policy considerations underlying it. This may explain why (pre-)trial chambers, at least,

---

[402] *Prosecutor v Lubanga* (Decision on the press interview with Ms Le Fraper du Hellen) ICC-01/04-01/06, T Ch I (12 May 2010) para 52.

[403] Ibid., para 53.

have continued to adopt 'abuse of process' terminology when ruling in applications for the proceedings to be stayed. Both the ad hoc Tribunals and the ICC distinguish between permanent and non-permanent (or 'conditional') stays of proceedings; while a permanent stay of proceedings bars prosecution for the same charges at a later date, a non-permanent stay does not, at least, not initially. A non-permanent stay is only available if it is clear, at the outset, that the problem that necessitated the imposition of the stay in the first place is resolvable. This necessarily limits the circumstances in which a non-permanent stay of proceedings could be considered to be an appropriate form of relief; not all problems are resolvable.

The fundamental reasoning behind a stay of proceedings at the ICC is comparable to that at the ad hoc Tribunals. At the ICC, a stay may, according to the ICC Appeals Chamber, be imposed on grounds of unfairness, whereby 'unfairness' in this context goes beyond the notion of 'trial fairness', i.e. the ability of the accused to defend him- or her-self properly, and, by extension the ability of a chamber to determine guilt accurately. Indeed, the ICC Appeals Chamber has emphasized that the right to a fair trial is a concept to be 'broadly perceived and applied', as 'embracing the judicial process in its entirety'. At the ad hoc Tribunals, a stay may, according to the shared Appeals Chamber, be imposed in two 'distinct' situations: where delay has made a fair trial for the accused impossible; and where in the circumstances of a particular case, proceeding with the trial of the accused would contravene the court's sense of justice, due to pre-trial impropriety or misconduct. While the ICC Appeals Chamber has continued to employ 'fair trial' terminology in this context, ICC trial chambers have interpreted the 'fair trial' test originally set forth in *Lubanga* as providing for two distinct grounds on which to stay the proceedings: where it would be 'odious' or 'repugnant' to the administration of justice to allow the proceedings to continue; and where the accused's rights have been breached to the extent that a fair trial has been rendered impossible. While the Appeals Chamber has, to date, not expressly endorsed this interpretation, it has not disapproved of it either.[404] It seems, therefore, that the 'fair trial' test originally set forth in *Lubanga* encompass both limbs of the abuse of process doctrine, as it applies at the ad hoc Tribunals; certainly the two grounds identified by the Trial Chamber in *Lubanga* correspond to the two 'situations' set out in *Barayagwiza*. Nevertheless, the (appellate) case law of the ad hoc Tribunals is clearer than that at the ICC as regards the circumstances that may lead to a permanent stay of proceedings.[405] While both the ad hoc Tribunals and the ICC purport to recognize two 'distinct' grounds for staying the proceedings (broadly speaking: 'impossibility of fair trial' and 'integrity of the court'), chambers at both the ad hoc Tribunals and the ICC have not always treated them as such, sometimes 'mixing' the two categories.

At the ad hoc Tribunals, chambers have entertained and ruled on (numerous) applications for the proceedings to be stayed, brought for varying reasons and

---

[404] See *Prosecutor v Lubanga* (Judgment on the appeal of Mr. Thomas Lubanga Dyilo against his conviction) ICC-01/04-01/06, A Ch (1 December 2014) paras 154, 156 and 168.

[405] See similarly Taylor and Jalloh 2013, 320.

alleging the violation of different rights. While it is true that chambers have repeatedly referred to 'serious mistreatment' when setting out the law on the abuse of process doctrine,[406] it is clear from the (appellate) case law that other 'egregious' violations of the accused's rights may also suffice for the purpose of the determination to be made under the doctrine. It is fair to assume that, once such a violation is established, the room for a chamber to decide *not* to stay the proceedings is extremely limited, if not non-existent.[407] Nevertheless, it is important to recall that in case of conduct other than 'serious mistreatment', the question of whether there has been an egregious violation of the suspect's or accused's rights *in the first place* is likely to depend on such factors as whether the Tribunal was involved. By contrast, 'serious mistreatment' would appear *per se* to constitute an egregious violation of the suspect's or accused's rights. Regarding the 'impossibility of a fair trial' limb, the wording of the test formulated by the Appeals Chamber in *Barayagwiza* for a stay of proceedings at the ad hoc Tribunals suggests that only where delay has made a fair trial impossible, will a stay of proceedings be warranted. However, it is reasonable to assume that *whenever* a fair trial has been made impossible, i.e. regardless of the cause, a stay will be warranted. As stated above, in formulating this test, the Appeals Chamber appears to have drawn on the test formulated by Lord Lowry in *R v Horseferry Road Magistrates' Court, Ex parte Bennett*, from which it is clear that the 'fair trial' limb of the abuse of process doctrine, as it applies in England and Wales, is not 'triggered' solely by delay.[408] The shared Appeals Chamber of the ad hoc Tribunals has emphasized that the abuse of process doctrine may be relied on 'as a matter of discretion'. While it has not clearly explained what it means to say so, it seems likely that what the Appeals Chamber is trying to convey is that the determination of an application for the proceedings to be stayed is a matter of fact and degree, whereby, clear cut cases aside, minds may well differ as to whether a stay of proceedings is necessary. As at the ad hoc Tribunals, chambers at the ICC have entertained applications brought for varying reasons. There are more concrete indications in the case law of the ICC as to what it means to frame the ability of chambers at the ICC to stay the proceedings in terms of 'discretion'. In *Lubanga*, the Trial Chamber said that, the question under

---

[406] See *Prosecutor v Nikolić* (Decision on Defence Motion Challenging the Exercise of Jurisdiction by the Tribunal) IT-94-2-PT, T Ch II (9 October 2002) para 114; *Prosecutor v Kajelijeli* (Judgement) ICTR-98-44A-A, A Ch (23 May 2005) para 206; *Prosecutor v Karemera, Ngirumpatse and Nzirorera* (Decision on Édouard Karemera's Motion Relating to his Right to be Tried without Undue Delay) ICTR-98-44-T, T Ch III (23 June 2009) para 6; *Prosecutor v Karadžić* (Decision on the Accused's Holbrooke Agreement Motion) IT-95-5/18-PT, T Ch III (8 July 2009) para 85; and *Prosecutor v Karadžić* (Decision on Karadžić's Appeal of Trial Chamber's Decision on Alleged Holbrooke Agreement) IT-95-5/18-AR73.4, A Ch (12 October 2009) para 47. This point is elaborated on in Chap. 6.

[407] In other words, the abuse of process doctrine (as it applies at the ad hoc Tribunals) is not a matter of discretion in the sense that it allows a chamber to do as it pleases, regardless of the circumstances.

[408] See n 52–53 and accompanying text, and, generally, Chap. 4, Sect. 4.4.1.1 under 'Stay of Proceedings'.

the 'integrity' limb of the test for a stay of proceedings 'is a matter of fact and degree'; moreover it suggested that this was inherent in the question that must be answered: whether it would be 'odious' or 'repugnant' to the administration of justice to allow the proceedings to continue.[409] In addition, the ICC Appeals Chamber has held that a chamber that has determined an application for the proceedings to be stayed 'enjoys a margin of appreciation' in this regard. In sum, then, at both the ad hoc Tribunals and the ICC, the determination of whether to stay the proceedings is considered to entail the exercise of discretion, in the sense that, clear cases aside, such determination is dependent on the particular facts and circumstances of the case, whereby it is accepted at the outset that reasonable minds may well differ as to whether a stay is required. This appears to be inherent in the standards that must be met in order for a chamber to be justified in doing so. At the ICC at least, this is reflected in the fact that the Appeals Chamber will not lightly interfere with a trial chamber's decision to stay, or as the case may be, to not stay the proceedings. In the paragraphs that follow, the facts and circumstances to which chambers of the ad hoc Tribunals and the ICC have attached importance in the exercise of their discretion are addressed.

When ruling on applications for the proceedings to be stayed, both the ad hoc Tribunals and the ICC look to whether the accused's rights have been violated, and, if so, 'how seriously'. At the ad hoc Tribunals, the Appeals Chamber has treated the question of whether there have been 'serious and egregious violations of the accused's rights' as relevant to the second, 'court's sense of justice' or 'integrity' limb of the abuse of process doctrine (as it applies at the ad hoc Tribunals) alone.[410] At the ICC also, the 'gravity of the violation of the rights of the suspect or accused' seems to be of particular relevance to the 'integrity' or 'odious' and 'repugnant' to the administration of justice' limb of the test for staying the proceedings. Nevertheless, chambers at both the ad hoc Tribunals and the ICC have emphasized the need for grave violations of suspect's or accused's rights in the context of applications for stays *more generally*, which may be explained by the fact that the impossibility of a fair trial (the concern under the first limb of the abuse of process doctrine at the ad hoc Tribunals, and the concern under the second limb of the test for staying the proceedings at the ICC) may, in a general sense, be denoted as 'a grave violation of the accused's rights'; after all, the impossibility of a fair trial may be taken to mean the violation of the accused's right to a fair trial.

In the determination of whether to stay the proceedings, chambers of both the ad hoc Tribunals and the ICC have emphasized the ability of the trial process to 'remedy' prejudice. Typically, they have done so where what has been at stake is 'trial fairness'. At both the ad hoc Tribunals and the ICC, the ability of the trial process to remedy (forensic) prejudice is an argument weighing *against* the imposition of a stay of proceedings, where the concern is that it will not be possible to hold a fair trial.

---

[409] See n 256 and accompanying text.

[410] See n 56, 90–91 and accompanying text.

At the ad hoc Tribunals, the Appeals Chamber has held that, in case of egregious violations of the accused's rights, it is irrelevant which entity was involved. However, it has also suggested that not all violations of the accused's rights will, on their own, be sufficiently serious as to warrant the imposition of a stay, while collusion by (an organ of) the relevant Tribunal has the capacity to elevate a serious violation of the accused's rights to an 'egregious' one. Nevertheless, it appears that, at the ad hoc Tribunals, involvement of the Tribunal need not always be shown in order to justify the imposition of a stay of proceedings. Seemingly by contrast, there are (strong) indications that, at the ICC, attribution to an organ thereof must (always) be shown in order for the proceedings to be stayed. Regarding the ICC case law, it is unclear whether the aforementioned findings suggesting that attribution must always be shown pertain only to the 'integrity' (or "odious' or 'repugnant' to the administration of justice') limb of the test for staying the proceedings, or, rather, to both limbs. It is worth recalling that in one case in which a stay of proceedings was sought on the basis that a fair trial could not, according to the defence, be held, in light of the difficulties it was experiencing in conducting investigations in the Sudan, the Trial Chamber expressly refrained from answering the question of whether 'prosecutorial fault' was necessary in order to stay the proceedings, focusing instead on the question of whether the accused was prejudiced by such difficulties.[411] In another case in which the availability of a stay of proceedings was considered amid concerns that a fair trial could not be held, the Trial Chamber expressly held that, in order to stay the proceedings, it was not necessary to establish bad faith on the part of the prosecution.[412] These cases suggest that 'attribution' need not (always) be shown in order to stay the proceedings; it may depend on the particular ground on which the stay is sought.

Chambers of both the ad hoc Tribunals and the ICC have suggested that the fact that the crimes with which the accused is charged are very serious may inform the decision on whether to stay the proceedings. More generally, they have suggested that the determination of whether to stay the proceedings involves the performance of a balancing exercise, whereby the rights or interests of the accused are pitted against the public interest in the prosecution of crimes of concern to the international community, i.e. of very serious crimes. In general terms, such a balancing exercise involves taking into account various factors, as relevant to one or both of the competing interests underlying it. The fact that the crimes with which the accused is charged are very serious, clearly underscores the latter interest and militates against the imposition of a stay. At the ad hoc Tribunals, the Appeals Chamber seems to endorse the performance of such a balancing exercise in the context of the 'integrity' limb of the abuse of process doctrine only.[413] At the ICC

---

[411] See n 278–280 and accompanying text.

[412] See n 281–283 and accompanying text.

[413] See n 88–89 and accompanying text. In the *Nikolić* case also, the Appeals Chamber suggested that the determination of whether to stay the proceedings entails the performance of a balancing exercise. In that case, it was the second, 'integrity', limb of the test at the ad hoc Tribunals for staying the proceedings that was at stake. See n 69–81 and accompanying text.

also, there are indications that it is only in the context of the 'integrity' (or the "odious' and 'repugnant' to the administration of justice') limb that a balancing exercise may be performed.[414] It is worth recalling here that in the *Lubanga* decision to stay the proceedings on account of the non-disclosure of a significant amount of potentially exculpatory material, the Trial Chamber acknowledged the public interest in the prosecution of crimes of concern to the international community only *after* it had determined that the fairness of the trial had been imperilled to such an extent as to necessitate a stay of proceedings. More will be said about 'discretion' and 'balancing' below, in Chap. 7.

Finally, on a more practical note, neither the ad hoc Tribunals nor the ICC consider applications for a permanent stay of proceedings to constitute challenges to jurisdiction in the narrow sense, i.e. as meant in the respective statutes of the ad hoc Tribunals and the ICC. A further similarity between the ad hoc Tribunals and ICC is that upon staying the proceedings permanently, the accused must be released unconditionally.

5.5.2 Exclusion of Evidence

Both the ad hoc Tribunals and the ICC expressly provide for the exclusion of unlawfully obtained evidence, i.e. for the exclusion of evidence on account of the improper manner in which it was obtained; the relevant provisions are Rule 95 of both the ICTY and ICTR RPEs and Article 69(7) of the ICC Statute. In addition, both the ad hoc Tribunals and the ICC provide for the exclusion of evidence where its probative value is (substantially) outweighed by its prejudicial or otherwise by the need to ensure a fair trial. While unlawfully obtained evidence may well be 'caught' by the latter exclusionary mechanism (as the case law of the ad hoc Tribunals demonstrates), it is clear that the improper manner in which evidence is obtained is *not* the primary concern under that mechanism. Therefore, that mechanism is of limited relevance for the purposes of this book.

Regarding the former exclusionary mechanism, while Rule 95 of the ICTY and ICTR RPEs does not specify the norm that needs to be violated, i.e. the manner in which the evidence must have been obtained, in order to trigger exclusion, Article 69(7) of the ICC Statute *does*; in order to trigger the exclusionary mechanism provided for under the latter provision, the evidence must have been obtained by violation of a provision of the ICC Statute, or of an internationally recognized human right. However, the *effects* that the manner in which the evidence was obtained must have in order to warrant exclusion are the same at the ad hoc Tribunals and ICC; the manner in which the evidence was obtained must either cast substantial doubt on the reliability of the evidence thereby obtained, or seriously damage the integrity of the proceedings.

---

[414] See n 256 and accompanying text.

Both Rule 95 and Article 69(7) are best understood as providing for an exclusionary *discretion* rather than an exclusionary *rule* (i.e. 'mandatory' or 'automatic' exclusion). The standards that must be met at both the ad hoc Tribunals and ICC in order to justify exclusion are cast in broad and flexible terms. This is particularly so as regards the second limb of the test for exclusion (i.e. the 'damage to integrity' limb). Given that, at both the ad hoc Tribunals and the ICC, the first, 'doubt as to reliability', limb of the test for exclusion appears to be concerned with hypothetical, rather than actual, unreliability, at these ICTs, the room for a discretionary approach under this limb would appear to be dependent on the extent to which the purpose of the underlying norm can be said to be the promotion of reliability. The clearer it is that the norm seeks to ensure the reliability of evidence, the less room there would appear to be for a discretionary approach.

At both the ad hoc Tribunals and the ICC, some procedural violations are more likely to lead to exclusion than others. Turning first to those that are less likely to lead to exclusion, at both the ad hoc Tribunals and the ICC, the violation of national law is not, by itself, sufficient to warrant exclusion under Rule 95 or Article 69(7), respectively. However, this should not be taken to mean that the exclusionary mechanism provided under such provisions is altogether unavailable when national authorities have gathered the evidence; chambers of both the ad hoc Tribunals and the ICC have entertained applications for the exclusion of evidence obtained by such authorities. Nor, it seems, will a violation of the internationally recognized human right to privacy, on its own, lead to exclusion. At both the ad hoc Tribunals and at the ICC, then, the fact that evidence has been obtained by violation of an internationally recognized human right will not necessarily require its exclusion. Put differently, neither the ad hoc Tribunals nor the ICC recognize an exclusionary *rule* entailing the automatic exclusion of evidence obtained by violation of an internationally recognized human right. For violations of the right to privacy and of national law, the determination of whether to exclude the evidence obtained thereby (under Rule 95 or Article 69(7)) entails a consideration of the particular facts and circumstances of the case. However, at the ICC, trial chambers have held that there are limitations on the factors that may be taken into account in this regard, whereas at the ad hoc Tribunals, no such restrictions appear to exist. More will be said about this below. As to the violations that are (more) likely to lead to exclusion of the evidence obtained thereby, at both the ad hoc Tribunals and the ICC, statements obtained in violation of the right to be assisted by counsel at the time of questioning and, it seems, by oppressive conduct such as to constitute a violation of the privilege against self-incrimination, are subject to automatic exclusion. In one ICTY case, this right (to be assisted by counsel) was found to have been violated, even though the relevant national law did not recognize such a right. Chambers have established the violation of this right on the basis of their own procedural frameworks, i.e. their respective Statutes and RPEs, where necessary, referring to the relevant case law of the ECtHR. And at both the ad hoc Tribunals and the ICC, the fact the statement was obtained by such a violation has been sufficient on its own to justify its exclusion. At both the ad hoc Tribunals and the ICC, then, the exclusionary discretion provided for under Rule 95 and Article 69(7), respectively, whereby a chamber may, in the determination of whether to exclude unlawfully obtained evidence, take into account the particular facts and circumstances of the case, appears to be *confined* to procedural violations that do not entail the violation of the right to legal assistance, or of the privilege against self-incrimination.

As stated above, for certain procedural violations (i.e. for violations that do not entail the violation of the right to legal assistance or of the privilege against self-incrimination), the determination of whether to exclude evidence obtained thereby pursuant to Rule 95 of the ICTY or ICTR RPE, or pursuant to Article 69(7) of the ICC Statute, entails a consideration of the particular facts and circumstances of the case. An important question at both the ad hoc Tribunals and the ICC relates to the nature of the (alleged) procedural violation: does it involve a violation of national law alone, or does it involve a violation of the relevant international criminal tribunal's own procedural framework, or of internationally recognized human rights? Violations of national law, it seems, are less likely to lead to exclusion than the latter category of violations. Insofar as the procedural violation constitutes a violation of an internationally recognised human right, chambers at the ICC have considered the 'gravity' of that violation to be a relevant consideration in this regard. The more grave the human rights violation, the more likely it is that evidence obtained thereby will be excluded. Moreover, at the ICC, one chamber has attached importance to the fact that it was not the accused's right that had been violated. This fact militated against exclusion of the evidence concerned. The fact that agents of the Tribunal were not involved in obtaining the evidence, or that, where they were 'involved', they were not 'in control' of the evidence-gathering process, is also a factor militating against exclusion. Conversely, the more involved such agents were, the more likely it is, it seems, that evidence obtained by the impropriety in which they were involved, will be excluded. At both the ad hoc Tribunals and the ICC, chambers have attached importance to the fact that the authorities concerned had acted in good faith, or not acted in bad faith. The presence of good faith or absence of bad faith also appears to militate against exclusion. Finally, at the ad hoc Tribunals at least, chambers have attached importance to the fact that the activities concerned were carried out in circumstances of urgency, emergency and/or necessity, whereby such circumstances militate against exclusion.

The aforementioned factors feature, in varying degrees of clarity and prominence, in the case law of both the ad hoc Tribunals and the ICC. Moreover, it is relatively clear from such case law that such factors are relevant under the second, 'damage to integrity', limb of the test for exclusion only.[415] However, regarding the practice of taking into account the particular facts and circumstances of the case in

---

[415] In considering whether to exclude the evidence, the chamber in each case referred to the second limb. See n 139, 153 and 346–350 and accompanying text.

order to determine whether to exclude evidence on account of how it was obtained, there are noteworthy differences between the case law of the ad hoc Tribunals, and that of the ICC. For example, while at the ad hoc Tribunals chambers have allowed the decision to be made under Rule 95 of the RPE to be informed by the probative value of the evidence, at the ICC, chambers have held that this factor may not inform the decision to be made under Article 69(7) of the ICC Statute. And while at ad hoc Tribunals it has been held that the fact that crimes with which the accused is charged are very serious may inform the determination to be made under Rule 95, at the ICC it has been held that it may not. More will be said about this discrepancy, and, more generally, about the meaning of taking into account (and of *not* taking into account) such factors, below, in Chap. 7.

Finally, insofar as Rule 95 of both the ICTY and ICTR RPEs and Article 69(7) might allow for other rationales of a non-epistemic nature to be pursued in the exclusion of evidence (other, that is, than the rationale expressly cited: that of 'integrity'), it is important to note that chambers of both the ad hoc Tribunals and the ICC have (seemingly) rejected the notion that evidence obtained (improperly) by national authorities should be excluded in order to deter such authorities from, and/or punish such authorities for, acting improperly in the future. As for the notion that evidence should be excluded in order to deter agents of the ICTs themselves from acting improperly in the future, it has been suggested by one ICC trial chamber that so long as such agents are not in control of the evidence-gathering process, exclusion will not be an effective deterrent (and therefore should not be employed for this purpose).

5.5.3   Financial Compensation

At both the ad hoc Tribunals and the ICC, financial compensation is available in case of procedural violations committed in the pre-trial phase of the proceedings. At the ICC, its availability appears to be limited to cases of unlawful arrest and detention. While at the ad hoc Tribunals, no express provision is made for such compensation in the respective Statutes or RPEs of the ICTY and ICTR, at the ICC, such compensation is expressly provided for in the ICC Statute and ICC RPE. The relevant provision in the ICC Statute adopts verbatim the wording of Article 9(5) of the ICCPR. This suggests that the rationale underlying this procedural step is to provide a personal remedy to victims of unlawful arrest and detention. At the ad hoc Tribunals also, the availability of financial compensation is linked to the need to provide a personal remedy for rights violations. At both the ad hoc Tribunals and the ICC, there are (strong) indications (in the case law) that attribution of the rights violation to the relevant international criminal tribunal is a prerequisite for such compensation.[416]

---

[416] This issue will be explored further in Chap. 6.

While at the ad hoc Tribunals, financial compensation may only be ordered upon acquittal of the accused, Article 85(1) of the ICC Statute does not appear to impose any such restriction. While the ICC provides for separate proceedings for requesting compensation, to be presided over by an altogether different panel of judges (designated by the Presidency especially for that purpose), at the ad hoc Tribunals, there is no such separation. Finally, it is worthy of note that neither the ad hoc Tribunals nor the ICC provide for a specific budget for the purposes of making an award of financial compensation, although this may be less problematic at the ICC than it has been at the ad hoc Tribunals.

5.5.4   Sentence Reduction

Neither the respective Statutes nor Rules of the ad hoc Tribunals provide for sentence reduction in case of procedural violations committed in the pre-trial phase of international criminal proceedings. Nevertheless, the reduction of sentence on account of such violations appears to be established practice at the ad hoc Tribunals, where it is linked to the need to provide a personal remedy for rights violations and where, it seems, the rights violation in question must be attributable to (an organ of) the relevant Tribunal in order to warrant such reduction.[417] As regards the ICC, the availability of sentence reduction in such circumstances has been recognized in the case law (albeit implicitly).

5.5.5   Express Acknowledgement

In cases in which procedural violations committed in the pre-trial phase of international criminal proceedings has resulted in minimal or no prejudice to the accused, chambers of both the ad hoc Tribunals and the ICC have resorted to express acknowledgement of such violations, in order to provide remedial relief to an accused, or to condemn official misconduct.

5.6   Conclusion

The purpose of this chapter was to set out the law and practice of the ICTs with respect to the question of how to address procedural violations committed in the pre-trial phase of the proceedings. In Sects. 5.3 and 5.4 the relevant law and

---

[417] This issue will be explored further in Chap. 6.

practice at the ad hoc Tribunals, and that at the ICC, was set out (respectively), while in the penultimate section of this chapter, such law and practice was compared. It was seen that the approaches of the ad hoc Tribunals and of the ICC to the question of how to address procedural violations committed in the pre-trial phase of international criminal proceedings are broadly similar, with a few notable differences. For example, the case law of the ad hoc Tribunals is clearer than that at the ICC as regards the circumstances that may lead to a permanent stay of proceedings. Further, while at the ad hoc Tribunals, involvement of the Tribunal need not always be shown in order to justify the imposition of a stay of proceedings, there are (strong) indications that, at the ICC, attribution to an organ thereof must (always) be shown in order for the proceedings to be stayed. Regarding the exclusion of unlawfully obtained evidence, while Rule 95 of the ICTY and ICTR RPEs does not specify the norm that needs to be violated, Article 69(7) of the ICC Statute *does*; in order to trigger the exclusionary mechanism provided for under the latter provision, the evidence must have been obtained by violation of a provision of the ICC Statute, or of an internationally recognized human right. In addition, it was seen that while at the ad hoc Tribunals chambers have allowed the determination to be made under Rule 95 of the RPE to be informed by the probative value of the evidence and the fact that crimes with which the accused is charged are very serious, at the ICC, chambers have held that this factor may *not* inform the determination to be made under Article 69(7) of the ICC Statute. Finally, in comparing the law and practice of the ICTs with respect to financial compensation, it was observed that while at the ad hoc Tribunals, financial compensation may only be ordered upon acquittal of the accused, at the ICC, no such restriction appears to apply. Further, while the ICC provides for separate proceedings for requesting compensation, to be presided over by an altogether different panel of judges (designated by the Presidency especially for that purpose), at the ad hoc Tribunals, there is no such separation.

In the next chapter, the law and practice of the ICTs with respect to the question set out at the beginning of this section will be addressed in two specific contexts: arrest and detention, and disclosure. This more 'contextual' chapter provides an opportunity to bring to light important issues that were not appropriately dealt with in the present chapter, for the reasons given above, in Sect. 5.1. The purpose of Chap. 6 is to complement the overview provided in the present chapter, and thereby provide a fuller picture of the law and practice of the ICTs with respect to the question of how to address procedural violations committed in the pre-trial phase of the proceedings. Ultimately, such law and practice will be evaluated in light of the human rights standards set out in Chap. 2, and compared to the national law and practice set out in Chaps. 3 and 4. It is there that a discussion will take place of, and conclusions will be drawn as to, the adequacy of the judicial response at the ad hoc Tribunals, and that at the ICC, to procedural violations committed in the pre-trial phase of the proceedings.

References

Alamuddin A (2010) Collection of Evidence. In: Khan KAA et al. (eds) Principles of Evidence in International Criminal Justice. Oxford University Press, Oxford, pp 231–305

Ambos K (2013) Treatise on International Criminal Law, vol 1. Oxford University Press, Oxford

Beresford S (2002) Redressing the Wrongs of the International Justice System: Compensation for Persons Erroneously Detained, Prosecuted, or Convicted by the Ad Hoc Tribunals. AJIL 96:628 et seq.

Bitti G (2001) Compensation to an Arrested or Convicted Person. In: Lee RS (ed) The International Criminal Court. Elements of Crimes and Rules of Procedure and Evidence. Transnational Publishers, Ardsley, NY, pp 623–636

Brady H, Jennings M (2001) Appeal and Revision. In: Lee RS (ed) The International Criminal Court. Elements of Crimes and Rules of Procedure and Evidence. Transnational Publishers, Ardsley, NY, pp 575–603

Cassese A (1998) On the Current Trends towards Criminal Prosecution and Punishment of Breaches of International Humanitarian Law. EJIL 9:2 et seq.

Choo AL-T (2008) Abuse of Process and Judicial Stays of Criminal Proceedings, 2nd edn. Oxford University Press, Oxford

Combs NA (2010) Evidence. In: Schabas WA, Bernaz N (eds) Handbook of International Criminal Law. Routledge, Abingdon, Oxon, pp 323–334

De Meester K (2014) The Investigation Phase in International Criminal Procedure. In Search of Common Rules. DPhil thesis, University of Amsterdam

De Meester K et al. (2013) Investigation, Coercive Measures, Arrest and Surrender. In: Sluiter G et al. (eds) International Criminal Procedure. Principles and Rules. Oxford University Press, Oxford, pp 171–379

Fairlie MA (2004) The Marriage of Common and Continental Law at the ICTY and its Progeny, Due Process Deficit. Int CLR 4:243 et seq.

Fairlie MA (2013) Miranda and its (More Rights-Protective) International Counterparts. UC Davis J Int'l L & Pol'y 20:1 et seq.

Gosnell C (2010) Admissibility of Evidence. In: Khan KAA et al. (eds) Principles of Evidence in International Criminal Justice. Oxford University Press, Oxford, pp 375–442

Gradoni L (2013) The Human Rights Dimension of International Criminal Procedure. In: Sluiter G et al. (eds) International Criminal Procedure. Principles and Rules. Oxford University Press, Oxford, pp. 74–95

Jackson JD, Summers SJ (2012) The Internationalisation of Criminal Evidence. Beyond the Common Law and Civil Law Traditions. Cambridge University Press, Cambridge

Khan KAA, Dixon R (2013) Archbold International Criminal Courts. Practice, Procedure and Evidence, 4th edn. Sweet & Maxwell, London

Klamberg M (2013) Evidence in International Criminal Trials: Confronting Legal Gaps and the Reconstruction of Disputed Events. Martinus Nijhoff, Leiden/Boston

Klamberg M (2013) General Requirements for the Admission of Evidence. In: Sluiter G et al. (eds) International Criminal Procedure. Principles and Rules. Oxford University Press, Oxford, pp 1016–1043

Mégret F (2008) In Search of the 'Vertical': An Exploration of What Makes International Criminal Tribunals Different (and Why). http://ssrn.com/abstract=1281546. Accessed 3 April 2016

Naqvi YQ (2010) Impediments to Exercising Jurisdiction over International Crimes. TMC Asser Press, The Hague

Nerenberg M, Timmermann W (2010) Documentary Evidence. In: Khan KAA et al. (eds) Principles of Evidence in International Criminal Justice. Oxford University Press, Oxford, pp 443–498

Orie AMM (1983) De Verdachte Tussen Wal en Schip Òf de Systeem-breuk in de Kleine Rechtshulp. In: De la Porte EA et al. (eds) Bij Deze Stand van Zaken. Bundel opstellen aangeboden aan A.L. Melai. Gouda Quint, Arnhem, pp 351–361

Paulussen C (2010) Male Captus Bene Detentus? Surrendering Suspects to the International Criminal Court. Intersentia, Antwerp

Piragoff DK (2008) Article 69. In: Triffterer O (ed) Commentary on the Rome Statute, 2nd edn. Verlag CH Beck/Hart Publishing/Nomos Verlagsgesellschaft, Munich/Oxford/Baden-Baden, pp 1301–1336

Pitcher KM (2013) Addressing violations of international criminal procedure. In: Abels D et al. (eds) Dialectiek van nationaal en internationaal strafrecht. Boom Juridische uitgevers, The Hague, pp 257–308

Ryngaert R (2008) The Doctrine of Abuse of Process: A Comment on the Cambodia Tribunal's Decisions in the Case against Duch. LJIL 21:719 et seq.

Safferling CJM (2003) Towards an International Criminal Procedure. Oxford University Press, Oxford

Schabas WA (2010) The International Criminal Court: A Commentary on the Rome Statute. Oxford University Press, Oxford

Sluiter G (2002) International Criminal Adjudication and the Collection of Evidence: Obligations of States. Intersentia, Antwerp

Sluiter G (2009) Human Rights Protection in the ICC Pre-Trial Phase. In: Stahn C, Sluiter G (eds) The Emerging Practice of the International Criminal Court. Martinus Nijhoff, Leiden, pp 459–475

Staker C (2008) Article 85. In: Triffterer O (ed) Commentary on the Rome Statute, 2nd edn. Verlag CH Beck/Hart Publishing/Nomos Verlagsgesellschaft, Munich/Oxford/Baden-Baden, pp 1499–1502

Summers SJ (2007) Fair Trials: The European Criminal Procedural Tradition and the European Court of Human Rights. Hart Publishing, Oxford

Swart B (2002) General Problems. In: Cassese A et al. (eds) The Rome Statute of the International Criminal Court. A Commentary, vol 2. Oxford University Press, Oxford, pp 1589–1605

Taylor M, Jalloh CC (2013) Provisional Arrest and Incarceration in the International Criminal Tribunals. Santa Clara J Int'l L 11:303 et seq.

Vanderpuye K (2005) The International Criminal Court and Discretionary Evidential Exclusion: Toeing the Mark? Tul J Int'l & Comp L 14:127 et seq.

Zahar A, Sluiter G (2008) International Criminal Law: A Critical Introduction. Oxford University Press, Oxford

Zappalà S (2002) Compensation to an Arrested or Convicted Person. In: Cassese A et al. (eds) The Rome Statute of the International Criminal Court. A Commentary, vol 2. Oxford University Press, Oxford, pp 1577–1585

Zappalà S (2003) Human Rights in International Criminal Proceedings. Oxford University Press, Oxford

Zeegers KJ (2016) International Criminal Tribunals and Human Rights Law. Adherence and Contextualization. TMC Asser Press, The Hague

Chapter 6
Law and Practice of the International Criminal Tribunals—Specific Contexts

Abstract In this chapter the law and practice of the international criminal tribunals (ICTs) with respect to the question of how to address procedural violations committed in the pre-trial phase of the proceedings is addressed in two specific contexts: arrest and detention, and disclosure. Indeed, this book is concerned with the judicial response to procedural violations committed in the pre-trial phase of international criminal proceedings, which covers not only what at the national level would be described as 'police illegality' or 'unlawfulness', of which unlawful arrest or detention is an obvious example, but also the violation by the prosecution of its pre-trial obligations, of which disclosure to the defence is a prime example. In this chapter also, the law and practice of the ad hoc Tribunals and that of the ICC are compared. The purpose of this 'contextual' chapter is to complement the (general) overview provided in the previous chapter, and thereby provide a fuller picture of the law and practice of the ICTs with respect to the question of how to address pre-trial procedural violations.

Keywords unlawful arrest · unlawful detention · stay of proceedings · impossibility of a fair trial · need to preserve the integrity of the proceedings · financial compensation · sentence reduction · right to an effective remedy · alternative remedies · late disclosure · non-disclosure · prejudice to the accused · sanctions · remedies

Contents

© T.M.C. ASSER PRESS and the author 2018

K. Pitcher, *Judicial Responses to Pre-Trial Procedural Violations in International Criminal Proceedings*, International Criminal Justice Series 16,
https://doi.org/10.1007/978-94-6265-219-4_6

6.1   Introduction

The purpose of this chapter is to set out the law and practice of the ICTs with respect to the question of how to address procedural violations committed in the pre-trial phase of the proceedings. Such law and practice will be addressed in two specific contexts, namely, arrest and detention, and disclosure.[1] At the ICTs, procedural violations have been (alleged to have been) committed in other contexts also, for example, the collection of evidence;[2] the purpose of this chapter is not, then, to provide an exhaustive overview of the types of procedural violation that the ICTs have been (or may be) called upon to rule on. Rather, it is to bring to light important issues relevant to the question set out above, that might be overlooked (or, at least, might not receive the attention they deserve) by examining the law and practice with respect to the aforementioned question from the perspective of the consequences that may be attached to procedural violations only.[3] One such important issue (as touched upon in the previous chapter) concerns the question of how the ICTs should address procedural violations physically committed by organs that are not institutionally connected to them (in the sense that they, the ICTs, do not form part of the same legal system as the national law enforcement authorities who carry out coercive measures on their behalf).[4] In this regard it should be recalled that the ICTs do not have their own enforcement agencies. The context of arrest and detention provides an opportunity to explore this issue, the ICTs being dependent on state cooperation (and that of international organizations) for the apprehension of persons suspected or accused of crimes falling within their jurisdiction. As to the other context under examination in this chapter, disclosure provides an opportunity to explore another important issue, namely the question of which rationale(s) should inform the determination of whether

---

[1] As stated in Chap. 1, this book is concerned with the judicial response to procedural violations committed in the pre-trial phase of international criminal proceedings, which covers not only what at the national level would be described as 'police illegality' or 'unlawfulness', of which unlawful arrest or detention is an obvious example, but also the violation by the prosecution of its pre-trial obligations, of which disclosure to the defence is a prime example.

[2] While this context is not addressed in this chapter, it has been dealt with, indirectly, in Chap. 5, in setting out the law and practice of the ICTs with respect to the exclusion of evidence.

[3] This was the approach taken in Chap. 5.

[4] It is submitted that the fact that states are under an obligation to cooperate with the ICTs (see Chap. 5, Sect. 5.2) does not make the two *institutionally* connected, i.e. does not make them part of the same legal system.

and how to address pre-trial procedural violations. The context of arrest and detention also provides an opportunity to do this, but whereas (cases involving long delays aside) the illegal or unlawful arrest or detention of a person suspected or accused of crimes falling within the jurisdiction of the relevant international criminal tribunal does not typically prevent such a person from receiving a fair trial, in the sense of being able to mount an effective defence, late or non-disclosure does potentially impact on the accused's ability to do so, and, importantly, on more besides. In other words, late or non-disclosure raises issues with respect to the accused's right to a fair trial as well as other fundamental values, such as respect for the rule of law and the preservation of the integrity of the proceedings, whereby different considerations are likely to apply under each, and whereby the key time at which each (such) rationale 'bites'[5] may differ. The contexts of arrest and detention, and disclosure, then, provide an opportunity to bring to light important issues relevant to the central research question of this book (as set out above).

By examining the law and practice with respect to the question of how to address procedural violations committed in the pre-trial phase of international criminal proceedings from the perspective of specific types of procedural violation, it will be possible provide to a fuller picture of the law and practice of the ICTs in this regard. Ultimately, such law and practice will be evaluated in light of the human rights standards set out in Chap. 2, and compared to the national law and practice set out in Chaps. 3 and 4. This will be done in Chap. 7; it is there that a discussion will take place of, and conclusions will be drawn as to, the adequacy of the judicial response at the ad hoc Tribunals, and that at the ICC, to procedural violations committed in the pre-trial phase of the proceedings. The present chapter, then, does not (purport to) adopt a normative approach to the aforementioned law and practice. In other words, it does not seek to argue what the law and practice at the ICTs with respect of the question of how to address procedural violations committed in the pre-trial phase of the proceedings *should* be; rather, the purpose of this chapter is to set out what it *is*, with a view to assessing its adequacy in Chap. 7 (where it *will* be argued what the aforementioned law and practice should be).

As to the structure of this chapter, in Sect. 6.2 the law and practice of the ICTs with respect to the question of how to address procedural violations committed in the context of arrest and detention will be set out, while in Sect. 6.3 the law and practice of the ICTs with respect to the question of how to address procedural violations committed in the context of disclosure will be set out. The make-up of each of these sections is as follows. First, the relevant law and practice at the ad hoc Tribunals will be set out (whereby the relevant case law will be set out more or less in chronological order); then that at the ICC will be set out. Next, the relevant law and practice at the ad hoc Tribunals will be compared to that at the ICC (and vice versa), whereby such law and practice will be analysed, and points of criticism in this regard will be set out (with a view to providing a more complete picture of the relevant law and practice, as well as to putting the reader on notice as to the issues

---

[5] To borrow from Mirfield 1997, 29.

that will be addressed in Chap. 7; not in order to argue what the law and practice should be). Thus, each section consists of a descriptive component, and a more analytical component. Finally, this chapter will conclude, in Sect. 6.4, with a brief summary of the main points of the analysis from Sects. 6.2 and 6.3.

6.2   Judicial Responses to Procedural Violations Connected to Arrest and Detention

The first context to be examined in this chapter is arrest and detention. The structure of this section is as follows. First the relevant law and practice at the ad hoc Tribunals will be set out, i.e. the law and practice with respect to the question of how to address procedural violations committed in the context of arrest and detention, which will be followed by an overview of the relevant law and practice at the ICC. Next, the law and practice at the ad hoc Tribunals and that at the ICC will be compared and (critically) analysed. In the next section (Sect. 6.3), the context of disclosure will be examined.

6.2.1   Ad Hoc Tribunals

At the ad hoc Tribunals, the arrest and detention of persons suspected or accused of crimes falling within their jurisdiction is governed by the tribunals' own governing documents and by relevant human rights standards.[6] The case law discussed here, then, concerns violations of the ad hoc Tribunals' Statutes and/or RPEs, and/or relevant human rights standards. It is worth recalling here[7] that the ad hoc Tribunals' governing documents say little about how requests for cooperation are to be executed by the authorities of the state to which they are directed. Thus, neither the Statutes nor the RPEs provide for a specific procedure for national authorities implementing an arrest warrant issued by the relevant ad hoc Tribunal,[8] or a request

---

[6] Regarding the latter, most obviously: the right to personal liberty, as provided for in Articles 9 and 5 of the ICCPR and ECHR, respectively. For a comprehensive overview of the standards governing arrest and detention at the ad hoc Tribunals, see De Meester 2014, Chap. 7.

[7] See in this regard Chap. 5.

[8] Pursuant to Article 19(2) ICTY Statute and Article 18(2) ICTR Statute, the judge who confirms the indictment 'may, at the request of the Prosecutor', issue a warrant for the arrest of the person concerned. Usually, warrants of arrest are executed by states, acting through their law enforcement authorities. This certainly seems to be the assumption underlying Rules 55–59 ICTY/ICTR RPE, which further regulate the arrest of persons suspected of crimes falling within the jurisdiction of the ad hoc Tribunals. However, pursuant to Rule 59bis of the ICTY RPE, warrants of arrest may also be transmitted to 'an appropriate authority or international body'; in this regard it may be observed that a significant number of ICTY arrest warrants have been executed by international organizations.

for provisional arrest pursuant to Rule 40 of the RPEs.[9] Nevertheless, the ad hoc Tribunals have recognized that suspects and accused persons have certain rights in the context of arrest and detention. For example, they have recognized that suspects or accused persons have the right to be informed properly of the reasons for arrest,[10] the right to be brought promptly before the judicial authorities,[11] and the right to challenge the lawfulness of detention.[12]

---

[9] Pursuant to Rule 40 of the ICTY/ICTR RPE, the Prosecutor may, in case of urgency, directly request any state to arrest a suspect 'provisionally'. In other words, both the ICTY and ICTR RPEs allow for the (provisional) arrest of a suspect or an accused without an arrest warrant, i.e. in the absence of judicial authorization. Rule 40bis of the ICTY and ICTR RPEs provides for the transfer to and provisional detention of suspects against whom no indictment has yet been confirmed in the premises of the detention unit of the relevant tribunal. Regarding the implementation of requests for provisional detention pursuant to Rule 40 ICTY/ICTR RPE, see *Prosecutor v Kajelijeli* (Judgement) ICTR-98-44A-A, A Ch (23 May 2005) para 219: 'The Appeals Chamber notes that the Statute and Rules of the Tribunal are silent with regard to the manner and method in which an arrest of a suspect is to be effected by a cooperating State under Rule 40 of the Rules at the urgent request of the Prosecution. For example, no mention is made of ensuring the suspect's right to be promptly informed of the reasons for his or her arrest or the right to be promptly brought before a Judge.'

[10] Article 20(2) ICTY Statute provides that: 'A person against whom an indictment has been confirmed shall, pursuant to an order or an arrest warrant of the International Tribunal, be taken into custody, immediately informed of the charges against him and transferred to the International Tribunal.' (Article 19(2) ICTR Statute contains almost identical wording). In relation to a person suspected of crimes falling within the jurisdiction of the ad hoc Tribunals but against whom no indictment has yet been confirmed, the shared Appeals Chamber of the ad hoc Tribunals has held that 'a suspect arrested at the behest of the Tribunal [that is, pursuant to Rule 40 ICTY/ICTR RPE] has a right to be promptly informed of the reasons for his or her arrest, and this right comes into effect from the moment of arrest and detention'. See *Prosecutor v Kajelijeli* (Judgement) ICTR-98-44A-A, A Ch (23 May 2005) para 226, referring to *Prosecutor v Semanza* (Decision) ICTR-97-23-A, A Ch (31 May 2000) para 78. Finally, in respect of arrests executed by international organizations, Rule 59bis(B) ICTY RPE confers on the accused a right to be informed promptly of the charges.

[11] The Appeals Chamber has confirmed that a person who has been arrested and detained pursuant to Rule 40 ICTY and ICTR RPEs, i.e. by national authorities at the request of the ad hoc Tribunals, has the right to be brought promptly before a national judge. See *Prosecutor v Kajelijeli* (Judgement) ICTR-98-44A-A, A Ch (23 May 2005) paras 231–233. In respect of suspects transferred to, and provisionally detained, at the relevant ad hoc Tribunal pursuant to Rule 40bis of the ICTY and ICTR RPEs, the right to be brought promptly before the judicial authorities is provided for in Rule 40bis(F) ICTY RPE and Rule 40bis(J) ICTR RPE. Otherwise, upon transfer to the ad hoc Tribunals, whether through state cooperation or by international organizations pursuant to Rule 59bis, Rule 62 ICTY/ICTR RPE provides for the swift initial appearance of the accused, into which the right may be read. See e.g. *Prosecutor v Barayagwiza* (Decision) ICTR-97-19-AR72, A Ch (3 November 1999) para 70.

[12] At the ad hoc Tribunals, challenges to the lawfulness of arrest and/or detention have been brought and/or construed as challenges to the exercise of jurisdiction. See e.g. *Prosecutor v Nikolić* (Decision on Defence Motion Challenging the Exercise of Jurisdiction by the Tribunal) IT-94-2-PT, T Ch II (9 October 2002); *Prosecutor v Nikolić* (Decision on Notice of Appeal) IT-94-2-AR72, A Ch (9 January 2003); and *Prosecutor v Tolimir* (Decision on Submissions of the Accused concerning Legality of Arrest) IT-05-88/2-PT, T Ch II (18 December 2008) para 12. While the consequence of a successful challenge to the lawfulness of detention within the meaning

In setting out the law and practice of the ad hoc Tribunals with respect to the question of how to address procedural violations arising in the context of arrest and detention, it is instructive to draw a distinction between unlawful *arrest* cases, whereby 'arrest' refers to 'the *act* of depriving personal liberty' and whereby 'unlawful arrest' usually denotes the circumvention of established procedures for depriving a person of their liberty or an arrest that is otherwise arbitrary, and unlawful *detention* cases, whereby 'detention' refers to 'the *state* of deprivation of liberty and whereby 'unlawful detention' denotes the violation of procedural rights that pertain to this state.[13] It may be noted at the outset that the Statutes and RPEs of the ad hoc Tribunals are silent on the question of how to address (allegations of) procedural violations in the context of arrest and detention.

§ Arrest

Allegations of unlawful arrest have been made in several cases before the ad hoc Tribunals. In a number of early ICTR decisions on defence motions for relief in respect of alleged illegality or unlawfulness on the part of national authorities in the execution of a request from the ICTR Prosecutor for the provisional arrest of a person pursuant to Rule 40 of the ICTR RPE, it was held that the ICTR has no jurisdiction over the conditions of an arrest carried out by a sovereign state at the request of the ICTR.[14] According to the Trial Chamber in *Kajelijeli*, in the context of an arrest of a 'suspect', i.e. of a (provisional) arrest within the meaning of Rule 40 of the ICTR RPE,[15] the 'manner and execution of arrest is an area within the

---

(Footnote 12 continued)

of Articles 9(4) ICCPR and 5(4) ECHR—'release'—should be distinguished from the consequence of a successful challenge to jurisdiction on the basis of unlawful arrest or detention—permanent stay of proceedings—such challenges and consequences are 'related'. As Paulussen points out, 'although the release of [Articles 9(4) ICCPR and 5(4) ECHR] does not preclude re-arrest, a serious violation of [the right to personal liberty] may nevertheless lead to a [permanent stay of proceedings], not because these provisions say so but because the judge may decide so in his discretion in finding the most appropriate remedy'. See Paulussen 2010, 169–170.

[13] Nowak 2005, 221.

[14] See e.g. *Prosecutor v Ngirumpatse* (Decision on the Defence Motion Challenging the Lawfulness of the Arrest and Detention and Seeking Return or Inspection of Seized Items) ICTR-97-44-I, T Ch II (10 December 1999) paras 56–57; *Prosecutor v Karemera* (Decision on the Defence Motion for the Release of the Accused) ICTR-98-44-I, T Ch II (10 December 1999) 6–7, *Prosecutor v Kajelijeli* (Decision on the Defence Motion Concerning the Arbitrary Arrest and Illegal Detention of the Accused and on the Defence Notice of Urgent Motion to Expand and Supplement the Record of 8 December 1999 Hearing) ICTR-98-44-I, T Ch II (8 May 2000) paras 34–35; and *Prosecutor v Nzirorera* (Decision on the Defence Motion Challenging the Legality of the Arrest and Detention of the Accused and Requesting the Return of Personal Items Seized) ICTR-98-44-T, T Ch II (7 September 2000) para 27. See also *Prosecutor v Rwamakuba and others* (Decision on the Defence Motion Concerning the Illegal Arrest and Illegal Detention of the Accused) ICTR-98-44-T, T Ch II (12 December 2000) para 22, in which the Trial Chamber referred to the aforementioned ICTR authorities, although in that case there had, according to the Trial Chamber, not been a request pursuant to Rule 40 ICTR RPE (see ibid., para 27).

[15] See in this regard n 9 and accompanying text.

States' responsibility'.[16] It further held that: 'When the Prosecutor makes a request for the *arrest* of [a suspect], the matter falls within the domain of the requested State and it is that State which organizes, controls and carries out the *arrest* in accordance with their domestic law.'[17] In *Ngirumpatse*, the Trial Chamber held that '[i]t is a sovereign State ... against whom the person arrested may seek a remedy against the arrest ... under the laws of the ... State [requested to cooperate]'.[18] It seems that ICTR trial chambers have divested themselves of jurisdiction over the circumstances of an arrest carried out by national authorities at the request of the Prosecutor *because* the Statute and RPE 'are silent with regard to the manner and method in which an arrest of a suspect is to be effected by a cooperating State under Rule 40 of the Rules at the urgent request of the Prosecution'.[19] In *Semanza*, the Trial Chamber appeared to apply similar reasoning in respect of the *ongoing detention* of a person being held at the behest of the ICTR: '[A]n accused, before his transfer to the custody of the Tribunal, has no remedy under the Statute and Rules for the detention and acts by sovereign States over which the Tribunal does not exercise control'.[20] However, in a number of subsequent decisions issued shortly thereafter, the Appeals Chamber rejected such reasoning; these decisions are set out below, under 'Detention'. According to the Trial Chamber in *Rwamakuba*, these decisions do not affect the principle set forth in the arrest cases referred to above, i.e. that the ICTR has no jurisdiction over the conditions of an arrest carried out by a sovereign state at the request of the ICTR. However, immediately after referring to such arrest cases, having seemingly cited them with approval, the Trial Chamber held that:

> As far as detention in a State is concerned, ... [the *arrest* cases] have to be read in the light of the Barayagwiza Decision of 3 November 1999, where the Appeals Chamber, seized of allegations of the Appellant's detention in the State of Cameroon, held that "under the facts of this case, Cameroon was holding [him] in the "constructive custody" of the Tribunal by virtue of the Tribunal's lawful process or authority". Although the notion of one's "constructive custody" was not explicitly referred to in its subsequent Semanza Decision of 31 May 2000, which addressed in essence the same issues, the Appeals Chamber applied *some* of the consequences drawn from the notion of constructive custody in its Barayagwiza

---

[16] *Prosecutor v Kajelijeli* (Decision on the Defence Motion Concerning the Arbitrary Arrest and Illegal Detention of the Accused and on the Defence Notice of Urgent Motion to Expand and Supplement the Record of 8 December 1999 Hearing) ICTR-98-44-I, T Ch II (8 May 2000) para 34.

[17] Ibid., para 34 (emphasis added).

[18] *Prosecutor v Ngirumpatse* (Decision on the Defence Motion Challenging the Lawfulness of the Arrest and Detention and Seeking Return or Inspection of Seized Items) ICTR-97-44-I, T Ch II (10 December 1999) para 56.

[19] See *Prosecutor v Kajelijeli* (Judgement) ICTR-98-44A-A, A Ch (23 May 2005) para 219.

[20] *Prosecutor v Semanza* (Decision on the "Motion to Set Aside the Arrest and Detention of Laurent Semanza as Unlawful") ICTR-97-20-I, T Ch III (6 October 1999) paras 30–31. See also *Prosecutor v Barayagwiza* (Decision on the Extremely Urgent Motion by the Defence for Orders to Review and/or Nullify the Arrest and Provisional Detention of the Suspect) ICTR-97-19- I, T Ch II (17 November 1998) 5.

Decision of 3 November 1999 in the Semanza Decision as well. Among these consequences are the responsibility of the Tribunal for *some* aspects of the detention of such an
individual detained at its behest, while *specific* timeframes under the Rules run with respect
to the "constructive detainee" of the Tribunal, prior to his transfer to the UNDF, notably
with respect to his right to promptly informed of the nature of the charges against him.[21]

Indeed, it is clear from the cases of *Barayagwiza*, *Semanza* and *Kajelijeli* that the
ICTR does have jurisdiction over the conditions of the *detention* of a suspect or
accused by national authorities where he or she was being held at the request of the
ICTR pursuant to Rule 40 of the ICTR RPE. In *Rwamakuba* itself, the Trial
Chamber did *not* have jurisdiction over the conditions of André Rwamakuba's
detention by the Namibian authorities, since he was not being detained at the
ICTR's behest, i.e. at the request of the ICTR Prosecutor.[22]

Allegations of unlawful arrest have also been made in several cases before the
ICTY. It is worth noting that '[m]ost arrests on behalf of the [ICTY] have been
followed by an immediate transfer of the suspect to The Hague.'[23] The first accused
to allege (before the ICTY) to have been illegally captured was Slavko
Dokmanović, who argued, among other things, that the method of his arrest (in
which the forces of UNTAES[24] had been involved, having earlier received an ICTY
warrant for Dokmanović's arrest, and which had involved the utilisation of the
mechanism provided for in Rule 59bis of the ICTY RPE)[25] was tantamount to
kidnapping.[26] As such, the ICTY did not have jurisdiction to try him.[27] According
to the ICTY Trial Chamber, however, the method of Dokmanović's arrest did not
constitute a violation of Article 9(1) of the ICCPR or Article 5(1) of the ECHR,[28]

---

[21] *Prosecutor v Rwamakuba and others* (Decision on the Defence Motion Concerning the Illegal
Arrest and Illegal Detention of the Accused) ICTR-98-44-T, T Ch II (12 December 2000) para 23
(emphasis added).

[22] Ibid., paras 30, 33 and 45: '[t]he Tribunal having no jurisdiction over the conditions of that
period of detention, any challenges in this respect are to be brought before the Namibian
jurisdictions'.

[23] DeFrancia 2001, 1403.

[24] The United Nations Transitional Administration for Eastern Slavonia, Baranja and Western
Sirmium.

[25] Regarding that mechanism, see n 8 and accompanying text.

[26] *Prosecutor v Mrksić, Radić, Šljivančanin and Dokmanović* (Decision on the Motion for Release
by the Accused Slavko Dokmanović) IT-95-13a-PT, T Ch II (22 October 1997) para 16.

[27] Ibid., para 19.

[28] Both provisions provide for the right to personal liberty. Article 9(1) provides that: 'Everyone
has the right to liberty and security of person. No one shall be subjected to arbitrary arrest or
detention. No one shall be deprived of his liberty except on such grounds and in accordance with
such procedure as are established by law.' Article 5(1) provides that: 'Everyone has the right to
liberty and security of person. No one shall be deprived of his liberty save in the ... [cases
provided for in subparagraphs (a) to (f) of Article 5(1) ECHR] and in accordance with a procedure
prescribed by law'.

since 'specific, established procedures' had not been circumvented[29] and since the deception and trickery used to lure the Accused into Eastern Slavonia, to which the Office of the Prosecutor freely conceded, did not amount to 'a forcible abduction or kidnapping' (and, therefore, was not 'manifestly arbitrary').[30] Since 'the particular method used to arrest and detain Mr. Dokmanović was justified and *legal*', it was not necessary for the Trial Chamber to 'decide ... whether the International Tribunal has the authority to exercise jurisdiction over a defendant *illegally* obtained from abroad'.[31] In *Todorović*, the Accused raised his alleged 'abduction, kidnapping and detention' in a number of motions before the ICTY.[32] Eventually, at the request of the Defence, the Trial Chamber ordered 'SFOR and its responsible authority, the North Atlantic Council' and the 'States participating in SFOR' to disclose to the Defence all material relevant to Todorović's arrest and detention.[33] However, a plea agreement was entered into between the Office of the Prosecutor and the Accused,[34] and the question of the consequences of an unlawful arrest on the exercise of jurisdiction remained unanswered. In *Milošević*, the Accused alleged that his transfer to the ICTY had been illegal and that the ICTY therefore had no jurisdiction over him on account of abuse of process.[35] Such illegality lay in the fact that the Accused had been arrested and transferred to the ICTY by the government of the Republic of Serbia, despite the fact that the ICTY had 'sent the arrest warrants to the authorities of the Federal Republic of Yugoslavia, not to the government of the Republic of Serbia'.[36] The Trial Chamber rejected this argument, holding that 'the transfer was effected in accordance with the provisions of the [ICTY] Statute'[37] and that 'the circumstances in which the accused was arrested and transferred—by the government of the Republic of Serbia, to whom no request was made, but which is a constituent part of the Federal Republic of Yugoslavia, to whom the request for arrest and transfer was made—are not such as to constitute an egregious violation of the accused's rights [and, by extension, not such as to undermine the court's integrity and require a stay of proceedings]'.[38]

---

[29] *Prosecutor v Mrksić, Radić, Šljivančanin and Dokmanović* (Decision on the Motion for Release by the Accused Slavko Dokmanović) IT-95-13a-PT, T Ch II (22 October 1997) paras 67 and 75.

[30] Ibid., paras 57 and 67.

[31] Ibid., para 78 (emphasis in original).

[32] For a detailed account of such motions, see Sloan 2003.

[33] *Prosecutor v Simić, Simić, Tadić, Todorović and Zarić* (Decision on Motion for Judicial Assistance to be Provided by SFOR and Others) IT-95-9-PT, T Ch III (18 October 2000) para 61 and the 'Disposition'.

[34] Sloan 2003, 92–93.

[35] *Prosecutor v Milošević* (Decision on Preliminary Motions) IT-99-37-PT, T Ch (8 November 2001) para 35.

[36] Ibid., paras 35 and 44.

[37] Ibid., para 46.

[38] Ibid., para 51. The reference to 'egregious violations' is a reference to the ICTR case of *Barayagwiza*, which is discussed in more detail below.

The ICTY case of *Nikolić* was the first case before the ad hoc Tribunals to shed light on the availability of a (permanent) stay of proceedings in case of unlawful *arrest*.[39] In that case, the Accused had been captured by unknown individuals in the Federal Republic of Yugoslavia (hereafter: FRY) before being handed over to SFOR in Bosnia and Herzegovina, who arrested and detained him, and ultimately to the ICTY.[40] Numerous warrants for his arrest had been issued and transmitted by the ICTY.[41] The Defence sought the dismissal of the indictment against the Accused (and the release of the Accused from the custody of the ICTY).[42] According to the Trial Chamber, the Defence's challenge to the exercise of jurisdiction was based on two lines of reasoning. First, the illegality of the acts of the unknown individuals (i.e. the abduction of the accused), were attributable to SFOR and, ultimately, the Prosecution.[43] According to the Defence, such acts were attributable to SFOR, because it 'had knowledge, actual or constructive, that the [A]ccused had been unlawfully apprehended and brought from Serbia against his free will'[44] and to the Prosecution, because 'SFOR must be considered both the de facto and de jure agent of the Prosecution … in apprehending indictees …'.[45] Second, 'the illegal character of the arrest *in and of itself*' barred the ICTY from exercising jurisdiction over the Accused (according to the principle, 'male captus, male detentus'),[46] since the manner of arrest entailed a violation of international law. The Defence seems to have argued that it entailed a violation of international law on three separate grounds: a violation of the principle of state sovereignty, a violation of international human rights law and a breach of the rule of law.[47] As to the first line of reasoning, although the Trial Chamber did not reject the Defence's account of the circumstances surrounding the arrest, it found that the acts of the unknown individuals could not be attributed to SFOR, 'for lack of acknowledgment or ratification',[48] or to the Prosecution, because the conduct of the unknown individuals

---

[39] However, it was not the first case to shed light on the availability of a permanent stay of proceedings in case of unlawful deprivation of liberty more generally; earlier, the ICTR case of *Barayagwiza* had shed light on the availability of a (permanent) stay of proceedings in case of unlawful *detention*. This case is discussed below; see n 82–109 and accompanying text.

[40] The Defence and Prosecution agreed on these facts. See *Prosecutor v Nikolić* (Decision on Defence Motion Challenging the Exercise of Jurisdiction by the Tribunal) IT-94-2-PT, T Ch II (9 October 2002) para 21.

[41] *Prosecutor v Nikolić* (Decision on Defence Motion Challenging the Exercise of Jurisdiction by the Tribunal) IT-94-2-PT, T Ch II (9 October 2002) paras 10–14.

[42] Ibid., para 2.

[43] Ibid., para 29.

[44] Ibid., paras 25 and 58.

[45] Ibid., para 25.

[46] Ibid., para 29 (emphasis added).

[47] Ibid., para 71.

[48] Ibid., para 68.

could not be attributed to SFOR.[49] In relation to the Defence's second line of reasoning, and, in particular, its argument with respect to the principle of state sovereignty, the Trial Chamber held that, in light of the fact that the model of cooperation at the ICTY is 'vertical' in nature,[50] 'sovereignty by definition cannot play the same role' as it does between states;[51] in this regard it observed that: 'As national jurisdictions function *concurrently* on an *equal* level, it is of utmost importance that any exercise of jurisdiction be exercised in full respect of other national jurisdictions.'[52] In addressing the Defence's argument with respect to state sovereignty, the Trial Chamber also attached importance to the fact that the Prosecutor had not been involved in the arrest (whereas the relevant national case law 'showed that in every case in which a court decided *not* to exercise jurisdiction the facts of the case demonstrate that executive authorities of the forum state had been involved in the disputed operation to transfer an accused from one state to another),[53] and to the lack of other available means for bringing an accused into the jurisdiction of the ICTY (no extradition treaties being applicable, in light of the vertical nature of the model of cooperation at the ad hoc Tribunals), which meant that 'no issues' arose 'as to possible circumvention of other available means for bringing the Accused into the jurisdiction of the Tribunal'. Accordingly, there had been no violation of state sovereignty.[54] Regarding the Defence's argument with respect to international human rights law, the Trial Chamber cited with approval the Appeals Chamber's finding in the ICTR case of *Barayagwiza* that 'the abuse of process doctrine may be relied on if "in the circumstances of a particular case, proceeding with the trial of the accused would contravene the court's sense of justice"', thereby stressing that in order to invoke the abuse of process doctrine (and to decline to exercise jurisdiction over the Accused) 'it needs to be clear that the rights of the Accused have been egregiously violated'.[55] As to what constitutes an

---

[49] Ibid., para 69. In other words, in light of its conclusion on the attribution of the illegal conduct to SFOR, the Trial Chamber did not find it necessary to discuss whether or not an agency relationship existed between SFOR and the Prosecution, such that such conduct could be attributed to the Prosecution. On appeal (*Prosecutor v Nikolić* (Decision on Interlocutory Appeal Concerning Legality of Arrest) IT-94-2-AR73, A Ch (5 June 2003)), the Appeals Chamber first considered the question of whether the facts of the case warranted the remedy sought, i.e. for the Tribunal to decline exercising of jurisdiction. Answering this question in the negative, the Appeals Chamber did not consider it necessary to assess whether the acts of the unknown individuals could be attributed to SFOR and by extension, the Prosecution.

[50] See in this regard Chap. 5, n 13–20 and accompanying text.

[51] *Prosecutor v Nikolić* (Decision on Defence Motion Challenging the Exercise of Jurisdiction by the Tribunal) IT-94-2-PT, T Ch II (9 October 2002) para 100.

[52] Ibid., para 100.

[53] Ibid., para 101 (emphasis added).

[54] Ibid., para 105.

[55] Ibid., para 111, referring to *Prosecutor v Barayagwiza* (Decision) ICTR-97-19-AR72, A Ch (3 November 1999) paras 77 and 73. In so doing, the Trial Chamber confirmed that it was the second, integrity', limb of the abuse of process doctrine, as it applies at the ad hoc Tribunals that was at stake in this case. See generally Chap. 5, Sect. 5.3.1.1.

egregious violation, the Trial Chamber held that 'in a situation where an accused is very seriously mistreated, maybe even subjected to inhuman, cruel or degrading treatment, or torture, before being handed over to the [ICTY], this may constitute a legal impediment to the exercise of jurisdiction over such an accused' and that even without the involvement of the Prosecution or SFOR, the Trial Chamber would find it 'extremely difficult to justify the exercise of jurisdiction over a person … after having been seriously mistreated'.[56] In addition, the Trial Chamber confirmed the Appeals Chamber's finding in *Barayagwiza* that, 'in cases of egregious violations of the rights of the Accused', it is irrelevant which entity was involved.[57] Further, in finding that the serious mistreatment of an accused prior to being surrendered to the ICTY might impede the exercise of jurisdiction over such an accused, the Trial Chamber noted that this would '*certainly* be the case if the Tribunal was somehow involved'.[58] Ultimately, the Trial Chamber found that, although the level of violence used against the accused did 'raise some concerns',[59] it did not amount to an *egregious* violation of his rights. This led the Trial Chamber to conclude that it 'must exercise jurisdiction over the Accused'.[60] The Appeals Chamber came to the same conclusion on (interlocutory) appeal. It found that the determination of whether to stay the proceedings on the grounds advanced by the Defence—a violation of the principle of state sovereignty and a violation of international human rights law—entailed the performance of a balancing exercise, whereby the 'legitimate expectation [of the international community] that those accused of … [Universally Condemned Offences, i.e. genocide, crimes against humanity and war crimes] will be brought to justice swiftly' is 'weighed against the principle of State sovereignty and the fundamental rights of the accused'.[61] Regarding the Defence's argument with respect to the principle of state sovereignty, the Appeals Chamber held as follows:

> … the damage caused to international justice by not apprehending fugitives accused of serious violations of international humanitarian law is comparatively higher than the injury, if any, caused to the sovereignty of a State by a limited intrusion in its territory, particularly when the intrusion occurs in default of the State's cooperation. Therefore, the Appeals Chamber does not consider that in cases of universally condemned offences, jurisdiction should be set aside on the ground that there was a violation of the sovereignty of a State,

---

[56] *Prosecutor v Nikolić* (Decision on Defence Motion Challenging the Exercise of Jurisdiction by the Tribunal) IT-94-2-PT, T Ch II (9 October 2002) para 114.

[57] Ibid., para 114 (emphasis added), referring to *Prosecutor v Barayagwiza* (Decision) ICTR-97-19-AR72, A Ch (3 November 1999) para 73 (which is discussed in more detail below, under 'Detention').

[58] *Prosecutor v Nikolić* (Decision on Defence Motion Challenging the Exercise of Jurisdiction by the Tribunal) IT-94-2-PT, T Ch II (9 October 2002) para 114 (emphasis added). See also para 106, where the involvement of the prosecuting forum is identified as a factor weighing in favour of finding that a human rights violation has occurred.

[59] Ibid., para 114.

[60] Ibid., para 115.

[61] *Prosecutor v Nikolić* (Decision on Interlocutory Appeal Concerning Legality of Arrest) IT-94-2-AR73, A Ch (5 June 2003) para 26.

when the violation is brought about by the apprehension of fugitives from international justice, whatever the consequences for the international responsibility of the State or organisation involved. This is all the more so in cases such as this one, in which the State whose sovereignty has allegedly been breached has not lodged any complaint and thus has acquiesced in the International Tribunal's exercise of jurisdiction.[62]

Regarding the Defence's argument with respect to international human rights law, the Appeals Chamber confirmed that it was the second, 'integrity' limb of the abuse of process doctrine that was at stake in this case.[63] It found that, '[a]lthough the assessment of the seriousness of the human rights violation depends on the circumstances of each case and cannot be made *in abstracto*, certain human rights violations are of such a serious nature that they require that the exercise of jurisdiction be declined' and that, apart from such exceptional cases, the remedy of setting aside jurisdiction 'will … usually be disproportionate'.[64] According to the Appeals Chamber, the evidence did not show 'that the rights of the accused were *egregiously* violated in the process of his arrest'.[65] Finally, it is important to note that neither the Trial Chamber nor the Appeals Chamber considered any alternative remedies in this regard (at any stage of the proceedings).

In *Tolimir*, the Accused alleged that he had been forcibly abducted by 'illegal groups and individuals' from his apartment in Belgrade, Serbia, to the Republika Srpska, where he was surrendered to NATO forces and, ultimately, to the ICTY. Initially, the Accused sought a stay of proceedings on the grounds that the ICTY had 'no jurisdiction to try abducted persons'.[66] On 14 December 2007, however, the Trial Chamber denied the Accused's motion(s) seeking such relief. In relation to the issue of state sovereignty, the Trial Chamber held as follows (thereby drawing on Appeals Chamber's findings in this regard in the *Nikolić* case):

In the present case, the Accused is charged with genocide, crimes against humanity and war crimes. Assuming, without deciding, that a violation of state sovereignty occurred in the instant case, the Trial Chamber finds that given the serious crimes involved such a violation is not sufficient to justify the setting aside of jurisdiction by this Tribunal. Moreover, the Trial Chamber notes that Serbia did not lodge a complaint.[67]

Regarding the human rights issues raised by the alleged abduction, the Trial Chamber said that, 'the factual allegations of the Accused related to the initial phase of the arrest'—which, for the purposes of its analysis, it was prepared to accept— did 'not amount to a human rights violation of such a serious nature [i.e. an

---

[62] Ibid., para 26.

[63] Ibid., paras 29–30.

[64] Ibid., para 30. See also *Prosecutor v Kajelijeli* (Judgement) ICTR-98-44A-A, A Ch (23 May 2005) para 206.

[65] *Prosecutor v Nikolić* (Decision on Interlocutory Appeal Concerning Legality of Arrest) IT-94-2-AR73, A Ch (5 June 2003) para 32 (emphasis added).

[66] *Prosecutor v Tolimir* (Decision on Preliminary Motions on the Indictment pursuant to Rule 72 of the Rules) IT-05-88/2-PT, T Ch II (14 December 2007) para 8.

[67] Ibid., para 19.

egregious violation] as to require that the exercise of jurisdiction be declined'; even '[a]ssuming those allegations to be true ... that scenario was not so egregious as to merit declining jurisdiction over this Accused in relation to the grave crimes charged against him.'[68] Moreover, the Accused had not provided 'any evidence to show the involvement of either NATO or the Prosecution in the initial phase of his arrest', while the Prosecution 'had provided evidence to the contrary' in this regard.[69] Finally, the Trial Chamber found that '[o]nce the Accused came into contact with NATO and the Prosecution his arrest was carried out in a lawful manner and without any violations of his rights.'[70] In a subsequent motion, the Accused sought a ruling that his arrest had been unlawful and his rights violated, i.e. declaratory relief. According to the Trial Chamber, however, '[w]hile the Accused may have [had] remedies to pursue in national courts in relation to an alleged illegal arrest',[71] it was not for the Trial Chamber 'to examine the circumstances of the Accused's arrest for the purposes of providing some sort of declaration', since the circumstances surrounding the arrest of the accused were (only) 'relevant to the Trial Chamber to the extent that they may affect the jurisdiction of the Tribunal over [the Accused]'.[72] Consequently, the Defence's arguments would only be considered 'in the context of the impact on the jurisdiction of the Trial Chamber to adjudicate on [the Accused's case]'.[73] On appeal, the Defence maintained that a declaration that the circumstances of the accused's arrest violated his right as an accused could in itself be an adequate legal remedy (and that the Trial Chamber had erred in refusing to issue such a declaration).[74] However, the appeal was dismissed for technical reasons and the merits were not considered.[75]

Finally, in *Karadžić*, the Accused challenged his arrest and detention in Belgrade, Serbia, in July 2008. In doing so, he alleged that his arrest and 'incommunicado' and 'unacknowledged' detention had been arbitrary and further that certain Serbian rules of procedure had not been adhered to.[76] This, he argued, violated his right to personal liberty. In addition, he alleged that his right to be informed promptly of the reasons for arrest and his right to be brought promptly

---

[68] Ibid., para 25. For such factual allegations, see para 9.

[69] Ibid., para 26.

[70] Ibid., para 26.

[71] This reasoning is reminiscent of that adopted by ICTR trial chambers in the 'arrest cases'. See n 14–18 and accompanying text.

[72] *Prosecutor v Tolimir* (Decision on Submissions of the Accused concerning Legality of Arrest) IT-05-88/2-PT, T Ch II (18 December 2008) para 12.

[73] Ibid., para 12.

[74] *Prosecutor v Tolimir* (Decision on Zdravko Tolimir's Appeal Against the Decision on Submissions of the Accused Concerning Legality of Arrest) IT-05-88/2-AR72.2, A Ch (12 March 2009) para 7.

[75] Ibid., para 7.

[76] *Prosecutor v Karadžić* (Decision on the Accused's Motion for Remedy for Violation of Rights in Connection with Arrest) IT-95-5/18-PT, T Ch III (31 August 2009) para 2.

before the judicial authorities had been violated.[77] According to the Accused, the appropriate remedy was either financial compensation upon acquittal or sentence reduction upon conviction,[78] for which he relied on the relevant decisions in the ICTR cases of *Barayagwiza, Semanza* and *Kajelijeli*.[79] However, the Trial Chamber held that, because such remedies are 'dependent on the outcome of the trial and [are] to take effect following the issuing of the judgement', it was 'premature' to impose such a remedy at that point (i.e. in the pre-trial stages of the proceedings).[80] Rather, such matters 'should be dealt with during the trial, or rather towards the end of the trial'.[81] This case, and the ICTR cases of *Barayagwiza, Semanza* and *Kajelijeli*, are discussed in more detail below, under 'Detention'.

§ Detention

Perhaps the most infamous case to address the issue of unlawful *detention* at the ad hoc Tribunals is *Barayagwiza*, in which a plethora of violations was found to have been committed in the context of Jean-Bosco Barayagwiza's detention in Cameroon (at the ICTR's behest). To begin with, the Appellant's 'right to be promptly charged under Rule 40*bis*' was found to have been violated. During the relevant period (4 March to 23 October 1997), the Appellant was being held at the behest of the ICTR. Establishing this violation was challenging, given that Rule 40bis(C) provides that '[t]he provisional detention of the suspect may be ordered for a period not exceeding 30 days *from the day after the transfer of the suspect to the detention unit of the Tribunal*',[82] while the violation was alleged to have occurred prior to the Appellant's transfer to the ICTR detention facility. To this end, the Appeals Chamber considered, after noting that the Appellant had been detained 'since 21 February 1997 solely at the behest of the Prosecutor', that, 'if the Appellant were in the *constructive custody* of the Tribunal after the Rule 40*bis* Order was filed on 4 March 1997, the provisions of that Rule would apply'.[83] It then held that, '[i]n order to determine if the period of time that the Appellant spent in Cameroon at the behest of the Tribunal is attributable to the Tribunal pursuant to Rule 40*bis*, it is necessary to analyse the relationship between Cameroon and the Tribunal with respect to the detention of the Appellant.'[84] According to the Appeals Chamber, 'under the facts of the case, Cameroon was holding the Appellant in constructive custody for the

---

[77] Ibid., para 2.

[78] Ibid., para 1.

[79] Ibid., para 6.

[80] Ibid., para 5.

[81] Ibid., para 5.

[82] This period may be extended twice by 30 days (see Rules 40bis(F) and (G), whilst pursuant to Rule 40*bis*(H), the total period of provisional detention 'shall in no case exceed 90 days after the day of transfer of the suspect to the Tribunal'.

[83] *Prosecutor v Barayagwiza* (Decision) ICTR-97-19-AR72, A Ch (3 November 1999) para 54 (original footnote omitted, emphasis added).

[84] Ibid., para 54 (emphasis added).

Tribunal by virtue of the Tribunal's lawful process or authority'.[85] Finally, it held that 'the length of time that the Appellant was detained in Cameroon at the behest of the Tribunal without being indicted violates [the 90-day rule in] Rule 40*bis* and established human rights jurisprudence'.[86] As to such human rights jurisprudence, the Appeals Chamber observed that, 'in interpreting Article 9(2) of the ICCPR, [the HRC] has developed considerable jurisprudence with respect to the permissible length of time that a suspect may be detained without being charged'.[87] Next, the 'statutory requirement that the initial appearance is held without delay' was found to have been violated.[88] In this regard, the Appeals Chamber observed that, '[t]he international instruments have not established specific time limits for the initial appearance of detainees, relying rather on a requirement that a person should "brought promptly before a Judge" following arrest', thereby referring to Article 9 (3) of the ICCPR.[89] It then found that 'a 96-day delay between the transfer of the Appellant to the Tribunal's detention unit [on 19 November 1997] and his initial appearance [on 23 February 1998] to be a violation of his fundamental rights as expressed by Articles 19 and 20 [of the ICTR Statute], internationally-recognised human rights standards and Rule 62'.[90] According to the Appeals Chamber, these two violations, i.e. of the right to be charged promptly and the right to be brought promptly before the judicial authorities, which were both attributable to the ICTR (by virtue of the Prosecutor's failure to exercise due diligence to ensure their protection),[91] warranted a stay of proceedings pursuant to the abuse of process doctrine.[92] Having found that, pursuant to the doctrine, it is 'irrelevant which entity or entities were responsible for the alleged violations …',[93] the Appeals Chamber found that the Appellant's right to be informed promptly of the reasons for arrest and detention (within the meaning of Articles 9(2) of the ICCPR and 5(2) of the ECHR)[94] had been violated. Thus, the fact that 'only 35 days out of the 11-month total [i.e. the 11-month delay in this regard] are clearly attributable to the Tribunal' did not absolve the ICTR of responsibility for the violation.[95] Together with the other violations, the 11-month delay in notifying the Appellant of the reasons for arrest and detention was considered serious enough to justify a stay of proceedings

---

[85] Ibid., para 61.

[86] Ibid., para 67.

[87] Ibid., para 63.

[88] Ibid., para 69.

[89] Ibid., para 70.

[90] Ibid., para 71.

[91] Ibid., paras 71 and 91–99.

[92] Ibid., para 72.

[93] Ibid., paras 73–77.

[94] Ibid., paras 80–84.

[95] Ibid., para 85.

pursuant to the abuse of process doctrine.[96] Finally, the 'failure to resolve the *writ of habeas corpus* in a timely manner', i.e. the right to challenge the lawfulness of detention within the meaning of Articles 9(4) of the ICCPR and 5(4) of the ECHR, was found to have been violated on the basis that the Appellant's writ was never heard by the Trial Chamber. Specifically, the Appeals Chamber held that 'the fact that the indictment of the Appellant has been confirmed and that he has had his initial appearance does not excuse the failure to resolve the *writ*' and that 'the belated issuance of the indictment did not nullify that violation'.[97]

According to the Appeals Chamber, the cumulative effect of the aforementioned violations and the ICTR Prosecutor's failure to exercise due diligence warranted the application of the abuse of process doctrine and, by extension, a permanent stay of proceedings.[98] It held that, 'the abuse of process doctrine may be relied on in two distinct situations: (1) where delay has made a fair trial for the accused impossible; and (2) where in the circumstances of a particular case, proceeding with the trial of the accused would contravene the court's sense of justice, due to pre-trial impropriety or misconduct'.[99] It was the second limb that was at stake here,[100] and in order for proceedings to be stayed on that basis, the 'pre-trial impropriety or misconduct' would have to entail 'serious and egregious violations of the accused's rights'.[101] This was indeed the case. Regarding the Appeals Chamber's finding that pursuant to the abuse of process doctrine, it is 'irrelevant which entity or entities were responsible for the alleged violations …',[102] it should be noted that most of the violations established by the Appeals Chamber were attributable to the ICTR and, more specifically, to the Prosecutor.[103] Upon *review* of the Appeal Chamber's

---

[96] In other words, by the time the Appeals Chamber got around to considering the violation of the right to be informed promptly of the charges, it had already declared the abuse of process doctrine applicable on the basis of other rights violations that were clearly attributable to the ICTR. See *Prosecutor v Barayagwiza* (Decision) ICTR-97-19-AR72, A Ch (3 November 1999) paras 71–72.

[97] *Prosecutor v Barayagwiza* (Decision) ICTR-97-19-AR72, A Ch (3 November 1999) paras 87–90.

[98] Ibid., para 73.

[99] Ibid., para 77.

[100] Ibid., para 77. Nevertheless, it should be noted that the Appeals Chamber's decision is not a model of clarity as regards the rationales for staying the proceedings or the rationale that it was pursuing. More will be said about this in Chap. 7.

[101] Ibid., paras 73–75. See also the ICTY case of *Karadžić*, in which the Appeals Chamber confirmed that there are two limbs to the abuse of process doctrine (fair trial and integrity) and that the Appeals Chamber's finding in *Barayagwiza* that, invoking the abuse of process doctrine as a matter of discretion 'is a process by which Judges may decline to exercise the court's jurisdiction in cases where to exercise that jurisdiction in light of serious and egregious violations of the accused's rights would prove detrimental to the court's integrity' (ibid., para 74), refers to the second limb. See *Prosecutor v Karadžić* (Decision on Karadžić's Appeal of Trial Chamber's Decision on Alleged Holbrooke Agreement) IT-95-5/18-AR73.4, A Ch (12 October 2009) para 51.

[102] *Prosecutor v Barayagwiza* (Decision) ICTR-97-19-AR72, A Ch (3 November 1999) paras 73–77.

[103] See n 91 and n 96.

decision to stay the proceedings[104] (at the Prosecutor's request), however, the (newly constituted) Appeals Chamber considered that although the Appellant's rights had been violated, the 'new facts' submitted by the Prosecution 'diminish[ed] the role played by the failings of the Prosecutor *as well as* the intensity of the violation of the rights of the Appellant'.[105] Therefore, a dismissal of the indictment was no longer justified. Nevertheless, since 'all violations demand a remedy',[106] the Appellant was entitled either to financial compensation upon acquittal, or sentence reduction upon conviction.[107] In this regard it is important to note that the 'role played by the failings of the Prosecutor' had merely been diminished, not negated altogether; while some violations were, upon review, no longer attributable to the Prosecutor (in particular, the right to be brought promptly before the judicial authorities), others presumably were.[108] Upon conviction, Barayagwiza's sentence was reduced from one of life imprisonment to thirty-two years.[109]

The same approach was adopted in *Semanza*. In that case, the Appeals Chamber found that the right to be informed promptly of the reasons for arrest, as meant in Articles 9(2) of the ICCPR and 5(2) of the ECHR, had been violated on two separate occasions.[110] On both occasions, a lapse of 18-days between the time the Appellant was taken into custody pursuant to the ICTR Prosecutor's request and the moment he was informed of the nature of the charges brought against him by the Prosecutor was found to violate this right.[111] The Appeals Chamber did not,

---

[104] As based on Article 25 ICTR Statute and Rule 120 ICTR RPE.

[105] *Prosecutor v Barayagwiza* (Decision (Prosecutor's Request for Review or Reconsideration)) ICTR-97-19-AR72, A Ch (31 March 2000) para 71 (emphasis added). See also para 74.

[106] Ibid., para 74.

[107] Ibid., para 75.

[108] In respect of some violations, which in the original decision (*Prosecutor v Barayagwiza* (Decision) ICTR-97-19-AR72, A Ch (3 November 1999)) *were* attributable to the ICTR, the issue of attribution was not discussed at all upon review. As such, it is fair to assume that these violations *remained* attributable to the ICTR.

[109] *Prosecutor v Nahimana, Barayagwiza and Ngeze* (Judgement and Sentence) ICTR-99-52-T, T Ch I (3 December 2003) para 1107; *Prosecutor v Nahimana, Barayagwiza and Ngeze* (Judgement) ICTR-99-52-A, A Ch (28 November 2007) para 1097.

[110] The Appellant had been detained in Cameroon at the Prosecutor's request during 'two distinct periods': 'The first period ran from 15 April 1996, the date of the Prosecutor's first request under Rule 40, to 17 May 1996, when the Prosecutor informed the authorities in Cameroon that he was dropping his case against the Appellant. The second period of detention ran from 21 February 1997, the date of the Prosecutor's second Rule 40 request, to 19 November 1997, when the Appellant was transferred to the Tribunal's Detention Facility.' See *Prosecutor v Semanza* (Decision) ICTR-97-23-A, A Ch (31 May 2000) para 79.

[111] *Prosecutor v Semanza* (Decision) ICTR-97-23-A, A Ch (31 May 2000) paras 87 and 90. In relation to the 'second period of detention' the Appeals Chamber found that, although the lapse of 18 days between the date at which the Appellant's right to be informed of the reasons for arrest came into effect and the date on which he was informed of such reasons could be said to constitute a violation of that right, the violation was 'less serious [than the violation in the first period of detention] since the Appellant had been informed in substance of the nature of the Prosecutor's charges against him during his first period of detention'. See para 90.

however, specify whether such violations could be attributed to (an organ of) the ICTR. Regarding the alleged violation of the right to be promptly charged, as set forth in Rule 40*bis*, the Appeals Chamber revised its earlier findings in *Barayagwiza*, that such right 'becomes effective as soon as a Rule 40*bis* Order is filed'.[112] According to the Appeals Chamber, on the basis of the legislative history, it is 'unambiguously clear that the Rule 40*bis* time-limit runs not from the day the Order is filed but rather from the day the suspect is transferred to the Tribunal's Detention Facility'.[113] Given that the Appellant had been transferred to the ICTR's Detention Facility on 19 November 1997, while the indictment against the Appellant had been confirmed on 23 October 1997, i.e. prior to the transfer, the Appeals Chamber concluded that the Appellant's right to be promptly charged 'could not have been violated'.[114] '[I]n any event', the Appeals Chamber reasoned, 'the Tribunal is not responsible for the time elapsed before the Appellant was transferred to the Tribunal's Detention Facility', since, 'firstly ... Cameroon was not prepared to transfer the Appellant before ... 21 October 1997 [the date on which the decree granting leave for the transfer was signed by the President of the Republic of Cameroon] ... and, secondly ... the time which elapsed before the decree was signed 'was the result of factors unrelated to lack of diligence on the part of the Prosecutor' and 'consequently ... the Tribunal did not violate Rule 40*bis*'.[115] Next, the Appeals Chamber considered the alleged violation of the 'right of the [A] ccused to be brought before a Trial Chamber without delay and to be formally charged', as set forth in Rule 62 of the RPE.[116] While it noted that 89 days had elapsed before the Accused made his initial appearance and was formally charged and that such a delay could lead to a finding that the right had been violated,[117] it found that Counsel for the Appellant had 'contributed' to this delay, by requesting that the initial appearance be postponed.[118] According to the Appeals Chamber, this request had 'the import of waiving the Appellant's right to claim violation of his

---

[112] See n 83 and accompanying text.

[113] *Prosecutor v Semanza* (Decision) ICTR-97-23-A, A Ch (31 May 2000) para 97. See also paras 91–96. The Appeals Chamber did not, however, address the question of whether this Rule was in conformity with international human rights jurisprudence; it only appeared concerned with the legislative history: 'Although the interpretation whereby the time-limit is to be calculated from the day the Order is filed is of course in keeping with the spirit and letter of the Rule adopted on 15 May 1996, the [AC] must take into account the abrogative effect of any legislative amendment.' See para 96.

[114] Ibid., paras 99–100.

[115] Ibid., paras 101–104.

[116] Interestingly, the Appeals Chamber did not refer to international human rights law in this regard. See n 89 and accompanying text.

[117] *Prosecutor v Semanza* (Decision) ICTR-97-23-A, A Ch (31 May 2000) para 107.

[118] Ibid., paras 108–110.

right to be brought before a Trial Chamber without delay or formally charged'.[119] Finally, the Appeals Chamber considered the alleged violation of the right to challenge the lawfulness of detention, which, it may be noted, is not explicitly provided for in the Statutes or RPEs of the ad hoc Tribunals.[120] The Appeals Chamber found that the right had been violated in light of the fact that the Appellant's challenge to detention had never been heard by the Trial Chamber (having not been placed on the cause list by the Registrar).[121] Nevertheless, it found that the violation could be (partly) attributed to Counsel for the Appellant, due to his failure to exercise due diligence in following up the challenge.[122] Although no material prejudice was found to have been caused in this regard,[123] the Appeals Chamber found that 'any violation, even if it entails only a relative degree of prejudice, requires a proportionate remedy'.[124] However, the relief sought by the Appellant, release, was considered disproportionate in the circumstances.[125] Upon conviction of the Accused, the Trial Chamber found that 'it was appropriate to reduce the Accused's sentence by a period of six months' in view of the violations committed in the context of his pre-trial detention (including the violations referred to above).[126]

In *Kajelijeli*, the Appellant alleged various violations of his fundamental rights in connection with his detention in Benin at the behest of the ICTR Prosecutor.[127] In this regard, the Appeals Chamber held that,

> under Rule 40 of the Rules, the Prosecution and Benin had overlapping responsibilities during the first period of the Appellant's arrest and detention in Benin [until his transfer to the ICTR in Arusha, Tanzania]. This flows from the rationale that the international division of labour in prosecuting crimes must not be to the detriment of the apprehended person. Under the *prosecutorial duty of due diligence*, the Prosecution is required to ensure that, once it initiates a case, "the case proceeds to trial in a way that respects the rights of the accused." With regard to the responsibility of the Benin authorities, … a cooperating State,

---

[119] Ibid., para 111. The precise meaning of this statement is, however, unclear. Was the Appeals Chamber of the view that the violation could not be attributed to the ICTR for the purpose of providing a remedy?

[120] See n 27 and accompanying text.

[121] *Prosecutor v Semanza* (Decision) ICTR-97-23-A, A Ch (31 May 2000) para 114.

[122] Ibid., paras 116–121.

[123] Ibid., para 124.

[124] Ibid., para 125.

[125] Ibid., para 125. For the remedy sought, see para 59.

[126] *Prosecutor v Semanza* (Judgement and Sentence) ICTR-97-20-T, T Ch III (15 May 2003) paras 579–580 (although the Trial Chamber acknowledged that the violation of the right to challenge the lawfulness of detention had not caused the Appellant *material* prejudice), as upheld in *Prosecutor v Semanza* (Judgement) ICTR-97-20-A, A Ch (20 May 2005) paras 323–329.

[127] In total, the Appellant was in the custody of the authorities of Benin from the date of his initial arrest until his transfer to the custody of the Tribunal for 95 days. During this period, the Appellant was in the custody of Benin authorities for 85 days before being served with an arrest warrant or a confirmed indictment. See *Prosecutor v Kajelijeli* (Judgement) ICTR-98-44A-A, A Ch (23 May 2005) para 210.

when effecting an urgent arrest and detention pursuant to the Prosecution's request under Rule 40 of the Rules, must strike a balance between two different obligations under international law. First, the State is required under Security Council Resolution 955 and Article 28 of the Tribunal's Statute to comply fully without undue delay with any requests for assistance from the Tribunal in fulfilling the weighty task of investigating and prosecuting persons accused of committing serious violations of international humanitarian law. On the other hand, the cooperating State still remains under its obligation to respect the human rights of the suspect as protected in customary international law, in the international treaties to which it has acceded, as well as in its own national legislation.[128]

In relation to the Prosecution's responsibilities, the Appeals Chamber held that,

the Prosecution is under a two-pronged duty. The request to the authorities of the cooperating State has to include a notification to the judiciary, or at least, by way of the Tribunal's primacy, a clause reminding the national authorities to promptly bring the suspect before a domestic Judge in order to ensure that the apprehended person's rights are safeguarded by a Judge of the requested State as outlined above. In addition, the Prosecution must notify the Tribunal in order to enable a Judge to furnish the cooperating State with a provisional arrest warrant and transfer order.[129]

Although in making urgent Rule 40 requests the Prosecution need not provide the suspect with a copy of the arrest warrant, the Appeals Chamber held that a suspect arrested at the behest of the ICTR still has a right to be promptly informed of the reasons for his or her arrest (as set out in Article 9(2) of the ICCPR),[130] such right coming into effect from the moment of arrest and detention.[131] In the absence of any evidence to the contrary, the Appeals Chamber found that 'the Appellant's right to be informed of the reasons as to why he was being deprived of his liberty was not properly guaranteed'.[132] Regarding the alleged violation of the right to be informed promptly of the charges against him (as set out in Articles 14(3)(a) of the ICCPR and 6(3)(a) of the ECHR)[133] and of the right to be brought promptly before the judicial authorities (as set out in Article 9(3) of the ICCPR),[134] the Appeals Chamber found that the Trial Chamber had 'erred in failing to find that [the Appellant's] detention in

---

[128] *Prosecutor v Kajelijeli* (Judgement) ICTR-98-44A-A, A Ch (23 May 2005) para 220. For its finding that '[u]nder the prosecutorial duty of due diligence, the Prosecution is required to ensure that, once it initiates a case, "the case proceeds to trial in a way that respects the rights of the accused"', the Appeals Chamber relied on its earlier findings in the *Barayagwiza* case. In that case, it had held that: 'Because the Prosecutor has the authority to commence the entire legal process, through investigation and submission of an indictment for confirmation, the Prosecutor has been likened to the "engine" driving the work of the Tribunal. […] Consequently, once the Prosecutor has set this process in motion, she is under a duty to ensure that, within the scope of her authority, the case proceeds to trial in a way that respects the rights of the accused.' See *Prosecutor v Barayagwiza* (Decision) ICTR-97-19-AR72, A Ch (3 November 1999) para 92.

[129] *Prosecutor v Kajelijeli* (Judgement) ICTR-98-44A-A, A Ch (23 May 2005) para 222.

[130] Ibid., para 224.

[131] Ibid., paras 226–227.

[132] Ibid., para 227. See also para 251.

[133] Ibid., para 229. The Appeals Chamber also referred to Article 9(2) ICCPR.

[134] Ibid., para 230.

Benin for a total of 85 days without charge and [95 days] without being brought promptly before a Judge was clearly unlawful and was in violation of his rights under the Tribunal's Statute and [RPE] as well as international human rights law'.[135] Moreover, it found that 'the Prosecution [was] responsible for these violations because it [had] failed to make a request within a reasonable time under Rules 40 and 40*bis* for the Appellant's provisional arrest and transfer to the Tribunal.'[136] Although the violation of the right to be brought promptly before the judicial authorities was 'not solely attributable to the Prosecution', the Appeals Chamber recalled that 'it was the Prosecution, thus an organ of the Tribunal, which was the requesting institution responsible for triggering the Appellant's apprehension, arrest and detention in Benin'.[137] Regarding these rights violations, the Appeals Chamber found that 'irrespective of any responsibility of Benin for [such] violations', *'fault ... [was] attributable to the Prosecution* for [such] violations', since it had *'failed to effect its prosecutorial duties with due diligence* out of respect for the Appellant's rights following its Rule 40 request to Benin'; *'Thus*, the Appellant ... [was] entitled to a remedy from the Tribunal.'[138] Finally, the 'right to an initial appearance before a Trial Chamber or a Judge without delay',[139] as set forth in Rule 62 of the RPE, was found to have been violated in view of the 211-day delay between the Appellant's transfer to the ICTR and the initial appearance.[140] According to the Appeals Chamber, this violation was 'attributable to the Tribunal, notwithstanding any attribution of fault to the Appellant',[141] i.e. the Appellant's (alleged) contribution to the delay in assignment of counsel and, therefore, the delay in the initial appearance.[142] In this regard the Appeals Chamber noted that 'the Trial Chamber or Judge could [have] ordered the assignment of duty counsel to the Appellant for purposes of presentation at the initial appearance' and that 'the initial appearance was also delayed in part due to the fact that the Appellant had been jointly indicted with several other accused' as a result of which it was 'difficult ... to find a date acceptable to all ...'[143] Such violations, together with the violation of the Accused's other fundamental rights (the right to counsel),[144] meant that the Appellant was 'entitled to

---

[135] Ibid., para 231, referring to *Prosecutor v Kajelijeli* (Decision on the Defence Motion Concerning the Arbitrary Arrest and Illegal Detention of the Accused and on the Defence Notice of Urgent Motion to Expand and Supplement the Record of 8 December 1999 Hearing) ICTR-98-44-I, T Ch II (8 May 2000). See also paras 232–233 and 251.

[136] *Prosecutor v Kajelijeli* (Judgement) ICTR-98-44A-A, A Ch (23 May 2005) para 231. See also paras 232 and 251 in this regard.

[137] Ibid., para 232.

[138] Ibid., para 252 (emphasis added).

[139] Ibid., para 239.

[140] Ibid., para 250. According to the Appeals Chamber, this constituted 'extreme undue delay'.

[141] Ibid., para 253.

[142] Ibid., paras 247–249.

[143] Ibid., paras 248 and 249.

[144] Ibid., paras 243–245 and 253. This right is not discussed here since it is not sufficiently related to the topic of unlawful detention.

a remedy from the Tribunal',[145] since 'any violation of the accused's rights [requires] the provision of an effective remedy pursuant to Article 2(3)(a) of the ICCPR'.[146] On appeal from conviction, Juvénal Kajelijeli's original sentence (two life sentences and fifteen years) was converted into a single sentence consisting of a fixed term of imprisonment of 45 years.[147] The actual relief sought by the Defence (the dismissal of jurisdiction) was found to be disproportionate and dismissed for lack of 'egregiousness'.[148]

Regarding the case of *Rwamakuba*, it should be recalled that the Trial Chamber was not prepared to enquire into the conditions of the Accused's detention in Namibia, on the grounds that such detention had not been at the behest of the ICTR Prosecutor.[149] It was, however, prepared to enquire into alleged violations of the Accused's rights while in detention at the ICTR Detention Facility. Regarding the alleged delay in setting up the initial appearance of the Accused, the Trial Chamber held that, although the initial appearance had not been scheduled by Court Management without delay, as required under Rule 62 of the RPE, this delay was 'mainly attributable to the difficulties in having Counsel assigned to the Accused'.[150] Although the Registry was not responsible for the delay in assigning counsel to the Accused, the Trial Chamber found that the Registrar had failed 'to act pursuant to Rule 44*bis* so as to appoint a Duty Counsel for the Accused pending assignment of his Counsel pursuant to Rule 45 of the [RPE]'.[151] According to the Trial Chamber, '[t]his omission resulted in the absence of any legal assistance for the Accused over an extended period of time in contradiction with, notably Article 20(4)(c) of the [ICTR] Statute, and, further, in the delay of the Accused's initial appearance.'[152] However, the Trial Chamber did not consider that the 'delay in providing the Accused with legal representation and thus, in the initial appearance' had caused him 'serious and irreparable prejudice',[153] On interlocutory appeal, the

---

[145] Ibid., paras 252 and 253.

[146] Ibid., para 255.

[147] Ibid., paras 255 and 320–324.

[148] Ibid., para 255 in conjunction with para 206, referring to *Prosecutor v Barayagwiza* (Decision) ICTR-97-19-AR72, A Ch (3 November 1999) and *Prosecutor v Nikolić* (Decision on Interlocutory Appeal Concerning Legality of Arrest) IT-94-2-AR73, A Ch (5 June 2003).

[149] *Prosecutor v Rwamakuba and others* (Decision on the Defence Motion Concerning the Illegal Arrest and Illegal Detention of the Accused) ICTR-98-44-T, T Ch II (12 December 2000) paras 30, 33 and 45. See n 22 and accompanying text.

[150] Ibid., para 36.

[151] Ibid., paras 40 and 43.

[152] Ibid., para 43. According to the Appeals Chamber, Rwamakuba had not been offered the assistance of a duty counsel for a period of four months. See *Prosecutor v Rwamakuba* (Decision on Appeal against Decision on Appropriate Remedy) ICTR-98-44C-A, A Ch (13 September 2007) para 16.

[153] *Prosecutor v Rwamakuba and others* (Decision on the Defence Motion Concerning the Illegal Arrest and Illegal Detention of the Accused) ICTR-98-44-T, T Ch II (12 December 2000) para 44.

Appeals Chamber held that it would be 'open to the Appellant to invoke the issue of the alleged violation of his fundamental human rights *by the Tribunal* in order to seek reparation as the case may be, at the appropriate time'.[154] Upon acquittal,[155] André Rwamakuba sought such reparation before the Trial Chamber, which the Trial Chamber granted pursuant to its 'inherent power to give effect to an accused's or former accused's right to an effective remedy'.[156] Specifically, it ordered the Registrar to pay Rwamakuba financial compensation (US$2,000) on account of his responsibility for the violation of Rwamakuba's right to legal assistance in the initial months of detention.[157] The Trial Chamber's decision ordering financial compensation was confirmed on appeal.[158]

In addition to alleging the circumvention of prescribed national procedures,[159] the Accused in *Karadžić* alleged that his arrest by unknown individuals and subsequent *incommunicado* detention were 'arbitrary' and that his right to be informed promptly of the reasons for arrest and right to be brought promptly before the judicial authorities had been violated.[160] According to the Accused, the appropriate remedy was either financial compensation upon acquittal or sentence reduction upon conviction, for which he relied on the ICTR cases discussed above. However, the Trial Chamber was of the view that such matters had been raised prematurely and, therefore, it did not consider the merits. Nevertheless, it did make some observations on the issue of attribution (of the alleged violation of rights to the ad hoc Tribunals), in light of the arguments raised by the Accused in this regard. It 'noted' that,

> the major discussions and findings [in the relevant ICTR decisions in the cases of *Barayagwiza*, *Semanza* and *Kajelijeli*, as relied upon by the Accused Radovan Karadžić in support of his argument that rights violations need not be attributed to the *ad hoc* Tribunals] ultimately revolved around the Prosecution's responsibility for violations, rather than the responsibility of [S]tate authorities.[161]

According to the Trial Chamber there was 'substance in the Prosecution's submission that, before being able to obtain the remedy he seeks, the Accused has to be able to attribute the infringement of his rights to one of the organs of the Tribunal or show that at least some responsibility for that infringement lies with the

---

[154] *Prosecutor v Rwamakuba* (Decision (Appeal against Dismissal of Motion concerning Illegal Arrest and Detention)) ICTR-98-44-A, A Ch (11 June 2001) 4 (emphasis added).

[155] *Prosecutor v Rwamakuba* (Judgement) ICTR-98-44C-T, T Ch III (20 September 2006).

[156] *Prosecutor v Rwamakuba* (Decision on Appropriate Remedy) ICTR-98-44C-T, T Ch III (31 January 2007) para 58.

[157] Ibid., 23.

[158] *Prosecutor v Rwamakuba* (Decision on Appeal against Decision on Appropriate Remedy) ICTR-98-44C-A, A Ch (13 September 2007).

[159] See n 76 and accompanying text.

[160] *Prosecutor v Karadžić* (Decision on the Accused's Motion for Remedy for Violation of Rights in Connection with Arrest) IT-95-5/18-PT, T Ch III (31 August 2009) para 2.

[161] Ibid., para 6 n 17.

Tribunal'.[162] In this regard, the Trial Chamber noted that the ICTY 'does not have an enforcement agency, such as its own police force, which could effectuate arrest of persons against whom an indictment has been issued and confirmed by the Tribunal's organs' and, therefore, that 'it must rely on the international community for the arrest and transfer of such persons'.[163] The Trial Chamber further noted that the ICTR cases relied upon by the Accused, which 'concerned facts where suspects were detained by various states pursuant to requests from the Prosecution under Rule 40 [of the ICTR RPE], and then were left to languish in those states for months, while the Prosecution was preparing to issue an indictment against them', could be distinguished from (and, as such, are not directly applicable to) cases in which an 'arrest warrant [was] issued and executed pursuant to Rule 55 [of the ICTY RPE]'. The distinction appears to be based on the definition of the Tribunal's obligations in each of the aforementioned rules,[164] whereby the argument appears to be that, the more clearly defined the obligations of the Tribunal are, and, crucially, where such obligations have been complied with, the less likely violations of a suspect's or an accused's rights at the national level will be attributed to the Tribunal (and, accordingly, the less inclined the ad hoc Tribunals will be to accept responsibility for, i.e. to attach (legal) consequences to, such violations).[165] Accordingly, the Trial Chamber advised the Accused to present any 'material proving that the arrest took place on 18 July 2008 and that the actions of the Serbian authorities could be attributed to the Prosecution or any other Tribunal's organ' in his possession *at trial*.[166]

6.2.2 ICC

Having set out the relevant law and practice at the ad hoc Tribunals, i.e. the law and practice with respect to the question of how to address procedural violations committed in the context of arrest and detention, it is time to turn to that at the ICC. At the ICC, the arrest and detention of persons suspected or accused of crimes

---

[162] Ibid., para 6. Nevertheless, the Trial Chamber's language appears cautious in this regard.

[163] Ibid., para 6, referring to, *inter alia*, *Prosecutor v Barayagwiza* (Decision) ICTR-97-19-AR72, A Ch (3 November 1999) para 42.

[164] According to the Trial Chamber, while Rule 55 ICTR (and ICTY) RPE clearly defines such obligations, Rule 40 ICTR (and ICTY) RPE does not. See *Prosecutor v Karadžić* (Decision on the Accused's Motion for Remedy for Violation of Rights in Connection with Arrest) IT-95-5/18-PT, T Ch III (31 August 2009) para 6.

[165] Now that the obligations of the Prosecution under Rule 40 have been 'aligned ... with the obligations outlined in Rule 55', such argument would also appear to apply to Rule 40. See *Prosecutor v Karadžić* (Decision on the Accused's Motion for Remedy for Violation of Rights in Connection with Arrest) IT-95-5/18-PT, T Ch III (31 August 2009) para 6, referring to *Prosecutor v Kajelijeli* (Judgement) ICTR-98-44A-A, A Ch (23 May 2005) paras 220–223.

[166] *Prosecutor v Karadžić* (Decision on the Accused's Motion for Remedy for Violation of Rights in Connection with Arrest) IT-95-5/18-PT, T Ch III (31 August 2009) para 6 (emphasis added).

falling within its jurisdiction is governed by the ICC Statute and RPE,[167] as well as by relevant human rights standards.[168] The case law discussed here, then, concerns violations of the ICC's governing documents and/or relevant human rights standards.

Unlike the ad hoc Tribunals' governing documents, the ICC Statute does provide for a procedure for national authorities implementing an official request for 'provisional arrest *or* for arrest and surrender' by the ICC. Article 59 of the ICC Statute provides (in relevant part) that:

1. A State Party which has received a request for provisional arrest or for arrest and surrender shall immediately take steps to arrest the person in question in accordance with its laws and the provisions of Part 9 [of the ICC Statute].
2. A person arrested shall be brought promptly before the competent judicial authority in the custodial State which shall determine, in accordance with the law of that State, that:

   a. The warrant applies to that person;
   b. The person has been arrested in accordance with the proper process; and
   c. The person's rights have been respected.

The procedure provided for in Article 59 raises several questions that bear, directly or indirectly, on the question of how procedural violations committed in the pre-trial phase of international criminal proceedings should be addressed which are worth addressing briefly, before setting out the case law. For example, the question arises as to what options are available to the *national judicial authority* upon finding that the person has not been arrested in accordance with the proper process, or that that person's rights have not been respected. Article 59 is silent on this issue, and the case law does not provide an answer in this regard. It is therefore unclear whether a requested state is entitled to decline to surrender a person suspected of crimes falling within the jurisdiction of the ICC on the basis of an illegal or unlawful arrest. In the literature, the prevailing view seems to be that states could only exceptionally decline to surrender such a person to the ICC.[169] According to Currie, it is likely that

---

[167] Pursuant to Article 55(1)(d) ICC Statute, any deprivation of liberty of persons under investigation by the ICC be carried out 'on such grounds and in accordance with such procedures as are established in [the ICC Statute]'. The relevant 'procedures as are established' in the ICC Statute can be found in Article 58 (which is concerned with the issuance of warrants for arrest or provisional arrest and summonses to appear), Article 59 (which 'covers the intermediate stage', i.e. the arrest and surrender by the custodial state) and Article 60 (which is concerned with the continued detention at the seat of the ICC) ICC Statute. At the ICC, no provision is made for the arrest of a person *without* judicial authorization, i.e. a warrant of arrest issued by the Pre-Trial Chamber (see Article 58(5) ICC Statute), which may be contrasted to the law of the ad hoc Tribunals. See in this regard n 9 and accompanying text. However, '[i]n urgent cases, the Court may request the provisional arrest of the person sought, pending presentation of the request for surrender and the documents supporting the request as specified in … [the ICC Statute]', whereby a time-limit of 60 days applies. For a comprehensive overview of the standards governing arrest and detention at the ICC, see De Meester 2014, Chap. 7.

[168] Regarding the latter, most obviously: the right to personal liberty, as provided for in Articles 9 and 5 of the ICCPR and ECHR, respectively.

[169] See in this regard De Meester 2014, 647.

the 'intention is for ICC to deal with any arrest irregularities *itself*, which he argues is apparent from the provision in Article 85(1) of the ICC Statute,[170] which provides that: 'Anyone who has been the victim of unlawful arrest or detention shall have an enforceable right to compensation.' The fact that the ICC Statute provides for a procedure for national authorities implementing an official ICC request for provisional arrest or for arrest and surrender, whereby the national judicial authority is *required* to make certain determinations,[171] implies that the ICC has a supervisory role in relation to this procedure. While the ICC Statute is silent on this matter, the Appeals Chamber has confirmed that the ICC has such a role, whereby it is the Court's task to 'see that the *process envisaged by ... [national] law* was duly followed and that the rights of the arrestee were properly respected'.[172] However, according to the Appeals Chamber, it 'does not sit in on the process ... as a court of appeal' on the decision of the national judicial authority.[173] This suggests that the review to be conducted by the Court is marginal in nature. Indeed, it seems that it is for '*national authorities* to have primary jurisdiction for interpreting and applying national law', which presumably encompasses the human rights obligations that flow from the treaties to which the state concerned is a party,[174] while the Court retains 'a degree of jurisdiction over how the national authorities interpret and apply *national law* when such an interpretation and application relates to matters which ... are referred directly back to that national law by the Statute'.[175] In another case, it was held that the Court's role with respect to Article 59 proceedings in the custodial state 'is limited to verifying that the basic safeguards envisaged *by national law* have been made available to the arrested person'.[176] More will be said about the procedure in Article 59 and the supervisory role of the ICC in this regard below.

Turning now to the case law, allegations of illegal or unlawful arrest and/or detention have been made in several cases before the ICC.[177] In *Lubanga*, it was

---

[170] Currie 2007, 374.

[171] Indeed, Article 59(2) provides that 'the custodial State ... *shall*' make such determinations.

[172] *Prosecutor v Lubanga* (Judgment on the Appeal of Mr. Thomas Lubanga Dyilo against the Decision on the Defence Challenge to the Jurisdiction of the Court pursuant to Article 19(2)(a) of the Statute of 3 October 2006) ICC-01/04-01/06, A Ch (14 December 2006) para 41 (emphasis added).

[173] Ibid., para 41.

[174] Nevertheless, De Meester laments that the Appeals Chamber does not expressly refer to rights in this context. See De Meester 2014, 645 n 189.

[175] *Prosecutor v Lubanga* (Decision on the Defence Challenge to the Jurisdiction of the Court pursuant to Article 19(2)(a) of the Statute) ICC-01/04-01/06, P T Ch I (3 October 2006) 6 (emphasis added).

[176] *Prosecutor v Gbagbo* (Decision on the "Corrigendum of the challenge to the jurisdiction of the International Criminal Court on the basis of Articles 12(3), 19(2), 21(3), 55 and 59 of the Rome Statute filed by the Defence for President Gbagbo (ICC-02/11-01/11-129)") ICC-02/11-01/11, P T Ch I (15 August 2012) para 104 (emphasis added).

[177] While in setting out the law and practice of the ad hoc Tribunals with respect to the question of how to address procedural violations arising in the context of arrest and detention it was instructive to distinguish between unlawful *arrest* cases and unlawful *detention* cases (see in this regard n 31

alleged that procedural violations were committed during two distinct periods, namely, (i) the arrest by the DRC authorities on 13 August 2003 and subsequent detention of Thomas Lubanga Dyilo in the DRC prior to 16 March 2006, in connection with proceedings before the DRC military courts; and (ii) the execution of the ICC's request for the arrest and surrender of Lubanga, sent to the DRC on 14 March 2006. In relation to the first period, the Defence alleged, in particular, that Lubanga's rights to be informed promptly of the reasons for arrest and to be brought promptly before the judicial authorities had been violated, as well as various other irregularities in the process of arresting and detaining him. In relation to the second period, the Defence alleged violations of Article 59 of the ICC Statute, including that, in executing the ICC's request for arrest and surrender, the DRC (enforcement) authorities had failed to comply with the relevant national law, that Lubanga had not been brought before the proper national judicial authority and, finally, that such authority failed to determine that he had not been arrested in accordance with the relevant national law and that his rights had not been respected. The relief sought in respect of such violations was the setting aside of jurisdiction, i.e. a permanent stay of proceedings. Turning first to the Pre-Trial Chamber's consideration of the second period of detention, it found that Lubanga had been promptly brought before the proper judicial authority, who had notified Lubanga that he was under arrest pursuant to an arrest warrant issued by the ICC, provided him with all materials attached to the ICC's request for cooperation (and, seemingly, read the arrest warrant to him), including a copy of the arrest warrant and a copy of the relevant provisions of the ICC Statute and RPE, including those relating to his rights, and heard his challenge to the arrest (and subsequent detention). It found 'no material breach of [A]rticle 59(2) of the Statute ... in the procedure followed by the competent Congolese national authorities during the execution of the ... [ICC's request for cooperation]'.[178] These findings were upheld on interlocutory appeal; the Appeals Chamber found as follows:

> In this case, the Pre-Trial Chamber determined that the process followed accorded with Congolese law. There is nothing to contradict this statement in light of the fact that the suspect was in custody for crimes coming within the purview of the military authorities. The suspect was afforded an opportunity to voice his views before the judicial authority that examined the request for his surrender. Moreover, there is nothing to indicate that his arrest or appearance before the Congolese authority involved or entailed any violation of his rights.[179]

As to the first period (i.e. the period *prior to* the execution of the ICC request for arrest and surrender), the Pre-Trial Chamber noted that 'Article 21(3) of the [ICC] Statute states that the "application and interpretation of law pursuant to this article must be

---

(Footnote 177 continued)

and accompanying text), the distinction is less visible in the case law of the ICC. Accordingly, in setting out the relevant law and practice of the ICC, no such distinction will be made.

[178] *Prosecutor v Lubanga* (Decision on the Defence Challenge to the Jurisdiction of the Court pursuant to Article 19(2)(a) of the Statute) ICC-01/04-01/06, P T Ch I (3 October 2006) 9.

[179] *Prosecutor v Lubanga* (Judgment on the Appeal of Mr. Thomas Lubanga Dyilo against the Decision on the Defence Challenge to the Jurisdiction of the Court pursuant to Article 19(2)(a) of the Statute of 3 October 2006) ICC-01/04-01/06, A Ch (14 December 2006) para 41.

consistent with internationally recognized human rights"', which meant that any violations of Lubanga's rights in relation to this period would be 'examined by the Court only once it has been established that there has been *concerted action* between the Court and the DRC authorities'.[180] In the absence of such 'concerted action', the abuse of process doctrine could lead to the setting aside of jurisdiction, upon showing that Lubanga had been subjected to 'torture or serious mistreatment' by the DRC authorities.[181] According to the Pre-Trial Chamber, the application of the abuse of process doctrine at the ICTs had been 'confined to instances of torture or serious mistreatment by national authorities of the custodial State in some way related to the process of arrest and transfer of the person to the relevant international criminal tribunal'.[182] However, according to the Pre-Trial Chamber, 'no issues … [had] arisen [as] to any alleged act of torture or serious mistreatment' of the Accused; nor was there any evidence to indicate that the arrest and detention in the first period was the result of any concerted action between the ICC and the DRC. Accordingly, the remedy sought by the Defence was denied.[183] These (factual) findings were upheld by the Appeals Chamber,[184] following a consideration of the availability of a permanent stay of proceedings at the ICC.[185] In this regard the Appeals Chamber held that:

> Where fair trial becomes impossible because of breaches of the fundamental rights of the suspect or the accused by his/her accusers, it would be a contradiction in terms to put the person on trial. Justice could not be done. A fair trial is the only means to do justice. If no fair trial can be held, the object of the judicial process is frustrated and the process must be stopped.[186]

Further down in the (same) decision, it held that:

> Where the breaches of the rights of the accused are such as to make it impossible for him/her to make his/her defence within the framework of his rights, no fair trial can take place and the proceedings can be stayed. … Unfairness in the treatment of the suspect or the accused may rupture the process to an extent making it impossible to piece together the constituent elements of a fair trial.[187]

---

[180] *Prosecutor v Lubanga* (Decision on the Defence Challenge to the Jurisdiction of the Court pursuant to Article 19(2)(a) of the Statute) ICC-01/04-01/06, P T Ch I (3 October 2006) 9 (emphasis added). Earlier on in the decision, it had held that Article 59(2) ICC Statute did not impose an obligation on the national authorities to review the lawfulness of the arrest and detention of Lubanga in the period prior to the execution of the ICC request for arrest and surrender (ibid., 6).

[181] Ibid., 10.

[182] Ibid., 10.

[183] Ibid., 10–11.

[184] *Prosecutor v Lubanga* (Judgment on the Appeal of Mr. Thomas Lubanga Dyilo against the Decision on the Defence Challenge to the Jurisdiction of the Court pursuant to Article 19(2)(a) of the Statute of 3 October 2006) ICC-01/04-01/06, A Ch (14 December 2006) paras 42–43.

[185] See generally Chap. 5, Sect. 5.3.1.1.

[186] *Prosecutor v Lubanga* (Judgment on the Appeal of Mr. Thomas Lubanga Dyilo against the Decision on the Defence Challenge to the Jurisdiction of the Court pursuant to Article 19(2)(a) of the Statute of 3 October 2006) ICC-01/04-01/06, A Ch (14 December 2006) para 37.

[187] Ibid., para 39.

As stated in the previous chapter, it appears that the references to 'fair trial' in at least the first of the statements are to be 'perceived and applied' broadly, to '[embrace] the judicial process in its entirety'.[188] Accordingly, it seems that a fair trial may become impossible due to 'violations of the rights of the accused *in the process of bringing him/her to justice*', i.e. in the process of exercising jurisdiction over the accused,[189] even if such violations do not affect the ability of the accused to mount an effective defence and, in this sense, prevent an accused from receiving a fair trial.[190] The first statement suggests that, in order for breaches of the accused's rights to lead to a (permanent) stay of proceedings, (an organ of) the ICC must have been involved in the violation in some way; after all, the question that needs to be answered is whether a fair has become impossible due to 'breaches of the fundamental rights of the suspect or the accused *by his/her accusers*'. In *Lubanga*, it seems, the Prosecutor had *not* been involved in the investigations carried out by the Congolese authorities (in connection with proceedings before the DRC military courts), so that the Pre-Trial Chamber's finding regarding the lack of concerted action between the ICC and the Congolese authorities could not be said to be erroneous in any way. Accordingly, the Appeals Chamber seemed to confirm the Pre-Trial Chamber's finding that violations committed prior to the transmission of the official request for cooperation would be examined by the ICC only once it has been established that there has been *concerted action* between the ICC and the relevant national authorities.[191] According to the Appeals Chamber, the 'material before the Pre-Trial Chamber … [regarding] communications between the Prosecutor and the … [Democratic Republic of Congo] did not reveal any *impropriety* on the part of the former'.[192] In this regard the Appeals Chamber observed that '[m]ere knowledge on the part of the Prosecutor of the investigations carried out by the Congolese authorities is no proof of involvement on his part in

---

[188] Ibid., para 37. See also *Prosecutor v Lubanga* (Judgment on the appeal of Mr. Thomas Lubanga Dyilo against his conviction) ICC-01/04-01/06, A Ch (1 December 2014) para 147.

[189] *Prosecutor v Lubanga* (Judgment on the Appeal of Mr. Thomas Lubanga Dyilo against the Decision on the Defence Challenge to the Jurisdiction of the Court pursuant to Article 19(2)(a) of the Statute of 3 October 2006) ICC-01/04-01/06, A Ch (14 December 2006) paras 36 and 44.

[190] See Chap. 5, n 246–252 and accompanying text.

[191] Essentially, this means that, in cases in which torture or serious mistreatment are alleged aside (see n 182–183 and accompanying text, and see *Prosecutor v Lubanga* (Judgment on the Appeal of Mr. Thomas Lubanga Dyilo against the Decision on the Defence Challenge to the Jurisdiction of the Court pursuant to Article 19(2)(a) of the Statute of 3 October 2006) ICC-01/04-01/06, A Ch (14 December 2006) para 43), the 'Court is not responsible for detention in the custodial State which was not at the behest of the tribunal'. See De Meester 2014, 650. He argues that: the 'inherent risk' of such a position is that 'it may lead to a situation whereby the ICC Registrar postpones the sending of the request for arrest and surrender until such time that he or she knows that the person can immediately be surrendered'. In this way 'the Court can avoid incurring responsibility for pre-transfer violations of the suspect'. Ibid., 652.

[192] *Prosecutor v Lubanga* (Judgment on the Appeal of Mr. Thomas Lubanga Dyilo against the Decision on the Defence Challenge to the Jurisdiction of the Court pursuant to Article 19(2)(a) of the Statute of 3 October 2006) ICC-01/04-01/06, A Ch (14 December 2006) para 42 (emphasis added).

the way they were conducted or the means including detention used for the pur-pose', and said that it was worth recalling 'that the crimes for which Mr. Lubanga Dyilo was detained by the Congolese authority were separate and distinct from those which led to the issuance of the warrant for his arrest'.[193] In the end, the Appeals Chamber concluded that the Appellant had failed to show any breaches of his rights as to warrant 'halting the process'.[194]

In *Katanga and Ngudjolo*, counsel for the Accused Germain Katanga had alleged numerous rights violations in the context of his detention in the DRC, both before and after the issuance by the ICC of the arrest warrant against him. The relief sought was 'a stay or termination of the proceedings' or, alternatively, financial compensation and/or (in the event of a conviction only) sentence reduction. The Defence *first* raised the alleged violations (and sought the aforementioned relief) just prior to the com-mencement of trial; however, according to the Trial Chamber, such allegations had been raised, and the relief sought, at too late a stage in the proceedings.[195] Accordingly, the Defence motion was dismissed, without considering the merits of the parties' submissions. The Appeals Chamber upheld the Trial Chamber's decision.[196] Some of the Chambers' observations and findings are worth noting here. First, this was 'the first case before [the ICC] where the question of the timing for motions alleging unlawful pre-surrender arrest and detention and seeking a stay of proceedings arises'.[197] Regarding such timing, the Trial Chamber held that 'a challenge to the lawfulness of the arrest and detention of an accused, in particular where such a challenge is accompanied by an application to stay or terminate the proceedings, must be submitted in the initial phase of the proceedings'.[198] According to the Trial Chamber, it was 'in the interests of all, and primarily of the suspects who have been deprived of their liberty, that the issue of the possible unlawfulness of their detention be raised and addressed as early as possible during the pre-trial phase'.[199] This approach was confirmed on appeal, with the Appeals Chamber holding that '[i]t is consistent with the role of the Pre-Trial Chamber and the purpose of the confirmation proceedings that, in the absence of any provision to the contrary, motions alleging

---

[193] Ibid., para 42.

[194] Ibid., para 44.

[195] See *Prosecutor v Katanga and Ngudjolo* (Public redacted version of the "Decision on the Motion of the Defence for Germain Katanga for a Declaration on Unlawful Detention and Stay of Proceedings" of 20 November 2009 (ICC-01/04-01/07-1666-Conf-Exp)) ICC-01/04-01/07, T Ch II (3 December 2009).

[196] *Prosecutor v Katanga and Ngudjolo* (Judgment on the Appeal of Mr. Katanga Against the Decision of Trial Chamber II of 20 November 2009 Entitled "Decision on the Motion of the Defence for Germain Katanga for a Declaration on Unlawful Detention and Stay of Proceedings") ICC-01/04-01/07, A Ch (12 July 2010).

[197] Ibid., para 51.

[198] *Prosecutor v Katanga and Ngudjolo* (Public redacted version of the "Decision on the Motion of the Defence for Germain Katanga for a Declaration on Unlawful Detention and Stay of Proceedings" of 20 November 2009 (ICC-01/04-01/07-1666-Conf-Exp)) ICC-01/04-01/07, T Ch II (3 December 2009) para 39.

[199] Ibid., para 40.

unlawful pre-surrender arrest and detention and seeking a stay of proceedings should be brought during the pre-trial phase of the proceedings.'[200] Only in exceptional circumstances will the accused be permitted to raise his or her alleged unlawful arrest, surrender or pre-trial detention at the trial stage.[201] Second, the Appeals Chamber's findings regarding the 'principle of proportionality' are of interest. According to the Defence, the Trial Chamber's decision (not to consider the merits of the Defence's allegations) was disproportionate 'given the importance of the issue he sought to litigate', and because the Trial Chamber 'could have decided his request for compensation and/or mitigation of his sentence in case of conviction without "effecting the process"'.[202] Regarding the first allegation of disproportionality, the Appeals Chamber found that the Trial Chamber had 'appropriately balanced Mr. Katanga's rights and the need for expeditiousness'.[203] Regarding the second, the Appeals Chamber held that 'Mr. Katanga had [had] an adequate and effective opportunity to present [his allegations of unlawful arrest and/or detention]'and that, in this context, 'it is irrelevant … that he sought several remedies'.[204] Following Katanga's conviction on 7 March 2014,[205] the Defence raised the (alleged) violations of his rights while detained in the DRC (again, both before and after the issuance by the ICC of the arrest warrant against him) in the context of the sentencing proceedings. It argued that such violations warranted a reduction of sentence. It is worth reproducing the Trial Chamber's findings in this regard:

> The Chamber considers that, should it be established that the convicted person's fundamental rights were violated, it would indeed be appropriate to take that into account in mitigation of the sentence to be imposed on him. However, it considers that the Statute in no way authorises the Court to rule on the legality of Congolese detention procedures or to consider whether they were flawed by violations. As a result, the Chamber cannot rule on alleged violations of Germain Katanga's rights to which he was subjected in the DRC *while he was not in detention on behalf of the Court.*[206]

---

[200] *Prosecutor v Katanga and Ngudjolo* (Judgment on the Appeal of Mr. Katanga Against the Decision of Trial Chamber II of 20 November 2009 Entitled "Decision on the Motion of the Defence for Germain Katanga for a Declaration on Unlawful Detention and Stay of Proceedings") ICC-01/04-01/07, A Ch (12 July 2010) para 41.

[201] Ibid., para 48.

[202] Ibid., para 24.

[203] Ibid., para 64.

[204] Ibid., para 66.

[205] See *Prosecutor v Katanga* (Judgment pursuant to Article 74 of the Statute) ICC-01/04-01/07, T Ch II (7 March 2014).

[206] *Prosecutor v Katanga* (Decision on Sentence pursuant to Article 76 of the Statute) ICC-01/04-01/07, T Ch II (23 May 2014) para 136 (emphasis added, footnotes in original omitted). See also para 138: 'In the case in point, and as elaborated upon hereunder, the Court considers that Germain Katanga's detention on behalf of the Court commenced on 18 September 2007. The Court therefore considers that the time in detention in the DRC before this date was not spent on behalf of the Court and it will therefore analyze possible violations only as from 18 September 2007.'

Next the Trial Chamber held that:

> However, regarding the period during which Germain Katanga was in detention on its behalf, the Chamber considers that violations may be imputable to the Court only where they concern a procedure undertaken before it. The Chamber will not entertain any violations of Germain Katanga's rights where such violations are unconnected to proceedings before it, even if they were committed during his detention on behalf of the Court.[207]

According to the Trial Chamber, Katanga's detention on behalf of the ICC 'commenced on 18 September 2007'.[208] The Defence had argued that, during the interview preceding his transfer on 17 October 2007, Katanga was not assisted by counsel. However, the Trial Chamber found that, contrary to the Defence submissions, he *had* been assisted by counsel at the time of his arrest and surrender to the ICC.[209]

In *Gbagbo*, counsel for the Accused Laurent Gbagbo alleged that he had been 'subjected to arbitrary arrest and detention by the Ivorian authorities' in the period between 11 April 2011 and 29 November 2011 (including the period between the receipt by the Ivorian authorities of the ICC request for arrest and surrender on 25 November 2011, and Gbagbo's transfer to The Hague on 29 November 2011) and that, during this time, he had been 'subjected to conditions of detention amounting to inhuman and degrading treatment as well as torture', all in violation of Article 55 of the ICC Statute.[210] In addition, the surrender proceedings that took place on 29 November 2011 before an Ivorian judicial authority had been tainted by various procedural irregularities, in violation of Article 59(2) of the ICC Statute.[211] Regarding the period between 11 April and 29 November 2011, the Defence alleged, *inter alia*, that lawful procedures had been circumvented in arresting Gbagbo, that he had not been informed of the reasons for his arrest or detention, that he had not been brought before the judicial authorities to challenge the lawfulness of his detention, and that during this period he had been denied (adequate) access to counsel.[212] Furthermore, the Defence alleged that the condition of Gbagbo's detention in Côte d'Ivoire constituted inhuman and degrading treatment, and torture.[213] As to the surrender proceedings and the alleged violation of Article 59(2), the Defence submitted that 'the arrest to be taken into account pursuant to [A]rticle 59(2) of the [ICC] Statute is … the one which took place on 11 April 2011', i.e. prior to the receipt by the Ivorian authorities of the ICC request for arrest

---

[207] Ibid., para 137 (footnotes in original omitted).

[208] Ibid., para 138.

[209] Ibid., para 139.

[210] *Prosecutor v Gbagbo* (Decision on the "Corrigendum of the challenge to the jurisdiction of the International Criminal Court on the basis of Articles 12(3), 19(2), 21(3), 55 and 59 of the Rome Statute filed by the Defence for President Gbagbo (ICC-02/11-01/11-129)") ICC-02/11-01/11, P T Ch I (15 August 2012) para 68.

[211] Ibid., para 70.

[212] Ibid., para 71.

[213] Ibid., para 72.

and surrender on 25 November 2011.[214] In addition, the Defence alleged certain 'flagrant' rights violations by the Ivorian authorities in this context, which the Pre-Trial Chamber summed up as follows: 'lack of time to prepare for [the surrender hearing]; the lack of any possibility for Mr. Gbagbo's lawyers to make submissions on the legality of the surrender; the lack of proper reasoning and he incorrect legal basis used by the Ivorian court in its decision; the lack of impartiality by the Ivorian Judges during the hearing and in the course of their deliberations'; and the fact Gbagbo's 'immediate transfer ... to The Hague ... was inconsistent with the suspensive effect of an appeal against a surrender decision under Ivorian law'.[215] According to the Defence, the violations in period between 11 April and 29 November 2011 could be attributed to the Prosecutor,[216] while the violations connected to the surrender proceedings could be attributed to the Registry.[217] In view of the fact that the cumulative effect of such violations rendered the proceedings against Gbagbo unfair, and undermined the integrity and the legitimacy of international justice, the Defence sought a permanent stay of proceedings.[218] Turning first to the relief sought, the Pre-Trial Chamber confirmed the Appeals Chamber's findings in *Lubanga* regarding the availability of a permanent stay of proceedings at the ICC,[219] and reiterated that 'a permanent stay of proceedings is a remedy of an exceptional nature' and that 'not every infraction of the law or breach of the rights of the suspect will give rise to abuse of process'.[220] Most significantly, the Pre-Trial Chamber held that attribution of the violation(s) to the ICC is a prerequisite for a permanent stay of proceedings. According to the Pre-Trial Chamber,

> violations of fundamental rights, however serious, can have the requisite impact on the proceedings to constitute an abuse of process *only insofar as they can be attributed to the Court*. Attribution in this sense means that the act of violation of fundamental rights is: (i) either directly perpetrated by persons associated with the Court; or (ii) perpetrated by

---

[214] Ibid., para 73.

[215] Ibid., para 74.

[216] Ibid., paras 75 and 111.

[217] Ibid., para 75.

[218] Ibid., para 76.

[219] Ibid., para 89, referring to *Prosecutor v Lubanga* (Judgment on the Appeal of Mr. Thomas Lubanga Dyilo against the Decision on the Defence Challenge to the Jurisdiction of the Court pursuant to Article 19(2)(a) of the Statute of 3 October 2006) ICC-01/04-01/06, A Ch (14 December 2006) para 37. The Pre-Trial Chamber also referred to other 'tests' developed at the *national* level and referred to by the Appeals Chamber in *Lubanga*, but which the Appeals Chamber did not adopt as such. See ibid., paras 89 n 135, 91 n 137 and n 138.

[220] *Prosecutor v Gbagbo* (Decision on the "Corrigendum of the challenge to the jurisdiction of the International Criminal Court on the basis of Articles 12(3), 19(2), 21(3), 55 and 59 of the Rome Statute filed by the Defence for President Gbagbo (ICC-02/11-01/11-129)") ICC-02/11-01/11, P T Ch I (15 August 2012) para 91.

third persons in collusion with the Court. Conversely, when a violation of the suspect's fundamental rights, however grave, is established, but demonstrates no such link with the Court, the exceptional remedy of staying the proceedings is not available.[221]

In so holding, the Pre-Trial Chamber suggested that, as far as a permanent stay of proceedings is concerned, the gravity of the violation(s) cannot make up for a lack of involvement of the ICC or otherwise for the inability to attribute the violation to the ICC. Equally, being able to attribute the rights violation in question to the ICC is not sufficient for a stay of proceedings; the violation(s) must be *grave*.[222] In ascertaining whether Gbagbo's rights had been violated, the Pre-Trial Chamber turned first to Articles 55 and 59 of the ICC Statute, which confer on suspects certain rights during the investigation and arrest proceedings, respectively, and which the Defence alleged had been violated. In this regard, it pointed out that 'not every violation of Articles 55 and 59 … would lead, per se, to the Court being required to decline to exercise jurisdiction, but only such violations that would amount, by themselves, or in combination with other circumstances, to an abuse of process'.[223] It then found that Article 55, which is applicable 'in respect of an investigation under [the ICC Statute]', did not apply to the period in question.[224] Similarly, Article 59 was only found to apply from the moment Gbagbo was notified by the Ivorian authorities of the arrest warrant against him;[225] in respect of the period to which Article 59 did apply, the Pre-Trial Chamber found that Gbagbo's rights had been respected.[226] It then turned to the question of whether there had been 'any other breach of Mr. Gbagbo's fundamental rights', i.e. whether a violation of Gbagbo's rights could be established other than through Articles 55 and 59, 'that … [could] be attributed to the Court and that … [was] so odious and repugnant to the rule of law as to make a fair trial impossible'.[227] In answering this question, the Pre-Trial Chamber focussed exclusively on the issue of attribution. It held that:

> [N]othing in the material brought before the Chamber shows any involvement on the part of the Court in the detention of Mr Gbagbo in Côte d'Ivoire *following his arrest on 11 April 2011. With respect to the period of detention prior to the notification of the request for arrest and surrender of Mr Gbagbo*, the Chamber notes that Mr Gbagbo was not detained at the behest of Court nor did the Court have any involvement with the domestic proceedings of the Ivorian authorities.[228]

In this regard it referred to the Appeals Chamber's finding in *Lubanga* that '[m]ere knowledge on the part of the Prosecutor of the investigations carried out by the

---

[221] Ibid., para 92.

[222] Ibid., para 93.

[223] Ibid., para 93.

[224] Ibid., paras 96–97.

[225] Ibid., paras 99–102.

[226] Ibid., paras 103–106.

[227] Ibid., para 107.

[228] Ibid., para 108.

[national] authorities is no proof of involvement on his part in the way they were conducted or the means including detention used for the purpose,' and added that, '[i]n the same vein, the mere fact that the Prosecutor was in contact with the Ivorian authorities does not suggest that there was any involvement of the Prosecutor in the detention of Mr. Gbagbo'.[229] In relation to the period between the notification of the request for arrest and surrender of Gbagbo and his transfer to The Hague, the Pre-Trial Chamber held that:

> During this period, he was still detained by the Ivorian authorities and the conditions of his detention were within their competence. In particular, while the organs of the Court were involved in the process of surrender of Mr Gbagbo to the Court, there is no evidence indicating any violation of Mr Gbagbo's fundamental rights that can in any way be attributed to the Court.[230]

Regarding the Defence's argument that the Prosecutor was under a 'duty of care' as concerns the Accused while he was being detained in Côte d'Ivoire, the Pre-Trial was 'unpersuaded' by it; in its view, 'the powers of the Prosecutor may only be exercised in the context of, or in relation to, proceedings before the Court'.[231] According to the Pre-Trial Chamber, 'in the absence of any involvement on the part of the Court in the detention of Mr. Gbagbo in Côte d'Ivoire' it could not 'proceed to a determination of any particular violation of Mr. Gbagbo's fundamental rights during his detention'.[232] As such, it was 'unnecessary [for it] to address the remaining requirements for [a permanent stay of proceedings] …'[233] The Defence application for a permanent stay of proceedings was rejected.

Finally, the Trial Chamber's findings in *Muthaura and Kenyatta* are worth noting here. In that case, an individual had alleged that he had been unlawfully arrested by Kenyan authorities on suspicion of the intimidation of prosecution witnesses in two ICC cases. The Trial Chamber held that 'in order for the Chamber to make a finding of unlawful arrest pursuant to Article 85(1) of the Statute, a domestic arrest must breach *a provision of the Court's statutory framework and be attributable in some way to the Court.*'[234] In its view,

---

[229] Ibid., para 109, referring to *Prosecutor v Lubanga* (Judgment on the Appeal of Mr. Thomas Lubanga Dyilo against the Decision on the Defence Challenge to the Jurisdiction of the Court pursuant to Article 19(2)(a) of the Statute of 3 October 2006) ICC-01/04-01/06, A Ch (14 December 2006) para 42.

[230] *Prosecutor v Gbagbo* (Decision on the "Corrigendum of the challenge to the jurisdiction of the International Criminal Court on the basis of Articles 12(3), 19(2), 21(3), 55 and 59 of the Rome Statute filed by the Defence for President Gbagbo (ICC-02/11-01/11-129)") ICC-02/11-01/11, P T Ch I (15 August 2012) para 110.

[231] Ibid., para 111.

[232] Ibid., para 112.

[233] Ibid., para 112.

[234] *Prosecutor v Muthaura and Kenyatta* (Decision on the application for a ruling on the legality of the arrest of Mr. Dennis Ole Itumbi) ICC-01/09-02/11, T Ch V (19 November 2012) para 6. Article 85(1) ICC Statute provides that: 'Anyone who has been the victim of unlawful arrest or detention shall have an enforceable right to compensation.'

[a]lthough Article 85(1) is broadly framed … its meaning and application must be interpreted in light of other relevant provisions of the [ICC] Statute. In particular … Article 85 (1) must in this case be read together with Article 55(1)(d) of the Statute, which protects persons from arbitrary arrest or detention "in respect of an investigation under this Statute". Furthermore, the Chamber considers that the right guaranteed under Article 55(l)(d) does not extend to every arrest or detention that related in any way to an investigation by the Court. Rather, in the view of the Chamber, in order for an arrest or detention to be "in respect of an investigation" within the meaning of Article 55(l)(d), it would need to be demonstrated, at minimum, that there is concerted action between the Court and national authorities.[235]

Regarding the last point, it ruled that 'in order to obtain a finding under Article 85 (1) of the Statute it is insufficient to establish that a person's arrest is merely "connected with Court proceedings" in the absence of concerted action',[236] whereby '[m]ere knowledge on the part of the Prosecutor of the investigations carried out by the Congolese authorities is no proof of involvement on his part in the way they were conducted or the means including detention used for the purpose.'[237] On the facts, there was no 'concerted action': the Trial Chamber was not satisfied that the arrest and detention by the Kenyan authorities, even assuming that it had taken place as alleged, was '"instigated" or otherwise requested by the prosecution or any other organ of the Court', and while there was evidence that the Applicant was being investigated by Kenyan authorities 'for matters connected with this Court's proceedings', this was insufficient for the purposes of Article 85(1) of the ICC Statute.[238] In other words, the Applicant had not been 'arrested in a manner attributable to the Prosecution or any other organ of the ICC'; accordingly, the application had to be rejected.[239]

6.2.3   Comparison and Analysis

Having set out the relevant law and practice with respect to the question of how to address procedural violations committed in the context of arrest and detention at the ad hoc Tribunals, and that at the ICC, respectively, the question that now needs to be answered is how the law and practice at the ad hoc Tribunals compares to that at the ICC (and vice versa). The purpose of the present subsection, then, is to compare

---

[235] *Prosecutor v Muthaura and Kenyatta* (Decision on the application for a ruling on the legality of the arrest of Mr. Dennis Ole Itumbi) ICC-01/09-02/11, T Ch V (19 November 2012) para 7.

[236] Ibid., para 9.

[237] Ibid., para 8, where the Trial Chamber refers to *Prosecutor v Lubanga* (Judgment on the Appeal of Mr. Thomas Lubanga Dyilo against the Decision on the Defence Challenge to the Jurisdiction of the Court pursuant to Article 19(2)(a) of the Statute of 3 October 2006) ICC-01/04-01/06, A Ch (14 December 2006) para 42.

[238] *Prosecutor v Muthaura and Kenyatta* (Decision on the application for a ruling on the legality of the arrest of Mr. Dennis Ole Itumbi) ICC-01/09-02/11, T Ch V (19 November 2012) para 9.

[239] Ibid., para 10.

the approaches of the ad hoc Tribunals and the ICC to the aforementioned question, and to (critically) analyse such law and practice (with a view to providing a more complete picture of the law and practice with respect to the question of how to address procedural violations committed in the context of arrest and detention, not in order to argue what the law and practice *should* be). DeFrancia has observed that, '[w]hen a Tribunal with no enforcement powers relies on the assistance of States to arrest and detain suspects, the question will inevitably arise as to *who is responsible* for due process violations committed while the detainee is not squarely in the custody of the requesting institution.'[240] This question of 'responsibility' is inevitably tied up with the question of how procedural violations committed in the pre-trial phase of international criminal proceedings should be addressed. Indeed, in a very general sense, the attachment of consequences to such violations may be seen to signify the acceptance of responsibility for them. However, in order for an international criminal tribunal to be able to accept *responsibility* for such violations, it would seem necessary for it to *enquire* into the circumstances surrounding the alleged violation, i.e. to examine the legality or lawfulness of the measure in question. The concepts of 'responsibility' and 'enquiry' provide useful tools by which to analyse the case law of the ICTs with respect to (alleged) unlawful arrest and detention, and in order to facilitate the comparison referred to above, they will be employed here. It may be observed at the outset that, in order to accept responsibility for a violation, more may be required than that which justified an enquiry into the (alleged) violation in the first place, or (than) the fact that a violation has occurred.

It was stated above that the Statutes and RPEs of the ad hoc Tribunals are silent on how national authorities are to implement an arrest warrant, or a request for provisional arrest and detention (as provided for in Rule 40 of the ICTY and ICTR RPEs) emanating from such a tribunal.[241] However, as was seen above, this has not prevented accused persons from bringing alleged illegality or unlawfulness in the course of their arrest or ongoing detention by national authorities to the ad hoc Tribunals' attention, or from seeking relief in this regard. The position of the ad hoc Tribunals with respect to such applications may be summed up as follows. At the ICTR at least, trial chambers appear to be unwilling to enquire into the circumstances surrounding an alleged illegal or unlawful *arrest* implemented by national authorities at the request (pursuant to Rule 40 of the ICTR RPE) of the ICTR Prosecutor, for the purpose of determining an application for relief in this regard.[242] The argument appears to be that they lack jurisdiction over the conditions of an arrest carried out by a sovereign state (even if carried out pursuant to the ICTR's request). By contrast, they *have* been willing to enquire into the circumstances

---

[240] DeFrancia 2001, 1404 (emphasis added).

ICTs have also relied on the cooperation of international organizations to obtain custody of persons suspected of having committed international crimes. For a detailed review of this practice, see Zhou 2006.

[241] See n 8–9 and accompanying text.

[242] See n 14–19 and accompanying text.

surrounding the alleged illegal or unlawful *detention* of a suspect by national authorities at the ICTR Prosecutor's request for this purpose.[243] In the cases concerned, it seems that the cause for enquiry into the circumstances surrounding the alleged illegal or unlawful detention in the first place was that, at the time of the alleged violation(s), the accused was being detained at the behest of the ICTR; conversely, it seems that where an accused was *not* being held at the behest of the ICTR, this is a reason *not* to enquire into the conditions of detention at the national level. According to DeFrancia, the 'divestiture-of-jurisdiction' decisions regarding arrest may be reconcilable with the latter (and later) decisions regarding the violation of detention rights, since the reasoning in the former decisions

> appears to be restricted to matters involving the execution of the arrest as opposed to the conditions of detention. In one case, for example, the question was whether the requested State used a warrant in its arrest of the suspect. Such technical matters *within the jurisdiction of the arrested State arguably* do not implicate fundamental due process rights of suspects.[244]

In any case, the (later) decisions regarding the violation of detention rights do not appear to have affected the import of the (earlier) decisions on arrest. In *Rwamakuba* the Trial Chamber seems to have cited *both* sets of decisions with approval; in relation to the detention decisions, it emphasized that the basis for accepting responsibility in such cases is the notion of 'constructive custody'.[245] Beyond this, however, chambers have not sought to explain why it is exactly that a distinction may be drawn between arrest and detention as far as applications for relief in respect of alleged illegality of unlawfulness on the part of national authorities in this regard are concerned.[246] None of this is to say that the ad hoc Tribunals will *never* enquire into the circumstances surrounding an alleged unlawful *arrest* of a person suspected or accused of crimes falling within their jurisdiction, with a view to attaching consequences to it. Indeed, in a number of ICTY cases chambers have been willing to enquire into alleged illegality or unlawfulness in the process of bringing the suspect or accused into the Tribunal's jurisdiction. In such cases, the method of arrest was alleged to be tantamount to abduction or kidnapping; such methods may be considered to be 'manifestly' or 'inherently' arbitrary,[247] and cannot be reduced to matters falling within the jurisdiction of a state (particularly where an international organisation has been

---

[243] See n 21 and accompanying text.

[244] DeFrancia 2001, 1408 (emphasis added, footnote in original omitted). The author refers to *Prosecutor v Kajelijeli* (Decision on the Defence Motion Concerning the Arbitrary Arrest and Illegal Detention of the Accused and on the Defence Notice of Urgent Motion to Expand and Supplement the Record of 8 December 1999 Hearing) ICTR-98-44-I, T Ch II (8 May 2000) para 35.

[245] See n 21 and accompanying text.

[246] DeFrancia himself does not appear to be convinced by the distinction; on the basis of the distinction, he observes that 'the ad hoc Tribunals are clearly not wholly committed to taking full responsibility for the due process rights of the suspects from the moment of enforcement'. See DeFrancia 2001, 1408. See also Sluiter 2003, 942–943.

[247] See n 30 and accompanying text.

involved in the apprehension of the suspect or accused); they raise issues that go beyond the circumvention of national procedure. However, where the method of arrest is 'merely' alleged to entail the circumvention of national procedure, it seems unlikely that the ICTY (or ICTR) would be willing to enquire into the circumstances surrounding the arrest for the purpose of determining an application for relief in this regard. As Sluiter has observed, in the law of the ad hoc Tribunals, the implementation of arrest warrants is '*essentially* perceived as an obligation of result for the State receiving the warrant', which is 'underlined by Rule 56 of the ICTY and ICTR RPEs obliging the State concerned to execute the arrest warrant' and by Rule 58 stipulating 'that the obligation to execute the warrant shall prevail over 'extradition obstacles'.[248]

As to the question of when the ad hoc Tribunals will *accept responsibility* for, i.e. attach legal consequences to, illegality of unlawfulness in the context of the arrest or detention of a person suspect or accused of crimes falling within their jurisdiction, the question of whether the illegality of unlawfulness is attributable to a particular organ of the tribunal in question has played an important role in this regard. Indeed, it appears that some level of attribution to an organ of the ad hoc Tribunal in question (that goes beyond the fact that the person concerned was being detained at the behest of the tribunal in question, or that the arrest was executed pursuant to a warrant of arrest issued and transmitted by the relevant tribunal)[249] is required in order for the tribunal to accept responsibility for the illegality or unlawfulness. Turning first to the ICTR *detention* cases, many of the rights violations established therein could be attributed to the ICTR by virtue of the Prosecution's *failure to exercise due diligence* in discharging its duties. In other cases, it could be attributed to the ICTR through (the failings of) other organs, for example the Registrar or trial chambers, or in a more general sense. Regarding the *Barayagwiza* case, it should be recalled that, while upon review of the Appeals Chamber's decision to stay the proceedings the 'new facts' submitted by the Prosecution 'diminish[ed] the role played by the failings of the Prosecutor *as well as* the intensity of the violation of the rights of the Appellant' (which meant that a stay of proceedings was no longer appropriate), the 'role played by the failings of the Prosecutor' had not been negated altogether. While some violations were, upon review, no longer attributable to the Prosecutor (in particular, the right to be brought promptly before the judicial authorities), others presumably were.[250] In that case also, then, the acceptance of responsibility on the part of the ICTR (as apparent from the Appeals Chamber's finding that the Appellant would be entitled to

---

[248] Sluiter 2009, 467 (emphasis added).

[249] That is, that goes beyond that which is required to justify an enquiry into the circumstances surrounding an alleged illegal or unlawful detention or an alleged illegal or unlawful arrest, respectively.

[250] In respect of some violations, which in the original decision (*Prosecutor v Barayagwiza* (Decision) ICTR-97-19-AR72, A Ch (3 November 1999)) *were* attributable to the ICTR, the issue of attribution was not discussed at all upon review. As such, it is fair to assume that these violations *remained* attributable to the ICTR.

financial compensation upon acquittal or sentence reduction upon conviction) appears to have been based on the involvement of an organ of the Tribunal in the violations in question. Turning now to the *arrest* cases, there are strong indications in the case law that the ad hoc Tribunals will, in principle, only accept responsibility for an unlawful arrest where the illegality of unlawfulness can be attributed to them. Only 'in cases of *egregious* violations of the rights of the [a]ccused', is it *'irrelevant* which entity was involved'.[251] In other words, only the abuse of process doctrine can constitute a basis for accepting responsibility where it is impossible to attribute the violation to the relevant ad hoc Tribunal. This applies to unlawful arrest cases as well as to unlawful detention cases. It seems that under this doctrine, the inability to attribute the violation(s) to an organ of the Tribunal can be 'compensated' by human rights violations that are, in and of themselves, very serious; in particular, it would seem that such inability can be 'compensated' by the torture or serious mistreatment of the suspect of the accused. In other words, in case of such mistreatment, attribution (i.e. a showing of involvement of an organ of the ad hoc Tribunal in question that goes beyond the fact that the person concerned was being detained at the behest of the tribunal in question, or that the arrest was executed pursuant to a warrant of arrest issued and transmitted by the relevant tribunal) need not be shown. The abuse of process doctrine, it should be recalled, can lead to one consequence only: a stay of proceedings. It is only in the context of this legal consequence, then, that it may be irrelevant which entity was involved.

Unlike the Statutes and RPEs of the ad hoc Tribunals, the governing documents of the ICC are *not* silent on how national authorities are to implement an official request for 'provisional arrest or for arrest and surrender' by the ICC (which, it may be noted, must be based on an arrest warrant);[252] indeed, the ICC Statute provides for a procedure for national authorities implementing an official ICC request for provisional arrest or for arrest and surrender, whereby the national judicial authority is *required* to make certain determinations in respect of the arrest. This implies that the ICC has a supervisory role in relation to this procedure. Such a role has been confirmed in the (appellate) case law. It is apparent from such case law that the nature of review to be carried out by the ICC in this regard is marginal; it is limited to seeing that the process envisaged by *national law* was duly followed and that the rights of the person to have been arrested were respected, whereby the ICC does not sit in on the process as a court of appeal. It is questionable whether, in reviewing an

---

[251] See e.g. *Prosecutor v Nikolić* (Decision on Defence Motion Challenging the Exercise of Jurisdiction by the Tribunal) IT-94-2-PT, T Ch II (9 October 2002) paras 56–69, 113–114 and 116; *Prosecutor v Nikolić* (Decision on Interlocutory Appeal Concerning Legality of Arrest) IT-94-2-AR73, A Ch (5 June 2003) para 33; *Prosecutor v Tolimir* (Decision on Preliminary Motions on the Indictment pursuant to Rule 72 of the Rules) IT-05-88/2-PT, T Ch II (14 December 2007) para 26; *Prosecutor v Karadžić* (Decision on the Accused's Holbrooke Agreement Motion) IT-95-5/18-PT, T Ch III (8 July 2009) para 85; and *Prosecutor v Karadžić* (Decision on the Accused's Motion for Remedy for Violation of Rights in Connection with Arrest) IT-95-5/18-PT, T Ch III (31 August 2009) para 6.

[252] See in this regard n 167 and accompanying text.

Article 59 procedure, the ICC would test whether the national law itself (or what happened in practice) accords with internationally protected human rights (or at least with those which flow from the treaties to which the state in question is a party).[253] Nevertheless, it is clear that, at the ICC, chambers will entertain applications for relief on the basis (of allegations) that the national authorities have circumvented their own national procedures in this regard (although, the fact that the review carried out by the ICC is marginal in nature suggests that states will be accorded a margin of appreciation in applying its own law). At the ad hoc Tribunals, it seems, they will *not* entertain applications for relief on this basis.[254] Only where it is alleged that the *arrest* was manifestly arbitrary, will they enquire into the circumstances surrounding an arrest for the purpose of determining an application for relief in this regard. Further, at the ad hoc Tribunals, chambers will not enquire into the conditions of *detention* where the accused was not being detained at the behest of the relevant Tribunal. Similarly, it seems, at the ICC, chambers will not enquire into the circumstances of an arrest and/or detention for the purpose of ascertaining whether it was illegal or unlawful, where 'concerted action' between the ICC and the state authorities in question cannot be shown.[255] However, the threshold at the ad hoc Tribunals for enquiring into the circumstances surrounding the accused's detention for the purpose of ascertaining its lawfulness appears to be lower than that at the ICC; at the ad hoc Tribunals it is sufficient that there was a request for provisional arrest pursuant to Rule 40 of the RPE (in such circumstances, it can be said that the person concerned was being held at the behest of the tribunal), whereas at the ICC, there must be concerted action, whereby it seems that the Prosecutor must have acted *improperly*.[256] At the ad hoc Tribunals, the question of how the Prosecutor conducted him- or herself is relevant to the question of whether the tribunal ought to accept responsibility for an illegal or unlawful detention (rather than the question of whether it ought to enquire into the conditions of detention in the first place, for the purpose of ascertaining whether it was illegal or unlawful), whereby the failure of the Prosecutor to act with due diligence (i.e. the Prosecutor's failure to act) may be sufficient.[257] It is unclear whether this would be sufficient for the ICC to accept responsibility for an illegal or unlawful arrest and/or detention.[258] At both the ad hoc Tribunals and the ICC, then,

---

[253] Sluiter 2009, 473.

[254] See n 17 and accompanying text.

[255] See n 180–181, 191 and 232 and accompanying text.

[256] See n 192 and accompanying text.

[257] See n 128 and 138 and accompanying text.

[258] Neither the Pre-Trial Chamber nor the Appeals Chamber in *Lubanga* properly addressed this issue. Taylor and Jalloh are highly critical in this regard: 'It is ... arguable that, by failing to set out standards of prosecutorial due diligence [within the context of the rights of suspects who have been apprehended and detained by national authorities] and effectively looking the other way, the Appeals Chamber placed its imprimatur on the practice of detaining possible ICC suspects in domestic prisons indefinitely or until such time that the Prosecutor decided to file an application for an ICC arrest warrant against the suspect in question. The impact this had ... is exemplified by

where there is an official request for cooperation (a Rule 40 request or a request based on an arrest warrant, at the ad hoc Tribunals, and a request for provisional arrest or for arrest and surrender, at the ICC), chambers will enquire into the period covered by the request, with a view to ascertaining whether it was lawful and, ultimately, to determining an application for relief in this regard. However, at both the ad hoc Tribunals and the ICC, this fact alone, i.e. the fact that an accused was being held at the relevant international criminal tribunal's behest, will not automatically lead to the acceptance of responsibility for any procedural violations committed in that context.

As to the consequences that may be attached to an illegal or unlawful arrest and/or detention, both the ad hoc Tribunals and the ICC accept that irregularities in the process of bringing a person into their jurisdiction, i.e. the arrest and transfer, and/or detention of a person suspected or accused of crimes falling within their jurisdiction, may require the proceedings to be stayed (permanently). While at the ad hoc Tribunals, the permanent stay of proceedings is the one judicial response for which attribution of the violation to an organ of the relevant tribunal need not always be shown, at the ICC, there are strong indications that attribution is *always* required in this regard.[259] It seems that at the ad hoc Tribunals, the inability to attribute the violation(s) in question to an organ of the tribunal can be 'compensated' by human rights violations that are, in and of themselves, very serious (of which torture or serious mistreatment is an important example), whereas at the ICC, it cannot. There, violations must be attributable to an organ of the ICC, *and* be grave. Regarding the circumstances that might require a permanent stay of proceedings, both the ad hoc Tribunals and the ICC have been criticised for focusing too much on 'serious mistreatment', whereas (it may be argued that) other serious human rights violations might also warrant such a response. According to Paulussen, the abuse of process doctrine 'is not only about physical mistreatment' and a suspect's rights may be violated 'even if he is not mistreated', as for example, when he or she is abducted[260] (which is contrary to the requirement of lawfulness under Articles 9(1) of the ICCPR and 5(1) of the ECHR and, arguably, manifestly arbitrary, and, moreover, often involves a degree of physical abuse and a threat to personal integrity).

In a number of cases before the ad hoc Tribunals, chambers have confirmed the availability of, and awarded, *alternative* remedies to persons whose rights had been violated, including those that occurred in the context of arrest and detention. In such cases, a permanent stay of proceedings was considered disproportionate. Thus,

---

(Footnote 258 continued)

the decision of the Prosecutor not to apply for an arrest warrant against Germain Katanga until June 25, 2007, even though the Prosecution was aware that he had been in detention since March 2005.' Taylor and Jalloh 2013, 321.

It is worth noting that in *Gbagbo*, the Pre-Trial Chamber seemed to reject the duty of care argument. See n 231 and accompanying text.

[259] See also Chap. 5, n 267–280 and accompanying text.

[260] Paulussen 2010, 460. See also 479–480.

upon conviction, the person concerned may be entitled to sentence reduction, while upon acquittal, the person concerned may be entitled to financial compensation, despite neither of these procedural steps being provided for in the ad hoc Tribunals' Statutes or RPEs. It appears that some level of attribution of the violation (or, where there are numerous violations, of *most* of the violations) to an organ of the ad hoc Tribunal is required in order to accept responsibility in this manner. The ICC Statute explicitly provides for financial compensation in case of unlawful arrest or unlawful detention, and there are indications in the case law that attribution of such unlawfulness to an organ of the ICC is a requirement in this regard.[261] While at the ad hoc Tribunals the case law confirms that other remedies (than a permanent stay of proceedings) may be available in case of unlawful arrest and/or detention, they— and, in particular, the ICTY—have been criticised for not always considering alternative remedies for violations that did not 'egregiously' violate the rights of the suspect or accused, i.e. that did not warrant the setting aside of jurisdiction. In relation to the *Nikolić* case, Sloan has said that,

> although the facts … clearly implied that illegality had occurred, the Trial Chamber [in *Nikolić*] concocted several arguments to the effect that there had been no breach of sovereignty or human rights [at all] and therefore no illegal capture. By making such improbable findings … the Trial Chamber was able to sidestep the difficult issue of what remedy would be required.[262]

Another explanation for the Trial Chamber's failure to consider alternative remedies is that, since it had already established that the acts of the unknown individuals (who had allegedly captured Nikolić) could not be attributed to an organ of the ICTY, it did not consider it necessary to consider such alternative remedies, which, it should be recalled, appear to require some level of attribution. However, the Trial Chamber did not say as much in its decision. Other explanations for the failure to consider alternative remedies may be sought in the stage at which the remedies were sought (where the consideration of alternative remedies such as financial compensation or sentence reduction would have been premature),[263] or the fact that such relief had not been expressly sought. Regarding the latter explanation, Sluiter has argued that, at the ICTY, 'the Chamber is not limited to the application of the parties' in responding to rights violations.[264] In *Tolimir* the Trial Chamber refused to consider alternative remedies, seemingly because the Accused had remedies to pursue in national courts. The ICC has also been criticized in this regard.[265] Although the Appeals Chamber in *Lubanga* noted that '[b]reach of the right to [personal liberty] by illegal arrest or detention confers a right to compensation to the victim' and that 'evidence obtained in breach of internationally recognized human rights [is] inadmissible in the circumstances specified by [A]rticle

---

[261] See n 234–239 and accompanying text, and see Chap. 5, n 375–380 and accompanying text.

[262] Sloan 2006, 341.

[263] See n 80 and accompanying text.

[264] Sluiter 2005, 245–246.

[265] See e.g. Taylor and Jalloh 2013, 320–321.

69(7) of the ICC Statute',[266] it did not consider such remedies in the case at hand. According to Sluiter, the ICTY case of *Nikolić* and the ICC case of *Lubanga* 'suffer … from the same flaw': '[w]ith the focus being on the ultimate remedy [the permanent stay of proceedings] … the core of the matter—have violations occurred?— and the need for alternative remedies, tend to be overlooked.'[267] He argues that, for the ICC, this is 'especially problematic', in view of the fact that the ICC's system is 'more inquisitorial in nature' than that of the ad hoc Tribunals, which may require chambers 'to explore issues *ultra petitum* and address violations *proprio motu* …'[268] Moreover, it raises the question of 'whether any violation … concerning the arrest or detention of an individual should … by definition be assessed in accordance with Article 85 of the [ICC] Statute'.[269] More will be said about these criticisms below, in Chap. 7.

6.3 Judicial Responses to Procedural Violations Connected to Disclosure

The second context to be examined in this chapter is disclosure. Disclosure may be defined as the process by which one party to the proceedings makes available to the other party (certain) information relevant to the case. In light of the subject matter of this book—pre-trial procedural violations—for the remainder of this section, the focus will be on the disclosure obligations of the *prosecution*.[270] The structure of this section is as follows. First the relevant law and practice at the ad hoc Tribunals will be

---

[266] *Prosecutor v Lubanga* (Judgment on the Appeal of Mr. Thomas Lubanga Dyilo against the Decision on the Defence Challenge to the Jurisdiction of the Court pursuant to Article 19(2)(a) of the Statute of 3 October 2006) ICC-01/04-01/06, A Ch (14 December 2006) para 37.

[267] Sluiter 2009, 471

[268] Ibid., 471–472.

[269] Ibid., 472.

[270] As stated in Chap. 1, this book is concerned with the judicial response to procedural violations committed in the pre-trial phase of international criminal proceedings, which covers not only what at the national level would be described as 'police illegality' or 'unlawfulness', of which unlawful arrest or detention is an obvious example, but also the violation by the prosecution of its pre-trial obligations, of which disclosure to the defence is a prime example. The fact that, at the ICTs, disclosure is an *ongoing* obligation, meaning that, 'as new material comes into the possession of the [p]rosecution, it should be assessed as to its potentially exculpatory nature and disclosed accordingly' (*Prosecutor v Karadžić* (Decision on Prosecution's Request for Reconsideration of Trial Chamber's 11 November 2010 Decision) IT-95-5/18, T Ch III (10 December 2010) para 11; thus, it does not mean that the prosecution 'can delay the disclosure of such material already in its possession, or identify and disclose potentially exculpatory material on a "rolling basis"' (ibid.)), does not alter the fact such disclosure should, in principle, be effected prior to the commencement of trial, i.e. that prosecution disclosure is, essentially, a pre-trial obligation. Some of the cases below concern the late disclosure of 'new material'; they have been included on the basis their instructiveness for the question of how violations of the prosecution's pre-trial disclosure obligations should be addressed.

set out, i.e. the law and practice with respect to the question of how to address procedural violations committed in the context of disclosure, which will be followed by an overview of the relevant law and practice at the ICC. Next, the law and practice at the ad hoc Tribunals and that at the ICC will be compared and (critically) analysed.

6.3.1 Ad Hoc Tribunals

At the ad hoc Tribunals disclosure is governed by the tribunals' own governing documents,[271] and by relevant human rights standards.[272] The case law discussed below, then, concerns violations of the ad hoc Tribunals' Statutes and/or RPEs, and/or relevant human rights standards. In setting out the law and practice at the ad hoc Tribunals with respect to the question of how to address procedural violations committed in the context of disclosure, it is instructive to draw a distinction between *late* disclosure, whereby the issue is that material that falls within the scope of a disclosure obligation on the part of the prosecution has been, or will have been, disclosed outside of the time limits prescribed or otherwise out of time, and *non-*disclosure, whereby the issue is that material that falls within the scope of such an obligation is being *withheld* in connection with some public or other interest. Further, it may be noted at the outset that the while the Statutes of the ad hoc Tribunals are silent on the question of how to address (allegations of) procedural violations in the context of disclosure, the ICTY RPE contains an express provision

---

[271] The principle disclosure obligations of the prosecution can be found in Rules 66 and 68 of both the ICTY and ICTR RPEs (both of which are subject to restrictions). While the purpose of the obligation under Rule 66(A) ICTY/ICTR RPE is, essentially, to put the defence on notice as to the case against the accused and allow it to prepare its defence accordingly, Rule 68 imposes on the prosecution an obligation to disclose to the defence 'as soon as practicable, any material which in the actual knowledge of the Prosecutor may suggest the innocence or mitigate the guilt of the accused or affect the credibility of Prosecution evidence'. In other words, Rule 68 provides for the disclosure of (potentially) exculpatory material (as well as other material). For a comprehensive overview of the standards governing disclosure at the ad hoc Tribunals, see Gibson and Lussiaà-Berdou 2010; and Fiori 2015.

[272] A failure on the part of the prosecution to disclose to the defence information relevant to the case against the accused may raise issues under the right to a fair trial, as provided for in, inter alia, Articles 14 ICCPR and 6 ECHR. Neither of these provisions expressly provides for a 'right to disclosure'; however, such a right has been read into the provisions. A right to disclosure has been read into Article 14(3)(b) ICCPR, i.e. the right of everyone charged with a criminal offence to have 'adequate time and facilities for the preparation of his defence', and linked to the principle of equality of arms (see in this regard HRC 'General Comment no 32. Article 14: Right to equality before courts and tribunals and to a fair trial' (23 August 2007) UN Doc CCPR/C/GC/32, para 33). At the ECtHR, the right to disclosure has been expressly linked to the principle of the equality of arms and that of adversarial proceedings, both of which are inherent in the 'fair hearing' requirement of Article 6(1) ECHR. In addition, it has been linked to the more specific rights under Article 6(3), and especially the right provided for under Article 6 (3)(b) of the ECHR, which provides that: 'Everyone charged with a criminal offence has the … [right] … to have adequate time and facilities for the preparation of his defence'. See generally Harris et al. 2014, 416–418.

in this regard, namely Rule 68bis. Rule 68bis (entitled 'Failure to Comply with Disclosure Obligations') was introduced into the ICTY RPE in 2001, and provides that: 'The pre-trial Judge or the Trial Chamber may decide *proprio motu*, or at the request of either party, on sanctions to be imposed on a party which fails to perform its disclosure obligations pursuant to the Rules.'[273] How this provision has been interpreted in practice is addressed below, in setting out the law and practice at the ad hoc Tribunals with respect to the question of how to address procedural violations committed in the context of disclosure.

§ *Late disclosure*

The ad hoc Tribunals have addressed the issue of late disclosure on numerous occasions. In the (early) ICTY case of *Furundžija*, the Trial Chamber addressed this issue against the backdrop of what the Trial Chamber itself described as 'a consistent pattern of non-compliance with the orders of the Trial Chamber, failure to comply with obligations imposed by the ... [ICTY RPE], late and/or last minute filing of substantial motions and failure to provide the Trial Chamber with satisfactory reasons for such conduct'.[274] This included the failure of the Prosecution to comply with its Rule 66 disclosure obligations[275] (that is, with the time-limits set therein; it seems that it was not seeking to withhold material from the Defence altogether); the Trial Chamber was 'particularly concerned that ... ten days before the commencement of trial, the Prosecution [had] filed a motion seeking the guidance of the Trial Chamber on disclosure to the Defence of transcripts from other proceedings before the ... [ICTY]', considering that the relevant witnesses had testifies *months* before the commencement of trial.[276] Moreover, a witness statement from the 'main witness against Anto Furundžija' was only disclosed to the Defence two weeks prior to the commencement of trial.[277] While the Accused had not been prejudiced by such failures, or, in any case, any prejudice caused thereby had been remedied,[278] according to the Trial Chamber, such conduct warranted the issuance of a formal complaint to the Prosecutor (which it did proprio motu). While having 'no express powers of discipline over members of the Prosecution', the Trial Chamber expressed 'its dismay at the conduct of the Prosecution' and referred the matter to the Prosecutor 'to be dealt with as she determines fit'.[279] According to the Trial

---

[273] The ICTR RPE does not contain such a rule. However, ICTR chambers have responded to disclosure violations in much the same way as the ICTY has.

[274] *Prosecutor v Furundžija* (The Trial Chamber's Formal Complaint to the Prosecutor Concerning the Conduct of the Prosecution) IT-95-17/1-PT, T Ch II (5 June 1998) para 2.

[275] For the nature of such obligations, see n 271 and accompanying text.

[276] *Prosecutor v Furundžija* (The Trial Chamber's Formal Complaint to the Prosecutor Concerning the Conduct of the Prosecution) IT-95-17/1-PT, T Ch II (5 June 1998) 6.

[277] Ibid., 6.

[278] Ibid., para 8.

[279] Ibid., para 12. A similar approach was taken in *Karemera, Ngirumpatse and Nzirorera*. According to the Trial Chamber, 'the lack of diligence in the Prosecution's compliance with its disclosure obligations' was 'unacceptable', 'offensive', obstructed the proceedings and was

Chamber, such conduct did not rise to the level required for contempt within the meaning of Rule 77 of the ICTY RPE.[280] Further disclosure violations in that case, consisting of the disclosure of Rule 68 material (that is, material that falls under the prosecution's obligation to disclose to the defence (potentially) exculpatory material) *after* the trial proceedings had closed and which, according to the Trial Chamber, amounted to serious misconduct on the part of the Prosecution in light of the fact that the material—including a witness statement recorded by the Office of the Prosecutor from of a psychologist concerning an important Prosecution witness and the treatment she had received as a result of the allegations which formed he subject matter of the indictment against the Accused—had pre-dated the disclosure by almost three years, led the Trial Chamber to order that the proceedings be reopened in connection to issues related to a specific witness, in order to cure the prejudice to the Defence.[281] This meant that the Defence could further cross-examine any Prosecution witness, and call further Defence witnesses.[282] It is worth noting that the Defence strongly opposed the reopening of the proceedings. It was of the view that only a new trial would suffice in this regard; alternatively, the evidence of the Prosecution witness in question was to be 'struck off'.[283] According to the Defence, the prejudice suffered was not limited to a particular witness but extended to trial strategy more generally; had it been aware of this information, its trial strategy may have been different. However, according to the Trial Chamber, it did not have the jurisdiction to order a new trial, and regarding the alternative, it was of the view that this was 'a procedural error specifically in the hands of the Prosecution', which had 'nothing to do with an error committed by a witness'. Therefore, the witness could not 'be made to suffer as a consequence'.[284]

In *Brđanin*, it was alleged by the Defence that the Prosecution had failed to discharge its disclosure obligations pursuant to Rule 68 of the ICTY RPE (which imposes on the prosecution an obligation to disclose to the defence 'as soon as practicable, any material which in the actual knowledge of the Prosecutor may suggest the innocence or mitigate the guilt of the accused or affect the credibility of Prosecution evidence'). An interview containing exculpatory material had been

---

(Footnote 279 continued)

'contrary to the interests of justice'. It therefore found that 'a sanction should be imposed against the Prosecution, by formally drawing the attention of the Prosecutor himself, as the disciplinary body, to this misconduct'. *Prosecutor v Karemera, Ngirumpatse and Nzirorera* (Decision on Defence Motion for Disclosure of RPF Material and for Sanctions Against the Prosecution) ICTR-98-44-T, T Ch III (19 October 2006) para 17.

[280] *Prosecutor v Furundžija* (The Trial Chamber's Formal Complaint to the Prosecutor Concerning the Conduct of the Prosecution) IT-95-17/1-PT, T Ch II (5 June 1998) para 11.

[281] *Prosecutor v Furundžija* (Oral Decision) IT-95-17/1-T, T Ch II (14 July 1998) 729–730. See also *Prosecutor v Furundžija* (Judgement) IT-95-17/1-T, T Ch II (10 December 1998) para 22.

[282] *Prosecutor v Furundžija* (Oral Decision) IT-95-17/1-T, T Ch II (14 July 1998) 741.

[283] Ibid., 729–730.

[284] Ibid., 729–730. The Defence argued that striking off the evidence was intended to punish the Prosecution, not the witness. See ibid., 736.

disclosed to the Defence *weeks* after it had been conducted, and even then, only in the form of a summary. According to the Defence, the Prosecution had deliberately taken their time to disclose the material, 'waiting for certain witnesses to complete their testimony'.[285] In this regard, the Defence pointed out that this was not the first time the issue of late disclosure had been raised before the Trial Chamber. In addition, the Defence alleged that the Prosecution had conducted a substantial number of other interviews without ever supplying the Defence with Rule 68 material.[286] Before addressing the specific allegations of the Defence, the Trial Chamber set out a number of general principles related to Rule 68 of the ICTY RPE, and the question of how to address violations thereof. It observed that, pursuant to the case law of the ICTY, 'if the Defence believes that the Prosecution has not complied with Rule 68, the Defence must first establish that the requested information is indeed in the possession of the Prosecution, and must second "present a prima facie case which would make probable the exculpatory nature of the materials sought"'.[287] It then noted that, '[i]f the Defence satisfies the Trial Chamber that there has been a failure by the Prosecution to comply with Rule 68, the Trial Chamber in addressing the aspect of appropriate remedies will examine whether or not the Defence has been prejudiced by non-compliance and will pro-vide accordingly pursuant to Rule 68*bis*',[288] and that 'in this context the "sanction approach" is not the primary option',[289] thereby citing an early ICTY decision in the *Blaškić* case, in which the Trial Chamber had held, amid allegations that the Prosecution had violated its disclosure obligations under Rule 68 of the ICTY RPE, that 'in general ... the possible violations of Rule 68 are governed less by a system of "sanctions" than by the Judges' definitive evaluation of the evidence presented

---

[285] *Prosecutor v Brđanin* (Decision on "Motion for Relief from Rule 68 Violations by the Prosecutor and for Sanctions to Be Imposed Pursuant to Rule 68*bis* and Motion for Adjournment while Matters Affecting Justice and a Fair Trial Can Be Resolved") IT-99-36-T, T Ch II (30 October 2002) para 5.

[286] Ibid., para 6.

[287] *Prosecutor v Brđanin* (Decision on "Motion for Relief from Rule 68 Violations by the Prosecutor and for Sanctions to Be Imposed Pursuant to Rule 68*bis* and Motion for Adjournment while Matters Affecting Justice and a Fair Trial Can Be Resolved") IT-99-36-T, T Ch II (30 October 2002) para 23. At the ICTR, *Prosecutor v Ndindiliyimana, Bizimungu, Nzuwonemeye and Sagahutu* (Decision on Defence Motions Alleging Violation of the Prosecutor's Disclosure Obligations Pursuant to Rule 68) ICTR-00-56-T, T Ch II (22 September 2008) para 13.

[288] *Prosecutor v Brđanin* (Decision on "Motion for Relief from Rule 68 Violations by the Prosecutor and for Sanctions to Be Imposed Pursuant to Rule 68*bis* and Motion for Adjournment while Matters Affecting Justice and a Fair Trial Can Be Resolved") IT-99-36-T, T Ch II (30 October 2002) para 23. See also *Prosecutor v Blaškić* (Judgement) IT-95-14-A, A Ch (29 July 2004) para 268 and *Prosecutor v Orić* (Decision on Urgent Defence Motion Regarding Prosecutorial Non-Compliance with Rule 68) IT-03-68-T, T Ch II (27 October 2005) 3.

[289] *Prosecutor v Brđanin* (Decision on "Motion for Relief from Rule 68 Violations by the Prosecutor and for Sanctions to Be Imposed Pursuant to Rule 68*bis* and Motion for Adjournment while Matters Affecting Justice and a Fair Trial Can Be Resolved") IT-99-36-T, T Ch II (30 October 2002) para 23.

by either of the parties, and the possibility which the opposing party will have had to contest it'.[290] Regarding Rule 68 more generally, it held that,

> the meaning of Rule 68 must … be placed in the broader context of securing the fair trial rights of the accused as enshrined in Articles 20 and 21 of the Statute of the Tribunal. The fair trial concept demands not only that the Prosecution, pursuant to the plain language of the Rule, disclose to the Defence in sufficient time "the existence of evidence", but also … that it actually provide the Defence with all of the exculpatory evidence in question "as soon as practicable".[291]

Regarding the specific allegations of the Defence, the Trial Chamber noted in relation to the first allegation that the Prosecution had 'acknowledged the delayed disclosure' and 'provided the Trial Chamber with an explanation for it'; on the basis thereof, it was convinced that the Prosecution had not acted maliciously or deliberately in this regard.[292] Regarding the second allegation, the Trial Chamber noted that the Prosecution had firmly refuted it, although it the Prosecution—had admitted that it had yet to disclose other exculpatory material to the Defence.[293] Regarding such delayed disclosure, the Trial Chamber held that the heavy workload of the Prosecution was not a justification for any further delay. It therefore instructed the Prosecution, pursuant to Rule 68bis, to disclose, within one week, the exculpatory material in question, in its original, unsummarized, form.[294] Finally, the Trial Chamber held that:

> … the decision to instruct the Prosecution to disclose Rule 68 material in its original form is being taken without prejudice to the rights of the Defence to recall witnesses for additional cross-examination, if it establishes to the satisfaction of this Trial Chamber that the lateness of the disclosure of the said documents prejudiced the preparation or presentation of his defence.[295]

---

[290] *Prosecutor v Brđanin* (Decision on "Motion for Relief from Rule 68 Violations by the Prosecutor and for Sanctions to Be Imposed Pursuant to Rule 68bis and Motion for Adjournment while Matters Affecting Justice and a Fair Trial Can Be Resolved") IT-99-36-T, T Ch II (30 October 2002) para 23, referring to *Prosecutor v Blaškić* (Decision on the Defence Motion for Sanctions for the Prosecutor's Continuing Violation of Rule 68) IT-95-14-T, T Ch I (28 September 1998) 3. See also *Prosecutor v Orić* (Decision on Urgent Defence Motion Regarding Prosecutorial Non-Compliance with Rule 68) IT-03-68-T, T Ch II (27 October 2005) 3 and *Prosecutor v Orić* (Decision on Ongoing Complaints about Prosecutorial Non-Compliance with Rule 68 of the Rules) IT-03-68-T, T Ch II (13 December 2005) para 32.

[291] *Prosecutor v Brđanin* (Decision on "Motion for Relief from Rule 68 Violations by the Prosecutor and for Sanctions to Be Imposed Pursuant to Rule 68bis and Motion for Adjournment while Matters Affecting Justice and a Fair Trial Can Be Resolved") IT-99-36-T, T Ch II (30 October 2002) para 24. See also *Prosecutor v Orić* (Decision on Urgent Defence Motion Regarding Prosecutorial Non-Compliance with Rule 68) IT-03-68-T, T Ch II (27 October 2005) 4.

[292] *Prosecutor v Brđanin* (Decision on "Motion for Relief from Rule 68 Violations by the Prosecutor and for Sanctions to Be Imposed Pursuant to Rule 68bis and Motion for Adjournment while Matters Affecting Justice and a Fair Trial Can Be Resolved") IT-99-36-T, T Ch II (30 October 2002) para 28.

[293] Ibid., para 29.

[294] Ibid., paras 29–30.

[295] Ibid., para 31.

In the ICTY case of *Krstić*, the Defence alleged, on appeal from conviction, that the Prosecution had violated its disclosure obligations under Rule 68 of the ICTY RPE, inter alia, by failing to disclose in a timely manner a number of witness statements, based on interviews conducted by the Prosecution prior to the Trial Chamber issuing its judgment, containing exculpatory material, and by failing to make two disclosures as soon as practicable. Regarding the first alleged violation of Rule 68, the Defence had earlier sought the admission of such statements as 'additional evidence' on appeal under Rule 115 of the ICTY RPE. The Appeals Chamber confirmed that any prejudice caused by a breach of Rule 68 could, where appropriate, be remedied through the admission of additional evidence under Rule 115.[296] Earlier on in the judgment, the Appeals Chamber had held that:

> [W]here the Defence seeks a remedy for the Prosecution's breach of its disclosure obligations under Rule 68, the Defence must show (i) that the Prosecution has acted in violation of its obligations under Rule 68, and (ii) that the Defence's case suffered *material prejudice* as a result. In other words, if the Defence satisfies the Tribunal that there has been a failure by the Prosecution to comply with Rule 68, the Tribunal - in addressing the aspect of appropriate remedies - will examine whether or not the Defence has been *prejudiced* by that failure to comply before considering whether a remedy is appropriate.[297]

It had further held that: 'The disclosure of exculpatory material is fundamental to the fairness of proceedings before the Tribunal, and considerations of fairness are the overriding factor in any determination of whether the governing Rule [Rule 68 of the ICTY RPE] has been breached.'[298] Regarding the second alleged violation of Rule 68, the Appeals Chamber seemed to accept as true the Defence's submission that some of the disclosures 'occurred over two years after the Prosecution came into possession of the evidence, and more than three months after the trial had begun', while others occurred 'over three months after the Prosecution came into possession of the evidence'.[299] While the Appeals Chamber was 'sympathetic' to the Prosecution's argument that 'in most instances material requires processing,

---

[296] *Prosecutor v Krstić* (Judgement) IT-98-33-A, A Ch (19 April 2004) para 187.

[297] Ibid., para 153 (emphasis added, footnotes in original omitted), referring to, inter alia, *Prosecutor v Brđanin* (Decision on "Motion for Relief from Rule 68 Violations by the Prosecutor and for Sanctions to Be Imposed Pursuant to Rule 68*bis* and Motion for Adjournment while Matters Affecting Justice and a Fair Trial Can Be Resolved") IT-99-36-T, T Ch II (30 October 2002). Other decisions to emphasize this point include: *Prosecutor v Blaškić* (Judgement) IT-95-14-A, A Ch (29 July 2004) para 295; *Prosecutor v Kordić and Čerkez* (Judgement) IT-95-14/2-A, A Ch (17 December 2004) para 179; *Prosecutor v Kajelijeli* (Judgement) ICTR-98-44A-A, A Ch (23 May 2005) para 262; *Prosecutor v Karemera, Ngirumpatse and Nzirorera* (Decision on Joseph Nzirorera's Interlocutory Appeal) ICTR-98-44-AR73.6, A Ch (28 April 2006) para 7; *Prosecutor v Ndindiliyimana, Bizimungu, Nzuwonemeye and Sagahutu* (Decision on Defence Motions Alleging Violation of the Prosecutor's Disclosure Obligations Pursuant to Rule 68) ICTR-00-56-T, T Ch II (22 September 2008) para 14.

[298] *Prosecutor v Krstić* (Judgement) IT-98-33-A, A Ch (19 April 2004) para 180. See also *Prosecutor v Orić* (Decision on Ongoing Complaints about Prosecutorial Non-Compliance with Rule 68 of the Rules) IT-03-68-T, T Ch II (13 December 2005) para 20.

[299] *Prosecutor v Krstić* (Judgement) IT-98-33-A, A Ch (19 April 2004) para 196.

translation, analysis and identification as exculpatory material', in its view, the Prosecution had taken 'an inordinate amount of time before disclosing material in this case', and had 'failed to provide a satisfactory explanation for the delay'.[300] However, the Defence had not established that it had suffered prejudice as a result of the breach of Rule 68.[301] Nevertheless, since the Prosecution had not met its obligations under the RPE, the Appeals Chamber was prepared to consider whether such breaches fell to be addressed under the 'disciplinary avenues' of Rules 46 and 68bis of the ICTY RPE.[302] In the end, the Appeals Chamber did not issue a formal sanction against the Prosecution for the violations of its disclosure obligations under Rule 68. It seems to have attached importance to the fact that it had been unable to determine whether the Prosecution had *deliberately* breached such obligations, and that, on the whole, the Prosecution had 'acted in good faith in the implementation of a systematic disclosure methodology'.[303] It also attached importance to the fact that the Defence had not been materially prejudiced by the breach.[304] It did order the Prosecutor to investigate the allegations of misconduct made against the Prosecution in that case and take appropriate action, since 'the Appeals Chamber will not tolerate anything short of strict compliance with disclosure obligations'; it considered its discussion of the issue in its judgment to be 'sufficient to put the Office of the Prosecutor on notice for its conduct in future proceedings'.[305]

Allegations of non-compliance with Rule 68 of the ICTY RPE were a 'recurrent feature' in the ICTY case of *Orić*.[306] On one occasion, the Prosecution had failed to disclose to the Defence in a timely manner a number of statements based on interviews conducted by the Office of the Prosecutor with a Defence witness. According to the Trial Chamber, such statements should have been disclosed to the Defence under Rules 66(B) and 68 of the ICTY RPE.[307] Nevertheless, the Trial Chamber declined to impose a sanction against the Prosecution (other than 'admonishing' it), given that there was no indication that the Prosecution had acted maliciously or in bad faith, that 'only minor differences exist[ed] between the contents of … [two of the three statements] and the evidence given by … [the Defence witness in question]' and that the Defence already had in its possession the other statement, and that there was no indication that the Defence had suffered prejudice as a result of the late

---

[300] Ibid., para 197.

[301] Ibid., para 199.

[302] Ibid., paras 200 and 210.

[303] Ibid., paras 213–214.

[304] Ibid., para 214.

[305] Ibid., para 215.

[306] *Prosecutor v Orić* (Decision on Ongoing Complaints about Prosecutorial Non-Compliance with Rule 68 of the Rules) IT-03-68-T, T Ch II (13 December 2005) para 2.

[307] *Prosecutor v Orić* (Decision on Alleged Prosecution Compliance with Disclosure Obligations under Rules 66(B) and 68(i)) IT-03-68-T, T Ch II (29 September 2005) 3.

disclosure.[308] In other cases involving the violation of Rule 66 of the RPEs,[309] chambers of the ad hoc Tribunals have, where the violation in question has prejudiced the accused, responded by postponing the testimony of the witness concerned, and, occasionally, allowing the Defence to request that certain prosecution witnesses be recalled, or by otherwise mooting such possibilities.[310] In so doing, chambers have emphasized that the exclusion of evidence[311] is an extreme response to such violations, and will be resorted to in exceptional circumstances only,[312] for example, where the prosecution has acted in bad faith.[313] This is because chambers would 'prefer to hear relevant testimony', provided the accused has the opportunity to test it.[314] In some cases, chambers have censured the prosecution for its failure to discharge its disclosure obligations under Rule 66 of the RPE.[315]

Upon being called to address the Prosecution's failure to comply with its Rule 68 disclosure obligations for the *fifth* time in *Orić*, the Trial Chamber, pursuant to Rules 68(i) and 68bis of the ICTY RPE, ordered the Prosecution to 'conduct a thorough and complete search for Rule 68(i) material relevant to the Defence' and to provide the Trial Chamber, by a certain date, with a 'declaration stating what searches have been made, where they have been made and the results of such searches', and the immediate disclosure of the Rule 68 material in question to the Defence, and invited the Defence 'to indicate … the names of any witnesses of the Prosecution that the Defence may wish to call for further cross-examination' in light

---

[308] Ibid., 3.

[309] See in this regard n 271 and accompanying text.

[310] *Prosecutor v Nahimana, Ngeze and Barayagwiza* (Decision on the Prosecutor's Oral Motion for Leave to Amend the List of Selected Witnesses) ICTR-99-52-T, T Ch I (26 June 2001) para 32; *Prosecutor v Bagosora, Kabiligi, Ntabakuze and Nsengiyumva* (Decision on the Defence for Bagosora's Motion for Postponement or Quashing of the Testimonies of Witnesses Ruggiu, XAM and ZF) ICTR-98-41-T, T Ch III (30 September 2002) para 13; and *Prosecutor v Zigiranyirazo* (Decision on Rule 66 of the Rules of Procedure and Evidence) ICTR-01-73-T, T Ch III (10 October 2005) 2.

[311] That is, of prosecution evidence not properly disclosed or evidence relating to facts to which the exculpatory material pertains. See Zappalà 2004, 627.

[312] *Prosecutor v Karemera, Ngirumpatse and Nzirorera* (Decision on Defence's Motion to Report Government of a Certain State to United Nations Security Council and on Prosecution Motions under Rule 66(C) of the Rules) ICTR-98-44-T, T Ch III (15 February 2006) para 25; and *Prosecutor v Zigiranyirazo* (Decision on Rule 66 of the Rules of Procedure and Evidence) ICTR-01-73-T, T Ch III (10 October 2005) 2.

[313] *Prosecutor v Bagosora, Kabiligi, Ntabakuze and Nsengiyumva* (Decision on Defence Motion to Preclude Certain Portions of the Anticipated Testimony of Prosecution Witnesses DCH, for the Postponement of Witness DCH's Testimony, and for the Appointment of Defence Counsel for DCH) ICTR-98-41-T, T Ch I (29 March 2004) para 6.

[314] Ibid., para 7. See also *Prosecutor v Zigiranyirazo* (Decision on Rule 66 of the Rules of Procedure and Evidence) ICTR-01-73-T, T Ch III (10 October 2005) 2.

[315] See e.g. *Prosecutor v Bagosora, Kabiligi, Ntabakuze and Nsengiyumva* (Decision on the Defence for Bagosora's Motion for Postponement or Quashing of the Testimonies of Witnesses Ruggiu, XAM and ZF) ICTR-98-41-T, T Ch III (30 September 2002).

of the disclosure of the material.[316] The Trial Chamber had previously noted that in addressing what is the appropriate remedy for a violation of Rule 68 of the ICTY RPE, 'the Trial Chamber *has* to examine whether or not the Defence has been prejudiced by ... [the breach], and rule accordingly pursuant to Rule 68bis',[317] and that the violation of Rule 68 is 'governed less by a system of "sanctions" than by the Judges' definitive evaluation of the evidence presented by either of the parties, and the possibility which the opposing party will have had to contest it'.[318] The Trial Chamber also noted that it was its responsibility to ensure that the Prosecution's obligation under Rule 68 'is fully observed at all times because it goes to the heart of the Accused's right to a fair trial', and also because it had the overall responsibility of preserving the integrity of the proceedings.[319] In the circumstances, the Defence had been prejudiced by the breach of Rule 68: there was nothing to show that the Defence was aware of the existence of the material in question 'until the time the Prosecution rested its case', and the material had therefore not been available to the Accused 'for potential cross-examination of Prosecution witnesses during the Prosecution's case-in-chief'.[320] However, the Prosecution had not intentionally violated its disclosure obligations.[321] Following the Trial Chamber's decision, the Defence filed a motion in which it submitted that at that stage of the proceedings (the Prosecution's case-in-chief had been completed, and the Defence case was well underway) 're-calling Prosecution witnesses would not only disrupt the orderly presentation of Defence evidence, it would even amount to a de facto re-trial because it considered that all Prosecution witnesses

---

[316] *Prosecutor v Orić* (Decision on Urgent Defence Motion Regarding Prosecutorial Non-Compliance with Rule 68) IT-03-68-T, T Ch II (27 October 2005) 4–5. Regarding the order to conduct a search for Rule 68 material relevant to the Defence and to provide the Trial Chamber with a declaration in this regard, see similarly *Prosecutor v Krnojelac* (Decision on Motion by Prosecution to Modify Order for Compliance with Rule 68) IT-97-25-PT, T Ch II (1 November 1999).

[317] *Prosecutor v Orić* (Decision on Urgent Defence Motion Regarding Prosecutorial Non-Compliance with Rule 68) IT-03-68-T, T Ch II (27 October 2005) 3 (emphasis added). The language of the Trial Chamber in this regard is stronger than that of the Trial Chamber in *Brđanin* (see n 288 and accompanying text). See also the language of the Appeals Chamber in *Prosecutor v Blaškić* (Judgement) IT-95-14-A, A Ch (29 July 2004) para 268.

[318] *Prosecutor v Orić* (Decision on Urgent Defence Motion Regarding Prosecutorial Non-Compliance with Rule 68) IT-03-68-T, T Ch II (27 October 2005) 3, referring to *Prosecutor v Blaškić* (Decision on the Defence Motion for Sanctions for the Prosecutor's Continuing Violation of Rule 68) IT-95-14-T, T Ch I (28 September 1998) 3 and *Prosecutor v Brđanin* (Decision on "Motion for Relief from Rule 68 Violations by the Prosecutor and for Sanctions to Be Imposed Pursuant to Rule 68*bis* and Motion for Adjournment while Matters Affecting Justice and a Fair Trial Can Be Resolved") IT-99-36-T, T Ch II (30 October 2002) para 23.

[319] *Prosecutor v Orić* (Decision on Urgent Defence Motion Regarding Prosecutorial Non-Compliance with Rule 68) IT-03-68-T, T Ch II (27 October 2005) 4.

[320] Ibid., 4.

[321] Ibid., 4.

would have to be re-called'.[322] According to the Defence, violations by the Prosecution of its obligations under Rule 68 were 'ongoing, and therefore, witnesses would need to be re-called on a rolling basis, which would be unacceptable in view of the imperative to secure an expeditious trial'.[323] It also raised further instances of non-compliance on the part of the Prosecution with its disclosure obligations under Rule 68. In responding to these submissions, the Trial Chamber again stated that the violation of Rule 68 is 'governed less by a system of "sanctions" than by the Judges' definitive evaluation of the evidence presented by either of the parties, and the possibility which the opposing party will have had to contest it'.[324] Having expressly noted the reasons provided by the Defence for not calling or re-calling further witnesses,[325] it found that 'disclosure practice adopted by the Prosecution during the proceedings … [had] not been satisfactory'. In light of this, it would 'consider the possibility of drawing the reasonable inferences in favour of the Accused with respect to specific evidence which has been the subject of a Rule 68 violation'.[326] It seems, therefore, that this would be an appropriate remedy 'where the violation of the disclosure violation is so extensive or occurs at such a late stage of the proceedings that it would violate the right of the accused to trial without undue delay, or where it would be impossible or impractical to recall prosecution witnesses without effectively reopening the case in its entirety'.[327] Finally, it is worth noting that in relation to one of the further instances of non-disclosure raised by the Defence, the Trial Chamber held that: 'As a general rule, if Rule 68 material is known and reasonably accessible to the defence, material prejudice cannot be shown.'[328]

In the ICTR case of *Karemera, Ngirumpatse and Nzirorera*, the Defence had requested the Trial Chamber to sanction the Prosecution for its failure to comply with an order for disclosure of potentially exculpatory material. The Prosecution did not deny this failure, but argued that the disclosure in question would put certain

---

[322] *Prosecutor v Orić* (Decision on Ongoing Complaints about Prosecutorial Non-Compliance with Rule 68 of the Rules) IT-03-68-T, T Ch II (13 December 2005) para 7.

[323] Ibid., para 7.

[324] Ibid., para 32.

[325] Ibid., para 33.

[326] Ibid., para 35. It is worth noting that *nowhere* in the decision does the Trial Chamber refer to Rule 68bis ICTY RPE. See also *Prosecutor v Orić* (Judgement) IT-03-68-T, T Ch II (30 June 2006) paras 76–77.

[327] *Prosecutor v Ndindiliyimana, Bizimungu, Nzuwonemeye and Sagahutu* (Decision on Defence Motions Alleging Violation of the Prosecutor's Disclosure Obligations Pursuant to Rule 68) ICTR-00-56-T, T Ch II (22 September 2008) para 14.

[328] *Prosecutor v Orić* (Decision on Ongoing Complaints about Prosecutorial Non-Compliance with Rule 68 of the Rules) IT-03-68-T, T Ch II (13 December 2005) para 27, referring to *Prosecutor v Blaškić* (Decision on the Appellant's Motions for the Production of Material, Suspension or Extension of the Briefing Schedule, and Additional Filings) IT-95-14-A, A Ch (26 September 2000) para 38. See also *Prosecutor v Karemera, Ngirumpatse and Nzirorera* (Oral Decision on Stay of Proceedings) ICTR-98-44-T, T Ch III (16 February 2006).

witnesses in danger and that it was obliged to protect their safety.[329] The Trial
Chamber first observed that where the Prosecution fears for the safety of a witness,
it may apply to the Trial Chamber for protective measures for that witness; it then
noted that the Prosecution had not requested any such measures.[330] Noting that it
had previously found a 'lack of diligence in the Prosecution's compliance with its
disclosure obligations', whereby it had concluded that this obstructed the proceedings and was contrary to the interests of justice' and imposed a 'warning
against the Prosecution', the Trial Chamber found that the failure to effect the
disclosure ordered by it was 'unacceptable', 'offensive', obstructed the proceedings
and was 'contrary to the interests of justice'. It therefore found that 'a sanction
should be imposed against the Prosecution, by formally drawing the attention of the
Prosecutor himself, as the disciplinary body, to this misconduct', pursuant to Rule
46(A) of the ICTR RPE.[331] In *Ndindiliyimana and others*, the Trial Chamber found
that the Prosecution had 'persistently violated its disclosure obligation under Rule
68' and that, in light of the stage of the proceedings at which some disclosures had
been made, and at which others had yet to be made (the Prosecution case had
closed, as had some of the Defence cases, while another was underway and yet
another had yet to commence), all of the Defence teams had been prejudiced by the
violations in the preparation of their defences.[332] The Prosecution had shown a lack
of diligence in discharging its disclosure obligations (some of the material had been
in the possession of the Prosecution for years)[333,334] and all of the Accused had
been deprived of the opportunity of using the exculpatory material to test the
credibility of Prosecution witnesses.[335] Moreover, two of the Accused (whose
Defence cases had closed) had been 'denied the opportunity of considering the
exculpatory material and deciding whether or not to call any of the witnesses to
testify on their behalf'.[336] According the Trial Chamber, the Prosecution's conduct
violated the Accused's right to a fair trial;[337] specifically, it 'flagrantly infringed

---

[329] *Prosecutor v Karemera, Ngirumpatse and Nzirorera* (Decision on Defence Motion for
Disclosure of RPF Material and for Sanctions Against the Prosecution) ICTR-98-44-T, T Ch III
(19 October 2006) para 13.

[330] Ibid., paras 14–15.

[331] Ibid., para 17.

[332] *Prosecutor v Ndindiliyimana, Bizimungu, Nzuwonemeye and Sagahutu* (Decision on Defence
Motions Alleging Violation of the Prosecutor's Disclosure Obligations Pursuant to Rule 68)
ICTR-00-56-T, T Ch II (22 September 2008) para 59.

[333] Ibid., paras 27, 31 and 33.

[334] Ibid., para 59.

[335] Ibid., para 59.

[336] Ibid., para 59.

[337] Earlier on in the decision the Trial Chamber had observed that the 'Prosecution's obligation to
disclose exculpatory material is essential to a fair trial'. *Prosecutor v Ndindiliyimana, Bizimungu,
Nzuwonemeye and Sagahutu* (Decision on Defence Motions Alleging Violation of the
Prosecutor's Disclosure Obligations Pursuant to Rule 68) ICTR-00-56-T, T Ch II (22 September
2008) para 12.

upon 'the rights of the Accused to examine or have examined the witnesses against them or to obtain the attendance and examination of witnesses on their behalf'.[338] Such a violation could not go without a remedy. According to the Trial Chamber, there were 'a large number of remedial options … available to the Chamber' in this regard, including: 'recalling relevant prosecution witnesses for further cross-examination, allowing the Defence teams to call additional defence witnesses, excluding relevant parts of the prosecution evidence, drawing necessary inferences from the exculpatory material, dismissing charges touched upon by the exculpatory material, and ordering a stay of proceedings'.[339] In determining which of these options is most suitable, the Trial Chamber had to 'take into account the nature and significance of the Prosecution's violations in light of the current stage of proceedings, the rights of the Accused, the need to preserve the integrity of the proceedings, and its obligation to discover the truth about the events that happened in Rwanda in 1994'.[340] In addition, the Trial Chamber noted that the last four of those options 'are severe forms of remedy that should be invoked only in exceptional circumstances where less severe measures reasonably capable of remedying the Prosecution's violation are unavailable'.[341] In the circumstances, it was sufficient to 'recall certain Prosecution witnesses for further cross-examination and, if necessary, to call additional Defence witnesses'. According to the Trial Chamber, this was 'the most practical way of remedying the Prosecution's disclosure violations while preserving the rights of the Accused to a full and fair defence and maintaining the integrity of the trial proceedings'.[342] Earlier on in the decision, the Trial Chamber had held that, '[b]efore granting a remedy for a breach of Rule 68 obligations, the Chamber must ascertain that material prejudice has been caused to the accused'.[343] In finding that the appropriate remedy was to recall certain Prosecution witnesses for further cross-examination and, if necessary, to call additional Defence witnesses, the Trial Chamber was mindful of the effect this would have on the length of the trial; it had to 'balance the competing interests of the Accused to a trial without undue delay, with their right to examine witnesses called for and against them bearing in mind the ultimate objective of ensuring a fair trial'.[344] According to the Trial Chamber, in light of the stage of the proceedings, the remedy proposed by it struck the right balance in this regard.[345] In addition to that remedy, the Trial Chamber issued a reprimand to the ICTR Prosecutor in respect of the Prosecution's lack of diligence in the disclosure of exculpatory material in this case.[346] In this

---

[338] Ibid., para 59.

[339] Ibid., para 61.

[340] Ibid., para 61.

[341] Ibid., para 62.

[342] Ibid., para 63.

[343] Ibid., para 14.

[344] Ibid., para 64.

[345] Ibid., para 64.

[346] Ibid., the disposition.

regard it is worth noting that, earlier on in the decision, the Trial Chamber had found that, 'where the Prosecution shows persistent disregard or lack of diligence in discharging its Rule 68 obligation to such an extent that he could be deemed to be obstructing the proceedings or interests of justice, the Trial Chamber may consider imposing sanctions against the Prosecutor'.[347] Pursuant to the Trial Chamber's decision, the Defence filed a motion for certain Prosecution witnesses to be recalled, and for additional Defence witnesses to be called, which the Trial Chamber granted in part. However, some of the witnesses whom the Defence wanted to recall or call were not available to testify, and so the Trial Chamber admitted a number of witness statements containing exculpatory material into evidence, in order to address the prejudice that the Accused Augustin Ndindiliyimana had suffered as a result of the Prosecution's disclosure violations.[348]

In the ICTY case of *Karadžić*, the Trial Chamber has on numerous occasions found the Prosecution to be in breach of its disclosure violations under Rules 66 and 68 of the ICTY RPE.[349] In relation to such violations, and in light of the 'strain which the stream of disclosure placed on the Accused's resources',[350] the Trial Chamber has ordered the Prosecution to take measures to ensure that the pattern of disclosure violations was brought to an end, suspended the trial in order to enable to Accused to review material disclosed late[351] and postponed the testimony of certain witnesses, in order to ensure that the Accused had sufficient time to review the disclosed material, and incorporate, if necessary, into his defence strategy and cross-examination of the affected witnesses.[352] It has also granted declaratory relief in respect of such violations, where there was no prejudice to the Accused. In a partially dissenting opinion on this matter, however, Judge Kwon opined that 'when the Accused does not suffer any prejudice resulting from the Prosecution's violation of Rule 68 … it is unnecessary, moot or even frivolous to issue a declaratory finding that the Prosecution has violated Rule 68 of the Rules. It serves no purpose.'[353] He further stated that:

---

[347] Ibid., para 14.

[348] *Prosecutor v Ndindiliyimana, Bizimungu, Nzuwonemeye and Sagahutu* (Decision on Ndindiliyimana's Motion to Recall Identified Prosecution Witnesses and to Call Additional Defence Witnesses) ICTR-00-56-T, T Ch II (4 December 2008).

[349] See e.g. *Prosecutor v Karadžić* (Decision On Accused's Eighteenth To Twenty-First Disclosure Violation Motions) IT-95-5/18-T, T Ch III (2 November 2010).

[350] *Prosecutor v Karadžić* (Decision on Accused's Motion for New Trial for Disclosure Violations) IT-95-5/18-T, T Ch III (3 September 2012) para 15.

[351] *Prosecutor v Karadžić* (Decision On Accused's Eighteenth To Twenty-First Disclosure Violation Motions) IT-95-5/18-T, T Ch III (2 November 2010) para 42.

[352] Ibid., para 43. See also *Prosecutor v Stanišić and Simatović* (Decision on Defence Motion for Exclusion of Prosecution Witnesses Due to Late Disclosure of Their Unredacted Statements) IT-03-69-PT, T Ch III (6 March 2008) 3.

[353] *Prosecutor v Karadžić* (Decision on Accused's Thirty-Seventh to Forty-Second Disclosure Violation Motions with Partially Dissenting Opinion of Judge Kwon) IT-95-5/18-T, T Ch III (29 March 2011), Partially Dissenting Opinion of Judge Kwon, para 4.

The jurisprudence clearly states that "if the Defence satisfies the Tribunal that there has been a failure by the Prosecution to comply with Rule 68, the Tribunal . . . will examine whether or not the Defence has been prejudiced by that failure to comply before considering whether a remedy is appropriate[.]" Accordingly, in the absence of prejudice, the Accused will not be given any remedy, including a declaration that the Prosecution has violated Rule 68.[354]

Judge Kwon's argument is best understood in light of his observations towards the end of the opinion:

> In a trial of this size and scope, where hundreds of witnesses are being called and tens of thousands of pages of documents are being tendered, it is unwarranted to seek a declaratory finding of disclosure violation every time that a potentially exculpatory document is belatedly disclosed in violation of Rule 68 without demonstrating any prejudice on the part of the Accused. *Otherwise, it would only encourage the Accused to continue filing unnecessary motions.*[355]

Nevertheless, the Trial Chamber has continued to grant declaratory relief where the violation has caused no, or minimal prejudice, to the accused.[356] Later on in the proceedings, the Accused sought an order granting a 'new trial' in light of the numerous disclosure obligations committed by the Prosecution in that case. The Accused sought such an order as a sanction against the Prosecution or, alternatively, as a remedy for the prejudice he had suffered. Regarding his request for a *sanction*, he argued that 'a new trial should be ordered as a sanction for the Prosecution's cumulative disclosure violations which continued with "impunity" despite the repeated warnings of the Chamber'.[357] Regarding his request for a *remedy*, he argued that the late disclosure of a significant amount of exculpatory material had 'affected his ability to plan a coherent defence and forced him to conduct "exploratory, rather than focused cross examinations"', and was contrary to the notion of a fair trial.[358] In setting out the applicable law in this regard, the Trial Chamber referred to Rule 68bis of the ICTY RPE (which provides that: 'A Trial Chamber may, *proprio motu* or at the request of either party, decide on sanctions to be imposed on a party which fails to comply with its disclosure obligations under the Rules') and, relying on appellate authorities, noted that, '[i]n determining the appropriate remedy (if any), the Chamber has to examine whether or not the accused has been prejudiced by the relevant breach'.[359] In this regard it observed that, up until the point, the Accused had not been found to have been prejudiced by any of the disclosure violations established by the Trial Chamber, although it remarked that such violations, which were numerous, 'reflected badly on the Prosecution, its knowledge of what it holds in its evidence

---

[354] Ibid., para 5.

[355] Ibid., para 7 (emphasis added).

[356] See e.g. *Prosecutor v Karadžić* (Decision on Accused's Sixtieth, Sixty-First, Sixty-Third, and Sixty-Fourth Disclosure Violation Motions) IT-95-5/18-T, T Ch III (22 November 2011) para 37 n 68.

[357] *Prosecutor v Karadžić* (Decision on Accused's Motion for New Trial for Disclosure Violations) IT-95-5/18-T, T Ch III (3 September 2012) para 3.

[358] Ibid., para 4.

[359] Ibid., para 12.

collection and its approach to disclosure'.[360] Throughout the case the Trial Chamber had taken various measures in response to disclosure violations committed by the Prosecution, which included the suspension of the proceedings 'to allow the Accused time to review and incorporate large batches of newly disclosed material into his preparations', the postponement of witness testimony, the imposition of 'deadlines for the Prosecution to review and disclose material' and requiring the Prosecution to 'provide detailed reports on their disclosure practices and to implement additional measures to rectify identified problems'.[361] Accordingly, there was 'no basis for the Accused's renewed claim that the Prosecution's disclosure violations, even in a cumulative sense, have caused him prejudice'.[362] In the absence of prejudice, there was 'no basis to order the exceptional measure of a new trial as a remedy'.[363] As for the request for a new trial as a *sanction*, the Trial Chamber observed that the Accused had requested such a measure 'even though the Chamber … [had] previously rejected such requests given that the Accused *had not been prejudiced by the violation*'.[364] Apart from arguing that the 'cumulative effect of the violations' warranted such a measure, the Accused had not provided any other reason for the Trial Chamber to order a new trial.[365] In light of the measures already taken by the Trial Chamber in the course of the trial aimed at ensuring its fairness, and of the absence of prejudice to the Accused, the sanction requested by the Accused was not warranted.[366]

Finally, in the *Haradinaj Balaj and Brahimaj* retrial, the Trial Chamber found that the Prosecution had committed 'several serious violations of Rule 68 [of the ICTY RPE] by failing to disclose, in a timely fashion' materials relevant to assessment of the credibility of a particular Prosecution witness. In setting out the applicable law in this regard, the Trial Chamber said that, where the Prosecution has breached its disclosure obligations under Rule 68, 'a Chamber must examine whether the Defence has been prejudiced by the violation before considering whether a remedy is appropriate'.[367] It also referred to Rule 68bis of the ICTY RPE, which allows a trial chamber to impose sanctions on a party found to have breached its disclosure obligations.[368] In the circumstances, the Defence had been prejudiced by the 'improperly late' disclosure; however such prejudice had been remedied by the Trial Chamber's decision to adjourn the Prosecution witness's testimony to

---

[360] Ibid., para 14.

[361] Ibid., paras 14–16.

[362] Ibid., para 17.

[363] Ibid., para 17.

[364] Ibid., para 19.

[365] Ibid., para 19.

[366] Ibid., para 19.

[367] *Prosecutor v Haradinaj, Balaj and Brahimaj* (Decision on Joint Defence Motion for Relief from Rule 68 Violations by the Prosecution and for Sanctions pursuant to Rule 68*bis*) IT-04-84bis-T, T Ch II (12 October 2011) para 42.

[368] Ibid., para 43.

allow the Defence to prepare its cross-examination.[369] Nevertheless, the Trial Chamber considered that a reprimand was warranted, which was issued to the Prosecution's Senior Trial Attorney pursuant to Rule 68bis of the ICTY RPE, on account of his 'serious failure to abide by Rule 68 and his unwillingness to recognise his violations of the rule'.[370] According to the Trial Chamber, the Senior Trial Attorney 'could not have reasonably believed that he had no duty to disclose that … [the witness in question had] requested and actually received assistance in his asylum case as a result of being a Prosecution witness'.[371] In addition, it ordered the Prosecution to file a report confirming that it had 'comprehensively searched for Rule 68 material in its possession, in relation to all its witnesses in … [that] trial, specifying what searches have been made, where they have been made, and the results of such searches'.[372] Shortly after the Trial Chamber issued its decision, the Prosecution filed a motion seeking vacation of the personal reprimand. The motion was granted by the Trial Chamber, on the basis that 'an individual reprimand could only have been administered … pursuant to Rule 46 and with the procedural safeguards provided therein';[373] according to the Trial Chamber, the Defence had not invoked Rule 46 in requesting that sanctions be imposed in respect of the disclosure violations in question, and it was not inclined to invoke that rule proprio motu.[374] Earlier on in the decision the Trial Chamber had held that, while the purpose of both Rule 68bis and Rule 46 is to

> … provide for possible responses, by the Chamber, to conduct which adversely affects the proper administration of justice … within the context of disclosure violations, Rule 46 is *lex specialis* as to responses to such conduct by an individual counsel, whereas Rule 68*bis* is *lex generalis* on sanctions for disclosure violations, and that by addressing, on the basis of Rule 68*bis*, an issue which is within the purview of Rule 46, the object and purpose of Rule 46 is frustrated.[375]

In this regard it observed that:

> If it were permissible to reprimand an individual counsel on the basis of Rule 68bis, a sanction could be imposed which is materially identical to a measure under Rule 46 without the requirement of Rule 46 that the Chamber be satisfied that the conduct of counsel is offensive, abusive, obstructive, negligent or otherwise fails to meet the standard of professional competence and ethics, having been met, thus rendering Rule 46 redundant.[376]

---

[369] Ibid., paras 56–57.

[370] Ibid., paras 64 and 20.

[371] Ibid., para 60.

[372] Ibid., para 66.

[373] *Prosecutor v Haradinaj, Balaj and Brahimaj* (Decision on Prosecution's Motion for Reconsideration of Relief Ordered pursuant to Rule 68bis with Partially Dissenting Opinion of Judge Hall) IT-04-84bis-T, T Ch II (27 March 2012) para 42.

[374] Ibid., para 43.

[375] Ibid., para 36.

[376] Ibid., para 37.

Further, it observed that, '[w]hile Rule 68bis prescribes no particular procedure, Rule 46 requires that any sanction may be imposed only "after giving counsel due warning"'.[377]

§ *Non-disclosure*

Having set out the case law concerning the question of how to address *late* disclosure, whereby the issue is that material that falls within the scope of a disclosure obligation on the part of the prosecution has been, or will have been, disclosed outside of the time limits prescribed or otherwise out of time, the case law with respect to the question of how to address *non*-disclosure, whereby the issue is that material that falls within the scope of such an obligation is being *withheld* in connection with some public or other interest, will now be set out.

Rule 70(B) of the ICTY RPE provides that:

> If the Prosecutor is in possession of information which has been provided to the Prosecutor on a confidential basis and which has been used solely for the purpose of generating new evidence, that initial information and its origin shall not be disclosed by the Prosecutor without the consent of the person or entity providing the initial information and shall in any event not be given in evidence without prior disclosure to the accused.[378]

It is not difficult to see how this provision might come into conflict with the Prosecutor's disclosure obligations under Rule 68 of the ICTY RPE. Until 2003, the year in which Rule 68 underwent substantial modifications, and based upon the formulation of that Rule as it read then, the position seemed to be that exculpatory material obtained by the prosecution pursuant to Rule 70 *had* to be disclosed to the accused.[379] Certainly, this was the position adopted by the Trial Chamber in the ICTY case of *Brđanin and Talić*; it held that Rule 70(B) did 'not relieve the Prosecution of the obligation, pursuant to Rule 68, to disclose to the Defence "the existence of material known to the Prosecutor which in any way tends to suggest the innocence of mitigate the guilt of the accused or may affect the credibility of prosecution evidence"'.[380] Following this decision, and as stated, Rule 68 was amended in 2003, seemingly in order to create a mechanism by which conflicts between Rule 70 and Rule 68 could be resolved. A new paragraph (C) was added (now paragraph (iii)), which provides that: 'The Prosecutor shall take reasonable steps, if confidential information is provided to the Prosecutor by a person or entity under Rule 70(B) and contains material referred to in paragraph (A) above, to obtain the consent of the

---

[377] Ibid., para 38.

[378] Rule 70(B) ICTR RPE contains almost identical wording.

[379] O'Sullivan and Montgomery 2010, 529. At the time, Rule 68 ICTY RPE read as follows: 'The Prosecutor shall, as soon as practicable, disclose to the defence the existence of material known to the Prosecutor which in any way tends to suggest the innocence or mitigate the guilt of the accused or may affect the credibility of prosecution evidence.'

[380] *Prosecutor v Brđanin and Talić* (Public Version of the Confidential Decision on the Alleged Illegality of Rule 70 of 6 May 2002) IT-99-36-T, T Ch II (23 May 2002) para 19. See also paras 20–21.

provider to disclosure of that material, or the fact of its existence, to the accused.' And a new paragraph (D) was added (now paragraph (iv)), which provides that:

> The Prosecutor shall apply to the Chamber sitting in camera to be relieved from an obli-
> gation under the Rules to disclose information in the possession of the Prosecutor, if its
> disclosure may prejudice further or ongoing investigations, or for any other reason may be
> contrary to the public interest or affect the security interests of any State, and when making
> such application, the Prosecutor shall provide the Trial Chamber (but only the Trial
> Chamber) with the information that is sought to be kept confidential.

This effectively boiled down to the following: the Prosecution would attempt to obtain consent from the information provider to disclose the confidential 'lead' information, and, if it could not, it would apply to the trial chamber to be relieved from its obligation to disclose.[381] What the mechanism did *not* provide for, how-ever, was the situation in which the Prosecution could *not* obtain consent from the information providers to disclose for the purpose of providing *to the Trial Chamber*, let alone to the accused.[382] Shortly after the 2003 amendment, Rule 68 was amended *again*, so that the disclosure obligation provided for therein is now expressly subject to the provisions of Rule 70, thereby implying that it would be up to the Prosecution to resolve conflicts between Rules 70 and 68 (i.e. to, itself, address its failure to discharge its disclosure obligations under Rule 68), where it could not gain consent from information providers for the purpose of providing it to the Trial Chamber. Indeed, this is what the Prosecution in *Brđanin and Talić* had proposed: if it—the Prosecution—could not obtain consent for disclosure, it would either 'withdraw the Prosecution evidence materially contradicted [by the material that it could not disclose], or … withdraw the charges for which an Accused was exonerated [by the material in question]'.[383] And, this solution appears to have been endorsed in a trial decision in the ICTY case of *Karadžić*:

> It is incumbent upon the Prosecution to ensure fulfilment of its disclosure-related obliga-
> tions under the Rules and Statute of the Tribunal, and there is a presumption that it is doing
> so in good faith. Pursuant to the language of Rule 70(B) and Rule 68(iii), the Accused is not
> entitled to disclosure of the existence of confidential information absent the consent of its
> provider. Where the Prosecution's confidentiality obligations under Rule 70(B) compete
> with its disclosure obligations under Rule 68, it is for the Prosecution to take measures to
> resolve those concerns without falling in breach of either provision, with the supervision of
> the Trial Chamber if necessary-for example, under Rule 68(iv).[384]

According to Whiting, in reality, conflicts between Rule 70(B) and Rule 68 have rarely arisen at the ICTY, 'because the Prosecution was usually able to obtain

---

[381] Whiting 2009, 212.

[382] Ibid., 212.

[383] *Prosecutor v Brđanin and Talić* (Public Version of the Confidential Decision on the Alleged Illegality of Rule 70 of 6 May 2002) IT-99-36-T, T Ch II (23 May 2002) para 12.

[384] *Prosecutor v Karadžić* (Decision on Accused's Application for Certification to Appeal Decision on Rule 70(B)) IT-95-5/18-PT, T Ch III (12 February 2009) para 8.

permission from providers to disclose potentially exculpatory material obtained through Rule 70(B)'.[385]

6.3.2 ICC

Having set out the law and practice at the ad hoc Tribunals with respect to the question of how to address procedural violations arising in the context of disclosure, it is time now to turn to that at the ICC. At the ICC disclosure is governed by the ICC's own governing documents,[386] and by relevant human rights standards.[387] The case law discussed below, then, concerns violations of the ad hoc Tribunals' Statutes and/or RPEs, and/or relevant human rights standards. As with the ad hoc Tribunals, in setting out the relevant law and practice at the ICC, a distinction will be drawn between *late* disclosure, whereby the issue is that material that falls within the scope of a disclosure obligation on the part of the prosecution has been, or will have been, disclosed outside of the time limits prescribed or otherwise out of time, and *non*-disclosure, whereby the issue is that material that falls within the scope of such an obligation is being *withheld* in connection with some public or other interest. It may be noted at the outset that the ICC Statute and RPE are silent on how such issues should be addressed.[388]

---

[385] Whiting 2009, 213–214.

[386] It should be noted that, at the ICC, provision is made for an elaborate confirmation of charges procedure, which (unlike at the ad hoc Tribunals) takes place after the issuance of an arrest warrant or summons to appear, and at which the suspect will, 'as a general rule', be present. Moreover, the suspect can 'participate actively in the proceedings', by, inter alia, presenting his or her own evidence and challenging the evidence relied on by the prosecution for the purposes of such proceedings. For the purpose of this procedure, the ICC Statute and ICC RPE provide for the *disclosure* of information to the defence (Article 61(3)(b)). In addition, the ICC Statute and ICC RPE contain disclosure provisions that apply to the proceedings in their entirety (including the confirmation stage), e.g. Article 67(2) ICC Statute. The latter provision imposes on the prosecution an obligation to disclose to the defence (potentially) exculpatory material. While on the one hand it may be observed that the level of disclosure required at the confirmation stage of the proceedings is lower than that required at the trial stage (in light of the different evidentiary thresholds applicable at each stage), on the other, it is important to note that 'the bulk of disclosure will take place *before* the confirmation of charges' (see Tochilovsky 2013, 1089 (emphasis added)). For a comprehensive overview of the standards governing disclosure at the ICC, see Gibson and Lussiaà-Berdou 2010; and Fiori 2015.

[387] See in this regard n 272 and accompanying text.

[388] Aside from the procedural step envisaged in Rule 121(8) ICC RPE: 'The Pre-Trial Chamber shall not take into consideration charges and evidence presented after the time limit, or any extension thereof, has expired.'

§ Late disclosure

Allegations of late disclosure have been raised on numerous occasions before the ICC. In *Lubanga*, the Defence had, towards the end of the trial, sought another stay of proceedings[389] on account of, inter alia, a number of instances of late disclosure on the part of the Prosecution, which the Defence alleged had been deliberate.[390] While the Prosecution conceded that 'on occasion, mistakes … [had] been made', it denied that any such delays had been deliberate.[391] In addressing the Defence's arguments, the Trial Chamber noted that throughout the trial, it had taken various measures to ensure its fairness, including the ordering of additional disclosure to the Defence.[392] After finding that a stay of proceedings was not appropriate,[393] the Trial Chamber said that, at the end of the case, it would review the instances in which it was suggested that the Prosecution had failed in its duty to disclose in a timely manner certain materials in its possession, and that if it found that this had indeed occurred, 'the appropriate remedy … [would] lie in the Court's approach to the evidence in question, and particularly the extent to which the relevant testimony and other materials … [were] to be relied on'.[394] According to the Trial Chamber, '[a] failure to ensure that the accused received all the material to which he is entitled (at an appropriate stage of the proceedings, or at all) may affect the Chamber's conclusions on the area or issue in question.'[395] Regarding the Defence's allegations that the Prosecution had acted deliberately, the Trial Chamber said that if any of the (limited number of) instances of late disclosure was found to have been committed deliberately, 'an appropriate sanction would fall to be imposed, but on the facts and examples advanced by the defence, this issue … would be resolved properly at the end of the trial, and the relatively limited instances of alleged deliberate non-disclosure relied on … [did] not make it unfair it repugnant to continue the trial'.[396] Earlier on in the trial, the Trial Chamber had responded to an instance of late disclosure on the part of the Prosecution by granting a defence request for the Prosecution witness to whom the material pertained to be recalled for further cross-examination by the Defence.[397] In other cases, the possibility of recalling prosecution witness for the purpose of allowing the defence to conduct (limited) further cross-examination in light of late disclosure has been expressly

---

[389] On two earlier occasions, a stay was imposed in this case. See n 434 and 459–460 and accompanying text.

[390] *Prosecutor v Lubanga* (Redacted Decision on the "Defence Application Seeking a Permanent Stay of the Proceedings") ICC-01/04-01/06, T Ch I (7 March 2011) para 206.

[391] Ibid., para 207.

[392] Ibid., paras 210–211.

[393] Ibid., para 212.

[394] Ibid., para 212.

[395] Ibid., para 212.

[396] Ibid., para 212.

[397] *Prosecutor v Lubanga* (Judgment pursuant to Article 74 of the Statute) ICC-01/04-01/06, T Ch I (14 March 2012) para 122.

mooted. In *Ntaganda*, for example, the Trial Chamber did so in the context of a defence request for the postponement of the cross-examination of the prosecution witness to whom the belatedly disclosed material pertained; in rejecting the request, the Trial Chamber found that the late disclosure concerned 'a very limited volume of information on a confined aspect', and noted that this decision was without prejudice to the aforementioned possibility.[398]

In *Kenyatta*, an affidavit of a witness on whose evidence the Prosecution had relied at the hearing on the confirmation of charges, and some other documents pertaining to this witness, which all fell within the scope of Article 67(2) of the ICC Statute (i.e. were potentially exculpatory), had been disclosed to the Defence only after the hearing, despite being in the Prosecution's possession before that time.[399] According to the Defence, the Prosecution had acted in bad faith in this regard; it alleged that the Prosecution had purposely withheld the affidavit until after the decision on the confirmation of charges was issued. According to the Trial Chamber, the Prosecution had made a 'grave mistake' in this regard, which was the 'result of a deficient review system in place (at the time) within the Prosecution, where—apparently—persons without knowledge of the overall state of the evidence against the accused, or at a minimum the overall evidence provided by the witness concerned, performed a review of the [affidavit]',[400] and where 'no member of the Prosecution appears to have adequately re-reviewed the [a]ffidavit and noticed the mistake'.[401] The Trial Chamber considered the Prosecution's failure to disclose the affidavit and other documents pertaining to the witness in question 'to be a cause for serious concern, both in terms of the integrity of the proceedings and the rights of Mr. Kenyatta'.[402] However, the prejudice caused by the breach could be 'rectified at trial', since the Prosecution no longer intended to call the witness in question, and the Defence would be able to 'challenge the credibility of other evidence relied upon by the Prosecution at confirmation in corroboration of ... [the relevant witness'] evidence'.[403] Moreover, according to the Trial Chamber, there was 'no conclusive information of bad faith on the part of the Prosecution in failing to disclose the document'.[404] Accordingly, a stay of proceedings was not an appropriate remedy. Instead, the Trial Chamber 'reprimanded' the Prosecution 'for its conduct', and ordered it to 'conduct a complete review of its case file and certify the Trial Chamber that it has done so in order to ensure that no other materials in its

---

[398] *Prosecutor v Ntaganda* (Public redacted version of 'Decision on Defence requests seeking disclosure orders in relation to witness P-0901 and seeking the postponement of the witness's cross-examination', ICC-01/04-02/06-840-Conf-Exp, issued on 18 September 2015') ICC-01/04-02/06, T Ch VI (5 October 2015) para 64.

[399] *Prosecutor v Kenyatta* (Decision on defence application pursuant to Article 64(4) and related requests) ICC-01/09-02/11, T Ch V (26 April 2013) paras 93–94.

[400] Ibid., para 93.

[401] Ibid., para 94.

[402] Ibid., para 95.

[403] Ibid., para 96.

[404] Ibid., para 96.

possession that ought to have been disclosed to the Defence, are left undisclosed'.[405] In addition, it conveyed its expectation that the Prosecution would make appropriate changes to its internal procedures.[406]

In *Bemba*, materials collected during the Prosecution's investigation related to offences under Article 70 of the ICC Statute (i.e. 'offences against the administration of justice'), in the case of *Bemba and others*, and which fell under Rule 77 of the ICC RPE,[407] had not been disclosed to the Defence promptly. However, according to the Trial Chamber, the Accused had not been prejudiced by the Prosecution's failure to disclose certain materials in a timely manner.[408] In so finding, the Trial Chamber attached importance to the fact that the Defence had not made 'timely submissions' on the materials once disclosed, including on any prejudice suffered by the late disclosure.[409] Regarding an earlier instance of late disclosure, the Trial Chamber found that the Defence had not been prejudiced thereby, since it had been given the opportunity to make additional submissions in its closing brief and to submit additional material into evidence.[410] Moreover, it had been able to address certain issues during the recall of one of the prosecution witnesses concerned.[411] In an earlier decision still, the Trial Chamber held in relation to a request for relief in respect of a late disclosure of Rule 77 material to the Defence (after the Defence had commenced its examination of a defence witness to whom the material pertained and which the Prosecution sought to use during cross-examination) that, while it '[disfavoured] late disclosure in principle', in the event of late disclosure which occurred for 'justifiable reasons', it would 'analyse the items at issue on a case-by-case basis in order to determine whether such late disclosure is unfairly prejudicial to the defence', whereby it would pay 'particular attention to the nature of the disclosed documents and the reasons justifying the late disclosure, and especially the reasons why it could not have been disclosed earlier'.[412] Earlier on in the decision, the Trial Chamber had said that:

[i]n exceptional cases, a document which was not previously subject to disclosure under …
[Article 67(2) of the ICC Statute or Rule 77 of the ICC RPE] may become disclosable on the

---

[405] Ibid., para 97.

[406] Ibid., para 97.

[407] Rule 77 ICC RPE provides that: 'The Prosecutor shall, subject to the restrictions on disclosure as provided for in the Statute and in Rules 81 and 82, permit the defence to inspect any books, documents, photographs and other tangible objects in the possession or control of the Prosecutor, which are material to the preparation of the defence or are intended for use by the Prosecutor as evidence for the purposes of the confirmation hearing or at trial, as the case may be, or were obtained from or belonged to the person.'

[408] *Prosecutor v Bemba* (Decision on "Defence Request for Relief for Abuse of Process") ICC-01/05-01/08, T Ch III (17 June 2015) para 90.

[409] Ibid., paras 90 and 84.

[410] Ibid., para 118.

[411] Ibid., para 118.

[412] *Prosecutor v Bemba* (Decision on "Defence Motion Regarding Prosecution Disclosure") ICC-01/05-01/08, T Ch III (3 September 2012) para 12.

basis of the testimony of a witness. In such a situation, the need for disclosure of the document may not have been foreseen before the commencement of the relevant testimony.[413]

In light of this, the Trial Chamber was 'not convinced that ordering the prosecution to conduct a full review of all relevant databases and archives and to provide the defence with any additional disclosable material in its possession, by a certain date, would serve any purpose or address the issue of unavoidable late disclosure'.[414] Similarly, it saw 'no merit in ordering the prosecution to certify that it has fulfilled its disclosure obligations as regards Article 67(2) items and Rule 77 material, since … such disclosure obligations are ongoing during the defence's presentation of evidence.'[415]

In *Ruto and Sang*, the Prosecution had failed to disclose a number of documents to the Defence in a timely manner,[416] in respect of which the Defence sought relief. In considering how to address such disclosure violations, the Trial Chamber attached importance to the fact that the majority of these violations were the result of 'human error', while the others stemmed from 'the Chamber's overruling the Prosecution position on the disclosability of certain materials'.[417] In concluding that the Prosecution's disclosure violations revealed '*imperfections* in the Prosecution's disclosure system rather than *systematic failures indicating lack of fitness for purpose*', the Trial Chamber found that, when viewed against the backdrop of the material already disclosed to the Defence, the violations were limited in number.[418] As to the relief sought by the Defence, the Trial Chamber found that the arguments presented by it did not 'reveal the specific systemic problems which would justify significant Chamber intervention into the Prosecution's disclosure process'.[419] Nevertheless, the Trial Chamber ordered the Prosecution 'to certify no later than the end of its case that no disclosable materials remain undisclosed.'[420] It did so '*[i] rrespective* of whether the established disclosure shortcomings [had] caused any *prejudice* to the Defence', having earlier observed that the determination of how to address disclosure violations was not simply matter of determining whether or not the defence was prejudiced thereby; according to the Trial Chamber, the 'ultimate question engaged' [was] this: what else may have been left undisclosed if the Prosecution's disclosure system is truly unsatisfactory?'[421] The Trial Chamber did

---

[413] Ibid., para 11.

[414] Ibid., para 13.

[415] Ibid., para 13.

[416] *Prosecutor v Ruto and Sang* (Decision on Ruto Defence Request for the Appointment of a Disclosure Officer and/or the Imposition of Other Remedies for Disclosure Breaches of 9 January 2015 (ICC-01/09-01/11-1774-Conf) ICC-01/09-01/11, T Ch V(A) (16 February 2015) paras 26, 52 and 55.

[417] Ibid., para 55.

[418] Ibid., para 55 (emphasis added).

[419] Ibid., para 57.

[420] Ibid., para 59.

[421] Ibid., paras 59 and 9.

not consider it necessary to appoint a disclosure officer,[422] who would be responsible for certifying that 'all disclosable materials have been provided to the Defence and, for future disclosures, to provide reasons why such material was not disclosed previously'.[423]

§ Non-disclosure

Having set out the case law concerning the question of how to address *late* disclosure, the case law with respect to the question of how to address *non*-disclosure, whereby the issue is that material that falls within the scope of such an obligation is being *withheld* in connection with some public or other interest, will now be set out.

Prior to the commencement of the *Lubanga* trial (but after the confirmation of charges), the Prosecution had indicated that it had Article 54(3)(e) material in its possession, which it had identified as potentially exculpatory or otherwise material to the Defence.[424] Initially, the Trial Chamber responded by ordering that the entirety of the Prosecution's evidence, including all exculpatory material in its possession, be served by a particular date the disclosure by a certain date.[425] In addition, it indicated that, if the prosecution had in its possession any exculpatory material which it was unable to disclose and which may materially impact on the Court's determination of guilt or innocence, it was under an obligation to withdraw any charges which the non-disclosed exculpatory material impacted upon, and that if the prosecution was in doubt as to whether or not the material fell into this category, it should be put before the bench for the Trial Chamber's determination.[426] Effectively, this boiled down to allowing the Prosecution to resolve conflicts between Articles 54(3)(e) and 67(2) of the ICC Statute itself, i.e. to, itself, address its failure to discharge its disclosure obligations under Article 67(2) of the ICC Statute.[427] In the months that followed, various attempts were made to obtain consent from the Article 54(3)(e) information providers to lift the confidentiality agreements, but with little success.[428] Having initially indicated that the documents that it was unable to disclose contained potentially exculpatory material, the Prosecution now argued that 'none of the undisclosed evidence "in fact" materially

---

[422] Ibid., para 62.

[423] Ibid., para 61.

[424] The same issue arose in the case of *Katanga and Ngudjolo*, but *prior to* the confirmation of charges. For how the Pre-Trial Chamber addressed the situation, see *Prosecutor v Katanga and Ngudjolo* (Decision on Article 54(3)(e) Documents Identified as Potentially Exculpatory or Otherwise Material to the Defence's Preparation for the Confirmation Hearing) ICC-01/04-01/07, P T Ch I (20 June 2008).

[425] *Prosecutor v Lubanga* (Decision Regarding the Timing and Manner of Disclosure and the Date of Trial) ICC-01/04-01/06, T Ch I (9 November 2007) para 25.

[426] Ibid., para 28.

[427] See also Whiting 2009, 215–217.

[428] *Prosecutor v Lubanga* (Decision on the consequences of non-disclosure of exculpatory materials covered by Article 54(3)(e) agreements and the application to stay the prosecution of the accused, together with certain other issues raised at the Status Conference on 10 June 2008) ICC-01/04-01/06, T Ch I (13 June 2008) paras 17, 19, 36–41, 49, 67 and 69.

impacted on the Chamber's determination of the guilt or innocence of the accused',[429] and that the similar, alternative materials it had provided to the Defence would allow the Defence to prepare for trial.[430] Upon ordering the Prosecution to provide to the Trial Chamber the undisclosed materials, in order for it to be able to review the material and determine whether the non-disclosure constituted a breach of the accused's right to a fair trial, the Prosecution indicated that it would be unable to comply (due to lack of consent on the part of the information providers).[431] The Trial Chamber then directed the Prosecution to provide it with descriptions of the undisclosed material, together with explanations as to why each document was not, in the Prosecution's view, exculpatory; however, the Prosecution indicated that it was also unable to comply with this order.[432] According to the Prosecution, the trial could commence as planned; the Defence had been provided with similar, alternative materials (which was limited in volume) and, in any case, none of the undisclosed potentially exculpatory material would impact on the guilt or innocence of the accused.[433] In addition, it argued that, since Article 67(2) directed the Prosecution to disclose materials which it 'believed' to be potentially exculpatory, the implication was that it would be trusted to deal with evidence in this area appropriately, and that disclosure, as an ongoing obligation, necessitated the defence accepting that disclosure of exculpatory materials would continue throughout the trial.[434] Instead, the Trial Chamber stayed the proceedings,[435] thereby abandoning its 'original approach of allowing the Prosecution to determine the remedy if it could not disclose the potentially exculpatory materials'.[436] In staying the proceedings, the Trial Chamber emphasized that *it* was the arbiter of whether or not materials fell to be disclosed under Article 67(2), and that the confidential agreements between the Prosecution and information providers (as meant in Article 54(3)(e) of the ICC Statute) undermined the Trial Chamber's role in this regard.[437] It also held that the Prosecution had 'given Article 54(3)(e) [of the ICC Statute] a broad and incorrect interpretation: it has utilized the provision routinely, in inappropriate circumstances, instead of resorting to it exceptionally, when particular, restrictive circumstances apply.[438] The Prosecution had conceded

---

[429] Ibid., para 20. See further paras 21–22 and 51.

[430] Ibid., paras 42, 50 and 51.

[431] Ibid., para 44.

[432] Ibid., para 44.

[433] Ibid., para 51.

[434] Ibid., para 51.

[435] Ibid., para 51.

[436] Whiting 2009, 217.

[437] *Prosecutor v Lubanga* (Decision on the consequences of non-disclosure of exculpatory materials covered by Article 54(3)(e) agreements and the application to stay the prosecution of the accused, together with certain other issues raised at the Status Conference on 10 June 2008) ICC-01/04-01/06, T Ch I (13 June 2008) paras 61–62.

[438] Ibid., para 72. See also para 73.

in open court that agreements reached under Article 54(3)(e) had been 'used generally to gather information, unconnected with its springboard or lead potential'.[439] According to the Trial Chamber, '[i]n light of the prosecution's *inappropriate* use of these confidentiality agreements, and the resulting inability to effect proper disclosure to the defence, it is manifest that the agreements should not be allowed to operate in a way that subverts the Statute.'[440] Nevertheless, it observed that in circumstances in which Article 54(3)(e) has been used *appropriately*, i.e. the Prosecution has made only limited use of it, 'it is likely that a mechanism ... [will be able to be] established which facilitates all necessary disclosure'.[441] According to the Trial Chamber, the failure to disclose a 'significant body' of potentially exculpatory evidence to the accused, which 'improperly ... [inhibited] the opportunities for the accused to prepare his defence', coupled with the inability of the Trial Chamber to review the material in question and determine whether the non-disclosure constituted a breach of the accused's right to a fair trial, meant that 'the trial process has been ruptured to such a degree that it is now impossible to piece together the constituent elements of a fair trial'.[442] According to the Trial Chamber, in order stay the proceedings, it was not necessary to establish bad faith —'mala fides'—on the part of the prosecution; it was sufficient to show that 'the essential preconditions of a fair trial are missing' and that 'there is no sufficient indication that this will be resolved during the trial process'; in such circumstances 'it is necessary—indeed, inevitable—that the proceedings should be stayed'.[443]

The stay of proceedings was upheld on appeal, with the Appeals Chamber confirming that the stay imposed by the Trial Chamber was not permanent, but rather halted the proceedings indefinitely. More specifically, the stay imposed by the Trial Chamber could—according to the Appeals Chamber—be characterized as 'conditional'.[444] In other words, the stay was subject to the condition that the obstacles that led to the imposition of the stay remain in place, whereby such obstacles were, from the outset, understood to be of such a nature that a fair trial might become possible at a later stage. In characterizing the stay imposed by the Trial Chamber as conditional, the Appeals Chamber does not appear to have envisaged a different response to that envisaged by the Trial Chamber. Indeed, according to the Appeals Chamber it was clear that the Trial Chamber intended to

---

[439] Ibid., para 72.

[440] Ibid., para 75 (emphasis added).

[441] Ibid., para 76.

[442] Ibid., paras 92–93.

[443] Ibid., paras 90–91.

[444] *Prosecutor v Lubanga* (Judgment on the appeal of the Prosecutor against the decision of Trial Chamber I entitled "Decision on the consequences of non-disclosure of exculpatory materials discovered by Article 54(3)(e) agreements and the application to stay the prosecution of the accused, together with certain other issues raised at the Status Conference on 10 June 2008") ICC-01/04-01/06, A Ch (21 October 2008) paras 4, 75 and 80.

impose a stay that was conditional and therefore potentially only temporary, referring to the Trial Chamber's explicit acknowledgment that the stay might be lifted.[445] Regarding the potential tension between Article 54(3)(e) and Article 67(2) of the ICC Statute, the Appeals Chamber observed that there might be circumstances in which it can be resolved by, for example, the prosecution providing 'new, exculpatory material' to the defence, providing the non-disclosable material in 'summarised form', stipulating relevant facts, or amending or withdrawing the charges.[446] In this case, however, material had been collected 'on a large scale',[447] as a consequence of which, it seems, the aforementioned measures would not have been appropriate. According to the Appeals Chamber, the last sentence of Article 67(2) of the ICC Statute ('[i]n case of doubt as to the application of ... [Article 67 (2)], the Court shall decide'), indicates that 'the final assessment as to whether material in the possession or control of the Prosecutor has to be disclosed under that provision will have to carried out by the Trial Chamber and that therefore the Chamber should receive the material', which 'coincides with the overall role ascribed to the Trial Chamber in Article 64(2) of the Statute to guarantee that the trial is fair and expeditious, and that the rights of the accused are fully respected'.[448] The Prosecution's approach to Article 54(3)(e) of the ICC Statute had, therefore, not been correct.[449] The Appeals Chamber concluded as follows:

> as of 13 June 2008, the Trial Chamber was faced with a situation in which a *large number of documents* containing potentially exculpatory information or information relevant to the

---

[445] Ibid., para 75.

[446] *Prosecutor v Lubanga* (Judgment on the appeal of the Prosecutor against the decision of Trial Chamber I entitled "Decision on the consequences of non-disclosure of exculpatory materials discovered by Article 54(3)(e) agreements and the application to stay the prosecution of the accused, together with certain other issues raised at the Status Conference on 10 June 2008") ICC-01/04-01/06, A Ch (21 October 2008) para 44 in conjunction with para 28. See also *Prosecutor v Banda and Jerbo* (Public redacted version of the "Second Decision on Article 54(3) (e) documents") ICC-02/05-03/09, T Ch IV (26 October 2012) para 9; and *Prosecutor v Banda and Jerbo* (Public Redacted Version of the "Third Decision on Article 54(3)(e) documents") ICC-02/05-03/09, T Ch IV (21 June 2013) para 12.

[447] *Prosecutor v Lubanga* (Judgment on the appeal of the Prosecutor against the decision of Trial Chamber I entitled "Decision on the consequences of non-disclosure of exculpatory materials discovered by Article 54(3)(e) agreements and the application to stay the prosecution of the accused, together with certain other issues raised at the Status Conference on 10 June 2008") ICC-01/04-01/06, A Ch (21 October 2008) para 44.

[448] Ibid., para 46. According to the Appeals Chamber, this approach has been confirmed by the ECtHR, e.g. in the cases of *Jasper v UK* App no 27052/95 (ECtHR, 16 February 2000) and *Rowe and Davis v UK* App no 28901/95 (ECtHR, 16 February 2000) (ibid., paras 46–47). Whiting is critical in this regard, noting also that this marks a shift from the relevant case law at the ICTY, and from the approach initially adopted by the Trial Chamber in *Lubanga*. Whiting 2009, 220–221.

[449] *Prosecutor v Lubanga* (Judgment on the appeal of the Prosecutor against the decision of Trial Chamber I entitled "Decision on the consequences of non-disclosure of exculpatory materials discovered by Article 54(3)(e) agreements and the application to stay the prosecution of the accused, together with certain other issues raised at the Status Conference on 10 June 2008") ICC-01/04-01/06, A Ch (21 October 2008) para 49.

preparation of the defence was in the possession of the Prosecutor, but could not be disclosed to Mr. Lubanga Dyilo. Nor could the Trial Chamber have access to the documents in order to assess whether a fair trial could be held even without the disclosure of the documents. … the Appeals Chamber has no reason to fault the assessment of the Trial Chamber on 13 June 2008 that this situation would continue. If the trial of Mr. Lubanga Dyilo had taken place in such circumstances, there would always have been a lurking doubt as to whether the disclosure of the documents in question would have changed the course of the trial.[450]

On 18 November 2008, the Trial Chamber lifted the stay in an oral decision, having (finally) been provided with the materials.[451]

In *Banda and Jerbo*, the Prosecution had also indicated that it had Article 54(3) (e) materials in its possession that were subject to Article 67(2) of the ICC Statute, i.e. were potentially exculpatory, or to Rule 77 of the ICC RPE, i.e. were material to the preparation of the defence. After the Trial Chamber had itself reviewed the documents and instructed the Prosecution to seek the consent of the information providers to disclose the documents to the Defence,[452] it became clear that such consent would not be granted (at least, not for the time being).[453] According to the Trial Chamber, in light of the fact that 'only a small number of documents' were concerned, it was sufficient to adopt appropriate 'counter-balancing measures'.[454] In the circumstances, this included the provision of narrative summaries instead of the original documentation, entering into admissions of fact relating to the undisclosed documents, and the provision of alternative evidence.[455] In so ruling, the Trial Chamber relied on the Appeals Chamber's findings in the *Lubanga* case, regarding the question of how to resolve a conflict between Article 67(2) and Article 54(3)(e) of the ICC Statute.[456] Regarding the admissions of fact into which the Prosecution had already entered, the Trial Chamber found that the 'concession' was 'sufficiently broad in scope and, together with the alternative evidence, … [covered] for the essential elements in the confidential documents', and that the Defence 'should be able to rely on … [the] admission from the [P]rosecution rather than having to seek to establish the facts through the unavailable material'.[457] Even

---

[450] Ibid., para 97 (emphasis added).

[451] *Prosecutor v Lubanga* (Oral Decision) ICC-01/04-01/06, T Ch I (18 November 2008) 3–4. The oral decision was followed by a written decision: *Prosecutor v Lubanga* (Reasons for Oral Decision lifting the stay of proceedings) ICC-01/04-01/06, T Ch I (23 January 2009).

[452] *Prosecutor v Banda and Jerbo* (Decision on Article 54(3)(e) documents) ICC-02/05-03/09, T Ch IV (23 November 2011) para 17.

[453] *Prosecutor v Banda and Jerbo* (Public redacted version of the "Second Decision on Article 54 (3)(e) documents") ICC-02/05-03/09, T Ch IV (26 October 2012) para 8.

[454] Ibid., para 9.

[455] Ibid., paras 11–21. See also *Prosecutor v Banda and Jerbo* (Public Redacted Version of the "Third Decision on Article 54(3)(e) documents") ICC-02/05-03/09, T Ch IV (21 June 2013) paras 10–18.

[456] See n 446 and accompanying text.

[457] *Prosecutor v Banda and Jerbo* (Public redacted version of the "Second Decision on Article 54 (3)(e) documents") ICC-02/05-03/09, T Ch IV (26 October 2012) para 19.

though the admission was not binding on the Trial Chamber, the Defence was put in a 'more favourable evidential position that it would have been otherwise'.[458]

The Appeals Chamber's findings in relation to the second stay of proceedings imposed by the Trial Chamber in the *Lubanga* case are also worth noting here. Two years after the imposition of the first stay of proceedings, the Trial Chamber imposed another stay on the basis of the Prosecutor's refusal to comply with its repeated orders to disclose to the Defence (in 'highly restricted circumstances')[459] the identity of an 'intermediary' used by the Prosecution in that case to contact witnesses that it intended to call, who the Defence alleged had influenced individuals to give false testimony (and who the Defence alleged the Prosecution had knowingly employed, or made use of),[460] *and* of the 'Prosecutor's clearly evinced intention not to implement the Chamber's orders that are made in … [the context of Article 68 of the ICC Statute, which provides for the protection of victims and witnesses and their participation in the proceedings], if he considers they conflict with his interpretation of the prosecution's other obligations'.[461] The Trial Chamber held that '[w]hilst these circumstances endure, the fair trial of the accused is no longer possible, and justice cannot be done, not least because the judges will have lost control of a significant aspect of the trial proceedings as provided under the Rome Statute framework.'[462] Accordingly, it was necessary to stay the proceedings. On appeal, the Appeals Chamber found that,

> in the present case, the Prosecutor's refusal to comply with or to be bound by the orders of the Trial Chamber extended to a significant part of the trial and concerned issues of the trial's fundamental fairness. It threatened not only Mr Lubanga Dyilo's right to be tried without undue delay but also the fairness of the proceedings as a whole. If a Trial Chamber loses control of such a significant and fundamental part of proceedings because of the Prosecutor's refusal to comply with its orders, it would indeed be impossible to ensure a fair trial, and a stay of proceedings would then be justified.[463]

---

[458] Ibid., para 19.

[459] *Prosecutor v Lubanga* (Judgment on the appeal of the Prosecutor against the decision of Trial Chamber I of 8 July entitled "Decision on the Prosecution's Urgent Request for Variation of the Time-Limit to Disclose the Identity of Intermediary 143 or Alternatively to Stay Proceedings Pending Further Consultations with the VWU") ICC-01/04-01/06, A Ch (8 October 2010) para 20.

[460] *Prosecutor v Lubanga* (Redacted Decision on the Prosecution's Urgent Request for Variation of the Time-Limit to Disclose the Identity of Intermediary 143 or Alternatively to Stay Proceedings Pending Further Consultations with the VWU) ICC-01/04-01/06, T Ch I (8 July 2010) para 20.

[461] Ibid., para 31. See also para 21. See *Prosecutor v Lubanga* (Judgment on the appeal of the Prosecutor against the decision of Trial Chamber I of 8 July entitled "Decision on the Prosecution's Urgent Request for Variation of the Time-Limit to Disclose the Identity of Intermediary 143 or Alternatively to Stay Proceedings Pending Further Consultations with the VWU") ICC-01/04-01/06, A Ch (8 October 2010) para 57.

[462] *Prosecutor v Lubanga* (Judgment on the appeal of the Prosecutor against the decision of Trial Chamber I of 8 July entitled "Decision on the Prosecution's Urgent Request for Variation of the Time-Limit to Disclose the Identity of Intermediary 143 or Alternatively to Stay Proceedings Pending Further Consultations with the VWU") ICC-01/04-01/06, A Ch (8 October 2010) para 31.

[463] Ibid., para 58.

However, the stay of proceedings imposed by the Trial Chamber had *not* been justified, since 'the Trial Chamber had not yet lost control of the proceedings'. In this regard, the Appeals Chamber noted that: '[A]rticle 71 of the [ICC] Statute [provides] Trial Chambers with a specific tool to maintain control of proceedings and, thereby, to ensure a fair trial when faced with the deliberate refusal of a party to comply with its directions', whereby the purpose of such sanctions 'is not merely … to punish the offending party, but also to bring about compliance'.[464] While, strictly speaking, these observations pertained to the Prosecution's refusal to comply with court orders more generally (and, ultimately, to the ability of the Trial Chamber to control the proceedings),[465] the underlying refusal to comply with court orders in this instance meant certain information not being disclosed to the Defence. Accordingly, it seems that where a refusal by the prosecution to comply with court orders involves certain material not being disclosed to the defence, the measures in Article 71 of the ICC Statute may be employed in order to bring about disclosure. In determining that the Trial Chamber had not yet lost control of the proceedings, the Appeals Chamber held that:

> Recourse to sanctions enables a Trial Chamber, using the tools available within the trial process itself, to cure the underlying obstacles to a fair trial, thereby allowing the trial to proceed speedily to a conclusion on its merits. Doing so, rather than resorting to the significantly more drastic remedy of a stay of proceedings, is in the interests, not only of the victims and of the international community as a whole who wish to see justice done, but also of the accused, who is potentially left in limbo, awaiting a decision on the merits of the case against him by the International Criminal Court or another court.[466]

According to the Appeals Chamber, there had, in the circumstances, been

> … no obstacle to imposing sanctions and allowing them a reasonable opportunity to induce compliance and, therefore, to change the very circumstances which made a fair trial prospectively impossible. In the view of the Appeals Chamber, the Trial Chamber therefore exceeded its margin of appreciation when it found that it had lost control of the proceedings and that, consequently, a fair trial had become impossible and a stay of proceedings was required. It is the view of the Appeals Chamber that, before ordering the stay of proceedings, the Trial Chamber should have imposed sanctions and given such sanctions a reasonable time to bring about their intended effects.[467]

6.3.3 Comparison and Analysis

Having set out the relevant law and practice with respect to the question of how to address procedural violations committed in the context of disclosure at the ad hoc

---

[464] Ibid., para 59.

[465] Ibid., paras 57–58.

[466] Ibid., para 60.

[467] Ibid., para 61.

Tribunals, and that at the ICC, respectively, the question that now needs to be answered is how such law and practice compares. The purpose of the present sub-section, then, is to compare the approaches of the ad hoc Tribunals and the ICC to the aforementioned question, and to (critically) analyse such law and practice, with a view to providing a more complete picture of the law and practice with respect to the question of how to address procedural violations committed in the context of disclosure (not in order to argue what the law and practice *should* be; it is in Chap. 7 that that arguments are made as to what the law and practice of the ICTs with respect to the question how to address pre-trial procedural violations ought to be).

Turning first to the issue of *late* disclosure, it was seen that the ad hoc Tribunals have consistently held that in the determination of how to address a disclosure violation on the part of the prosecution, it is necessary to examine whether the accused was prejudiced by the violation, that is, whether the accused has been hampered in his or her ability to challenge prosecution witnesses effectively, and, by extension, to mount an effective defence, such as to infringe on the accused's right to a fair trial. At the ICC also, chambers have, when called upon to rule on disclosure violations on the part of the prosecution, consistently examined whether the accused was prejudiced by the violation. At the ad hoc Tribunals, chambers have responded to such prejudice in a variety of ways. In a case in which the disclosure had been effected after both the Prosecution and Defence cases had closed, the case was partially reopened.[468] Where the (late) disclosure has been effected after the prosecution case has closed, and the (potentially exculpatory) material in question pertains to a prosecution witness, it seems that there will, by definition, be prejudice to the accused; the defence will have been prevented from effectively examining witnesses *against* him or her. In such circumstances, the response has been to allow the defence to apply for prosecution witnesses to be recalled for further cross-examination, and/or for additional defence witnesses to be called. In a case in which it was not possible to (re)call certain witnesses, because they were unavailable, while the Defence had shown good cause to (re)call them, the chamber admitted into evidence certain material from the bar table, that is, not through a witness.[469] Recalling or calling (additional) witnesses may not be an option in light of the delay that it would cause and/or in light of fact that it would mean reopening the case in its entirety. In one case in which this was deemed to be the case, the chamber reserved the right to draw inferences in favour of the Accused with respect to specific evidence that has been the subject of a disclosure violation.[470] As Gibson and Lussiaà-Berdou observe, this is probably most far-reaching consequence to have been attached to disclosure violations at the ad hoc Tribunals;[471] while other, more far-reaching consequences, such as a stay of proceedings and the exclusion of (prosecution) evidence (i.e. prosecution evidence not

---

[468] See n 281–282 and accompanying text.

[469] See n 348 and accompanying text.

[470] See n 326 and accompanying text.

[471] Gibson and Lussiaà-Berdou 2010, 336.

properly disclosed or evidence relating to facts to which the exculpatory material pertains),[472] have been mooted, they have not been applied in practice. Where the (late) disclosure is effected during the prosecution case, the response has been to postpone the testimony of the witness concerned, or to allow the defence to apply for prosecution witnesses to be recalled for further cross-examination, or where the (late) disclosure is more substantial, adjourning the case for a more prolonged period. At the ICC also, chambers have responded to 'prejudice to the accused' resulting from a disclosure violation on the part of the prosecution in a variety of ways, depending on, among other things, the stage of the proceedings at which the disclosure was, belatedly, effected. Like their counterparts at the ad hoc Tribunals, ICC chambers have allowed the defence to apply for prosecution witnesses to be recalled for further cross-examination (or have otherwise indicated their willingness to entertain such applications), and have granted the defence extra time in order to review material disclosed belatedly. In a case in which the disclosure violations had been brought to light at the end of the trial, it was held that if any of the allegations proved to be true, the chamber would take this into account in its evaluation of the evidence to which the disclosure pertained.[473] At both the ad hoc Tribunals and the ICC, such 'remedial' measures have been taken regardless of the nature of the disclosure violation in question, i.e. regardless of whether it constitutes a failure to disclose (potentially) exculpatory material, or simply incriminating material on which the prosecution seeks to rely. Further, at both the ad hoc Tribunals and the ICC, if the material to have been disclosed belatedly has already been disclosed to the defence in one way or another, or is otherwise in the defence's possession, there will, as a rule, be no prejudice to the accused, and, if there is prejudice to the accused, the disclosure violation in question need not have been committed deliberately, let alone in bad faith, in order to justify such a remedial measure.

The tendency of both the ad hoc Tribunals and the ICC to focus on the question of whether the accused has been prejudiced by the failure on the part of the prosecution to discharge its disclosure obligations has been roundly criticized in the literature. Fiori argues that while such an approach may be appropriate in respect of isolated disclosure violations, 'a more robust solution' is required where there is a 'consolidated pattern of non-disclosure or late disclosure, which plagues the proceedings'.[474] The argument appears to be that repeated disclosure violations have the ability to impact on more than 'just' the ability of the defence to test the evidence of the particular witness or particular witnesses in question; they may hamper the ability of the accused to develop a coherent trial strategy for responding to the prosecution's case and for presenting its own, and, by extension to mount an effective defence. A further point of criticism is that, in adopting remedial measures such as granting extra time for preparation or allowing the defence to (re)call witnesses, chambers have not always been mindful of (and in any case have not

---

[472] Zappalà 2004, 627.

[473] See n 394–395 and accompanying text.

[474] Fiori 2015, 238.

expressly addressed) the potential impact thereof on the right of an accused to an *expeditious* trial.

In a number of decisions at the ad hoc Tribunals, the aforementioned *remedial* measures have been brought within the scope of Rule 68bis of the ICTY RPE, which, it may be recalled, provides that chambers 'may decide proprio motu, or at the request of either party, on *sanctions* to be imposed on a party which fails to perform its disclosure obligations pursuant to the Rules' (emphasis added). Such decisions appear to treat Rule 68bis as an umbrella provision, covering both remedial measures, which are aimed at curing prejudice suffered by the party to whom the material should have been disclosed (in a timely manner), in this case the defence, and 'sanctions *proper*',[475] which are aimed at punishing or disciplining the violating party, in this case the prosecution.[476] In other decisions, no reference is made to Rule 68bis in this regard. Here it may be observed that Rule 68bis was only introduced in 2001, and that before this, chambers had been taking measures to remedy prejudice.[477] Where (then) it is alleged that disclosure violations impact on the accused's right to a fair trial, chambers at the ad hoc Tribunals have held that it is necessary to examine whether there is prejudice to the accused. In one decision at least, the question of whether or not there was prejudice to the accused was taken into account in the determination of whether to impose a *sanction* on the prosecution for its failure to discharge its disclosure obligations; in that case a sanction was not imposed, *because* there was no prejudice to the accused.[478] However, it is not at all obvious why there must be prejudice to the accused as a result of the particular disclosure violation in question, in order to justify the imposition of a sanction; the purpose of a sanction is to punish the party responsible for the disclosure violation, or to deter such conduct in the future. It is arguable that disclosure violations always raise the risk of prejudice to the accused, even if in the particular circumstances that risk has not materialized; it is the risk that disclosure violations pose to the accused's right to a fair trial that calls for sanctions to be imposed, particularly where the prosecution has repeatedly failed to discharge its disclosure obligations. In other decisions at the ad hoc Tribunals, it has been suggested that, if

---

[475] Khan and Dixon 2013, 490.

[476] De los Reyes similarly distinguishes between remedies and sanctions in the context of disclosure. See De los Reyes 2005, 595.

[477] See e.g. the ICTY case of *Furundžija*, as set out above (see n 281–282 and accompanying text).

[478] See n 304 and accompanying text. In other decisions, chambers have held that for remedies, prejudice must be shown, in the same breath as referring to Rule 68 bis. See e.g. *Prosecutor v Brđanin* (Decision on "Motion for Relief from Rule 68 Violations by the Prosecutor and for Sanctions to Be Imposed Pursuant to Rule 68*bis* and Motion for Adjournment while Matters Affecting Justice and a Fair Trial Can Be Resolved") IT-99-36-T, T Ch II (30 October 2002) para 23; *Prosecutor v Blaškić* (Judgement) IT-95-14-A, A Ch (29 July 2004) para 268; and *Prosecutor v Orić* (Decision on Urgent Defence Motion Regarding Prosecutorial Non-Compliance with Rule 68) IT-03-68-T, T Ch II (27 October 2005) 3. However, given that these decisions also seem to treat Rule 68bis as an 'umbrella' provision, covering both remedial measures and 'sanctions proper' (see n 475–476 and accompanying text), it may be that the point regarding prejudice is only meant to apply to the 'remedial aspect' of that rule.

no prejudice is shown, chambers may nevertheless impose sanctions on account of disclosure violations.[479] Put differently, it has been suggested that in order to impose a sanction, prejudice to the accused need not be shown. Examples of sanctions at ad hoc Tribunals include judicial condemnation and (personal) reprimands, and/or referring the matter to the Prosecutor. In addition, chambers of the ad hoc Tribunals have mooted the possibility of holding prosecution counsel in contempt under Rule 77 of the RPE. A relevant consideration in the context of sanctions is whether the violation was the result of an oversight or, rather, was deliberate, and whether it stood alone or formed part of a pattern. The ICC also recognizes that there are other ways to respond to disclosure violations committed by the prosecution, i.e. irrespective of whether there is prejudice to the accused.[480] At the ICC also, the question of whether the disclosure violation was deliberate, or formed part of a wider pattern of late disclosure, is relevant to the question of whether a sanction is warranted.

Both the ad hoc Tribunals and the ICC, then, recognize that there are different ways to respond to disclosure violations committed by the prosecution; by way of measures aimed at remedying prejudice to the accused, and/or by way of measures aimed at punishing or disciplining the prosecution, with a view to deterring such conduct in the future. While they do not always clearly distinguish between such theoretical foundations, it is reasonable to conclude that, at both the ad hoc Tribunals and the ICC, in practice, disclosure violations are (indeed) governed more by a system of remedies, i.e. measures aimed at curing prejudice to the accused in terms of his or her ability to mount an effective defence, than by a system of sanctions aimed at punishing or disciplining the prosecution for failing to discharge its disclosure obligations. This state of affairs has been subject to much criticism in the literature. Several authors have called for more robust measures to be taken in relation to disclosure violations committed by the prosecution, to ensure compliance with disclosure obligations, often arguing that only more far-reaching measures such as the exclusion of evidence are capable of constituting an effective deterrent to failure to discharge such obligations.[481] In focusing on 'prejudice to the accused', the ad hoc Tribunals and the ICC have effectively side-stepped such questions as which sanctions are available to chambers faced with deliberate and/or repeated disclosure violations on the part of the prosecution, and under what conditions each sanction may be imposed. Another point worth noting here is that, in addressing late disclosure, chambers have rarely expressly considered how such conduct might reflect on *them*; they have considered the impact of such conduct on the defence and the possible ramifications thereof for, and how it reflects on, the

---

[479] See e.g. the ICTY cases of *Furundžija*, as set out above (see n 274–280 and accompanying text), *Krstić*, as set out above (see n 301 302 and accompanying text, but see also n 304 and 478 and accompanying text) and *Haradinaj, Balaj and Brahimaj*, as set out above (see n 369–370 and accompanying text).

[480] See n 393–396 and 421 and accompanying text.

[481] See e.g. Zappalà 2004, Gibson and Lussiaà-Berdou 2010, 320–322, 327 and 335–338, and, most recently, Fiori 2015, 237–239, 292–293, 343–345.

prosecution, but only rarely have they considered how such violations might otherwise impact on the integrity of the proceedings. More will be said about these issues below, in Chap. 7.

Turning now to *non*-disclosure, whereby the issue is that material that falls within the scope of a disclosure obligation on the part of the prosecution is being withheld in connection with some public or other interest, it seems that while at the ad hoc Tribunals it is up to the prosecution itself to address a failure to discharge its disclosure obligations, at the ICC, this is a matter for the trial chamber. At the ad hoc Tribunals, there are a number of options open to the prosecution to address a failure to discharge its disclosure obligations, where necessary, under the supervision of the trial chamber under Rule 68(iv): prosecution evidence that is materially contradicted by the information that cannot be disclosed may be withdrawn, or charges may be withdrawn. However, the RPEs do not provide for the situation in which judicial supervision is deemed to be necessary, but the prosecution is unable to disclose the confidential material to the trial chamber for this purpose, on account of a lack of consent on the part of the information providers; nor is the case law clear on what options are available to the trial chamber in this regard.[482] At the ICC, where material that is subject to disclosure cannot be disclosed on account of a lack of consent on the part of the information providers, there are a number of options; *under the supervision of the trial chamber*, i.e. upon the trial chamber having reviewed the material in question, the prosecution may provide alternative evidence or summaries of the evidence, or stipulate relevant facts, or amend or withdraw the charges. Where the chamber is unable to supervise the resolution of a conflict between confidential 'lead' evidence provisions on the one hand and the prosecution's disclosure obligations on the other, there are a number of options available to the chamber, depending on, among other things, the nature and volume of the material that cannot be disclosed: where the material has been identified as being potentially exculpatory and is substantial in volume, the trial chamber may stay the proceedings conditionally. In less serious cases, a less far-reaching response is warranted, such as the judicial disciplinary measures provided for in Article 71 of the ICC Statute.

6.4 Conclusion

The purpose of this chapter was to set out the law and practice of the ICTs with respect to the question of how to address procedural violations committed in the pre-trial phase of the proceedings from the perspective of specific types of procedural violation. In Sect. 6.2, the law and practice at the ICTs with respect to the

---

[482] This may be because, at the ICTY at least, the prosecution has generally been able to obtain consent from the information providers to disclose potentially exculpatory material to the defence. See n 385 and accompanying text.

question of how to address procedural violations committed in the context of arrest and detention was set out, while in Sect. 6.3, the law and practice of the ICTs with respect to the question of how to address procedural violations committed in the context of disclosure was set out. In this section, the main points of analysis are summarised.

Regarding the question raised in the introduction to this chapter of how the ICTs should address procedural violations physically committed by organs that are not institutionally connected to them, it was seen, in setting out and analysing the law and practice with respect to the question of how to address procedural violations committed in the context of arrest and detention, that the ICTs are prepared to entertain applications for relief in relation to an alleged illegal or unlawful deprivation of liberty carried out by national authorities (although the conditions for doing so differ as between the ad hoc Tribunals and the ICC). However, it seems that they will not attach consequences to such violations when it cannot be shown that the relevant international criminal tribunal was somehow involved in the violation(s) (the abuse of process doctrine being an exception to this rule at the ad hoc Tribunals). It was also seen that the threshold for enquiring into the circumstances surrounding an alleged illegal or unlawful deprivation of liberty in the first place for the purpose of determining an application for relief in this regard differs as between the ad hoc Tribunals and the ICC, as does what is understood by 'involvement' of the international criminal tribunal in the violation(s). Another point to emerge from the examination of the law and practice with respect to the question of how to address procedural violations committed in the context of arrest and detention is that, in determining an application for a certain type of relief in respect of an alleged illegal or unlawful deprivation of liberty, for example a stay of proceedings, chambers have not always considered 'alternative' and less far-reaching, forms of relief.

Another important point to emerge more clearly in the current chapter (than in the previous one), and in particular, in the context of arrest and detention, is that both the ad hoc Tribunals and the ICC are willing to attach consequences to procedural violations that do not impact on the accused's right to a fair trial in the sense of being able to mount an effective defence. Here it should be recalled that, cases involving long delays aside, the illegal or unlawful arrest or detention of a person suspected or accused of crimes falling within the jurisdiction of the relevant international criminal tribunal does not typically prevent such a person from being able to mount an effective defence. This point goes to the question raised in the introduction to this chapter of which rationale(s) should inform the determination of whether and how to address pre-trial procedural violations. It was observed above that, unlike illegal or unlawful arrest and detention (cases involving long delays aside), late or non-disclosure (i.e. procedural violations committed in the context of disclosure) raises issues with respect to the accused's right to a fair trial *as well as* other fundamental values, such as respect for the rule of law and the preservation of the integrity of the proceedings, whereby different considerations are likely to apply under each. This may raise the question of which rationale should 'prevail', i.e. what the primary rationale should be, when addressing such procedural violations (bearing in mind that to pursue one rationale may well be to give effect to another). In setting out and analysing the law and practice with respect to the question of how to address procedural violations committed in the context of disclosure, it was seen that ensuring the accused's right to a fair trial is the primary rationale in this regard, which chambers have sought to achieve by remedying established prejudice to the accused, largely on a piecemeal basis. While other fundamental values, i.e. respect for the rule of law and the preservation of the integrity of the proceedings, may well be served by the more remedial measures (aimed at curing established prejudice to the accused), they do not appear to be at the forefront of the ICTs' thinking with respect to the question of how to address procedural violations committed in the context of disclosure. While the ICTs have purported to impose sanctions against the prosecution for a failure to discharge its disclosure obligations, and have consistently mooted the possibility of doing so, they have done so sparingly, both in the sense that chambers more often resort to remedial measures, and in the sense that, when they do, they tend not to opt for the more far-reaching measures, such as exclusion of evidence, but rather the less far-reaching ones, such as judicial condemnation and referrals to the Prosecutor. An explanation for this may lie in chambers' findings that in failing to discharge its disclosure obligations, the prosecution did not act maliciously or in bad faith; in numerous decisions chambers have, in declining to sanction the prosecution for its failure to disclose in a timely manner, or in opting for a less far-reaching sanction, attached importance to this fact. Of course, the reluctance to impose more far-reaching sanctions may also be explained by a commitment to truth-finding, even if chambers do not always expressly acknowledge this. More will be said about the aforementioned issues below, in Chap. 7.

In the next chapter, the law and practice of the ICTs with respect to the question of how to address procedural violations committed in the pre-trial phase of the proceedings, as set out in Chap. 5 and in the current chapter, will be evaluated in light of the human rights standards set out in Chap. 2, and compared to the national law and practice set out in Chaps. 3 and 4. It is there that a discussion will take place of, and conclusions will be drawn as to, the adequacy of the judicial response at the ad hoc Tribunals, and that at the ICC, to procedural violations committed in the pre-trial phase of international criminal proceedings.

References

Currie RJ (2007) Abducted Fugitives Before the International Criminal Court: Problems and Prospects. Crim LF 18:349 et seq.

DeFrancia C (2001) Due Process in International Criminal Courts: Why Procedure Matters. Va L Rev 87:1381 et seq.

De los Reyes C (2005) Revisiting Disclosure Obligations at the ICTR and Its Implications for the Rights of the Accused. Chinese JIL 4:583 et seq.

De Meester K (2014) The Investigation Phase in International Criminal Procedure. In Search of Common Rules. DPhil thesis, University of Amsterdam

Fiori BM (2015) Disclosure of Information in Criminal Proceedings. A comparative analysis of national and international criminal procedurals and human rights law. Wolf Legal Publishers, Oisterwijk

Gibson K, Lussiaà-Berdou C (2010) Disclosure of Evidence. In: Khan KAA et al. (eds) Principles of Evidence in International Criminal Justice. Oxford University Press, Oxford, pp 306–372

Harris DJ et al. (2014) Harris, O'Boyle & Warbrick. Law of the European Convention on Human Rights, 3rd edn. Oxford University Press, Oxford

Khan KAA, Dixon R (2013) Archbold International Criminal Courts. Practice, Procedure and Evidence, 4th edn. Sweet & Maxwell, London

Mirfield P (1997) Silence, Confessions and Improperly Obtained Evidence. Oxford University Press, Oxford

Nowak M (2005) U.N. Convention on Civil and Political Rights: CCPR Commentary, 2nd edn. NP Engel Verlag, Kehl

O'Sullivan E, Montgomery D (2010) The Erosion of the Right to Confrontation under the Cloak of Fairness at the ICTY. JICJ 8:511 et seq.

Paulussen C (2010) Male Captus Bene Detentus? Surrendering Suspects to the International Criminal Court. Intersentia, Antwerp

Sloan J (2003) Prosecutor v. Todorović: Illegal Capture as an Obstacle to the Exercise of International Criminal Jurisdiction. LJIL 16:85 et seq.

Sloan J (2006) Breaching International Law to Ensure its Enforcement: The Reliance by the ICTY on Illegal Capture. In: McCormack T, McDonald A (eds) Yearbook of International Humanitarian Law, TMC Asser Press, The Hague, pp 319–344

Sluiter G (2003) International Criminal Proceedings and the Protection of Human Rights. New Eng L Rev 37:935 et seq.

Sluiter G (2005) Commentary. In: Klip A, Sluiter G (eds) Annotated Leading Cases of International Criminal Tribunals. Volume VII: The International Criminal Tribunal for the Former Yugoslavia 2001. Intersentia, Antwerp, pp 243–247

Sluiter G (2009) Human Rights Protection in the ICC Pre-Trial Phase. In: Stahn C, Sluiter G (eds) The Emerging Practice of the International Criminal Court. Martinus Nijhoff, Leiden, pp 459–475

Taylor M, Jalloh CC (2013) Provisional Arrest and Incarceration in the International Criminal Tribunals. Santa Clara J Int'l L 11:303 et seq.

Tochilovsky V (2013) Defence Access to the Prosecution Material. In: Sluiter G et al. (eds) International Criminal Procedure. Principles and Rules. Oxford University Press, Oxford, pp 1083–1098

Whiting A (2009) Lead Evidence and Discovery Before the International Criminal Court: The Lubanga Case. UCLA J Int'l L Foreign Aff 14:207 et seq.

Zappalà S (2004) The Prosecutor's Duty to Disclose Exculpatory Materials and the Recent Amendment to Rule 68 ICTY RPE. JICJ 2:620 et seq.

Zhou H (2006) The Enforcement of Arrest Warrants by International Forces. From the ICTY to the ICC. JICJ 4:202 et seq.

Chapter 7
Assessment of the International Criminal Tribunals' Law and Practice

Abstract In this chapter, the law and practice of the international criminal tribunals (ICTs) with respect to the question of how to address procedural violations committed in the pre-trial phase of the proceedings, as set out in Chaps. 5 and 6, is evaluated in light of the human rights standards set out in Chap. 2, and compared to the national law and practice (and the theoretical accounts thereof) set out in Chaps. 3 and 4, in an assessment of its soundness; compliance with human rights law, and the quality of reasoning of the ICTs in this regard, in terms of cogency, coherence and consistency. Points of concern are identified and suggestions for improvement are made, and conclusions are drawn as to the most suitable rationale(s) for responding to procedural violations committed in the pre-trial phase of international criminal proceedings, the merits of a discretionary approach to the question of how to address such violations and to the impact of certain particularities of international criminal proceedings on the determination of this question.

Keywords compliance with human rights law · comparative criminal procedure · right to a fair trial · right to an effective remedy · right to compensation in case of unlawful arrest or detention · inter-state cooperation in criminal matters · non-enquiry · shared responsibility · due diligence · exclusion of evidence · stay of proceedings · sentence reduction · financial compensation · express acknowledgement · integrity rationale · public attitude integrity · court-centred integrity · seriousness of the offence · seriousness of the procedural violation · consequentialist reasoning · right to an effective remedy · factors · (judicial) discretion · balancing · goals of international criminal justice · features/goals of international criminal procedure

Contents

© T.M.C. ASSER PRESS and the author 2018   437
K. Pitcher, *Judicial Responses to Pre-Trial Procedural Violations in International Criminal Proceedings*, International Criminal Justice Series 16, https://doi.org/10.1007/978-94-6265-219-4_7

7.1 Introduction

The purpose of this chapter is to evaluate the law and practice of the ICTs with respect to the question of how to address procedural violations committed in the pre-trial phase of the proceedings, as set out in Chaps. 5 and 6, in light of the human rights standards set out in Chap. 2, and to compare it to the national law and practice set out in Chaps. 3 and 4, with a view to being able to answer the central research question of this book: how should judges at the ICTs respond to procedural violations committed in the pre-trial phase of the proceedings? As observed in Chap. 1, answering this (normative) question requires an assessment of the 'soundness' of the existing law and practice of the ICTs in this regard.[1] In the following—final—chapter of this book (Chap. 8), a final answer to the central research question will be provided, based on the analysis provided in the current chapter.

The structure of this chapter is as follows. First the law and practice of the ICTs with respect to the question of how to address procedural violations committed in the pre-trial phase of the proceedings will be evaluated in light of the relevant human rights standards, then it will (separately) be compared to the national law and practice examined in this book, i.e. that of the Netherlands and England and Wales. Where points of concern are identified, suggestions will be made for improvement, which are addressed primarily to the ICC; in this regard it should be recalled that the ICTR closed its doors on 31 December 2015, while the ICTY is expected to do so at the end of 2017.[2] Further analysis will be provided at the end of

---

[1] Parts of the assessment undertaken in this chapter are based on those undertaken in an earlier written piece. See De Meester et al. 2013. Due to a mistake on the part of the publisher, this chapter was presented as a co-authored chapter. However, part 5 of this chapter ('Remedies') is to be attributed to the present author. This will be corrected with the next edition. Further, some of the (normative) arguments made in this chapter were put forward, in a very rudimentary form, in an earlier article. See Pitcher 2013.

[2] A precise date has not been given, but at the end of 2015, the President of the ICTY submitted a request to the UN Secretary-General for the extension of the terms of 17 judges until dates ranging

the section, to complement the human rights evaluation and the comparison to the relevant national law and practice.

7.2 Evaluation in Light of Human Rights Standards

It was seen in Chap. 2 that several rights enshrined in the ICCPR and the ECHR are relevant to the question of how judges at the ICTs should respond to procedural violations committed in the pre-trial phase of the proceedings. The right to a fair trial, provided for in Articles 14 and 6 of the ICCPR and ECHR, respectively, is an obvious starting point for addressing the aforementioned question; it sheds light on whether it is necessary to address pre-trial procedural violations *within the criminal trial*. Other rights are also relevant to the question of how judges at the ICTs should address procedural violations committed in the pre-trial phase of the proceedings, although they do not require a response within the criminal trial. These are the right to an effective remedy and the right to compensation in case of unlawful arrest or detention. It was also seen that there is case law at the ECtHR to shed light on the question of how to address procedural violations committed in an international context, i.e. in the context of inter-state cooperation in criminal matters. In the paragraphs below, the compatibility of the ICTs' law and practice with respect to the question of how to address procedural violations committed in the pre-trial phase of the proceedings with the aforementioned human rights standards will be addressed.

7.2.1 The Right to a Fair Trial

Turning first the ECtHR's case law with respect to the right to a fair trial provided for in Article 6 of the ECHR,[3] it was seen in Chap. 2 that in cases in which unlawfulness on the part of public authorities in the pre-trial phase of criminal proceedings is alleged to engage Article 6(1) of the ECHR, the ECtHR attaches significant importance to the use of the evidence so obtained. Put differently, it is *the use of evidence* obtained unlawfully, that is, in violation of a Convention right,

---

(Footnote 2 continued)

from 31 March 2016 to 30 November 2017, based on projections for the completion of the Tribunal's remaining work. See 'Letter dated 1 October 2015 from the President of the International Tribunal for the Former Yugoslavia addressed to the Secretary-General', annexed to 'Identical letters dated 28 October 2015 from the Secretary-General addressed to the President of the General Assembly and the President of the Security Council' (10 November 2015) UN Doc S/2015/825.

[3] For the reasons set out in Chap. 2 (see n 15–18 and accompanying text), in setting out the human rights standards on the right to a fair trial, the focus will be on the ECHR (and, specifically, Article 6 thereof).

that triggers the protection of Article 6 of the ECHR; on its own, unlawfulness on the part of public authorities in the pre-trial phase of criminal proceedings, even when it amounts to torture, is not sufficient to do so. While the ECtHR recognizes that an accused person may, on account of unlawfulness on the part of public authorities in the pre-trial phase, be 'definitively' deprived of a fair trial 'right from the outset',[4] it has only done so in the context of entrapment, where evidence will by definition have been used. At the ICTs, the judicial response within the criminal trial to procedural violations committed in the pre-trial phase is not limited to those procedural violations that have generated evidence which is now being sought for admission. Put differently, in case of procedural violations in the pre-trial phase, it is not only where the prosecution is proposing to rely on evidence obtained thereby that the ICTs will entertain applications for relief in respect thereof. Both the ad hoc Tribunals and the ICC will entertain applications for relief in respect of alleged procedural violations that do not, typically, entail the collection of evidence. Thus, they have entertained applications for relief in respect of (alleged) unlawful arrest or detention. Moreover, notably, and in contrast to the case law of the ECtHR, at the ICTs, the fact that a suspect or accused has been tortured or otherwise seriously mistreated in the process of bringing him or her into the jurisdiction of the international criminal tribunal in question, may, regardless of whether the prosecution is proposing to rely on evidence obtained thereby, warrant a response within the criminal trial: a stay of proceedings.

More generally, it is worth noting that both the ad hoc Tribunals and the ICC will entertain applications for relief in respect of a wide range of procedural violations, not just the violation of internationally recognized human rights. At the ad hoc Tribunals, the test for a stay of proceedings provides that the proceedings may be stayed not only on account of delay which prevents the accused from receiving a fair trial, but also 'pre-trial impropriety or misconduct' which 'contravenes the court's sense of justice' (of which serious human rights violations are, of course, an obvious example), and, at the ICTY, the title of Rule 95 of the ICTY RPE, which provided for the exclusion of evidence on account of the manner in which it was obtained, was amended precisely in order to widen the scope of the rule's application. At the ICC, it is not only the violation of an 'internationally recognized human right' that is capable of leading to exclusion under Article 69(7) of the ICC Statute, but also a violation of the ICC Statute. And, under Article 85(1) of the ICC Statute, which provides for financial compensation in case of unlawful arrest or detention, an arrest or detention will be considered 'unlawful' if it was carried out in breach of the 'Court's statutory framework'. Accordingly, at the ICTs, the judicial response within the trial is *available* in respect of a wide range of procedural violations, i.e. not just those that constitute rights violations. Nevertheless, it is clear from the case law that the question of whether internationally recognized rights were violated is a pertinent consideration in the determination of whether to attach a consequence to procedural violations in the pre-trial phase.

---

[4] *Teixeira de Castro v Portugal* App no 25829/94 (ECtHR, 9 June 1998), para 39.

In the ECtHR case of *Teixeira de Castro v Portugal*, it was found that the Applicant had been 'definitively' deprived of a fair trial 'right from the outset', on the basis of police incitement and of the fact that the evidence obtained thereby had been used in criminal proceedings.[5] The ECtHR's findings in *Teixeira* have been interpreted in the literature as prescribing a stay of proceedings (or a judicial response akin to it)[6] in the context of *entrapment*. The ICTs also recognize that there may be circumstances in which it would be inappropriate to put an accused on trial *at all*, although the issue of entrapment has not been considered at the ICTs; the issue has not arisen and it is unlikely to do so in the future, in light of the nature of the crimes falling within their jurisdiction. While it is only in the context of entrapment that the ECtHR recognizes that an accused may be 'definitively' deprived of a fair trial 'right from the outset', i.e. that it may not be fair to put an accused on trial at all, both the ad hoc Tribunals and the ICC have recognized that the proceedings may be stayed in case of other forms of impropriety also. In particular (and as stated), they have found that where a suspect or accused has been tortured or otherwise seriously mistreated in the process of bringing him or her into the jurisdiction of the international criminal tribunal in question, it might not be fair to put him or her on trial at all, i.e. this might warrant a stay of proceedings. This is so even where no evidence has been obtained as a result of the torture, or where any evidence obtained thereby is not being sought for admission.

While in the case law of the ECtHR the use of evidence obtained unlawfully triggers the protection of Article 6, it will not automatically result in a violation of Article 6 of the ECHR. Accordingly, under the ECHR, there is no automatic exclusion, i.e. no blanket exclusionary rule, for evidence obtained by violation of the suspect's or accused's Convention rights, let alone for evidence obtained by procedural violations committed by public authorities in the context of a criminal investigation more generally. Similarly, at both the ad hoc Tribunals and the ICC, there is no automatic exclusion for evidence obtained by violation of an internationally recognized human right, let alone for evidence obtained by another type of procedural violation. Indeed, the exclusionary mechanisms provided for under Rule 95 of the ICTY and ICTR RPEs and under Article 69(7) of the ICC Statute, which allow for the exclusion of evidence on account of how it was obtained, provide for an exclusionary *discretion*, rather than an exclusionary *rule*. Therefore, as at the ECtHR, at ICTs, the 'protective' or 'remedial' rationale, which sees the judicial response within the criminal trial to procedural violations committed by public authorities in the pre-trial phase of criminal proceedings (and, in particular, the exclusion of evidence obtained thereby) as a way of protecting rights, is not the primary rationale.[7] Nevertheless, it was seen in Chap. 2 that the ECtHR does

---

[5] *Teixeira de Castro v Portugal* App no 25829/94 (ECtHR, 9 June 1998), para 39.

[6] The ECtHR itself has stated that it must lead to the exclusion of all evidence obtained as a result of the police incitement or a similar consequence (see Chap. 2, n 171–172 and accompanying text).

[7] See in this regard Jackson 2012, 138; and Jackson and Summers 2012, 182.

recognize automatic, or near automatic, exclusionary rules for certain rights violations; the use of evidence obtained by such rights violations always, or nearly always, renders the trial unfair, i.e. violates Article 6(1) of the ECHR. Thus, the ECtHR recognizes an automatic exclusionary rule for evidence obtained by torture within the meaning of Article 3 of the ECHR, whereby it matters not by whom, i.e. by which authorities—domestic or foreign—it was obtained.[8] In addition, the ECtHR recognizes a near automatic exclusionary rule for evidence obtained in violation of the right of access to a lawyer at the time of questioning under Article 6 (3)(c) of the ECHR, which, it was observed in Chap. 2, is likely to extend to statements obtained by the authorities of another state.[9] The ICTs also recognize an automatic, or near automatic exclusionary rule for some procedural violations. While the ICTs have not expressly addressed the admissibility of evidence obtained by torture, it is fair to assume that they do recognize an automatic exclusionary rule in respect of such evidence, also given that they purport to do so for statements which have been obtained by *oppressive conduct* or otherwise in violation of the privilege against self-incrimination (although this is not to suggest that the sole reason for excluding torture evidence is to uphold the privilege against self-incrimination).[10] The ICTs also recognize an automatic exclusionary rule for statements obtained in violation of the right of access to a lawyer at the time of questioning, whereby it matters not that the statement was taken by national authorities.[11] In the ICC case of *Katanga and Ngudjolo*, the statement of the Accused Germain Katanga had been taken by national authorities, which had not been acting on behalf of the ICC Prosecutor; nevertheless, the statement, which was obtained in violation of the right of access to a lawyer at the time of questioning, was excluded in the trial proceedings before the ICC. In respect of violations of the right of access to a lawyer at the time of questioning and/or the privilege against self-incrimination, the ICTs have not looked to other facts and circumstances (such as the probative value of the evidence, the seriousness of the offence with which the accused has been charged,[12] or the good faith of the public authorities concerned) in order to determine whether the evidence obtained thereby should be excluded. This is consistent with ECtHR case law.

---

[8] See Chap. 2, n 345–347 and accompanying text.

[9] See Chap. 2, n 348–350 and accompanying text.

[10] See e.g. the following decisions: *Prosecutor v Martić* (Decision Adopting Guidelines on the Standards Governing the Admission of Evidence) IT-95-11-T, T Ch I (19 January 2006) para 9; and *Prosecutor v Katanga and Ngudjolo* (Decision on the Prosecutor's Bar Table Motions) ICC-01/04-01/07, T Ch II (17 December 2010) paras 63–65.

[11] See in particular *Prosecutor v Delalić, Mucić, Delić and Landžo* (Decision on Zdravko Mucić's Motion for the Exclusion of Evidence) IT-96-21-T, T Ch II (2 September 1997); and *Prosecutor v Katanga and Ngudjolo* (Decision on the Prosecutor's Bar Table Motions) ICC-01/04-01/07, T Ch II (17 December 2010).

[12] At the ICC, chambers may not take these factors into account anyway. More will be said about this later on in the chapter.

Having said this, it is a cause for concern that evidence obtained by oppressive conduct such as to violate the privilege against self-incrimination or by violation of the right of access to a lawyer at the time of questioning seems to fall within the scope of Rule 95 of the RPE at the ad hoc Tribunals, and Article 69(7) of the Statute at the ICC, whereby such unlawfulness is deemed to automatically satisfy one or both of the prongs thereunder: 'substantial doubt as to reliability' or 'serious damage to the integrity of the proceedings'. Both of these provisions, it should be recalled, provide for an exclusionary *discretion*. In order to avoid confusion in this regard, i.e. in order to remove any temptation on the part of judges to look beyond the fact that the evidence was obtained by torture, oppressive conduct such as to violate the privilege against self-incrimination or, as the case may be, violation of the right of access to a lawyer at the time of questioning, when ruling on the admissibility of such evidence, it would be preferable to keep evidence obtained by such violations (i.e. the rights violations in respect of which the ECtHR prescribes automatic exclusion of evidence obtained thereby)[13] outside of the scope of the exclusionary mechanisms under Rule 95 of the ICTY and ICTR RPEs and under Article 69(7) of the ICC Statute.[14] This might be achieved by 'superimposing' onto such provisions exclusionary rules[15] for the aforementioned violations, i.e. by the development of strong appellate case law in this regard, which clearly confines the discretion provided therein to evidence not already subject to one of the (automatic) exclusionary rules and which explains *why* evidence obtained by such violations is subject to automatic exclusion.[16] Such an approach would have the advantage of flexibility; over time, it may be necessary to alter the scope of such exclusionary rules, or to develop altogether new ones. The disadvantage of such an approach is that it is dependent the parties bringing such issues to the Appeals Chambers' attention, and on the passing of time; strong appellate case law is not developed overnight. Another option would be to introduce into the governing documents of the international criminal tribunals automatic exclusionary rules for such violations. In other words, it might be achieved by *codifying* the automatic exclusion of evidence obtained by torture, oppressive conduct such as to violate the privilege against self-incrimination or violation of the right of access to a lawyer at the time of questioning, whereby it is clear from such provisions that it matters *not* which authorities obtained the evidence. The advantage of such an approach would be (immediate) clarity. However, such an approach has the disadvantage of

---

[13] Strictly speaking, the ECtHR does not set forth rules on the admissibility evidence. See in this regard *Schenk v Switzerland* App no 10862/84 (ECtHR, 12 July 1988), para 46. In any case, according to the ECtHR, the use at trial of evidence obtained by the aforementioned violations will automatically, or nearly so, lead to a violation of Article 6(1) ECHR.

[14] Judge Meron made a similar argument in respect of statements obtained in violation of the provision at the ad hoc Tribunals that the questioning of suspects be audio- or video-recorded. See Chap. 5, n 175–176 and accompanying text.

[15] To borrow from Choo; see in this regard Choo 2015, 189.

[16] See in this regard Chap. 5, Sect. 5.3.2, where it was observed that chambers have not explained *why* certain evidence is subject to automatic exclusion.

inflexibility, in light of what is necessary to amend such governing documents; as stated, over time it may be necessary to alter the scope of the exclusionary rules, or to introduce altogether new ones. Moreover the texts of the existing exclusionary provisions referred to above would need to be amended, in order to clarify that the exclusionary discretion provided therein only applies to, i.e. is confined to, evidence not already subject to one of the (codified) automatic exclusionary rules.

Turning back again to the human rights law, for other Convention violations committed in the pre-trial phase of criminal proceedings (other, that is, than torture and the right of access to a lawyer at the time of questioning), the impact of the use of evidence obtained thereby on the fairness of the proceedings depends on such factors as whether the rights of the defence were observed, *how* it was used, the probative value (or 'quality') of the evidence and/or the public interest in the investigation and prosecution of offence in question. In other words, the use at trial of evidence obtained by such violations does not necessarily constitute a violation of Article 6(1) of the ECHR. The ECtHR's practice of taking into account such factors is often referred to as 'balancing'; indeed, this is an apt term for an approach that allows for factors to be taken into account that seemingly have nothing to do with that which made the evidence problematic in the first place, and which militate towards admission of the evidence. Similarly, and as already noted, at the ICTs, the violation of an internationally recognized human right does not automatically lead to the exclusion of the evidence obtained thereby. There are, indeed, strong indications in the case law of the ICTs that a violation of the right to privacy would not lead to the exclusion obtained thereby. Here it should be recalled that, at the ad hoc Tribunals at least, there has been a reluctance to, in cases in which the manner in which the evidence is alleged to have been obtained raises issues under the internationally recognized human right to privacy, determine whether that right was actually violated (about which more will be said below, in evaluating the ICTs' law and practice in light of the right to an effective remedy).[17] The ECtHR's approach to the use of evidence obtained by violation of Article 8 of the ECHR has been criticized in the literature for coming (too) close to 'embracing the discredited 'separation thesis'', and in doing so implying that 'how the evidence was obtained is immaterial to its admissibility'.[18] As Ashworth explains:

> The Court's prevailing view seems to be that violations of Article 8 and the requirements of Article 6 are two entirely *separate* matters. The appropriate way to deal with Article 8 breaches is to provide a remedy to the person whose right was infringed, a remedy that might be found in an award of damages or perhaps a reduction of sentence. But the criminal trial is something *separate*, with its own fairness criteria, and the questionable provenance of the prosecution's evidence will not compromise trial fairness just because other substantive human rights have been breached.[19]

---

[17] See generally Zeegers 2016, Chap. 4.

[18] Jackson 2012, 138.

[19] Ashworth 2012, 157 (emphasis added).

At the ICTs (and, more generally, in the context of inter-state cooperation in criminal matters), the separation thesis may be at its strongest; this is so because the ICTs are reliant on state-cooperation for such activities as the apprehension of persons suspected or accused of crimes falling within their jurisdiction and for the carrying out of investigations. Thus, it is *national authorities* that violate the right to privacy. Accordingly, it might be argued that, with the alleged misconduct being by an agent of a state, to which the ICTs are not institutionally 'connected' in the sense that they, the ICTs, do not form part of the same legal system as national law enforcement authorities, 'there is little possibility of deterrence', and the ICTs 'could hardly be said to have a responsibility for the conduct of investigations in that state'.[20] Given that, at both the ad hoc Tribunals and the ICC, violation of the right to privacy is unlikely to lead to the exclusion of evidence obtained thereby, it may be argued, by analogy with the analysis of the ECtHR's approach in this regard, that they also endorse the 'separation thesis' (at least as regards violations of the right to privacy); nevertheless, there may be more to it than the notion (central to the separation thesis) that 'there is no real connection between the actions of the police in investigating the crime and the court's verdict'.[21] In a purely domestic context, it can at least be said that the investigative authorities to have acted unlawfully, and the judicial authorities now seized of an application to exclude the evidence obtained thereby, form part of the same legal (and criminal justice) system (even if the judicial authorities are independent of the investigative (law enforcement) authorities and vice versa); the same cannot be said for the judicial authorities at the ICTs and the national authorities on which they are dependent for the aforementioned activities. This is not to say that the ICTs would be (more) justified in embracing the separation thesis; however, more may be required (by way of argumentation) to overcome the separation thesis in the context of international criminal proceedings than would be in a purely domestic context. More will be said about this issue below, in addressing the question as to the most suitable rationale for responding within the criminal trial to procedural violations committed in the context of international criminal proceedings.

Turning now to the specific factors that the ECtHR takes into account in the determination of whether the use of evidence obtained by violation of Convention rights other than the prohibition of torture and the right of access to a lawyer at the time of questioning, and, in particular, to the ability of the defence to challenge the use of the impugned evidence, it may be observed that the scope of application of the exclusionary mechanisms at each international criminal tribunal that allow for the exclusion of evidence on account of the manner in which it was obtained (Rules 95 of the ICTY and ICTR RPEs and Article 69(7) of the ICC Statute) is broad. It is open to the defence to challenge the proposed use of evidence obtained by employees of the ICTs themselves,[22] as well as by national authorities, and they

---

[20] Ashworth and Redmayne 2010, 362.

[21] Redmayne 2009, 305.

[22] See in this regard Chap. 5, n 22–23 and accompanying text.

may challenge the proposed use of evidence obtained by violation of internationally recognized human rights, as well as by other procedural standards.[23] However, in several early ICTR decisions concerning defence motions for relief in respect of alleged illegality or unlawfulness on the part of *national authorities* in the execution of a request for cooperation from the ICTR Prosecutor (including the following measures: arrest, custody, search, and seizure), the chamber declined even to enquire into the circumstances surrounding the execution of the measure in question, on the basis that the ICTR was not competent to supervise the legality thereof; only the state in question was competent to do so. The approach adopted in these cases resembles that commonly adopted by states in the context of inter-state cooperation in criminal matters: an approach based on the principle of non-enquiry. At first glance, an approach of non-enquiry would seem to be inconsistent with the ECtHR's case law addressing the fairness of the use at trial of evidence obtained unlawfully, from which it is apparent that the ability of the defence to challenge evidence obtained unlawfully is an important factor in the determination of whether Article 6 has been violated as a result thereof; it may offset any risk to fairness presented by the use of evidence obtained unlawfully. As to how an approach based on the rule of non-enquiry might affect the ability of the defence to challenge evidence, it should first be noted that the consequences of a court declining to enquire into the circumstances surrounding the collection of the evidence sought for admission may be that the provenance of such evidence remains unaccounted for. And, as Van Hoek and Luchtman observe, '[w]hen the provenance of information is not accounted for, it cannot be tested—neither by the defence, nor by the court'.[24] They argue, convincingly, that evidence whose provenance is unaccounted for, which cannot therefore be tested by the defence or the court, should not be used, which they argue 'would seem to be the simple and straightforward consequence of the responsibility of the receiving state for upholding Article 6'.[25] However, it was seen in Chap. 2 that, in the context of inter-state cooperation in criminal matters, the ECtHR seems to endorse a rule of '*qualified* non-enquiry':

---

[23] At the ad hoc Tribunals, the norm that must have been violated in order to trigger the exclusionary mechanism under Rule 95 is not defined; in principle, therefore, it is open to the defence to challenge evidence obtained by violation of national law (although on its own, such a violation will not lead to the exclusion of evidence obtained thereby). At the ICC, the norm that must have been violated in order to trigger the exclusionary mechanism under Article 69(7) ICC Statute *is* defined; it seems therefore that it is not open to the defence to challenge evidence obtained by violation of national law *alone*.

[24] Van Hoek and Luchtman 2005, 24.

[25] Van Hoek and Luchtman 2005, 24 and 38.

> ... the Court considers that the Convention does not preclude reliance, *at the investigating stage*, on information obtained by the investigating authorities from sources such as foreign criminal investigations. Nevertheless, the *subsequent* use of such information can raise issues under the Convention where there are reasons to assume that in this foreign investigation defence rights guaranteed have been disrespected.[26]

This would seem to boil down to the following: (1) in principle, it may be assumed that the manner in which evidence was obtained abroad, by the authorities of that state, was lawful, such that the trial court in the 'requesting' state need not enquire into the circumstances surrounding the collection of evidence in the 'requested' state; (2) however, the way in which it was obtained must not 'disrespect' the rights of the defence; (3) where there are reasons to assume that the evidence was so obtained (either because the court, of its own accord, believes this to be the case or because the defence has made it sufficiently plausible that the evidence was obtained in such a manner), the trial court in the requesting state may not turn a blind eye to the manner of the evidence's obtaining on the basis of the rule of non-enquiry. Accordingly, only where there are reasons to assume that the evidence was obtained in a manner which *disrespected defence rights*,[27] does the ECtHR require the trial court in the requesting state to enquire into the circumstances surrounding the collection of the evidence concerned, whereby the defence would be in a position to challenge the evidence. The ECtHR's case law may be criticized on this basis, but the point is that, insofar as the ICTs may be said to have embraced an approach of non-enquiry, this may not be incompatible with human rights law. More will be said about this issue below, in evaluating the ICTs' law and practice in light of the human rights standards with respect to the question of how to address procedural violations committed in the context of inter-state cooperation in criminal matters.

As stated above, for *other* Convention violations committed in the pre-trial phase of criminal proceedings (other, that is, than torture or violation of the right of access to a lawyer at the time of questioning), the impact of the use of evidence obtained thereby on the fairness of the proceedings also depends on the probative value (or quality) of the evidence and/or the public interest in the investigation and prosecution of the offence in question. Indeed, in the context of the violation of the prohibition of inhuman or degrading treatment (within the meaning of Article 3 of the ECHR), the ECtHR will look to both of these factors (although it is important to note that the probative value of the evidence will not be a decisive factor,[28] and that consideration of the latter factor may well work in favour of the Applicant in

---

[26] *Echeverri Rodriguez v Netherlands* App no 3286/98 (ECtHR, Decision of 27 June 2000), 8 (emphasis added).

[27] The ECtHR does not explain what falls under 'defence rights'; here the assumption is that what is meant here is the specific fair trial rights enumerated in or otherwise flowing from Article 6 ECHR.

[28] In *Jalloh v Germany* (App no 54810/00 (ECtHR, 11 July 2006)), it should be recalled, the evidence obtained by violation of Article 3 ECHR was highly probative; nevertheless, the ECtHR founded a violation of Article 6 ECHR.

proceedings before the ECtHR).[29] In the context of the violation of the right to privacy (within the meaning of Article 8 of the ECHR), it will look to the probative value of the evidence; while the ECtHR rarely refers expressly to the public interest in the investigation and prosecution of the offence in question in this context,[30] as was observed in Chap. 2, public interest considerations may already enter the fair trial analysis via consideration of the probative value of the evidence.[31] At the ad hoc Tribunals also, such factors may inform the determination to be made under Rule 95 of the RPE, i.e. whether to exclude evidence on account of the manner of its obtaining (in case of other rights violations than torture, oppressive conduct such as to violate the privilege against self-incrimination or violation of the right of access to a lawyer at the time of questioning, that is). Accordingly, the ad hoc Tribunals *also* take into account factors that seemingly have nothing to do with that which made the evidence problematic in the first place, and which tend to militate towards admission of the evidence. As at the ECtHR, then, the ad hoc Tribunals adopt a 'balancing' approach towards certain types of unlawfully obtained evidence. By contrast, at the ICC, the focus of the determination to be made under Article 69(7) of the ICC Statute, which provides for the exclusion of evidence on account of the manner in which it was obtained, is precisely that: the manner in which it was obtained and whether it was serious enough to warrant exclusion. There, it seems, neither the probative value of the evidence nor the seriousness of the offence(s) with which the accused is charged may inform that determination. Below, in comparing the ICTs' law and practice to that of the domestic jurisdictions examined in this book, it will be argued the ICC's approach is to be preferred over that of the ad hoc Tribunals.

7.2.2 The Right to an Effective Remedy

It was seen in Chap. 2 that, while on its own (that is, unaccompanied by the use of evidence obtained thereby), unlawfulness on the part of public authorities in the pre-trial phase is not sufficient to trigger the protection of Article 6 of the ECHR, under the ECHR (and under the ICCPR) the victim of such unlawfulness nevertheless has remedies to pursue in this regard. Articles 2(3)(a) and 13 of the ICCPR and ECHR, respectively, provide for the right to an effective remedy, and Articles 9 (5) and 5(5) of the ICCPR and ECHR, respectively, provide for the right to compensation in case of unlawful arrest or detention, whereby the latter right may be viewed as a specific manifestation of the former. The focus of the current subsection

---

[29] This seems to have been the case in *Jalloh*. See *Jalloh v Germany* App no 54810/00 (ECtHR, 11 July 2006), para 119.

[30] For an example of such a case, see *Heglas v Czech Republic* App no 5935/02 (ECtHR, 1 March 2007), para 87.

[31] See Chap. 2, n 246 and accompanying text.

is on the (general) right to an effective remedy, while the more specific manifestation thereof is dealt with separately, below.

In the context of inter-state cooperation in criminal matters, the question arises as to whether a suspect or accused may invoke the right to an effective remedy in the requesting, adjudicating, state in respect of violations committed in the requested state. While the wording of Article 13 does not appear to preclude this, the fact that the effectiveness of the remedy depends on the ability of the national authority to properly 'deal with the substance of the complaint' raises obvious difficulties in this regard: is the requesting state really in a position to properly deal with the substance of a complaint concerning a violation committed by foreign officials, abroad? The same may, arguably, be said for the requested state. As has been observed, 'the requested state is ... often not in a position to fully test the facts of the case'.[32] The point is that, in the context of inter-state cooperation in criminal matters, it may well be compatible with the right to an effective remedy for the requesting, trial, state to 'refer an investigation into the evidence [sought to be used in the case against the accused in that state] to the state of origin [i.e. the state in which the evidence was obtained]—provided a local remedy is available there'.[33] However, even if referral by the requesting, trial, state of a complaint regarding the lawfulness of the execution of a request for cooperation to the state whose authorities executed the request is not incompatible with the right to an effective remedy, there may still be good reason to have the requesting, trial, state to provide a remedy in respect of rights violations committed abroad. An oft-cited argument in this regard is that from efficiency; it would be more *efficient* to have the requesting, trial, state to address any unlawfulness in the execution by the authorities of the requested state of a request for cooperation (though not necessarily by means of the exclusion of evidence obtained thereby). As Van Hoek and Luchtman observe, this would 'require a willingness to share information on the part of the state of origin of the information involved'.[34]

In the context of inter-state cooperation in criminal matters, it may, then, be compatible with the right to an effective remedy for a state to refer a complaint regarding the lawfulness of the execution of a request for cooperation to the state whose authorities executed the request (provided that a domestic remedy is available, and provided moreover that the allegation does not concern a flagrant rights violation such as to require a response within the trial itself). Inter-state cooperation in criminal matters, it should be recalled, while different from the cooperation between states and the ICTs, has greatly influenced the latter, such that the human rights law in respect thereof may be employed as an evaluative tool in respect of the ICTs' law and practice in this regard. Turning now to such law and practice, at the ad hoc Tribunals, and, in particular, the ICTR, chambers have relied on the right to an effective remedy to justify granting financial compensation or sentence reduction

---

[32] Van Hoek and Luchtman 2005, 25–26.

[33] Ibid., 38.

[34] Ibid., 38.

to persons whose rights were violated in the pre-trial phase of the proceedings, in particular, for the violation of procedural rights pertaining to the state of deprivation of liberty, i.e. for unlawful detention. Such rights violations were established on the basis of the ICTR's own procedural framework (i.e. the ICTR Statute and/or ICTR RPE), as well as on international human rights standards. Moreover, such rights violations could be attributed to the ICTR by virtue of the ICTR Prosecutor's failure to exercise due diligence in discharging its duties in respect of persons being held at his or her behest, or through other organs of the ICTR. At the ICC, the right to compensation in case of unlawful arrest or detention is expressly provided for in the ICC Statute, in Article 85(1) thereof. In order to make a finding of unlawful arrest or detention within the meaning of that provision, a provision of the ICC Statute must have been breached, and, moreover, the unlawful arrest or detention must be attributable to the ICC in some way. Accordingly, neither the ad hoc Tribunals nor the ICC appear willing to provide effective, personal remedies in respect of any rights violation, let alone any procedural violation, committed in the execution of a request for cooperation. At first glance, this would seem not to be *in*compatible with human rights law, i.e. the right to an effective remedy. After all, in the context of inter-state cooperation in criminal matters, it may be compatible with the right to an effective remedy for a state to refer a complaint regarding the lawfulness of the execution of a request for cooperation to the state whose authorities executed the request (provided that a domestic remedy is available, and provided moreover that the allegation does not concern a flagrant rights violation such as to require a response within the trial itself). More will be said about this below, in arguing *when* the ICTs *should* provide effective, personal remedies to persons whose rights have been violated by national authorities in the execution of a request from them for cooperation.

As stated, ICTR chambers have relied on the right to an effective remedy to justify granting financial compensation or sentence reduction to persons whose rights were violated in the pre-trial phase of the proceedings, in particular, for unlawful detention (although in the one case at the ad hoc Tribunals in which financial compensation was granted as a personal remedy for rights violations, the underlying rights violation did not, strictly speaking, concern a procedural right pertaining to the state of deprivation of liberty; André Rwamakuba was granted financial compensation for the violation of his right to legal assistance in the initial months of detention, while he was being detained in the ICTR Detention Facility). At the ICC, financial compensation is available in respect of an unlawful arrest or detention; in addition, it appears that sentence reduction may be granted in respect thereof. Nevertheless, there are indications at both the ad hoc Tribunals and ICC that personal remedies may be available in case of *other* rights violations than those pertaining to the deprivation of liberty. Insofar as the ICTs (purport to) provide effective, personal remedies for rights violations, it is worth noting that such remedies entail a *judicial* remedy (it is the judges themselves who grant remedies, not some other organ of the relevant tribunal), which goes further than that which is required under human rights law.[35]

At first glance, the ICTs' practice with respect to the right to an effective remedy appears to be inconsistent, in that the ICTs have seemingly provided (or otherwise mooted the possibility of providing) personal remedies for some rights violations, but not for others. It was seen in Chap. 6, that while the ad hoc Tribunals are prepared to provide personal remedies for unlawful *detention*, they have often been unwilling even to enquire into the circumstances surrounding an unlawful *arrest* for the purpose of determining an application for relief in this regard. The reason for this is that they consider themselves to lack jurisdiction over the conditions of an arrest carried out by a sovereign state (even where executed pursuant to a request by the relevant tribunal). Only where the method of arrest is alleged to be 'manifestly' or 'inherently' arbitrary, as is the case for kidnapping, and cannot be reduced to matters falling within the jurisdiction of a state, will they enquire into the circumstances surrounding the arrest for this purpose. And, in the literature, the ICTs have been criticized for not providing personal remedies for violations of the right to privacy in the course of (for example) search and seizure operations carried out at their request.[36] To an extent, the apparent inconsistency in the case law as regards the practice of providing effective, personal remedies for rights violations can be explained (if not *justified*) by the fact that the ICTs' statutory frameworks are altogether silent as regards the actual execution of certain coercive measures. At the ad hoc Tribunals, for example, the statutory frameworks are silent on how a request for arrest is to be executed. In a number of early ICTR decisions, chambers seemed to have declined to enquire into the circumstances surrounding an arrest executed at the ICTR Prosecutor's request *precisely because* the ICTR's governing documents did not regulate this matter. And at both the ad hoc Tribunals and the ICC, they are silent on, among other things, how a search and seizure operation is to be carried out, and what rights the accused has in this regard. Accordingly, the failure of the ICTs to provide effective, personal remedies in respect of certain rights violations may be connected to the absence of clear, written standards for the execution of coercive measures. However, this absence has not stopped chambers from establishing rights violations in respect of the execution of coercive measures. At the ICC, it may be recalled, the Trial Chamber in *Lubanga* found that a search and seizure operation carried out by the Congolese national authorities (at which an ICC investigator had been present) had violated the internationally recognized human right to privacy—specifically, the principle of proportionality—although the evidence obtained thereby did not need to be excluded pursuant to Article 69(7)(b) of

---

[35] See Chap. 2, n 297 and accompanying text. By contrast, the right to compensation in case of unlawful arrest or detention, which may be viewed as a specific manifestation of the right to an effective remedy, does require a judicial remedy.

[36] Zeegers 2016, 175–179.

the ICC Statute.[37] However, it did not then consider whether the accused was entitled to an effective, personal remedy thereof; this is understandable, given that it was not *the accused's* right to privacy that had been violated (but a third party's).[38] It is interesting to speculate as to whether, if it *had* been the accused's right to privacy that had been violated, whether he—the Accused—would have been considered to be entitled to an effective remedy in respect thereof (and if so, what such a remedy would have entailed).

It is indeed arguable that the ICTs *should* provide effective, personal remedies to persons whose rights have been violated by national authorities in the execution of a request from them for cooperation. However, it is submitted that any requirement that they do so should reflect the *shared responsibility* of the ICTs and the national authorities that carry out requests for cooperation in ensuring that suspect's or accused's rights are protected. In the ICTR case of *Kajelijeli*, in which the Appellant had alleged various rights violations in connection with his detention in Benin at the behest of the ICTR Prosecutor, the Appeals Chamber said that the notion of shared responsibility flowed from the 'rationale that the international division of labour in prosecuting crimes must not be to the detriment of the apprehended person'.[39] Regarding the Prosecution's responsibility, it referred to the 'prosecutorial duty of due diligence', under which the 'Prosecution is required to ensure that, once it initiates a case, "the case proceeds to trial in a way that respects the rights of the accused"'.[40] As to the responsibility of a cooperating state, it stated that while it is obliged to 'comply fully without undue delay with any requests for assistance from the Tribunal', it still remained under 'its obligation to respect the human rights of the suspect as protected in customary international law, in the international treaties to which it has acceded, as well as its own national legislation'.[41] On this basis it may be argued that, the fact that rights have been violated in the execution of a request from the ICTs for cooperation, does not mean that it is for *the ICTs* to provide remedies in respect thereof. After all, states also bear responsibility for the protection of the suspect's or accused's rights. Such a set-up would seem not to be incompatible with human rights law, i.e. the right to an effective remedy; indeed, it was seen above that, in the context of inter-state cooperation in criminal matters, it may be compatible with the right to an effective remedy for a state to refer a complaint regarding the lawfulness of the execution of a request for cooperation to the state whose authorities executed the request (provided that a domestic remedy is available, and provided moreover that the allegation does not

---

[37] See *Prosecutor v Lubanga* (Decision on the admission of material from the "bar table") ICC-01/04-01/06, T Ch I (24 June 2009), and the discussion of this decision in Chap. 5 (see n 339–360 and accompanying text).

[38] However, as will be explained below, it not obvious why the fact it was not the accused's right that had been violated should be a reason not to exclude evidence. See n 107 and accompanying text.

[39] *Prosecutor v Kajelijeli* (Judgement) ICTR-98-44A-A, A Ch (23 May 2005), para 220.

[40] Ibid., para 220.

[41] Ibid., para 220.

concern a flagrant rights violation such as to require a response within the trial itself).[42] While the fact that a state has failed in this protection (i.e. has not respected the rights of the suspect 'as protected in customary international law, in the international treaties to which it has acceded', or has not adhered to its own national laws) need not mean that the ICTs should not seek to provide effective, personal remedies in respect of rights violations, in order to justify their doing so, it is reasonable to require that the rights violation be attributable to them in some way.[43] In *Kajelijeli* itself, the rights violations in question were attributable to the ICTR (such as to warrant the provision of an effective, personal remedy in respect thereof) by virtue of the ICTR Prosecutor's failure to exercise due diligence in ensuring that the case proceeded to trial in a way that respected the rights of the accused (having failed to make a request within reasonable time for the Appellant's transfer to the Tribunal). It is submitted that such a failure *should be* sufficient in order to be able to attribute a rights violation to the ICTs, such as to warrant the provision of an effective, personal remedy in respect thereof. In other words, such a failure, and not a higher degree of involvement on the part of the ICTs in the rights violation, should be sufficient for such purposes; this is in keeping with the argument that 'the international division of labour in prosecuting crimes must not be to the detriment of the apprehended person'. A lower degree (or lack) of involvement might undermine the notion of *shared responsibility* as between the ICTs and the national authorities that carry out requests for cooperation for ensuring that suspect's or accused's rights are protected. At the ad hoc Tribunals, it may be easier to pinpoint the moment at which a duty of due diligence arises. The governing documents of those tribunals allow for the provisional arrest of persons while the indictment is being prepared for confirmation (that is, the arrest of persons without judicial authorization); the moment at which the aforementioned duty arises is (at least) that at which the request for provisional arrest is transmitted to the state authorities in question. The ICC does not allow for the arrest of persons without judicial authorization, but, as Taylor and Jalloh observe, neither the ICC Statute nor RPE 'prohibit the [ICC] Prosecutor from informally communicating … a wish [that a suspect be provisionally arrested and/or detained pending the issuance of an arrest warrant by the ICC] to national authorities'.[44] Despite this possibility (which in all likelihood has already been,[45] and will (continue to) be exploited by the ICC Prosecutor) the ICC has thus far failed to address the issue of prosecutorial due diligence in the context of the apprehension and detention of persons suspected of

---

[42] This is the approach adopted in the Netherlands. See in this regard the following decision of the Dutch Supreme Court: HR 5 October 2010, ECLI:NL:HR:2010:BL5629, r.o. 4.4.1, *NJ* 2011/169 m.nt. TM Schalken.

[43] An argument *in favour* of the ICTs providing effective, personal remedies in respect of rights violations *that are not attributable to them* is that states may be disinclined to address rights violations committed by their own authorities in the execution of a request for cooperation, in light of the fact that they will have provided such assistance as a matter of legal obligation.

[44] Taylor and Jalloh 2013, 319.

[45] See in this regard Taylor and Jalloh 2013, 321.

crimes falling within the jurisdiction of the ICC, let alone set standards in this regard.[46] In the context of Article 85(1) of the ICC Statute (which provides for the right of compensation in case of unlawful arrest or detention, and (more to the point) which may be seen as a specific manifestation of the right to an effective remedy), chambers have spoken of the need for 'concerted action' between an organ of the ICC and the national authorities concerned, whereby 'mere knowledge on the part of the Prosecutor' that a person suspected of crimes falling within the jurisdiction of the ICC is being detained at the national level is 'no proof' of his involvement in any unlawfulness to arise in the context of such detention.[47]

Insofar as the ICTs *are* required to provide an effective, personal remedy for rights violations, the question arises as to what remedy ought to be provided. It may be recalled that, the fact that a suspect's rights have been violated in the context of a criminal investigation, and/or that the violation of such rights in this context has resulted in a criminal prosecution (incriminating evidence having been obtained and subsequently adduced), does not mean that an effective, personal remedy (within the meaning of the right to an effective remedy) need be given within the criminal trial for that violation (although this fact may warrant a response within the criminal trial for *other* reasons). The right to an effective remedy simply requires the provision of a remedy allowing the competent authority 'both to deal with the substance of the relevant Convention complaint and to grant appropriate relief',[48] whereby the authority need not be a judicial one. The right to an effective remedy does not, then, require that evidence obtained by a rights violation in the context of a criminal investigation be excluded from evidence (exclusion being a classic 'trial' remedy). This is not to say that evidence obtained by such a violation should not be excluded from evidence, only that it *need* not be under the right to an effective remedy; moreover, there may be good reasons not to base exclusion on the right to an effective remedy. To construe the exclusion of evidence as a personal, effective remedy may be to overlook the 'institutional' dimension of exclusion, i.e. the fact that it is required not (only) in the interests of the individual accused, but in the interest of the public in the integrity of the criminal justice system (more will be said about this below, in addressing the question as to the most suitable rationale for responding within the criminal trial to procedural violations committed in the context of international criminal proceedings). Further, it is questionable whether the exclusion of evidence can really be said to provide an effective, personal remedy for rights violations within the meaning of the internationally recognized human right to an effective remedy. It may, of course, serve to 'vindicate' rights in a more general sense; this ability of the exclusion of evidence to vindicate rights lies at the heart of what, in the national literature, has been referred to as the 'protective' (or

---

[46] See also Taylor and Jalloh 2013, 320.

[47] See *Prosecutor v Muthaura and Kenyatta* (Decision on the application for a ruling on the legality of the arrest of Mr. Dennis Ole Itumbi) ICC-01/09-02/11, T Ch V (19 November 2012) paras 7–9.

[48] *Goranova-Karaeneva v Bulgaria* App no 12739/05 (ECtHR, 8 March 2011), para 57, referring to *Khan v UK* App no 35394/97 (ECtHR, 12 May 2000), para 44.

'remedial' or 'vindicatory') rationale.[49] However, this rationale should be distinguished from the right to an effective remedy; rather than seeking to provide a tailored response to the particular right to have been violated, an approach based on the former rationale seeks to vindicate rights in a more general sense, whereby the exclusion of evidence obtained by a rights violation is the chief (if not only) mechanism by which to achieve this. In respect of some rights violations, as for example in case of unlawful arrest or detention (which does not typically entail the generation of evidence) the issue of exclusion will not usually arise; in such cases compensation may be an appropriate remedy. In case of privacy violations (subject to what was said above),[50] it is questionable whether the provision of a procedural remedy (the exclusion of evidence) can constitute an effective, personal remedy in respect of the violation of a substantive right (the right to privacy); more generally, it is questionable whether the criminal trial is the right place to seek to provide effective, personal remedies in respect of rights violations.[51] Again, none of this is to say that evidence obtained by violation of the right to privacy should not be excluded; only that, under the right to an effective remedy, it *need* not be (and, as stated, there may be good reasons not to base exclusion on the right to an effective remedy). Below it will be argued that such violations should, under certain circumstances, lead to the exclusion of evidence obtained thereby.

7.2.3 The Right to Compensation in Case of Unlawful Arrest or Detention

Turning now to the more specific manifestation of right to an effective remedy in the context of violations of the right to personal liberty, it was seen in Chap. 2 that, under the comprehensive human rights treaties, there is a right to compensation in case of unlawful arrest or detention, whereby the compensation to be provided is usually financial, but need not be. On the basis of this right, the shared Appeals Chamber of the ad hoc Tribunals has held that, in case of unlawfulness in the detention of persons at such tribunals' request, such a person is entitled to sentence reduction upon conviction, and financial compensation upon acquittal. At the ICC, Article 85(1) of the ICC Statute, referred to above, adopts *verbatim* the wording of Article 9(5) of the ICCPR; it is available to 'anyone who has been the victim of unlawful arrest or detention'. In other words, it is not only available to persons to have been acquitted by the ICC. While, on the face of it, the granting of sentence reduction as a means of compensation for unlawful arrest or detention does not appear to be inconsistent with the relevant human rights law (since such law does

---

[49] See Chap. 4, Sect. 4.3.3.

[50] See n 17 and accompanying text.

[51] This issue is addressed further, in the following subsection on the right to compensation in case of unlawful arrest or detention.

not require that the compensation be financial), a cause for concern in this regard is the time that it takes to provide such compensation (such compensation only being available at the end of the trial). At the ICTs, trials can take years, and, accordingly, it could take years for a remedy to be provided in respect of a rights violation, which might undermine its effectiveness. The ICC's procedure is to be preferred in this regard; as stated, the remedy under Article 85(1) is available to all persons, not only those to have been acquitted, meaning that it is not only available upon acquittal, i.e. at the end of the trial. Moreover, the fact that the procedure envisaged thereunder is separate to the trial proper, may mean that there is more room to bring to light issues relevant to the determination of the amount of compensation to be provided, for example, the 'damage' suffered by the person concerned, which might not otherwise receive the attention they deserve. In this regard it should be recalled that the right to an effective remedy (of which the right to compensation in case of unlawful arrest or detention is a specific manifestation) consists of a procedural and a substantive component, whereby pursuant to the former, the competent authority must be able to deal with the substance of the complaint. In other words, it is not sufficient to provide substantive relief; moreover, in the absence of a procedural remedy that allows the national authority to deal with the *substance* of the complaint, it is questionable whether any consequence to be attached to a rights violation can properly be called *substantive* relief. The fact that the ICC provides for a separate procedure in this regard has been subject to criticism in the literature. Zappalà argues that it would have been preferable for the procedure relating to Article 85(1) of the ICC Statute to allow the same chamber to have determined that the arrest or detention was unlawful, determine the request for compensation: 'This solution would have ensured more speed in doing justice to the victim of an unlawful arrest [or detention]... Moreover, it would have had the interest of speeding up the activities of the Court as a whole, as it does not seem appropriate to burden the system of the Court with several micro-proceedings unrelated to the main object of its jurisdiction'.[52] Such criticism is understandable (indeed, as noted above, the failure to provide a speedy remedy may detract from its effectiveness), but if the ICC is committed to providing effective, personal remedies for rights violation committed in the pre-trial phase of the proceedings, it must do so properly; and it is questionable whether it is possible to do so within the trial itself.

Another cause for concern as regards the question of compatibility of the ICTs' law and practice with the internationally recognized human right to compensation in case of unlawful arrest or detention is the fact that, while the ad hoc Tribunals and the ICC both purport to recognize that right, neither provide for a designated budget in this regard. The lack of a designated budget for providing compensation in case of unlawful arrest or detention has the ability to render the aforementioned right theoretical and illusory and is, therefore, problematic from a human rights perspective. It was seen in Chap. 5 that in the one case at the ad hoc Tribunals in which financial compensation was ordered, the ICTR Registrar initially refused to

---

[52] Zappalà 2002, 1584.

do so. At the ICC there may be more possibilities than there were/are at the ad hoc Tribunals; it may be that such compensation will be paid out of the 'Contingency Fund' established by the Assembly of States Parties. The fact that at the ICC the right to compensation in case of unlawful arrest or detention has an express, statutory, basis cannot be underestimated in this regard.

7.2.4 *Procedural Violations in the Context of Inter-State Cooperation in Criminal Matters*

As stated, in the context of inter-state cooperation in criminal matters, the ECtHR seems to endorse an approach of '*qualified* non-enquiry', which seems to boil down to the following: (1) in principle, it may be assumed that the manner in which evidence was obtained abroad, by the authorities of that state, was lawful, such that the trial court in the 'requesting' state need not enquire into the circumstances surrounding the collection of evidence in the 'requested' state; (2) however, the way in which it was obtained must not 'disrespect' the rights of the defence; (3) where there are reasons to assume that the evidence was so obtained (either because the court, of its own accord, believes this to be the case or because the defence has made it sufficiently plausible that the evidence was obtained in such a manner), the trial court in the requesting state may not turn a blind eye to the manner of the evidence's obtaining on the basis of the principle of non-enquiry.[53] Accordingly, only where there are reasons to assume that the evidence was obtained in a manner which *disrespected defence rights*, does the ECtHR require the trial court in the requesting state to enquire into the circumstances surrounding the collection of the evidence concerned (and presumably make necessary orders for disclosure and see to it that relevant witnesses are heard), whereby the defence would be in a position to challenge the evidence. In this regard it may be observed that in order to show that evidence was unlawfully obtained, it is necessary to have knowledge of the circumstances, and that in most cases the defence will be dependent on the court for acquiring such knowledge (which is a reason for not requiring too much from the defence by way of substantiation in order to justify an enquiry into the manner of the evidence's obtaining). At both the ad hoc Tribunals and the ICC, disrespect at the national level for certain defence rights, whether or not the investigative measure in question was carried out at their request, requires the exclusion of the evidence obtained thereby. Thus, violation of the right of access to counsel at the time of questioning, or of the right not to incriminate oneself (by means of oppression) by national authorities, automatically leads to the exclusion of statements obtained thereby. By contrast, and as already observed above, violations of *other* rights by national authorities, do not automatically lead to exclusion of the evidence obtained thereby. As to the requirement in the case law of the ECHR that

---

[53] See also n 367 and accompanying text.

there be reasons to assume unlawfulness in the investigation abroad (specifically, that the evidence was obtained in a manner that disrespected *defence rights*), in *Mucić and others*, in which, it should be recalled, a statement obtained by Austrian authorities from the Accused was excluded from evidence on the basis that the Accused had not had access to counsel at the time of questioning, the cause for the enquiry into the circumstances in which the statement was taken may have been the fact that Austrian law actually *prohibited* access to counsel at the time of questioning, although the chamber did not make any express findings as to what is required from the Defence in order to justify an enquiry by the court into the circumstances surrounding the collection of evidence whose admission it opposes. Similarly, in *Katanga and Ngudjolo*, in which a statement obtained by the Congolese authorities was excluded on the basis of concerns that the privilege against self-incrimination had been breached, no such findings were made (and it appears that Congolese law did not prohibit access to counsel at the time of questioning). In cases in which other (non-defence) rights have been implicated, chambers have required the defence to *establish* or *show* unlawfulness either under the governing documents or international law.[54]

In sum, the law and practice of the ICTs does not appear to be incompatible with human rights case law on this point. However, as suggested above, the human rights law may itself be inconsistent, or otherwise flawed. On the one hand, the ECtHR's case law addressing the fairness of the use at trial of evidence obtained unlawfully shows that the ability of the defence to challenge the evidence obtained unlawfully is an important factor in the determination of whether Article 6 has been violated as a result thereof. It may offset any risk to fairness presented by the use of evidence obtained unlawfully; conversely, the inability of the defence to challenge the evidence obtained unlawfully may lead the ECtHR to found a violation of Article 6(1) of the ECHR. On the other hand, in the context of inter-state cooperation in criminal matters, the ECtHR seems to endorse an approach of 'qualified non-enquiry', whereby it was observed above that the consequences of a court declining to enquire into the circumstances surrounding the collection of the evidence sought for admission may be that the provenance of such evidence remains unaccounted for, and that when the provenance of information is not accounted for, it cannot be challenged. Even if a refusal on the part of the ICTs to enquire into the circumstances surrounding the collection of evidence cannot be said to be incompatible with human rights law (or, at least, even if it can be said that there is case law to support such an approach), it is certainly problematic from the perspective of the notion that the fairness (within the meaning of the right to a fair trial) of the use

---

[54] See *Prosecutor v Muvunyi* (Decision on the Prosecutor's Motion Pursuant to Trial Chamber's Directives of 7 December 2005 for the Verification of the Authenticity of Evidence Obtained Out of Court Pursuant to Rules 89(C) and (D)) ICTR-2000-55A-T, T Ch II (26 April 2006) para 23, referring to *Prosecutor v Stakić* (Decision) IT-97-24-AR73.5, A Ch (10 October 2002). At the ICC, similar statements have been made in the context of confirmation proceedings; see *Prosecutor v Mbarushimana* (Decision on the confirmation of charges) ICC-01/04-01/10, P T Ch I (16 December 2011), paras 58–65.

of evidence obtained unlawfully depends on the ability of the defence to challenge it (whereby it is acknowledged that the ECtHR has not been consistent in applying this notion). Non-enquiry may result in the provenance of the evidence remaining unaccounted for. It is submitted that evidence whose provenance is unaccounted for, and which, by extension, cannot be challenged by the defence, should not be used. This applies just as much to the context of cooperation between states and the ICTs, as to the context of inter-state cooperation in criminal matters. The issue is one of fundamental fairness.

In the context of inter-state cooperation in criminal matters, it has been argued that the obligation of states to ensure that the accused receives a fair trial necessitates a 'rethink' of the traditional approach of non-enquiry, whereby states decline to enquire into the lawfulness of investigative measures executed abroad.[55] An oft-cited justification for an approach of non-enquiry is respect for state sovereignty. At the ICTs, the argument from state sovereignty would appear to hold less sway than in the inter-state context, in light of the nature of the cooperation between states and the ICTs; whereas inter-state cooperation is shaped by 'reciprocity, statutory exceptions, and sovereign discretion', the 'vertical' relationship between ICTs and states is defined by 'stricter obligations, non-reciprocity, and the right of the requesting party to interpret and determine the content and scope of a request for cooperation'.[56] While the ICC cooperation regime is arguably more sensitive to issues related to sovereignty than that of the ad hoc Tribunals, it may still be described as 'a (weak) *vertical* cooperation regime'.[57] Indeed, '[n]otwithstanding differences in detail, the ad hoc Tribunals and the ICC are equipped with a robust legal framework in order to secure cooperation', whereby '[i]t is less a question of whether certain acts of cooperation may be demanded or whether judicial requests may be challenged, but rather a question of deficiencies in enforcement that weaken the regime overall'.[58] Pragmatic arguments may also underlie an approach of non-enquiry; in the context of inter-state cooperation in criminal matters, Bachmaier Winter refers to 'the factual impossibility of checking whether ... [the request for cooperation] has been executed according to the law of the executing state', only to refute it, on the basis of the ready accessibility (at least within the European Union) of national codes of criminal procedure, and on the basis that there is nothing to prevent a state from requesting information about the manner in which the requested measure was executed.[59] In this regard it is worth noting that in many cases, the ICTs *have*, apparently, been able to access relevant national laws and to obtain information about the manner in which the request for cooperation

---

[55] See e.g. Bachmaier Winter 2013, 139–140.

[56] Reisinger-Coracini 2013, 96–97.

[57] Ibid., 97 (emphasis added).

[58] Ibid., 97 and 115.

[59] Bachmaier Winter 2013, 139.

was executed.[60] Finally, while the practice at the ICTs of requiring that the defence establish or show unlawfulness (at least in cases in which the unlawfulness alleged does not concern defence rights) may not be incompatible with human rights law, it is, arguably, unreasonable. It is reasonable to require the defence to substantiate its applications for relief in respect of alleged unlawfulness in the pre-trial phase, but to place on it a *burden of proof* in this regard, i.e. a burden of establishing or showing unlawfulness, would seem excessive. It may be more difficult for the *defence* to request (and certainly for it to obtain) information regarding the manner in which a request for cooperation was executed. As observed above, in most cases the defence will be dependent on the court for acquiring knowledge of the circumstances of the evidence's obtaining (which, again, is a reason for not requiring too much from the defence by way of substantiation in order to justify an enquiry into such circumstances).

Finally, it is worth noting that any obligation to allow the defence to challenge the use of evidence (alleged to have been) obtained unlawfully in the execution of a request for cooperation is not tantamount to an obligation to exclude the evidence once it has been established that it was obtained unlawfully. Indeed, the exclusion of unlawfully obtained evidence is not a requirement of 'fairness', at least not under the notion of fairness propounded by the (majority at the) ECtHR. Below an approach to unlawfully obtained evidence will be advocated that envisages the exclusion of evidence for a broader range of rights violations than does the ECtHR, though not on the basis of 'fairness' or of the right to an effective remedy, but rather of judicial integrity.

7.3   Comparison to National Law and Practice

Having evaluated the law and practice of the ICTs with respect to the question of how to address procedural violations committed in the pre-trial phase of the proceedings in light of the relevant human rights standards, such law and practice will now be compared to the national law and practice examined in this book, that of the Netherlands and that of England and Wales. As stated in Chap. 1 (and as has been emphasized throughout this book), while the ICTs are not bound by the national law or practice of domestic jurisdictions, such law and practice (and the theoretical accounts thereof) provides a tool by which to assess the quality of the ICTs' reasoning in this regard, in terms of cogency, coherence and consistency, and may also provide inspiration and guidance to the ICTs in the application of their own law. Logically, then, the 'point of departure' in the comparison below is the law and

---

[60] See e.g. *Prosecutor v Delalić, Mucić, Delić and Landžo* (Decision on Zdravko Mucić's Motion for the Exclusion of Evidence) IT-96-21-T, T Ch II (2 September 1997); and *Prosecutor v Katanga and Ngudjolo* (Decision on the Prosecutor's Bar Table Motions) ICC-01/04-01/07, T Ch II (17 December 2010); see, however, *Prosecutor v Renzaho* (Decision on Exclusion of Testimony and Admission of Exhibit) ICTR-97-31-T, T Ch I (20 March 2007) para 16.

practice of the ICTs. Specifically, the comparison will be carried out from the perspective of the specific consequences that judges at the ICTs may attach to procedural violations (whereby, for the purposes of the analysis, it is instructive to start with the exclusion of evidence), and the procedural issues that arise in this regard.

7.3.1 Exclusion of Evidence

7.3.1.1 No Blanket Exclusionary Rule; a Matter of Discretion, Clear-Cut Cases Aside

As stated above, at the ad hoc Tribunals and the ICC, there is no automatic exclusion, i.e. no blanket exclusionary rule, for evidence obtained by violation of an internationally recognized human right, let alone for evidence obtained by another type of procedural violation. At both the ad hoc Tribunals and the ICC there are two grounds for excluding evidence on account of the manner in which it was obtained: 'substantial doubt as to reliability' and 'serious damage to the integrity of the proceedings'.[61] Under both grounds, exclusion is a matter of discretion, i.e. a matter of fact and degree. Nevertheless, the room to take into account the particular facts and circumstances of the case appears to differ as between the grounds; each ground is addressed below, including the extent to which it entails the exercise of judgement. As also stated above, the ICTs recognize an automatic, or near automatic, exclusionary rule for certain procedural violations, in particular, for certain rights violations; thus, they appear to provide for the automatic exclusion of evidence obtained by torture, by oppressive conduct such as to violate the privilege against self-incrimination and by violation of the right of access to a lawyer at the time of questioning. It seems that such violations will automatically satisfy one or both of the grounds referred to above.[62] At the ICTs, the 'exclusion of evidence', then, is characterized by the absence of a 'blanket' exclusionary rule, the existence of several specific, i.e. narrowly defined, exclusionary rules and broad discretion for the judges. Similarly, neither of the domestic jurisdictions examined in this book—the Netherlands, and England and Wales—provide for the automatic exclusion of evidence obtained by a right (a Convention right[63] or otherwise), let alone for evidence obtained by another type of procedural violation. In neither of these jurisdictions, then, is the 'protective' (or 'remedial') rationale, which sees the judicial response within the criminal trial to procedural violations committed by public authorities in the pre-trial phase of criminal proceedings (and, in particular, the exclusion of evidence obtained thereby) as a way of protecting rights, the

---

[61] See Rule 95 ICTY/ICTR RPE and Article 69(7) ICC Statute.

[62] Although as was seen in Chap. 5, this is not entirely clear. See Chap. 5, n 170–172 and accompanying text.

[63] Both of the domestic jurisdictions examined in this book are signatories to the ECHR.

primary rationale for excluding evidence, whereby it may recalled that the same conclusion was drawn above with respect to the ICTs (as well as in respect of the ECtHR).

In both of the domestic jurisdictions examined in this book the overriding criterion for exclusion reflects the discretionary (rather than mandatory) nature of the determination of whether to exclude evidence obtained by a pre-trial procedural violation. In the Netherlands the overriding question is whether an important provision or principle (of criminal procedure) has been *seriously* breached, whereby the evidence must have been obtained by the breach,[64] while in England and Wales it is whether 'admission of the evidence would have *such* an adverse effect on the *fairness of the proceedings* that it ought not to be admitted'.[65] At the ICTs, as well as in the Netherlands and England and Wales, the discretionary nature of the determination of whether to exclude evidence allows the judge(s) to take into account the particular facts and circumstances of the case. However, in each of these jurisdictions, the ability of the judge(s) to do so is restricted in one way or another. At the ICTs, evidence obtained by torture, evidence obtained by oppression such as to violate the privilege against self-incrimination and evidence obtained by violation of the right of access to a lawyer at the time of questioning are subject to automatic exclusion. In the Netherlands, the exclusionary discretion is 'confined' in at least one noteworthy way: there is little to no room to consider facts and circumstances that might militate against a (certain) response once it is established that the right of the accused to a fair trial, within the meaning of Article 6 of the ECHR and, importantly, as also interpreted by the ECtHR, is at stake. In England and Wales, provision is made for exclusionary *rules* in respect of confessions, and in respect of evidence obtained by torture. And it seems that there is less room for the judge to take into the facts and circumstances of the case in respect of 'significant and substantial' breaches of a provision of PACE and/or its codes of practice.

In the Netherlands, at least, the ability of the judge to, in the determination of whether to exclude evidence on account of the manner in which it was obtained, take into account the particular facts and circumstances of the case is restricted in another sense, also. It was seen in Chap. 3 that, in the Netherlands, Article 359a of the Dutch Code of Criminal Procedure, which, it should be recalled, governs the Dutch judicial response within the criminal trial to pre-trial procedural violations, sets forth the factors that may inform the determination of whether to attach a consequence to a procedural violations committed in the course of the criminal investigation; these are the interest that the violated provision purports to protect, the seriousness of the violation and the prejudice caused by it. It was also seen that, pursuant to the case law of the Dutch Supreme Court, such factors are not to serve

---

[64] See HR 30 March 2004, ECLI:NL:HR:2004:AM2533, *NJ* 2004/376 m.nt. Y Buruma, para 3.6.4, as repeated in HR 19 February 2013, ECLI:NL:HR:2013:BY5322, *NJ* 2013/308 m.nt. BF Keulen, para 2.4.2.

[65] See s 78(1) PACE.

as guidelines, which may be set aside if the trial judges deems that the circumstances so require, but as cumulative criteria, in the sense that any of the responses envisaged in Article 359a of the CCP, and therefore also the exclusion of evidence, must be justified by a combination of these factors, and, significantly, therefore also the existence of prejudice, which, moreover, is defined narrowly. Moreover, any freedom conferred by the legislator on the trial judge as regards the determination of whether to exclude evidence (and as regards the determination of whether to attach consequences to procedural violations committed in the course of the criminal investigation *more generally*) has been (further) curtailed by the introduction of a number of categories which (narrowly) define the circumstances under which evidence may (or must) be excluded. In light of this, it was questioned whether the Dutch judicial response within the criminal trial to pre-trial procedural violations, as envisaged by the Supreme Court, can accurately be depicted as discretionary in nature. In England and Wales, neither Section 78(1) of PACE itself nor the appellate case law interpreting that provision *comprehensively* sets forth the factors that may inform the determination to be made by the trial judge thereunder. There calls have been made for more 'structured' decision-making in the context of Section 78(1) of PACE, whereby the rationale to be pursued, and the factors to which the trial judge should attach importance, are clearly identified.[66] It is submitted that the ICTs could also benefit from a (more) structured approach to the determination of applications for the exclusion of evidence on account of the manner of its obtaining, at least under the 'serious damage to the integrity of the proceedings' limb of the exclusionary mechanism provided for in Rule 95 of the ICTY and ICTR RPE and Article 69(7) of the ICC Statute (the relevant case law hardly being a model of clarity as regards the rationale to be pursued or the factors to which chambers should attach importance in this regard), and that lessons may be drawn from both of these systems for this purpose. On the face of it, the Dutch system ensures clarity, predictability and legal certainty in the context of the determination of whether evidence obtained by a procedural violation committed in the course of a criminal investigation should be excluded. However, it significantly hampers the ability of the judge to do justice according to the needs of the case, whatever its complications.[67] The English system allows for flexibility and individualized judgments, but the lack of structured decision-making in the context of Section 78(1) gives rise to ambiguity, unpredictability and uncertainty.[68] The solution, it seems, lies somewhere in between: the determination at the ICTs of whether to exclude evidence obtained by a procedural violation committed in the pre-trial phase of the proceedings should be sufficiently structured so as to ensure clarity and predictability, but not 'over-structured' so as to undermine the discretionary nature of that determination. Identifying the factors to which a chamber should attach importance would be a step in the right direction. However, in order

---

[66] More will be said about this below, in addressing the merits of judicial discretion.

[67] See n 66.

[68] See n 66.

to be able to do so, it is necessary to obtain a better understanding of the rationale that underlies the determination of whether to exclude evidence; after all, the question of which factors should inform that determination inevitably depends on the rationale that is being pursued. As stated, at the ICTs, there are two grounds on which to exclude evidence on account of the manner of its obtaining: 'substantial doubt as to reliability' and 'serious damage to the integrity of the proceedings'. Each ground is addressed (separately) below. It is worth noting that at the ICTs, the governing documents identify more expressly *and* clearly the rationale(s) that should underlie the determination of whether to exclude evidence on account of the manner of its obtaining than do the Dutch provision governing this determination— Article 359a of the CCP—which is altogether silent on the matter, and the relevant English provision—Section 78(1) of PACE—which, while not silent on the matter, cites the need to preserve the 'fairness of the proceedings' as the rationale for excluding evidence, a criterion that has been subject to much criticism in the English literature for its vagueness.[69]

7.3.1.2 Substantial Doubt as to Reliability

It was observed in Chap. 5 that the inclusion of an 'unreliability' limb under the mechanism for excluding evidence on account of the manner of its obtaining sits somewhat uneasily with the notion seemingly underlying that mechanism, namely that chambers will refuse to admit evidence obtained by improper means, no matter how probative.[70] However, it was also observed that this need not be the case if the 'unreliability' limb is understood as being concerned with *hypothetical* rather than *actual* unreliability, whereby, under the former conception of unreliability, the chamber would have to ask itself whether any evidence (of the same type as the impugned evidence) that might have been obtained at the point at which the impugned evidence was in fact obtained, was likely to be unreliable as a result of the manner of obtaining (in other words, the chamber would have to make generalized predictions of unreliability in particular sets of circumstances). In England and Wales, Section 76(2)(b) of PACE, or the 'unreliability' head of the exclusionary rule in respect of confessions, is concerned with hypothetical rather than actual unreliability; for the purposes of that rule, an unreliable confession is not one which is *in fact* unreliable.[71]

---

[69] See e.g. Ormerod and Birch 2004.

[70] When the content of Rule 95 ICTY RPE was amended in January 1995 to how it currently reads, the ICTY said that the amendment was made to '[put] parties on notice that although a Trial Chamber is not bound by national rules of evidence, it will refuse to admit evidence—no matter how probative—if it was obtained by improper methods'. See ICTY 'Second Annual Report of the International Tribunal for the Prosecution of Persons Responsible for Serious Violations of International Humanitarian Law Committed in the Territory of the Former Yugoslavia Since 1991' (23 August 1995) UN Doc A/50/365–S/1995/728, 45.

[71] See Chap. 4, n 205–208 and accompanying text.

It was observed that the fact that what matters under the 'reliability' limb of the test for the exclusion (whereby it should be recalled that the effects that the manner in which the evidence was obtained must have in order to warrant exclusion —'substantial doubt as to reliability' and 'serious damage to the integrity of the proceedings'—are exactly the same at the ad hoc Tribunals and the ICC) is whether the procedural violation in question *casts doubt* on the reliability of the evidence suggests that what this limb is concerned with (at both the ad hoc Tribunals and the ICC) is *hypothetical* rather than *actual* unreliability. In addition, there are indications in the case law (at the ad hoc Tribunals, at least) that this is indeed the concern under the 'unreliability' limb of the test for exclusion.[72] The matter is of some importance, since it determines whether a chamber may look to information already admitted into evidence for the purposes of the determination to be made under that limb of the test for exclusion. If hypothetical unreliability is indeed the concern under the 'unreliability' limb of the test for exclusion, it would be inappropriate for the chamber to look to such information,[73] whereas if actual unreliability was the concern, it would be no more than reasonable for it to do so. What would be appropriate for the chamber to consider if hypothetical unreliability was the concern under the 'unreliability' limb of that test is the *purpose* of the provision (alleged) to have been violated, i.e. whether it is to ensure, or is otherwise concerned with, reliability. The room for a discretionary approach under the 'substantial doubt as to reliability' limb of the test for exclusion, then, may be tied up with the norm (alleged) to have been violated; the clearer it is that the norm seeks to ensure the reliability of the evidence, the less room there would appear to be for a discretionary approach under this limb.

Not all procedural violations will affect the reliability of the evidence obtained thereby, or raise issues under the 'substantial doubt as to reliability' limb of the test for exclusion. As stated, there is, at the ICTs, another ground on which to exclude evidence: 'serious damage to the integrity of the proceedings'. It is to that ground that we now turn.

7.3.1.3 Serious Damage to the Integrity of the Proceedings

Neither of the domestic jurisdictions examined in this book adopt the integrity rationale in the context of the exclusion of evidence, in the statutory framework or otherwise. However, in England and Wales, it *has* been embraced in the context of the abuse of process doctrine, and, moreover, it is widely accepted (in the English literature, at least) that preservation of the integrity of the proceedings is *a* (if not

---

[72] See Chap. 5, n 174 and 337 and accompanying text.

[73] See in this regard Dennis' comments regarding s 76(2)(b) PACE in England and Wales: 'because the court is dealing only with the hypothetical issue at the particular moment in the interview, the prosecution cannot overcome problems about the reliability of a confession by using extrinsic evidence that is likely to be true'. See Dennis 2013, 234–235.

the) reason to exclude unlawfully obtained evidence.[74] In Chap. 4, in setting out the English theory with respect to how to address pre-trial procedural violations, it was seen that there are a number of variations of the rationale. In order to better understand the rationale that underlies the determination at the ICTs of whether to exclude unlawfully obtained evidence (with a view to identifying the factors to which the ICTs should attach importance in this regard), it is instructive to consider the ICTs' law and practice in light of such theory.

A. The meaning of integrity

It was seen in Chap. 5 that in cases not involving torture or oppressive conduct such as to violate the privilege against self-incrimination, or the violation of the right of access to a lawyer at the time of questioning, whereby any evidence obtained thereby is subject to automatic exclusion, chambers at both the ad hoc Tribunals and the ICC will consider the facts and circumstances of the case in order to determine whether the evidence needs to be excluded (under the 'serious damage to the integrity of the proceedings' limb of the exclusionary mechanism, at least). At the ad hoc Tribunals, such factors include whether the public authorities involved acted in good faith, the probative value of the evidence and the seriousness of the crimes with which the accused is charged. Accordingly, and as observed above, in cases in which the procedural violation in question does not lead to automatic exclusion, the ad hoc Tribunals allow for factors to be taken into account that seemingly have nothing to do with that which made the evidence problematic in the first place—i.e. the manner in which it was obtained—and which tend to militate towards admission of the evidence. In other words, they seem to adopt a 'balancing' approach towards unlawfully obtained evidence (at least insofar as it concerns evidence not subject to one of the automatic exclusionary rules). It was seen in Chap. 4, that there are three variations of the integrity rationale: 'court-centred integrity', 'public conduct integrity' and 'public attitude integrity',[75] whereby the latter—public attitude—variation requires the court to perform a balancing exercise involving competing public interests (the public interest in the conviction of the 'factually guilty' against whom there is reliable evidence and the public interest in the judiciary not condoning the unlawful action of law enforcement agencies), which entails the consideration of factors relevant to each of the public interests involved, while the first—court-centred—variation does not. Put differently, while under the 'public attitude' variation of the integrity rationale a judge may take into account the seriousness of the procedural violation, i.e. that which made the evidence problematic in the first place, *as well as* the seriousness of the crime(s) with which the accused is charged, under the first, the concern should solely be with the seriousness of the violation. The ad hoc Tribunals' case law (at least insofar as it concerns evidence *not* subject to automatic exclusion) is in line with, and reflects,

---

[74] It is also worth noting that (one version or another of) the integrity rationale has been adopted as the primary rationale for exclusion in a number of jurisdictions, e.g. Canada and Australia.

[75] See Chap. 4, Sect. 4.3.4.

the *public attitude* variation of the integrity rationale.[76] At the ICC, it seems, a chamber may *not* take into account the probative value of the evidence or the seriousness of the crime(s) with which the accused is charged (although it bears emphasizing that the matter has yet to be addressed by the ICC Appeals Chamber). In *Lubanga*, the Trial Chamber said that this was due 'in part ... [to] the *lex specialis* nature of Article 69(7) vis-à-vis the general admissibility provisions set out in the [ICC] Statute'. An approach to unlawfully obtained evidence that does not take into account these factors is consistent with the *court-centred* variation of the integrity rationale. And the fact that the Trial Chamber's finding that such factors could not inform the determination to be made under Article 69(7) was due (only) 'in part' to the lex specialis nature of Article 69(7) vis-à-vis the general admissibility provisions suggests that there may be another explanation for it; it may suggest that the ICC made this finding as a matter of principle.[77] In this regard it is worth noting that the Trial Chamber's findings regarding the 'probative value of the evidence' and the 'seriousness of the alleged crimes committed by the accused' were (immediately) preceded by the following passage:

> When deciding whether there has been serious damage to the "integrity of the proceedings" as provided in Article 69(7) (b), *it has been stressed that* "the respect for the integrity of the proceedings is necessarily made up of respect for the core values which run through the Rome Statute'". *It has been suggested that* applying this provision involves balancing a number of concerns and values found in the Statute, including "respect for the sovereignty of States, respect for the rights of the person, the protection of victims and witnesses and the effective punishment of those guilty of grave crimes". In respect of the latter, the effective punishment of serious crimes *has been said to* render it "utterly inappropriate to exclude relevant evidence due to procedural considerations, as long as the fairness of the trial is guaranteed".[78]

As observed in Chap. 5,[79] *insofar* as they would require such factors as the probative value of the evidence and the seriousness of the offence(s) with which the accused is charged to inform the decision to be made under Article 69(7), the Trial Chamber seems to have rejected the propositions that 'respect for the integrity of the proceedings [within the meaning of Article 69(7)(b) of the ICC statute] is necessarily made up of respect for the core values which run through the Rome Statute' and that 'applying this provision [i.e. Article 69(7)(b)] involves balancing a number of concerns and values found in the Statute, including "respect for the

---

[76] See in particular *Prosecutor v Brđanin* (Decision on the Defence "Objection to Intercept Evidence") IT-99-36-T, T Ch II (3 October 2003) para 63; as was seen in Chap. 5, this decision has been cited with approval in numerous decisions at the ad hoc Tribunals.

[77] Nevertheless, it is important to note that, in the context of the ('preservation of the integrity of the proceedings' limb of the test for a) stay of proceedings, the Trial Chamber seemed to approve taking the seriousness of crime with which the accused is charged into account. See in this regard n 163 and accompanying text.

[78] *Prosecutor v Lubanga* (Decision on the admission of material from the "bar table") ICC-01/04-01/06, T Ch I (24 June 2009) para 42 (footnotes in original omitted; emphasis added).

[79] See Chap. 5, n 359 and accompanying text.

sovereignty of States, respect for the rights of the person, the protection of victims and witnesses and the effective punishment of those guilty of grave crimes'. At the very least, it is clear from the manner in which those propositions are set out (whereby the Trial Chamber made sure to make clear that such propositions emanated from *other* sources) that the Trial Chamber was not necessarily agreeing with them.

It is submitted that the ICC's approach, which does not allow the probative value of the evidence or the seriousness of the charges(s) with which the accused is charged to inform the determination of whether to exclude the evidence on account of the manner in which it was obtained, is preferable. More generally, as far as the rationale for excluding evidence on account of how it was obtained is concerned, the court-centred variation of the integrity rationale is to be preferred over the public attitude variation thereof, and it is worth noting at the outset that such an understanding of the integrity rationale is consistent with the wording the exclusionary mechanism in Rule 95 of the ICTY and ICTR RPEs and Article 69(7)(b) of the ICC Statute. Under the court-centred variation of the integrity rationale, the court acts for reasons that are independent of (predicted) public reaction, and must 'apply its own standards of propriety and decency in this respect';[80] under this variation of the integrity rationale, the judge acts for moral reasons stemming from his or her *own* conscience. By contrast, under the public attitude variation thereof, the court acts on the basis of predicted public reaction. Of course, it may be argued that, under the public attitude variation of the integrity rationale, the likely public reaction should be determined by reference to the 'views of the hypothetical, reasonable, well-informed and dispassionate person in the community',[81] which are 'a construction of the judiciary themselves'.[82] Put differently, it might be argued that that variation of the integrity rationale does not, actually, require the courts to 'pander to public mood'.[83] If that is so, then there may not be much between the public attitude variation of the integrity rationale and the court-centred variation thereof at all. Where they distinguish themselves is in the factors that may taken into account under each; while the seriousness of the procedural violation is a pertinent consideration under both variations, the probative value of the evidence

---

[80] Mirfield 1997, 24.

[81] Dennis 2013, 108.

[82] Ibid., 108. Mirfield is sceptical in this regard: 'it would seem strange to regard the disrepute in which the administration of justice would be held as properly to be assessed by those who themselves administer it; one's reputation is a reflection of what others think of one'. Mirfield 1997, 369.

[83] Choo 2008, 112. See also Duff 2004, 175: '... courts in operating a moral legitimacy rationale [which may be equated to the public attitude variation of the integrity rationale; see in this regard Mirfield 1997, 27–28] need not simply reflect the allegedly right wing, "law and order" reflexes of the general citizenry but can take a more rational and liberal approach.' Nevertheless, according to Duff, if courts 'are to pay more than lip-service to the moral legitimacy rationale, they must attach considerable importance to the likely views of the body politic.' Ibid. The notion that a population can be depicted as a single group is questionable, however, and in the context of *international* criminal adjudication this problem is exacerbated.

and the seriousness of the offence are relevant considerations under the latter but not the former. And herein lies a major objection to the public attitude variation of the integrity rationale. It allows for the probative value of the evidence, and the fact that the offence with which the accused is charged is a serious one, to be taken into account,[84] which must indeed 'signify a tendency towards ... "ends justifies the means" reasoning'.[85] In other words, the public attitude variation of the integrity rationale opens the door to, if not invites, consequentialist reasoning. And consequentialist reasoning is unacceptable, once it is accepted that reliably convicting the guilty and ensuring the protection of the innocent from conviction is not the sole function of the criminal trial; for example, as Duff, Farmer, Marshall and Tadros explain,

> What matters ... is not just that the truth be established, but that it be established by an appropriate process of calling the defendant to answer the charge—by a process that addresses the defendant as a responsible citizen. This is not just a side-constraint on a system whose positive aim is the discovery of the truth; it is integral to the very aims of the criminal trial. On such a view, serious breaches of due process, serious failures to address the defendant as a responsible citizen, undermine the legitimacy of the trial as a process that calls citizens to answer charges of wrongdoing, and thus also undermine the legitimacy of the verdict as a judgement that is to emerge from such a process.[86]

This applies no less to the trials held at the ICTs than to those held at the domestic level.[87] It is for this reason that it would be inappropriate for the ICTs (as it would for domestic courts) to adopt an approach to unlawfully obtained evidence based on the reliability rationale,[88] which, it may be recalled, posits that 'determining the truth of the criminal charges is the sole purpose of the criminal trial, and [that] evidence should be admitted or excluded solely on that basis'.[89]

It is worth noting that in Canada, where the public attitude variation of the integrity rationale lies at the heart of the exclusionary discretion provided for under Section 24(2) of the Canadian Charter of Rights and Freedoms, safeguards have been built in to the determination to be made under that provision, which might prevent such reasoning. Section 24(2) of the Charter provides that:

> Where, in proceedings under subsection (1), a court concludes that evidence was obtained in a manner that infringed or denied any rights or freedoms guaranteed by this Charter, the evidence shall be excluded if it is established that, having regard to all the circumstances,

---

[84] See Chap. 4, n 93 and 95 and accompanying text.

[85] Grevling 1997, 681.

[86] Duff et al. 2004, 25.

[87] Admittedly, the descriptor 'citizen' is somewhat awkward in the context of international criminal adjudication; the term '(responsible) agent' may be more fitting in this context.

[88] See in this regard Ormerod and Birch 2004, 782, where the authors argue, in relation to s 78 PACE, that: 'a reliability-centered discretion is problematic... the trial is not merely about reliably convicting the guilty and ensuring the protection of the innocent from conviction; there is an important judicial responsibility to maintain the moral integrity of the process'.

[89] Ashworth 1977, 723.

the admission of it in the proceedings would bring the administration of justice into disrepute.

In a leading decision on that provision, the Supreme Court of Canada held that:

The phrase "bring the administration of justice into disrepute" must be understood in the long-term sense of maintaining the integrity of, and public confidence in, the justice system. Exclusion of evidence resulting in an acquittal may provoke immediate criticism. But s. 24 (2) *does not focus on immediate reaction to the individual case*. Rather, it looks to whether the overall repute of the justice system, *viewed in the long term*, will be adversely affected by admission of the evidence. The inquiry is objective. It asks whether a reasonable person, informed of all relevant circumstances and the values underlying the Charter, would conclude that the admission of the evidence would bring the administration of justice into disrepute.[90]

Also in the same decision, the Supreme Court held that:

while the seriousness of the alleged offence may be a valid consideration, it has the potential to cut both ways. Failure to effectively prosecute a serious charge due to excluded evidence may have an immediate impact on how people view the justice system. Yet ... it is the long-term repute of the justice system that is s. 24(2)'s focus. ... *The short-term public clamour for a conviction in a particular case must not deafen the s. 24(2) judge to the longer-term repute of the administration of justice.* Moreover, while the public has a heightened interest in seeing a determination on the merits where the offence charged is serious, it also has a vital interest in having a justice system that is above reproach, particularly where the penal stakes for the accused are high.[91]

If safeguards can be built into the determination to be made under a given exclusionary discretion, which make it more difficult for a judge to resort to 'ends justifies the means' reasoning,[92] the question arises as to whether the court-centred variation of the integrity rationale is still to be preferred over the public attitude variation thereof. It might be argued that adoption of the latter variation of the integrity rationale has the advantage of 'locating the issues presented by ... [unlawfully] obtained evidence in a wider context', by treating the determination of whether to exclude evidence on account of how it was obtained as a 'broad question of public policy',[93] and thereby 'informing the public of the difficulty of choosing between admissibility and inadmissibility'.[94] While these pursuits may be commendable, it should be recalled that, under the public attitude variation of the integrity rationale, public opinion may be *ignored* insofar as it requires something that runs contrary to the court's sense of justice; after all, under that rationale, it is the 'views of the

---

[90] *R v Grant* [2009] 2 SCR 353 [68] (emphasis added).

[91] Ibid., [84] (emphasis added).

[92] See in this regard also the Canadian Supreme Court's findings in *R v Harrison* [2009] 2 SCR 494 [34]: 'While the charged offence is serious, this factor must not take on disproportionate significance.'

[93] See Dennis 2013, 107–108.

[94] Zuckerman 1987, 59.

hypothetical, reasonable, well-informed and dispassionate person in the community' that count, which are 'a construction of the judiciary themselves'.[95] And if that is so, it may be argued the court-centred variation of the integrity rationale, which, as stated, entails the judge acting for moral reasons stemming from his or her *own* conscience, better reflects what the court is actually doing. It goes without saying that courts should properly explain their decisions to exclude or admit evidence that has been obtained by a procedural violation; it should not simply be assumed that the general public, including victim populations, are incapable of the understanding the moral reasons underlying their decisions. And even where (or, perhaps, *especially* where) a negative public reaction to a decision to exclude evidence obtained by a procedural violation may reasonably be expected, the judge has a moral obligation to explain his or her decision; if the judge is not obliged to be guided by the public opinion (and it is submitted that the judge should not be so obliged), he or she may nevertheless be expected to play a role in shaping it.

There are, then, several reasons for preferring the court-centred variation of the integrity rationale over the public attitude variation thereof, but the most compelling argument for doing so is that it—the court-centred variation of the integrity rationale—does not allow the probative value of the evidence or the fact that the crime (s) with which the accused is charged is a serious one to inform the determination of whether to exclude evidence obtained by a procedural violation. Adoption of this rationale as the primary rationale for excluding evidence on account of the manner in which it was obtained would send the *unequivocal* message that, in the determination of whether to exclude unlawfully obtained evidence, chambers will not allow themselves to be guided by consequentialist thinking. Of course, adoption of this rationale could not prevent chambers from allowing that determination to be guided by consequentialist thinking altogether. The primary consideration under the court-centred variation of the integrity rationale is the seriousness of the procedural violation; as will be demonstrated below, this consideration may give rise to a whole host of lines of enquiry, and creates sufficient scope for a judge so inclined to allow the determination of whether to exclude unlawfully obtained evidence to be guided by consequentialist thinking. While not for a moment suggesting that the judges in that case were so inclined, the *Lubanga* decision addressing the lawfulness of a search and seizure operation carried out by the Congolese national authorities[96] demonstrates just how flexible an approach based on the court-centred variation of the integrity rationale potentially is; after finding that the probative value of the evidence and the fact that the crime with which the accused is charged is serious could not inform the decision to be made under Article 69(7) of the ICC Statute (which, as stated above, is in line with the court-centred variation of the

---

[95] See n 81–82 and accompanying text.

[96] *Prosecutor v Lubanga* (Decision on the admission of material from the "bar table") ICC-01/04-01/06, T Ch I (24 June 2009).

integrity rationale), it pointed to three factors, two of which at least properly went to the seriousness of the violation, which justified admission of the evidence.[97] The court-centred variation of the integrity rationale, then, is manipulable; however, it is submitted that the public attitude variation thereof (like the cost-benefit analysis that criminal courts in the Netherlands may (in the second category of case in which evidence may be excluded) or must (in the third category thereof) perform when applying Article 359a of the CCP)[98] is significantly more so.[99]

B. Pertinent factors

The preferred rationale as regards the exclusion of unlawfully obtained evidence, then, is the court-centred variation of the integrity rationale; the question that now needs to be answered is: to which factors should judges at the ICTs attach (significant) importance in this regard?[100] First of all, it is worth reiterating that under this rationale, they may not take into account, let alone attach importance to, the probative value of the evidence, or the fact that the crime with which the accused is charged is a serious one. In both of the jurisdictions examined in this book—the Netherlands, and England and Wales—the fact that the offence with which the accused is charged is (very) serious may be taken into account in the determination of whether to exclude evidence on account of the manner of its obtaining, at least in cases in which the underlying violation is not such that the use of the evidence obtained thereby would automatically render the trial unfair, or, as the case may be, in cases in which the underlying violations does not constitute a significant and substantial breach of PACE and/or its codes of practice. It was seen in Chap. 3 that, in the Netherlands, this factor has been read into the second paragraph Article 359a of the Dutch Code of Criminal Procedure (the central provision in the Netherlands for responding to procedural violations committed in the course of the criminal investigation within the criminal trial), which sets forth the factors that the court is required to take into account when determining whether to attach consequences to procedural violations committed in the course of a criminal investigation (and, if so, which), and now also 'enters the equation' via the cost-benefit analysis that the court is, according to the Supreme Court, permitted (in case of the second category of exclusion) and required (in case of the third category) to undertake in the determination of whether to exclude an item of evidence on account of the manner in which it was obtained. In Chap. 4 it was seen that, in England and Wales, this factor has been allowed to enter the analysis on the basis that, under Section 78(1) of the Police and Criminal Evidence Act, which, it may be recalled, provides for a discretion to exclude evidence if its admission 'would have such an adverse effect on the fairness of the proceedings that the court ought not

---

[97] Ibid., para 47. It is not obvious why the fact that it was not the accused's, but a third person's, right to privacy that had been violated would make the violation less serious.

[98] See Chap. 3, n 309–315 and accompanying text.

[99] See in this regard Kamisar 1987, 18.

[100] Or, in other words, 'at what point does moral scruple properly obtrude?' See Mirfield 1997, 25. See also n 80 and accompanying text.

to admit it', fairness is owed to 'both sides': the defence *and* prosecution. In both jurisdictions, the ability of the court to, in the determination of whether to exclude evidence on account of the manner of its obtaining, take into account the fact that the offence with which the accused is charged is (very) serious has been criticized in the literature,[101] and, it is submitted, rightly so.

As stated, the focus of the enquiry under the court-centred variation of the integrity rationale is the seriousness of the procedural violation. The reason for this is that, under that variation of the integrity rationale, 'the essence of the objection is to the court joining hands, so to speak, with the officer who conducted himself as he did', so that the 'key time at which the principle bites, is the time of the unlawful or improper investigative step', whereas, under the public attitude variation of the integrity rationale, the key time at which the principle bites is at trial, when the decision of whether or not to exclude the evidence is made.[102] As suggested above, any approach to the question of how to address pre-trial procedural violations in which the seriousness of the procedural violation(s) is the focus may properly be said to entail the exercise of *discretion*, if not the performance of a balancing exercise. In a purely domestic context, relevant considerations under the court-centred variation of the integrity rationale are, for example, whether the procedural violation constitutes a rights violation and, if so, how serious it was, whether the officers acted in bad or in good faith and whether it was committed in circumstances of urgency, emergency or necessity. In the international context, the fact that the ICTs and the national authorities of the state who execute a request for cooperation do not form part of the same legal system (i.e. the fact that the ICTs are not institutionally connected to the national authorities actually carry out coercive measures) may complicate matters; put differently, the 'separation thesis', which posits that 'there is no real connection between the actions of the police in investigating the crime and the court's verdict',[103] is at its strongest in this context, so that the question may arise as to whether a chamber of an international criminal tribunal *could* even 'join hands' with those who physically committed the violation (i.e. whether, in declining to exclude any evidence obtained thereby, they may be held to be condoning such conduct).[104] Adjusting the court-centred variation of the integrity rationale to the international context, the essence of the objection *should*, arguably, be to the international criminal tribunal in question joining hands with the national public authorities that conducted themselves as they did *with the involvement of the ICTs*. At the ICTs, a pertinent consideration under the court-centred variation of the integrity rationale, then, should be whether the ICTs were involved in the violation, at least insofar as the evidence concerned is not

---

[101] See Chap. 3, n 292–297 and accompanying text, and Chap. 4, n 412–413 and accompanying text.

[102] See Mirfield 1997, 29.

[103] See n 18–21 and accompanying text.

[104] More will be said about this issue below, in addressing the question as to the most suitable rationale for responding within the criminal trial to procedural violations committed in the pre-trial phase context of international criminal proceedings.

subject to automatic exclusion, i.e. was not obtained by torture or oppressive conduct such as to violate the privilege against self-incrimination, or by violation of the right of access to a lawyer at the time of questioning; in such cases the question of involvement is not, and in any case, *should* not be a pertinent consideration. More will be said about this consideration below.

Another pertinent consideration under that rationale should be whether the procedural violation in question constituted a violation of an internationally recognized human right. After all, such a violation must surely cause damage to the integrity of the proceedings, regardless of the internationally recognized human right to have been violated.[105] That, of course, is not the standard for exclusion under Rule 95 of the ICTY and ICTR RPEs or Article 69(7)(b) of the ICC Statute: rather, the question is whether the admission of the evidence would *seriously* damage the integrity of the proceedings. As stated, certain rights violations (torture, violation of the privilege against self-incrimination and violation of the right of access to a lawyer at the time of questioning) will automatically lead to exclusion of the evidence obtained thereby, seemingly because the admission of evidence obtained by such a violation would automatically satisfy one or both prongs of the test for the exclusion of evidence on account of the manner of its obtaining ('substantial doubt as to reliability' and 'serious damage to the integrity of the proceedings'). In respect of *other* internationally recognized human rights, which do not automatically lead to exclusion of the evidence obtained thereby, it might be argued that not all rights violations are equally serious (i.e. a rights violation may be trivial or serious), and that this is a factor to which the international criminal tribunal in question is entitled to attach importance in the determination of whether to exclude the evidence obtained thereby. In *Lubanga*, it may be recalled, in declining to exclude evidence obtained by Congolese national authorities in the course of a search and seizure operation, the Trial Chamber argued (among other things) that the rights violation in question (violation of the internationally recognized human right to privacy—specifically, of the principle of proportionality) 'was not of a particularly grave kind', although it did not explain why this was the case. It is submitted that where a violation is of a particularly grave kind, this is a reason to automatically exclude the evidence obtained thereby; at the ICTs, it certainly seems to be a reason to do so. However, it does not follow that where a violation is not of a particularly grave kind, this is a reason *not* to exclude the evidence obtained thereby. There may, however, be other reasons not to exclude (i.e. to admit) the evidence obtained by violation of an internationally recognized human right that is not of a 'particularly grave kind', for example, when the ICTs cannot be said to have been involved in the violation. Conversely, combined with a certain level of involvement on the part of the ICTs therein, it is arguable that the violation of an internationally recognized human right

---

[105] Various authors have argued or otherwise acknowledged that the (use of evidence obtained by the) violation of human (or constitutional) rights in particular is problematic from the perspective of the integrity rationale. See in this regard Chap. 4, n 88–90 and accompanying text, and also Roberts 2012 and Safferling 2003, 295 ('every human rights violation must ... hamper the integrity of the proceedings.').

(that is *not* of a particularly grave kind) should make a compelling case for exclusion. Before turning to the issue of involvement, one final observation is in order regarding the ability of rights violations to impact on the integrity of the proceedings: it is not obvious why the fact that it was not the accused's, but a third party's internationally recognized human rights that were violated, should be a reason *not* to exclude the evidence obtained thereby. In *Lubanga*, it may be recalled, this was one of the factors cited by the Trial Chamber as justifying the evidence's admission, notwithstanding that it had been obtained by violation of the internationally recognized human right to privacy.[106] As has been observed, 'even if it is a third party's, and not the defendant's, rights which have been violated ... it may still be morally unacceptable for the court, as a body responsible for upholding values, to handle the 'soiled goods' generated'.[107]

The fact that the ICTs have, in their case law, attached importance to the matter of involvement in determining whether to exclude unlawfully obtained evidence (and in determining whether to attach other consequences to procedural violations), is, it is submitted, not unreasonable or illogical. Before explaining why this is so, it bears recalling that in case of certain rights violations, the ICTs do not attach importance to the matter of involvement at all; it was seen above that in case of violation of the right of access to a lawyer at the time of questioning, it matters not that the statement was taken by national authorities, for example.[108] Similarly, in the Netherlands, where the manner in which the evidence was obtained undermines the accused's right to a fair trial, under whose responsibility (the Dutch authorities or foreign authorities) the conduct in question was carried out is irrelevant. Turning back to the point raised at the beginning of the paragraph, it is worth pointing out that, at the national level, when principled calls for exclusion are made (for example, when it is argued that the fact that evidence has been obtained by a *rights* violation, this is a reason to exclude it), this is on the understanding that the investigative authorities to have acted unlawfully, and the judicial authorities now seized of an application to exclude the evidence obtained thereby, form part of the same legal system, such that they can be said to be institutionally connected (even if they are independent of one another) and, more importantly, such that the judicial authorities may be argued to have a responsibility for the conduct of the investigative authorities (although presumably adherents of the separation thesis[109] would disagree with this). By contrast, the judicial authorities at the ICTs and the national authorities on which they are dependent for such activities as the apprehension of persons suspected or accused of crimes falling within their jurisdiction and the carrying out of investigations, do not form part of the same legal system. It is understandable, then, that they have attached importance to the matter of the ICTs

---

[106] *Prosecutor v Lubanga* (Decision on the admission of material from the "bar table") ICC-01/04-01/06, T Ch I (24 June 2009) para 47.

[107] Choo 2008, 110.

[108] See n 11 and accompanying text.

[109] See in this regard n 18–21 and accompanying text.

involvement in the violation; in case of involvement, the ICTs may reasonably be argued to have a responsibility for the conduct the national authorities to have acted unlawfully in the execution of a request for cooperation. However, their approach to the matter of involvement may be too narrow. In the determination of applications for relief for an (alleged) unlawful arrest or detention, chambers have spoken of the need for 'concerted action' between an organ of the ICC and the national authorities concerned, whereby 'mere knowledge on the part of the Prosecutor' that a person suspected of crimes falling within the jurisdiction of the ICC is being detained at the national level is 'no proof' of his involvement in any unlawfulness to arise in the context of such detention.[110] In the determination of applications for the exclusion of evidence also, it appears that what is required is concerted or 'collusive' action between the ICC and the national authorities carrying out the coercive measure in question. In *Lubanga*, it may be recalled, in declining to exclude evidence obtained by Congolese national authorities in the course of a search and seizure operation, the Trial Chamber argued (among other things) that the 'illegal acts [i.e. the acts that violated the internationally recognized human right to privacy—specifically, of the principle of proportionality] were committed by the Congolese authorities, albeit in the presence of an investigator from the prosecution'.[111] While the Trial Chamber did not use the term, the argument seems to have been that there was no 'concerted action' between the Congolese national authorities and the ICC (on account of the ICC investigator having merely been present). In the first place it may be observed that there are indications that the ICC investigator had not merely been present; earlier on in the decision, the Trial Chamber had found that 'the search was the sole responsibility of the Congolese authorities', and that they had carried it out, whereas 'the prosecution's investigator was only "permitted to *assist*"'.[112] And in an earlier ruling on the matter (made in the context of the confirmation of charges proceedings) the Pre-Trial Chamber noted that the Prosecution's investigator's 'presence [had] *influenced* the conduct of the search and seizure'.[113] However, the more important point is that the Trial Chamber's apparent conclusion that there had been no concerted action between the Congolese authorities and the ICC was based solely on the conduct of the prosecution's

---

[110] See e.g. *Prosecutor v Lubanga* (Judgment on the Appeal of Mr. Thomas Lubanga Dyilo against the Decision on the Defence Challenge to the Jurisdiction of the Court pursuant to Article 19(2)(a) of the Statute of 3 October 2006) ICC-01/04-01/06, A Ch (14 December 2006) para 42; *Prosecutor v Gbagbo* (Decision on the "Corrigendum of the challenge to the jurisdiction of the International Criminal Court on the basis of Articles 12(3), 19(2), 21(3), 55 and 59 of the Rome Statute filed by the Defence for President Gbagbo (ICC-02/11-01/11-129)") ICC-02/11-01/11, P T Ch I (15 August 2012) para 109; and *Prosecutor v Muthaura and Kenyatta* (Decision on the application for a ruling on the legality of the arrest of Mr. Dennis Ole Itumbi) ICC-01/09-02/11, T Ch V (19 November 2012) paras 7–9.

[111] *Prosecutor v Lubanga* (Decision on the admission of material from the "bar table") ICC-01/04-01/06, T Ch I (24 June 2009) para 47.

[112] Ibid., para 46.

[113] *Prosecutor v Lubanga* (Decision on Confirmation of Charges) ICC-01/04-01/06, P T Ch I (29 January 2007) para 80 (emphasis added).

investigator at the time of the search; it was not based on the conduct of the *prosecution* more generally, including its conduct in the lead up to the search. Presumably, the ICC investigator's presence at the search was not coincidental. The prosecution might have played an active role in the lead up to the search, orchestrating or coordinating it perhaps, or otherwise steering or facilitating it, and ensuring that one of its investigators was present in order to ensure that certain materials were seized or otherwise to receive the materials seized. If that had been the case, it could not sincerely be said that there had been no concerted action between the national authorities and the ICC. And if it played such a role, i.e. if there was concerted action, and it was aware or could have been aware that there was a significant chance that internationally recognized human rights would be violated in the execution of the coercive measure in question (and such rights were, in fact, violated in the execution thereof), there may be good reason to exclude any evidence obtained thereby, on the basis that not doing so would cause *substantial* damage to the integrity the proceedings (whereby it should be recalled that violation of an internationally recognized right must necessarily cause damage to the integrity of the proceedings).

By contrast, if there is no concerted action, i.e. the prosecution is merely the fortunate recipient of tainted evidence, for example, evidence obtained by violation of an internationally recognized human right, it may be reasonable to admit the evidence. This raises the question of *when* the prosecution may be said to have merely been the fortunate recipient of tainted evidence; in particular, if the prosecution has requested cooperation, formally or informally, but has not otherwise played an active role, i.e. it has left the matter entirely to the national authorities, can it really be said to have merely been the fortunate recipient of the evidence? After all, such an approach may amount to a failure to exercise due diligence. It was argued above that a failure on the part of the prosecution to exercise due diligence to ensure that, once it initiates a case, the case proceeds to trial in a way that respects the rights of the accused, should be sufficient in order to be able to attribute a rights violation to the international criminal tribunal in question, such as warrant the provision of an effective, personal remedy in respect thereof; the question is whether this should be sufficient to justify *exclusion of the evidence* obtained by such a rights violation. It is certainly arguable that if it were to transpire that the prosecution was making a *habit* of making requests for cooperation and not following them up, whereby it knew or could have known that in the state in question there was a significant chance that internationally recognized human rights would be violated in the execution of the coercive measure in question, this should lead to the exclusion of evidence obtained in such a manner in the case at hand. In sum, if 'concerted action' is to be the standard of involvement under the 'substantial damage to integrity' limb of the test for exclusion, it is important that chambers of the ICC address the issue *properly*. Where it is clear that officials of the international criminal tribunal in question were in fact involved at some stage of the operation (whether it was in the lead up to, or during the execution of the measure), the ICTs should conduct a thorough examination into the facts in order to determine the nature and degree of that involvement, and, where necessary, make relevant orders for disclosure. Not doing so may result in the provenance of the evidence not being properly accounted for and the inability of the defence to challenge it.

A consideration frequently cited as relevant to the determination of whether to exclude evidence on account of the manner of its obtaining is whether the public authorities involved acted in bad or in good faith; whereas bad faith on the part of the public authorities militates towards *exclusion* of the evidence, good faith on the part of such authorities militates towards *admission*. If it is the integrity rationale that underlies the exclusionary mechanism (regardless of the variation thereof: court-centred integrity or public attitude integrity) it is clear that good faith on the part of the investigative authorities will decrease the need for the court to dissociate itself from the conduct concerned, while bad faith on their part will increase the need to do so. In the context of international criminal proceedings, the question may arise as to *whose* bad faith or good faith should matter: that of the national authorities, or rather that of the prosecution, and the issue might be further complicated if an investigator for the prosecution was involved in the actual execution of the coercive measure, as was the case in the ICC case of *Lubanga*. Good faith on the part of *the prosecution* is, arguably, a reason *not* to exclude evidence obtained by violation of an internationally recognized human right. The question as to good faith on the part of the prosecution might involve asking whether, in seeking state cooperation, or in seeking to benefit from it, the prosecution did everything that it could to ensure that the execution of the request would comply with internationally recognized human rights, for example, by checking the relevant national law and human rights treaties applicable to the country in question and, where, notwithstanding the legal framework in place, there are concerns about the national practice in this regard (in light of, for example, reports by the bodies charged with supervising the compliance with, and implementation of, the applicable human rights treaty, or reports by NGOs), it has made efforts to ensure that the legal framework is properly implemented. However, if good faith is to have any meaning in this regard, it is submitted that chambers should not be too quick to accept good faith on the part of the prosecution; as has been argued at the national level in the context of the question of when unlawfully obtained evidence should be excluded, 'ignorance ... must not be rewarded or encouraged and negligence or wilful blindness cannot be equated with good faith'.[114] Similarly, the absence of bad faith should not automatically be equated to the presence of good faith. As to the national authorities, there may be good reason to presume the good faith of the national authorities concerned where they were acting pursuant to a duty to cooperate with the international criminal tribunal in question,[115] while it is difficult to see how this could negate a finding of bad faith on the part of the prosecution or otherwise offset the damage caused to the integrity of the proceedings where the violation of an internationally recognized human right was the result of concerted action between the prosecution and the national authorities. At the same time, it is questionable

---

[114] *R v Grant* [2009] 2 SCR 353 [75].

[115] Regarding the issue of cooperation, see n 56–58 and accompanying text.

whether a deliberate flouting of local laws by the national authorities could (or, at least, should) negate the good faith of the prosecution (where it is found to have been present), such as to necessitate exclusion of the evidence.

Another consideration that may, arguably, be taken into account under the integrity rationale, is whether the evidence was obtained (unlawfully) in circumstances of urgency, emergency or necessity. Such factors militate towards admission under the court-centred variation of the integrity rationale, because they make it less offensive for the court to join hands with the errant law enforcement officer. In the ICTY case of *Brđanin*, in declining to exclude several intercepted telephone conversations which the Defence alleged had been obtained unlawfully, the Trial Chamber attached importance to the fact that 'at the time, [Bosnia and Herzegovina was] on the brink of armed conflict and the purpose of the proposed interceptions was to uncover the extent of the threat to the internal security of Bosnia and Herzegovina'.[116] That would seem to be a valid consideration under the court-centred variation of the integrity rationale. If this factor is to have any meaning or value in this regard, it is submitted that chambers should not be too quick to accept that the evidence was obtained in circumstances of urgency, emergency or necessity. In particular, the fact that the ICTs are to a large extent reliant on state-cooperation for the collection of evidence, and the fact the state concerned was obliged to cooperate, should not be sufficient to found 'necessity'.

In sum, pertinent considerations under the integrity limb of the test for exclusion of evidence on account of the manner of its obtaining (at least insofar as evidence *not* subject to automatic exclusion is concerned) are: whether there was a violation of an internationally recognized human right, whether the international criminal tribunal in question was involved (and, in particular, whether there was concerted action between an organ of the international criminal tribunal in question and the national authorities), whether the prosecution acted in good or bad faith and whether the evidence was obtained (unlawfully) in circumstances of urgency, emergency or necessity. Such factors go to the seriousness of the procedural violation, which, as stated above, is the primary consideration under the court-centred variation of the integrity rationale (in light of the 'key time at which the principle bites'). It is submitted that, combined with concerted action (which, if it is to be the standard of involvement under the substantial damages to the integrity of the proceedings limb, should not be approached disingenuously), the violation of an internationally recognized human right should make a compelling case for exclusion of the evidence obtained thereby. Nevertheless, the good faith of the *prosecution*, or the fact that the evidence was obtained in circumstances of urgency, emergency or necessity might, exceptionally, warrant a different conclusion. Factors which should not be taken into account are the probative value of the evidence or the fact that the offence(s) with which the accused has been charged are very serious; in light of the 'key time' at which the court-centred variation of the

---

[116] *Prosecutor v Brđanin* (Decision on the Defence "Objection to Intercept Evidence") IT-99-36-T, T Ch II (3 October 2003) para 63.

integrity rationale 'bites', it would not be appropriate to take such factors into account. Aside from this, to allow such factors to be taken into account is to open the door to, if not invite, 'ends justifies the means' reasoning.

7.3.2   Stay of Proceedings

7.3.2.1   A Matter of Discretion, Clear-Cut Cases Aside

Having analysed the ICTs' law and practice with respect to the exclusion of evidence, the stay of proceedings will now be turned to. At the ad hoc Tribunals and the ICC, the proceedings may be stayed (permanently) in exceptional circumstances. Similarly, in England and Wales, a stay of proceedings, and, in the Netherlands, a declaration that the prosecution is inadmissible (a procedural step akin to a stay of proceedings), are exceptional measures. At the ICTs, the determination of an application for a stay of proceedings is a matter of discretion, or, put differently, a matter of fact and degree, whereby, clear-cut cases aside, minds may well differ as to whether a stay of proceedings is necessary. One such clear-cut case would appear to be where the suspect or accused has been tortured or seriously mistreated in the process of being brought into the jurisdiction of the international criminal tribunal in question (more will be said about this below). In England and Wales, the determination of an application for a stay of proceedings also entails the exercise of discretion, in the sense that the standard to be applied is 'open-textured' in nature, and affords the judge a good deal of latitude in its application to a given set of facts. By contrast, the test in the Netherlands for declaring the prosecution inadmissible is more rule-like in nature; it consists of several components which appear to be cumulative: the public authorities must have committed serious violations of principles of proper administration of justice, either intentionally or by gross negligence, as a result of which the suspect is prevented from receiving a fair trial. It was seen in Chap. 3 that, in practice, the test is not always applied strictly; in particular, if the procedural violation in question clearly prevents the accused from receiving a fair trial, whether the public authorities committed the violation intentionally or by gross negligence may be of less importance. However, bad faith or gross-negligence on the part of the public authorities in committing 'serious violations of principles of proper administration of justice' is not, by itself, sufficient to justify a declaration that the prosecution is inadmissible; the violation must impact on the ability of the accused to receive a fair trial. In the Netherlands, then, there is, effectively, one ground on which to declare the prosecution inadmissible: the impossibility of a fair trial. And it appears that the notion of fair trial is to be construed narrowly here, in the sense of being concerned with accurate truth-finding and the protection of the innocent from wrongful conviction. At the ICTs, the impossibility of fair trial is one of *two* grounds on which the proceedings may be stayed. The other ground is to maintain the integrity of the proceedings. In England and Wales also, there are two categories of case in which a court has a discretion to stay the proceedings on the ground that to try those proceedings will amount to an abuse of its own process: 'either (1) because it will be impossible (usually by reason of delay) to give the accused a fair trial or (2) because it offends the court's sense of justice and propriety to be asked to try the accused in the circumstances of a particular case'.[117] More will be said about these grounds in the next subsections; for now it may be noted that, at the ICTs, as in England and Wales, the test for staying the proceedings reflects the notion that the court has responsibilities that go beyond reliably convicting the guilty and ensuring the protection of the innocent from wrongful conviction.

As stated, at the ICTs, the determination of whether to stay the proceedings is a matter of discretion, or, put differently, a matter of fact and degree, whereby, clear-cut cases aside, minds may well differ as to whether a stay of proceedings is necessary. Similarly, in England and Wales, the determination of whether to stay the proceedings entails the exercise of discretion, in the sense that the standard to be applied is 'open-textured' in nature, and affords the judge a good deal of latitude in its application to a given set of facts. In England and Wales, calls have been made for a more 'structured' approach to the exercise of the abuse of process discretion, i.e. to the determination of an application for a stay of proceedings, especially to the determination to be made under the 'integrity' limb of that discretion (the second limb referred to above), which would entail identification of the rationale and of the factors to which courts should attach (significant) importance in this regard. The ICTs could also benefit from a more structured approach to the discretion to stay the proceedings; the case law is not a model of clarity as regards the rationales that are to be pursued or the factors that may be taken into account in this regard. In order to identify the factors to which chambers should attach significant importance in exercising said discretion, it is necessary to obtain a better understanding of the rationales that underlie the determination of whether to stay the proceedings; it is to such rationales that we now turn.

7.3.2.2 Different Grounds

As stated, there are two grounds for staying the proceedings at the ICTs. At the ad hoc Tribunals, a stay may, according to the shared Appeals Chamber, be imposed in two 'distinct' situations: where delay has made a fair trial for the accused impossible; and where in the circumstances of a particular case, proceeding with the trial of the accused would contravene the court's sense of justice, due to pre-trial impropriety or misconduct.[118] In setting out this test, the Appeals Chamber appears to have drawn heavily on Lord Lowry's formulation of the categories of case in which a court in England has a discretion to stay the proceedings as an abuse of process in the (English) case of *R v Horseferry Road Magistrates' Court, Ex parte*

---

[117] *R v Horseferry Road Magistrates' Court, Ex parte Bennett* [1994] 1 AC 42, 74.

[118] *Prosecutor v Barayagwiza* (Decision) ICTR-97-19-AR72, A Ch (3 November 1999) para 77.

Bennett.[119] At the ICC, a stay may, according to the ICC Appeals Chamber, be imposed '[w]here fair trial becomes impossible because of breaches of the fundamental rights of the suspect or the accused by his/her accusers', in which case 'it would be a contradiction in terms to put the person on trial', given that 'a fair trial is the only means to do justice'.[120] Accordingly, at the ICC, a stay of proceedings may be imposed on grounds of unfairness, whereby the references to 'fair trial' in at least the first of the statements are to be 'perceived and applied' broadly, to '[embrace] the judicial process in its entirety'.[121] Such references appear to denote something more than just 'trial fairness', i.e. the ability of the accused to defend him- or herself properly (which, it should be noted, may be compromised by the failure to respect the accused's fair trial rights in the pre-trial phase of proceedings). Accordingly, it seems that a fair trial may become impossible due to the violation of *other* rights (than fair trial rights), such as 'violations of the rights of the accused in the process of bringing him/her to justice', i.e. in the process of exercising jurisdiction over the accused,[122] even if such violations do not affect the ability of the accused to mount an effective defence and, by extension, the ability of the judges to determine guilt accurately. In other words, in such cases the question is not whether the suspect or accused can receive a fair trial in the narrow sense of the term, but whether in the circumstances it would be fair to *put them on trial at all*. ICC trial chambers have interpreted the 'fair trial' test originally set forth in *Lubanga*[123] as providing for two *distinct* grounds on which to stay the proceedings: where it would be 'odious' or 'repugnant' to the administration of justice to allow the proceedings to continue; and where the accused's rights have been breached to the extent that a fair trial has been rendered impossible.[124] While the Appeals Chamber has, to date, not expressly endorsed this interpretation, it has not disapproved of it either. It seems, therefore, that the fair trial test originally set forth in *Lubanga* encompass both limbs of the abuse of process doctrine, as it applies at the ad hoc Tribunals; certainly the two grounds identified by the Trial Chamber in *Lubanga* correspond to the two 'situations' set out in *Barayagwiza*. Nevertheless, the appellate case law at the ad hoc Tribunals is clearer than that at the ICC as regards the circumstances that

---

[119] See n 117 and accompanying text.

[120] *Prosecutor v Lubanga* (Judgment on the Appeal of Mr. Thomas Lubanga Dyilo against the Decision on the Defence Challenge to the Jurisdiction of the Court pursuant to Article 19(2)(a) of the Statute of 3 October 2006) ICC-01/04-01/06, A Ch (14 December 2006) para 37.

[121] Ibid., para 37. See also *Prosecutor v Lubanga* (Judgment on the appeal of Mr. Thomas Lubanga Dyilo against his conviction) ICC-01/04-01/06, A Ch (1 December 2014) para 147.

[122] *Prosecutor v Lubanga* (Judgment on the Appeal of Mr. Thomas Lubanga Dyilo against the Decision on the Defence Challenge to the Jurisdiction of the Court pursuant to Article 19(2)(a) of the Statute of 3 October 2006) ICC-01/04-01/06, A Ch (14 December 2006) para 36.

[123] See n 120 and 228–229 and accompanying text.

[124] *Prosecutor v Lubanga* (Redacted Decision on the "Defence Application Seeking a Permanent Stay of the Proceedings") ICC-01/04-01/06, T Ch I (7 March 2011) paras 165–166.

may lead to a permanent stay of proceedings.[125] As stated, the ICC Appeals Chamber has not expressly endorsed the interpretation of its fair trial test by trial chambers; indeed, it continues to employ 'fair trial' terminology in this context. Here it may be recalled that in England and Wales also, the abuse of process doctrine is sometimes rationalized solely in terms of 'fairness'; thus, it has been held that proceedings can be stayed on the basis of the abuse of process doctrine in cases where it is impossible to give the accused a fair trial, *and* in cases 'where the court concludes that it would be *unfair for the defendant to be tried*'.[126] Insofar as the second category may be said to be concerned with 'fairness to try', the question is whether it would be fair to try someone *at all*, even if they can be given a fair trial. But the 'fairness to try' terminology has been subject to criticism in the literature (as well as in the case law) and rightly so. According to Choo,

> It is confusing, to say the least, to use the term 'unfair trial' to connote a trial that has the potential to result in a factually incorrect guilty verdict, and to say that it would be 'unfair to try' a defendant in circumstances where, even if a 'fair trial' can be held, it will nevertheless be inappropriate to try the defendant because of considerations of moral integrity. To make matters even more confusing, the courts sometimes display lack of care in their use of these terms.[127]

The ICC Appeals Chambers' rationalization of the stay of proceedings solely in terms of 'fairness' is a cause for concern. It is indeed confusing. In order to ensure that the two grounds for staying the proceedings remain conceptually distinct, it is important that the Appeals Chamber adopt clear and appropriate terminology in this regard, for which it may, it is submitted (and subject to the comments made below), draw on ICC trial chambers' interpretation of the 'fair trial' test originally set forth in *Lubanga*, as providing for two distinct grounds on which to stay the proceedings: where it would be 'odious' or 'repugnant' to the administration of justice to allow the proceedings to continue; and where the accused's rights have been breached to the extent that a fair trial has been rendered impossible. And it is important that chambers at the ICC treat such grounds as distinct, whereby they are mindful of the fact that different considerations apply under each.

---

[125] See similarly Taylor and Jalloh 2013, 320.

[126] *R v Beckford* [1996] 1 Cr App R 94 at 100–101. See also *R (Ebrahim) v Feltham Magistrates' Court* [2001] 1 WLR 1293 [20].

[127] Choo 2008, 187. As to the case law, in *Warren*, Lord Dyson was similarly critical of the 'fairness to try' terminology: 'It is unhelpful and confusing to say that this category [the second category of case under the abuse of process doctrine] is founded on the imperative of avoiding unfairness to the accused. It is unhelpful because it focuses attention on what is fair to the accused, rather than on whether the court's sense of justice and propriety is offended or public confidence in the criminal justice system would be undermined by the trial. It is confusing because fairness to the accused should be the focus of the first category of case.' See *Warren and others v Attorney General for Jersey* [2012] 1 AC 22 [35].

7.3.2.3 Impossibility of a Fair Trial

In both of the national jurisdictions examined in this book, the impossibility of a fair trial is a ground for staying the proceedings or, as the case may be, declaring the prosecution inadmissible (a procedural step akin to a stay of proceedings). In England and Wales, a stay of proceedings imposed on this ground seeks to 'ensure that the defendant does not in some way suffer from forensic prejudice or disadvantage at trial with the result that he or she may be unable to defend him- or herself properly, leading to the danger of a factually inaccurate verdict of guilty ensuing',[128] and is accordingly concerned with 'considerations of intrinsic policy',[129] or *epistemic* considerations. In terms of broader objectives of criminal justice, a stay imposed on this ground seeks to protect the accused from wrongful conviction. Similarly, in the Netherlands, a declaration that the prosecution is inadmissible seeks to protect the accused from wrongful conviction in circumstances in which the inability of the defence to exercise its fair trial rights has seriously hampered the court in 'establishing the truth'. At the ICTs also, the impossibility of a fair trial is a ground for staying the proceedings. At the ad hoc Tribunals, it may be recalled, the Appeals Chamber has stated that it is a reason to stay the proceedings permanently 'where ... a fair trial for the accused [has been made] impossible', and confirmed that this limb of the abuse of process doctrine (the basis at the ad hoc Tribunals for staying the proceedings) is concerned with protecting the accused from wrongful conviction.[130] At the ICC, it may be recalled, the Appeals Chamber has held that:

> Where fair trial becomes impossible because of breaches of the fundamental rights of the suspect or the accused by his/her accusers, it would be a contradiction in terms to put the person on trial. Justice could not be done. A fair trial is the only means to do justice. If no fair trial can be held, the object of the judicial process is frustrated and the process must be stopped.[131]

Also in the same decision, the Appeals Chamber held that:

> Where the breaches of the rights of the accused are such as to make it impossible for him/her to make his/her defence within the framework of his rights, no fair trial can take place and the proceedings can be stayed. ... Unfairness in the treatment of the suspect or the accused may rupture the process to an extent making it impossible to piece together the constituent elements of a fair trial.[132]

---

[128] Choo 2008, 18.

[129] Ibid., 18.

[130] See *Prosecutor v Barayagwiza* (Decision) ICTR-97-19-AR72, A Ch (3 November 1999) para 77 and *Prosecutor v Stanišić and Župljanin* (Decision on Mićo Stanišić's Motion Requesting a Declaration of Mistrial and Stojan Zupljanin's Motion to Vacate Trial Judgement) IT-08-91-A, A Ch (2 April 2014) para 35.

[131] *Prosecutor v Lubanga* (Judgment on the Appeal of Mr. Thomas Lubanga Dyilo against the Decision on the Defence Challenge to the Jurisdiction of the Court pursuant to Article 19(2)(a) of the Statute of 3 October 2006) ICC-01/04-01/06, A Ch (14 December 2006) para 37.

[132] Ibid., para 39.

And, as stated, trial chambers have interpreted this test as providing for two separate bases on which to stay the proceedings: (1) where it would be '"odious" or "repugnant" to the administration of justice to allow the proceedings to continue', or (2) where 'the accused's rights [have] been breached to the extent that a fair trial has been rendered impossible'.[133] Looking at the tests, it is noticeable that while at the ICC the impossibility of a fair trial is expressly linked to the non-observance of rights, at the ad hoc Tribunals, it is not (at least, at first glance it is not). The strong rights-focus at the ICC as regards the 'impossibility of a fair trial' limb of the test for a stay of proceedings[134] is understandable. To begin with, there is an obvious link between the fairness of the trial and the ability of the defence to exercise 'defence' or 'fair trial' rights, i.e. the more specific rights that flow from the broader right to a fair trial, such that the impossibility of a fair trial is likely to be the result of the inability of the defence to exercise such (specific) rights. Moreover, the impossibility of a fair trial may, in a general sense, be denoted as a violation of the accused's rights; after all, the impossibility of a fair trial may be taken to mean the violation of the accused's right to a fair trial. At the ad hoc Tribunals also, chambers have, in the determination of whether to stay the proceedings on the ground that a fair trial has been rendered impossible, sometimes referred to the need for serious violations of the accused's rights.[135] While understandable, the ICTs' tendency to import into the 'impossibility of a fair trial' analysis the need for serious violations of the accused's rights is a cause for concern, because it has the potential to distract chambers from the question that they must ultimately answer: whether, in circumstances in which the accused has suffered forensic prejudice, to proceed to verdict would be to expose the defendant to an unacceptably high risk of wrongful conviction. As has been put: '*Any* defendant should be afforded adequate protection from a wrongful conviction; it does not matter, for example, that no serious breach of a right of the defendant was involved, or that the police or prosecution did not act in bad faith, or that the offence charged was a relatively serious one.'[136] Here it may be recalled that the test in the Netherlands for declaring the prosecution inadmissible (a procedural step akin to a stay of proceedings) has been criticized for suggesting that it is not sufficient for making such a declaration that the accused is prevented from receiving a fair trial.[137] That test, it may be recalled, provides as follows: the public authorities must have committed serious violations of principles of proper administration of justice, either intentionally or by gross negligence, as a result of which the suspect is prevented from receiving a fair trial. And it was seen in Chap. 3, where the Dutch

---

[133] *Prosecutor v Lubanga* (Redacted Decision on the "Defence Application Seeking a Permanent Stay of the Proceedings") ICC-01/04-01/06, T Ch I (7 March 2011) paras 165–166.

[134] See Chap. 5, n 254 and 264–266 and accompanying text.

[135] See Chap. 5, n 90–91 and accompanying text.

[136] Choo 2008, 189 (emphasis added).

[137] See e.g. Knigge 2003, 194; and Kuiper 2014, 368. See more generally Chap. 3, n 248–254 and accompanying text.

judicial response to procedural violations was examined, that there are indications in the case law of the Dutch Supreme Court that if the procedural violation in question clearly prevents the accused from receiving a fair trial, whether the public authorities committed such violation intentionally or by gross negligence is of less importance.[138] While consideration of whether the accused's (defence or fair trial) rights have been violated may well assist a chamber in answering the aforementioned question, it should not form the primary focus of its enquiry. Rather, it is the *effects* of the procedural violation in question with which the chamber should be concerned, i.e. the extent to which the defence has been prejudiced.[139] Logically, then, a relevant consideration under the 'impossibility of a fair trial' limb of the test for staying the proceedings is 'whether some lesser remedy, such as the exclusion of certain prosecution evidence ... would suffice to provide ... protection [against wrongful conviction]'.[140] As has been put, 'we will always want to recognize ... [the] jurisdiction [to stay the proceedings where a fair trial has been rendered impossible], if not through respect for the importance of fair trials, then at least for the pragmatic reason that stopping the trial before it inevitably leads to an unsafe conviction spares the expense of the trial and appeal process'.[141] Indeed, it may be helpful to think of a stay of proceedings imposed on this basis as 'nothing more than the weapon of last resort to all judges ... when no lesser means of ensuring a fair trial is sufficient'.[142]

In the ICC case of *Lubanga*, the Trial Chamber seems to have had the above well in mind when it stayed the proceedings in circumstances in which the Prosecution had indicated that it had in its possession a large amount of material which it had identified as potentially exculpatory or otherwise material to the Defence, but which it was unable to disclose to the Defence or provide to the Trial Chamber in light of the confidentiality agreements under which it had been obtained.[143] According to the Trial Chamber, the failure to disclose a 'significant body' of potentially exculpatory evidence to the accused, which 'improperly ... [inhibited] the opportunities for the accused to prepare his defence', coupled with the inability of the Trial Chamber to review the material in question and determine whether the non-disclosure constituted a breach of the accused's right to a fair trial, meant that 'the trial process has been ruptured to such a degree that it is now impossible to piece together the constituent elements of a fair trial'.[144] According to

---

[138] See Chap. 3, n 252 and accompanying text.

[139] See in this regard Martin 2005, 181.

[140] Choo 2008, 189–190.

[141] Rogers 2008, 291.

[142] Ibid., 291.

[143] For a more comprehensive overview of the facts, see Chap. 6, n 424–441 and accompanying text.

[144] *Prosecutor v Lubanga* (Decision on the consequences of non-disclosure of exculpatory materials covered by Article 54(3)(e) agreements and the application to stay the prosecution of the accused, together with certain other issues raised at the Status Conference on 10 June 2008) ICC-01/04-01/06, T Ch I (13 June 2008) paras 92–93.

the Trial Chamber, in order stay the proceedings, it was not necessary to establish bad faith—'mala fides'—on the part of the prosecution; it was sufficient to show that 'the essential preconditions of a fair trial are missing' and that 'there is no sufficient indication that this will be resolved during the trial process'. In such circumstances 'it is necessary—indeed, inevitable—that the proceedings should be stayed'.[145] *After* concluding that a stay of proceedings was warranted, the Trial Chamber said that:

> Although the Chamber has no doubt that this stay of proceedings is necessary, it has nonetheless imposed it with great reluctance, not least because it means the Court will not make a decision on issues which are of significance to the international community, the peoples of the Democratic Republic of the Congo, the victims and the accused himself. When crimes, particularly of a grave nature, are alleged it is necessary for justice that, whenever possible, a final determination is made as to the guilt or innocence of the accused. The judicial process is seriously undermined if a court is prevented from reaching a verdict on the charges brought against an individual. One consequence is that the victims will be denied an opportunity to participate in a public forum, in which their views and concerns were to have been presented and their right to receive reparations will be affected. The judges are acutely aware that by staying these proceedings the victims have, in this sense, been excluded from justice.[146]

In other words, the Trial Chamber acknowledged the public interest in the prosecution of crimes of concern to the international community only *after* it had determined that the fairness of the trial had been imperilled to such an extent as to necessitate a stay of proceedings. And that, it is submitted, is the right approach.[147] As has been put (in the context of the Trial Chamber's decision to stay the proceedings, as it happens): '[N]o non-adjudicative goal can ever justify countenancing an unfair trial that is unfair because a violation of the defendant's rights prevents accurate adjudication'.[148,149]

---

[145] Ibid., paras 90–91.

[146] Ibid., para 95.

[147] It is worth noting in this regard that the Trial Chamber's decision was upheld on appeal, with the Appeals Chamber observing that: 'If the trial of Mr. Lubanga Dyilo had taken place in such circumstances, there would always have been a lurking doubt as to whether the disclosure of the documents in question would have changed the course of the trial.' See *Prosecutor v Lubanga* (Judgment on the appeal of the Prosecutor against the decision of Trial Chamber I entitled "Decision on the consequences of non-disclosure of exculpatory materials discovered by Article 54(3)(e) agreements and the application to stay the prosecution of the accused, together with certain other issues raised at the Status Conference on 10 June 2008") ICC-01/04-01/06, A Ch (21 October 2008) para 97.

[148] Heller KJ, 'NYU JILP Symposium: The Rhetoric of Remedies' (Opinio Juris, 5 April 2013), http://opiniojuris.org/2013/04/05/nyu-jilp-symposium-the-rhetoric-of-remedies/ Accessed 1 March 2017.

[149] It would therefore be misleading to describe the Trial Chamber's decision to stay the proceedings in this case as 'absolutist'. See Heller 2013 (n 148), referring to Iontcheva Turner 2012.

7.3.2.4   The Need to Preserve the Integrity of the Proceedings

As stated, there are two grounds on which the proceedings may be stayed at the ICTs: the impossibility of a fair trial and the need to preserve of the integrity of the proceedings. Having examined the first ground, it is to the latter ground that we now turn. As stated, there are at least three different variations of the integrity rationale, whereby different considerations apply under each. The purpose of the next subsection is to obtain a better understanding of the (more specific) rationale that underlies the 'non-epistemic' limb of the test at the ICTs for staying the proceedings (the 'impossibility of a fair trial' limb being the 'epistemic' limb),[150] with a view to identifying the factors to which chambers at the ICTs should attach (significant) importance in the determination of whether a stay of proceedings is required in order to preserve the integrity of the proceedings.

A. The meaning of integrity

As stated, in the Netherlands there is, effectively, only one ground on which to declare the prosecution inadmissible (a procedural step akin to a stay of proceedings): the impossibility of a fair trial. However, in England and Wales, there are two categories of case in which a court has a discretion to stay the proceedings on the ground that to try those proceedings will amount to an abuse of its own process: 'either (1) because it will be impossible (usually by reason of delay) to give the accused a fair trial or (2) because it offends the court's sense of justice and propriety to be asked to try the accused in the circumstances of a particular case'.[151] In one of the jurisdictions examined in this book, then, the integrity rationale is a rationale for staying the proceedings. As stated, there are three variations of the integrity rationale: 'court-centred integrity', 'public conduct integrity' and 'public attitude integrity',[152] whereby the latter—public attitude—variation requires the court to perform a balancing exercise involving competing public interests (the public interest in the conviction of the 'factually guilty' against whom there is reliable evidence and the public interest in the judiciary not condoning the unlawful action of law enforcement agencies), which entails the consideration of factors relevant to each of the public interests involved, while the first—court-centred—variation does not. Accordingly, while under the public attitude variation of the integrity rationale a judge may take into account the seriousness of the procedural violation *as well as* the seriousness of the crime(s) with which the accused is charged, under the first, the concern should solely be with the seriousness of the violation. It was observed in Chap. 4 that, in England and Wales, the public attitude variation of the integrity rationale seems to be at the forefront of the appellate courts' thinking as regards the second limb of the abuse of process discretion.[153] The question that now needs to be

---

[150] See in this regard n 105–129 and accompanying text.

[151] See n 117 and accompanying text.

[152] See n 75 and accompanying text.

[153] See Chap. 4, n 441–446 and accompanying text.

answered is how the ICTs' case law is to be appreciated in this regard, and, ultimately, which variation of the integrity rationale *should* underlie the determination to be made under this non-epistemic limb of the test for staying the proceedings.

Turning first the ad hoc Tribunals, the Appeals Chamber's approach to the matter in the ICTR case of *Barayagwiza* is most in line with the court-centred variation of the integrity rationale; the focus of the Appeals Chamber's enquiry in that case was on the seriousness of the procedural violations. While it did allude to the public interest in the investigation and prosecution of crime, it did not expressly factor it into the analysis.[154] Nevertheless, it should be noted that the Appeals Chamber's decision is not a model of clarity as regards the rationales for staying the proceedings or the rationale that it was pursuing, which was not helped by the fact that 'delay'—the underlying issue in that case—may raise issues under both limbs of the abuse of process doctrine. While the Appeals Chamber purported to recognize two 'distinct' grounds for staying the proceedings ('(1) where delay has made a fair trial for the accused impossible; and (2) where in the circumstances of a particular case, proceeding with the trial of the accused would contravene the court's sense of justice, due to pre-trial impropriety or misconduct'),[155] it also seemed to suggest that the existence of forensic prejudice to the accused is a pertinent consideration under the second ground for staying the proceedings.[156] The Appeals Chamber added to the confusion by finding that a stay of proceedings was not only necessary in order to preserve the integrity of the proceedings, but that it was the only 'effective remedy' for the violation of the accused's rights and might well deter the commission of such violations in the future.[157]

In the ICTY case of *Nikolić*, the Appeals Chamber seemed to suggest that the second limb of the abuse of process doctrine (as set out in *Barayagwiza*) entails the performance of a balancing exercise, which in that particular case entailed weighing the 'legitimate expectation that those accused of ... ['crimes such as genocide, crimes against humanity and war crimes which are universally recognized and condemned as such'] will be brought to justice swiftly' against 'the principle of State sovereignty and the fundamental human rights of the accused'.[158] In finding

---

[154] See in this regard *Prosecutor v Barayagwiza* (Decision) ICTR-97-19-AR72, A Ch (3 November 1999) paras 106, 108 and 112.

[155] Ibid., para 77.

[156] The Appeals Chamber held that: 'Considering the lengthy delay in the Appellant's case, "it is quite impossible to say that there was no prejudice to the applicant in the continuance of the case". The following discussion, *therefore*, focuses on whether it would offend the Tribunal's sense of justice to proceed to the trial of the accused.' See *Prosecutor v Barayagwiza* (Decision) ICTR-97-19-AR72, A Ch (3 November 1999) para 77 (emphasis added). In making this finding, the Appeals Chamber relied on an English 'undue delay' case (*R v Oxford City Justices, ex parte Smith* (1982) 75 Cr App R 200) in which the concern was with *forensic* prejudice.

[157] *Prosecutor v Barayagwiza* (Decision) ICTR-97-19-AR72, A Ch (3 November 1999) para 108.

[158] *Prosecutor v Nikolić* (Decision on Interlocutory Appeal Concerning Legality of Arrest) IT-94-2-AR73, A Ch (5 June 2003) paras 24–26. See also *Prosecutor v Tolimir* (Decision on Preliminary Motions on the Indictment pursuant to Rule 72 of the Rules) IT-05-88/2-PT, T Ch II (14 December 2007) paras 19 and 25.

that the evidence did not show 'that the rights of the accused were *egregiously* violated in the process of his arrest',[159] and in concluding that there was 'no basis upon which jurisdiction should not be exercised',[160] the Appeals Chamber made no further reference to the balancing exercise it had set out earlier on in the decision. It seems, therefore, that this balancing exercise is *inherent* in the determination of whether there has been an egregious violation of the accused's rights. Put differently, insofar as the second limb of the abuse of process doctrine at the ad hoc Tribunals does entail the performance of a balancing exercise, what is not envisaged is 'ad hoc' balancing; the chamber need only determine whether there has been an egregious violation of the accused's rights. In the ICTY case of *Karadžić* also, the Appeals Chamber implied that the second limb of the abuse of process doctrine entails the performance of a balancing exercise in which 'the public interest in the prosecution of an individual accused of ... [genocide, crimes against humanity and war crimes], [which are] universally condemned' is weighed against the interests of the accused.[161] These decisions appear to be more in line with the public attitude variation of the integrity rationale, although it is worth reiterating that what is not envisaged, it seems, is the performance of a balancing exercise on an 'ad hoc' basis. Rather, the chamber need only determine whether there has been an egregious violation of the accused's rights; the performance of the balancing exercise is, in other words, inherent in the determination of whether there has been such a violation. In *Barayagwiza* also, the Appeals Chamber had emphasized the need for 'egregious violations of the accused's rights' under the second limb of the abuse of process doctrine (although, as stated, it did not consider the determination under that limb to entail the performance of a balancing exercise). It may well be that the Appeals Chamber's incorporation of an abstract balancing exercise into the determination to be made under that limb in *Nikolić* was intended to ensure that that criterion—egregious violations of the accused's rights—is not construed too broadly (i.e. is not deemed to be satisfied too easily). In the Netherlands, this seems to be the purpose of the 'additional' balancing that the court 'may' undertake in the second category of case in which evidence may be excluded.[162]

As for the ICC, there is case law to suggest that the 'preservation of the integrity of the proceedings' limb of the test for staying the proceedings entails the performance of a balancing exercise, which is in line with the public attitude variation of the integrity rationale. According to the Trial Chamber in *Lubanga*, a chamber *must*, in the context of that limb of the test 'weigh the nature of the alleged abuse of process against the fact that only the most serious crimes of concern for the

---

[159] *Prosecutor v Nikolić* (Decision on Interlocutory Appeal Concerning Legality of Arrest) IT-94-2-AR73, A Ch (5 June 2003) para 32 (emphasis added).

[160] Ibid., para 33.

[161] *Prosecutor v Karadžić* (Decision on Karadžić's Appeal of Trial Chamber's Decision on Alleged Holbrooke Agreement) IT-95-5/18-AR73.4, A Ch (12 October 2009) para 49. See also *Prosecutor v Nikolić* (Decision on Interlocutory Appeal Concerning Legality of Arrest) IT-94-2-AR73, A Ch (5 June 2003) paras 25–26, and 30.

[162] See Chap. 3, n 315 and accompanying text.

international community as a whole fall under the jurisdiction of the Court.[163] The Trial Chamber's findings in this regard are at odds with its findings regarding the non-epistemic limb of the test for the exclusion of evidence in an earlier decision (which were discussed above);[164] in the decision in question, the Trial Chamber found that neither the probative value of the evidence nor the seriousness of the offence with which the accused is charged could inform the determination to be made under Article 69(7)(b) of the ICC Statute. As stated above, these are relevant factors under the public attitude variation of the integrity rationale, so that, implicitly, at least, in finding that they could not be taken into account, the Trial Chamber seemed to reject that variation of integrity rationale as the rationale for excluding evidence on account of the manner of its obtaining.

It is submitted that, as far as the (more specific) rationale for staying the proceedings in order to preserve the integrity of the proceedings (i.e. as far as the non-epistemic limb of the test for staying the proceedings) is concerned, the court-centred variation of the integrity rationale is to be preferred over the public attitude variation thereof, whereby it may be recalled that the same was argued in relation to the discretion at the ICTs to exclude evidence on account of the manner of its obtaining. Broadly speaking, the arguments that were advanced above as regards the exclusion of evidence apply equally here.[165] The main objection to the adoption of the public attitude variation of the integrity rationale as the rationale for staying the proceedings on grounds of integrity is that it allows for the fact that the offence with which the accused is charged is a serious one to be taken into account, which opens the door to 'ends justifies the means reasoning'. And, even though it is, in theory, possible to build into an approach based on the public attitude variation of the integrity rationale safeguards which would make it more difficult for a judge to resort to such reasoning,[166] an approach based on the court-centred variation of the integrity rationale is still preferable; indeed, adoption of the court-centred rationale in this context would send the *unequivocal* message that, in the determination of whether to stay the proceedings on grounds of integrity, chambers will not allow themselves to be guided by consequentialist thinking. Of course, adoption of this rationale could not prevent chambers from allowing that determination to be guided by consequentialist thinking altogether. The primary consideration under the court-centred variation of the integrity rationale is the seriousness of the procedural violation; as will be demonstrated below, this consideration may give rise to a whole host of lines of enquiry, and creates sufficient scope for a judge so inclined to allow the determination of whether to stay the proceedings to be guided by consequentialist thinking. The court-centred variation of the integrity rationale, then, is manipulable; however, it is submitted that the

---

[163] *Prosecutor v Lubanga* (Redacted Decision on the "Defence Application Seeking a Permanent Stay of the Proceedings") ICC-01/04-01/06, T Ch I (7 March 2011) para 195.

[164] See n 77–78 and accompanying text.

[165] See in this regard n 80–99 and accompanying text.

[166] See n 81–82 and 90–91 and accompanying text.

public attitude variation thereof is significantly more so.[167] While it may well be that the incorporation in the *Nikolić* case of an abstract balancing exercise into the determination to be made under the second limb of the abuse of process doctrine was solely intended to ensure that the criterion 'egregious violations of the accused's rights' is not construed too broadly (so that a stay of proceedings remains an exceptional remedy), the problem is that it—the incorporation of an abstract balancing exercise into the analysis—may also be construed as an invitation to chambers to interpret the criterion unduly narrowly. More will be said about the criterion 'egregious violations of the accused's rights' below.

B. Pertinent factors

The preferred rationale as regard the 'integrity' limb of the test at the ICTs for staying the proceedings then, is the court-centred variation of the integrity rationale; the question that now needs to be answered is: to which factors should judges at the ICTs attach (significant) importance in this regard? Broadly speaking, the factors that were identified above as pertinent considerations under the 'serious damage to the integrity of the proceedings' limb of the test at the ICTs for the exclusion of evidence on account of the manner in which it was obtained, may also be said to be pertinent considerations under the non-epistemic limb of the test for staying the proceedings. Before addressing such factors (further) in the specific context of the stay of proceedings, however, it bears emphasizing that under this rationale, chambers may not take into account, let alone attach importance to, the fact that crime with which the accused is charged is a serious one; in other words, under this rationale judges may not take into account the seriousness of the offence as a standalone factor. Again, the reason for this is that, under the court-centred variation of the integrity rationale, 'the essence of the objection is to the court joining hands, so to speak, with the officer who conducted himself as he did', so that the 'key time at which the principle bites, is the time of the unlawful or improper investigative step', whereas, under the public attitude variation of the integrity rationale, the key time at which the principle bites is the moment at which the decision of whether or not to stay the proceedings is made.[168] The fact that, under the court-centred variation of the integrity rationale, the seriousness of the offence with which the accused is charged may not be taken into account, does not take away from the discretionary nature of an approach based on this rationale. In light of the 'key time' at which the rationale bites, the focus of such an approach should be the seriousness of the procedural violation, which, as has been demonstrated, may give rise to a whole host of lines of enquiry, such that, any approach to the question of how to address procedural violations in which this 'factor' is the focus might properly be said to entail the exercise of discretion.

As with the exclusion of evidence, a pertinent consideration under the 'preservation of the integrity of the proceedings' limb of the test for staying the

---

[167] See in this regard n 96–99 and accompanying text.
[168] See n 102 and accompanying text.

proceedings should be whether the pre-trial misconduct violated internationally recognized human rights. Under the non-epistemic, 'preservation of the integrity of the proceedings', limb of the test for staying the proceedings at the ICTs it is the *nature* of the impugned conduct that should be the focus,[169] which is why it is appropriate under this limb to consider whether the conduct violated the accused's rights. By contrast, the epistemic, 'impossibility of a fair trial', limb is concerned with the *effects* of the procedural violation in question; accordingly, as stated, under that limb, the question of whether the conduct violated the accused's rights should not form the primary focus of the enquiry.[170] Both the ad hoc Tribunals and the ICC have treated the question of whether the impugned conduct constitutes a violation of the accused's rights as a pertinent consideration under the non-epistemic, 'preservation of the integrity of the proceedings', limb of the test for staying the proceedings. In particular, they have treated the question of how serious or 'grave' the violation of the accused's rights was as a pertinent consideration thereunder. The argument appears to be that advanced by the Appeals Chamber in the ICTY case of *Nikolić*, that '*certain* human rights violations are of such a serious nature that they require that the exercise of jurisdiction be declined', and that 'it would be inappropriate for a court of law to try the victims of these abuses'.[171] It is worth noting that the Appeals Chamber did not attempt to explain which human rights violations fall into this category, although it is likely that what it had in mind was serious mistreatment, i.e. 'inhuman, cruel or degrading treatment, or torture'; that was the example cited in the Trial Chamber's decision which the Appeals Chamber was reviewing, which the Appeals Chamber seemed to endorse.[172] The ability of human rights violations 'of a particularly serious nature' to impact on the integrity of the proceedings such as to require a stay of proceedings might be thought to be self-evident, but this is questionable. While on a very general, abstract, level, there may be said to be a connection between the observance of (basic) human rights in the pre-trial phase of criminal proceedings and the integrity of the court trying the case, it is not self-evident that human rights violations of a particularly serious nature should lead to the procedural step of staying the proceedings *in particular*, i.e. to a refusal of the chamber to take cognizance of the case. That is so even where an organ of the international criminal tribunal can be said to have been involved in

---

[169] See in this regard Martin 2005, 181.

[170] See n 139 and accompanying text.

[171] *Prosecutor v Nikolić* (Decision on Interlocutory Appeal Concerning Legality of Arrest) IT-94-2-AR73, A Ch (5 June 2003) para 30. See also *Prosecutor v Gbagbo* (Decision on the "Corrigendum of the challenge to the jurisdiction of the International Criminal Court on the basis of Articles 12(3), 19(2), 21(3), 55 and 59 of the Rome Statute filed by the Defence for President Gbagbo (ICC-02/11-01/11-129)") ICC-02/11-01/11, P T Ch I (15 August 2012) para 91; and *Prosecutor v Lubanga* (Redacted Decision on the "Defence Application Seeking a Permanent Stay of the Proceedings") ICC-01/04-01/06, T Ch I (7 March 2011) para 195.

[172] See *Prosecutor v Nikolić* (Decision on Interlocutory Appeal Concerning Legality of Arrest) IT-94-2-AR73, A Ch (5 June 2003) paras 28–33; and *Prosecutor v Nikolić* (Decision on Defence Motion Challenging the Exercise of Jurisdiction by the Tribunal) IT-94-2-PT, T Ch II (9 October 2002) para 114.

the violation. It is not self-evident, it is submitted, that a less far-reaching response would not suffice in this regard, such as the exclusion of evidence obtained thereby or sentence reduction. And the fact that no evidence has been obtained to exclude, is not a reason to resort to such a dramatic measure. There is, in other words, something missing from the equation. If human rights violations of a particularly serious nature are to lead to a stay of proceedings (assuming for the moment that only such human rights violations, i.e. human rights violations 'of a particularly serious nature', may do so), there is another factor to which chambers should have reference, and that is the extent to which the prosecution is, or the proceedings are, 'the product of' the human rights violation, or has or have 'been made possible by' the violation.[173] Put differently, chambers should ask themselves whether 'there is a reasonable likelihood that the prosecution would not be taking place *but for* the breach'.[174] This factor, then, concerns the 'causal connection' or 'causal link' between the human rights violation and the prosecution. Until recently, 'but for' causation seems to have been a pertinent consideration under the second limb of the abuse of process doctrine in England and Wales.[175] In *Mullen*, for example, in which the British authorities had 'initiated and subsequently assisted in and procured the deportation of the defendant, by unlawful means, in circumstances in which there were specific extradition facilities', and had, in so doing, acted 'in breach of public international law', the Court of Appeal had held that the proceedings had to be stayed, 'on the basis that, *but for* the unlawful manner of his deportation, he would not have been in this country to be prosecuted when he was, and there was a real prospect that he would never have been brought to this country at all'.[176]

While it is true that the only category of abuse to have been identified by the ICTs as constituting a human rights violation of such a serious nature that it would be inappropriate to try a victim thereof is serious mistreatment, i.e. 'inhuman, cruel or degrading treatment, or torture', it is clear from the (appellate) case law that other violations of the accused's rights may also suffice for the purpose of the determination to be made under the doctrine. Certainly chambers at both the ad hoc Tribunals and the ICC have entertained and ruled on applications for a stay of proceedings brought for varying reasons and alleging the violation of different rights, and the case law also contains more explicit indications that other rights violations are capable of leading to a stay,[177] in particular, where accompanied by the involvement by an organ of the international criminal tribunal in the violation[178]

---

[173] See in this regard Choo 2008, 126. See also 190.

[174] Choo 2008, 126.

[175] See, generally, Chap. 4, n 125–135 and accompanying text.

[176] *R v Mullen* [2000] QB 520 at 536 (emphasis added).

[177] *Prosecutor v Karadžić* (Decision on Karadžić's Appeal of Trial Chamber's Decision on Alleged Holbrooke Agreement) IT-95-5/18-AR73.4, A Ch (12 October 2009) para 47.

[178] See in this regard *Prosecutor v Nikolić* (Decision on Defence Motion Challenging the Exercise of Jurisdiction by the Tribunal) IT-94-2-PT, T Ch II (9 October 2002) para 114.

or where multiple violations have been committed.[179] By contrast, 'serious mistreatment' would appear *per se* to constitute an egregious violation of the suspect's or accused's rights. The point is that chambers at both the ad hoc Tribunals and the ICC do not seem to be content to limit the availability of a stay of proceedings to 'serious mistreatment'. That is understandable. Where a human rights violation is of a particularly serious nature, this may be a reason to stay the proceedings more or less automatically (subject to what was said above regarding the need, in principle, for 'but for' causation); but it does not follow that where a human rights violation is not of a particularly serious nature, this is a reason *not* to stay the proceedings. There may be *other* reasons not to stay the proceedings where it can otherwise be said that, but for the human rights violation (*any* human rights violation), the prosecution would not be taking place, for example, when the ICTs cannot be said to have involved in the violation. Conversely, combined with a certain level of involvement on the part of the ICTs therein, the fact that, but for the human rights violation (again, *any* human rights violation), the prosecution would not be taking place, should make for a compelling case for a stay. It is to the matter of involvement that we now turn.

At the ICC in particular, chambers have attached significant importance to the matter of involvement.[180] This, it is submitted, is not unreasonable or illogical. As with exclusion, when at the national level principled calls for stays of proceedings are made, this is on the understanding that the investigative authorities to have acted unlawfully, and the judicial authorities now seized of an application for a stay of proceedings, form part of the same legal system, such that they can be said to be institutionally connected (even if they are independent of one another) and, more importantly, such that the judicial may be argued to have a responsibility for the conduct of such authorities (although, again, presumably adherents of the 'separation thesis' would disagree with this). By contrast, the judicial authorities at the ICTs and the national authorities on which they are dependent for such activities as the apprehension of persons suspected or accused of crimes falling within their jurisdiction and the carrying out of investigations, do not form part of the same legal system. It is understandable, then, that they have attached importance to the matter of the ICTs' involvement in the violation; in case of involvement, the ICTs may reasonably be argued to have a responsibility for the conduct the national authorities to have acted unlawfully in the execution of a request for cooperation. However, as with the exclusion of evidence, they may have approached the matter of involvement too narrowly.[181] In the ICC case of *Gbagbo*, for example, in which the Defence had sought a stay of proceedings in connection with Laurent Gbagbo's arrest and detention in in Côte d'Ivoire (which it alleged had been unlawful), the Pre-Trial Chamber held that:

---

[179] As was the case in the ICTR case of *Barayagwiza*.

[180] See Chap. 5, n 267–280 and accompanying text.

[181] See the discussion above, in the context of the exclusionary discretion; n 110–113 and accompanying text.

violations of fundamental rights, however serious, can have the requisite impact on the proceedings to constitute an abuse of process *only insofar as they can be attributed to the Court*. Attribution in this sense means that the act of violation of fundamental rights is: (i) either directly perpetrated by persons associated with the Court; or (ii) perpetrated by third persons in collusion with the Court. Conversely, when a violation of the suspect's fundamental rights, however grave, is established, but demonstrates no such link with the Court, the exceptional remedy of staying the proceedings is not available.[182]

The Pre-Trial Chamber found that:

... nothing in the material brought before the Chamber shows any involvement on the part of the Court in the detention of Mr Gbagbo in Côte d'Ivoire following his arrest on 11 April 2011 [by the Ivorian authorities]. With respect to the period of detention prior to the notification of the [ICC] request for arrest and surrender of Mr Gbagbo, the Chamber notes that Mr Gbagbo was not detained at the behest of Court nor did the Court have any involvement with the domestic proceedings of the Ivorian authorities.[183]

In concluding that the ICC had not been involved in Gbagbo's detention, the Pre-Trial Chamber emphasized that "'[m]ere knowledge on the part of the Prosecutor of the investigations carried out by the [national] authorities is no proof of involvement on his part in the way they were conducted or the means used for the purpose'", and found that 'the mere fact that the Prosecutor was in contact with the Ivorian authorities does not suggest that there was any involvement of the Prosecutor in the detention of Mr. Gbagbo'.[184] There is something troubling about these statements; 'involvement' is given a strict interpretation, while, as observed above, there is nothing in the ICC Statute nor RPE that prohibits the ICC Prosecutor from informally seeking cooperation from state authorities, for example, to arrest and/or detain a suspect provisionally pending the issuance of an arrest warrant by the ICC (a possibility which in all likelihood has already been,[185] and will (continue to) be exploited by the ICC Prosecutor). Such circumstances, it is submitted, should warrant a thorough examination into the facts in order to determine the nature and degree of the involvement. If 'collusion of the ICC' with third persons, including

---

[182] *Prosecutor v Gbagbo* (Decision on the "Corrigendum of the challenge to the jurisdiction of the International Criminal Court on the basis of Articles 12(3), 19(2), 21(3), 55 and 59 of the Rome Statute filed by the Defence for President Gbagbo (ICC-02/11-01/11-129)") ICC-02/11-01/11, P T Ch I (15 August 2012) para 92. The Pre-Trial Chamber's decision was upheld on appeal, and while this was not an issue on appeal, the Appeals Chamber did not distance itself from the Pre-Trial Chamber's finding on attribution. See *Prosecutor v Gbagbo* (Judgment on the appeal of Mr. Laurent Koudou Gbagbo against the decision of Pre-Trial Chamber I on jurisdiction and stay of the proceedings) ICC-02/11-01/11 OA 2 (12 December 2012).

[183] *Prosecutor v Gbagbo* (Decision on the "Corrigendum of the challenge to the jurisdiction of the International Criminal Court on the basis of Articles 12(3), 19(2), 21(3), 55 and 59 of the Rome Statute filed by the Defence for President Gbagbo (ICC-02/11-01/11-129)") ICC-02/11-01/11, P T Ch I (15 August 2012) para 108.

[184] Ibid., para 109.

[185] See n 45 and accompanying text.

national authorities, is to be the 'lower limit' of involvement, it is important that chambers at the ICC address the issue properly.

The involvement of the international criminal tribunal in question should, then, be a pertinent consideration under the 'preservation of the integrity of the proceedings' limb of the test for staying the proceedings. However, at the ad hoc Tribunals it has been held that, under the abuse of process doctrine 'it is irrelevant which entity or entities were responsible for the alleged violations...';[186] how is the argument being advanced here (that the involvement of the international criminal tribunal in question should be a pertinent consideration under the 'preservation of the integrity of the proceedings' limb of the test for staying the proceedings) to be reconciled with this finding? Here it is worth noting that in the case to first argue the point, the ICTR case of *Barayagwiza*, the argument seems to have been *not* that the ad hoc Tribunal in question need not have been involved in, or 'be responsible' for, the violation *at all*, but rather that, in order to justify application of the abuse of process doctrine (and by extension, the imposition of a stay of proceedings), it is not necessary to say where *exactly*, i.e. with which organ of the ad hoc Tribunal, the responsibility lies, and the ad hoc Tribunal in question need not be *solely* responsible for the violations.[187] In the ICTY case of *Nikolić*, the accused, Dragan Nikolić, had been captured by unknown individuals in the Federal Republic of Yugoslavia before being handed over to the NATO-led Stabilisation Force (SFOR) in Bosnia and Herzegovina, who arrested and detained him, and ultimately to the ICTY; in that case, in which the Defence sought a stay of proceedings on the basis of unlawful apprehension, the Trial Chamber endorsed the Appeals Chamber's finding in *Barayagwiza* that under the abuse of process doctrine 'it is irrelevant which entity or entities were responsible for the alleged violations...', and held that:

> in a situation where an accused is very seriously mistreated, maybe even subjected to inhuman, cruel or degrading treatment, or torture, before being handed over to the Tribunal, this may constitute a legal impediment to the exercise of jurisdiction over such an accused. This would certainly be the case where persons acting for SFOR or the Prosecution were involved in such very serious mistreatment. But even without such involvement this Chamber finds it extremely difficult to justify the exercise of jurisdiction over a person if that person was brought into the jurisdiction of the Tribunal after having been seriously mistreated.[188]

It is indeed arguable that some human rights violations are so serious that where it can be said that, but for the violation, the prosecution would not be taking place, whether the international criminal tribunal in question was involved in the violation,

---

[186] See *Prosecutor v Barayagwiza* (Decision) ICTR-97-19-AR72, A Ch (3 November 1999) para 73, and *Prosecutor v Nikolić* (Decision on Defence Motion Challenging the Exercise of Jurisdiction by the Tribunal) IT-94-2-PT, T Ch II (9 October 2002) para 114.

[187] See *Prosecutor v Barayagwiza* (Decision) ICTR-97-19-AR72, A Ch (3 November 1999) paras 73 and 75.

[188] *Prosecutor v Nikolić* (Decision on Defence Motion Challenging the Exercise of Jurisdiction by the Tribunal) IT-94-2-PT, T Ch II (9 October 2002) para 114.

i.e. colluded with the authorities that inflicted the mistreatment, is immaterial. It will be interesting to see how the ICC approaches this issue; it was seen in Chap. 5 that, at present, it is unclear whether, in case of torture or serious mistreatment of a suspect or an accused by national authorities or unknown individuals, it is necessary to establish concerted action between such authorities or individuals and the ICC in order to justify a stay of proceedings.[189]

Finally, further (pertinent) considerations under the 'preservation of the integrity of the proceedings' limb of the test for staying the proceedings concern the bad or good faith of the prosecution in particular,[190] and whether the impugned conduct took place in circumstances of urgency, emergency or necessity.[191]

In sum, pertinent considerations under the 'preservation of the integrity of the proceedings' limb of the test for staying the proceedings are: whether there was a violation of an internationally recognized human right, whether it can be said that, but for the human rights violation (*any* human rights violation), the prosecution would not be taking place, whether the international criminal tribunal in question was involved (whereby 'collusion of the ICC' with third persons, including national authorities, is the 'lower limit' of involvement), whether the prosecution acted in bad or good faith and whether the impugned conduct took place in circumstances of urgency, emergency or necessity. Such factors go to the seriousness of the procedural violation, which, as stated above, is the primary consideration under the court-centred variation of the integrity rationale. It is submitted that, combined with a certain level of involvement on the part of the ICTs therein, the fact that, but for the human rights violation (*any* human rights violation), the prosecution would not be taking place, should make for a compelling case for a stay. Nevertheless, as with exclusion, the good faith of the prosecution, or the fact that the conduct took place in circumstances of urgency, emergency or necessity might, exceptionally, warrant a different conclusion. A factor which should not be taken into account under the 'preservation of the integrity of the proceedings' limb of the test for staying the proceedings is the seriousness of the offence, i.e. the fact that the offence with which the accused is charged is very serious. Aside from the fact that it would not be appropriate to take this factor into account under the court-centred variation of the integrity rationale, this factor opens the door to 'ends justifies the means' reasoning.

7.3.3 Other Responses

At the ICTs, as in the two domestic jurisdictions examined in this book, the exclusion of evidence and a stay of proceedings are not the only responses to

---

[189] See, generally, Chap. 5, n 270–272 and accompanying text.

[190] See in this regard n 114–115 and accompanying text.

[191] See n 116 and accompanying text.

procedural violations committed in the pre-trial phase of the proceedings; other judicial responses to such violations within the criminal trial are sentence reduction and express acknowledgement of the violation. At the ICTs, financial compensation is another such response. There, the purpose of financial compensation, and of sentence reduction, is to provide a personal remedy for rights violations. In the Netherlands, this appears to be the rationale underlying sentence reduction, which, it may be recalled, is one of the consequences listed in Article 359a of the CCP—the central provision in the Netherlands for responding to procedural violations committed in the course of the criminal investigation within the criminal trial—that a judge may attach to an established procedural violation. In none of the jurisdictions examined in this book will judges automatically grant sentence reduction where an application for a more far-reaching judicial response, i.e. a stay of proceedings or the exclusion of evidence, fails. In other words, in none of these jurisdictions is sentence reduction a 'residual' category. At the ICTs, as in the Netherlands, the purpose of sentence reduction (and of financial compensation) is the provision of a personal remedy for rights violations, whereby specific requirements apply. At the ICTs, for instance, the rights violation must be attributable to the international criminal tribunal in question in some way.[192] One of the points to emerge in the examination of the law and practice at the ICTs with respect to question of how to address procedural violations committed in the context of arrest and detention in Chap. 6, was that, in determining an application for a certain type of relief in respect of an alleged illegal or unlawful deprivation of liberty, for example a stay of proceedings, chambers have not always considered 'alternative' and less far-reaching forms of relief in circumstances in which the impugned conduct, while not being grave enough to warrant the more far-reaching remedy, might have amounted to a violation of the accused's rights and warranted the provision of a personal remedy in respect thereof.[193] It was argued above that the ICTs *should* provide personal remedies to persons whose rights have been violated by national authorities in the execution of a request from them for cooperation, but only insofar as the rights violation is attributable to the international criminal tribunal in question. However, the level of attribution required for the purpose of providing a personal remedy may be lower than that (which may reasonably be) required for more far-reaching responses (it was argued above that a failure on the part of the prosecution to exercise due diligence to ensure that that the case proceeds to trial in a way that respect the rights of the accused should suffice for such purposes), so that rejection of an application for a stay of proceedings on the basis that the international criminal tribunal in question was not sufficiently involved should not prevent the consideration of personal remedies for rights violations.

---

[192] For the ad hoc Tribunals, see Chap. 5, n 197–204 and 212–213 and accompanying text, and for the ICC, see n 47 and accompanying text.

[193] See Chap. 6, Sect. 6.2.3.

In the Netherlands, under Article 359a of the CCP, sentence reduction may only be granted if, among other things, the accused has suffered 'actual prejudice' and this prejudice lends itself to compensation by way of sentence reduction. Regarding this last requirement, it was seen in Chap. 3 that prejudice to the accused's *defence* (or *fair trial*) rights, such as the right to counsel, typically does *not* lend itself to such compensation.[194] In the one case at the ICTs in which financial compensation has been granted as a personal remedy—the ICTR case of *Rwamakuba*—the rights violation concerned a violation of the right to legal assistance in the initial months of detention, which the Trial Chamber granting the remedy expressly linked to the right of an accused to a fair trial.[195] In that case, the remedy was granted after André Rwamakuba was acquitted, so that the choice of remedy may be understandable. But it is important that chambers remain mindful of the 'limitations of financial compensation and sentence reduction as remedies for rights violations; in general, these are not appropriate responses to procedural violations that hamper the ability of the accused to mount an effective defence.[196] Regarding the requirement (in the Netherlands) that there be 'actual prejudice' in order to justify sentence reduction, it was seen in Chap. 3 that what is envisaged is not 'expressive harm', i.e. the harm that is done when government actors disrespect individual rights, whereby such disrespect sends 'demeaning messages about human worth',[197] but concrete, non-material damage to the individual accused, for example, physical pain, emotional distress and suffering and/or injury to honour. The ICTs have not focused on this factor in the context of chambers' determination of whether to provide personal remedies for rights violations (although they do refer to it), and this, it is submitted, is preferable to the Dutch approach; in the Netherlands, the inability to pinpoint the damage suffered is a reason not to provide sentence reduction. While there is human rights case law to suggest that states are free to make an award of a personal remedy for rights violations dependent upon the ability of the person concerned to show damage resulting from the breach and upon the person concerned having suffered pecuniary or non-pecuniary damage,[198] there is also case law to suggest that an overly formalistic approach to, in particular, the question of whether non-pecuniary damage has been suffered is problematic from the perspective of the right to an effective remedy.[199] In the Netherlands, the way in which the notion of 'prejudice' has been interpreted (narrowly), coupled with the fact that it is a *requirement* and

---

[194] See Chap. 3, n 186 and accompanying text.

[195] *Prosecutor v Rwamakuba* (Decision on Appropriate Remedy) ICTR-98-44C-T, T Ch III (31 January 2007).

[196] Nevertheless, in a recent ruling, the Dutch Supreme Court held that sentence reduction would be an appropriate response to a violation of the right to legal assistance *during* questioning, where the accused's right to legal assistance prior to questioning has been observed. See HR 22 December 2015, ECLI:NL:HR:2015:3608, para 6.4.2.

[197] Starr 2009, 1534–1535.

[198] *Wassink v Netherlands* App no 12535/86 (ECtHR, 27 September 1990), para 38.

[199] *Danev v Bulgaria* App no 9411/05 (ECtHR, 2 September 2010), para 35. See also *Georgi Marinov v Bulgaria* App 36103/04 (ECtHR, 15 March 2011), paras 47–48.

not merely a relevant consideration, appears calculated to ensure that procedural violations committed in the pre-trial phase of criminal proceedings do not interfere with the court's truth-finding objective, i.e. the determination of the criminal responsibility of the accused, and, where there is such responsibility, with the imposition a sanction that is commensurate therewith.

Finally, turning to the response of 'express acknowledgement', it was seen in Chap. 5 that, in cases in which procedural violations committed in the pre-trial phase of the proceedings has resulted in minimal or no prejudice to the accused, chambers of both the ad hoc Tribunals and the ICC have resorted to express acknowledgement of such violations, in order to provide remedial relief to an accused, or to condemn official misconduct. In the Netherlands, this the most common response to procedural violations committed in the course of a criminal investigation, while in England and Wales, appellate courts have also referred to the ability of courts to respond to procedural violations in this way. In light of what has been said thus far about how ICTs should respond to procedural violations committed in the pre-trial phase of the proceedings, it is submitted that express acknowledgement may indeed be an appropriate response where the procedural violation has resulted no or minimal prejudice to the accused, although chambers should always be mindful of the expressive harm that is done when rights are violated. Put differently, chambers should not be too quick to conclude that there is no prejudice to the accused, and, perhaps more importantly, to conclude that, *therefore*, nothing more than express acknowledgement is required. Express acknowledgement may also be an appropriate response where the prosecution cannot be said to have failed in its duty of due diligence to ensure that, once it initiates a case, the case proceeds to trial in a way that respects the rights of the accused, in circumstances in which the rights violation was committed in the execution of a request for cooperation by the international criminal tribunal in question.

7.3.4 Procedural Issues

Having examined the specific consequences that judges at the ICTs may attach to procedural violations in light of relevant domestic law and practice, it is time to turn to the procedural issues that arise in this regard. It was seen in Chap. 5 and above, that the ICTs have sometimes sought (or purported) to impose on the defence a burden of proof of sorts relating to the relief sought by it in respect of alleged procedural violations. At the ad hoc Tribunals, the Appeals Chamber has held the defence seeks a stay of proceedings, it bears the 'burden' of 'showing that there has been an abuse of process'. And, as observed above (in evaluating the law and practice of the ICTs in light of the human rights case law regarding procedural violations in the context of inter-state cooperation in criminal matters), in cases not involving 'flagrant' rights violations (i.e. rights violations that on their face pose a high risk to the fairness of the trial), chambers at both the ad hoc Tribunals and the ICC have required the defence to 'establish' or 'show' unlawfulness for the purposes of their applications for the exclusion of evidence on account of the manner of its obtaining.[200] In England and Wales, Section 78 of PACE (pursuant to which courts have the power to exclude evidence if its admission 'would have such an adverse effect on the fairness of the proceedings that the court ought not to admit it') does not appear to impose on the defence a burden of proof; nor would there appear to rest on the defence a burden of proof in the context of the abuse of process doctrine.[201] In this regard it may be recalled that, at the ICC, one trial chamber at least seems to have rejected the notion that, in seeking a stay of proceedings, there rests on the defence a burden of proof.[202] That same trial chamber said that, in seeking a stay of proceedings, the defence is required to 'properly substantiate' its application. In other ICC cases also, chambers have also referred to the need for the defence to properly substantiate its applications for such relief. It is worth noting that in some of these cases, the chamber itself does not appear to have had a firm grip on the law regarding stays of proceedings (and, in particular, that there are two grounds on which the proceedings may be stayed, which are distinct, and in respect of which different considerations may apply); in this regard it may be noted (again) that the test originally formulated by the ICC Appeals Chamber for staying the proceedings is not a model of clarity.[203] If the defence is to properly substantiate an application for the proceedings to be stayed, the law on this matter should be clear. And while it is not, it would be inappropriate to impose on the defence onerous substantiation obligations. In this regard it may be recalled that, in the Netherlands, only where an application for relief pursuant to Article 359a of the CCP is properly motivated is the court required to rule on it. Moreover, according to the Dutch Supreme Court, failure to properly motivate an application for relief pursuant to Article 359a of the CCP (whereby the defence must have reference to all of the statutory weighing factors and explain how such factors warrant the relief sought) means that the court may refuse to grant the relief sought or simply declare that an irreparable procedural violation has occurred (i.e. it may refuse to take, in a general sense, *responsibility* for procedural violations) without otherwise *enquiring* into the factual circumstances that, according to the defence, warrant such relief.[204] There, the onerous substantiation requirements imposed on the defence have been criticized (in the academic literature), seemingly on the basis that the regulation of certain aspects of the criminal investigation is too underdeveloped to expect the

---

[200] See n 54 and accompanying text.

[201] See in this regard Choo 2008, 166–167.

[202] See *Prosecutor v Lubanga* (Redacted Decision on the "Defence Application Seeking a Permanent Stay of the Proceedings") ICC-01/04-01/06, T Ch I (7 March 2011) para 169.

[203] See n 126–127 and accompanying text.

[204] See Chap. 3, n 174–175 and accompanying text.

defence to motivate their applications for relief in any great detail and, by extension, to justify the rejection of an application for relief on the basis that it is not sufficiently detailed.[205] A similar argument may be made in the context of the ICTs, where 'criminal procedure' is still very much in development.

It was seen in Chap. 5 that, at the ICC at least, the likely success of an application for a stay of proceedings may depend on when it is made. For applications for the proceedings to be stayed on basis that a fair trial has been rendered impossible, it would seem not to matter when an application is made. However, for applications for a stay based on an alleged unlawful arrest or unlawful detention, for example, timing does appear to matter. According to the ICC Appeals Chamber, such applications should be made during the pre-trial phase of the proceedings (although, exceptionally, they may be made at the trial stage).[206] That finding appears to have been primarily motivated by considerations of efficiency and judicial economy,[207] but there may be other reasons for requiring that applications for a stay of proceedings be made, and ruled on, at an early stage of the proceedings: 'The very act of allowing the trial to proceed and evidence to be heard may run the risk of judicial condonation of abusive conduct... Judges should generally be in a position before they hear much evidence on the merits, to decide whether hearing the case will harm judicial integrity by condoning a serious abuse.'[208]

7.4   Further Analysis

In this subsection further analysis will be provided to complement the human rights evaluation and the comparison to the relevant national law and practice. The purpose is to highlight and expand on certain aspects of the analysis provided above, outside of the confines of the aforementioned analytical frameworks. One issue worth expanding on is the question as to the most suitable rationale for responding within the criminal trial to procedural violations committed in the context of international criminal proceedings. It was argued above, in the context of specific judicial responses to procedural violations that the *court-centred* variation of the integrity rationale is to be preferred over the public attitude variation thereof, as far as the 'non-epistemic' limb of the tests for each of these responses are concerned, but it is also important to explain why the (court-centred) integrity rationale is to be preferred over other rationales also, in the particular context of international criminal proceedings. Another issue worth exploring further is the notion of

---

[205] Ölçer 2008, 518.

[206] See Chap. 5, n 285−287 and accompanying text.

[207] *Prosecutor v Katanga and Ngudjolo* (Judgment on the Appeal of Mr. Katanga Against the Decision of Trial Chamber II of 20 November 2009 Entitled "Decision on the Motion of the Defence for Germain Katanga for a Declaration on Unlawful Detention and Stay of Proceedings") ICC-01/04-01/07 OA 10, A Ch (12 July 2010) para 40.

[208] Roach 1998, 411.

discretion. In the analysis above, the determinations of whether to stay the proceedings and to exclude evidence were depicted as discretionary (as opposed to mandatory) in nature, and suggestions were made as to how to structure this discretion, but it remains to be explained why judicial discretion is to be welcomed in the context of these determinations and to be preferred over 'blanket' *rules*. Finally, it was argued above that under the court-centred variation of the integrity rationale, it is inappropriate to take into account the seriousness of the offence, i.e. the fact that the offence with which the accused is charged is very serious, whereby it bears recalling that *that* rationale was argued to be the preferred rationale for excluding evidence and for staying the proceedings (so far as the non-epistemic limbs thereof are concerned, at least), but it is important to consider the likely counterarguments in this regard, which have to do with the distinctive features of international criminal procedure, or of international criminal justice more generally.

7.4.1   The Most Suitable Rationale for Responding to Procedural Violations

Above, it was argued why at the ICTs, in the context of the determination of whether to exclude evidence on account of how it was obtained, or of whether to stay the proceedings permanently, the *court-centred* variation of the integrity rationale is to be preferred over the public attitude variation thereof, as far as the 'non-epistemic', i.e. integrity-based, limb of the tests for each of these responses are concerned.[209] Here, it will be explained why at the ICTs, the (court-centred variation of the) integrity rationale is to be preferred in general, i.e. over other rationales also.

As observed above, the judicial authorities at the ICTs and the national authorities on which the ICTs are dependent for such activities as the apprehension of persons suspected or accused of crimes falling within their jurisdiction and the carrying out of investigations, do not form part of the same legal system, such that they cannot be said to be institutionally connected.[210] This fact alone suggests that the disciplinary or deterrence rationale is ill-suited to the context of international criminal proceedings. The lack of institutional connectedness means that it is not appropriate for an international criminal tribunal to *seek* to discipline the national authorities that carried out the coercive measure in question and/or deter them from acting unlawfully in the future; in other words, it means that it is not an international criminal tribunal's function to deter and/or punish unlawful conduct on the

---

[209] As was seen above, at the ICTs, there two grounds for excluding evidence on account of the manner in which was obtained—'substantial doubt as to reliability' and 'serious damage to the integrity of the proceedings'—and two grounds for staying the proceedings—'impossibility of a fair trial' and 'preservation of the integrity of the proceedings'.

[210] It is submitted that the fact that states are under an obligation to cooperate with the ICTs (see in this Chap. 5, Sect. 5.2) does not make the two *institutionally* connected, i.e. does not make them part of the same legal system.

part of national authorities. This has been recognized by the ICTs in their case law.[211] For similar reasons, the approach advocated by some Dutch authors to the question of how to address pre-trial procedural violations based on the notion inherent to the concept of the rule of law that the authorities must *also* abide by the law, would also seem ill-suited to the context of international criminal proceedings.[212] Aside from the issue of institutional disconnectedness, it is questionable whether disciplining the public authorities for unlawful conduct, or deterring from acting this way in the future, can be said to be a proper function of *any* criminal court;[213] in this regard it may be recalled that in one of the jurisdictions examined in this book, the Netherlands, one of the primary rationales for exclusion is deterrence,[214] whereas in the other, England and Wales, courts have expressly distanced themselves from this rationale as regards both the discretion to stay the proceedings and the discretion to exclude unlawfully obtained evidence.[215] This is not to deny that the exclusion of evidence or a stay of proceedings may have the *effect* of deterring public authorities charged with the investigation of crime from conducting themselves in a certain way; they may well do, and criminal courts may have this well in mind when they resort to such measures (albeit in pursuit of other rationales). The point is that deterring and/or disciplining the public authorities charged with investigating crime ought not be the primary *pursuit* of such measures (in light of the argument that they cannot be considered to be proper functions of a criminal court), which means, among other things, that the extent to which the measure in

---

[211] See *Prosecutor v Brđanin* (Decision on the Defence "Objection to Intercept Evidence") IT-99-36-T, T Ch II (3 October 2003) para 63 and *Prosecutor v Lubanga* (Decision on the admission of material from the "bar table") ICC-01/04-01/06, T Ch I (24 June 2009) para 45.

[212] Indeed, it was seen in Chap. 3 that it may be a reason to exclude evidence (or, in particularly serious cases, to declare the prosecution inadmissible (a procedural step akin to a stay of proceedings)) that, in obtaining the evidence in question, the public authorities violated the norms that govern the exercise of the powers conferred on them for the purpose of investigating and prosecuting crime; in other words, it may be a reason to exclude evidence that, in obtaining the evidence in question, the public authorities charged with the investigation and prosecution of crime failed to observe the norms that bind them. Aside from the fact that this argument would seem ill-suited to the context of international criminal proceedings, it would appear to have particular force in systems which have a codified (and more or less closed) system of standards for the conduct of criminal investigation. In such systems it is easier to argue that non-observance by the authorities of the standards that bind them should lead to the nullification or invalidation of the unlawful act and its results (which may be achieved by the exclusion of evidence obtained thereby). For this reason also, the argument from the rule of law is unlikely to present a forceful argument for exclusion in the context of international criminal proceedings. As observed in Chap. 5, a feature of international criminal procedure is the broad attribution of powers and the absence of detailed rules in respect of the investigation. Thus, the ICTs governing documents confer on the ICTs broad coercive powers, but, in general, say little about the actual execution of coercive measures.

[213] Ashworth 1977, 725.

[214] See Chap. 3, n 216–236 and accompanying text.

[215] See Chap. 4, n 114–117 and 457 and accompanying text.

question can be said to actually deter should not be a pertinent consideration in determining whether to resort to it.[216] The question may arise as to whether it *is* a proper function of the court to discipline the *prosecution* for its own procedural violations, and/or deter it from engaging in similar conduct in the future. In this regard it may be recalled that, in the literature concerning the ICTs' law and practice, calls have repeatedly been made for a more robust response to late disclosure on the part of the prosecution, in order to deter it from doing so in the future. Even if it cannot be said to be the proper or primary function of the court (specifically, chambers of the ICTs) to discipline the prosecution for its own procedural violations, and/or deter it from engaging in similar conduct in the future, surely it is a proper function of the court to ensure the integrity of the proceedings, which might be undermined in case of (ongoing) failure to disclose certain material to the defence in a timely manner. Here it may be recalled that in addressing late disclosure, chambers at the ICTs rarely expressly consider how such conduct might reflect on *them* as *judicial* authorities; they have considered the impact of such conduct on the defence and the possible ramifications thereof for, and how it reflects on, the prosecution, but rarely do they expressly consider how such violations might otherwise impact on the integrity of the proceedings. It is against the backdrop of the need to protect the integrity of the proceedings that calls for a more robust judicial response to late disclosure (which might include a stay of proceedings and the exclusion of (prosecution) evidence (i.e. prosecution evidence not properly disclosed or evidence relating to facts to which the exculpatory material pertains), and the availability at both the ICTY and ICC of judicial disciplinary measures,[217] are best understood. Focusing on the extent to which an accused has been prejudiced by late disclosure may be too narrow an approach to the question of how to address a failure on the part of the prosecution to discharge its disclosure obligations; such an enquiry goes to the question of whether the accused's has been hampered in his or her ability to mount an effective defence, whereas that is not all that is at stake in case of such failure.

Turning now to the protective rationale, which, it may be recalled, sees the judicial response within the criminal trial as (a way of) protecting rights,[218] it is *possible* to construct an argument for exclusion at the ICTs on the basis thereof. In the context of international criminal proceedings, it is national authorities that carry

---

[216] In the Netherlands, this *is* a pertinent consideration under the third category of exclusion, at least, where the underlying rationale for exclusion is 'deterrence'. See Chap. 3, n 232 and accompanying text. The focus on this rationale to the exclusion of other rationales has been subject to criticism in the Dutch literature, also on the basis that it wrongly assumes that it is a task of the criminal court to 'police the police', whereas this is the task of the public prosecutor. See T Schalken in his annotation to HR 9 September 2014, ECLI:NL:HR:2014:2650, *NJ* 2014/420.

[217] For an overview of such measures, and of non-judicial—administrative—measures at the ICTs, see Iontcheva Turner 2012, 232–244.

[218] See Chap. 4, Sect. 4.3.3.

out investigative measures and national authorities that violate internationally recognized human rights,[219] but if the prosecution can be shown to have been involved in the violation, it might be argued that the relevant international criminal tribunal itself carried out the investigative measure in question and, by extension, committed a rights violation, such that the exclusion of the evidence obtained thereby is warranted. However, there is something artificial about this argument. Moreover, to describe an approach in which a rights violation is not in itself (always) sufficient to warrant exclusion (whereby it may be recalled that it was argued above that involvement of an organ of the international criminal tribunal in question in the procedural violation may, in principle, be required for exclusion)[220] as one based on the protective or remedial rationale may be misleading; certainly such an approach could not be said to entail a 'strictly protective' or 'strictly remedial' approach to the question of exclusion, especially in light of what may be required by way of examination and argumentation to establish 'involvement' and, by extension, to justify exclusion. Aside from the particular challenges that the context of international criminal proceedings may pose to the proper application of this rationale, the rationale itself suffers from a number of weaknesses such as to outweigh its (obvious) attractions. To begin with, if the goal of a protective or remedial approach is to 'vindicate' rights, it is not immediately obvious why rights violations should 'trigger an exclusionary remedy, rather than providing the accused with direct redress through tort liability, human rights legislation, criminal injuries compensation, or by subjecting individual miscreants to penal or disciplinary sanctions'.[221] And where the rights violation does not concern a procedural right, but a substantive one, for example, it is not immediately obvious why that right could not be vindicated by other trial remedies, such as sentence reduction. Put differently, it not entirely clear why, when evidence has been obtained by way of a rights violation, the right in question can only be vindicated by the exclusion of the evidence obtained thereby;[222] it may well be fitting or natural to exclude the evidence, but it would not seem to be *necessary* to do so (at least, not where the rights

---

[219] It is submitted that (internationally recognized human) rights violations *should* be able to be established on the basis of the acts of national authorities alone. To argue that rights should only be considered to have been violated when an organ of the international criminal tribunal in question was involved would be to distort the analysis and is apt to mislead.

[220] See n 108–113 and accompanying text.

[221] Roberts 2012, 180–181.

[222] It has been argued that the adoption of a (strong and inflexible) rights-based exclusionary *rule* might have the opposite effect of vindicating rights, or, at least, might undermine human rights enforcement, since, in light of the 'high costs' of such an exclusionary rule (whereby 'costs' would appear to cover both financial costs, e.g. the costs of a retrial, and non-financial costs, i.e. the reputation of the criminal justice system being undermined), courts might be driven 'to circumvent those costs by narrowing their substantive interpretations of rights'. See generally Starr 2008. Another 'manifestation' of 'remedial deterrence', according to which notion 'if it is more costly to recognize a remedy, courts will be less likely to do so' (ibid., 695 and 715, 'borrowing from' Levinson 1999), is where the court finds 'some procedural reason to avoid reaching the merits of a rights claim in the first place', for example, lack of jurisdiction.

violation concerns a substantive right), and doing so, or staying the proceedings on the basis of the protective rationale, might lead to the perception that the accused is being made 'better off than he would have been absent the violation'.[223] And if it is not necessary to vindicate the accused's rights by way of exclusion, it may not be unreasonable to require a suspect or an accused whose (substantive) rights were violated by the national authorities in the execution of a request by an international criminal tribunal for cooperation to seek a remedy in the state whose authorities were involved; surely, under the protective rationale, any relevant 'remedy' would presumably involve the defendant vis-à-vis the state (or, more generally, the entity) directly responsible for the violation.[224]

None of this is to say that evidence obtained by a rights violation need not be excluded at the ICTs; rather, the point is that (ironically, perhaps) the protective rationale may not provide the most convincing argument to do so (quite apart from the fact that this is not, in fact, the primary rationale for exclusion at the ICTs; see in this regard the wording of Rule 95 of the ICTY RPE and Article 69(7)(b) of the ICC Statute). Nor is it being argued that where rights violations have been committed by national authorities in the execution of a request by an international criminal tribunal for cooperation the accused should seek a remedy from the state whose authorities were involved; rather, the point is that the need to provide effective, personal remedies (which may be understood as a type of remedial rationale, if not *the* remedial or protective rationale)[225] does not explain why *the international criminal tribunal* in question should provide such a remedy for rights violations committed by the national authorities, for example, by way of financial compensation or sentence reduction. Indeed, as observed above, in the context of inter-state cooperation in criminal matters it may well be compatible with the right to an effective remedy for a state to refer a complaint regarding the lawfulness of the execution of a request for cooperation to the state whose authorities executed the request (provided that a domestic remedy is available, and provided moreover that the allegation does not concern a flagrant rights violation such as to require a response within the trial itself). It was argued above that, while the fact that a state can be said to bear responsibility for a rights violation (because it has not respected the rights of the suspect 'as protected in customary international law' or 'in the international treaties to which it has acceded', or it has not adhered to its own national laws) need not mean that the ICTs should *not* seek to provide effective, personal remedies in respect of rights violations, in order to justify their doing so, it is reasonable to require that the rights violation be attributable to them in some way, whereby a failure on the part of the prosecution to exercise due diligence to ensure that the case proceeds to trial in a way that respects the rights of the accused should suffice. And in light of the need, in principle, for attribution (whereby it is again submitted that such a requirement is only reasonable), i.e. in light of the fact that a

---

[223] See in this regard Starr 2008, 703–704.

[224] See similarly Choo 2008, 110–111.

[225] See in this regard n 48–51 and accompanying text.

rights violation is not, by itself, sufficient to warrant the provision by an international criminal tribunal of a personal remedy for rights violations, the depiction of an approach in which a rights violation is not in itself sufficient to warrant financial compensation or sentence reduction (involvement of an organ of the international criminal tribunal in question being necessary) in terms of *a* type of protective or remedial rationale (i.e. the right to an effective remedy) may be misleading.

Aside from the fact that the integrity rationale *is* in fact the rationale (or, rather, one of the two primary rationales) for excluding evidence and for staying the proceedings at the ICTs, it is submitted that it also provides the best 'fit' for the context of international criminal proceedings. As observed in Chap. 4, the separation thesis, which posits that 'there is no real connection between the actions of the police in investigating the crime and the court's verdict',[226] poses particular problems for the integrity rationale, and appears to be at its strongest where the alleged unlawful conduct is committed by an agent of a foreign state,[227] or, more generally, by an agent foreign to the system in which the trial is being held. However, there are several, compelling (if not foolproof), responses to the separation thesis. For example, it may be argued that the different stages of the criminal process cannot, or in any case should not, be treated in isolation in view of the *purpose* of (many of) the pre-trial activities of police and prosecutors, which is 'to obtain evidence, or 'leads' that may produce evidence, with a view to constructing a case against a suspect ... that will either yield sufficient evidence for a prosecution or lead the defendant to plead guilty'.[228] Put differently, it may be argued that the 'whole apparatus of the administration of criminal justice should be viewed as a single system'.[229] Further, it may be argued that 'for a court to act on the fruits of evidence [whether the evidence consists of a single item or the case as a whole] resulting from the breach of a fundamental right is to *condone* that breach'.[230] According to Ashworth, this argument 'depend[s] on attributions of symbolic significance to court decisions': 'By their actions, as much as (or even more than) by their words, judicial decisions carry a certain message. If a judge says that the violation of a fundamental right was a terrible thing, but that the court takes the view that it has no bearing on the overall fairness of the trial, it is *not unreasonable* to infer that the court has condoned the violation.'[231] Perhaps the most compelling response to the separation thesis is the notion of 'contamination'. Indeed, it seems possible that even if it cannot convincingly be argued that the 'whole apparatus of the administration of criminal justice should be viewed as a single system', and even if a decision not to exclude evidence, or not to stay the proceedings does not

---

[226] See Chap. 4, n 31–33 and accompanying text.

[227] Ashworth and Redmayne 2010, 362.

[228] Ashworth 2003, 113–114.

[229] Ibid., 116.

[230] Ibid., 117 (emphasis added).

[231] Ibid., 118 (emphasis added).

condone the conduct in question, 'the court will still be compromised'.[232] In support of this argument, Ashworth and Redmayne point to the language adopted by some of the Law Lords in the English case of *A v Secretary of State for the Home Department (No 2)*.[233] In that case the question was whether evidence obtained by torture is inadmissible in judicial proceedings in England and Wales; in the case at hand, the evidence had been obtained by the authorities of a foreign state, without the complicity of any British official. Lord Hoffmann argued that, if the purpose of the 'rule excluding evidence obtained by torture' is to uphold the integrity of the administration of justice, 'the rule must exclude statements obtained by torture anywhere, since the stain attaching to such evidence will *defile* an English court whatever the nationality of the torturer',[234] while Lord Carswell argued that to allow the admission of evidence obtained by torture 'would shock the conscience, abuse or degrade the proceedings and involve the state in moral *defilement*'.[235] They also point to a recent empirical study conducted in the US which suggests that the Fourth Amendment's exclusionary rule is, in fact, perceived as a means of protecting the judicial system from 'dirty' evidence, and that the integrity rationale might better serve the ends of the rule than the deterrence rationale.[236] The Fourth Amendment to the United States Constitution prohibits unreasonable searches and seizures; accordingly, the metaphor of contamination would appear to have a wider application than just to the context of torture.[237] The integrity rationale provides the best 'fit' for the context of the ICTs, then, because it allows chambers to exclude evidence, or to stay the proceedings, when, despite the institutional disconnectedness between the ICTs and the national authorities that actually carry out investigations, their sense of justice is (nevertheless) offended by unlawful conduct on the part of such national authorities. And it provides a better fit for the context of the ICTs in light of the need, in principle, for attribution of the procedural violation(s) in question to the international criminal tribunal in question, also.[238] Quite apart from the fact that the integrity rationale is well-suited to the specific context of the ICTs, the integrity rationale, properly applied, requires internationally recognized human rights to be taken seriously,[239] and better captures (than do the

---

[232] Ashworth and Redmayne 2010, 362.

[233] *A v Secretary of State for the Home Department (No 2)* [2005] 3 WLR 1249.

[234] Ibid., [91] (Lord Hoffmann, emphasis added).

[235] Ibid., [150] (Lord Carswell, emphasis added).

[236] Ashworth and Redmayne 2010, 362, referring to an earlier version of Bilz 2012.

[237] Ashworth and Redmayne 2010, 362.

[238] It may be recalled that it was argued above, in discussing the suitability of the 'protective' or 'remedial' rationale to the particular context of the ICTs, that precisely in light of the need, in principle, for attribution of the procedural violation to the international criminal tribunal in question, i.e. the need for some level of involvement in the violation, it may be misleading to construe the judicial response to such violations (where the fact that rights violations have been committed is not, by itself, sufficient to warrant a judicial response) in terms of that rationale.

[239] See similarly Choo 2008, 190.

other rationales referred to above) the 'institutional' harm that is caused when the rights of a person to have been drawn into the criminal process are violated.

There is one rationale that has not yet received attention in this chapter, and that is the reliability rationale. Pursuant to that rationale, it may be recalled, 'determining the truth of the criminal charges is the sole purpose of the criminal trial, and evidence should be admitted or excluded solely on that basis'.[240] Thus, pursuant to the reliability rationale, if evidence is rendered unreliable by the (unlawful) manner in which it was obtained, it should be excluded; if, however, the reliability of the unlawfully obtained evidence is not in question, that evidence should *not* be excluded, i.e. it should be admitted. It may also be recalled that the reliability rationale has been described as 'not so much a genuine 'principle' as a hard-headed pragmatic preference for receiving relevant information bearing on the issues at trial, almost irrespective of its provenance'.[241] There is a clear connection then, between the reliability rationale, and what in the Dutch literature is referred to as the argument from the primacy of crime control. And such an approach is, it is submitted, unacceptable once it is accepted (as, it is submitted, it *should* be) that reliably convicting the guilty and ensuring the protection of the innocent from conviction is not the sole function of the criminal trial.[242]

Finally, it is worth pointing out that to pursue one rationale or principle in addressing procedural violations may well be to give effect to another. However, as different considerations are likely to apply under each rationale, it is of paramount importance that chambers distinguish between the primary rationale that is being pursued and the rationales that may or may not be served by pursuing the primary rationale. The Appeals Chamber's lumping together of the integrity rationale, the remedial rationale and the deterrence rationale in the ICTR case of *Barayagwiza*[243] is unfortunate in this regard, even if the point was merely that other rationales might well be served by staying the proceedings in order to protect the court's integrity. Clear identification of the rationale that is being pursued is essential for 'structured' decision-making and for the justification of judicial discretion more generally. It is to these matters that we now turn.

7.4.2 The Merits of Judicial Discretion

Throughout this chapter and, in particular, the comparative analysis above, the judicial response at the ICTs to procedural violations committed in the pre-trial phase of the proceedings has been depicted in terms of 'discretion' and 'rules'. It was said that, at the ICTs, the 'exclusion of evidence' is characterized by the

---

[240] Ashworth 1977, 723.

[241] Roberts 2012, 172.

[242] See n 86–89 and accompanying text.

[243] *Prosecutor v Barayagwiza* (Decision) ICTR-97-19-AR72, A Ch (3 November 1999) para 108.

absence of a 'blanket' exclusionary *rule*, the existence of several specific, i.e. narrowly defined, exclusionary *rules* and (otherwise) broad *discretion* for the judges, and it was said that, at the ICTs, the determination of an application for the proceedings to be stayed is a matter of discretion, i.e. a matter of fact and degree, whereby, clear cut cases aside, minds may well differ as to whether a stay of proceedings is necessary. In respect of both procedural steps it was argued that the ICTs could benefit from a more structured approach to the discretion to be exercised in this regard, which would entail identification of the rationale and of the factors to which chambers should attach significant importance. The particular rationale that chambers should pursue (in respect of both procedural steps), it was argued, is the court-centred variation of the integrity rationale, whereby it was observed that, under an approach based on this rationale, the focus is on the seriousness of the procedural violation(s), and to this end, a number of factors were identified which would give structure to the discretion (whereby it was also observed that any approach to the question of how to address pre-trial procedural violations in which the seriousness of the procedural violation(s) is the focus may properly be said to entail the exercise of discretion, if not the performance of a balancing exercise). Implicit in this analysis is the argument that the exercise of judicial discretion is to be welcomed in the context of the determination of applications for the exclusion of evidence or for the proceedings to be stayed; it is worth addressing this issue more explicitly, and explaining why the exercise of judicial discretion is to be welcomed in this context.

It was seen in Chap. 4 that there are two possible interpretations of judicial discretion. The first 'treats judicial discretion as signifying totally unfettered power on the part of the ... judge', whereby a judge would be 'at liberty to reach conclusion B even though an application of the relevant test or standard requires that conclusion A be reached',[244] while the second interpretation 'relates to the open-texturedness of the test or standard to be applied in reaching a conclusion'.[245] In England and Wales, both the abuse of process discretion and the exclusionary mechanism under Section 78 of PACE provide for discretion in the latter sense; this means that once it is established that the standard in question has been satisfied, the judge must stay the proceedings, or, as the case may be, exclude the evidence. This, it is submitted, is how the notion of judicial discretion is to be understood at the ICTs also; as signifying the open-texturedness of the test or standard to be applied in reaching a conclusion, i.e. a 'legal standard, cast in broad and flexible terms, which gives the judge a good deal of latitude in its application to a given set of facts',[246] rather than as signifying 'totally unfettered power' on the part of the ... judge',[247] i.e. 'a power of

---

[244] Choo 2008, 156.

[245] Ibid., 156–157. For these two interpretations, Choo draws on Dworkin's *Taking Rights Seriously*, in which a distinction is drawn between 'discretion' in a weak sense and 'discretion' in a strong sense. See Dworkin 1977, 31–32.

[246] Dennis 2013, 89.

[247] Choo 2008, 156.

the judge to act in any way that he thinks fit on the facts before him'. [248] In order to explain why the exercise of judicial discretion is to be welcomed in the context of the determination at the ICTs of applications for the exclusion of evidence or for the proceedings to be stayed, it is necessary to contrast it to the application of a 'rule'; it was seen in Chap. 4 that 'rules' are 'traditionally more rigid, often prescribing that, where certain conditions are satisfied, a particular consequence will automatically follow'.[249] Thus, whereas 'rules' are characterized by rigidity, the exercise of discretion is characterized by flexibility. More generally, the exercise of judicial discretion would seem to allow judges to '[tailor] results to unique facts and circumstances of particular cases', i.e. to dispense 'individualized justice',[250] or provide 'individualized solutions' to problems,[251] which is the principle attraction of (the exercise of) judicial discretion, over (the application of) 'blanket' rules. As has been put: '… that the public believe justice is done is no less important than that it be done with the greatest possible *precision*'.[252] Understood as the provision of 'individualized solutions', judicial discretion, then, has intrinsic value. Indeed, 'rules may serve only to hamper the strong judge and to prevent application of the full measure of his good sense and sound judgment to the case in hand. Such a magistrate may know how to take account of some things, which could not be included in a rule, which nevertheless may be more or less controlling in the individual cause.'[253]

Having said this, it is important to note that the concept of judicial discretion has been met with considerable scepticism in the academic literature, and has been criticized on the basis that it gives rise to uncertainty and unpredictability of application, and may result in arbitrary decisions.[254] However, as has been observed, 'the fact that a discretion exists does not mean that the … judge is free to act arbitrarily in exercising it', and the aforementioned concerns can be met by 'confining' and 'structuring' discretion.[255] According to Choo, '[t]he purpose of confining discretion is to keep it within designated boundaries, while the purpose of structuring it is to control the manner of its exercise within these boundaries',[256] whereby discretion may be structured 'through the recognition of guidelines for its exercise', and/or the recognition of 'factors' to which the judge may attach importance in exercising the discretion.[257] However, in order to ensure that

---

[248] Dennis 2013, 89.

[249] Choo 2015, 14–15. See also Choo 2008, 156–157, drawing on Pound's *Jurisprudence*. Pound defines a rule as 'a legal precept attaching a definite detailed legal consequence to a definite detailed state of fact'. Pound 1959, 124.

[250] Davis 1969, 17.

[251] See Choo 2008, 157.

[252] Pound 1959, 367.

[253] Ibid., 367–368.

[254] For a concise overview of the objections to judicial discretion, see Choo 2008, 158–162.

[255] See Choo 2008, 161–166, drawing on, among other works, Davis 1969.

[256] Choo 2008, 163.

[257] Ibid., 163–165.

discretion is exercised in order to provide 'individualized solutions', such guidelines and factors 'should not be applied rigidly and mechanically in every case';[258] in other words, they should not be treated as *rules* which are never to be departed from.[259] The 'structuring' of discretion, then, involves striking a compromise: 'On the one hand guidelines must be developed, but on the other hand they must not be applied rigidly to every case'.[260]

In this chapter, it has been suggested that it is (indeed) appropriate to confine the exclusionary discretion to procedural violations that do not constitute torture or oppressive conduct such as to violate the privilege against self-incrimination, or a violation of the right of access to counsel at the time of questioning (all of which may be said to constitute flagrant rights violations, i.e. rights violations that on their face pose a high risk to the fairness of the proceedings or are obviously offensive to other fundamental values), and suggestions have been made to structure the discretion, entailing the identification of the rationale that should be pursued and the factors to which chambers should attach importance on this basis. That rationale, it was argued, is the court-centred variation of the integrity rationale, and the factors identified all go to the 'seriousness of the procedural violation', which, it was observed, should be the focus of an approach based on the aforementioned rationale. In addition, it was suggested that certain combinations of such factors should make a compelling case for exclusion.[261] In respect of stays of proceedings also, (similar) suggestions were made to structure the discretion. In light of what was said above, the following observations are in order, regarding the aforementioned arguments and suggestions. The recognition of a limited number of specific, narrowly defined, exclusionary rules need not take away from the overall discretionary nature of the determination of the admissibility of evidence to have been obtained illegally or unlawfully, i.e. the ability of the judge to provide individualized solutions. Similarly, the recognition that certain combinations of factors should make for a compelling case for exclusion, or, as the case may be, for a stay proceedings, need not take away from the overall discretionary nature of the determination in question. What matters is attention to the circumstances of the individual case, whereby (such) 'guidelines' should not be construed as rules, and factors should not be 'applied rigidly and mechanically in every case',[262] i.e. they should not be treated as cumulative criteria, but should rather serve as a basis for an enquiry into the circumstances of the individual case. And chambers should be willing to depart from these guidelines where there is good reason to do so.

---

[258] Ibid., 165.

[259] Ibid., 164.

[260] Ibid., 164.

[261] Thus, it was argued that, combined with a certain level of involvement on the part of the ICTs therein, the violation of an internationally recognized human right should make a compelling case for exclusion.

[262] See Choo 2008, 165.

7.4.3 The Distinctive Features of International Criminal Procedure

It was stated in Chap. 5 that several distinctive features of international criminal procedure have the potential to lead to a more restrained or restrictive approach by the ICTs to the question of how to address procedural violations committed in the pre-trial phase of the proceedings, or, otherwise, to complicate the determination by the ICTs of the consequences, if any, to be attached to pre-trial procedural violations (as compared to that made in a purely national context). Such features, which are interrelated, are: the nature of the regulation of the investigation in international criminal procedure (i.e. the broad attribution of powers and absence of detailed rules in respect of the investigation), the lack of an own enforcement agency to execute investigative measures (and the resulting reliance on state-cooperation) and the fragmentation of the investigation over several jurisdictions. While it can be confirmed that such features do indeed raise challenging questions of both a conceptual and practical nature in the context of the determination of how to address procedural violations committed in the pre-trial phase of international criminal proceedings, it is equally clear that such features can be factored into the equation easily enough, due in no small part to the flexibility of the (court-centred variation of the) integrity rationale, and the notion of contamination that would seem to underlie it, so that the fact that such features raise challenging questions should not be a reason at the outset to adopt a restrained or restrictive approach to the question of how to address procedural violations committed in the pre-trial phase of international criminal proceedings. The (court-centred variation of) integrity rationale, it may be recalled, allows chambers at the ICTs to attach legal consequences to procedural violations despite the institutional disconnectedness between the ICTs and the national authorities actually commit such violations.

It was seen above that, under the court-centred variation of the integrity rationale, it is inappropriate to take into account the seriousness of the offence, i.e. the fact that the offence with which the accused is charged is very serious. The question may arise as to whether the fact that the goals of international criminal justice are not limited to 'ordinary' goals of criminal justice, i.e. the conviction of the guilty and (correspondingly), the acquittal of the innocent, but include such 'special' or 'idiosyncratic' (socio-political) goals as 'reconciliation and restoration of peace and security', 'establishment of a historical record', 'promoting international rule of law' and 'justice for victims',[263] warrants a different conclusion; it might be argued that such goals warrant taking into account the seriousness of the offence and attaching importance to it as an argument in favour of admitting illegally or unlawfully obtained evidence, or, as the case may be, of allowing the trial to proceed to verdict despite serious misconduct in the pre-trial phase. It is surely true that the goals of international criminal justice are not limited to 'ordinary' goals of

---

[263] Vasiliev 2014, 174–182.

criminal justice, i.e. the conviction of the guilty and (correspondingly), the acquittal of the innocent.[264] However, it is difficult to see why the aforementioned 'special' goals of international criminal justice should lead to a different approach to that advocated in this book, whereby, among other things, the seriousness of the offence may not be taken into account. More generally, it is difficult to see why they should (a priori) lead to a restrained or restrictive judicial response within the criminal trial to pre-trial procedural violations. They are goals of international criminal *justice*, 'institutional' objectives as it were, *not* goals or functions of international criminal *procedure* or the international criminal *process*. As Vasiliev observes, goals of international criminal justice are 'not directly pursued by the process as such', the latter is 'but a tool or mechanism through which such outcomes can be brought about.'[265] He points to the danger of conflating procedural objectives with goals of punishment and sentencing rationales and/or goals of criminal justice:[266]

> Retribution, deterrence, rehabilitation and other similar purposes may not be regarded as the proper objectives a (liberal) criminal process is to pursue. Those should be neutral and inconclusive when it comes to determining the optimal procedural arrangements. If they are not, the criminal procedure itself mutates into a penal tool which retributes, deters, or incapacitates, thereby conjuring the imagery of trials by ordeal and mediaeval inquisition. While substantive criminal law is a legitimate tool for the realization of crime-control policies through criminalization of conduct, employing criminal procedure as a mechanism for implementing those policies is contrary to the presumption of innocence and fundamental notions of a fair trial. In liberal criminal justice, the procedure may not be punitive in and by itself. It precedes punishment and makes its imposition possible and legitimate but it never amounts to it… Nor should the objectives of international criminal procedure be equated or aligned with substantive … goals of international criminal justice.[267]

The goals of international criminal justice (special or ordinary) should not, then, be confused with the goals of international criminal procedure. As to how the former and latter sets of goals do (or ought to) relate to one another, one ICTY Trial Chamber has very succinctly put it as follows (whereby it bears recalling that 'reconciliation and restoration of peace and security' may be said to be a special goal of international criminal justice):

> The International Tribunal was established to aid in the restoration and maintenance of peace in the former Yugoslavia. *As a criminal court,* its primary obligation is to provide a fair and expeditious trial and to guarantee the rights of the accused. This adjudicatory process strengthens the rule of law, a fundamental principle shared by all members of the international community. If effective, this *may contribute to* reconciliation, which is a precondition for lasting peace.[268]

---

[264] Ibid., 167–168, in particular. See also Ohlin 2013, 55–68.
For a critical overview of the special goals, see ibid., 171–182.

[265] Vasiliev 2014, 170.

[266] Ibid., 170. Thus, Vasiliev argues that the goals of criminal justice should be distinguished from goals of punishment and sentencing rationales. Ibid., 168.

[267] Vasiliev 2014, 170.

[268] *Prosecutor v Blaškić* (Decision on the Objection of the Republic of Croatia to the Issuance of Subpoenae Duces Tecum) IT-95-14-PT, T Ch II (18 July 1997) para 154 (emphasis added).

To allow the aforementioned special goals of international criminal justice to 'enter the analysis' would be to suggest that socio-political goals form a legitimate constraint on the procedural objectives referred to by the ICTY Trial Chamber, or, put differently, that the criminal process may be utilized to pursue socio-political objectives. It is one thing to say that, through their processes, the ICTs may contribute to the achievement of such goals (in the long-term), it is quite another to say that they may be utilized for such purposes. The argument that the special goals of international criminal justice warrant taking into account the seriousness of the offence as an argument in favour of admitting illegally or unlawfully obtained evidence, or, as the case may be, of allowing the trial to proceed to verdict despite serious misconduct in the pre-trial phase, appears to conflate procedural objectives with goals of criminal justice with all that this entails; accordingly, it must be rejected.

Other features of international criminal procedure that might be argued to require a restrictive judicial response within the criminal trial to procedural violations committed in the pre-trial phase of international criminal proceedings are the formal recognition of victim participatory rights at the ICC and the fact that the ICTs are dependent on the state-cooperation for such activities as the apprehension of persons suspected or accused of crimes falling within their jurisdiction and for the carrying out of investigations. Regarding the former feature, it may simply be observed that the fact that at the ICC Statute provides for 'real participatory rights' for victims, which allow such persons 'whose personal rights are affected to present their views and concerns at appropriate stages of the proceedings',[269] does not mean that victims have a right to demand punishment,[270] or to demand that judges refrain from taking procedural steps (aimed at ensuring a fair trial or protecting the integrity of the proceedings) that might prevent effective punishment. As to the latter feature of international criminal procedure—the dependence of the ICTs on state-cooperation for such activities as the apprehension of persons suspected or accused of crimes falling within their jurisdiction and for the carrying out of investigations—it bears recalling that the Appeals Chamber's decision in the ICTR case of *Barayagwiza* to stay the proceedings in connection with the accused's detention in Cameroon, whereby the accused's detention rights had been violated, was met with widespread condemnation in Rwanda, whereby the Rwandan government is reported to have 'reacted adversely' to the decision, threatening 'to suspend all cooperation with the ICTR'.[271] In light of this, it would indeed be 'difficult to maintain that outside wishes and interests, be they attributed to the form of a U.N. organ, an individual State, or even the international community at large, fail to influence the activities of the [international criminal tribunals]'.[272] However, this does not mean that it would be *appropriate* for judges at the ICTs to, in the determination of an application for the proceedings to be stayed, take into account

---

[269] De Brouwer and Heikkilä 2013, 1300.

[270] Seibert-Fohr 2009, 283.

[271] Schabas 2000, 565. See also Zappalà 2003, 256.

[272] Fairlie 2003, 59.

the likelihood of 'political backlash', i.e. treat it as a legitimate interest in this regard. So long as the accusations remain unproven, any such backlash would necessarily be motivated by illegitimate interests.[273] In addition to posing problems for the presumption of innocence, consideration of this factor would be inconsistent with the independence with which the judiciary is required to perform its functions.

7.5 Concluding Remarks

In this chapter, the law and practice of the ICTs with respect to the question of how to address procedural violations committed in the pre-trial phase of international criminal proceedings was evaluated in light of relevant human rights standards and compared to the relevant national law and practice of the jurisdictions examined in this book, with a view to being able to answer the central research question: how should judges at the ICTs respond to procedural violations committed in the pre-trial phase of international criminal proceedings? The soundness of the existing law and practice of the ICTs was assessed against the aforementioned benchmarks, whereby points of concern were identified and suggestions were made for improvement, and further analysis was provided to complement that provided in the human rights evaluation and the comparison with national law and practice. Together, these elements provide an answer to the question of how judges at the ICTs should respond to procedural violations committed in the pre-trial phase of international criminal proceedings. In the following—final—chapter of this book, the main points of analysis will be summarized, and a final answer to the central research question will be provided.

References

Ashworth AJ (1977) Excluding Evidence as Protecting Rights. Crim LR 723 et seq.

Ashworth A (2003) Exploring the Integrity Principle in Evidence and Procedure. In: Mirfield P, Smith R (eds) Essays for Colin Tapper. LexisNexis UK, London/Edinburgh, pp 107–125

Ashworth A (2012) The Exclusion of Evidence Obtained by violating a Fundamental Right: Pragmatism Before Principle in Strasbourg Jurisprudence. In: Roberts P, Hunter J (eds) Criminal Evidence and Human Rights: Reimagining Common Law Procedural Traditions. Hart Publishing, Oxford, pp 145–161

Ashworth A, Redmayne M (2010) The Criminal Process, 4th edn. Oxford University Press, Oxford

Bachmaier Winter L (2013) Transnational Criminal Proceedings, Witness Evidence and Confrontation: Lessons from the ECtHR's Case Law. Utrecht LR 9:127 et seq.

Bilz K (2012) Dirty Hands or Deterrence? An Experimental Examination of the Exclusionary Rule. JELS 9:149 et seq.

---

[273] Starr 2008, 761.

Choo AL-T (2008) Abuse of Process and Judicial Stays of Criminal Proceedings, 2nd edn. Oxford University Press, Oxford

Choo AL-T (2015) Evidence, 4th edn. Oxford University Press, Oxford

Davis KC (1969) Discretionary Justice: A Preliminary Inquiry. Louisiana State University, Baton Rouge

De Brouwer A-M, Heikkilä M (2013) Victim Issues: Participation, Protection, Reparation, and Assistance. In: Sluiter G et al. (eds) International Criminal Procedure. Principles and Rules. Oxford University Press, Oxford, pp 1299–1374

De Meester K et al. (2013) Investigation, Coercive Measures, Arrest, and Surrender. In: Sluiter G et al. (eds) International Criminal Procedure. Principles and Rules. Oxford University Press, Oxford, pp 171–379

Dennis IH (2013) The Law of Evidence, 5th edn. Sweet & Maxwell, London

Duff A et al. (2004) Introduction: Towards a Normative Theory of the Criminal Trial. In: Duff A et al. (eds) The Trial on Trial. Volume One: Truth and Due Process. Hart Publishing, Oxford, pp 1–28

Duff P (2004) Admissibility of Improperly Obtained Physical Evidence in the Scottish Criminal Trial: The Search for Principle. Edin LR 8:152 et seq.

Dworkin R (1977) Taking Rights Seriously. Duckworth, London

Fairlie MA (2003) Due Process Erosion: The Diminution of Live Testimony at the ICTY. Cal W Int'l L J 34:47 et seq.

Grevling K (1997) Fairness and the exclusion of evidence under section 78(1) of the Police and Criminal Evidence Act. LQR 667 et seq.

Iontcheva Turner J (2012) Policing International Prosecutors. NYU J Int'l L & P 45:175 et seq.

Jackson J (2012) Human Rights, Constitutional Law and Exclusionary Safeguards in Ireland. In: Roberts P, Hunter J (eds) Criminal Evidence and Human Rights: Reimagining Common Law Procedural Traditions. Hart Publishing, Oxford, pp 119–143

Jackson JD, Summers SJ (2012) The Internationalisation of Criminal Evidence. Beyond the Common Law and Civil Law Traditions. Cambridge University Press, Cambridge

Kamisar Y (1987) "Comparative Reprehensibility" and the Fourth Amendment Exclusionary Rule. Mich L Rev 86:1 et seq.

Knigge G (2003) Het Zwolsman-criterium op de helling. RM Themis 2003, afl 4, pp 193–195

Kuiper R (2014) Vormfouten. Juridische Consequenties van Vormverzuimen in Strafzaken. Kluwer, Deventer

Levinson DJ (1999) Rights Essentialism and Remedial Equilibration. Colum L Rev 99:857 et seq.

Martin S (2005) Lost and destroyed evidence: The search for a principled approach to abuse of process. 9 E&P 158 et seq.

Mirfield P (1997) Silence, Confessions and Improperly Obtained Evidence. Oxford University Press, Oxford

Ohlin JD (2013) Goals of International Criminal Justice and International Criminal Procedure. In: Sluiter G et al. (eds) International Criminal Procedure. Principles and Rules. Oxford University Press, Oxford, pp 55–68

Ölçer FP (2008) Eerlijk Proces en Bijzondere Opsporing. Wolf Legal Publishers, Nijmegen

Ormerod D, Birch D (2004) The evolution of the discretionary exclusion of evidence. Crim LR 767 et seq.

Pitcher KM (2013) Addressing violations of international criminal procedure. In: Abels D et al. (eds) Dialectiek van nationaal en internationaal strafrecht. Boom Juridische uitgevers, The Hague, pp 257–308

Pound R (1959) Jurisprudence (Vol II). West Publishing Co, St Paul, Minn

Redmayne M (2009) Theorizing the Criminal Trial. New Crim L Rev 12:287 et seq.

Reisinger-Coracini A (2013) Cooperation from States and Other Entities. In: Sluiter G et al. (eds) International Criminal Procedure. Principles and Rules. Oxford University Press, Oxford, pp 95–116

Roach K (1998) The Evolving Tests for Stays of Proceedings. Crim LQ 40:400 et seq.

Roberts P (2012) Excluding Evidence as Protecting Constitutional or Human Rights? In: Zedner L, Roberts JV (eds) Principles and Values in Criminal Law and Criminal Justice: Essays in Honour of Andrew Ashworth. Oxford University Press, Oxford, pp 171–190

Rogers J (2008) The Boundaries of Abuse of Process in Criminal Trials. CLP 61:289 et seq.

Safferling CJM (2003) Towards an International Criminal Procedure. Oxford University Press, Oxford

Schabas WA (2000) International Decisions: Barayagwiza v. Prosecutor (Decision, and Decision (Prosecutor's Request for Review or Reconsideration)). AJIL 94:563 et seq.

Seibert-Fohr A (2009) Prosecuting Serious Human Rights Violations. Oxford University Press, Oxford

Starr SB (2008) Rethinking "Effective Remedies": Remedial Deterrence in International Courts. NYU L Rev 83:693 et seq.

Starr SB (2009) Sentence Reduction as a Remedy for Prosecutorial Misconduct. Geo LJ 97:1509 et seq.

Taylor M, Jalloh CC (2013) Provisional Arrest and Incarceration in the International Criminal Tribunals. Santa Clara J Int'l L 11:303 et seq.

Van Hoek AAF, Luchtman MJJP (2005) Transnational Cooperation in Criminal Matters and the Safeguarding of Human Rights. Utrecht LR 1:1 et seq.

Vasiliev S (2014) International Criminal Trials. A Normative Theory. Volume 1: Nature. DPhil thesis, University of Amsterdam

Zappalà S (2002) Compensation to an Arrested or Convicted Person. In: Cassese A et al. (eds) The Rome Statute of the International Criminal Court. A Commentary, vol 2. Oxford University Press, Oxford, pp 1577–1585

Zappalà S (2003) Human Rights in International Criminal Proceedings. Oxford University Press, Oxford

Zeegers KJ (2016) International Criminal Tribunals and Human Rights Law. Adherence and Contextualization. TMC Asser Press, The Hague

Zuckerman AAS (1987) Illegally-Obtained Evidence—Discretion as a Guardian of Legitimacy. CLP 55 et seq.

Chapter 8
Conclusion

Abstract In this chapter, the main points of analysis to have emerged in the previous chapters are summarized, including the points of concern identified in the penultimate chapter as well as the suggestions for improvement made therein, and a final answer to the central research question is provided.

Keywords compliance with human rights law · comparative criminal procedure · right to a fair trial · right to an effective remedy · inter-state cooperation in criminal matters · non-enquiry · shared responsibility · due diligence · exclusion of evidence · stay of proceedings · sentence reduction · financial compensation · express acknowledgement · integrity rationale · public attitude integrity · court-centred integrity · seriousness of the offence · seriousness of the procedural violation · consequentialist reasoning · right to an effective remedy · factors · (judicial) discretion · balancing · goals of international criminal justice · features/goals of international criminal procedure

Contents

The purpose of this book is to provide an in-depth examination of the judicial response at the international criminal tribunals to pre-trial procedural violations, with a view to answering the central research question of this book: how should judges at the ICTs respond to procedural violations committed in the pre-trial phase of the proceedings? Underlying this (normative) question was the assumption that certain particularities of international criminal proceedings may warrant a different approach to the matter—how to address pre-trial procedural violations—than at the national level. While the potential for controversy when a court attaches legal consequences to the violation of procedural standards in the pre-trial phase of

K. Pitcher, *Judicial Responses to Pre-Trial Procedural Violations in International Criminal Proceedings*, International Criminal Justice Series 16,
https://doi.org/10.1007/978-94-6265-219-4_8

criminal proceedings is not unique to the context of the ICTs, the questions raised thereby—should the (predicted) public reaction to the judicial response be taken into account in the determination of how to address such violations? Should the seriousness of the offence with which the accused is charged inform the judge's decision in this regard?—may take on a different meaning at the international level, in light of the fact that goals of international criminal justice include such 'special' goals as 'reconciliation and restoration of peace and security', 'history-writing', 'promoting international rule of law' and 'justice for victims', and in light of the ICTs' dependence on state cooperation for their proper functioning (thereby making them vulnerable to political backlash). Moreover, the fact that the ICTs do not have their own enforcement agencies, coupled with the fact that their governing documents are (largely) silent on how such activities are to be executed, may raise challenging questions on both a conceptual and practical level for a judge faced with an application for relief in respect of procedural violations committed in the pre-trial phase of international criminal proceedings.

In order to answer the central research question, which is normative in nature, it was necessary to set out what the law and practice of the ICTs with respect to the question of how to address procedural violations committed in the pre-trial phase of the proceedings *is* (which was the purpose of Chaps. 5 and 6) and also to assess the soundness of the existing law and practice (which was the purpose of Chap. 7, as well as to argue what the law and practice *ought to be*). For the purpose of said assessment, two analytical tools were employed: human rights law (in particular, that pertaining to the position of the suspect or accused), and national criminal procedure (whereby the former tool was set out in Chap. 2, and the latter in Chaps. 3 and 4). In this final chapter, the main points of analysis to have arisen from the examination (that is, the description and assessment of the existing law and practice, as well as the normative analysis thereof) are summarized, including the points of concern to have been identified and the suggestions made for improvement, in order to provide a more succinct answer to the central research question.

In Chaps. 5 and 6, the existing law and practice of the ICTs with respect to the question how to address procedural violations committed in the pre-trial phase of the proceedings was set out. In the former chapter, this was done by means of an overview of the consequences that the judge may attach to such violations, while in the latter, such law and practice was addressed in two specific contexts: arrest and detention, and disclosure. There are, broadly speaking, five possible responses to procedural violations committed in the pre-trial phase of international criminal proceedings: a stay of proceedings (a procedural step by which the proceedings are brought to a halt), the exclusion of evidence obtained thereby, financial compensation, sentence reduction and express acknowledgement of the violation. Each of these responses is available at both the ad hoc Tribunals and the ICC, and the manner in which the responses have been applied or interpreted is broadly similar at both, with a few notable differences. Turning first to the similarities, at both the ad hoc Tribunals and the ICC the test for a stay of proceedings consists of two non-cumulative limbs: the impossibility of a fair trial and the need to preserve the integrity of the proceedings. Further, at both the ad hoc Tribunal and the ICC, there are two grounds on which to exclude evidence on account of the manner of its obtaining: substantial doubt as to reliability and serious damage to the integrity of the proceedings. And at both the ad hoc Tribunals and the ICC, financial compensation and sentence reduction are available for rights violation committed in the pre-trial phase of the proceedings. As to the (most notable) differences, at the ad hoc Tribunals, the appellate case law is clearer than that at the ICC as regards the circumstances that may lead to a stay of proceedings. Further, while at the ad hoc Tribunals, involvement of the Tribunal need not always be shown in order to justify the imposition of a stay of proceedings, there are (strong) indications that, at the ICC, attribution to an organ thereof must (always) be shown in order for the proceedings to be stayed. Regarding the exclusion of unlawfully obtained evidence, while at the ad hoc Tribunals chambers have allowed the determination to be made under Rule 95 of the RPE—the central provision at both of the ad hoc Tribunals for excluding evidence on account of the manner of its obtaining—to be informed by the probative value of the evidence and the fact that the crimes with which the accused is charged are very serious, at the ICC, it has been held that this factor may *not* inform the determination to be made under Article 69(7) of the ICC Statute— the central provision at the ICC for excluding evidence on account of the manner of its obtaining. Finally, while at the ad hoc Tribunals, financial compensation may only be ordered upon acquittal of the accused, at the ICC, no such restriction appears to apply. And while the ICC provides for separate proceedings for requesting compensation (separate, that is, from the trial proper), at the ad hoc Tribunals, there is no such separation.

As to the assessment of the ICTs' law and practice with respect to the question of how to address procedural violations committed in the pre-trial phase of the proceedings, it was seen in Chap. 7 that, overall, the ICTs' law and practice is not incompatible with the relevant human rights standards (those pertaining to the position of the suspect or accused), i.e. the right to a fair trial (which sheds light on whether it is necessary to address pre-trial procedural violations *within the criminal trial*), the right to an effective remedy, the right to compensation in case of unlawful arrest or detention (which may be viewed as a specific manifestation of the right to an effective remedy) and the case law regarding the question of how to address procedural violations committed in the context of inter-state cooperation in criminal matters. However, some points of concern were identified.

In conformity with human rights law, the ICTs recognize several specific, i.e. narrowly defined, exclusionary rules for certain, 'flagrant', rights violations— torture, oppressive conduct such as to violate the privilege against self-incrimination or violation of the right of access to a lawyer at the time of questioning—(while for other procedural violations exclusion is a matter of discretion for the judge), however it is a cause for concern that evidence obtained by such rights violations still seems to fall with the scope of Rule 95 of the ICTY and ICTR RPEs and Article 69(7) of the ICC Statute. Those provisions, it may be recalled, provide for an exclusionary *discretion*, whereby the determination to be made thereunder is a matter of fact and degree, entailing consideration of the particular circumstances of the case (although the extent of the discretion may differ as between the two different grounds for excluding evidence: substantial doubt as to reliability and serious damage to the integrity of the proceedings). In order to avoid confusion in this regard, i.e. in order to remove any temptation on the part of judges to look beyond the fact that the evidence was obtained by such a violation, evidence obtained by such violations should be kept outside of the scope of the aforementioned provisions. This might be achieved by the development of strong appellate case law in this regard, which clearly confines the discretion provided therein to evidence not already subject to one of the (automatic) exclusionary rules and which explains why evidence obtained by such violations is subject to automatic exclusion, or by codifying (in the governing documents of the ICTs) the automatic exclusion of evidence obtained by torture, oppressive conduct such as to violate the privilege against self-incrimination or violation of the right of access to a lawyer at the time of questioning.

It is commendable that the ICTs have sought to provide, or have mooted the possibility of providing, accused persons with personal remedies (within the meaning of the right to an effective remedy) for rights violations committed by national authorities acting upon a request for cooperation by an international criminal tribunal, in the form of financial compensation and sentence reduction. However, as observed in Chap. 7, there are inconsistencies in the practice, in that the ICTs have seemingly provided (or otherwise mooted the possibility of providing) personal remedies for some rights violations but not for others, and in that the ad hoc Tribunals and the ICC seemingly require differing levels of involvement of the international criminal tribunal in question in the rights violation in order to justify the provision of a personal remedy in respect thereof. Neither the ad hoc Tribunals nor the ICC, then, seem willing to provide remedies for *any* rights violation to have been committed in the context of the execution of a request for cooperation. This may not be incompatible with human rights law; after all, in the context of inter-state cooperation in criminal matters, it may be compatible with the right to an effective remedy for a state to refer a complaint regarding the lawfulness of the execution of a request for cooperation to the state whose authorities executed the request,[1] provided that the allegation does not concern a flagrant rights violation such as to require a response within the trial (state) itself and provided, moreover, that a domestic remedy is available. It is this last point (regarding the availability of domestic remedies) that warrants a more 'willing' attitude on the part of the ICTs towards the issue of remedies. They should seek to ensure that the 'international division of labour in prosecuting crimes' does not operate to the 'detriment of the apprehended person';[2] therefore, in attaching importance to the involvement of the international criminal tribunal in question in the rights violation (which, it is

---

[1] As stated above, while inter-state cooperation in criminal matters is different from the cooperation between states and the ICTs, the former has greatly influenced the latter, so that the human rights law in respect thereof (inter-state cooperation in criminal matters, that is) may be employed as an evaluative tool in respect of the ICTs' law and practice in this regard.

[2] To borrow from the Appeals Chamber in *Prosecutor v Kajelijeli* (Judgement) ICTR-98-44A-A, A Ch (23 May 2005), para 220.

submitted, the ICTs are entitled to do in light of the notion *shared responsibility* as between the ICTs and the national authorities that carry out requests for cooperation for ensuring that the suspect's or accused's rights are protected), a failure to exercise due diligence in ensuring that the case proceeds to trial in a way that respects the rights of the accused, and not a *higher* degree of involvement (whereby it may be recalled that for the exclusion of evidence and for stays, a higher degree of involvement may reasonably be required), should be sufficient in order to be able to attribute a rights violation to the ICTs such as to warrant the provision of an effective, personal remedy in respect thereof. Other points of concern regarding the ICTs' practice concerning the right to an effective remedy are the time that it takes to provide (personal) remedies (whereby it may be recalled that both the ad hoc Tribunals and the ICC consider sentence reduction to be capable of providing an effective, personal remedy for rights violations), which may undermine the effectiveness thereof, and the fact that the ICTs purport to provide such remedies within the trial itself. Regarding this last point, it is questionable whether the criminal trial is the right place to deal with the substance of the complaint, as is required under the right to an effective remedy. A separate procedure may be more appropriate, modelled on the procedure at the ICC for claiming compensation for unlawful arrest or detention.

A final point of concern to have arisen in the human rights evaluation relates to the ability of the defence to challenge evidence in the proceedings in which they are sought for admission; this, it was seen, is an important factor for the ECtHR in the determination of whether the right to a fair trial has been violated as a result of the use at trial of evidence obtained unlawfully. In some cases, ICTs have, effectively, adopted a stance of non-enquiry, declining to enquire into the circumstances surrounding the execution of an investigative measure for the purpose of determining an application for relief in this regard. While there is human rights case law to support such an approach (at least insofar as what is not being alleged is that defence rights have been disrespected), that case law may itself be criticized on the basis that it is inconsistent with the case law addressing the fairness of the use at trial of evidence obtained unlawfully, whereby the ability of the defence to challenge the evidence is an important factor in the determination of whether the right to a fair trial has been violated. Non-enquiry may result in the provenance of the evidence remaining unaccounted for, and evidence whose provenance is unaccounted for, and which, by extension, cannot be challenged by the defence, should not be used; not in the inter-state context, and not at the ICTs. The issue is one of fundamental fairness.

Turning now to the comparative criminal procedure analysis, it was seen in Chap. 7 that the ICTs' approach to unlawfully obtained evidence, characterized as it is by the absence of a 'blanket' exclusionary rule, the existence of several specific, i.e. narrowly defined, exclusionary rules and (otherwise) broad discretion for the judges (although, again, the extent of the discretion may differ as between the two different grounds for excluding evidence: substantial doubt as to reliability and serious damage to the integrity of the proceedings), is not dissimilar to the respective approaches of the two national jurisdictions examined in this book—the

Netherlands, and England and Wales—to such evidence. In observing that, at the national level, efforts have been made (or calls have been made *for* efforts to be made) to ensure a more 'structured' approach to the determination of applications to exclude evidence, it was argued that the ICTs could also benefit from a more structured approach in this regard, particularly as regards the 'serious damage to the integrity of the proceedings' limb of the exclusionary discretion, whereby the rationale being pursued would be defined more clearly, which would in turn enable identification of the factors to which the court ruling on the application should attach significant importance. It was argued that the court-centred variation of the integrity rationale, whereby the judge acts for moral reasons stemming from his own conscience, is to be preferred over the public attitude variation thereof, which requires the judge to perform a balancing exercise involving competing public interests (the public interest in the conviction of the 'factually guilty' against whom there is reliable evidence and the public interest in the judiciary not condoning the unlawful action of law enforcement agencies) and to consider factors relevant to each of the public interests involved,[3] in this regard. On this basis, whereby it may be recalled that the focus of an approach based on the former rationale is the seriousness of the *procedural violation*, the factors to which the court should have reference were identified. The most glaring omission from this list is, perhaps, the seriousness of the offence with which the accused is charged. Aside from the fact that it would not be appropriate to take this factor into account under the court-centred variation of the integrity rationale (in light of the 'key time' at which the rationale 'bites'),[4] this factor, it is submitted, should not be allowed to guide the determination of an application for the exclusion of evidence any way, on the basis that it would open the door to, if not invite, consequentialist reasoning. For similar reasons, the probative value of the evidence has been omitted from the list. The factors to which chambers *may* have reference in the determination to be made under the 'serious damage to the integrity of the proceedings' limb of the exclusionary discretion are: whether there was a violation of an internationally recognized human right, whether there was concerted action between an organ of the international criminal tribunal in question and the national authorities (a question that the ICTs are entitled to ask given that the ICTs and the national authorities on which they are dependent for such activities as the apprehension of persons suspected or accused of crimes falling within their jurisdiction and the collection of evidence do not form part of the same legal system, on the assumption that they do not approach the issue too narrowly, i.e. disingenuously), whether the prosecution acted in good or bad faith and whether the evidence was obtained (unlawfully) in circumstances of urgency, emergency or necessity. Combined with a certain level of involvement on the part of the ICTs therein, it is arguable that the violation of an internationally recognized human right should make a compelling case for exclusion.

---

[3] For an overview and discussion of these rationales, see Chap. 4, Sect. 4.3.4.

[4] To borrow from Mirfield. See Mirfield 1997, 29.

At the ICTs, there are two, distinct grounds for staying the proceedings: the impossibility of a fair trial and the need to preserve the integrity of the proceedings. In England and Wales also, there are two categories of case in which a court has a discretion to stay the proceedings, on the ground that to try those proceedings will amount to an abuse of its process; by contrast, in the Netherlands there is, effectively, only one ground on which to declare that the prosecution is inadmissible: the impossibility of a fair trial. It was observed in Chap. 7 (and in Chap. 5, also) that the appellate case law at the ad hoc Tribunals is clearer than that at the ICC as regards the distinction between the two grounds for staying the proceedings, and that the ICC Appeals Chamber's rationalization of a stay of proceedings solely in terms of 'fairness' is a cause for concern in this regard. Accordingly, it was argued that the ICC Appeals Chamber should adopt clear and appropriate terminology in this regard, in order to ensure that the two grounds remain conceptually distinct. Regarding the 'impossibility of a fair trial' limb of the test for staying the proceedings, it was argued that it may be more helpful to think of a stay of proceedings imposed on this basis as a 'weapon of last resort', 'where there is no hope that any conviction would be seen as a factually accurate verdict which was fairly reached',[5] than as a means of upholding rights. The question that a chamber should ask itself is whether the defence has been prejudiced to such an extent as to make a fair trial impossible, i.e. as to lead to the danger of a factually inaccurate verdict; while consideration of whether the accused's (defence or fair trial) rights have been violated may well assist a chamber in answering this question, it should not form the primary focus of the enquiry. Put differently, chambers should not approach the question too formalistically. Regarding the 'preservation of the integrity proceedings' limb, it was argued that the ICTs could benefit from a more structured approach to the determination to be made thereunder, whereby the rationale being pursued would be defined more clearly, which would (in turn) enable identification of the factors to which the court ruling on the application should attach significant importance. In this context also it was argued that the court-centred variation of the integrity rationale is to be preferred over the public attitude variation thereof, for the same reasons as under the exclusionary discretion. The factors to which the court may have reference under the 'preservation of the integrity of the proceedings' limb of the test for staying the proceedings are: whether there was a violation of an internationally recognized human right, whether it can be said that, but for the human rights violation, the prosecution would not be taking place (a question which is distinct to this particular judicial response and would seem to require an affirmative answer in order to justify something so far-reaching as a stay or proceedings, i.e. a refusal to take cognizance of the case), whether the international criminal tribunal in question was involved, whether the prosecution acted in bad or good faith and whether the impugned conduct took place in circumstances of urgency, emergency or necessity. Combined with a certain level of involvement on the part of the ICTs therein, it is arguable that the fact that, but for the human rights

---

[5] See Rogers 2008, 290–291.

violation, the prosecution would not be taking place, should make for a compelling case for a stay. However, as with the exclusion of evidence, in the determination of an application for the proceedings to be stayed, chambers should not take into account the fact that the crime with which the accused is charged is a serious one.

In reflecting *further* on the ICTs' the law and practice with respect to the question of how to address procedural violations committed in the pre-trial phase of the proceedings, it was argued in Chap. 7 that the court-centred variation of the integrity rationale is not only to be preferred over the public attitude variation thereof, as far as the 'non-epistemic' limb of the exclusionary discretion and the tests for staying the proceedings are concerned; in the particular context of inter-national criminal proceedings, it is to be preferred over other rationales also, such as the disciplinary or deterrence rationale and the protective rationale (which sees the judicial response to procedural violations as (a way of) protecting rights). The (court-centred variation of the) integrity rationale provides the best 'fit' for the context of the ICTs because it allows chambers to exclude evidence, or to stay the proceedings, when, despite the institutional disconnectedness between the ICTs and the national authorities that actually carry out investigations, their sense of justice is (nevertheless) offended by unlawful conduct on the part of such national authorities. This is due to the notion of contamination that seems to underlie it. More generally, the integrity rationale, properly applied, requires internationally recognized human rights to be taken seriously,[6] and better captures (than do the other rationales) the 'institutional' harm that is caused when the rights of a person to have been drawn into the criminal process are violated.

Another feature of the court-centred variation of the integrity rationale is that it allows for a *discretionary* approach to the determination of an application for the exclusion of evidence on account of the manner of its obtaining, or, as the case may be, for the proceedings to be stayed. This is so, because the focus of an approach based on this rationale is the seriousness of the procedural violation; this factor, it was seen in Chap. 7, may give rise to a whole host of lines of enquiry, such that, any approach to the question of how to address procedural violations in which this factor is the focus might properly be said to entail the exercise of discretion. A discretionary approach, it was argued, has intrinsic value; it allows a judge to provide 'individualized solutions' to problems, to do 'justice' with 'the greatest possible precision'.[7] Nevertheless, in order to ensure that the discretionary nature of the determination of applications for the exclusion of evidence and stays of pro-ceedings does not give rise to uncertainty, unpredictability and/or arbitrary decision-making, *structure* is required; it is in this light also, then, that the argument for clearer identification of the rationale that is being pursued, and of the factors that should inform the determination to be made, is to be understood. At the same time, care should be taken to not 'over-structure'. The recognition of a limited number of

---

[6] See in this regard Choo 2008, 190.

[7] To borrow from Pound, Davis and Choo. See Pound 1959, 367; Davis 1969, 17; and Choo 2008, 157. See generally Chap. 7, Sect. 7.4.2.

specific, narrowly defined, exclusionary rules (which, it was suggested in Chap. 7, is appropriate insofar as the underlying procedural violation constitutes a flagrant rights violations, i.e. a rights violation that on its face poses a high risk to the fairness of the proceedings or is obviously offensive to other fundamental values) need not take away from the overall discretionary nature of the determination of the admissibility of evidence to have been obtained illegally or unlawfully, i.e. the ability of the judge to provide individualized solutions. Similarly, the recognition that certain combinations of factors should make for a compelling case for exclusion, or, as the case may be, for a stay of proceedings (as was recommended in Chap. 7), need not take away from the overall discretionary nature of the determination in question. What matters is attention to the circumstances of the individual case, whereby such 'guidelines' should not be construed as rules, and factors should not be 'applied rigidly and mechanically in every case',[8] i.e. they should not be treated as cumulative criteria, but should rather serve as a basis for an enquiry into the circumstances of the individual case. And chambers should be willing to depart from these guidelines where there is good reason to do so.

Finally, it was argued in Chap. 7 that while several, distinctive features of international criminal procedure—the nature of the regulation of the investigation in international criminal procedure, the lack of an own enforcement agency to execute investigative measures (and the resulting reliance on state-cooperation) and the fragmentation of the investigation across several jurisdictions—raise challenging questions as regards the question of how judges at the ICTs should respond to procedural violations committed in the pre-trial phase of the proceedings, such features can be factored into the equation easily enough, due in no small part to the flexibility of the (court-centred variation of the) integrity rationale, and the notion of contamination that would seem to underlie it. Accordingly, the fact that such features raise challenging questions should not be a reason to, at the outset, adopt a restrained or restrictive approach to the question of how to address procedural violations committed in the pre-trial phase of international criminal proceedings. It is, furthermore, difficult to see how *other* features of international criminal procedure, such as the formal recognition of victim participatory rights (at the ICC, at least), and the fact that the ICTs are dependent on state cooperation for such activities as the apprehension of persons suspected or accused of crimes falling within their jurisdiction and the carrying out of investigations, should lead to such an approach. Regarding the former feature, it was observed in Chap. 7 that the recognition of such rights does not equate to a right to demand punishment. Regarding the latter, it was argued that the idea of judges taking into account the likelihood of 'political backlash' in the determination of an application for the proceedings to be stayed is deeply problematic, from the perspective of the presumption of innocence, and in light of the fact that the ICTs are supposed to be independent judicial bodies (and need to be perceived as such). As for the fact that the goals of international criminal justice are not limited to 'ordinary' goals of

---

[8] See Choo 2008, 165.

criminal justice (the conviction of the guilty and (correspondingly) the acquittal of the innocent), but include such 'special' goals as 'reconciliation', 'history-writing' and 'justice for victims', it was argued that such 'special' goals do not warrant taking into account the seriousness of the offence with which the accused is charged as an argument *against* excluding unlawfully obtained evidence, or, as the case may be, staying the proceedings for serious misconduct. To allow such goals to enter the analysis in *any* way would seem to be inherently problematic, suggesting as it does that socio-political goals form a legitimate constraint on procedural objectives, i.e. the provision of fair and expeditious trials and protection of the rights of the accused, or, put differently, that the criminal process may be utilized to pursue socio-political objectives.

Having summarized the main points of analysis to have arisen from the examination of the judicial response at the ICTs to procedural violations committed in the pre-trial phase of the proceedings (that is, the description and assessment of the existing law and practice, as well as the normative analysis thereof), we may return to the questions raised in Chap. 1—the introduction to this book—and above, at the beginning of this chapter. The questions of whether the (predicted) public reaction to the judicial response should be taken into account in the determination of how to address such violations and whether the seriousness of the offence with which the accused is charged should inform the judge's decision in this regard may be answered in the negative, and the fact that goals of international criminal justice are not limited to the conviction of the guilty (and, correspondingly, the acquittal of the innocent), but include such 'special' goals as 'reconciliation and restoration of peace and security', 'history-writing', 'promoting international rule of law' and 'justice for victims' does not alter this. Nor does the fact that the ICTs are dependent on state cooperation for such essential activities as the apprehension of persons suspected or accused of crimes falling within their jurisdiction and for the carrying out of investigations. While it can be confirmed that the fact that the ICTs do not have their own enforcement agencies, coupled with the fact that their governing documents are (largely) silent on how such activities are to be executed, raises challenging questions for a judge faced with an application for relief in respect of procedural violations committed in the pre-trial phase of international criminal proceedings, this is not a reason to, at the outset, adopt a restrained or restrictive approach to the question of how to address pre-trial procedural violations. Again, such features can be factored into the equation easily enough.

Of course, in order to be able to do so, chambers should have a clear idea of what the equation is. In other words, they should have a clear idea of the rationale underlying the determination to be made. And this is perhaps the most problematic aspect of the ICTs' case law regarding the question of how to address procedural violations committed in the pre-trial phase of international criminal proceedings: the lack of clarity as regards, and of due regard for, the rationale(s) to be pursued (particularly as regards the exclusion of evidence on account of the manner of its obtaining and the stay of proceedings), inconsistency in the case law in this regard, as between chambers of the same institution, as well as in the selection of factors to be taken into account. At the same time, it is relatively clear that at the ICTs, the determination of an application for the exclusion of evidence, or, as the case may be, for a stay of proceedings, is a matter of discretion, i.e. a matter of fact and degree. Such an approach lends itself to the provision of 'individualized solutions' or 'tailored responses', and, to this extent, the ICTs' approach is to be commended. What is required, however, is more 'structure' in the decision-making process, in order to ensure that the notion of judicial discretion does not become synonymous with vagueness, uncertainty and unpredictability. This calls for the clear identification of the rationale that is being pursued, and of the factors that may be taken into account, whereby the latter 'correspond' to the former. What should also be borne in mind is that discretion is *not* synonymous with 'balancing'; the latter may be a manifestation of the former, but the exercise of judicial discretion need not entail the performance of a balancing exercise involving competing public interests. In this book it has been argued that, in the context of addressing procedural violations committed in the pre-trial phase of criminal proceedings, it should not.

References

Choo AL-T (2008) Abuse of Process and Judicial Stays of Criminal Proceedings, 2nd edn. Oxford University Press, Oxford

Davis KC (1969) Discretionary Justice: A Preliminary Inquiry. Louisiana State University, Baton Rouge

Mirfield P (1997) Silence, Confessions and Improperly Obtained Evidence. Oxford University Press, Oxford

Pound R (1959) Jurisprudence (Vol II). West Publishing Co, St Paul, Minn

Rogers J (2008) The Boundaries of Abuse of Process in Criminal Trials. CLP 61:289 et seq.

Bibliography

Books and Monographs, Book Chapters and Journal Articles

(2008) Entrapment: incitement to commit an offence - state officials acting in a private capacity – Art 6. EHRLR 3:410 et seq.

Alamuddin A (2010) Collection of Evidence. In: Khan KAA et al. (eds) Principles of Evidence in International Criminal Justice. Oxford University Press, Oxford, pp 231–305

Ambos K (2009) The Transnational Use of Torture Evidence. Is LR 42:362 et seq.

Ambos K (2013) Treatise on International Criminal Law, vol 1. Oxford University Press, Oxford

Ashworth AJ (1977) Excluding Evidence as Protecting Rights. Crim LR 723 et seq.

Ashworth A (1999) Defending the entrapped. Arch. News 5 et seq.

Ashworth A (2003) Exploring the Integrity Principle in Evidence and Procedure. In: Mirfield P, Smith R (eds) Essays for Colin Tapper. LexisNexis UK, London/Edinburgh, pp 107–125

Ashworth A (2012) The Exclusion of Evidence Obtained by violating a Fundamental Right: Pragmatism Before Principle in Strasbourg Jurisprudence. In: Roberts P, Hunter J (eds) Criminal Evidence and Human Rights: Reimagining Common Law Procedural Traditions. Hart Publishing, Oxford, pp 145–161

Ashworth A (2014) A decade of human rights in criminal justice. Crim LR 325 et seq.

Ashworth A, Redmayne M (2010) The Criminal Process, 4th edn. Oxford University Press, Oxford

Baaijens-Van Geloven YGM (2004) De rechtsgevolgen (sanctionering) van onrechtmatigheden in het opsporingsonderzoek. In: Groenhuijsen MS, Knigge G (eds) Afronding en Verantwoording. Eindrapport onderzoeksproject Strafvordering 2001. Kluwer, Deventer, pp 341–420

Bachmaier Winter L (2013) Transnational Criminal Proceedings, Witness Evidence and Confrontation: Lessons from the ECtHR's Case Law. Utrecht LR 9:127 et seq.

Baldiga WR (1983) Excluding Evidence to Protect Rights: Principles Underlying the Exclusionary Rule in England and the United States. BC Int'l & Comp L Rev 6:133 et seq.

Beresford S (2002) Redressing the Wrongs of the International Justice System: Compensation for Persons Erroneously Detained, Prosecuted, or Convicted by the Ad Hoc Tribunals. AJIL 96:628 et seq.

Bilz K (2012) Dirty Hands or Deterrence? An Experimental Examination of the Exclusionary Rule. JELS 9:149 et seq.

Bitti G (2001) Compensation to an Arrested or Convicted Person. In: Lee RS (ed) The International Criminal Court. Elements of Crimes and Rules of Procedure and Evidence. Transnational Publishers, Ardsley, NY, pp 623–636

Blom T (2002) De meest passende sanctie: de Hoge Raad en onrechtmatig verkregen bewijs. *DD* 2002/32, afl 9, pp 1049–1055

© T.M.C. Asser Press and the author 2018
K. Pitcher, *Judicial Responses to Pre-Trial Procedural Violations in International Criminal Proceedings*, International Criminal Justice Series 16,
https://doi.org/10.1007/978-94-6265-219-4

Blom T (2008) Vormverzuimen. In: Cleiren CPM et al. (eds) Jurisprudentie Strafrecht Select, 3rd edn. Sdu Uitgevers, The Hague, pp 113–133

Blom T (2011) Vormen verzuimd bij het politieverhoor. Vossiuspers UvA, Amsterdam

Blom T (2015) Bespreking van: R. Kuiper (2014) Vormfouten: juridische consequenties van vormverzuimen in strafzaken, thesis. *RM Themis* 2015, afl 3, pp 116–120

Bloom RM, Dewey E (2011) When rights become empty promises: Promoting an exclusionary rule that vindicates personal rights. IJ 46:38 et seq.

Borgers MJ (2012) De toekomst van artikel 359a Sv. *DD* 2012/25, afl 4, pp 257–273

Borgers MJ, Kooijmans T (2013) Alternatieven voor rechterlijke controle op vormverzuimen. In: Groenhuijsen MS et al. (eds) Roosachtig strafrecht: Liber amicorum Theo de Roos. Kluwer, Deventer, pp 17–36

Brady H, Jennings M (2001) Appeal and Revision. In: Lee RS (ed) The International Criminal Court. Elements of Crimes and Rules of Procedure and Evidence. Transnational Publishers, Ardsley, NY, pp 575–603

Brants CH et al. (2003) Op zoek naar grondslagen. In: Brants CH et al. (eds) Op zoek naar grondslagen. Strafvordering 2001 ter discussie. Boom Juridische uitgevers, The Hague, pp 1–27

Brinkhoff S (2016) De toepassing van artikel 359a Sv anno 2016. Een pleidooi voor herstel van balans en de terugkeer naar echte rechterlijke vrijheid. *DD* 2016/8, afl 2, pp 101–116

Buruma Y (2008) Onprofessioneel politieoptreden. *DD* 2008/8, afl 1, pp 87–104

Buruma Y (2013) Strafrechtelijke rechtsvorming. *Strafblad* 2013/3, afl 1, pp 6–14

Buruma Y (2013) Als de politie zich niet aan de wet houdt… *NJB* 2013/494, afl 10, p 595

Cameron JD, Lustiger R (1984) The Exclusionary Rule: A Cost-Benefit Analysis. FRD 101:109 et seq.

Cassese A (1998) On the Current Trends towards Criminal Prosecution and Punishment of Breaches of International Humanitarian Law. EJIL 9:2 et seq.

Chedraui AMT (2010) An analysis of the exclusion of evidence obtained in violation of human rights in light of the jurisprudence of the European Court of Human Rights. Tilburg LR 15:205 et seq.

Choo AL-T (2006) Evidence. Oxford University Press, Oxford

Choo AL-T (2008) Abuse of Process and Judicial Stays of Criminal Proceedings, 2nd edn. Oxford University Press, Oxford

Choo AL-T (2012) 'Give us what you have'—Information, Compulsion and the Privilege Against Self-Incrimination as a Human Right. In: Roberts P, Hunter J (eds) Criminal Evidence and Human Rights: Reimagining Common Law Procedural Traditions. Hart Publishing, Oxford, pp 239–258

Choo AL-T (2013) The Privilege Against Self-Incrimination and Criminal Justice. Hart Publishing, Oxford

Choo AL-T (2015) Evidence, 4th edn. Oxford University Press, Oxford

Clapham A (2006) Human Rights Obligations of Non-State Actors. Oxford University Press, Oxford

Cleiren CPM (2015) Art 1 Sv, aant 11. *Tekst & Commentaar Strafvordering*. Kluwer, Deventer (online, last updated 1 July 2015)

Cleiren CPM, Mevis PAM (1995) Beoordeling van strafvorderlijk overheidsoptreden. *DD* 1995/25, afl 7, pp 700–713

Cleiren CPM, Mevis PAM (1996) Het dubbelzijdig karakter van onrechtmatig strafvorderlijk overheidsoptreden. In: Cleiren CPM et al. (eds) Voor risico van de overheid? Vooruitzichten van de aansprakelijkheid van de overheid in bestuurs-, straf- en civielrechtelijk perspectief. Gouda Quint, Deventer, pp 187–205

Cogan JK (2002) International Criminal Courts and Fair Trials: Difficulties and Prospects. Yale J Int'l L 27:111 et seq.

Combs NA (2010) Evidence. In: Schabas WA, Bernaz N (eds) Handbook of International Criminal Law. Routledge, Abingdon, Oxon, pp 323–334

Corstens GJM (ed) (1993) Rapporten herijking strafvordering 1993. Gouda Quint, Arnhem

Corstens GJM (2014) In: Borgers MJ (ed) Het Nederlands strafprocesrecht, 8th edn. Kluwer, Deventer

Corstens G, Kuiper R (2013) Niet-ontvankelijkverklaring van het openbaar ministerie als reactie op een vormverzuim. In: Groenhuijsen MS et al. (eds) Roosachtig strafrecht: Liber amicorum Theo de Roos. Kluwer, Deventer, pp 125–140

Crijns JH, Van der Meij PPJ (2005) Over de grenzen van de materiële waarheidsvinding. In: Haveman RH, Wiersinga HC (eds) Langs de randen van het strafrecht. Wolf Legal Publishers, Nijmegen, pp 45–69

Currie RJ (2000) Human Rights and International Mutual Legal Assistance: Resolving the Tension. Crim LF 11:143 et seq.

Currie RJ (2007) Abducted Fugitives Before the International Criminal Court: Problems and Prospects. Crim LF 18:349 et seq.

Davis KC (1969) Discretionary Justice: A Preliminary Inquiry. Louisiana State University, Baton Rouge

De Brouwer A-M, Heikkilä M (2013) Victim Issues: Participation, Protection, Reparation, and Assistance. In: Sluiter G et al. (eds) International Criminal Procedure. Principles and Rules. Oxford University Press, Oxford, pp 1299–1374

De Jong DH (1985) Bewijsuitsluiting kent meer dan één rechtsgrond. In: Balkema JP et al. (eds) Liber Amicorum Th.W. van Veen. Opstellen aangeboden aan Th.W. van Veen ter gelegenheid van zijn vijfenzestigste verjaardag. Gouda Quint, Arnhem, pp 97–111

De los Reyes C (2005) Revisiting Disclosure Obligations at the ICTR and Its Implications for the Rights of the Accused. Chinese JIL 4:583 et seq.

De Meester K (2014) The Investigation Phase in International Criminal Procedure. In Search of Common Rules. DPhil thesis, University of Amsterdam

De Meester K et al. (2013) Investigation, Coercive Measures, Arrest and Surrender. In: Sluiter G et al. (eds) International Criminal Procedure. Principles and Rules. Oxford University Press, Oxford, pp 171–379

DeFrancia C (2001) Due Process in International Criminal Courts: Why Procedure Matters. Va L Rev 87:1381 et seq.

Dennis IH (1989) Reconstructing the Law of Criminal Evidence. CLP 42:21 et seq.

Dennis I (2003) Fair Trials and Safe Convictions. CLP 56:211 et seq.

Dennis IH (2013) The Law of Evidence, 5th edn. Sweet & Maxwell, London

Doorenbos DR (1990) Een absolute relativiteitstheorie?. DD 1990/20, afl 1, pp 21–34

Dubelaar MJ (2009) Betrouwbaarheid versus rechtmatigheid in strafzaken. RM Themis 2009, afl 3, pp 101–114

Duff A et al. (2004) Introduction: Towards a Normative Theory of the Criminal Trial. In: Duff A et al. (eds) The Trial on Trial. Volume One: Truth and Due Process. Hart Publishing, Oxford, pp 1–28

Duff A et al. (2007) The Trial on Trial, Vol. Three. Hart Publishing, Oxford

Duff P (2004) Admissibility of Improperly Obtained Physical Evidence in the Scottish Criminal Trial: The Search for Principle. Edin LR 8:152 et seq.

Dworkin R (1977) Taking Rights Seriously. Duckworth, London

Embregts MCD (2003) Uitsluitsel over bewijsuitsluiting. Een onderzoek naar de toelaatbaarheid van onrechtmatig verkregen bewijs in het strafrecht, het civiele recht en het bestuursrecht. Kluwer, Deventer

Fairlie MA (2003) Due Process Erosion: The Diminution of Live Testimony at the ICTY. Cal W Int'l L J 34:47 et seq.

Fairlie MA (2004) The Marriage of Common and Continental Law at the ICTY and its Progeny, Due Process Deficit. Int CLR 4:243 et seq.

Fairlie MA (2013) Miranda and its (More Rights-Protective) International Counterparts. UC Davis J Int'l L & Pol'y 20:1 et seq.

Fiori BM (2015) Disclosure of Information in Criminal Proceedings. A comparative analysis of national and international criminal procedurals and human rights law. Wolf Legal Publishers, Oisterwijk

Fokkens JW (1991) Enkele gedachten over de sanctie op onrechtmatige bewijsgaring. In: Corstens GJM et al. (eds) Met hoofd en hart: Opstellen aangeboden aan prof. mr. J.C.M. Leijten ter gelegenheid van zijn afscheid als hoogleraar aan de Katholieke Universiteit Nijmegen. Tjeenk Willink, Zwolle, pp 227–234

Friedman D (2002) From due deference to due process: human rights litigation in the criminal law. EHRLR 2:216 et seq.

Giannoulopoulos D (2007) The Exclusion of Improperly Obtained Evidence in Greece: Putting Constitutional Rights First. E&P 11:181 et seq.

Gibson K, Lussiaà-Berdou C (2010) Disclosure of Evidence. In: Khan KAA et al. (eds) Principles of Evidence in International Criminal Justice. Oxford University Press, Oxford, pp 306–372

Gosnell C (2010) Admissibility of Evidence. In: Khan KAA et al. (eds) Principles of Evidence in International Criminal Justice. Oxford University Press, Oxford, pp 375–442

Goss R (2014) Criminal Fair Trial Rights. Article 6 of the European Convention on Human Rights. Hart Publishing, Oxford

Gradoni L (2006) International Criminal Courts and Tribunals: Bound by Human Rights Norms … or Tied Down? LJIL 19:847 et seq.

Gradoni L (2013) The Human Rights Dimension of International Criminal Procedure. In: Sluiter G et al. (eds) International Criminal Procedure. Principles and Rules. Oxford University Press, Oxford, pp 74–95

Grevling K (1997) Fairness and the exclusion of evidence under section 78(1) of the Police and Criminal Evidence Act. LQR 667 et seq.

Groenhuijsen MS (1996) Het niet realiseren van gegronde materieelrechtelijke aanspraken in het strafprocesrecht. In: Van de Griend ESGNAI, De Waard BWN (eds) Rechtsvinding. Gedachtenwisseling over het nieuwe Algemeen Deel** van de Asser-serie. Tjeenk Willink, Zwolle, pp 9–20

Groenhuijsen MS, Knigge G (2001) Algemeen deel. In: Groenhuijsen MS, Knigge G (eds) Het onderzoek ter zitting. Eerste interimrapport onderzoeksproject Strafvordering 2001. Gouda Quint, Deventer, pp 1–55

Haazen OA (2007) Precedent in the Netherlands. EJCL 11. http://www.ejcl.org/111/art111-12.pdf. Accessed 2 April 2016

Harris DJ et al. (2009) Harris, O'Boyle & Warbrick. Law of the European Convention on Human Rights, 2nd edn. Oxford University Press, Oxford

Harris DJ et al. (2014) Harris, O'Boyle & Warbrick. Law of the European Convention on Human Rights, 3rd edn. Oxford University Press, Oxford

Hodgson JS (2011) Safeguarding Suspects' Rights in Europe: A Comparative Perspective. New Crim L Rev 14:611 et seq.

Hoyano L (2014) What is balanced on the scales of justice? In search of the essence of the right to a fair trial. Crim LR 4 et seq.

Iontcheva Turner J (2012) Policing International Prosecutors. NYU J Int'l L & P 45:175 et seq.

Jackson J (2012) Human Rights, Constitutional Law and Exclusionary Safeguards in Ireland. In: Roberts P, Hunter J (eds) Criminal Evidence and Human Rights: Reimagining Common Law Procedural Traditions. Hart Publishing, Oxford, pp 119–143

Jackson JD, Summers SJ (2012) The Internationalisation of Criminal Evidence. Beyond the Common Law and Civil Law Traditions. Cambridge University Press, Cambridge

Jacobs D (2012) Puzzling over Amnesties: Defragmenting the Debate for International Criminal Tribunals. In: Van den Herik L, Stahn C (eds) The Diversification and Fragmentation of International Criminal Law. Martinus Nijhoff Publishers, Leiden/Boston, pp 305–345

Jörg N (1989) De exclusionary rule als drijfveer achter normering van bevoegdheden. DD 1989/19, afl 7, pp 654–670

Kamisar Y (1987) "Comparative Reprehensibility" and the Fourth Amendment Exclusionary Rule. Mich L Rev 86:1 et seq.

Keane A, McKeown P (2014) The Modern Law of Evidence, 10th edn. Oxford University Press, Oxford

Keulen BF, Knigge G (2010) Strafprocesrecht, 12th edn. Kluwer, Deventer

Khan KAA, Dixon R (2013) Archbold International Criminal Courts. Practice, Procedure and Evidence, 4th edn. Sweet & Maxwell, London

Klamberg M (2013) Evidence in International Criminal Trials: Confronting Legal Gaps and the Reconstruction of Disputed Events. Martinus Nijhoff, Leiden/Boston

Klamberg M (2013) General Requirements for the Admission of Evidence. In: Sluiter G et al. (eds) International Criminal Procedure. Principles and Rules. Oxford University Press, Oxford, pp 1016–1043

Klip A (2012) European Criminal Law: An Integrative Approach, 2nd edn. Intersentia, Antwerp

Knigge G (2003) Het Zwolsman-criterium op de helling. *RM Themis* 2003, afl 4, pp 193–195

Kooijmans T (2011) Elk nadeel heb z'n voordeel? Artikel 359a Sv en de ontdekking van het strafbare feit. *DD* 2011/78, afl 9, pp 1091–1108

Koopmans FAJ (2001) Art. 359a. In: Cleiren CPM, Nijboer JF (eds) Tekst & Commentaar Strafvordering. Kluwer, Deventer, pp 886–888

Krikke A (1983) De rechtsgrond van de bewijsuitsluiting in strafzaken. In: De la Porte EA et al. (eds) Bij deze stand van zaken. Bundel opstellen aangeboden aan A.L. Melai. Gouda Quint, Arnhem, pp 273–294

Kuiper R (2009) Strafvermindering als reactie op vormverzuimen. Van Via della Conciliazione tot Afvoerpijp en verder. In: Duker MJA et al. (eds) Welberaden. Beschouwingen over de rechtsontwikkeling in de rechtspraak van de Hoge Raad der Nederlanden. Wolf Legal Publishers, Nijmegen, pp 35–59

Kuiper R (2014) Vormfouten. Juridische Consequenties van Vormverzuimen in Strafzaken. Kluwer, Deventer

Leeuw BJG (2013) Grondwet en eerlijk proces. Een onderzoek naar de eventuele meerwaarde van het opnemen van het recht op een eerlijk proces in de Nederlandse Grondwet. Wolf Legal Publishers, Oisterwijk

Levinson DJ (1999) Rights Essentialism and Remedial Equilibration. Colum L Rev 99:857 et seq.

Loof R (2011) Obtaining, adducing and contesting evidence from abroad: a defence perspective on cross-border evidence. Crim LR 40 et seq.

Macovei M (2002) Human rights handbooks, No. 5. The right to liberty and security of the person. A guide to the implementation of Article 5 of the European Convention on Human Rights. Council of Europe, Strasbourg

Martin S (2005) Lost and destroyed evidence: The search for a principled approach to abuse of process. 9 E&P 158 et seq.

Mégret F (2008) In Search of the 'Vertical': An Exploration of What Makes International Criminal Tribunals Different (and Why). http://ssrn.com/abstract=1281546. Accessed 3 April 2016

Mégret F (2013) The Sources of International Criminal Procedure. In: Sluiter G et al. (eds) International Criminal Procedure. Principles and Rules. Oxford University Press, Oxford, pp 68–73

Mevis PAM (1995) De rechtsgevolgen van onrechtmatigheden in het vooronderzoek. In: Balkema JP et al. (eds) Dynamisch strafrecht. Opstellen ter gelegenheid van het afscheid van Prof.mr. G.J.M. Corstens van de Katholieke Universiteit van Nijmegen. Gouda Quint, Arnhem, pp 251–268

Mevis PAM et al. (2001) Rechtmatigheidstoetsing in het nieuwe millennium. In: Brants CH et al. (eds) Legitieme Strafvordering. Rechten van de mens in de 21ste eeuw. Intersentia, Antwerp/Groningen, pp 37–55

Mirfield P (1997) Silence, Confessions and Improperly Obtained Evidence. Oxford University Press, Oxford

Mowbray AR (2004) The Development of Positive Obligations under the European Convention on Human Rights by the European Court of Human Rights. Hart Publishing, Oxford

Naqvi YQ (2010) Impediments to Exercising Jurisdiction over International Crimes. TMC Asser Press, The Hague

Nash S, Choo AL-T (1999) What's the matter with Section 78? Crim LR 929 et seq.

Naymark D (2008) Violations of the Rights of the Accused at International Criminal Tribunals: The Problem of Remedy. JILIR 4:1 et seq.

Nerenberg M, Timmermann W (2010) Documentary Evidence. In: Khan KAA et al. (eds) Principles of Evidence in International Criminal Justice. Oxford University Press, Oxford, pp 443–498

Nowak M (2005) U.N. Convention on Civil and Political Rights: CCPR Commentary, 2nd edn. NP Engel Verlag, Kehl

Ochoa-Sanchez JC (2013) The Rights of Victims in Criminal Justice Proceedings for Serious Human Rights Violations. Martinus Nijhoff Publishers, Leiden/Boston

O'Connor P (2012) "Abuse of process" after Warren and Maxwell. Crim LR 672 et seq.

Oderkerk M (2001) The Importance of Context: Selecting Legal Systems in Comparative Legal Research NILR 48:293 et seq.

Ohlin JD (2013) Goals of International Criminal Justice and International Criminal Procedure. In: Sluiter G et al. (eds) International Criminal Procedure. Principles and Rules. Oxford University Press, Oxford, pp 55–68

Ölçer FP (2008) Eerlijk Proces en Bijzondere Opsporing. Wolf Legal Publishers, Nijmegen

Ölçer FP (2013) The European Court of Human Rights: The Fair Trial Analysis Under Article 6 of the European Convention of Human Rights. In: Thaman SC (ed) Exclusionary Rules in Comparative Law. Springer, Dordrecht/Heidelberg/New York/London, pp 371–399

Orie AMM (1983) De Verdachte Tussen Wal en Schip Òf de Systeem-breuk in de Kleine Rechtshulp. In: De la Porte EA et al (eds) Bij Deze Stand van Zaken. Bundel opstellen aangeboden aan A.L. Melai. Gouda Quint, Arnhem, pp 351–361

Ormerod D (2003) ECHR and the exclusion of evidence: Trial remedies for Article 8 breaches? Crim LR 61 et seq.

Ormerod D, Birch D (2004) The evolution of the discretionary exclusion of evidence. Crim LR 767 et seq.

O'Sullivan E, Montgomery D (2010) The Erosion of the Right to Confrontation under the Cloak of Fairness at the ICTY. JICJ 8:511 et seq.

Ovey et al. (2014) Jacobs, White & Ovey. The European Convention on Human Rights, 6th edn. Oxford University Press, Oxford

Pattenden R (2006) Admissibility in criminal proceedings of third party and real evidence obtained by methods prohibited by UNCAT. E&P 10:1 et seq.

Paulussen C (2010) Male Captus Bene Detentus? Surrendering Suspects to the International Criminal Court. Intersentia, Antwerp

Peters AAG (1973) Illegale radiozender 'de Marconist'. AA 1973, afl 5, pp 236–253

Piragoff DK (2008) Article 69. In: Triffterer O (ed) Commentary on the Rome Statute, 2nd edn. Verlag CH Beck/Hart Publishing/Nomos Verlagsgesellschaft, München/Oxford/Baden-Baden, pp 1301–1336

Pitcher KM (2013) Addressing violations of international criminal procedure. In: Abels D et al. (eds) Dialectiek van nationaal en internationaal strafrecht. Boom Juridische uitgevers, The Hague, pp 257–308

Pound R (1959) Jurisprudence (Vol II). West Publishing Co, St Paul, Minn

Redmayne M (2009) Theorizing the Criminal Trial. New Crim L Rev 12:287 et seq.

Reijntjes JM et al. (2008) Wederzijdse rechtshulp. In: Van Sliedregt E et al. (eds) Handboek Internationaal Strafrecht. Kluwer, Deventer, pp 245–301

Reisinger-Coracini A (2013) Cooperation from States and Other Entities. In: Sluiter G et al. (eds) International Criminal Procedure. Principles and Rules. Oxford University Press, Oxford, pp 95–116

Roach K (1998) The Evolving Tests for Stays of Proceedings. Crim LQ 40:400 et seq.

Roberts P (2012) Normative Evolution in evidentiary Exclusion: Coercion, Deception and the Right to a Fair Trial. In: Roberts P, Hunter J (eds) Criminal Evidence and Human Rights: Reimagining Common Law Procedural Traditions. Hart Publishing, Oxford, pp 163–193

Roberts P (2012) Excluding Evidence as Protecting Constitutional or Human Rights? In: Zedner L, Roberts JV (eds) Principles and Values in Criminal Law and Criminal Justice: Essays in Honour of Andrew Ashworth. Oxford University Press, Oxford, pp 171–190

Rogers J (2008) The Boundaries of Abuse of Process in Criminal Trials. CLP 61:289 et seq.

Rogers J (2011) Abuse of process reconsidered. Arch Rev 6 et seq.

Röttgering AEM (2013) Cassatie in strafzaken. Een rechtsbeschermend perspectief. Sdu uitgevers, The Hague

Ryngaert R (2008) The Doctrine of Abuse of Process: A Comment on the Cambodia Tribunal's Decisions in the Case against Duch. LJIL 21:719 et seq.

Safferling CJM (2003) Towards an International Criminal Procedure. Oxford University Press, Oxford

Samadi M (2016) Policing the police: het toezicht op de opsporing. *DD* 2016/37, afl 6, pp 406–418

Schabas WA (2000) International Decisions: Barayagwiza v. Prosecutor (Decision, and Decision (Prosecutor's Request for Review or Reconsideration)). AJIL 94:563 et seq.

Schabas WA (2010) The International Criminal Court: A Commentary on the Rome Statute. Oxford University Press, Oxford

Schalken TM (1981) Zelfkant van de rechtshandhaving. Over onrechtmatig verkregen bewijs in strafzaken. Gouda Quint, Arnhem

Schalken TM (1989) Schending van wettelijke voorschriften en het redelijke belang van de verdachte: een redelijk criterium? Enkele inleidende opmerkingen. In: Schalken TM, Hofstee EJ (eds) In zijn verdediging geschaad. Over vormverzuimen en het belang van de verdachte. Gouda Quint, Arnhem, pp 3–15

Schalken TM (2013) Een renaissance van vormverzuimen in het strafrecht? *NJB* 2013/1301, afl 21, pp 1391–1394

Schleker C (2009) Reparations. In: Forsythe DP (ed) Encyclopedia of Human Rights, Vol. 4. Oxford University Press, Oxford, pp 330–341

Schoep GK (2015) Art 359a Sv, aant 3. *Tekst & Commentaar Strafvordering*, Kluwer, Deventer (online, last updated 1 July 2015)

Seibert-Fohr A (2009) Prosecuting Serious Human Rights Violations. Oxford University Press, Oxford

Shelton D (2005) Remedies in International Human Rights Law, 2nd edn. Oxford University Press, Oxford

Sloan J (2003) Prosecutor v. Todorović: Illegal Capture as an Obstacle to the Exercise of International Criminal Jurisdiction. LJIL 16:85 et seq.

Sloan J (2006) Breaching International Law to Ensure its Enforcement: The Reliance by the ICTY on Illegal Capture. In: McCormack T, McDonald A (eds) Yearbook of International Humanitarian Law 2003, TMC Asser Press, The Hague, pp 319–344

Sluiter G (2002) International Criminal Adjudication and the Collection of Evidence: Obligations of States. Intersentia, Antwerp

Sluiter G (2003) International Criminal Proceedings and the Protection of Human Rights. New Eng L Rev 37:935 et seq.

Sluiter G (2005) Commentary. In: Klip A, Sluiter G (eds) Annotated Leading Cases of International Criminal Tribunals. Volume VII: The International Criminal Tribunal for the Former Yugoslavia 2001. Intersentia, Antwerp, pp 243–247

Sluiter G (2009) Human Rights Protection in the ICC Pre-Trial Phase. In: Stahn C, Sluiter G (eds) The Emerging Practice of the International Criminal Court. Martinus Nijhoff, Leiden/Boston, pp 459–475

Staker C (2008) Article 85. In: Triffterer O (ed) Commentary on the Rome Statute, 2nd edn. Verlag CH Beck/Hart Publishing/Nomos Verlagsgesellschaft, München/Oxford/Baden-Baden, pp 1499–1502

Starr SB (2008) Rethinking "Effective Remedies": Remedial Deterrence in International Courts. NYU L Rev 83:693 et seq.

Starr SB (2009) Sentence Reduction as a Remedy for Prosecutorial Misconduct. Geo LJ 97:1509 et seq.

Strasser W (1988) The relationship between substantive rights and procedural rights guaranteed by the European Convention on Human Rights. In: Matscher F, Petzold H (eds) Protecting Human Rights: The European Dimension. Carl Heymanns Verlag KG, Cologne, pp 595–604

Summers SJ (2007) Fair Trials: The European Criminal Procedural Tradition and the European Court of Human Rights. Hart Publishing, Oxford

Swart B (2002) General Problems. In: Cassese A et al. (eds) The Rome Statute of the International Criminal Court. A Commentary, vol 2. Oxford University Press, Oxford, pp 1589–1605

Tapper C (2010) Cross & Tapper on Evidence, 12th edn. Oxford University Press, Oxford

Taylor M, Jalloh CC (2013) Provisional Arrest and Incarceration in the International Criminal Tribunals. Santa Clara J Int'l L 11:303 et seq.

Ter Haar R, Meijer GH (2011) Vormverzuimen. Kluwer, Deventer

Thienel T (2006) The Admissibility of Evidence Obtained by Torture under International Law. EJIL 17:349 et seq.

Tochilovsky V (2013) Defence Access to the Prosecution Material. In: Sluiter G et al. (eds) International Criminal Procedure. Principles and Rules. Oxford University Press, Oxford, pp 1083–1098

Trechsel S (2006) Human Rights in Criminal Proceedings. Oxford University Press, Oxford

Van de Westelaken R (2010) Het EVRM als Wapen tegen Straffeloosheid: Over het Recht van Slachtoffers van Ernstige Mensenrechtenschendingen op een Effectieve Strafrechtelijke Aanpak van de Dader. NTM/NJCM-Bull 2010, afl 2, pp 135–152

Van der Meij PPJ (2008) De raadsman bij het politieverhoor en de audiovisuele registratie. De verdedigingsrol bij de materiële waarheidsvinding in het strafrechtelijk vooronderzoek. In: Crijns JH et al. (eds) De waarde van waarheid. Opstellen over waarheidsvinding in het strafrecht. Boom Juridische uitgevers, The Hague, pp 57–93

Van der Meij PPJ (2010) De driehoeksverhouding in het strafrechtelijk vooronderzoek. Een onverminderde zoektocht naar evenwicht in de rolverdeling tussen rechter-commissaris, de officier van justitie en de verdediging. Kluwer, Deventer

Van Hoek AAF, Luchtman MJJP (2005) Transnational Cooperation in Criminal Matters and the Safeguarding of Human Rights. Utrecht LR 1:1 et seq.

Van Leijen G (1994) Sanctionering van normverzuimen en de betekenis van vormvoorschriften in het strafproces. Recht en kritiek 1994/20, afl 3, pp 227–247

Van Sliedregt E, Sjöcrona JM (2008) Algemene inleiding. In: Van Sliedregt E et al. (eds) Handboek Internationaal Strafrecht. Kluwer, Deventer, pp 1–27

Van Woensel AM (2004) Sanctionering van onrechtmatig verkregen bewijsmateriaal. Preadvies voor de Vereniging voor de vergelijkende studie van het recht van België en Nederland. DD 2004/10, afl 2, pp 119–171

Vanderpuye K (2005) The International Criminal Court and Discretionary Evidential Exclusion: Toeing the Mark? Tul J Int'l & Comp L 14:127 et seq.

Vasiliev S (2014) International Criminal Trials. A Normative Theory. Volume 1: Nature. DPhil thesis, University of Amsterdam

Vasiliev S et al. (2013) Introduction. In: Sluiter G et al. (eds) International Criminal Procedure. Principles and Rules. Oxford University Press, Oxford, pp 1–37

Vellinga-Schootstra F, Vellinga WH (2008) 'Positive Obligations' en het Nederlandse Straf (proces)recht. Kluwer, Deventer

Vogler R (2013) Transnational Inquiries and the Protection of Human Rights in the Case-Law of the European Court of Human Rights. In: Ruggeri S (ed) Transnational Inquiries and the Protection of Fundamental Rights in Criminal Proceedings. Springer-Verlag, Berlin/Heidelberg, pp 27–40

Ward R, Akhtar A (2011) Walker & Walker's English Legal System, 11th edn. Oxford University Press, Oxford

Whiting A (2009) Lead Evidence and Discovery Before the International Criminal Court: The Lubanga Case. UCLA J Int'l L Foreign Aff 14:207 et seq.

Zahar A, Sluiter G (2008) International Criminal Law: A Critical Introduction. Oxford University Press, Oxford

Zander M (1985) The Police and Criminal Evidence Act 1984. Sweet & Maxwell, London

Zappalà S (2002) Compensation to an Arrested or Convicted Person. In: Cassese A et al. (eds) The Rome Statute of the International Criminal Court. A Commentary, vol 2. Oxford University Press, Oxford, pp 1577–1585

Zappalà S (2003) Human Rights in International Criminal Proceedings. Oxford University Press, Oxford

Zappalà S (2004) The Prosecutor's Duty to Disclose Exculpatory Materials and the Recent Amendment to Rule 68 ICTY RPE. JICJ 2:620 et seq.

Zeegers KJ (2013) De invloed van mensenrechten op het internationaal strafprocesrecht. In: Abels D et al. (eds) Dialectiek van nationaal en internationaal strafrecht. Boom Juridische uitgevers, The Hague, pp 353–400

Zeegers KJ (2016) International Criminal Tribunals and Human Rights Law. Adherence and Contextualization. TMC Asser Press, The Hague

Zhou H (2006) The Enforcement of Arrest Warrants by International Forces. From the ICTY to the ICC. JICJ 4:202 et seq.

Zuckerman AAS (1987) Illegally-Obtained Evidence—Discretion as a Guardian of Legitimacy. CLP 55 et seq.

Zuckerman AAS (1989) The Principles of Criminal Evidence. Clarendon Press, Oxford

NGO Reports and Publications

International Commission of Jurists (2006) The Right to a Remedy and to Reparation for Gross Human Rights Violations. A Practitioners' Guide. https://www.icj.org/wp-content/uploads/2012/08/right-to-remedy-and-reparations-practitioners-guide-2006-eng.pdf. Accessed 28 February 2017

News Items

Hirondelle News Agency, 'ICTR Compensates Genocide Acquitted Person For Legal Discrepancy', 27 February 2008, http://www.hirondellenews.com/ictr-rwanda/363-trials-ended/rwamakuba-andre/21559-en-en-270208-ictrrwamakuba-ictr-compensates-genocide-acquitted-person-for-legal-discrepancy1061010610 Accessed 15 November 2015

Hirondelle News Agency, 'The ICTR Registrar Is Unable to Enforce a Judgment of the ICTR', 18 September 2007, http://www.hirondellenews.com/ictr-rwanda/363-trials-ended/rwamakuba-andre/20846-en-en-180907-ictrrwamakuba-the-ictr-registry-is-unable-to-enforce-a-judgment-of-the-ictr98979897 Accessed 15 November 2015

Online Resources and Blogposts

Blackburn R, 'Britain's unwritten constitution', https://www.bl.uk/magna-carta/articles/britains-unwritten-constitution Accessed 1 March 2017

Heller KJ, 'NYU JILP Symposium: The Rhetoric of Remedies' (Opinio Juris, 5 April 2013) http://opiniojuris.org/2013/04/05/nyu-jilp-symposium-the-rhetoric-of-remedies/ Accessed 1 March 2017

List of Cases

International Courts and Tribunals, and Treaty Bodies

European Commission on Human Rights

Bozano v France App no 9990/82 (ECnHR, 15 May 1984)
Chinoy v UK App no 15199/89 (ECnHR, 4 September 1992)
S v Austria App no 12592/86 (ECnHR, 6 March 1989

European Court of Human Rights

Al-Khawaja and Tahery v UK App no 26766/05 and 22228/06 (ECtHR, 15 December 2011)
Al-Skeini and Others v UK App no 55721/07 (ECtHR, 7 July 2011)
Alchagin v Russia App no 20212/05 (ECtHR, 17 January 2012)
Aleksandr Zaichenko v Russia App no 39660/02 (ECtHR, 18 February 2010)
Allan v UK App no 48539/99 (ECtHR, 5 November 2002)
Amann v Switzerland (App no 27798/95 (ECtHR, 16 February 2000)
Atalay v Turkey App no 1249/03 (ECtHR, 18 September 2008)
Austrianu v Romania App no 16117/02 (ECtHR, 12 February 2013), para 74
Bannikova v Russia App no 18757/06 (ECtHR, 4 November 2010)
Baran and Hun v Turkey App no 30685/05 (ECtHR, 20 May 2010)
Bayram Güçlü v Turkey App no 31535/04 (ECtHR, 18 February 2014)
Beganović v Croatia App no 46423/06 (ECtHR, 25 June 2009)
Bektaş and Özalp v Turkey App no 10036/03 (ECtHR, 20 April 2010)
Budayeva and Others v Russia App nos 15339/02, 21166/02, 20058/02, 11673/02 and 15343/02
    (ECtHR, 20 March 2008)
Bykov v Russia App no 4378/02 (ECtHR, 10 March 2009)
Cēsnieks v Latvia App no 9278/06 (ECtHR, 11 February 2014)
Chalkley v UK App no 63831/00 (ECtHR, 12 June 2003)
Danev v Bulgaria App no 9411/05 (ECtHR, 2 September 2010)
Dayanan v Turkey App no 7377/03 (ECtHR, 13 October 2009)
Echeverri Rodriguez v Netherlands App no 3286/98 (ECtHR, Decision of 27 June 2000)
Edwards v UK App no 13071/87 (ECtHR, 16 December 1992)
Edwards and Lewis v UK App nos 39647/98 and 40461/98 (ECtHR, 27 October 2004)
El Haski v Belgium App no 649/08 (ECtHR, 25 September 2012)

© T.M.C. Asser Press and the author 2018
K. Pitcher, *Judicial Responses to Pre-Trial Procedural Violations in International
Criminal Proceedings*, International Criminal Justice Series 16,
https://doi.org/10.1007/978-94-6265-219-4

Öneryıldız v Turkey App no 48939/99 (ECtHR, 30 November 2004)
Osman v UK App no 23452/94 (ECtHR, 28 October 1998)
Osmanov and Husseinov v Bulgaria App no 54178/00 (ECtHR, Decision of 4 September 2003)
Othman (Abu Qatada) v UK App no 8139/09 (ECtHR, 17 January 2012)
Panovits v Cyprus App no 4268/04 (ECtHR, 11 December 2008)
Pavlenko v Russia App no 42371/02 (ECtHR, 1 April 2010)
PG and JH v UK App no 44787/98 (ECtHR, 25 September 2001)
PV v FRG App no 11853/85 (ECnHR, 13 July 1987)
Quinn v Ireland App no 36887/97 (ECtHR, 21 December 2000)
Ramanauskas v Lithuania App no 74420/01 (ECtHR, 5 February 2008)
Ramsahai and Others v The Netherlands App no 52391/99 (ECtHR, 15 May 2007)
Rotaru v Romania App no 28341/95 (ECtHR, 4 May 2000)
Rowe and Davis v UK App no 28901/95 (ECtHR, 16 February 2000)
Ryabtsev v Russia App no 13642/06 (ECtHR, 14 November 2013)
Saadi v Italy App no 37201/06 (ECtHR, 28 February 2008)
Salduz v Turkey App no 36391/02 (ECtHR, 27 November 2008)
Sari v Turkey and Denmark App no 21889/93 (ECtHR, 8 November 2001)
Saunders v UK App no 19187/91 (ECtHR, 17 December 1996)
Schenk v Switzerland App no 10862/84 (ECtHR, 12 July 1988)
Sebalj v Croatia App no 4429/09 (ECtHR, 28 June 2011)
Shannon v UK App no 67537/01 (ECtHR, 6 April 2004)
Shannon v UK App no 6563/03 (ECtHR, 4 October 2005)
Shishkin v Russia App no 18280/04 (ECtHR, 7 July 2011)
Silver and Others v UK App nos 5947/72; 6205/73; 7052/75; 7061/75; 7107/75; 7113/75; and
    7136/75 (ECtHR, 25 March 1983)
Simons v Belgium App no 71407/10 (ECtHR, 28 August 2012)
Şiray v Turkey App no 29724/08 (ECtHR, 11 February 2014)
Smith and Grady v UK App nos 33985/96 33986/96 (ECtHR, 27 September 1999)
Smolik v Ukraine App no 11778/05 (ECtHR, 19 January 2012)
Soering v UK App no 14038/88 (ECtHR, 7 July 1989)
Sorokins and Sorokina v Latvia App no 45476/04 (ECtHR, 28 May 2013)
Stanimirović v Serbia App no 26088/06 (ECtHR, 18 October 2011)
Tangiyev v Russia App no 27610/05 (ECtHR, 11 December 2012)
Teixeira de Castro v Portugal App no 25829/94 (ECtHR, 9 June 1998)
Uğur v Turkey App no 37308/05 (ECtHR, 13 January 2015)
Veselov and Others v Russia App nos 23200/10, 24009/07 and 556/10 (ECtHR, 2 October 2012)
Wassink v Netherlands App no 12535/86 (ECtHR, 27 September 1990)
Weh v Austria App no 38544/97 (ECtHR, 8 April 2004)
X and Y v Netherlands App no 8978/80 (ECtHR, 26 March 1985)
Zdravko Petrov v Bulgaria App no 20024/04 (ECtHR, 23 June 2011)

Human Rights Committee (United Nations)

Bautista de Arellana v Colombia Comm no 563/1993 (HRC, 27 October 1995)
Boucherf v Algeria Comm no 1196/2003 (HRC, 30 March 2006)
El Alwani v Libya App no 1295/2004 (HRC, 11 July 2007)
Grioua v Algeria Comm no 1327/2004 (HRC, 10 July 2007)
HCMA v Netherlands Comm no 213/1986 (HRC, 30 March 1989)
Horvath v Australia Comm no 1885/2009 (HRC, 27 March 2014)
Kulomin v Hungary Comm no 521/1992 (HRC, 16 March 1994)

MS v Netherlands Comm no 396/1990 (HRC, 22 July 1992)
Njaru v Cameroon Comm no 1353/2005 (HRC, 19 March 2007)
Rajapakse v Sri Lanka Comm no 1250/2004 (HRC, 14 July 2006)
RAVN and others v Argentina Comm nos 43, 344 and 345/1988 (HRC, 26 March 1990)
Rizvanović and Rizvanović v Bosnia and Herzegovina Comm no 1997/2010 (HRC, 21 March 2014)
Rodríguez v Uruguay Comm no 322/1988 (HRC, 19 July 1994)
SE v Argentina Comm no 275/1988 (HRC, 26 March 1990)
Vicente and others v Colombia Comm no 612/1995 (HRC, 29 July 1997)
Zheikov v Russian Federation Comm no 889/1999 (HRC, 17 March 2006)

Inter-American Court of Human Rights

Blake v Guatemala Series C no 36 (IACtHR, 24 January 1998)
Castillo-Páez v Peru Series C no 34 (IACtHR, 3 November 1997)
Goiburú and others v Paraguay Series C no 153 (IACtHR, 22 September 2006)
Velásquez Rodríguez v Honduras Series C no 4 (IACtHR, 29 July 1988)

International Court of Justice

Case Concerning the Factory at Chorzów (Germany v Poland) (Merits) PCIJ Rep Series A No 17.

International Criminal Court

Prosecutor v Lubanga (Decision on the Defence Challenge to the Jurisdiction of the Court pursuant to Article 19(2)(a) of the Statute) ICC-01/04-01/06, P T Ch I (3 October 2006)
Prosecutor v Lubanga (Decision on the Practices of Witness Familiarisation and Witness Proofing) ICC-01/04-01/06, T Ch (8 November 2006)
Prosecutor v Lubanga (Judgment on the Appeal of Mr. Thomas Lubanga Dyilo against the Decision on the Defence Challenge to the Jurisdiction of the Court pursuant to Article 19(2)(a) of the Statute of 3 October 2006) ICC-01/04-01/06, A Ch (14 December 2006)
Prosecutor v Lubanga (Decision on Confirmation of Charges) ICC-01/04-01/06, P T Ch I (29 January 2007)
Prosecutor v Lubanga (Decision Regarding the Timing and Manner of Disclosure and the Date of Trial) ICC-01/04-01/06, T Ch I (9 November 2007)
Prosecutor v Katanga and Ngudjolo (Decision on the admissibility for the confirmation hearing of the transcripts of interview of deceased Witness 12) ICC-01/04-01/07, P T Ch I (18 April 2008)
Prosecutor v Lubanga (Decision on the admissibility of four documents) ICC-01/04-01/06, T Ch I (13 June 2008)
Prosecutor v Lubanga (Decision on the consequences of non-disclosure of exculpatory materials covered by Article 54(3)(e) agreements and the application to stay the prosecution of the accused, together with certain other issues raised at the Status Conference on 10 June 2008) ICC-01/04-01/06, T Ch I (13 June 2008)
Prosecutor v Katanga and Ngudjolo (Decision on Article 54(3)(e) Documents Identified as Potentially Exculpatory or Otherwise Material to the Defence's Preparation for the Confirmation Hearing) ICC-01/04-01/07, P T Ch I (20 June 2008)

Prosecutor v Lubanga (Decision on the release of Thomas Lubanga Dyilo) ICC-01/04-01/06, T Ch I (2 July 2008)

Prosecutor v Katanga and Ngudjolo (Decision on the confirmation of charges) ICC-01/04-01/07, P T Ch I (30 September 2008)

Prosecutor v Lubanga (Judgment on the appeal of the Prosecutor against the decision of Trial Chamber I entitled "Decision on the consequences of non-disclosure of exculpatory materials covered by Article 54(3)(e) agreements and the application to stay the prosecution of the accused, together with certain other issues raised at the Status Conference on 10 June 2008") ICC-01/04-01/06 OA 13, A Ch (21 October 2008)

Prosecutor v Lubanga (Judgment on the appeal of the Prosecutor against the decision of Trial Chamber I entitled "Decision on the release of Thomas Lubanga Dyilo") ICC-01/04-01/06 OA 12, A Ch (21 October 2008)

Prosecutor v Lubanga (Oral Decision) ICC-01/04-01/06, T Ch I (18 November 2008)

Prosecutor v Lubanga (Reasons for Oral Decision lifting the stay of proceedings) ICC-01/04-01/06, T Ch I (23 January 2009)

Prosecutor v Lubanga (Decision on the admission of material from the "bar table") ICC-01/04-01/06, T Ch I (24 June 2009)

Prosecutor v Katanga and Ngudjolo (Public redacted version of the "Decision on the Motion of the Defence for Germain Katanga for a Declaration on Unlawful Detention and Stay of Proceedings" of 20 November 2009 (ICC-01/04-01/07-1666-Conf-Exp)) ICC-01/04-01/07, T Ch II (3 December 2009)

Prosecutor v Lubanga (Decision on the press interview with Ms Le Fraper du Hellen) ICC-01/04-01/06, T Ch I (12 May 2010)

Prosecutor v Bemba (Decision on the Admissibility and Abuse of Process Challenges) ICC-01/05-01/08, T Ch III (24 June 2010)

Prosecutor v Lubanga (Redacted Decision on the Prosecution's Urgent Request for Variation of the Time-Limit to Disclose the Identity of Intermediary 143 or Alternatively to Stay Proceedings Pending Further Consultations with the VWU) ICC-01/04-01/06, T Ch I (8 July 2010)

Prosecutor v Katanga and Ngudjolo (Judgment on the Appeal of Mr. Katanga Against the Decision of Trial Chamber II of 20 November 2009 Entitled "Decision on the Motion of the Defence for Germain Katanga for a Declaration on Unlawful Detention and Stay of Proceedings") ICC-01/04-01/07 OA 10, A Ch (12 July 2010)

Prosecutor v Lubanga (Judgment on the appeal of the Prosecutor against the decision of Trial Chamber I of 8 July 2010 entitled "Decision on the Prosecution's Urgent Request for Variation of the Time-Limit to Disclose the Identity of Intermediary 143 or Alternatively to Stay Proceedings Pending Further Consultations with the VWU") ICC-01/04-01/06 OA 18, A Ch (8 October 2010)

Prosecutor v Lubanga (Redacted Decision on the Prosecution's Urgent Request for Variation of the Time-Limit to Disclose the Identity of Intermediary 143 or Alternatively to Stay Proceedings Pending Further Consultations with the VWU) ICC-01/04-01/06, T Ch I (8 July 2010)

Prosecutor v Katanga and Ngudjolo (Decision on the Prosecutor's Bar Table Motions) ICC-01/04-01/07, T Ch II (17 December 2010)

Prosecutor v Lubanga (Redacted Decision on the "Defence Application Seeking a Permanent Stay of the Proceedings") ICC-01/04-01/06, T Ch I (7 March 2011)

Prosecutor v Mbarushimana (Decision on the "Defence request for a permanent stay of proceedings") ICC-01/04-01/10, P T Ch I (1 July 2011)

Prosecutor v Banda and Jerbo (Decision on Article 54(3)(e) documents) ICC-02/05-03/09, T Ch IV (23 November 2011)

Prosecutor v Mbarushimana (Decision on the Confirmation of Charges) ICC-01/04-01/10, P T Ch I (16 December 2011)

Prosecutor v Lubanga (Judgment pursuant to Article 74 of the Statute) ICC-01/04-01/06, T Ch I (14 March 2012)

Prosecutor v Lubanga (Decision on Sentence pursuant to Article 76 of the Statute) ICC-01/04-01/06, T Ch I (10 July 2012)

Prosecutor v Gbagbo (Decision on the "Corrigendum of the challenge to the jurisdiction of the International Criminal Court on the basis of Articles 12(3), 19(2), 21(3), 55 and 59 of the Rome Statute filed by the Defence for President Gbagbo (ICC-02/11-01/11-129)") ICC-02/11-01/11, P T Ch I (15 August 2012)

Prosecutor v Bemba (Decision on "Defence Motion Regarding Prosecution Disclosure") ICC-01/05-01/08, T Ch III (3 September 2012)

Prosecutor v Banda and Jerbo (Decision on the defence request for a temporary stay of proceedings) ICC-02/05-03/09, T Ch IV (26 October 2012)

Prosecutor v Banda and Jerbo (Public redacted version of the "Second Decision on Article 54(3)(e) documents") ICC-02/05-03/09, T Ch IV (26 October 2012)

Prosecutor v Muthaura and Kenyatta (Decision on the application for a ruling on the legality of the arrest of Mr. Dennis Ole Itumbi) ICC-01/09-02/11, T Ch V (19 November 2012)

Prosecutor v Gbagbo (Judgment on the appeal of Mr. Laurent Koudou Gbagbo against the decision of Pre-Trial Chamber I on jurisdiction and stay of the proceedings) ICC-02/11-01/11 OA 2 (12 December 2012)

Prosecutor v Kenyatta (Decision on defence application pursuant to Article 64(4) and related requests) ICC-01/09-02/11, T Ch V (26 April 2013)

Prosecutor v Banda and Jerbo (Public Redacted Version of the "Third Decision on Article 54(3)(e) documents") ICC-02/05-03/09, T Ch IV (21 June 2013)

Prosecutor v Kenyatta (Decision on Defence application for a permanent stay of the proceedings due to abuse of process) ICC-01/09-02/11, T Ch V (5 December 2013)

Prosecutor v Katanga (Judgment pursuant to Article 74 of the Statute) ICC-01/04-01/07, T Ch II (7 March 2014)

Prosecutor v Katanga (Decision on Sentence pursuant to Article 76 of the Statute) ICC-01/04-01/07, T Ch II (23 May 2014)

Prosecutor v Lubanga (Judgment on the appeal of Mr. Thomas Lubanga Dyilo against his conviction) ICC-01/04-01/06, A Ch (1 December 2014)

Prosecutor v Lubanga (Judgment on the appeals of the Prosecutor and Mr. Thomas Lubanga Dyilo against the "Decision on Sentence pursuant to Article 76 of the Statute") ICC-01/04-01/06 A 4 A 6, A Ch (1 December 2014)

Prosecutor v Ruto and Sang (Decision on Ruto Defence Request for the Appointment of a Disclosure Officer and/or the Imposition of Other Remedies for Disclosure Breaches of 9 January 2015 (ICC-01/09-01/11-1774-Conf) ICC-01/09-01/11, T Ch V(A) (16 February 2015)

Prosecutor v Bemba (Decision on "Defence Request for Relief for Abuse of Process") ICC-01/05-01/08, T Ch III (17 June 2015)

Prosecutor v Bemba (Decision on "Defence Request for Leave to Appeal the 'Decision on Defence Request for Relief for Abuse of Process'") ICC-01/05-01/08, T Ch III (24 July 2015)

Prosecutor v Bemba, Kilolo, Mangenda, Babala and Arido (Decision on Kilolo Defence Motion for Inadmissibility of Material) ICC-01/05-01/13, T Ch VII (16 September 2015)

Prosecutor v Lubanga (Decision on the review concerning reduction of sentence of Mr. Thomas Lubanga Dyilo) ICC-01/04/01/06 (22 September 2015)

Prosecutor v Bemba, Kilolo, Mangenda, Babala and Arido (Decision on Request to declare telephone intercepts inadmissible) ICC-01/05-01/13, T Ch VII (24 September 2015)

Prosecutor v Ntaganda (Public redacted version of 'Decision on Defence requests seeking disclosure orders in relation to witness P-0901 and seeking the postponement of the witness's cross-examination', ICC-01/04-02/06-840-Conf-Exp, issued on 18 September 2015') ICC-01/04-02/06, T Ch VI (5 October 2015)

International Criminal Tribunal for the Former Yugoslavia (United Nations)

Prosecutor v Delalić, Mucić, Delić and Landžo (Decision on Zdravko Mucić's Motion for the Exclusion of Evidence) IT-96-21-T, T Ch II (2 September 1997)

Prosecutor v Mrksić, Radić, Šljivančanin and Dokmanović (Decision on the Motion for Release by the Accused Slavko Dokmanović) IT-95-13a-PT, T Ch II (22 October 1997)

Prosecutor v Blaškić (Judgement on the Request of the Republic of Croatia For Review of the Decision of Trial Chamber II of 18 July 1997) IT-95-14, A Ch (29 October 1997)

Prosecutor v Delalić, Mucić, Delić and Landžo (Decision on the Tendering of Prosecution Exhibits 104 - 108) IT-96-21-T, T Ch II (9 February 1998)

Prosecutor v Furundžija (The Trial Chamber's Formal Complaint to the Prosecutor Concerning the Conduct of the Prosecution) IT-95-17/1-PT, T Ch II (5 June 1998)

Prosecutor v Furundžija (Oral Decision) IT-95-17/1-T, T Ch II (14 July 1998)

Prosecutor v Blaškić (Decision on the Defence Motion for Sanctions for the Prosecutor's Continuing Violation of Rule 68) IT-95-14-T, T Ch I (28 September 1998)

Prosecutor v Delalić, Mucić, Delić and Landžo (Judgement) IT-96-21-T, T Ch (16 November 1998)

Prosecutor v Furundžija (Judgement) IT-95-17/1-T, T Ch II (10 December 1998)

Prosecutor v Krnojelac (Decision on Motion by Prosecution to Modify Order for Compliance with Rule 68) IT-97-25-PT, T Ch II (1 November 1999)

Prosecutor v Brđanin (Decision on Petition for a Writ of Habeas Corpus on Behalf of Radoslav Brđanin) IT-99-36-PT, T Ch II (8 December 1999)

Prosecutor v Aleksovski (Judgement) IT-95-14/1-A, A Ch (24 March 2000)

Prosecutor v Blaškić (Decision on the Appellant's Motions for the Production of Material, Suspension or Extension of the Briefing Schedule, and Additional Filings) IT-95-14-A, A Ch (26 September 2000)

Prosecutor v Simić, Simić, Tadić, Todorović and Zarić (Decision on Motion for Judicial Assistance to be Provided by SFOR and Others) IT-95-9-PT, T Ch III (18 October 2000)

Prosecutor v Kordić and Čerkez (Decision on Prosecutor's Submissions Concerning "Zagreb Exhibits" and Presidential Transcripts) IT-95-14/2-T, T Ch III (1 December 2000)

Prosecutor v Delalić, Mucić, Delić and Landžo (Judgement) IT-96-21-A, A Ch (20 February 2001)

Prosecutor v Brđanin and Talić (Decision on Second Motion by Brđanin to Dismiss the Indictment) IT-99-36-PT, T Ch II (16 May 2001)

Prosecutor v Kvočka, Kos, Radić, Žigić and Prcać (Decision on Zoran Zigić's Motion for Rescinding Confidentiality of Schedules Attached to the Indictment Decision on Exhibits) IT-98-30/1-T, T Ch I (19 July 2001)

Prosecutor v Milošević (Decision on Preliminary Motions) IT-02-54, T Ch III (8 November 2001)

Prosecutor v Brđanin and Talić (Public Version of the Confidential Decision on the Alleged Illegality of Rule 70 of 6 May 2002) IT-99-36-T, T Ch II (23 May 2002)

Prosecutor v Nikolić (Decision on Defence Motion Challenging the Exercise of Jurisdiction by the Tribunal) IT-94-2-PT, T Ch II (9 October 2002)

Prosecutor v Stakić (Decision) IT-97-24-AR73.5, A Ch (10 October 2002)

Prosecutor v Brđanin (Decision on "Motion for Relief from Rule 68 Violations by the Prosecutor and for Sanctions to Be Imposed Pursuant to Rule 68bis and Motion for Adjournment while Matters Affecting Justice and a Fair Trial Can Be Resolved") IT-99-36-T, T Ch II (30 October 2002)

Prosecutor v Nikolić (Decision on Notice of Appeal) IT-94-2-AR72, A Ch (9 January 2003)

Prosecutor v Nikolić (Decision on Interlocutory Appeal Concerning Legality of Arrest) IT-94-2-AR73, A Ch (5 June 2003)

Prosecutor v Brđanin (Decision on the Defence "Objection to Intercept Evidence") IT-99-36-T, T Ch II (3 October 2003)

Prosecutor v Blagojević (Public and Redacted Reasons for Decision on Appeal by Vidoje Blagojevic to Replace his Defense Team) IT-02-60-AR73.4, A Ch (7 November 2003)

International Criminal Tribunal for Rwanda (United Nations)

Special Tribunal for Lebanon

National Courts

The Netherlands

Dutch Supreme Court

HR 26 June 1962, NJ 1962/470 m.nt. W Pompe
HR 18 April 1978, ECLI:NL:HR:1978:AC6236, NJ 1978/365 m.nt. ThW van Veen
HR 12 December 1978, ECLI:NL:HR:1978:AC2751, NJ 1979/142 m.nt. GE Mulder
HR 23 September 1980, ECLI:NL:HR:1980:AC6987, NJ 1981/116 m.nt. GE Mulder
HR 7 April 1987, ECLI:NL:HR:1987:AB9733, NJ 1987/587 m.nt. ThW van Veen
HR 19 December 1995, ECLI:NL:HR:1995:ZD0328, NJ 1996/249 m.nt. TM Schalken
HR 18 February 1997, ECLI:NL:HR:1997:ZD0643, NJ 1997/484 m.nt. JM Reijntjes
HR 22 September 1998, ECLI:NL:HR:1998:ZD1277, NJ 1999/104 m.nt. J de Hullu
HR 20 October 1998, ECLI:NL:HR:1998:ZD1309, NJ 1999/122
HR 12 January 1999, ECLI:NL:HR:1999:ZD1402, NJ 1999/290
HR 1 June 1999, ECLI:NL:HR:1999:ZD1143, NJ 1999/567 m.nt. TM Schalken
HR 21 March 2000. http://uitspraken.rechtspraak.nl/inziendocument?id=ECLI:NL:HR:2000:AA5254.
    Accessed 1 March 2017
HR 19 June 2001, ECLI:NL:HR:2001:AB2202, NJ 2001/574 m.nt. JM Reijntjes
HR 3 July 2001, ECLI:NL:HR:2001:AB2732, NJ 2002/8 m.nt. TM Schalken
HR 25 June 2002, ECLI:NL:HR:2002:AD9204, NJ 2002/625 m.nt. TM Schalken
HR 14 January 2003, ECLI:NL:HR:2003:AE9038, NJ 2003/288 m.nt. Y Buruma
HR 18 March 2003, ECLI:NL:HR:2003:AF4321, NJ 2003/527
HR 1 July 2003, ECLI:NL:HR:2003:AF9417, NJ 2003/695 m.nt. PAM Mevis
HR 16 December 2003, ECLI:NL:HR:2003:AN7635
HR 30 March 2004, ECLI:NL:HR:2004:AM2533, NJ 2004/376 m.nt. Y Buruma
HR 28 March 2006, ECLI:NL:HR:2006:AU5471, NJ 2007/38 m.nt. TM Schalken
HR 13 June 2006, ECLI:NL:HR:2006:AV6195, NJ 2006/623 m.nt. AH Klip
HR 5 September 2006, ECLI:NL:HR:2006:AV4122, NJ 2007/336 m.nt. TM Schalken
HR 21 November 2006, ECLI:NL:HR:2006:AY9670, NJ 2006/653
HR 21 November 2006, ECLI:NL:HR:2006:AY9673, NJ 2007/233 m.nt. PAM Mevis
HR 24 April 2007, ECLI:NL:HR:2007:AZ8411, NJ 2008/145 m.nt TM Schalken
HR 29 May 2007, ECLI:NL:HR:2007:AZ8795, NJ 2008/14 m.nt. JM Reijntjes
HR 2 October 2007, ECLI:NL:HR:2007:BA5632, NJ 2008/374 m.nt. J Legemaate
HR 12 February 2008, ECLI:NL:HR:2008:BC3496, NJ 2008/248 m.nt. TM Schalken
HR 8 July 2008, ECLI:NL:HR:2008:BC5973, NJ 2009/440 m.nt. Y Buruma
HR 30 June 2009, ECLI:NL:HR:2009:BH3079, NJ 2009/349 m.nt. TM Schalken
HR 7 July 2009, ECLI:NL:HR:2009:BH8889, NJ 2009/399
HR 30 March 2010, ECLI:NL:HR:2010:BK4173, NJ 2011/603 m.nt. MJ Borgers
HR 29 June 2010, ECLI:NL:HR:2010:BL0656, NJ 2010/442 m.nt. TM Schalken
HR 5 October 2010, ECLI:NL:HR:2010:BL5629, NJ 2011/169 m.nt. TM Schalken
HR 4 January 2011, ECLI:NL:HR:2011:BM6673, NJ 2012/145 m.nt. MJ Borgers
HR 11 January 2011, ECLI:NL:HR:2011:BN2297, NJ 2012, 297 m.nt. MJ Borgers
HR 31 May 2011, ECLI:NL:HR:2011:BP1179, NJ 2011/412 m.nt. TM Schalken
HR 27 September 2011, ECLI:NL:HR:2011:BQ3765, NJ 2011/557 m.nt. TM Schalken
HR 13 December 2011, ECLI:NL:HR:2011:BT2173, NJ 2012/299 m.nt. JM Reijntjes
HR 7 February 2012, ECLI:NL:HR:2012:BU6784, NJB 2012/539
HR 3 July 2012, ECLI:NL:HR:2012:BV1800, NJB 2012/1772
HR 13 November 2012, ECLI:NL:HR:2012:BW9338, NJ 2013/413 m.nt. MJ Borgers
HR 29 January 2013, ECLI:NL:HR:2013:BY2814, NJ 2013, 415 m.nt. MJ Borgers

HR 19 February 2013, ECLI:NL:HR:2013:BY5322, NJ 2013/308 m.nt. BF Keulen
HR 9 April 2013, ECLI:NL:HR:2013:BX4439, NJ 2013/309 m.nt. BF Keulen
HR 17 September 2013, ECLI:NL:HR:2013:BZ9992, NJ 2014/91 m.nt. TM Schalken
HR 16 September 2014, ECLI:NL:HR:2014:2670, NJ 2014/461 m.nt. TM Schalken
HR 16 September 2014, ECLI:NL:HR:2014:2749, NJ 2014/462 m.nt. TM Schalken
HR 9 September 2014, ECLI:NL:HR:2014:2650, NJ 2014/420 m.nt. TM Schalken
HR 6 January 2015, ECLI:NL:HR:2015:4, NJ 2015/109 m.nt. TM Schalken
HR 22 December 2015, ECLI:NL:HR:2015:3608, NJ 2016/52 m.nt. AH Klip
HR 5 January 2016, ECLI:NL:HR:2016:9, NJ 2016/153 m.nt. F Vellinga-Schootstra
HR 1 November 2016, ECLI:NL:HR:2016:2454

Courts of Appeal

Hof Den Haag 21 March 2014. http://uitspraken.rechtspraak.nl/inziendocument?id=ECLI:NL:
  GHDHA:2014:1007. Accessed 1 March 2017
Hof Amsterdam 21 December 2015, ECLI:NL:GHAMS:2015:5307

United Kingdom

A v Secretary of State for the Home Department (No 2) [2005] 3 WLR 1249
A-G's Reference (No 2 of 2001) [2001] 1 WLR 1869
R v Horncastle [2009] UKSC 14
R v Horseferry Road Magistrates' Court, Ex parte Bennett [1994] 1 AC 42
R v Khan [1997] AC 558
R v Latif; R v Shahzad [1996] 1 WLR 104
R v Looseley [2001] 1 WLR 2060
R v Maxwell [2011] 1 WLR 1837
R v P [2002] 1 AC 146
R v Sang [1980] AC 402

England and Wales

A-G's Reference (No 3 of 1999) [2001] 2 AC 91
DPP v Hussain, The Times 1 June 1994
H v DPP [2007] EWHC 2192 (Admin)
R v Absolam (1989) 88 Cr App R 332
R v Alladice (1988) 87 Cr App R 380
R v Bailey [1993] 97 Cr App R 365
R v Barry [1992] 95 Cr App R 384
R v Beckford [1996] 1 Cr App R 94
R v Blackwell [1995] 2 Cr App R 625
R v Canale (1990) 91 Cr App R 1
R v Chalkley [1998] QB 848
R v Christou [1992] QB 979
R v Cooke [1995] 1 Cr App R 318
R v Crampton (1991) 92 Cr App R 369
R v Davis, Rowe and Johnson [2001] 1 Cr App R 8
R v Delaney (1989) 88 Cr App R 338

Other

Kuruma v R [1955] AC 197
Panday v Virgil (Senior Superintendent of Police) [2008] AC 1386
R v Grant [2009] 2 SCR 353
R v Harrison [2009] 2 SCR 494
Warren and others v Attorney General for Jersey [2012] 1 AC 22

List of Instruments

International and Regional Treaties and Conventions

Convention for the Protection of Human Rights and Fundamental Freedoms (European Convention on Human Rights (ECHR), 4 November 1950) ETS 5

International Covenant on Civil and Political Rights (ICCPR, adopted 16 December 1996, entered into force 23 March 1976) 999 UNTS 171

American Convention on Human Rights (Pact of San José (ACHR), adopted 22 November 1969, entered into force 18 July 1978) OASTS 36

Convention against Torture and other Cruel, Inhuman or Degrading Treatment or Punishment (United Nations Convention against Torture (UNCAT), adopted 10 December 1984, entered into force 26 June 1987) 1465 UNTS 85

Rome Statute of the International Criminal Court (adopted 17 July 1998, entered into force 1 July 2002) 2187 UNTS 38544

Resolutions, Reports and Regulations of International Organizations

Assembly of States Parties (ICC)

Rules of Procedure and Evidence (adopted 9 September 2002, entered into force 9 September 2002) ICC-ASP/1/3

Resolution ICC-ASP/3/Res.4. Programme budget for 2005, Contingency Fund, Working Capital Fund for 2005, scale of assessments for the apportionment of expenses of the International Criminal Court and financing of appropriations for the year 2005 (10 September 2004) ICC-ASP/3/Res.4

European Union

Directive 2013/48/EU of the European Parliament and of the Council of 22 October 2013 on the right of access to a lawyer in criminal proceedings and in European arrest warrant proceedings, and on the right to have a third party informed upon deprivation of liberty and to communicate with third persons and with consular authorities while deprived of liberty (2013) OJ L 294/1

© T.M.C. Asser Press and the author 2018
K. Pitcher, *Judicial Responses to Pre-Trial Procedural Violations in International Criminal Proceedings*, International Criminal Justice Series 16,
https://doi.org/10.1007/978-94-6265-219-4

Directive 2014/41/EU of the European Parliament and of the Council of 3 April 2014 regarding the
European Investigation Order in criminal matters (2014) OJ L 130/1

International Criminal Tribunal for the Former Yugoslavia (United Nations)

Rules of Procedure and Evidence, as amended

International Criminal Tribunal for Rwanda (United Nations)

Rules of Procedure and Evidence, as amended

Official Statements, Records, Reports, and Letters

International Criminal Tribunal for the Former Yugoslavia (United Nations)

'Second Annual Report of the International Tribunal for the Prosecution of Persons Responsible
for Serious Violations of International Humanitarian Law Committed in the Territory of the
Former Yugoslavia Since 1991' (23 August 1995) UN Doc A/50/365–S/1995/728

'Letter dated 19 September 2000 from the President of the International Criminal Tribunal for the
Former Yugoslavia Addressed to the Secretary-General', annexed to 'Letter Dated 26
September 2000 from the Secretary-General Addressed to the President of the Security
Council' (26 September 2000) UN Doc S/2000/904

'Letter dated 1 October 2015 from the President of the International Tribunal for the Former
Yugoslavia addressed to the Secretary-General', annexed to 'Identical letters dated 28 October
2015 from the Secretary-General addressed to the President of the General Assembly and the
President of the Security Council' (10 November 2015) UN Doc A/70/547–S/2015/825

International Criminal Tribunal for Rwanda
(United Nations)

'Letter dated 26 September 2000 from the President of the International Criminal Tribunal for
Rwanda Addressed to the Secretary-General', annexed to 'Letter dated 28 September 2000
from the Secretary-General Addressed to the President of the Security Council' (6 October
2000) UN Doc S/2000/925

United Nations Organs and Bodies

General Assembly

'Model Treaty on Mutual Legal Assistance in Criminal Matters', UNGA Res 45/117 and Annex
(14 December 1990) UN Doc A/RES/45/117

'Resolution adopted by the General Assembly on the report of the Sixth Committee (A/56/589 and Corr.1), Responsibility of States for Internationally Wrongful Acts', UNGA Res 56/83 and Annex (28 Jan 2002) UN Doc A/RES/56/83

Human Rights Committee

'Comments of the Human Rights Committee: Sri Lanka' (27 July 1995) UN Doc CCPR/C/79/Add.56

'General Comment no 13. Article 14 (Administration of justice)' in Compilation of General Comments and General Recommendations Adopted by Human Rights Treaty Bodies (1994) UN Doc HRI/GEN/1/Rev.1, 14

'General Comment no 20. Article 7 (Prohibition of torture, or other cruel, inhuman or degrading treatment or punishment)' in Compilation of General Comments and General Recommendations Adopted by Human Rights Treaty Bodies (1994) UN Doc HRI/GEN/1/Rev.1, 32

'General Comment no 31. The Nature of the General Legal Obligation Imposed on States Parties to the Covenant' (26 May 2004) UN Doc CCPR/C/21/Rev.1/Add. 13

'General Comment no 32. Article 14: Right to equality before courts and tribunals and to a fair trial' (23 August 2007) UN Doc CCPR/C/GC/32

'Summary record of the 1519th meeting: Peru' (1 November 1996) UN Doc CCPR/C/SR.1519

National Legislation

The Netherlands

Criminal Code [Wetboek van Strafrecht], Act of 3 March 1881 [Wet van 3 maart 1881], Stb. 1881, 35

Code of Criminal Procedure [Wetboek van Strafvordering], Act of 15 January 1921 [Wet van 15 januari 1921], Stb. 1921, 14

Constitution [Grondwet], Act of 24 August 1815 [Wet van 24 augustus 1815], Stb. 1815, 45

Opium Act [Opiumwet], Act of 12 May 1928 [Wet van 12 mei 1928], Stb. 1928, 167

Weapons and Ammunition Act [Wet wapens en munitie], Act of 5 July 1997 [Wet van 5 juli 1997], Stb. 1997, 292

General Act on Entry into Dwellings [Algemene wet op het binnentreden], Act of 22 June 1994 [Wet van 22 juni 1994], Stb. 1994, 572

United Kingdom

Magistrates' Courts Act 1980 c. 43, 1 August 1980

Police and Criminal Evidence Act (PACE) 1984 c. 60 and the supplementing Codes of Conduct, 31 October 1984

Road Traffic Act 1988 c. 52, 15 November 1988

Police Act 1997 c. 50, 21 March 1997

Human Rights Act 1998 c. 42, 9 November 1998

Regulation of Investigatory Powers Act 2000 c. 23, 28 July 2000
Criminal Justice Act 2003 c. 44, 20 November 2003
Constitutional Reform Act 2005 c. 4, 24 March 2005

England and Wales

Criminal Appeal Act 1968 c. 19, 8 May 1968
Senior Courts Act 1981 c. 54, 28 July 1981

Other

Canadian Charter of Rights and Freedoms, Part I of the Constitution Act, 1982, enacted as
    Schedule B to the Canada Act 1982 (UK), c. 11, 29 March 1982
Fourth Amendment to the Constitution of the United States of America, proposed 25 September
    1789, ratified fully as of 15 December 1791

Index

© T.M.C. Asser Press and the author 2018
K. Pitcher, *Judicial Responses to Pre-Trial Procedural Violations in International
Criminal Proceedings*, International Criminal Justice Series 16,
https://doi.org/10.1007/978-94-6265-219-4

Printed by Printforce, the Netherlands